Market Research and Analysis

Market Research and Analysis

Donald R. Lehmann
Columbia University

1989 Third Edition

Homewood, IL 60430
Boston, MA 02116

Sponsoring editor: Elizabeth J. Schilling
Production manager: Irene H. Sotiroff
Cover design: Jeanne Regan
Compositor: Science Typographers, Inc.
Type face: 10/12 Times Roman
Printer: R. R. Donnelley & Sons Company

Library of Congress Cataloging-in-Publication Data

Lehmann, Donald R.
Market research and analysis/Donald R. Lehmann.—3rd ed.
p. cm.
Includes bibliographies and index.
ISBN 0-256-07038-5
1. Marketing research. 2. Marketing research—Problems, exercises, etc. I. Title
HF5415.2.L388 1989
658.8′3—dc19 88–15734
CIP

Printed in the United States of America

3 4 5 6 7 8 9 0 DO 5 4 3 2 1

To my family, teachers, and friends

Preface

The third edition of this book represents a refinement of the approach taken in the first two editions. The book is based on the premises that (a) research is useful, (b) research skills can be learned, and (c) not everyone reading this book does so voluntarily. Consequently the book attempts to convey some of the fun as well as the agony involved in doing and using marketing research, while still providing a fairly complete coverage of technical issues. Some basic features of the book are:

1. While there are descriptive sections, the basic writing style is instructive rather than encyclopedic. The reason for this is the assumption that most people need to follow a learning process in understanding marketing research which is more than just memorization of facts.
2. The author feels that the best way to learn the nuances of research is by doing some. He has found that a simple project (define a problem, make up a questionnaire, go get 150 respondents, analyze the data, and write a report) is the best learning experience in the course. Next to that, analysis of results seems to be the best way to increase understanding. For that reason, the analysis chapters contain studies already analyzed so the reader can see how inferences can be drawn from actual results.
3. A common data base involving 940 female heads of households' responses to a 1975 survey about usage of and attitudes toward foods is used throughout much of the book as an ongoing case example. This provides readers with the opportunity to view a large survey as it is analyzed by several methods and to compare the methods in a concrete situation.
4. The "fancy" analytical techniques are discussed mainly in words in the chapters. Mathematics are generally banished to appendixes. (How's that for market segmentation?)
5. Sample computer output from the SPSS and SAS programs is reproduced in the appendixes to the analysis chapters. This allows practice in interpreting essential results from actual output.

6. The target reader is a user rather than a producer of marketing research. Still, in order to be a good user, one must know enough about the subject to ask good questions. Therefore, the book will try to explain how or at least why many of the basic procedures are used.
7. The writing style will be, at times, light. This is based on the assumptions that (a) some readers may not be passionately interested in the subject and need to be kept awake, (b) it is dangerous for an author to take himself too seriously, and (c) this book should help introduce the subject but cannot possibly say everything relevant about it.

The major changes from the second edition include:

1. A study concerned with durable ownership and life styles is added to illustrate the techniques. Sample outputs (from both SPSSX and SAS) are included in the instructor's manual which can be copied to provide additional hands-on experience in interpreting output.
2. Chapter 8, which deals with supplier services, has been completely redone.
3. The discussion of factor analysis in Chapter 14 has been restructured (and hopefully made simpler).
4. Somewhat greater attention has been paid to qualitative procedures.
5. Via appendixes, a few useful technical issues such as testing for the equality of regression coefficients have been added.

In addition, the entire volume has been tightened, and painful though it was, some sections were actually removed.

The author would like to thank many people for their assistance and encouragement on the revision including Gary Gaeth of the University of Iowa and David Schmittlein of the University of Pennsylvania, as well as the faculty members at Columbia and his family. Unfortunately, the blame for any shortcomings is not as easily conveyed.

Special thanks are due my wife, Kris, without whose efforts at editing, typing, drawing figures, etc., this book would not have been completed.

Donald R. Lehmann

Contents

PART THREE
Analytical Methods 387

Part 1

Basic Concepts

Chapter 1

The Role of Marketing Research

The term *marketing research* means different things to different people. For this book, the following definition is used:

> Marketing research is the collection, processing, and analysis of information on topics relevant to marketing. It begins with problem definition and ends with a report and action recommendations.

This is purposely a broad definition and is intended to include the large variety of things done under the name of marketing research. One thing this definition excludes are marketing/sales gimmicks which masquerade as marketing research (e.g., the old opening gambits of many encyclopedia or real estate salespersons, see McDaniel, Verille, and Madden, 1985).

An expanded version of this definition was adopted by the American Marketing Association in 1987:

> Marketing Research is the function which links the consumer, customer, and public to the marketer through information—information used to identify and define marketing opportunities and problems; generate, refine, and evaluate marketing actions; monitor marketing performance; and improve understanding of marketing as a process.
>
> Marketing Research specifies the information required to address these issues; designs the method for collection information; manages and implements the data collection process; analyzes the results; and communicates the findings and their implications.

In order to understand what marketing research is about, it is useful to understand where it comes from. Set in a business environment, marketing research is practically oriented. Aligned as it is with marketing, producing results which "sell" (are accepted) is very important. Yet, in juxtaposition with this pragmatic framework is the connotation of research—scientific, scholarly, logical pursuit of truth. As will be seen, this juxtaposition leads to perpetual conflict between the demands of expediency and truth seeking.

As an applied field, marketing research has been a large importer of methodologies and concepts from other fields. These "benefactors" have included the following:

Psychology and sociology, from which most of the theories about how consumers think and process information have been drawn. Particularly relevant is the field of social psychology.

Microeconomics, from which utility theory and related concepts have been appropriated.

Statistics, from which most of the analytical procedures have been borrowed.

Experimental design, from which the fundamental concepts of testing and research design have largely been drawn.

As would be expected in such a hybrid field, the terminology also is drawn from separate areas, and learning the jargon can be a nontrivial barrier to understanding the subject (as the reader may already be aware).

The term *research* encompasses widely disparate approaches to gaining and analyzing information. Some of the major contrasts are as follows:

Orientation. This can range from tightly focused research (e.g., what would be the effect on sales of a 10 percent price cut) to very general, scholarly styled investigations (e.g., finding out what our customers think about when they use our product).

Formality. While most people associate research with studies which are structured with budgets, time schedules, and computerized analysis, both introspection and informal contacts with customers or salespersons are excellent ways to gain information.

Amount of data collection. Again, a common stereotype of marketing research is that it involves extensive data collection, usually in the form of either an experiment or a survey. Not only are there many other kinds of data collection, but much of marketing research involves analysis of data which is already available.

Complexity of analysis. Research can include nothing more complicated than counts of the responses to a single question (i.e., how many people bought blue shirts) or "fancy" multivariate statistical procedures which simultaneously examine several variables in a variety of ways.

Marketing research and analysis is thus something of a hodgepodge of different approaches and heritages.

WHO DOES MARKETING RESEARCH?

The people who do marketing research are a widely disparate group. There are no marketing research schools, no certification exams, and very few schools where even a marketing research major exists. Hence, the academic backgrounds of those in research tend to be varied, with psychology and statistics the two most common courses of study of those in research. Many people enter research on rotational assignments from line marketing positions. Hence, it may be somewhat surprising that there is considerable colleagueality among members of the research business. Job movement between suppliers (companies that provide research services to other companies for a fee), advertising agencies, and marketing companies is common.

The research function is traditionally a staff function, often aligned with the planning function. In the past, this has been synonymous with dead-end jobs and a certain lack of respect. Recently, this has begun to change as job mobility and integration have increased. Still, in many organizations, research is something of a stepchild.

Another view of marketing research can be gained by viewing who it reports to and what the pay scale is. The results of surveys done every five years by the American Marketing Association (Twedt, 1983), appear in the table below.

Position	*1968*	*1973*	*1978*	*1983*
Immediate Boss of Marketing Research Director (percent of occurrence)				
President, executive vice president, divisional vice president	30%	45%	37%	27%
Sales/marketing management	54	46	54	53
Other	14	9	11	20
Average Annual Compensation ($000)				
Marketing research director	$19.5	$24.6	$35.8	$51.0
Assistant director	15.7	20.0	31.1	44.7
Statistician	11.5	16.5	22.6	30.7
Senior analyst	13.6	16.3	24.2	34.0
Analyst	10.2	13.0	18.2	25.1
Junior analyst	7.6	12.7	13.9	18.8
Librarian	7.2	12.1	13.9	20.8
Clerical supervisor	7.0	13.6	14.0	16.8
Field work director	7.2	11.9	15.8	23.5
Interviewer	7.0	10.2	10.0	13.1
Clerical/tabulating	5.5	11.4	10.0	14.0

Source: Dik Warren Twedt, *Survey of Marketing Research* (Chicago: American Marketing Association, 1983), pp. 4, 25, 57.

These results are hard to interpret because they are aggregated across many types of companies of vastly different sizes. They do point up two key results, however. First, marketing research is very likely to report to a general, rather than a marketing, manager—which means it often functions in somewhat of a watchdog capacity with respect to marketing. Second, there are a variety of jobs in research—with living wages. Actually the wages for those with advanced degrees at some firms are noticeably higher than these, and it is possible to earn $100,000 or above in the business.

WHAT IS MARKETING RESEARCH?

The problems addressed by marketing research are as varied as its methods. Some of the most common include the following:

Forecasting. Forecasting sales is one of the most obvious tasks of marketing research. Unfortunately, how to get good forecasts is much less obvious.

Buyer analysis/segmentation. Studying buyers to find the characteristics of users of different brands in order to more efficiently allocate resources (i.e., advertising dollars) is another common type of research.

Choice processes and information processing. Studying how buyers get information and make choices is probably the most common form of basic research done in marketing.

Factor testing. The focus of a large portion of marketing research is selecting among different combinations and levels of the various factors which make up the marketing mix: price, advertising level and copy, promotion, packaging, and so forth.

It is also interesting to realize how the research business differs in various situations. Consumer packaged goods research often involves large sample surveys or experiments as well as frequently employing multivariate statistical procedures. Industrial marketing research is much more likely to use existing data or small samples of key accounts along with relatively simple analytical procedures. Research in the developing nations is most likely to be a struggle to collect reliable data, although recently the ability to get research done in remote (from the United States point of view) areas of the world has improved markedly. The "moral" of this discussion, then, is that marketing research is many things to many people.

THE ROLE OF MARKETING RESEARCH IN A BUSINESS

Understanding the role of marketing research requires some conception of how a business operates. One useful way of portraying a business is as a collection of three principle activities: intelligence, operations, and strategy development. Intelligence consists of any activity devoted to collecting or portraying information for use in operating or strategic decisions. Accounting, which is primarily internally focused (e.g., reporting sales, inventory), and marketing research, which is externally oriented (primarily to customers and competitors) are two major intelligence functions. Operations consists of the current focus of a business, including manufacturing, marketing programs (e.g., sales), finance, etc. The strategic element of a business is concerned with the long run and includes such activities as long-range planning and research and development.

Marketing research thus exists to serve the information needs of both operations and strategy development. At its most basic level, monitoring sales and market shares provides data for evaluating operations. More imaginative research might focus on alternative program evaluation (e.g., advertising testing). Finally, the most ambitious types of marketing research attempt to assess future markets in terms of customer preferences and competitive actions.

In the past, marketing research has often been confined both by the narrow perspective of its producers and an unenlightened view on the part of its users to providing information related to operational needs. As an extreme example, the term *marketing research* in one major airline referred to a single task: periodic surveys of passengers of the airline. Pricing decisions were studied in a separate organization, and volume forecasting in still another unit. The position of this book is that all these activities are correctly considered as part of the task of marketing research. Moreover, it also is appropriate for marketing research to be involved in longer run and hence, in some sense, more important decisions (e.g., providing input to R & D). As can be seen from Table 1–1, in the past, marketing research has concentrated on forecasting and potential estimation, new product testing, and market description.

A more recent survey (Hardin, 1983) showed increasing emphasis on marketing strategy studies and decreased emphasis on product and advertising testing. The reduction in product testing may be a result of the general slowing in innovations caused partly by high interest rates and recession. In terms of what is done, 9 of 10 firms reported using WATS phone interviewing, shopping mall intercept studies, and focus groups. By contrast, in-home personal interviews and direct-mail surveys decreased in frequency of use.

The likelihood that managers pay attention to research findings depends on several factors. One study (Deshpande and Zaltman, 1982) found that research which had impact tended to:

Be confirmatory rather than exploratory in nature.

Not produce surprising results. (See also Lee, Acito, and Day, 1987.)

Occur in a decentralized organization.

Have high interactions between researchers and managers.

Be of high technical quality.

TABLE 1–1 Research Activities of 599 Respondent Companies

	Percent Doing	*Done by Mkt. Res. Dept.*	*Done by Another Dept.*	*Done by Outside Firm*
Advertising Research				
A. Motivation research	47%	30%	2%	15%
B. Copy research	61	30	6	25
C. Media research	68	22	14	32
D. Studies of ad effectiveness	76	42	5	29
E. Studies of competitive advertising	67	36	11	20
Business Economics and Corporate Research				
A. Short-range forecasting (up to 1 year)	89	51	36	2
B. Long-range forecasting (over 1 year)	87	49	34	4
C. Studies of business trends	91	68	20	3
D. Pricing studies	83	34	47	2
E. Plant and warehouse location studies	68	29	35	4
F. Acquisition studies	73	33	38	2
G. Export and international studies	49	22	25	2
H. MIS (management information system)	80	25	53	2
I. Operations research	65	14	50	1
J. Internal company employees	76	25	45	6
Corporate Responsibility Research				
A. Consumers "right to know" studies	18	7	9	2
B. Ecological impact studies	23	2	17	4
C. Studies of legal constraints on advertising and promotion	46	10	31	5
D. Social values and policies studies	39	19	13	7
Product Research				
A. New product acceptance and potential	76	59	11	6
B. Competitive product studies	87	71	10	6
C. Testing of existing products	80	55	19	6
D. Packaging research design or physical characteristics	65	44	12	9
Sales and Market Research				
A. Measurement of market potentials	97	88	4	5
B. Market share analysis	97	85	6	6
C. Determination of market characteristics	97	88	3	6
D. Sales analysis	92	67	23	2
E. Establishment of sales quotas, territories	78	23	54	1
F. Distribution channel studies	71	32	38	1
G. Test markets, store audits	59	43	7	9
H. Consumer panel operations	63	46	2	15
I. Sales compensation studies	60	13	43	4
J. Promotional studies of premiums, coupons, sampling, deals, etc.	58	38	14	6

Source: Reprinted from Dik Warren Twedt, *1983 Survey of Marketing Research* (Chicago: American Marketing Association, 1983), p. 41.

In a follow-up study focusing on industrial firms, Deshpande and Zaltman (1987) again confirmed that surprising findings are less utilized (confirming the obvious but often overlooked fact that new ideas are rarely welcomed). They also found greater utilization in more formal organizations and when the objective was more exploratory. While a more complete discussion of organizational issues is not appropriate at this time, it is obvious that a marketing researcher has to worry about organizational as well as technical issues.

THE ROLE OF THE MARKETING RESEARCHER VIS-À-VIS THE MANAGER

The role of the company marketing researcher in a research project is essentially threefold. First, the researcher serves as a technical consultant who provides expertise in such areas as sampling and implementation (generally by knowing available suppliers, selecting an appropriate one, and working with the supplier during execution of data collection). Second, he or she is generally responsible for performing analysis of data and providing an initial interpretation of the results. Third, the researcher should act as a consultant to the manager in both the problem definition and action recommendation stages of the project.

By contrast, the manager is primarily responsible for defining the problem and the final recommendations. In order to be comfortable with the results, a manager must have at least a logical, nontechnical understanding of the research project, especially in terms of its basic design.

The manager must also maintain a reasonable perspective on what research can and can't do. Research cannot make a bad product sell nor can it exactly forecast sales in the year 2010. A manager who asks for a single estimate of, for example, sales, ignores the uncertainty associated with it. Knowing whether forecast sales of 1.2 million are reliable within 10,000 or 200,000 is critical to proper contingency planning. Also, the manager who sets unrealistic time schedules (e.g., two weeks for a study where data collection should take three) or budgets will end up with relatively unreliable research. Finally, managers should recognize that some apparently simple questions (e.g., What is the effect of advertising on sales?) are actually very complex. In addition to a variety of measurement issues (Do we measure sales in terms of units, dollars, or market share; advertising in terms of dollars, exposures, media used?), the basic nature of the cause and effect relationship among variables is often unclear (e.g., Does advertising cause sales, or is the advertising budget set as percent of sales?). In short, a manager must accept research projects as a useful but imperfect aid to decision making rather than a panacea.

HOW COMPANIES GET RESEARCH DONE

Where research is done is also interesting and occasionally surprising to the uninitiated. Few companies have the staff to actually do data collection. Rather, most companies contract data collection to a host of supplier companies ranging from large, well-known firms with offices in many major cities to small job shops with fewer than 10 people. While advertising agencies often serve as a vehicle for getting research done, typically they

FIGURE 1–1 General Foods' Organization before Downsizing

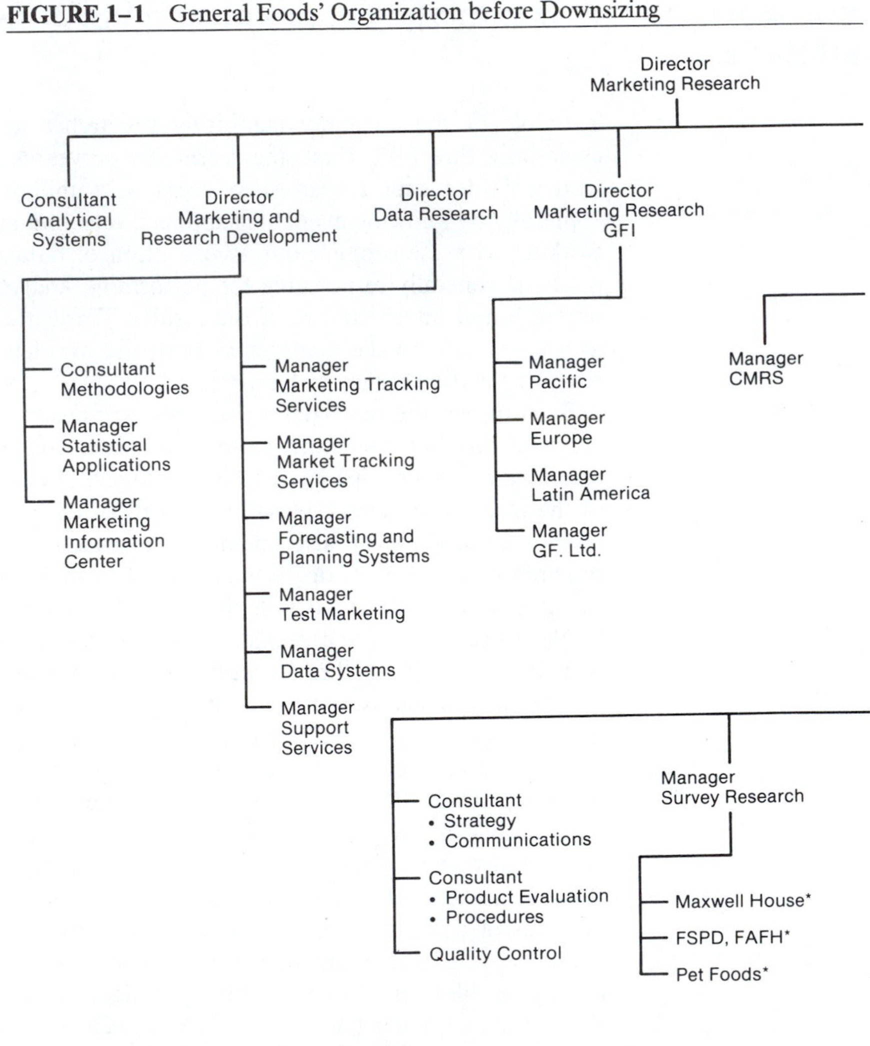

Source: *Marketing Review* 35 (March–April 1980), p. 12.

serve as conduits to the same suppliers. The suppliers in turn may subcontract data collection work to a network of field supervisors. Similarly, computer analysis is often handled by outside firms. Hence, data collection and analysis involves a whole series of subcontractors who work on various parts of a job.

The size of the research business in terms of revenue is relatively small. Typically, marketing research budgets run about 1 to 2 percent of sales at a consumer package goods company and far less than 1 percent (e.g., 0.2 percent) at a financial services company.

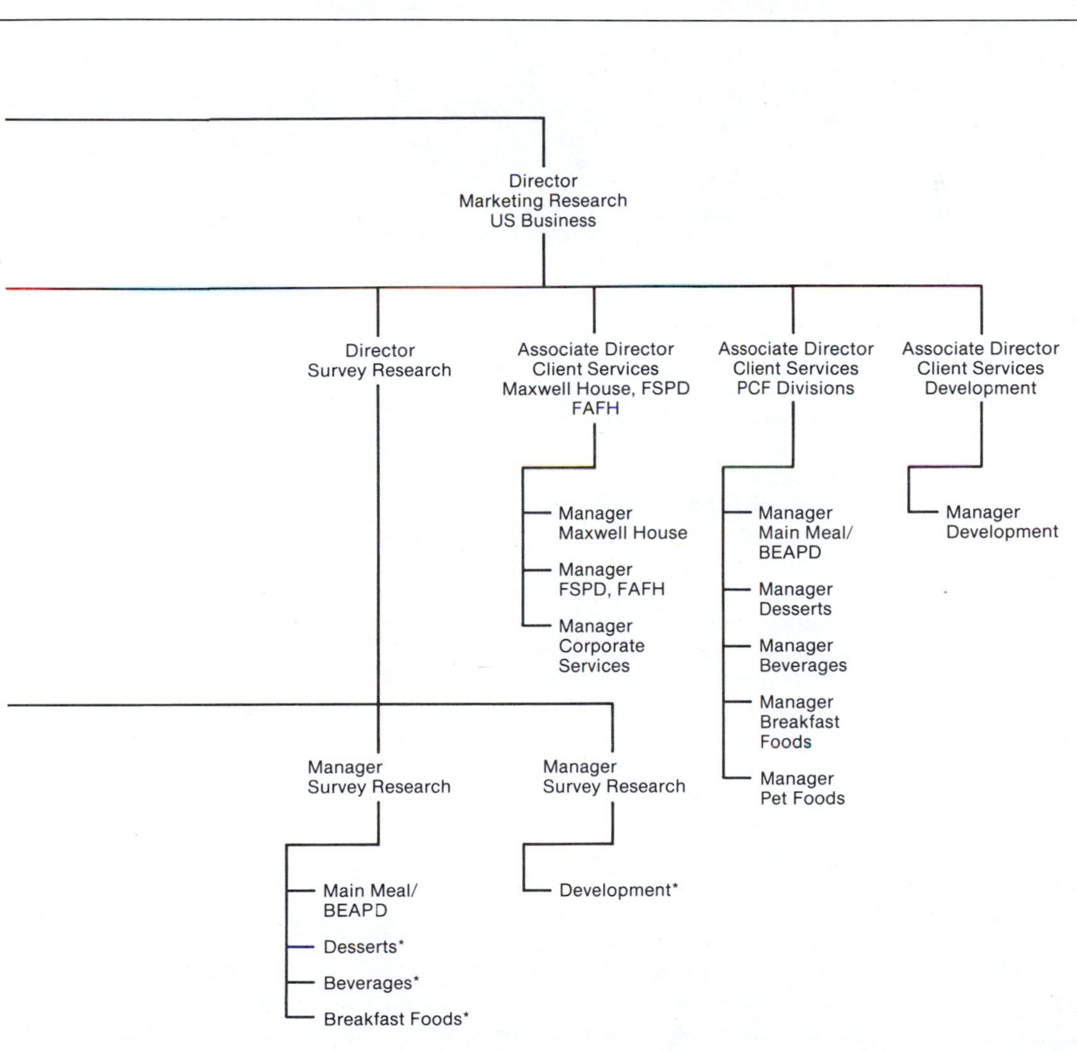

TABLE 1–2 How They Rank (1986 revenues—46 leading U.S. research organizations)

Rank 1986	Rank 1985	Organization	Total Research Revenues* ($ millions)	Percent Change vs. 1985†	Percent Revenues from Outside United States
1	1	A. C. Nielsen Co.	$615.0	+19.0%	approx. 60%
2	2	IMS International	245.4	+41.8	45.6
3	3	SAMI/Burke	174.5	+ 7.7	3.5
4	4	Arbitron Ratings Co.	137.2	+12.3	—
5	5	Information Resources	93.6	+21.2	4.0
6	—	MRB Group	52.0	+ 8.7	37.0
7	7	M/A/R/C	47.5	+ 2.6	—
8	9	NFO Research	36.7	+ 7.0	—
9	8	Market Facts	36.0	− 4.6	—
10	10	NPD Group	35.5	+ 7.3	1.4
11	12	Westat	35.2	+39.9	—
12	11	Maritz Marketing Research	32.9	+ 9.6	—
13	13	Elrick and Lavidge	26.7	+ 8.5	—
14	15	YSW/Clancy Shulman	22.0	+12.8	—
15	14	Walker Research	21.3	+ 2.6	—
16	16	Chilton Research	19.5	+ 2.1	—
17	19	ASI Market Research	17.1	+ 8.6	—
18	22	Decisions Center	15.6	+13.0	—
19	18	Louis Harris and Associates	15.5	− 2.0	43.0
20	20	Opinion Research Corp.	15.2	+ 4.8	—
21	23	Ehrhart-Babic Group	14.5	+ 5.1	—
22	27	National Analysts	13.3	+38.5	—
23	24	Harte-Hanks Marketing Services Group	12.2	+ 4.6	—
24	28	Mediamark Research	21.1	+26.6	—
25	25	Data Development Corp.	10.5	− 2.7	—
26	26	Custom Research	10.4	+ 7.2	—
27	36	Decision/Making/ Information	10.4	+55.2	—
28	35	Decision Research Corp.	9.8	+16.7	—
29	32	Gallup Organization	9.7	+13.1	—
30	37	Market Opinion Research	9.4	+45.0	—
31	29	Admar Research	9.4	+ 5.6	—
32	30	Starch INRA Hooper	9.1	+ 2.8	—
33	33	National Research Group	8.9	+ 9.9	11.0
34	31	McCollum/Spielman Research	8.4	− 2.3	—
35	38	Guideline Research	7.5	+15.4	—
36	34	Response Analysis	6.9	− 9.3	—
37	40	J.D. Power & Associates	6.1	+ 5.2	—

TABLE 1–2 *(concluded)*

Rank 1986	Rank 1985	Organization	Total Research Revenues* ($ millions)	Percent Change vs. 1985†	Percent Revenues from Outside United States
38	39	Ad Factors/Millward Brown	5.9	0	—
39	42	Marketing Research Services	5.8	+13.7	—
40	42	Oxtoby-Smith	5.8	+16.0	—
41	—	Birch Research	5.8	+25.4	—
42	—	Newman-Stein	5.3	+ 4.9	—
43	—	Field Research Corp.	5.2	+28.0	—
44	41	Lieberman Research West	5.2	−12.7	—
45	46	Kapuler Marketing Research	5.1	+ 6.0	—
46	—	Total Research Corp.	5.0	+48.4	—
		Subtotal, top 46	$1,911.2‡	+16.2 %	Approx. 26.8
		All other (90 CASRO companies not included in top 46)§	207.5	+ 6.6	
		Total (136 organizations)	$2,118.7	+15.1 %	

*Total revenues that include nonresearch activities, for some companies, are significantly higher. This information is given in the individual company profiles in the main article.

†Rate of growth from year to year has been adjusted so as not to include revenue gains from acquisition. See main article for explanation.

‡Rounded to nearest hundred thousand.

§Total revenues of 90 survey research firms—over and beyond those listed in top 46 list—that provide financial information, on a confidential basis, to CASRO.

Source: Jack J. Honomichl, "Top 46 Companies' Growth Is Partly Illusion" *Advertising Age*, May 11, 1987, p. S–2. Reprinted with permission by Crain Communications, Inc.

The internal organization of firms is quite variable. While some companies have large organizations (Figure 1–1 depicts General Foods in 1980; it has since downsized considerably), most are quite lean (e.g., Best Foods, with under 10 professional staff members).

The 1986 revenues of 136 leading U.S. research organizations were just over $2 billion (Table 1–2), with Nielsen the leader at $615 million and only four firms reporting revenues above $100 million (Honomichl, 1987). These revenues have been growing at about 14 percent per year over the last ten years. Interestingly, much of the growth in the research revenues is due to work done outside the United States. Yet the top 46 advertising agencies still have almost four times the revenue of the 46 largest research organizations ($7.1 versus $1.9 billion). Thus, research budgets are still relatively small, when compared to the presumed critical role of customer analysis in shaping marketing strategy.

WHAT RESEARCH DOES NOT DO

Research can possibly be best understood in terms of what it can't do. The following two major things research cannot do:

Make decisions. Research's role is not to make decisions. Rather, research takes data on a confusing/uncertain market and rearranges them into a different form which hopefully makes the market more understandable and consequently good decisions easier. However, researchers often make recommendations which become the decision after the appropriate approval is gained.

Guarantee success. Research at best can improve the odds of making a correct decision. Anyone who expects to eliminate the possibility of failure by doing research is both unrealistic and likely to be disappointed. The real value of research can be seen over the long run where increasing the percentage of good decisions should be manifested in improved bottom-line performance and in the occasional revelation which arises from research.

TABLE 1–3

*Estimated Size of Total Marketing/Advertising Research Market**

Country	*Annual Volume U.S. Dollars† (000,000)*	*Country*	*Annual Volume U.S. Dollars† (000,000)*
United States	$1,800	New Zealand	$14
United Kingdom	345	Ireland	13
Fed. Rep. Germany	325	Argentina	10
Japan	260	Venezuela	9
France	215	India	8
Canada	175	Hong Kong	7
Italy	150	Singapore	4
Australia	84	Thailand	4
The Netherlands	82	Greece	4
Mexico	70	South Korea	4
Switzerland	54	Saudi Arabia	4
Spain	29	Malaysia	4
Brazil	28	Philippines	3
Sweden	27	Taiwan	3
Austria	25	Indonesia	3
Belgium	22	All other Middle East	3
Finland	18	Kuwait	2
Norway	16	Egypt	1
Denmark	15	Pakistan	1
South Africa	15	All others‡	3
		Total	$3,859

THE INTERNATIONAL PERSPECTIVE

When one broadens the view of research beyond U.S. organizations, it appears currently most of the revenue and activity occurs in the developed world (Table 1–3). Also, when one expands the list of research organizations beyond the United States, only five of the top 15 are not based in the United States: AGB (Great Britain, fourth with revenue of $135 million), GGK (West Germany), Research International (Great Britain), Infratest (West Germany), and Video Research (Japan). While it seems inevitable that the importance of currently less-developed companies will increase in the research business as in all businesses, for the present most of the activity is in the United States.

This book thus has as its focus the types of research most commonly used in the United States. There are at least three reasons for this, other than the

TABLE 1–3 *(concluded)*

Number of Foreign Research Companies Conducting Research in Each Listed Country in the Past Two Years[§]

Country	Companies	Country	Companies
Germany (FRG)	283	Indonesia	51
France	262	Singapore	51
United Kingdom	223	Finland	44
Italy	183	Brazil	43
United States	176	Taiwan	43
Netherlands	163	Malaysia	42
Canada	156	Greece	38
Belgium	151	Thailand	37
Spain	106	Philippines	36
Switzerland	101	Korea (ROK)	35
Japan	100	South Africa	34
Sweden	87	Egypt	31
Denmark	71	Kuwait	29
Australia	69	Venezuela	22
Norway	65	Nigeria	17
Austria	61	Kenya	16
Hong Kong	59	Ivory Coast	15
Mexico	56	Yugoslavia	14
Saudi Arabia	52	Misc./Eastern Europe	7

**Advertising Age* compilation
†Rounded to nearest million dollars
‡Yugoslavia, Morocco, Ivory Coast, Nigeria, Kenya, Sri Lanka, Peru, Chile, Hungary, Central America and China
§Paper by Philip Bernard, Research International, presented to ESMOR

Source: Jack J. Honomichl, "Ranking Top Players in Growing Global Arena." *Advertising Age*, November 24, 1986, p. S-2. Reprinted with permission by Crain Communications, Inc.

current preponderance of work in the United States or by U. S. firms. First, the basic principles of design and analysis transfer across cultural boundaries, although many data collection procedures may not. Second, for better or worse, there seems to be a trend toward reproducing many of the "developed" world's procedures in the rest of the world. Third, the author doesn't know much about much of the world so it would be presumptuous (not to mention very difficult) for him to write about it. For those who don't buy the first two arguments (or condone the third), the book by Douglas and Craig (1983) might be worth pursuing.

THE APPROACH OF THIS BOOK

Many people argue that marketing research is more of an art than a science. Actually, it probably most resembles a craft in that it requires both adherence to some basic principles and some skill gained from experience. This book will approach the topic by attempting to explain the methods most commonly used: what they are, how they work, and what their weaknesses are. As much as possible, the book will be user oriented and will stress practicality over purity.

In the interest of practicality, it is important to recognize that there are other useful references available to anyone interested in the subject:

1. Aaker, D., and G. Day. *Marketing Research*. 3rd ed. New York: John Wiley & Sons, 1986.
2. Banks, S. *Experimentation in Marketing*. New York: McGraw-Hill, 1965.
3. Campbell, D. T., and J. C. Stanley. *Experimental Designs for Research*. Skokie, Ill.: Rand McNally, 1966.
4. Churchill, G. A., Jr. *Marketing Research*. 4th ed. Hindsale, Ill.: Dryden Press, 1987.
5. Cox, W. E. *Industrial Marketing Research*. New York: John Wiley & Sons, 1979.
6. Douglas, S. P., and C. S. Craig. *International Marketing Research*. Englewood Cliffs, N.J.: Prentice-Hall, 1983.
7. Ferber, R., ed. *Handbook of Marketing Research*. New York: McGraw-Hill, 1974. This book is worth its high price ($84.95) for the heavy user.
8. Green, P. E.; D. S. Tull; and G. Albaum. *Research for Marketing Decisions*. 5th ed. Englewood Cliffs, N.J.: Prentice-Hall, 1988. This is a competitive text which is very useful if the reader has reasonable experience and quantitative skill.
9. Kerlinger, F. N. *Foundations of Behavioral Research*. 2nd ed. New York: Holt, Rinehart & Winston, 1973.
10. Kinnear, T. C., and J. R. Taylor. *Marketing Research*. 3rd ed. New York: McGraw-Hill, 1987.
11. Lehmann, D. R., and R. S. Winer. *Analysis for Marketing Planning*. Plano, Tex:. Business Publications, 1987. This book really is designed for marketing planning, but a free plug is too good an opportunity to pass up.
12. Lilien, G. L., and P. Kotler. *Marketing Decision Making: A Model Building Approach*. New York: Harper & Row, 1983.

13. Payne, S. L. *The Art of Asking Questions*. Princeton, N.J.: Princeton University Press, 1951.
14. Shaw, M. E., and J. M. Wright. *Scales for the Measurement of Attitude*. New York: McGraw-Hill, 1967.
15. Sudman, S., and N. M. Bradburn. *Asking Questions*. San Francisco: Jossey-Bass, 1982.
16. Tull, D. S., and D. I. Hawkins. *Marketing Research*. New York: Macmillan, 1980.

The point of listing these books is not to convince you to use another book. Rather, the purpose is to list some of the sources where additional information and different perspectives are available. The rest of this book will then provide a Layman's (no one spells my name correctly) view of marketing research.

Stylistically, this means the book is hopefully both informal and informative. In terms of content, the book begins by discussing the need for and types of studies (Chapters 2 and 3) and the design of studies, with particular emphasis on survey design (Chapters 4–7). Suppliers are described in Chapter 8, with sampling covered in Chapter 9. Coding and basic analysis are covered in Chapters 10–12. More advanced analytical material appears in Chapters 13–16, and areas of application are briefly described in Chapters 17–19, chapters which are often skipped. Finally, some general comments on the future of research are provided in Chapter 20.

BIBLIOGRAPHY

Aaker, David and George Day. *Marketing Research*. 3rd ed. New York: John Wiley & Sons, 1986.

Banks, Seymour. *Experimentation in Marketing*. New York: McGraw-Hill, 1965.

Campbell, Donald T., and Julian C. Stanley. *Experimental Designs for Research*. Skokie, Ill.: Rand McNally, 1966.

Churchill, Gilbert A., Jr. *Marketing Research*. 4th ed. Hindsale, Ill.: Dryden Press, 1987.

Cook, Thomas D., and Donald T. Campbell. *Quasi-Experimentation: Design and Analysis Issues for Field Settings*. Chicago: Rand McNally, 1979.

Cox, William E. *Industrial Marketing Research*. New York: John Wiley & Sons, 1979.

Deshpande, Rohit, and Gerald Zaltman. "A Comparison of Factors Affecting Use of Marketing Information in Consumer and Industrial Firms." *Journal of Marketing Research* 24 (February, 1987), pp. 114–17.

______. "Factors Affecting the Use of Market Research Information: A Path Analysis." *Journal of Marketing Research* 19 (February 1982), pp. 14–24.

Dillon, William R.; Thomas J. Madden; and Neil H. Firtle. *Marketing Research in a Marketing Environment*. St. Louis: Times Mirror/Mosby, 1987.

Douglas, Susan P., and C. Samuel Craig. *International Marketing Research*. Englewood Cliffs, N.J.: Prentice-Hall, 1983.

Ferber, Robert, ed. *Handbook of Marketing Research*. New York: McGraw-Hill, 1974.

Green, Paul E.; Donald S. Tull; and Gerald Albaum. *Research for Marketing Decisions*. 5th ed. Englewood Cliffs, N.J.: Prentice-Hall, 1988.

Hardin, David K. "Inflation Adjusted Spending Is on Rise for Consumer Research." *Marketing News* 17 (May 27, 1983), p. 13.

Honomichl, Jack J. "Top 46 Companies' Growth Is Partly Illusion." *Advertising Age* 58 (May 11, 1987), pp. S-1 to S-26.

______. "Ranking Top Players in Growing Global Arena." *Advertising Age* 57 (November 24, 1986), pp. S-1 to S-10.

Kerlinger, Fred N. *Foundations of Behavioral Research*. 2nd ed. New York: Holt, Rinehart & Winston, 1973.

Kinnear, Thomas C., and James R. Taylor. *Marketing Research*. 3rd ed. New York: McGraw-Hill, 1987.

Lee, Hanjoon; Frank Acito; and Ralph L. Day. "Evaluation and Use of Marketing Research by Decision Makers: A Behavioral Simulation." *Journal of Marketing Research* 24 (May, 1987), pp. 187–96.

Lehmann, Donald R., and Russell S. Winer. *Analysis for Marketing Planning*. Plano, Tex.: Business Publications, 1987.

Lilien, Gary L., and Philip Kotler. *Marketing Decision Making: A Model Building Approach*. New York: Harper & Row, 1983.

McDaniel, Stephen W.; Perry Verille; and Charles S. Madden. "The Threats to Marketing Research: An Empirical Reappraisal." *Journal of Marketing Research* 22 (February, 1985), pp. 74–80.

Payne, Stanley L. *The Art of Asking Questions*. Princeton, N.J.: Princeton University Press, 1951.

Peterson, Robert A. *Marketing Research*. Plano, Tex.: Business Publications, 1988.

"The Reorganization in the Marketing Research Department at General Foods." *Marketing Review* 25 (March–April 1980), pp. 11–15.

Sellitz, Claire. *Research Methods in Social Relations*. New York: Holt, Rinehart & Winston, 1959.

Shaw, Marvin E., and Jack M. Wright. *Scales for the Measurement of Attitude*. New York: McGraw-Hill, 1967.

Sudman, Seymour, and Norman M. Bradburn. *Asking Questions*. San Francisco: Jossey-Bass, 1982.

Tull, Donald S., and Del I. Hawkins. *Marketing Research*. New York: Macmillan, 1976.

Twedt, Dik W. *Survey of Marketing Research*. Chicago: American Marketing Association, 1978; 1983.

______. "Six Trends in Corporate Marketing Research Show Budget, Productivity, Pay, and Opportunity Increases." *Marketing News* 9 (March 14, 1975), p. 3.

Chapter 2

The Value of Information

Information needs exist for both new and existing brands. For example, Kodak's Disc Camera was developed with marketing research as the driving force. While the impetus was provided by the peaking of Instamatic sales in 1978, the design was the result of research indicating that "trouble-free" photography in a broader range of situations than was possible with instamatics had appeal to the market. Moreover, actual design of features followed extensive customer testing. In some respects, the introduction of the Disc Camera represents a model blending of marketing, marketing research, and research and development personnel as partners in a new venture.

Research is often less dramatic but at least as prevalent among existing brands. Consider Gillette and its mature products; razors and razor blades. Their research includes annual national surveys of men and women, an annual interview of an existing panel, a national telephone brand awareness study, numerous consumer use tests, and their own as well as syndicated retail audits. Thus, the collection of information plays a crucial role in many companies.

The basic thrust of this chapter is that the value of information is related to the improvement it leads to in actual decisions. When considering the value of information, it is important to recognize that many uses of information are only indirectly related to decisions or profit and loss calculations, or both. Hence, in addition to aiding decision making, information also is collected for the following reasons:

Tradition. As is the case with any organization, patterns of behavior become established. A budget allocated to research is a budget that will be spent. While marketing research typically is a very weak competitor in the bureaucratic battles for funds, it does have a certain permanence: those involved in information collection and analysis tend to recommend further research.

To gain agreement. Often research is used not to influence the person who orders the research (who has already made a decision) but as a document to gain support for the decision within the organization. Here research serves both a legitimization and a quality control function.

To prepare a defense in case of failure. Research serves as a defense in case a decision goes awry. While there is a fairly low limit to the number of blunders a person can be associated with and still be employed, it is a lot easier to explain a decision if you can produce a report which said it was the right one.

To stall. One of the best ways to delay a decision is to postpone it by suggesting that it can be studied further.

Legal. An increasing amount of research is related to legal issues, such as claim substantiation and trademark infringement. Also, deceptive advertising complaints to the FTC create a demand for marketing research studies.

PR / advertising. Research often serves as the basis for advertising claims (e.g., "7 of 10 doctors..."). Here its role is to convince consumers of either the truth of a particular claim or of the trustworthiness and high-mindedness of the company in general.

Consciousness raising. In some cases, conducting a study is designed to focus attention of either respondents or interviewers on a topic. For example, a manager at a major computer manufacturer recently used a customer survey as a way of increasing the sensitivity of the sales force to particular nontechnical benefits and problems from the customer's perspective.

Obviously, all of these help explain why information is collected. Nonetheless, much information is collected for the express purpose of aiding a particular decision, and it is to those situations that this chapter most directly applies.

This chapter deals with the measurement of the value of information. There are many decisions where the situation is sufficiently clear that no additional information is likely to change the decision, and hence the value of information is very small. (For example, if the boss asks if you'd like to get coffee, the answer is, "How much?") On the other hand, some decisions cry out for information which may not be available at any price. (For example, secret information about the price of Polaroid stock six months in the future would be crucial to the decision whether to buy or sell the stock, except for certain legal issues.) More likely, however, is a situation where information will improve the odds of making a good decision (such as getting a better measure of the market potential for a new product).

The concept of the odds of making a good decision is crucial to the concept of the value of information. For example, assume that a decision maker is faced with a tough decision—one where there are two choices and each one seems about equally likely to be correct. By relying on experience the decision maker might be able to increase the odds of choosing the correct action from 50 : 50 to 60 : 40. By collecting the best available information, the odds might be increased from 60 : 40 to 80 : 20 in favor of making the correct decision. Hence, the value of information in this case comes in increasing the chance of the correct decision from three out of five to four out of five. Information is not perfect (there is still a one in five chance of making a wrong decision), and in fact it is possible that we will make the wrong decision after collecting information, whereas we would have made the correct decision without the information. Still, over the long run, one is clearly better off with information than without it whenever there is uncertainty about the consequences of alternative decisions.

Another point worth making is that unless a decision changes as the result of information, then the information has no value in this context. This truism has two separate levels of meaning. First, unless the manager is willing to change his or her mind based on data, then the data collection is an unnecessary expense. Second, if all the decisions after information collection are to go and the prior decision was also to go, the information has no value. For example, it could be relatively obvious that we wish to enter a market. If we collected further information, we might better pinpoint the size of the market but we would be so unlikely to find an inadequate market that for the purpose of the enter/not enter decision, the information would not be worth anything. This leads to two other key points. In general, information is most useful in cases (1) where we are most unsure what to do and (2) where there are extreme values (either huge losses or profits) which would be extremely important if they came to pass. What collecting information really does is lower the odds that you will go ahead with a flop or, conversely, fail to proceed with a success. Exactly how much information is worth depends on the following three basic things:

1. The amount the odds of making the correct decision increase when the information is collected and used.
2. The relative benefit (profitability) of the alternative decisions.
3. The cost of the information.

This chapter proceeds by presenting a formal framework for decision making and then for evaluating the worth of information. While this framework is rarely used in a formal sense, both the logical structure itself and concepts concerning the value of information are worth emphasizing. The chapter closes by reemphasizing some "real world" considerations in assessing the value of information. The reader is warned that the treatment that follows is at least semiformal. If such treatment leads to intimidation or frustration, the reader should concentrate on understanding the concept of the value of information since this is by far the most important concept in the chapter.

DECISION ANALYSIS AND INFORMATION VALUE: CONCEPT

Before discussing decision analysis and the value of information in detail, it is useful to highlight the concepts.

The concepts are illustrated by considering the case of whether to introduce a new product. New product introduction is a risky undertaking, with the risk varying by, among other things, the level of study prior to entering the market, the relative benefits and costs of the new product versus the products it competes with, and the general level of competitive activity.

In structuring the decision, one first needs to identify the possible decisions. Here we will assume the possible decisions are to go ahead and introduce the product, to not introduce the product, or to conduct a test of the product, and then either go ahead or not. Next we need to specify the possible results. While clearly there are an infinite number of results (e.g., sales = 0 units, 1 unit, 2 units, . . .), we can (over)simplify this by considering only two levels of sales: low and high.

The consequences of the various combinations of decisions and market results are pretty obvious. Introducing the product to a low sales level leads to a loss, while introducing it to a high level leads to a gain. Not proceeding has no cost or profit associated with it. Performing the test adds to the cost.

Notice that we are ignoring the very real possibility that the study would uncover information that would allow us to improve a product and thus improve the chances of a high sales level. This simplification is made solely to prevent the discussion from becoming any more complicated than it already is.

We now need to assess how likely each of the possible results is. In this case, we begin by assuming that the likelihood of a successful new product is so low that, if we directly introduce the product, sales are more likely to be low than high (i.e., the likelihood of low sales is high and high sales are low). Next we consider how likely a test is to produce a positive result. Since, at least for most new products which are relatively similar to existing ones, test results are likely to be better than market results, we assume the likelihoods of negative or positive results are both about 50 percent. Assuming we get a negative result, we know from experience that the chances of a low sales level are very high and those of a high sales level very low. On the other hand, if we get a positive result we have learned that there is a moderate chance of then achieving both a low and high level of sales.

FIGURE 2–1 Conceptual Example: Product Introduction and Testing

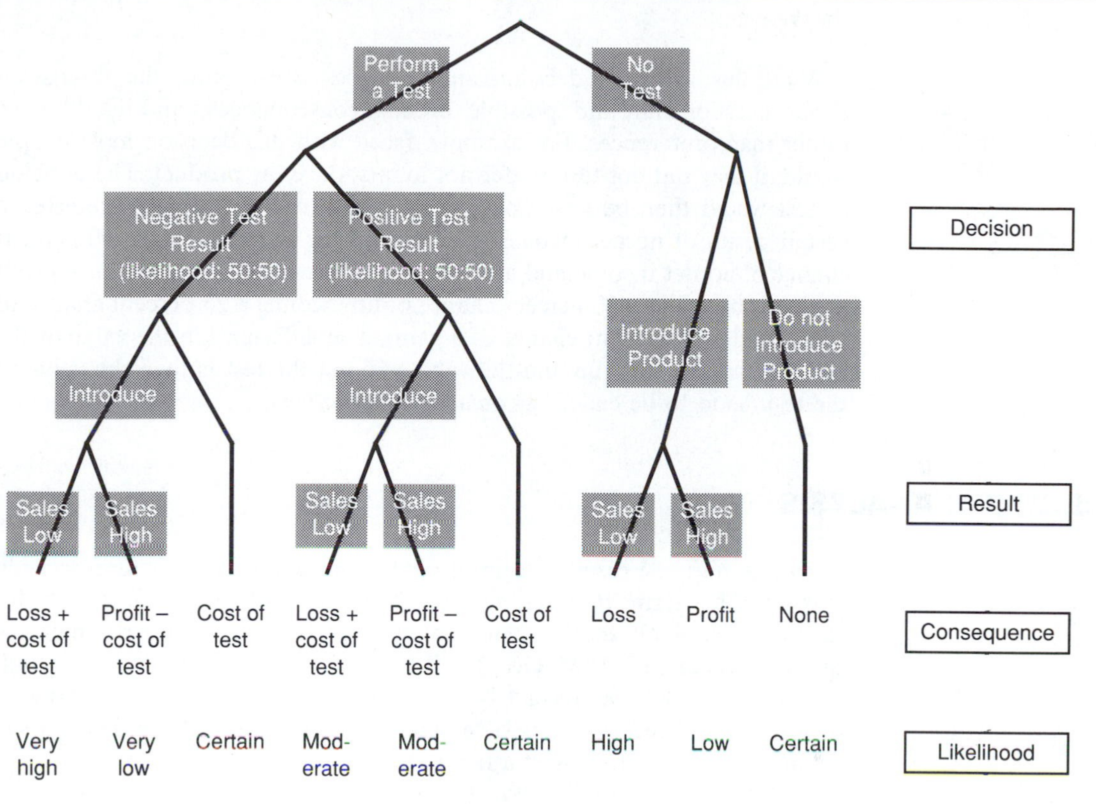

This information is summarized in the tree in Figure 2–1. The viable decisions are thus pretty clear: don't introduce, introduce without testing, or test and proceed to introduce if the test result is positive (it generally makes no sense to test and ignore the results, which going ahead after a negative test would imply). The impact of these decisions can be summarized as follows:

Do not introduce. You are certain that there will be no impact (loss or profit).

Introduce without test. The likelihood is high you will incur a loss and low you will produce a profit.

Test. There is about a 50 percent chance you will introduce the product with a moderate chance of a loss and a moderate chance of a gain, and a 50 percent chance you will decide, based on the negative test result, not to introduce the product. You are certain you have to pay for the test.

What this informal decision analysis does is structure the discussion about decisions around possible events, consequences, and likelihoods, rather than preferences. For example, faced with this decision most people would, if they did not test, prefer not to introduce the product. The decision to test would then be based on whether the decision maker(s) preferred a certain result of no net income or to pay for the test and have a 50 percent chance of no net income and a 50 percent chance of either a loss or a profit (which is basically a 50 percent chance of no income, a 25 percent chance of a loss, and a 25 percent chance of a gain). The difference in the value of the result if the test was run and the value without the test is then the value of the test (soon to be called *the value of information*).

DECISION ANALYSIS

In this section, we discuss decision analysis as a way to structure decision making. The term *decision analysis* refers to a logical framework for choosing among alternative courses of action. Much has been written on the subject (Assmus, 1977; MaGee, 1964; Raiffa, 1968; Schlaiffer, 1959) including a fairly readable recent book by Jones (1977). The framework is typically visualized in terms of a tree diagram (Figure 2–1). The typical method of constructing such a tree is as follows:

1. Delineate the possible courses of action.
2. List the possible results ("states of nature") of each course of action.
3. Estimate the payoff (usually in monetary terms) of each possible combination of courses of action and results.
4. Assign likelihoods of occurrence (probabilities) to the different possible results for each given course of action.
5. Select the course of action which seems to lead to the most desirable results.

Example

To see how decision analysis is used more formally, consider the following problem: The XYZ Transportation Company, which specializes in freight deliveries, is considering a new rate on its New York to Boston route. (For the moment, assume that government regulations, such as the Interstate Commerce Commission rules, do not apply.) In the past, there has been a two-tier pricing system for one-pound packages: $20 for "first class," which guarantees next-day delivery, and $10 for "regular," which typically takes two to three days. We are now considering instituting a same-day delivery service at the price of $30 or $40 (we have a thing about prices in $10 increments and will consider no other prices—boss's orders). After some preliminary analysis, we decide that one of three possible results is likely to occur if we price at $30: getting 100, 60, or 20 new packages per day. Similarly, if we price at $40, we can get either 50, 30, or 5 new packages per day.

Also, at the new prices, we expect some of our present customers to "trade up" to the new service. At the $30 price, we think either 20 or 30 packages per day will be sent same-day instead of first class, whereas at $40, either 10 or 20 will move to same-day.

The daily cost of setting up and running the new service will be $700. The variable costs to send a package by the three classes of service are: $18 for same-day, $12 for first class, and $8 for regular. What should we do?

Even though this is a fairly simple situation, the data are sufficiently extensive to make analyzing the decision in one's head fairly complicated. Hence, to provide a structure to the decision-making process, one could quite logically begin by drawing a tree to represent the situation (Figure 2–2).

Having delineated the situation faced by identifying (*a*) the courses of action and (*b*) the possible results (outcomes), one would now proceed to

FIGURE 2–2 Package Pricing Decision Tree

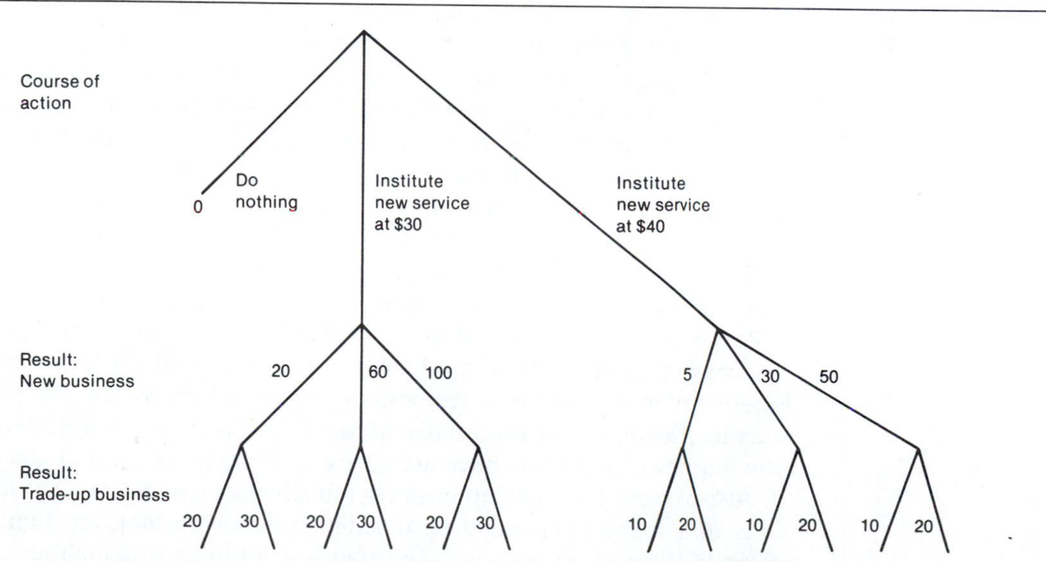

TABLE 2–1 Profit Results Given Different Market Results

Course of Action; New Service Price	*Result: New Business*	*Result: Trade-Up Business*	*Incremental Daily Profit**
None	—	—	0
$30	20	20	320 − 700 = −380
		30	360 − 700 = −340
	60	20	800 − 700 = 100
		30	840 − 700 = 140
	100	20	1,280 − 700 = 580
		30	1,320 − 700 = 620
40	5	10	250 − 700 = −450
		20	390 − 700 = −310
	30	10	800 − 700 = 100
		20	940 − 700 = 240
	50	10	1,240 − 700 = 540
		20	1,380 − 700 = 680

*For the $30 price, incremental profit is $12 × New Business + $4 × Trade-up business − $700; whereas for $40, incremental profit is $22 × New business + $14 × Trade-up business − $700.

estimate (*c*) the monetary consequences of each of the possible results. Consider the value of a single new piece of business at the $30 price. Since XYZ gets $30 and it costs them $18, they gain $12 for each new piece of business. Similarly, for everyone who trades up, they make $12 instead of $20 − $12 = $8 for a net gain of $4. Hence, for the result of 20 new packages plus 20 "trade-ups," they would make incrementally 20 × $12 + 20 × $4 = $320 per day. When the fixed cost of $700 per day is figured in, the incremental profit becomes $320 − $700 = −$380. (Note here that we are using the incremental profit compared with doing nothing. We could also have calculated actual profit but chose incremental because, quite frankly, the numbers are smaller.) One can get the profit results for each of the profit combinations in a similar manner (Table 2–1).

Having identified the profit implications of the various results, the next step is to estimate the relative likelihoods of the different possible results. This is typically done by assigning probabilities to each of the possible branches of the tree. These probabilities may be based on survey results, experience in analogous situations, or expert judgment. In the present situation, assume that the probabilities of the different possible levels of new business for the $30 price are 20 units, .2; 60 units, .5; and 100 units, .3. Also assume the trade-up business probabilities are 20 units, .6; and 30 units, .4. For the $40 price, the probabilities of new business are 5 units, .2; 30 units, .6; and 50 units, .2. The trade-up business probabilities are 10

FIGURE 2–3 Package Pricing Decision Tree with Probabilities and Profits

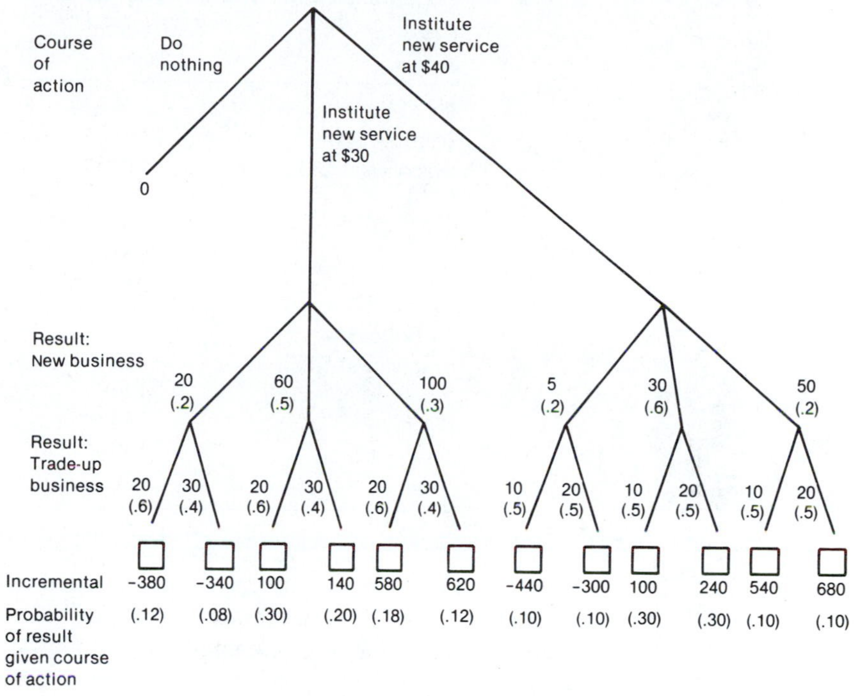

Course of action: Do nothing — 0; Institute new service at $30; Institute new service at $40

Result: New business

$30: 20 (.2) | 60 (.5) | 100 (.3)

$40: 5 (.2) | 30 (.6) | 50 (.2)

Result: Trade-up business

$30: 20 (.6) 30 (.4) | 20 (.6) 30 (.4) | 20 (.6) 30 (.4)

$40: 10 (.5) 20 (.5) | 10 (.5) 20 (.5) | 10 (.5) 20 (.5)

Incremental	-380	-340	100	140	580	620	-440	-300	100	240	540	680
Probability of result given course of action	(.12)	(.08)	(.30)	(.20)	(.18)	(.12)	(.10)	(.10)	(.30)	(.30)	(.10)	(.10)

units, .5; and 20 units, .5. The decision tree can then be redrawn with the appropriate probabilities[1] and profits (Figure 2–3).

In order to estimate the probability of a particular profit for a given course of action, simply multiply the probabilities of the results which must occur to produce the profit result. For example, 20 new packages and 20 trade-ups produce an incremental profit of −\$380. The probability of the result of 20 new and 20 trade-up packages for a \$30 price is thus $.2 \times .6 = .12$.

Thus each course of action produces a distribution of possible profits with probabilities attached to them (Table 2–2). Hence, the decision about

[1]The "appropriate" probabilities are called conditional probabilities. The probability of trade-up business being 20 when new business is 20 might well be different from the probability that trade-up business would be 20 if new business were 100. (This could happen if one believed that the service would either be a big success all around or a consistent failure.) Hence, the probability of 20 units of trade-up business could depend/be conditional on the level of new business. For the sake of simplicity, however, this example assumes the trade-up business achieved will be unrelated to/independent of the level of new business.

TABLE 2–2 Profit Distributions for Three Possible Courses of Action

Course of Action	*Incremental Profit*	*Probability of Profit*
Do nothing	0	1.0
Institute new service at $30	−380	.12
	−340	.08
	100	.30
	140	.20
	580	.18
	520	.12
Institute new service at $40	−450	.10
	−310	.10
	100	.30
	240	.30
	540	.10
	580	.10

which course of action to take has been converted to a decision about which distribution of results is more appealing. Several selection procedures are possible. Three of the most common are as follows:

1. Choose that decision which guarantees the best result if everything goes wrong. This criterion (known as *minimax*) is the most conservative procedure and leads to very conservative decisions—in this case, doing nothing since both the other decisions could lose money and doing nothing would keep profits constant.

2. Choose the decision which gives the chance for the best possible result. This is the gamble strategy (called *maximax*) which explains why people are willing to buy lottery tickets—they are willing to expect to lose a little money on the chance they will earn a lot. Since the $40 price offers the greatest potential gain ($680 if 50 packages are generated and 20 trade-up), the new service would be instituted at a $40 price under this criterion.

3. Choose that course of action which provides the largest expected monetary reward. This is the criterion most often associated with decision trees (although not necessarily the best one). It requires calculating the expected monetary consequences of each of the possible courses of action by "weighting" the possible monetary results by their probabilities of occurrence. In the present example, this involves the following:

a. Do nothing.

b. Institute the new service at $30 and expect to make $164 per day incremental profit (Table 2–3).

c. Institute the new service at $40 and expect to make $148 per day incremental profit (Table 2–4).

TABLE 2–3 Expected Incremental Profit of $30 Price

Result				
New Business	*Trade-Up Business*	*(A) Increment in Daily Profit: IP|R*	*(B) Probability of Result: P(R)*	*(A) × (B)*
20	20	−380	.12	$ −45.60
	30	−340	.08	−27.20
60	20	100	.30	+30.00
	30	140	.20	+28.00
100	20	580	.18	+104.40
	30	620	.12	+74.40
				$ 164.00

TABLE 2–4 Expected Incremental Profit of $40 Price

Result				
New Business	*Trade-Up Business*	*(A) Increment in Daily Profit: IP|R*	*(B) Probability of Result: P(R)*	*(A) × (B)*
5	10	−450	.10	$ −45.00
	20	−310	.10	−31.00
30	10	100	.30	+30.00
	20	240	.30	+72.00
50	10	540	.10	+54.00
	20	680	.10	+68.00
				$ 148.00

Since the $164 per day net incremental profit from instituting the service at the $30 price is the maximum of the three possibilities, we would institute the new service at $30.

Summary of the Problems with Using Decision Trees

Decision analysis has been around for a long time, and its pros and cons are fairly well known (MaGee, 1964; Villani and Morrison, 1976). There are a number of problems inherent in using decision trees. They are discussed in this section.

Specifying the Alternative Courses of Action and Their Consequences. In many situations the alternatives are fairly clear-cut. For example, the phone company's choices in raising pay-phone charges were/are pretty much limited to 15 cents, 20 cents, or 25 cents, given the equipment already in place. Similarly, a product manager at some stage may be faced with a choice between launching a new product nationally or regionally, test marketing it, doing further tests or refinements, or dropping it. What makes things complicated is the possible responses of competition or, as is becoming more important, regulatory bodies or lobbying groups. Since these responses can affect both the results (i.e., if the rate case finds against the phone company, they can't charge 25 cents) and their profitability (beating back consumer or competitive challenges is expensive), these potential responses can greatly complicate the tree. Even in the example used in this chapter, we would expect some probability that the rate would not be approved by the appropriate regulatory agency and a good likelihood that competition would react to the new service in some way. These would in turn lead to further actions by XYZ, Inc. In short a series of courses of action and results are needed to realistically represent most decisions.

Finally, it is important to recognize that for a "real" problem, no single tree is drawn. Rather, a first-cut tree is constructed to select those alternatives which seem most promising. Then the other branches of the tree are dropped and those which are retained are refined, sometimes by collecting data, until the "best" decision emerges.

Estimating Possible Results and Their Probabilities. There are three basic sources of the possible results of a decision and their probabilities: logic/deduction, past experience/empirical evidence, and subjective estimates.

1. *Logic/deduction.* In certain very simple situations, it is possible to deduce the probabilities of the results from the situation. For example, the probability of a head on the flip of a coin, a 7 on the roll of two dice, or a full house in a game of poker can be deduced from the situation and a few basic rules of probability and statistics (although students have a disarming tendency to do so incorrectly on tests). Unfortunately, in most marketing research situations, this method is not applicable.

2. *Past experience/empirical evidence.* Past experience is one source of estimates of the possible results and their probabilities. When Procter & Gamble introduces a new soap, it has a pretty sound idea of possible sales levels because it has introduced so many similar products in the past. Similarly, data analysis is often performed and sales levels forecast based on models using such variables as GNP, market growth rate, and so forth. The models in turn can be used to formally generate the probabilities of different results. Unfortunately, the past data and analyses rarely seem perfectly compatible with the situation under consideration. Hence, the analysis of past data typically only serves as a basis for subjective estimates of the possible results and their probabilities.

3. *Subjective estimates.* In the absence of hard data, a manager must make guesses about what the results will be. While these guesses should be based on as much analysis and experience as possible, they still involve some subjectivity. It is this subjectivity that, for many people, causes the greatest consternation over the use of decision analysis.

The first major issue in obtaining subjective estimates of the possible results and their probabilities is to decide from whom to collect the estimates. Aside from the obvious—finding someone who is knowledgeable, honest, and willing to provide estimates—knowing exactly who to talk to is something of an art. One obvious source is salespersons who are in direct contact with buyers and hopefully (but not always actually) in tune with the market. Another source is so-called experts, both inside and outside the organization. Since the responsibility for the decision under consideration will ultimately fall on someone, however, it is appropriate to involve the person or persons (i.e., the product manager) whose evaluation depends on the decision in estimating possible results and their probabilities. (A side benefit of this is that those people who give estimates will be involved in the analysis and, therefore, more committed to the results. This benefit can, of course, turn into a cost if individuals involved give false probabilities to affect the outcome of the analysis.)

The second major issue in assessing the possible results and their probabilities is how to obtain them. This turns out to be a very tricky task since most people don't understand probability concepts (Tversky and Kahneman, 1974). The most obvious approach is to directly ask an individual to list the possible results and their probabilities of occurring. Unfortunately, many people (and especially nonquantitatively oriented managers) don't respond well to such direct assessments of probabilities; and when they do respond, they are often inaccurate. Hence, a variety of devices are employed to get the probabilities less directly.

The most commonly used gambit to elicit probabilities involves asking an individual to indicate various levels which sales will exceed with a certain likelihood. For example, the individual might be asked to indicate:

1. What level will sales exceed 90 percent of the time (e.g., 5,000 units).
2. What level will sales exceed 50 percent of the time (e.g., 10,000 units).
3. What level will sales exceed only 10 percent of the time (e.g., 20,000 units).

By using the answers to these questions, a researcher can develop an entire distribution of possible results (Figure 2–4).

Alternatively, a researcher may ask a key individual to first list some possible results. Then the researcher can ask the individual to indicate the relative likelihood of occurrence (from which probabilities of the results can be deduced). Detailed discussion of methods for eliciting results and their probabilities is beyond the scope of this book. For further reading, see Hogarth, 1975; Jones, 1977; Sarin, 1978; Savage, 1971; Winkler, 1967a,b. Suffice it to say that elicitation of accurate probabilities is a doable but not a trivial task.

FIGURE 2–4 Derived Distribution of Possible Sales Levels

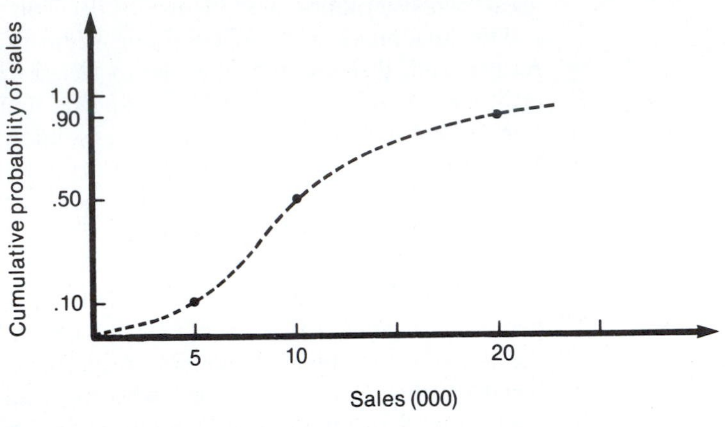

Considerable opposition exists to using subjective probabilities. This comes from two basic schools of thought. The first position of opposition is that anything based on subjective probabilities is essentially worthless. Assuming the person making the estimates has experience, the subjective estimates will in fact be based on data (experience in analogous situations, etc.). The difference between subjective and data-based estimates (which should be and typically are subjectively adjusted) is, thus, not as great as it first appears. The other major opposition to using subjective probabilities is that since they are not perfectly accurate or easy to obtain, they are not worthwhile. Development of the probabilities of results is a nontrivial task. It is, however, doable.

Assessing the Monetary Consequences of the Different Combinations of Courses of Action and Results. While this is possibly the easiest of the problems to deal with, it is by no means trivial. For example, estimating future costs of production given changes in energy costs, raw material prices, and so forth, is very difficult. Hence, the monetary consequences are really estimates whose effect on the decisions should usually be checked at least by sensitivity analysis if not by incorporating multiple monetary results and attendant probabilities into the decision tree.

Choosing an Appropriate Criterion. The most obvious criterion to apply is expected monetary value. Indeed, this is a good criterion to use only in the case of repetitive decisions which are independent of each other and are not so large as to greatly affect the organization depending on the results. The independence notion is rarely true, since the condition of the general economy alone dictates that either most things go well or many go sour together. Also, unfortunately, in many cases the decision will have sufficiently large impact that it will affect the organization, or at least the subpart of it with which the decision maker is associated. For example, certain possible results may seriously damage the financial position of the company, and decisions leading to these will typically be avoided in going concerns.

Another barrier to the expected value criterion is individual behavior. Since turning a profitable product into an unprofitable one may lead to being fired, whereas doubling profits may only lead to a 10 percent raise, the personal consequences of the results may be asymmetric and, hence, the expected value criterion inappropriate. In short, individuals may be understandably more cautious (risk averse) than is implied by the expected value criterion.

It is possible to develop a formula which translates the different monetary results into utilities and then to compute expected utilities. A more pragmatic approach, however, is to calculate the expected value and simply check to see if any of the likely results of the indicated decision are sufficiently bad to cause reconsideration and possibly a change to a less risky decision. It is also sometimes appropriate to check other decisions that result in lower expected values to see if there is a possible result under these decisions that is so desirable it is worth going against averages.

Sensitivity Analysis

Given the fact that any decision tree is typically at best a facsimile of the world, it is useful to examine the sensitivity of a decision to small changes in the tree. For example, would changing the new business demand estimates in Figure 2–3 change the decision? If changing the estimates in the tree does not change the decision, then the decision is relatively insensitive to those estimates, giving one more confidence that the decision is optimal. If, on the other hand, the decision changes as a result of small changes in the tree, then it is less easy to argue strongly that the optimal decision is known.

Whenever sensitivity analysis reveals something on which a decision does seem to depend, it suggests that this type of information is relatively crucial and is possibly worth further investigation. Put more simply, if a decision is portrayed as a tree, then those pieces of information which seem to affect the decision are those which should be further studied. While this sounds obvious, many dollars have been spent fine-tuning advertising copy when the major uncertainty was the possible entrance of a new competitor or a ban by the FDA. Hence, one should generally study those elements of a decision that (*a*) matter (no sense studying irrelevant material, as any student knows), (*b*) are uncertain (no sense studying something that is already known), and (*c*) can be learned about (if you can't reasonably expect to reduce uncertainty, it is not very intelligent to spend much money trying to do so).

Summary

Having spent considerable time pointing out the weaknesses of decision trees, it is important to indicate that they still are useful devices. Their major advantage is that they create structure in what appear to be largely unstructured situations. It seems far more constructive to have people debating the likely results in sales of a decision, rather than arguing whether they like the decision or not. (Such discussions are also more likely to be based on facts than on political clout or debating skills.) There is also some evidence which suggests that breaking a decision into small parts leads to better decisions. Decision trees also provide an indication of what key uncertainties exist. If the expected value criterion is used, it provides a very useful starting point for deciding what to do. In short, given an uncertain world, decision trees are a useful device for structuring a problem and getting an indication (relatively quickly and inexpensively) of what is the best decision to make. Since managers are ultimately judged more by results than by method, however, it is the managers' prerogative to make choices any way they choose.

VALUE OF INFORMATION: QUANTITATIVE ASSESSMENT

Before investing time and money in collecting information about a decision, most people make a judgment (at least implicitly) on whether the information will be worth the trouble. Consider, for example, an individual choosing a new dishwasher. That person may already have a choice in mind (e.g., I have a GE now that I bought from store A and it worked well, so I will buy a GE there next time). In deciding whether to gather more information (e.g., read *Consumer Reports*, shop around, etc.), several major considerations exist as follows:

1. Under what kind of time pressure is the individual? (For example, is the present dishwasher flooding the kitchen or just getting old? How much "free" time does the individual have?)
2. How easy is it to collect more information? (For example, does the individual subscribe to *Consumer Reports*, live in an area where shopping is easy, etc.?)
3. What is the cost of a bad decision? (To illustrate, what is the cost of buying another new machine, cost of a service contract, etc.?)

4. How different are the available alternatives? (For example, does which brand is bought make much difference in terms of either length of life or quality of service?)
5. How likely is it that more information will change the decision? (For example, if the individual is fairly certain that he or she will buy a GE at store A, then more information is probably irrelevant.)

Of these considerations, 1 and 2 are related to the cost of information, 3 and 4 to the relative results of the alternative decisions, and 5 to the relative odds of making a good decision with and without more information. If a sample of people were asked whether they would collect information in a set of situations/scenarios, we would expect more of them to collect information when (*a*) the cost of information was low, (*b*) there was a noticeable difference among alternatives, and (*c*) they felt a relative high degree of uncertainty about which decision alternative to select.

While the preceding seems sensible, it does not directly produce a quantitative assessment of the value of additional information. In order to get a quantitative assessment, one procedure uses decision trees. The procedure has three basic steps:

1. Build a decision tree for the situation assuming current information. Then calculate the optimal decision and its expected value (EV|CI).
2. Build a decision tree for the situation assuming that additional information were available. Then calculate the optimal decision given the additional information and its expected value (EV|AI).
3. Estimate the expected value of additional information (EVAI) as EVAI = EV|AI − EV|CI. Hence the value of information is the expected improvement in profit which would result if the information were obtained.

Example

A more complete discussion of the methodology appears in the Appendix to this chapter. However, for illustrative purposes a simpler example will be used here. Assume an individual is trying to decide whether to put money in the bank (and end up with $50) or to buy a stock (which will end up worth either $10 or $80). If the individual buys the stock, it seems equally likely it will be worth $10 or $80 given current information. Hence we get the picture in Figure 2–5. The expected values of the two decisions are as follows:

Put money in the bank: $50(1.0) = $50
Buy the stock: $10(.5) + $80(.5) = $45

FIGURE 2–5 Decision Tree with Current Information

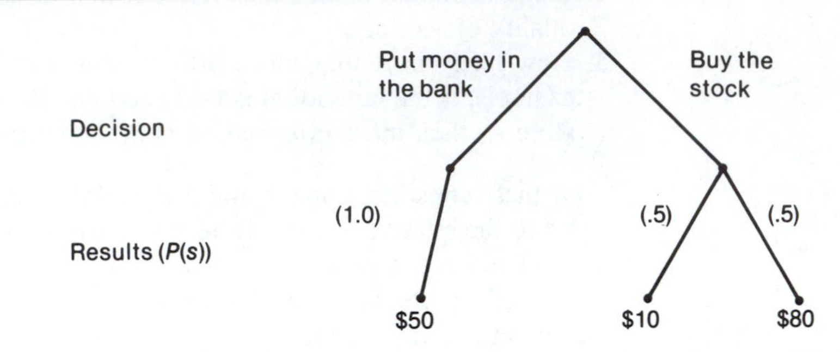

Hence, given current information, we would put the money in the bank and EV|CI = $50.

Now assume we could get a research report on the stock which would be either unfavorable (in which case, the probability that the stock value would be $10 increases to .66) or favorable (in which case, the probability that the stock value would be $10 decreases to .26). Also assume that we expect the probability of an unfavorable report is .60. We can represent the choices given this additional information by Figure 2–6.

FIGURE 2–6 Decision Tree with Additional Information

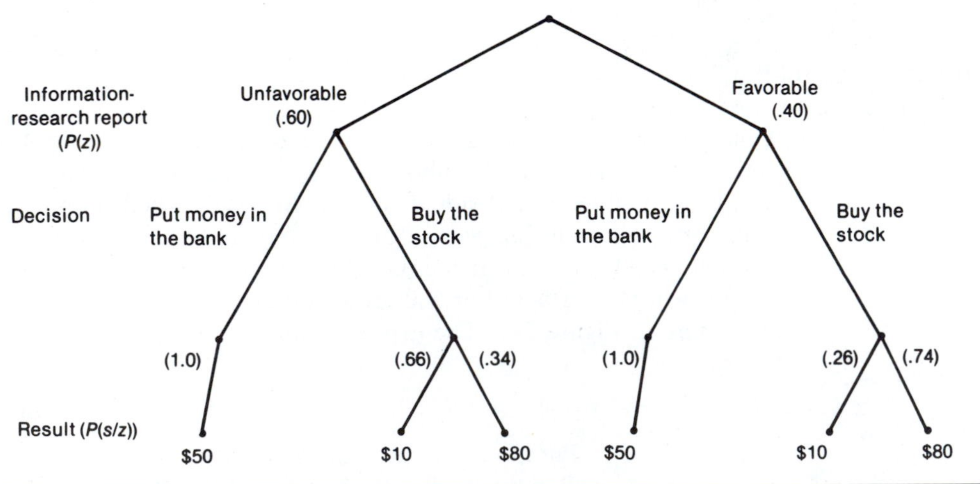

The results of the two decisions under the two possible research reports are determined as follows:

Unfavorable report:

Put money in the bank: \$50(1.0) = \$50
Buy the stock: \$10(.66) + \$80(.34) = \$33.80

Favorable report:

Put money in the bank: \$50(1.0) = \$50
Buy the stock: \$10(.26) + \$80(.74) = \$61.80

Hence, given an unfavorable report, we would, not surprisingly, put the money in the bank and make \$50; while given a favorable report we would buy the stock and expect to make \$61.80. Since 60 percent of the time we expect an unfavorable report, the expected value given additional information is given by:

$$\begin{aligned} EV|AI &= \$50(.60) + \$61.80(.40) \\ &= \$54.72 \end{aligned}$$

Thus, the expected value of the additional information (in this case the research report) is:

$$\begin{aligned} EVAI &= EV|AI - EV|CI \\ &= \$54.72 - \$50.00 \\ &= \$4.72 \end{aligned}$$

This approach is relatively easy to extend to more complex situations. The problem in applying the approach comes in obtaining reasonable estimates for the monetary results which are possible, the prior probabilities of these results, the probabilities of the various possible results of additional information, and the probabilities of each of the actual results given the information. In many situations, these probabilities are hard to deduce even with considerable effort. For this and other reasons, it is often useful to calculate an upper limit on the value of additional information.

To calculate the upper limit on the value of information, two steps are employed:

1. Calculate the optimal decisions given perfect information (i.e., the decision which you would make if you knew what the result would be in advance) and its expected value (EV|PI).

2. Calculate the expected value of perfect information (EVPI) as $EVPI = EV|PI - EV|CI$.

Returning to the example in Figure 2–5, we see that, if the stock value would go to $10, we would want our money in the bank (and make $50); while if the stock value would go to $80, then we would want to buy stock (and make $80). Since half the time the stock value will be $10 and half the time $80:

$$\begin{aligned} EV|PI &= \$50(.5) + \$80(.5) \\ &= \$65 \end{aligned}$$

Hence:

$$\begin{aligned} EVPI &= EV|PI - EV|CI \\ &= \$65 - \$50 \\ &= \$15 \end{aligned}$$

The most we would be willing to pay for information would be $15. If someone offered to sell us research for $20, we would politely decline the offer no matter how good the person's forecasting record was.

Limitations on Quantitatively Assessing the Value of Information

The methodology just described for quantitatively assessing the value of information, once learned, is relatively simple to apply. Its conceptual use is widespread. Yet its application in a formal sense is limited. There are several reasons for this limited use. They are as follows:

Difficulty in Application. It is possible to argue that the technique is not used because it is perceived to be hard to apply. This argument is, however, both largely incorrect and self-serving. The cost of using such procedures is fairly low; and its lack of use must be even lower, indicating other explanations are needed.

The Expected Value Criterion Does Not Apply. This limitation is an important one. For a small firm, operating on an expected value basis ignores the very real problem of bankruptcy. Similarly, the job security of an individual may require avoidance of bad results more than attainment of spectacular ones.

Prima Facie Decisions. Many apparent decisions may in fact be preordained. This can be due to the fact that the situation dictates the decision (i.e., if I'm a small firm producing a commodity, I may have to match price cuts). Alternatively, it may be that political realities dictate a decision. (We may all know that the idea is dumb; but if it is the boss's pet idea, we may prefer to have the market test tell the boss so.)

Company Policy. In many cases, it is company policy to proceed in a certain manner. For example, it may be policy to test commercials on samples of 100 in Albany, New York. Therefore, the value of information is not the issue—the only feasible course of action is to proceed. (It is, of course, possible to argue that the company policy is in need of revision. While this may make you a star, it is more likely to make you unpopular, unemployed, or both.)

INFORMATION NEED AND VALUE INFLUENCES

Having spent considerable effort on assessing the value of information, we concluded that it is the improvement in profit which would occur if the information were available. The value of information is related to several factors.

The accuracy of obtainable information. Obviously the more accurate the information, the greater its value.

The cost (both dollar and time) of information. Data already on hand or contracted for are relatively costless, while collecting new data is both costly and time-consuming.

The ability and willingness to accept information and act accordingly. The more receptive management is to information, the greater the value of the information.

The lack of clarity over what the right answer is. The more obvious the decision, the less the need for information.

The extreme results and their consequences. The more serious the extreme results are, the greater the need for information.

The degree of risk aversion both on a company and personal level. The greater the risk aversion, the greater the information need. On a personal level, getting the right information may protect one to some extent in case the decision is bad. (At least we can blame luck or some other factor rather than lack of diligence.)

Competitive reaction to information gathering in terms of "jamming" the information and being given more time to plan a counterattack. Competitors will often do their best to destroy the information value of data collection, especially test markets where tripling advertising, cutting price, and offering large trade deals to fill the channels of distribution are only a few of the common gambits. The motivation for this is to feed you bad information and make it harder for you to make the right decision. Also, the more time you spend gathering data, the more obvious it becomes to competitors what you are planning to do and the more time they have to react to it.

Company policy. Company policy often dictates the "need" for information collection.

The need to gain agreement. Information collection is perhaps most important in that it facilitates the establishment of reasonable agreement among the many parties to a decision about the advisability of the decision and the way to proceed.

The need to stall/build momentum. Often a decision is sufficiently controversial that people look for a way to postpone it. Opponents of a position who feel open opposition is unwise can and do line up in favor of gathering more data, a much less risky position. By the same logic, supporters of a proposal who believe they do not have sufficient support to push the proposal through at the present may suggest getting data (a "pilot" study) to determine feasibility as a means of getting a toe in the door.

SUMMARY

The formal determination of the value information can be a fairly tricky task. Nonetheless, the concept of comparing the value of information with its cost is a useful step. In doing so, it is essential to define both benefits and costs broadly enough to take into account the positions and proclivities of the various parties to the decision. Based on the assumption that at least occasionally one will find information of positive value (a hoped-for result if those individuals in market research positions are to continue to eat), the rest of this book is devoted to alternative means of collecting, analyzing, and utilizing information.

PROBLEMS

1. Assume you were considering changing the formulation of a food product by substituting one ingredient for an existing one.
   a. List the concerns you would have.
   b. Draw a decision tree to represent the problem.

2. What do you think would be the value of additional information in each of the following situations:
   a. A decision by P&G about whether to market Tide next year.
   b. A decision about which style dial to put on GE dishwashers this year.
   c. A decision whether or not to drill an oil well.
   d. A decision to launch a new packaged goods product.
   e. A decision to change the format of a ballet company's performances.
3. Bernie C. owns an ice truck. He sells ice cream on his lunch hour. When the weather is good, hot, and humid, he can net about $120 per day at the beach or about $60 per day if he sells ice cream around his home. When the weather is poor, cold, and rainy, his net at the beach is about $15 per day, and at home about $25 per day.

   In this area, there is a 20 percent chance of fair weather (and therefore an 80 percent chance of poor weather).
   a. What should Bernie do?
   b. How much should Bernie pay for a perfect forecast?
   c. How much should Bernie pay for an 80 percent reliable weather forecasting service? (The probability of forecast matching weather is .8.)
4. Draw a decision tree that would help the phone company assess the effect of raising the price of pay-phone calls 10 cents.
5. In consiering three different positioning strategies for Slurp, a new soft drink, I assume one of three possible market conditions can occur. These will influence the profits as follows:

Market Condition			
I	*II*	*III*	*Position*
12	14	18	Conservative
16	12	12	Moderate
4	8	30	Flaky

   My subjective estimates of the probabilities of the three market conditions are .5, .3, and .2 respectively.
   a. With no other information, what should I do?
   b. What is the most I would pay for information about which market condition will occur?
   c. A firm proposes to test what market condition will exist. It traditionally is right 80 percent of the time. When it is wrong, it is equally likely that anything else can happen. How much is this firm's research worth to me?

6. Assume demand for a machine I rent/lease is as follows:

Demand (units)	*Probability*
200	.05
220	.05
240	.10
260	.15
280	.20
300	.25
320	.15
340	.05

The item costs me $80 and I can rent it for $120.

a. How many should I stock?

b. What is EVPI?

c. If you were legally committed to stock 300, what would EVPI be?

7. Assume that I had a brilliant concept for a new product. It is company policty to test products sequentially. I estimate the probabilities of this idea passing each screen, given that it passes the previous screens, are as follows:

Stage	*P (pass)*	*Cost*
Initial screen	.5	1,000
Concept test	.8	10,000
Product test	.5	30,000
Economic analysis	.4	10,000
Test market	.5	400,000

If I pass the test-market stage, I will roll out nationally (fixed cost = $4 million) with three possible results: failure (net profit of $1 million), so-so (net profit $5 million), and success (net profit of $14 million). The probabilities of these three results are .4, .4, and .2, respectively.

a. What is my expected profit if I begin the process and proceed unless screened out?

b. What is the expected value of perfect information?

c. Assuming you had passed the concept test, what is the expected profit in proceeding?

8. I am considering changing my package design for Munch, my best-selling dog food. I suspect one of three market conditions will exist. The

expected profits associated with each of the possible results are as follows:

	Market Condition		
Packaging	*A*	*B*	*C*
Old	10	10	4
New	12	7	5

The probabilities of occurrence of the three market conditions are .5 for A, .3 for B, and .2 for C.

a. With no other information, what should I do?

b. What is the most I would pay for information about the future market condition?

c. My market research department has proposed a test to determine which market condition will hold. Its characteristics can be described as follows:

	Probability of Test Result Given Market Condition		
Market Condition	*X*	*Y*	*Z*
A	.8	.1	.1
B	.2	.7	.1
C	.2	.1	.7

What is the value of this test?

BIBLIOGRAPHY

Assmus, Gert. "Bayesian Analysis for the Evaluation of Marketing Research Expenditures: A Reassessment." *Journal of Marketing Research* 14 (November 1977), pp. 562–68.

Hogarth, Robin M. "Cognitive Processes and the Assessment of Subjective Probability Distributions." *Journal of the American Statistical Association* 70 (June 1975), pp. 271–89.

Jones, J. Morgan. *Introduction to Decision Theory*. Homewood, Ill.: Richard D. Irwin, 1977.

MaGee, John F. "Decision Trees for Decision Making." *Harvard Business Review* 42 (July–August 1964), pp. 126–38.

Raiffa, Howard. *Decision Analysis: Introductory Lectures on Choices under Uncertainty.* Reading, Mass.: Addison-Wesley, 1968.

Sarin, Rakesh Kumar. "Elicitation of Subjective Probabilities in the Context of Decision Making." *Decision Sciences* 9 (January 1978), pp. 37–48.

Savage, L. J. "Elicitation of Personal Probabilities and Expectations." *Journal of the American Statistical Association* 66 (December 1971), pp. 783–801.

Schlaiffer, Robert. *Probability and Statistics for Business Decisions.* New York: McGraw-Hill, 1959.

Tversky, Amos, and Daniel Kahneman. "Judgment under Uncertainty: Heuristics and Biases." *Science* 185 (September 1974), pp. 1124–31.

Villani, Kathryn, E. A., and Donald G. Morrison. "A Method for Analyzing New Formulation Decisions." *Journal of Marketing Research* 13 (August 1976), pp. 284–88.

Winkler, R. L. "The Quantification of Judgment: Some Methodological Suggestions." *Journal of the American Statistical Association* 62 (December 1967), pp. 1105–20.(a)

______. "The Assessment of Prior Distributions in Bayesian Analysis." *Journal of the American Statistical Association* 62 (September 1967), pp. 776–800.(b)

Appendix 2–A

An Example of Expected Information Value Calculations

Assume a supplier of parts to automotive manufacturers just developed a new van accessory. Tooling and other fixed costs would be $3 million. Sales would be through an established distribution channel, and the price to the distributors would be $110. The variable costs per unit are $70. Analysis indicates four possible levels of sales:

Sales (s)	*Probability of Market Result: P(s)*
5,000	.4
50,000	.2
100,000	.2
200,000	.2

Questions

1. With no other information, should the company market the accessory?
2. What is the most the company should pay for information about likely sales?

TABLE 2A–1 Probability of Test Result Given Actual Sales $P(z|s)$

	Test Result (z)		
Sales (s)	*Winner*	*Also-ran*	*Loser*
5,000	.2	.2	.6
50,000	.3	.6	.1
100,000	.6	.2	.2
200,000	.7	.2	.1

3. A firm specializing in projecting sales for products based on a scale which characterizes products as winners, also-rans, or losers offers to do research for the company. Based on their claims and discussions with former clients, their accuracy is estimated to be expressed as in Table 2A–1. How much is this survey worth?

Decision with No Further Information

The decision of what to do with no further information can be addressed by means of the decision tree approach of the previous section. First convert sales to profit figures:

$$\text{Profit} = \text{Sales } (110 - 70) - 3{,}000{,}000$$

Hence, we have the following:

Sales (s)	*Monetary Profit Given Sales: M(s)*	*Probability of Result: P(s)*
5,000	−2,800,000	.4
50,000	−1,000,000	.2
100,000	+1,000,000	.2
200,000	+5,000,000	.2

Next, compute an expected value given current information (EV|CI) by multiplying the profit given result times the probability of the result for each of the four results and summing the results:

$$\text{EV}|\text{CI} = \sum_{\text{all results}} (\text{profit result}) \cdot P(\text{result})$$

$$= \Sigma M(s)P(s)$$

$$= (-2{,}800{,}000)(.4) + (-1{,}000{,}000)(.2)$$

$$+ (1{,}000{,}000)(.2) + (5{,}000{,}000)(.2)$$

$$= -1{,}120{,}000 - 200{,}000 + 200{,}000 + 1{,}000{,}000$$

$$= -120{,}000$$

Since $-120{,}000$ is less than zero (which I could achieve by not marketing the accessory), my decision on an expected value basis would be not to go ahead at the present time. Still, the possibility of making $5 million is sufficiently intriguing that I may not want to completely drop the idea.

Expected Value of Perfect Information (EVPI)

The key to deciding whether to drop the concept or not is to find out *in advance* what market result I am facing. Obviously it is impossible for nonmystics or those who are not friends of the Delphic Oracle to know the results in the future. Still, it is a useful step to calculate the value of such perfect information.

The concept of getting perfect information is that one would know what sales were going to be in advance but could not alter them. (In other words, you would be omniscient but not omnipotent.) Therefore, what a decision maker would do would be to proceed whenever the profit were positive and not proceed (and hence have a zero, rather than a negative profit) whenever the profit would be negative. This is equivalent in poker to knowing what cards the opponents hold: You drop if they will beat you and stay if you will beat them (assuming no successful bluffing can be done). The expected profit given perfect information (EV|PI) would then be:

$$\text{EV}|\text{PI} = \sum_{\substack{\text{all results}\\ \text{where profit}\\ \text{is negative}}} P(s)(0) + \sum_{\substack{\text{all results}\\ \text{where profit}\\ \text{is positive}}} P(s)M(s)$$

In this case, that becomes:

$$\text{EV}|\text{PI} = (.4)(0) + (.2)(0) + (.2)(1{,}000{,}000) + (.2)(5{,}000{,}000)$$

$$= 1{,}200{,}000$$

The expected value of perfect information then is the *net* difference between the expected profit given perfect information and the expected profit under the optimal decision given current information:

$$\text{EVPI} = \text{EV}|\text{PI} - \text{EV}|\text{CI}$$

In this case, this becomes:

$$\begin{aligned}\text{EVPI} &= 1{,}200{,}000 - 0 \\ &= 1{,}200{,}000\end{aligned}$$

(Notice that we subtract 0, rather than a $-120{,}000$, since, under current information, the optimal policy is not to proceed.)

Thus, EVPI is an upper bound on the amount we would be willing to pay for additional information. If a firm offers to do a $2 million study for us, we can reject it out of hand since in expected value terms even perfect information is only worth $1.2 million. We also would be very leery of proposals close in cost to the EVPI, since most information is far from perfect.

Expected Value of Additional Information (EVAI)

The concept of the expected value of additional information is, like EVPI, a net value concept. EVAI is the difference between the expected profit given the additional information and the expected profit given current information. Calculating EVAI requires estimating the expected value given additional information, which in turn requires quantifying how accurate the information is likely to be.

To see this problem more clearly, it is useful to construct a decision tree to represent the situation (Figure 2A–1). In order to make a decision, we must attach monetary values to each of the results and probabilities to each of the branches of the trees. The monetary values are known and some probabilities are easily attached (Figure 2A–2). Thus, we see that we should either do the study or not sell the accessory. Unfortunately, to analyze the results of doing the study, we need two sets of probabilities: the probabilities of the study results ($P(z)$) and the probabilities of the sales given the study results ($P(s|z)$). There are two basic approaches to getting these:

Directly estimate them. It may in some cases be possible to directly estimate $P(z)$ and $P(s|z)$ based on experience. This is the exception rather than the rule, however.

Indirectly estimate them. In many cases it is not very easy to estimate the $P(s_i|z_j)$ and especially the $P(z_j)$ (as in the given example). However, $P(z_j|s_i)$ values may be more easily estimated. The method for transpos-

FIGURE 2A–1 Decision Tree Including Additional Information

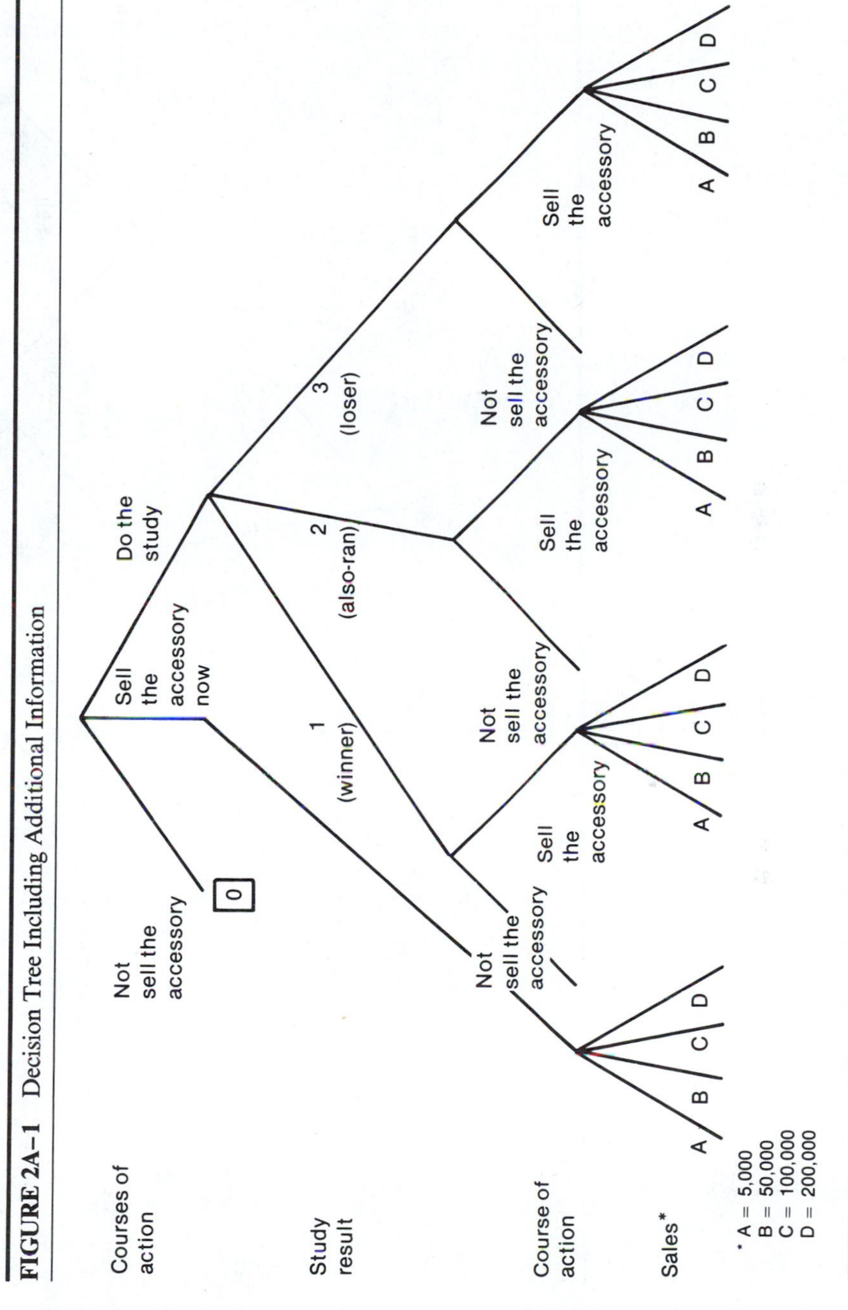

* A = 5,000
B = 50,000
C = 100,000
D = 200,000

FIGURE 2A–2 Decision Tree with Known Probabilities

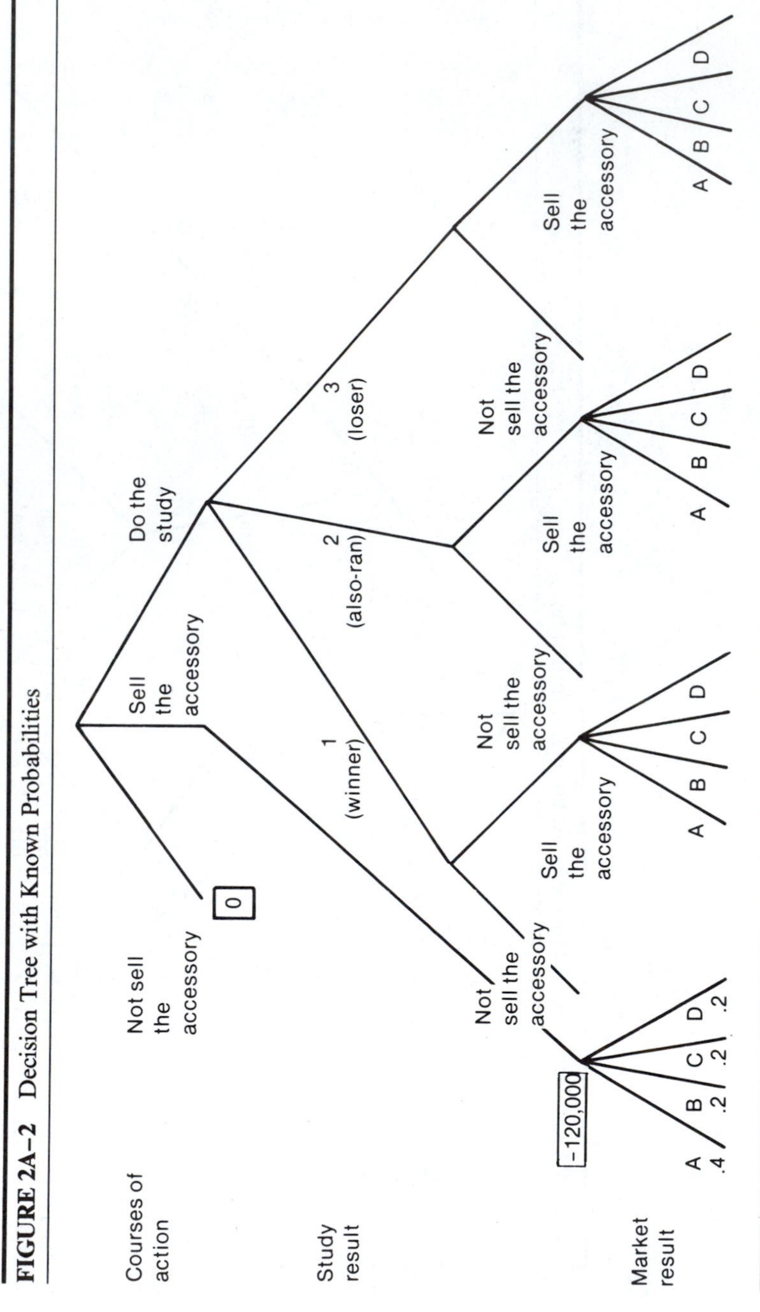

ing the $P(z_j|s_i)$ values into $P(z_j)$ and $P(s_i|z_j)$ values is based on something called *Bayes theorem.*

Bayes theorem is the result of the penchant of an English vicar for playing with probability theory. Its use has become synonymous to many with incorporating subjective probabilities in analysis (as well as so many four-letter words on the part of students that the good vicar would wonder what he had wrought). Nonetheless, the concept is simple enough that it can be applied fairly easily (if somewhat cumbersomely).

The basic notion is that the probability of a sales level given a test result is the probability of a sales level *and* the test result divided by the probability of the test result:

$$P(s_i|z_j) = \frac{P(z_j \cap s_i)}{P(z_j)} = \frac{P(\text{sales level and test result})}{P(\text{test result})}$$

By clever manipulation, this converts to:

$$P(s_i|z_j) = \frac{P(s_i)P(z_j|s_i)}{P(z_j)}$$

The secret then is to calculate $P(z)$ since the $P(z|s)$'s are already known. The procedure followed has three basic steps. First, we construct a table as follows: Since we know that $P(z_j \cap s_i) = P(s_i)(P(z_j|s_i)$, we can use the information originally given to calculate a table of the joint probability of a particular test result and a particular market result. Returning to the numerical example, the P(test result 1 and sales of 5,000) is calculated by P(sales of 5,000) · P(test result 1|sales of 5,000) = (.4)(.2) = .08. Similarly, we compute all the numbers in the table down through P(sales of 200,000 and test result 3) = (.2)(.1) = .02. We now have Table 2A–2, which represents all possible combinations of test results and sales levels.

TABLE 2A–2 Joint Probability of Test Result and Sales Level: $P(z_j \cap s_i)$

	Test Result (z)		
Sales (s)	*1*	*2*	*3*
5,000	.08	.08	.24
50,000	.06	.12	.02
100,000	.12	.04	.04
200,000	.14	.04	.02

TABLE 2A–3 $P(z_j)$

	Test Result (z)		
Sales (s)	*1*	*2*	*3*
5,000	.08	.08	.24
50,000	.06	.12	.02
100,000	.12	.04	.04
200,000	.14	.04	.02
$P(z_j)$	.40	.28	.32

The next step is to calculate the probability of the different test results—$P(z)$. Since a test-market result must occur in conjunction with one of the four sales levels, we can get $P(z)$ by simply summing numbers down the column of the previous table:

$$P(z_j) = \sum_{\text{all } i} P(z_j \cap s_i)$$

Hence, we get Table 2A–3.

The final step is to calculate the probabilities of the market given test results. This is done by using:

$$P(s_i|z_i) = \frac{P(s_i \cap z_j)}{P(z_j)}$$

For example, the probability of a sales level of 5,000, given test result 1, is:

$$\frac{P(\text{sales of 5,000 and test result 1})}{P(\text{test result 1})} = \frac{.08}{.40} = .20$$

Similarly, I can calculate all elements[2] $P(s_i|z_j)$ (Table 2A–4). We can now attach all the necessary probabilities to the decision tree as in Figure 2A–3.

The next step is to calculate the expected values of the decisions given the test results so we can determine the optimal decision based on the test information.

---

[2] In this case, by dividing each element in the $P(z_j \cap s_i)$ table by its column sum.

TABLE 2A–4 $P(s_i|z_j)$

	Test Result (z)		
Sales (s)	*1*	*2*	*3*
5,000	.20	.29	.75
50,000	.15	.43	.06
100,000	.30	.14	.13
200,000	.35	.14	.06
	1.00	1.00	1.00

Test result 1:

Expected profit given do not sell the accessory = 0

$$\begin{aligned}\text{Expected profit given sell} &= .20(-2{,}800{,}000) + .15(-1{,}000{,}000)\\ &\quad + .30(+1{,}000{,}000) + .35(+5{,}000{,}000)\\ &= -560{,}000 - 150{,}000 + 300{,}000\\ &\quad +1{,}750{,}000\\ &= +1{,}340{,}000\end{aligned}$$

Hence, given a test result of 1, we would go ahead.

FIGURE 2A–3 Decision Tree with Computed Probabilities

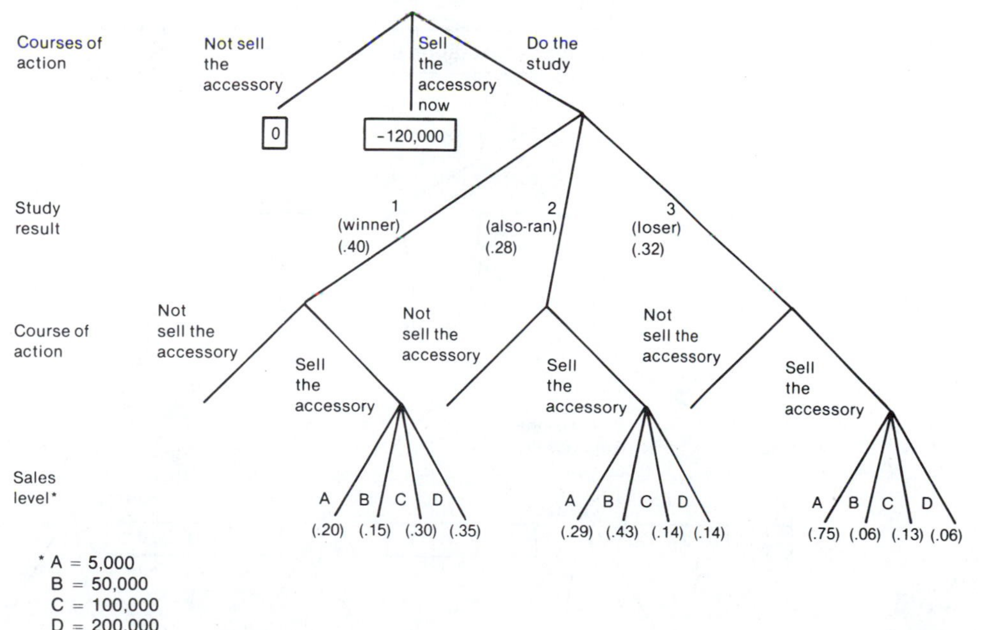

Test result 2:

Expected profit given do not sell the accessory = 0

Expected profit given sell = .29(−2,800,000) + .43(−1,000,000) + .14(1,000,000) + .14(5,000,000)
= −812,000 − 430,000 + 140,000 + 700,000
= −402,000

Given this test result, we will not market the accessory.

Test result 3:

Expected profit given do not sell the accessory = 0

Expected profit given sell = .75(−2,800,000) + .06(−1,000,000) + .13(1,000,000) + .06(5,000,000)
= −2,100,000 − 60,000 + 130,000 + 300,000
= −1,730,000

Here we also do not market the accessory. (Actually since result 2 indicated not to market and result 3 suggests a lower chance for success than 2, we could have saved ourselves the calculation time.)

We are now (finally) ready to calculate the expected value given additional information. Returning to the tree, we have Figure 2A–4. The

FIGURE 2A–4 Expected Profit—Consequences of Additional Information

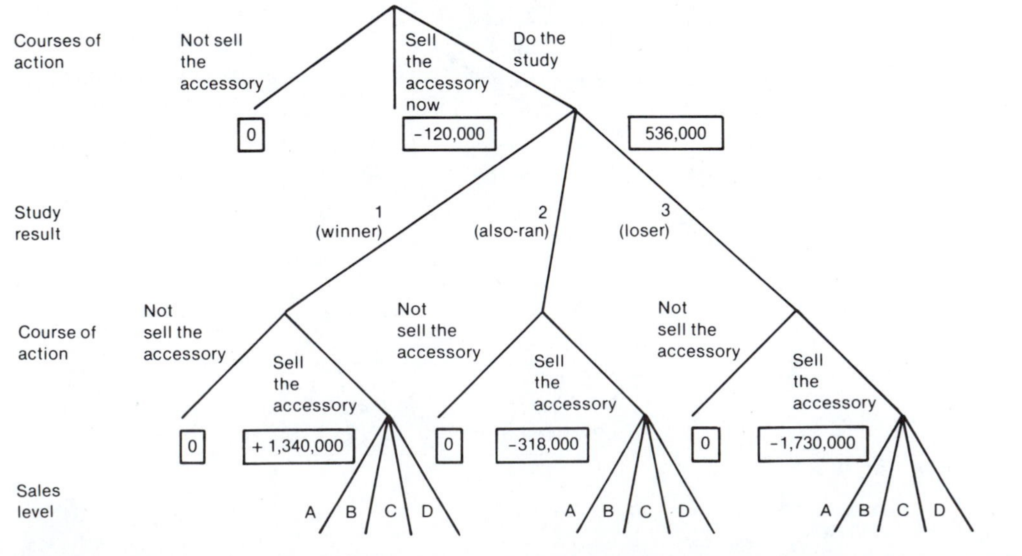

expected value given additional information is the weighted sum of the expected profit of the *optimal* decision given each of the test results:

$$EV|AI = .40(1{,}340{,}000) + .28(0) + .32(0) = \$536{,}000$$

We now calculate the value of additional information as the net increase in expected profit given the information:

$$\begin{aligned} EVAI &= EV|AI - EV|CI \\ &= \$536{,}000 \end{aligned}$$

What this means is that, if the cost of this particular study is less than $536,000, we should go ahead with the study. If the study's costs are greater, however, we should not do the study. While this process may seem tedious, it is actually quite straightforward (Figure 2A–5). It is also possible to convert these steps to a series of matrix operations. (See D. H. Mann, "A Matrix Technique for Finite Bayesian Decision Problems," *Decision Sciences* 3 (October 1972), pp. 129–36.)

Some Comments on the Methodology

In reviewing the methodology just presented, two points seem worth emphasis. First, the conclusions are only as good as the input data. Since suppliers will tend to be overly optimistic in their presentation of the accuracy of their service in predicting results, it is often necessary to tone down these predictions. Put differently, it is desirable to do sensitivity analysis by varying the input values—$P(z)$, $M(s)$, and $P(z|s)$—to see if the decision would change. If the decision is relatively sensitive to small changes in these input values, then it is often worth reconsidering the input values. A final point can be made concerning the relationship between information value and the accuracy of additional information. Since the accuracy of additional information is measured by $P(z|s)$, we can see how information value could be related to the $P(z|s)$ values for a hypothetical three equally likely states of nature, three test-result case. Perfect information would look like the following:

(Pz|s)

	Test Result (z)		
Sales Level (s)	*1*	*2*	*3*
A	1	0	0
B	0	1	0
C	0	0	1

FIGURE 2A-5 Steps to Calculate *EVAI*

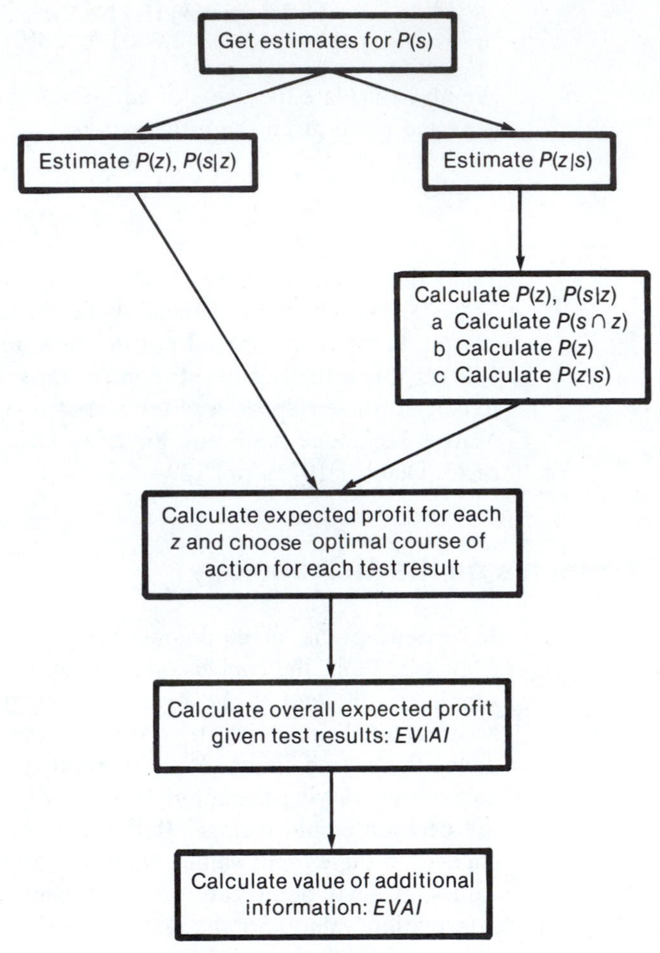

In other words, the test results will be a perfect match with the sales level. Information of no value, on the other hand, would appear as follows:

P(z|s)

	Test Result (z)		
Sales Level (s)	*1*	*2*	*3*
A	.33	.33	.33
B	.33	.33	.33
C	.33	.33	.33

TABLE 2A–5

I. Information Has No Value

Decision	*Market Result*	*Consequences (profit)*
1	A	20
	B	19
	C	18
2	A	14
	B	12
	C	−200
3	A	17
	B	9
	C	−300

II. Information Has Value

Decision	*Market Result*	*Consequences (profit)*
1	A	30
	B	10
	C	−15
2	A	8
	B	6
	C	4
3	A	−4
	B	2
	C	12

Put differently, if the test result is independent of the sales level, then the test results will have no information value. Clearly, the closer the situation is to the perfect information case (especially for extreme/serious market results), the greater will be the value of the information.

The concept of when information has value can be demonstrated further by considering the example in Table 2A–5. First, notice that variance alone does not mean information has value. In case I, the variation of the results under decisions 2 and 3 is much greater than it is in case II. Yet, decision 1 dominates decisions 2 and 3 in case I: the worst result under decision 1 (18) is better than the best result under either decision 2 or 3 (17). Consequently, decision 1 is optimal in case I, and information of which market condition will occur has no bearing on the optimal decision. Second, notice that the same market result may not produce the best results for all decisions (e.g., in case II, decision 1 works best in market condition A, whereas decision 3 works best in condition C). What gives information value in case II is the dependence of the optimal decision on the market condition (i.e., decision 1 produces under one market condition the best possible result (30), and under another the worst possible result (−15).

Chapter 3

The Research Process

Discussions of research design often appear to be a series of platitudes and caveats which, if taken together, would void almost all research actually done. Nowhere is the conflict between "scientific" and real-world considerations more apparent than in the selection of a research design. To be purely scientific is so costly that research becomes more of a cost than a benefit; to ignore sound research design may cut costs drastically but also cuts the value of the research to zero (or even negative if the results are sufficiently misleading). The key to research design, then, is to make an intelligent compromise between scientific correctness and easy doability.

This chapter gives an overview of the research process. The process can be viewed as a series of 10 steps:

1. Problem definition.
2. Determining information needs.
3. Setting research objectives.
4. Selection of type of research.
5. Design of data collection.
6. Development of a plan of analysis.
7. Data collection.
8. Analysis.
9. Drawing conclusions.
10. Reporting.

The first six steps encompass what is known as research design and the last four represent execution. Design is much broader than simply sampling or experiments, and it must fit into the context of the research process.

In a company, multiple research processes are in progress at any time in various stages of development. For a particular process, the stages of problem definition, determining information needs, and setting research

FIGURE 3–1

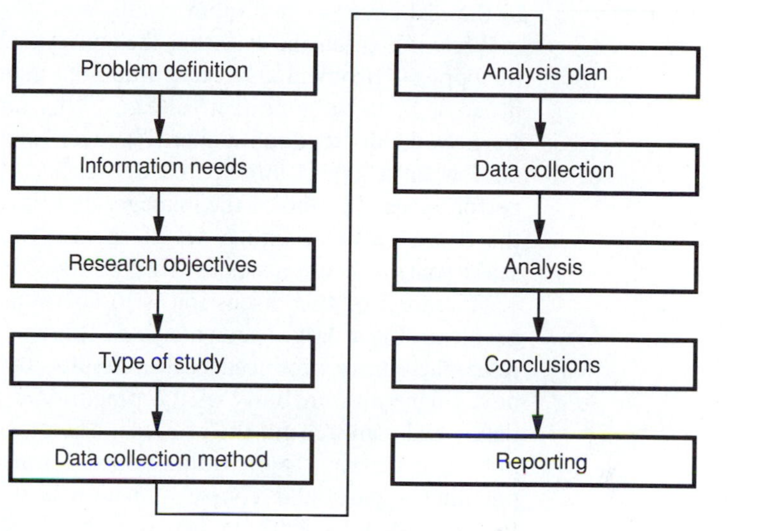

objectives require cooperation between manager and researcher. Selection of a type of research through analysis is typically primarily the task of the market researcher. Drawing conclusions and reporting also require cooperation between researcher and manager.

This chapter proceeds by briefly discussing each of these 10 steps (Figure 3–1). More detailed discussions appear in ensuing chapters.

PROBLEM DEFINITION

The most important phase of any research is the definition of the problem to be addressed. In spite of this, there is a tendency to spend very little time on this issue. Partially due to the pressure of busy schedules, partially because people assume that the stated problem is the real one, and partially from a reluctance to appear foolish by asking such a naive question as "What is the real problem?" a large percentage of research turns out to be of little or no value.

It is very easy to assume that the stated problem is the real one if it is worded as a research problem. If someone asks if a particular analysis can be performed (e.g., a regression analysis of price on sales), it is very easy to answer this technical question rather than inquire why you want to do the analysis (e.g., to set the price on a new product, choose a promotion plan for an existing product, or evaluate the decisions of a product manager).

Put differently, the stated problem is often the tip of the real problem iceberg (a mixed metaphor, but hopefully an informative one); its relation to the real issue is often quite small.

While it is often the case that the stated problem is the tip of the iceberg, the opposite problem also exists when the managerial problem is sufficently broad so as to be nondirective (e.g., "Why are sales sluggish?"; "What do we need to do to double share?"). Such managerial problems frequently arise when a gap is anticipated between actual and planned or budgeted performance. The job of the manager and the researcher is then to translate the broad problem into a set of specific information needs and then to select some of these needs as research objectives.

The moral of this discussion is to continually probe to uncover the real problem. In a large percentage of cases where practitioners feel that researchers have produced useless results, the source of this feeling is the unwillingness or inability of the practitioner and the researcher to jointly define and comprehend the problem. The problem can range from making a particular decision to providing political ammunition for convincing someone that a particular course of action is useful (and if it fails, at least logical), giving a learning experience or sense of prestige to the person whose budget is being tapped, or simply using up a budget so it isn't cut next year. It is not unusual for the problem definition to change in the mind of the person paying for the research as a study is in the field. Hence, it is strongly advisable to ask the question, "What is the real problem?" several different times and ways (including by observing what the person paying for the research is both personally interested in and rewarded for by the organization), and then put the agreed-upon problem in writing.

It is clearly preferable to ask "What is the problem?" in a probing, supportive, cooperative manner. Overtly blunt questioning can provoke hostility and defensiveness on the part of a manager. Hence, it is best to begin asking about general concerns and specific decisions that are important to the manager. In essence, then, the market researcher plays the role of consultant at this stage. However, it is important to continue one's questions about the nature of the problem, rather than suggesting solutions at this stage.

A key element in defining a problem is distinguishing a problem symptom from a problem situation. Put differently, it is easy to spend one's effort stopping a runny nose, rather than treating the flu which is causing it. This occurs because the person asking for research often states the symptom, rather than the underlying problem. Consider, for example, the following situations which have occurred:

1. *Stated problem:* To improve the motivation of the sales force.

Real problem: Sales were falling below quotas. As it turned out, the cause was a combination of a quality control problem in the company's product and aggressive competitive activities. Motivation was a symptom of the situation, not a cause.

2. *Stated problem:* To use regression analysis to forecast sales.

Real problem: A textile manufacturer was interested in developing a forecasting system for its many lines of fabrics and patterns. As it turned out, business was so volatile that regression analysis (or any other mechanical forecasting system) proved to be of limited value.

3. *Stated problem:* To study the relationship between price and sales for an ethical drug market.

Real problem: A pharmaceutical manufacturer was considering introducing a drug in the market. A key concern was what price it could charge for it, which was the result of someone's suggestion that a very high price could be set since prescriptions were insensitive to price. Investigation of the relation between the price of existing drugs and sales indicated that the higher-priced goods were in fact the major sellers, hence suggesting a high price was appropriate. Further study, however, indicated that the high-price/high-sales brands were the first to enter the product category as well as the most highly rated by doctors. Hence, studying the historical data relating price to sales was at best of little value and at worst misleading.

4. *Stated problem:* To evaluate methods of forecasting sales of a major new durable.

Real problem: A major manufacturer was in the process of developing a new durable for a potentially large but undeveloped market. The manufacturer needed to decide (*a*) whether to continue with development, (*b*) what particular features of the product would be most appealing and, hence, should be developed further by the R & D/engineering department, and (*c*) what level of sales to plan for. While describing different forecasting methodologies is interesting, it does not solve the basic problems facing the manufacturer.

5. *Stated problem:* To find out what consumers think of a company's advertising.

Real problem: A company faced a possible cease and desist order from the Federal Trade Commission concerning their advertising. The problem was to collect evidence (*a*) which showed whether the ads were in fact having a measurable and inappropriate affect on consumer perceptions of the product (obviously the "right" answer was no) and (*b*) which would be admissible and persuasive in legal proceedings. The outcome was a national probability sample done by Gallup, which surveyed consumers and became a key element in the company's defense. Knowing that the real problem was legal, rather than informational, led to a different approach to data collection, analysis, and result presentation.

6. *Stated problem:* To determine whether a new formulation of a product was perceived to be better than the old one.

Real problem: The major competitor was gaining share. In blind tests, the competitor's product was considered better by a majority of customers. Therefore, the question was whether a new formulation closer to the competitor's would be better.

The astute reader (in this case, anyone who contributed to my retirement fund by purchasing this book) will notice this last problem is the situation faced by Coke versus Pepsi prior to the introduction of new Coke. This managerial problem was translated into the research problem: which formulation tasted better. Since the new Coke formula was preferred in blind taste tests, the decision was made to replace the old ("Classic") formula with new Coke. The market results, however, did not match the test results. What apparently happened (I am also good at criticizing Sunday sports on Monday) was that, as a product, Coke involved image and association as much as taste. Hence, the publicized change in formula also had the effect of reducing the brand's goodwill and, hence, sales were disappointing. The moral of this story is that a product offering is much broader than the physical product, so blind product tests alone may not indicate how well a particular formulation will do.

Another key issue to be addressed along with problem definition is, When must the results be available? This is a question to which the first answer is typically unrealistic (i.e., yesterday), and some thought must be given to deciding what the real deadline is.

It is possible to spend so much time defining the problem that nothing is accomplished. It also may be uncomfortable for someone in a staff position or consultancy role to probe a "superior." Also, there is a limit to how long the "What is the problem?" game can be played. (Some people cover up inability or unwillingness to proceed by stalling with general questions.) Nonetheless, problem definition should receive more attention than it typically does.

INFORMATION NEEDS

Having satisfactorily defined a problem, the next step is to determine what types of information are most appropriate/useful for resolving the problem. It is generally useful to search for both broad descriptions and a relatively extensive list at this stage. The list of information needs becomes a starting point from which the specific research objectives are selected.

Generally, information needs can be uncovered as an extension of the process of defining the problem.

Consider the problem of explaining why sales are falling short of expectations. A number of information needs are apparent, including:

1. Industry sales.
2. Sales of competitors.
3. Competitive activity (pricing, advertising).
4. Attributes of products gaining and losing sales (e.g., are sales moving from lower- to higher-quality products?).
5. Behavior of past customers (are they switching to other brands or buying less?).
6. Distribution channel behavior.

Clearly a single study cannot hope to answer all these questions. Thus a decision must be made about which are (*a*) most important and (*b*) most researchable (i.e., can be addressed in a reasonable time period for a reasonable cost). The need(s) which are then the highest on both importance and researchability then become research objectives.

RESEARCH OBJECTIVES

By contrast to information needs, research objectives should be both specific and limited. One of the greatest causes of dissatisfaction with research is vaguely worded or overly optimistic objectives which are rarely achieved. For example, a research objective might be "to determine the effect on the market share of brand B of a 5-percent-off promotion run for two months." While the research is likely to provide other information, requiring it to serve too many masters will often result in a study being (*a*) expensive, (*b*) late, and (*c*) inconclusive. Put differently, if the goal is to develop segments of the market based on lifestyle measures, this should be agreed to in advance. Obviously any additional insights the research uncovers will only add value to the study.

TYPE OF STUDY

Deciding on research objectives first requires understanding of the type of research being done. The most common categorization ranges from exploratory (which assumes no preconceived notions) to causal (which assumes a very specific preconception of how one or more variables influence one or more other variables). A useful categorization is exploratory, descriptive, and causal.

Exploratory. This is a study which is designed to find out enough about a problem to usefully formulate hypotheses. It stems from general problem descriptions, such as finding out how consumers make decisions about life insurance. Typically, such studies have few if any formal hypotheses and use "soft" methods, such as in-depth interviews, focus groups, or employee testing.

Descriptive. Descriptive studies are part way along the continuum from exploratory to causal. These studies assume that relevant variables are known (e.g., for life insurance purchase, income, age, family status, and risk aversion). Hypotheses are of the general type: x and y are related (e.g., life insurance purchase is related to age). Results tend to be profiles of purchasers versus nonpurchasers and so forth.

Causal. These are the most demanding type of study. They assume that not only do we know what the relevant variables are but that we know (hypothesize) how they affect each other. Hence, we are concerned with two basic problems:

1. Confirming or disproving the hypothesized relationships.
2. If the hypotheses are so specific that the mathematical form of the relationship between variables is known (e.g., $Y = a + bx$), estimating the parameters and strength of the relationship.

Exploratory research is very important in that it prevents preconceived notions from excluding potentially useful results. It is easy for a researcher or brand manager to forget that they are not typical consumers. Pure exploratory research, however, is almost never done. By selecting who to get data from and the general form of that information, a researcher betrays his or her preconceptions about the problem. Also, though exploratory research is useful for generating ideas (hypotheses), it typically fails to be a good basis for decision making. The results of exploratory research also often defy statistical analysis. Because of this, there is substantial pressure to make research less exploratory and more causal. Nonetheless, qualitative methods are very useful and will be discussed at some length in the next chapter.

STATING HYPOTHESES

Partly because of its psychological and statistical heritage, marketing research often refines its research objectives into formal hypotheses. In stating hypotheses, we are really explicitly stating our preconceptions about the way the market we are concerned with works. While the hypotheses can be simply prejudices or hunches, they are more appropriately based on prior research or existing theories. It is possible and often useful to state hypotheses quite explicitly. For example, H_0: A 10 percent increase in advertising will generate an 8 percent increase in brand mentions. Such explicitivity is not necessary, however, and often is a symptom of pseudo-scientification. If the strongest reasonable guess you have is that increasing advertising will increase brand mentions, then your hypotheses should state that.

Stating hypotheses has two major advantages. First, it translates a problem statement into a series of assertions (questions) which can be addressed with data and, thus, largely determines the research design by specifying the data needed. Second, being forced to make implicit notions explicit is a healthy exercise which often leads to modifications of opinions even without data collection. It is possible to overly bureaucratize the hypothesis-generating process by demanding such things as a formal hypothesis for every question asked and a significance test and cutoff level in advance of data collection. In such a case, the form of the hypotheses may become more important than the substance, to the detriment of the research. Still, with the caveat of avoiding foolish rigor, explicit (as opposed to formal) statements of hypotheses are very beneficial.

SELECTION OF TYPE OF RESEARCH

Selection of a type of study depends heavily on the research objectives. It also depends on available data, budgets, time pressures, and the experience of the potential users. Actually, in many cases, a research objective will require multiple research approaches, often in sequence. For example, Frank (1983) describes an extensive approach for repositioning an existing brand of consumer package good, which has five stages:

1. Qualitative (focus groups, depth interviews).
2. Positioning study of the market.
3. Study of the potential for alternative positionings.
4. In-home use tests.
5. Advertising testing.

The discussion in this chapter, therefore, focuses on the approach to designing each stage in such an effort.

Using Existing versus New Data

Before spending the time, money, and effort to collect data, it is useful to see if usable data are already available. Existing data are more widespread and useful than most people realize and should be considered first. Some sources of secondary data are described in Chapter 4.

Method of Collection

Assuming new data are required (and can be justified in terms of a cost/benefit analysis), the following basic alternatives are available: observation, questioning, and simulation.

Observation. One of the most obvious ways to collect data is to simply observe behavior. This can be done in a natural setting (where people are allowed to go about their "normal" business) or a controlled (laboratory) situation. This can also be done either unobtrusively, so people are unaware they are being observed (i.e., with hidden cameras), or obtrusively, with either personal or mechanical observation.

The advantage of directly observing behavior is that one can directly obtain information which is "bottom line"—did they buy our brand, use the coupon, read the point-of-purchase ad? The disadvantages are, first, that it can be costly (try following an individual around with a videotape camera to observe a typical shopping trip or a salesperson to see which accounts he or she calls on). Second, the fact that a person is being observed may affect the behavior which is directly exhibited. (I rarely beat my kids in public and always support socially desirable causes.) There is also a very important indirect effect on behavior of any obtrusive measurement method. By focusing an individual's attention on a particular aspect of behavior, the individual may think about it more consciously, which may in turn cause a behavior change. Hence, measurement methods may be every bit as important agents of change as advertising or price promotions, and consequently care should be taken to be sure that the behavior being monitored is typical of the real world and not an artifact of the data collection process.

Questioning. By far, the most widely recognized method of collecting data is questioning. (Who hasn't been asked to fill out some survey at one time or another?) Market research is equivalent in many people's minds to survey research. Even when observation studies are done, it is common to supplement them with a questionnaire.

One advantage of surveys is they are generally much less expensive than observation. They also can cover areas which are not subject to direct observation, such as awareness, attitudes, and intentions. The major disadvantage of questions is that the responses may not be accurate. This can be true because of either a simple memory error (what brand of gas did I buy last?) or a conscious attempt to distort the facts (most people won't admit to being "against" ecology, good nutrition, etc.) In fact, the tendency to present socially desirable responses is a major problem with survey research. There are also some common results, such as the overstatement of intentions (of those who say they definitely will buy something in the next six months, typically less than half do so) which make interpreting survey responses difficult.

Simulation. One type of study which is very different is one that falls under the broad title "simulation." Simulation studies are not directed toward collecting data but rather at using existing (past) data and models to project the answer to "what if" questions. Based on a model of a situation (i.e., Sales = 2.73 + 4.12 advertising + log (percent distribution) + . . .), the results are projected for different hypothetical situations, simulating actual results. While simple models can be solved analytically, many models are sufficiently complex to defy easy analytical solution. In these situations, results are simulated over many trials, usually by means of a computer program. It is these large-scale computer models that are typically associated with the term *simulation*.

The advantage of these models is that they can be directed toward answering managerial questions without collecting new data. The disadvantage is that, if the model is faultily constructed or the past data which were used to calibrate the model are no longer relevant, the results will be misleading. Unfortunately, there is no mechanism built into simulation (or to any other projection method, for that matter) which will enable the user to know a priori when the results are bad. In general, simulation models are not used to generate marketing research data.

DESIGN OF DATA COLLECTION METHOD

The term *test instrument* is used here to signify the method by which data are actually secured. Hence, for a lab experiment involving placement of chips into piles to indicate the relative importance of attributes, the chips serve as the test instrument.

In the case of a survey, one issue which arises is that of direct versus indirect questions. Indirect may sometimes "trick" respondents into giving a more truthful answer about touchy subjects (i.e., the projective technique of asking what does your neighbor think about . . .). On the other hand, indirect questions may provide false information (my neighbor is a mechanic who likes working on cars, while I prefer Nautilus workouts). Another issue is whether to use aided/structured versus unaided/open-ended questions. Structured response questions get results which are easier for analysis, while unaided have less measurement effect built in but tend to be dominated by the verbal respondents and those with strong positions on the issues involved. The overall format of the questionnaire, the order of questions, and length are among numerous other issues which must be considered in designing a questionnaire.

One potential hazard of designing a test instrument is that it can become a catchall for many different individuals' research needs. Nice-to-know questions are interesting but usually not worth their cost. Questionnaires designed by committee are usually long and disjointed ones. While it is obviously desirable to piggyback questions on a study if the cost is low, the point is often reached where the costs are substantial and some brave soul must say "Enough," lest the instrument become so cumbersome that it no longer serves its original purpose.

Who Will Be Sampled

A key question in any study is, Who will be studied? If an industrial company has four major clients, then a sample of all four clients is often in order. For a consumer packaged good, however, there are obviously too many customers to include all in a study, and thus we must choose a sample to represent them. The question of who will be sampled really breaks down into the following four separate but related issues:

1. Who is the target population? This question requires specification of who are the subjects from whom you desire information (e.g., our five largest accounts, female heads of households between 21 and 39, . . .).
2. How many will be sampled? This question deals with trading off accuracy, which requires making the sample large, against cost constraints, which lead to making the sample smaller.
3. How will the subjects be contacted? While a variety of means exist for contacting target subjects, the vast majority of studies use either personal contact, phone contact, or mail.
4. How will sample points be selected from the target population? Another budget-constrained decision, the choice of sample points ranges from pure random selection (which is usually expensive and almost never employed) through methods designed to ensure representation of key groups (e.g., stratified or quota samples) to convenience sampling procedures.

Sampling can be considered as a separate step in the research process but here is considered jointly with the data collection method, since the two are related. For example, it doesn't make sense to design a detailed written questionnaire for the illiterate—which, incidentally, represents up to 20 percent of the U.S. population, depending on the definition used.

Who Will Do the Work

One of the first questions addressed is, Who will do the work? The answer is overwhelmingly a supplier/outside contractor. Next, the question of who will work on it both from the company and the supplier (a critical factor which is often overlooked) must be addressed.

How Much Will Be Spent

The amount of money to be spent has a (the) critical effect on the type of study chosen (i.e., budgets of $10,000 exclude complex field experiments). While in theory the amount of money budgeted should be the result of an analysis of the likely value of information, in practice it is more likely to be a predetermined figure.

ANALYSIS PLAN

Before data are actually collected, an analysis plan should be developed. Since most commercial research is done on a tight timetable, all relevant analyses should be prespecified. A side benefit of this prespecification is that it allows one to check to see if the data being collected are adequate for the form of analysis planned. This cuts down considerably on the after-the-fact "why didn't we..." questions.

It is also important to specify in advance what levels in the results lead to what actions. Prespecifying these "action standards" prevents a lot of agonizing over what the results mean as people with different desires interpret the results to suit their positions. For example, at this stage it is usually possible to agree on a target share for a new brand of, say, 10 percent. Specifying this as the cutoff prior to data collection makes the decision making, once the results are in, less subject to political persuasion. While it is important not to overlook unexpected events which affect the results of a study, it is also important to have predetermined decision cutoffs.

An example of a situation requiring predetermined action standards is the introduction of a new food product in test market. The key decision is whether to introduce the product nationally, and the key piece of information needed is what level of sales the product will attain nationally. Because the first months of sales will largely be pipeline (wholesale and retail trade stocking up), factory shipments are a poor indicator of sales. Hence, an indicator of retail sales (e.g., Nielsen) is needed.

To develop action standards, the national share needed to achieve a satisfactory rate of return must be calculated (assume it is 8 percent). Next, characteristics of the test market must be considered. These include advertising levels (likely to be higher than normal), prices (likely to be lower than normal), and so forth, which might be thought to affect market share (assume an inflation of 1 percent). Assuming a 9 percent share in the test market is needed to indicate profitability, the resulting action standards might be:

Test-Market Share	*Decision*
12% or more	Expand aggressively
10–12%	Limited expansion
8–10%	Continue to test
Under 7%	Reevaluate the product

A final point concerning analysis is that the availability and requirements of analytical routines (mainly computer programs) must be considered. If the planned analyses require certain forms of data, then those data must be included in the test instrument. Similarly, the availability of analytical procedures will influence which analyses are planned; only rarely is it worth developing a new procedure for a single application.

DATA COLLECTION

The data collection phase is one which typically is a period of waiting for the researcher. Having specified what is to be done, he or she sits back and lets the supplier work. This can be a mistake. Keeping in touch with the supplier both helps quality control and gives insights which often are unavailable from the summarized results. Also, the data collection phase is an opportunity to try out and debug the analytical procedures needed when the data become available.

It is crucial to pretest a procedure before going to a big sample. At the very least, researchers should force themselves and a few convenient subjects to go through the process. It is amazing how many poor questions can be screened out this way. It is also desirable to run a pilot of 50 to 100 typical subjects. This tests whether the procedure works on subjects in the target population and whether the data have any variability. (If everyone answers a question the same way, it is probably not worth asking.) While a pilot test has both time and monetary costs associated with it, its benefits usually far exceed its costs.

ANALYSIS AND INTERPRETATION

Analysis is, in one sense, the least interesting part of most research. The analyses prespecified by the analysis plan are simply (assuming computer gremlins are absent) carried out and the results reported. The

FIGURE 3–2 Historical Relation of Question Answers and Actual Sales Results

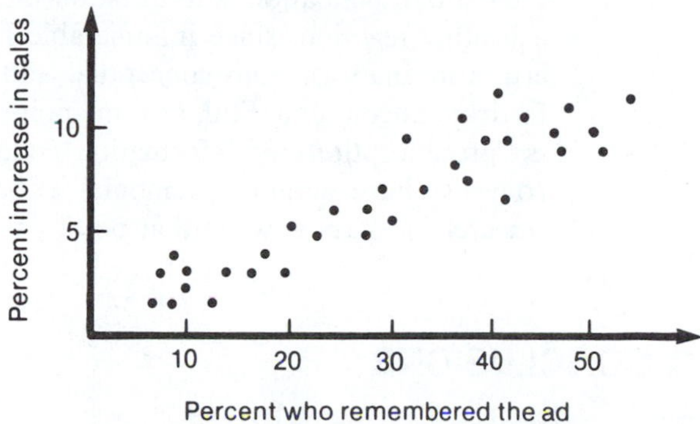

interesting/creative part of the analysis occurs when results from the initial phase suggest further work. However, conducting extensive further work usually indicates inadequate planning as well as the lack of budget and time constraints—a rare combination indeed (except, of course, for academic researchers).

Interpretation of the results is rarely literal. For example, 40 percent of a sample may say they remembered a given ad. While this sounds good in absolute terms, it is not clear what it would translate into in dollar sales. The key to interpretation is to gather information on a previously used scale. For example, assume in the past I ran 34 similar studies in which an ad was actually used and sales as well as ad recall were measured. These results could be portrayed graphically as in Figure 3–2. Given this background, a 40 percent favorable rating seems likely to produce between a 6 percent and 11 percent increase in sales. Hence, we might interpret the 40 percent recall as an indication that the ad, if run, would produce an 8 percent increase in sales.

So important is the calibration issue that design of the basic elements of the test instrument should almost always be restricted to previously used methods. Even such seemingly innocuous changes as going from five- to six-point intentions scales make interpretation of the results difficult (are 20 percent "top box" responses on a five-point scale the same as 17 percent "top box" responses on a six-point scale?). Similarly, to know 70 percent of respondents are satisfied with our brand is not very informative unless I know what percent are satisified with our major competitors. In short, absolute values in research are usually misleading. It is only by examining measured values relative to either historical data or concurrently gathered measures of competitive products that useful interpretations can be made.

The process of reconciling results with prior conceptions is very interesting. Whenever analysis of data conflicts with strongly held preconceptions, the natural inclination is to question the data, the analysis, or both. This is a healthy reaction, since innumerable biases may creep into a study and errors in analysis, both conceptual and computational/programming, are far from uncommon. Still, at some point, a manager must be willing to give up preconceptions or information collection loses its real value and becomes a bureaucratic ceremonial exercise. The art of using marketing research is to know when that point has been reached.

DRAWING CONCLUSIONS

The final step of a well-ordered research process is drawing conclusions. The ex post value of the conclusions depends on how well they assist in resolving the problem. Unfortunately, much research ends up by concluding (*a*) that the problem needs to be modified, (*b*) that the data don't address the problem, or (*c*) that more research is needed. (This is the favorite conclusion of both academic research and reports from consultants, for obvious reasons.)

THE RESEARCH REPORT

The reporting of research results is a marketing task and, hence, it requires understanding the talents and preferences of the readers. Nonetheless, for most situations "the" research report should be a series of reports in various stages of detail and technical language.

The basic report should be a one- to two-page memorandum with the following basic information:

1. Problem.
2. Method of study (e.g., a survey of 139 railroad workers).
3. Basic results (findings).
4. Conclusions.

The basic report should be written in nontechnical language and be readable by any reasonably intelligent person.

The next level of detail would be a 10- to 20-page version, which expands on the basic report by including more detail on study methods (e.g., a questionnaire, sampling plan and response rate). It can also contain key analytical results (e.g., cross-tabs or a crucial regression analysis) as well as a brief discussion of the limitations of the study.

The third level of detail is a complete record of what was done and of the results, including tabs on every question (if the study is a survey). This is supported by a fourth level, which includes the raw data and computer output and is typically stored in a basement until it rots due to age.

The purposes of the most general level are (*a*) to be widely circulated, (*b*) to summarize *the* key result, and (*c*) to make it possible to decide intelligently whether to read the longer (10- to 20-page) version. The second level of detail is written to be available to interested readers who are competent but not necessarily technical specialists. Put differently, this report should also be in the native tongue and not statistical jargon. The third level is for the few experts who both exist and care to examine the results in detail. The fourth level is designed to (*a*) make reanalysis possible and (*b*) give archaeologists a challenge in the future. The four levels can be summarized as follows:

Level of Detail	*Target Audience*	*Length*
1	Broad, managers	1–2 pages
2	Limited	10–20 pages
3	Research-oriented readers	"Longish" (e.g., 100 pages)
4	Rats and roaches, professors	Excessive

In producing these reports, a useful approach is to complete level 4 first, then 3, etc., so each report is essentially an abstract or synopsis of the previous one.

Oral Presentation of Findings

For better or worse, many people rely on an oral presentation of research findings to learn what happened in a study. The oral presentation, like the research report, should be available in several levels of detail. For maximum impact, nontechnical language and proper use of visual aids are invaluable. Put differently, it is best to (*a*) overprepare, (*b*) start out simply, and (*c*) be willing to accelerate or amplify the presentation, depending on audience reaction. The last point is especially crucial. Intelligent people are offended by slow, inflexible presentations. On the other hand, no one likes to feel they aren't smart enough to follow a presentation. Therefore, the pacing of a report is often as important as its content.

A TYPICAL APPROACH

The approach just outlined is a series of logical steps occurring in sequence. In practice, this approach is more goal than reality. In the first place, the sequence is typically attacked iteratively with problem definition, statement of hypothesis, selection of type of study, sample definition, and analysis plan all considered almost simultaneously. While not pure in an academic sense, this approach has much to recommend it when there are time and money constraints as well as established company procedures for certain types of research. What is often disastrous, however, is when the sequence is used out of order. For example, assume that using a particular analytic procedure is the goal of the study (i.e., "I want to do a market segmentation study using multidimensional scaling"). This is appropriate for basic research but certainly not for applied research. The effect of such bad priorities, where the analytical procedure dictates problem definition, is generally the production of research that is read and then appropriately filed but does nothing which aids management. Put differently, it is perfectly reasonable to build a data collection method or analytical technique into a study to assess its value for this and future problems; but it is generally wasteful to build a major study around a technique. This is especially true of fancy multivariate techniques, which make good "add-ons" but should rarely be used in the absence of more standard techniques which serve as the "fail-safe" in case the fancy techniques fail to uncover anything interesting.

The typical approach, then, is to see what approaches are feasible, given multiple constraints, such as the following:

1. Time (a two-month deadline eliminates many approaches).
2. Budget ($3,000 does not lend itself to probability samples and to personal interviewing).
3. Standard practice (standard procedures have big edges, in that they are easier to interpret because of comparability to past results and easier to communicate because of familiarity).

The culmination of any good research design is a time line summarizing when different stages will be completed. This time line is often/typically constructed with the ending date given (i.e., "We expect a report on March 1"). While it is possible to use elaborate CPM or PERT Chart procedures, the example in Figure 3–3 of the process for a survey is more typical. Notice that it is common to do several activities in parallel (simultaneously). Also notice that the entire process was scheduled for five months, indicating the need to plan well in advance. While this can be cut, the tendency to save six weeks by eliminating the pilot test stage is probably the worst bargain imaginable. It is also worth pointing out that large projects usually have built-in evaluation/exit points. These points provide the option to

FIGURE 3–3

Completion Date	*Duration (weeks)*	*Task*
February 1	4	Finalization of problem and data needs (hypothesis statements)
March 1	4	1. Development of questionnaire (test instrument) 2. Selection of sampling plan 3. Analysis plan
April 1	4	Pilot test and tabs
April 15	2	1. Revision of questionnaire 2. Final analysis of plan 3. Payment of federal taxes
June 1	6	Field work
June 15	2	Data coding, punching, and initial tabs
July 1	2	1. Complete analysis 2. Initial ("top-line") results produced
July 15	2	Final report presented

discontinue the research once the results become sufficiently clear without spending the entire budget.

AN EXAMPLE

This section describes a project which serves as a point of reference for the book (but not as a model of how to do research) and will be discussed in more detail later. The subject of the project was the nutritional knowledge, attitudes, and practices of U.S. households (Lehmann, 1976). The project was undertaken for two basic reasons: (*a*) the issue was interesting and important and (*b*) a budget was available to spend on it.

Obviously, a variety of approaches are available for studying this problem. A variety of constraints, however, largely dictated the following design:

1. A budget ceiling of $10,000.
2. A single principal researcher with no staff.
3. A five-month time frame in which to complete the research.
4. The principal researcher's familiarity with survey methodology and fondness for large data sets and multivariate procedures.

Given these constraints, the resulting design should have been no surprise. A series of notions about how nutritional knowledge would affect behavior were considered. Changes in behavior and perceptions were also deemed important pieces of data. To gather data, a survey of 1,200 female heads of households was undertaken. These respondents were chosen from an existing mail panel (thus guaranteeing both demographic information and a high response rate as well as removing the sample selection, mailing, and data punching jobs from the principal researcher). The analysis plan was to establish a simple question-by-question tabulation as the basic report for wide dissemination and to play with "fancy" techniques both to understand the determinants of weekly food expenditures and to see how various foods, nutrients, and parts of the body were perceived to relate to each other. A pilot test of 100 was also included, and it resulted in one major change in the questionnaire. While the results came in late (so much for the time line), the study provided some interesting findings, some of which will be discussed later.

SUMMARY

Research design is the crucial stage of research. As will be seen later in this book, many of the issues raised here have been well delineated and the alternative solutions examined. The six keys to a good research design are common sense, logic, knowledge of the problem, attention to detail, effort, and luck. No matter how good the first five elements, nature can provide surprises or changes (i.e., oil embargoes) which invalidate well-designed research.

This book will proceed as follows. The next chapter provides a basic overview of the types of studies which are available. Chapters 5 to 8 address in more detail issues related to specific kinds of studies. Chapter 9 focuses on sampling. Chapter 10 deals with coding and editing responses, and Chapters 11 to 16 focus on methods of analysis. Chapters 17 to 19 give examples of how the research methods developed earlier can be applied to particular problems.

PROBLEMS

1. Assume you had eight packages of a certain product and knew one had been short-weighted. Design the most efficient scheme for using a balancing scale (assume each use of the scale is expensive) to find the short-weighted package. (This is a classic logic problem.)
2. Mr. Smart has just been assigned the task of recommending a way to test the effect of shelf facings (2 versus 3 versus 4) and promotions (5-cent, 10-cent, and 20-cent discounts) on Slop-out, a new toilet bowl cleaner and sterling silver wash. Suggest three alternative approaches, list their pros and cons, and make a recommendation.

3. Estimating the effect of advertising on sales is a key problem in marketing.
   a. Suggest some alternative research designs for addressing this problem.
   b. Indicate why this problem is so elusive.
4. Assume you wanted to monitor food consumption patterns of 20- to 25-year-olds in the United States. What could be done?
5. A certain school points proudly to the average salaries of its graduates (highest in the country) and claims this proves it has the best program. What counterarguments might be made?
6. Assume you wanted to know whether attitude change preceded or followed behavior change for a new food product. What would you do?
7. Is it possible to prove causality? To disprove it?
8. A certain chemical manufacturer noted that its sales of a given compound were flat. It knew that its sales were distributed across several industries: utilities (60 percent), paper manufacturers (20 percent), chemical producers (15 percent), and miscellaneous others (5 percent). It wanted to know its market share, the share of its three major competitors, and how clients perceived its product versus those of its major competitors. What study would you design, given a $10,000 budget?

BIBLIOGRAPHY

Campbell, Donald T., and Julian C. Stanley. *Experimental Designs for Research*. Skokie, Ill.: Rand-McNally, 1966.

Frank, Newton. "An Approach to Repositioning Currently Marketed Brands." *Marketing Review* 38 (April–May 1983), pp. 21–25.

Lehmann, Donald R. "Nutritional Knowledge, Attitudes, and Food Consumption Patterns of U.S. Female Heads of Households." Columbia University Graduate School of Business, Research Paper no. 121, 1976.

Chapter 4

Sources of Information

The purpose of this chapter is to delineate the various sources of information available for marketing research. As will be seen, there are enough sources that keeping up with them is a full-time job. The extent of the job is such that most larger firms establish research libraries. A user of research should be careful to support a good library and librarian. Beyond that and keeping up in spare time, making friends with the librarian is probably the best way to keep informed about available information.

The chapter draws the distinction between secondary sources (those which already exist) and primary sources (those which require data collection). The rest of this chapter describes some of the most important sources of information (summarized in Table 4–1), with particular emphasis on secondary sources and qualitative information. More detail on some specific services offered by suppliers appears in Chapter 8.

SECONDARY SOURCES: INTERNAL

A major source of data is information available within the company. Sales records by territories, factory shipments, and marketing programs are all typically available. The problem comes in getting them in a form which is relevant for marketing. A discussion of some of the major problems follows.

Data Are Not Comparable

Much of the data available are gathered for accounting purposes. This implies that many of the profit figures, for example, will be based on fully allocated costs and may not be directly usable for abandonment decisions.

TABLE 4–1 Data Sources

Secondary
Internal
External:
Public domain
Private
Primary
Informal
Qualitative:
Introspection
Depth interviews
Focus groups
Observations
Surveys:
Personal
Phone
Mail
Panels:
Continuous reporting
Special purpose
Standby
Scanner
Experiments:
Laboratory
Field
Models/Simulations

It is also not unlikely to find production, sales, and profit figures all measured in slightly different time frames (as well as in some conflict with each other). In short, since much of the data are not gathered for marketing research purposes, they are often in a form which require adjustment before they are useful. They also tend to be at variance with external measures, such as those obtained from sales audits by firms such as Nielsen.

More Data Are Available than You Know Exist

Few companies have accurate filing systems on the information and research which has already been completed. Decentralized management and product management systems may be excellent for increasing incentives but are inefficient in terms of conveying information. It is not uncommon for essentially the same study to be done in two or more regions as well as at the corporate staff level. Therefore, it is advisable to have a central information clearing house in a large company. Failing that, it is usually a good investment to have occasional lunches with people outside your immediate group to find out what's going on elsewhere in the company.

The Data Are Overly Aggregated

To investigate a variety of issues (i.e., advertising's effect on sales), it is desirable to have data as disaggregated as possible (i.e., sales by regions, districts, or even individual consumers). Yet, much of the data collected is available only in summary form (i.e., national sales and advertising figures), and analyses which could be performed if the original data were accessible are often precluded by the retention of only aggregate information.

Report Formats Are Rigid

Most of the data available are in the form of periodic reports. These reports are typically imposing collections of tables in the form of computer output. These reports might, for example, break sales by region and income category. If someone wanted sales broken by educational background, this would entail a special report, a time delay, and a budget outlay. Because of this, many of the reports serve more to fill up empty shelves than to help make decisions.

Yet, in spite of these problems, internal data and past research reports are very useful forms of information. It is also possible to use internal data to generate the equivalent of primary data. For example, any company which bills its accounts on a periodic basis, such as a utility, can use its own billing records to set up a sample of accounts to act as a panel for monitoring customer behavior over time. One such panel was set up by AT & T, which monitored a sample of both business and residential customers on a monthly basis. (Since the billing system was already in place, the marginal cost of such a system was relatively low.) Hence, given some modest ingenuity, internal data can be put to use effectively.

SECONDARY SOURCES: EXTERNAL

Probably the most underutilized source of information is the library (both the company's, if a good one exists, and the public library). There seem to be two principal reasons for this. First, knowing something is in a library does not make finding it in an up-to-date form easy. Second, there is a feeling that each problem is sufficiently different to require special research (i.e., "that may be true for toothpaste, but we're talking about mouthwash").

The first point can best be addressed by getting to know a research librarian. (An excellent bibliography on external sources of data is contained in Daniells, 1980.) The second point is true, but only to a certain extent—surely something about toothpaste purchase behavior is relevant to mouthwash purchase behavior, at least to the extent that it suggests the kind of research which might be useful. This section, therefore, will proceed to suggest some of the most useful secondary sources. For a more complete discussion, see Stewart (1984).

Trade Associations

Trade associations often maintain extensive information on sales and profits. In addition, they often keep a file on reported research dealing with their industry. Finally, a few actually collect data from consumers, such as the Textile Manufacturers Association, which maintains a panel who report their clothing purchases. For a list of associations, see Fisk and Pair (1977). Another useful source of basic information is The Conference Board.

General Business Publications

In addition to specific industry-oriented publications (e.g., *Progressive Grocer*, *Steel*, *Chemical and Engineering News*) a variety of general publications often carry useful information. Among the most useful are: *Advertising Age*, *Business Week*, *Forbes*, *Fortune*, *Industrial Marketing*, and *Sales and Marketing Management*. Also, *The Wall Street Journal* and *New York Times* newspapers provide additional sources of general information. In addition to these publications, two sets of handbooks contain useful information. The Dartnell Corporation series of handbooks includes *Advertising Manager's Handbook*, *Direct Mail and Mail Order Handbook*, *Marketing Manager's Handbook*, and *Sales Promotion Handbook*. The McGraw-Hill Handbook Series includes *Handbook of Advertising Management*, *Handbook of Marketing Research*, and *Handbook of Modern Marketing*.

Academic Publications

A variety of "professional" journals exist which contain articles of value for marketing research. These journals provide a means of communication both between academics (usually the theoretically/quantitatively oriented ones) and other academics and between academics and practitioners. Those most directed toward practitioners include *Harvard Business Review*, *Journal of Marketing*, *Journal of Advertising Research*, *Journal of Advertising*, and

Journal of Retailing. The more theoretically/methodologically oriented include *Journal of Consumer Research*, *Journal of Marketing Research*, and *Marketing Science*.

Annual Reports

Annual reports provide substantial companywide information. Each company is also required to provide information about its various lines of business annually in a form known as a 10-K report. These reports are filed with the Securities and Exchange Commission and are available on request from the company. Since this type of reporting, in addition to being expensive, provides some useful competitive information, it is not surprising that companies are not eager to comply with this requirement.

Government Publications

Perhaps the most common source of information is the U.S. government. Since your taxes already have paid for it, it is strongly advisable to gather any possible benefit from the various government offices. Most of the data is aggregate in nature (product, rather than brand; region, rather than individual oriented). Its major value is often in assessing market potential.

Department of Commerce/Bureau of Census. The single most useful publication is the *Statistical Abstract of the United States*. This book contains tables of statistical data on income, sales by product categories, and so on. It also provides references to other sources and, hence, serves as an excellent starting point in any data collection process. Another useful reference guide is *Measuring Markets: A Guide to the Use of Federal and State Statistical Data*. Also see *Current Survey Statistics Available from the Bureau of Census*.

Much of the useful data available comes from the Commerce Department/Bureau of Census, so making contact with someone there is a wise move. Some of the most useful sources you are likely to be guided to include the following:

Survey of Current Business. Over 2,500 indicators are reviewed, including commodity prices, real estate, labor force, employment, earnings, foreign trade, and various raw material industries. In addition, a verbal review of the current situation and other articles are included. The data reported here is summarized every two years in *Business Statistics*.

Census of Business (Economic Censuses). For purposes of reporting, similar companies are grouped together by means of a Standard Industrial Classification (SIC) coding system. This system is described in detail by the

Standard Industrial Classification Manual. The grouping method is based on the principal product or service the company produces. Consequently, companies with multiple product lines and those companies that are vertically integrated are difficult to classify, as are many companies which end up in miscellaneous categories. Classification is done first by major groups (two-digit SIC code), then by subgroups, which are broadly defined industries (three-digit SIC code), and then by specific industry (four-digit SIC code). For example, Major Group 34 is Fabricated Metal Products, Group 344 is Fabricated Structural Metal Products, and Industry 3442 is metal doors, sash frames, molding, and trim.

Censuses of the following areas are prepared; Agriculture, Retail Trade, Wholesale Trade, Selected Service Industries, Construction Industries, Manufacturers, Mineral Industries, Transportation, and Government. For example, the census of manufacturers is a production-oriented report geared to measuring number of establishments, output, costs, value added, and wages. Reports are also available both on a product basis in the industry series (e.g., Fabricated Structural Metal Products SIC Group 344) and on a regional basis in the Area Series (e.g., New Jersey). Data are collected by mail canvass on employment, payrolls, man-hours, inventories, capital expenditures, and costs of materials, resales, fuels, electricity, and contract work. In addition, the *Annual Survey of Manufacturers* surveys 65,000 firms to update these data and also collects information on type of fuel consumed, supplemental labor costs, quantity of electricity, gross value of fixed assets, and rental payments. An excellent if dated summary of available reports is provided in *Guide to the* 1982 *Economic Censuses and Related Statistics*.

Current Industrial Reports. These are the periodically updated production statistics for the various product classifications (SIC codes). For example, in April 1976, a report on the "Pulp, Paper, and Board" industry was issued based on a sample of 650 firms.

Current Business Reports. These reports summarize business in different areas. Monthly retail trade by product category is a widely used form of this report.

County Business Patterns. These documents report data on employment and payroll for type of business (two- and four-digit SIC codes) and by geographic area (states, counties, and MSAs—Metropolitan Statistical Areas) as well as for total United States.

Census of Population and Housing. The census of individual households done every 10 years provides a wealth of consumer data on a regional basis. Two general guides are the *User's Guide to the* 1980 *Census of Population and Housing* (U.S. Department of Commerce) and *Making Sense of Census '80: A Marketing Guide* (Allard, 1983). The following are key points:

1. In addition to the questions everyone answered, one long form (which included extensive demographic and other information) went to 19

percent of the total population (with the sample selected to overrepresent rural areas).

2. Governmental areas include:
   a. The United States, Puerto Rico, and other areas under U.S. jurisdiction.
   b. States, counties, and county equivalents.
   c. Incorporated places (cities, villages) and minor civil divisions (MCDs), such as townships.
   d. Congressional districts and election precincts.
   e. American Indian reservations and Alaska native villages.
3. Statistical areas include:
   a. Census regions (Northeast, South, Midwest, and West) and divisions.
   b. Metropolitan statistical areas (MSAs), Primary MSAs (PMSAs), and Consolidated MSAs (CMSAs). These replaced the SMSAs and SCSAs used until 1983.
   c. County census divisions (CCDs).
   d. Census designated places (these used to be unincorporated places).
   e. Urbanized areas.
   f. Census tracts and block numbering areas (BNAs) averaging 4,000 people.
   g. Census blocks (usually city blocks).
   h. Block groups averaging 900 people.
   i. Enumeration districts (EDs) averaging 700. EDs are used when census blocks are not available.
   j. Neighborhoods.
   k. ZIP codes.
4. The pattern of data collection crosses governmental and statistical areas and is fairly complex, as Figure 4–1 indicates.
5. Data are available in several forms, including printed reports, microfiche, computer tapes, and are also accessible via remote computer terminals through CENDATA, an online service.

The census data are very useful for assessing potential by area. In spite of the massive effort entailed, however, it is not a true census in the sense of being completely accurate. Interviewing cheating is a factor, and so is the desire of some people to provide false data. For example, since welfare depends on the presence of a male head of household, there is an obvious incentive to falsify those responses. Hence, it is unfair to deify the census results or castigate other results too harshly which are at slight variance with census results.

Inquiries about Bureau of the Census programs should be directed to Data User Services Division, Customer Services, Bureau of the Census, Washington, DC 20233; (301) 763-4100.

FIGURE 4–1 Principal Hierarchical Relationships among Geographic Units

These figures illustrate the principal hierarchical or "nesting" relationships among census geographic areas. Note that the hierarchies overlap; for example, counties are subdivided into MCDs or CCDs (part A), into urban and rural components (part C), and, inside MSAs, also into census tracts (part B).

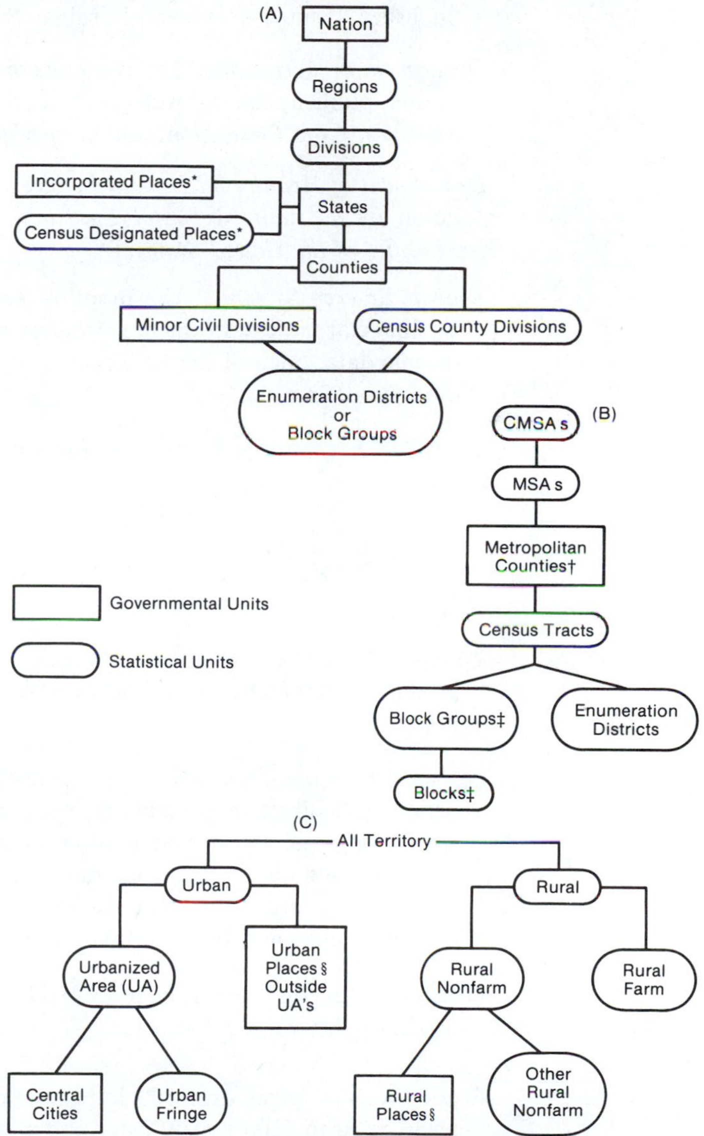

*Places are not shown in the county, MCD, and CCD hierarchy, since places may cross the boundaries of these areas. ED and BG summaries do, however, respect place boundaries.

†In New England, metropolitan towns (MCDs) and cities replace counties as the components of MSAs.

‡In MSAs, blocks and block groups generally cover only the urbanized area and places of 10,000 or more.

§Includes both incorporated places (governmental units) and census designated places (statistical units).

Source: 1980 Census of Population and Housing, modified.

Other Government Sources

Department of Labor. The Monthly Labor Review provides data on employment, wages, and consumer price indexes. The department also publishes "Employment and Earnings Statistics" annually.

Department of Agriculture. The Agriculture Department has monthly and special publications as well as such annual reports as *Agricultural Statistics*, *Crop Production*, and *Crop Values*.

Department of Health and Human Services. HHS provides data on population in the monthly *Vital Statistics Report* and the annual *Vital Statistics of the United States*.

Federal Reserve System. The monthly *Federal Reserve Bulletin* reports on financial indicators, such as interest rates, fund flows, and national income data. Each of the 12 Regional Federal Reserve banks also puts out periodic reports.

Council of Economic Advisors. Publishes the monthly "Economic Indicators."

Other Sources

Thomas Register of American Manufacturers contains information on products manufactured and services rendered by company, including brand names.

Standard Rate and Data Service publishes advertising rates and data for periodicals, direct mail, network, spot radio and TV, newspaper, and transit. Also, newspaper circulation is audited annually. In addition to rates, the newspaper and spot radio and TV reports include data by state, city, county, and metropolitan area on population, spendable income, retail sales, farm population, and farm income.

Other sources on media include *Ayer Directory of Publications and Standard Periodical Directory*.

Morton Reports gives over 500 industry fact reports. These reports cost about $100 to $200 per industry and go into some detail in describing an industry. Some other companies which provide industry reports include *Frost and Sullivan*, *Predicasts*, *Information Source*, and *Find/SVP*. Predicasts has an online data base which combines several sources of data.

Sales and Marketing Management Survey of Buying Power gives data for cities, counties, metropolitan areas, states, and total United States on population, number of households, per capita income, retail sales in total and nine categories, plus indexes of buying power and sales activities.

Editor and Publisher Market Guide profiles 1,500 newspaper markets in terms of a variety of standard measures (population, housing, transportation facilities, salaries, number employed) as well as such other measures as principal industries, utility meters, temperature, shopping days, and retail outlets.

A Guide to Consumer Markets contains census information plus population, prices, employment, and so forth, on statewide or larger regional unit bases. Ownership of durables and spending by categories, often cross-tabbed by income, age, and so forth, are given.

Rand-McNally Commercial Atlas and Marketing Guide contains population figures plus 40 statistics on each county in the United States.

United Nations Statistical Yearbook is a source of international statistical data.

Dun & Bradstreet's Market Identifiers provides data on various businesses.

Leading National Advertisers (LNA). A researcher interested in advertising expenditures would be likely to use LNA reports.

General Comments

Obviously, there are a variety of sources of information which may be useful for specific problems. The key is to know which are relevant. Guides to data sources are available. Two useful ones are the *Business Periodicals Index*, a cross-indexed source of 150 major business periodicals and the *Encyclopedia of Business Information Sources* (Gale Research Company). Other guides include:

Directory of Directories, 3rd ed. Detroit: Gale Research, 1985.

Encyclopedia of Associations. Detroit: Gale Research, published annually.

Computerized literature surveys are now also widely available.

Recently, many firms have begun providing computerized information search services. An example is Lockheed's DIALOG, which, for an hourly fee, will search databases, such as *Chemical Industry Notes* and *Standard & Poor's News* for information of interest (Fries, 1982). Given the amount of information extant, a computer-generated bibliography is often a good investment. There are several guides to computerized information, such as:

Kruzas, Anthony T. and Linda Varekamp Sullivan, eds., *Encyclopedia of Information Systems and Services*, 6th ed. (Detroit: Gale Research, 1985).

Finding the data is not the only problem, however. The accuracy of the data is often questionable, government sources included. Most of the data sources are good for relative comparisons (comparing current sales with last year's). On the other hand, almost no source (the census included) is perfectly accurate in an absolute sense. Accurately measuring, for example, the unemployment rate requires assumptions about how to compute the total labor force, what to do about so-called underemployment (e.g., a Ph.D. working as a waiter), and so forth. Also, frequently, apparently accurate statistics are really gross approximations. For example, the number of umbrellas bought in the United States could be estimated based on a sample of 1,000 in Buffalo, New York, and then projected to the United States as a whole. When the data are reported, however, the numbers take on a permanence and aura of truth which their estimation rarely justifies. Hence, care must be taken not to interpret reported data as perfectly accurate.

PRIMARY SOURCES: INFORMAL

It may seem strange to begin a discussion of primary sources of information for research by considering informal sources. Yet, much useful information can be gained from introspection, discussions with acquaintances, and listening to consumer comments and complaints. For example, while usually overlooked or downplayed by marketing research, some introspection about the problem in question is very useful. While no one can logically argue that brand managers, marketing researchers, or their associates and spouses are typical consumers, they are both consumers and (at least hopefully) fairly knowledgeable about the product/service in question. They also are observers of how others behave. Hence, "insiders" should have a fairly good notion about the product/service under investigation and may be able to list such things as alternative product uses, attributes important to the selection process, and so forth. While such "results" may not be perfectly projectable, they are an extremely useful starting point for further research. Introspection also has the potential to generate a genuinely new idea, something which rarely results from standard surveys. These ideas can either be applied directly or submitted to more formal research for substantiation or rejection. Given the cost of informal research, any good idea which emerges is a bargain.

A side benefit of conducting informal research is that it forces researchers and managers to address problems directly, rather than simply considering the information that is filtered through various reports. One often feels that many of the bad management and research decisions which are made could be avoided if someone had taken the simple step of directly talking to customers and/or looking at the problem from the customer's point of view.

QUALITATIVE METHODS

The research discussed in this book is largely directed toward generating quantitative measures of constructs for the purpose of aiding understanding of the market and, consequently, decision making. Since structured questions presuppose that the relevant responses are known and the only issue is their relative frequency, they are not amenable to first-cut analysis of a problem. Qualitative methods, on the other hand, provide such a starting point and are largely useful prior to the use of structured surveys. Interestingly, the use of "soft" methods seems more prevalent in Japan than in the United States (Johansson and Nonaka, 1987).

At one time, the author as well as many other researchers treated qualitative research as an interesting anachronism but as somehow less pure and useful than quantitative studies of large samples. Recently, due to cost considerations, a realization that big samples don't necessarily produce truth—and a feeling that one- and two-page summaries of large studies are relatively sterile in providing insights—qualitative research has reemerged as an important part of marketing research. In fact, one article suggested that the reason for the success of Japanese companies may be partly attributable to their use of more qualitative research techniques in general and of focus groups in particular (Trachtenberg, 1987). Thus, the only question in this edition was whether to devote an entire chapter to the topic. However, old habits die hard, so this edition contains expanded but by no means complete coverage of the topic.

Qualitative research is widely recognized as useful for structuring problems and helping design quantitative studies. Quantitative studies, on the other hand, are generally preferable when numerical counts or forecasts are needed. Hence, an obvious "do qualitative work first, then a quantitative study" suggestion emerges. Less obvious is the role both play in providing insight, the real goal of research. Quantitative studies often produce results (e.g., uncover a customer segment, find an unexpected correlate with behavior) which require further understanding, often by means of qualitative research. Thus, quantitative and qualitative methods are complementary tools. Moreover, since qualitative methods are essentially ways to engage customers in conversation on their terms, they are quite consistent with the normative dictum of "getting close to the customer." (Certainly, at least in form, qualitative methods seem more user-oriented than surveys, which appear closer to tests than friendly conversations to many respondents.)

The value of qualitative procedures depends almost totally on the insight and intuition of the researcher. Moreover, a portion of qualitative research is driven by the presumption that man is driven by emotions (Zajonc and Markus, 1982; Hirschman and Holbrook, 1982; Havlena and Holbrook, 1986) and by values and social systems (Rook, 1985; Mick, 1986) as much as "rational" economic factors. The combination makes many people uncomfortable, since the research seems "unscientific." However, since the goal of research is to provide information and insight (Langer, 1987), blanket rejection of any method seems inappropriate, especially one which can provide different perspectives.

Several qualitative methods are available and three will be discussed here: participant-observer, depth interviews, and focus group studies.

Participant-Observer

The use of a participant as the primary data source is common in such fields as anthropology (Hirschman, 1986). In this method, the observer (researcher) actually becomes a participant (e.g., a member of a buying committee) and after some time passes makes observations about how the group behaved. While such methods are subject to bias, it is hard to argue that skilled participant-observers do not produce meaningful insights. In fact, because they are involved in greater depth and over time in compiling information, they may be able to explain behavior which, based on a single survey, seems incomprehensible. It is the importance of "social context" that led Bonoma (1985) to call for the expanded use of case research in marketing. (This position is not surprising, given the fact that Bonoma is on the faculty of Harvard, where case research is clearly socially appropriate. Without knowing the context, however, one might find it harder to understand his position.) Still, the use of the classic participant-observer, who might live with the other subjects for from six months to several years, is rarely utilized in marketing research.

Depth Interviews

Depth interviews consist of probing questions being directed at a single subject by a single interviewer. These interviews often last over one hour and require a highly trained (and highly paid) interviewer. The purpose of a depth interview is to continually probe so superficial responses (e.g., "I use brand X because it is pretty") are translated into more specific responses (e.g., "I have a thing about pink, and brand X's wrappers are pink").

Depth interviews were borrowed from psychology and during the 50s enjoyed considerable popularity. People like Ernest Dichter specialized in probing respondents to uncover basic motives (which incidentally often proved to be Freudian/sexual in nature).

An example of a modified form of depth interviewing was provided by the so-called Consumer Behavior Odyssey project. Including such researchers as Russell Belk and Melanie Wallendorf, the odyssey traveled across the United States in a van, observing behavior and videotaping interviews with consumers. While the results are not projectable, some of these interviews are fairly startling in the deep emotional attachment some consumers have to their behavior. (A videotape of the odyssey is available from the Marketing Science Institute in Cambridge, Massachusetts.)

Focus Groups

Focus groups are basically open discussions between 6 to 12 people, with the focus provided by a trained moderator. These sessions typically cost about $1,500 each (for normal consumers) and run for one to one and a half hours. The moderator's role is to gently direct the group to discuss items of interest to the buyer of such research, probing what appear to be superficial answers and moving on when a topic seems to be exhausted.

Focus groups, including some of the best, are often conducted by single entrepreneurs operating out of their living rooms, although major firms have considerable experience in conducting focus group sessions. Focus groups can be used for a variety of purposes (Calder, 1977):

To generate hypotheses about the way consumers think or behave.

To structure questionnaires by uncovering relevant questions and appropriate response categories.

To overcome reticence on the part of subjects to respond. The group setting often encourages participants to say things they would not say in a one-to-one setting. This can result because of a "safety in numbers" effect or the snowballing/egging-on which occurs in group situations.

To generate or evaluate new ideas for products or product uses.

To find explanations for results of other studies.

Focus group sessions are handled in many different ways. However, a common approach when the focus is brand preference and use is to have members of the group progress through three stages. First, group members discuss products they use for a particular situation/need with very little intervention by the moderator. Second, the members are guided to discuss how they rate alternative products. Finally, the moderator probes their feelings in order to uncover why they favor one product over others.

TABLE 4–2 Focus Group Topics and Sample Questions

1. Definiton of significant classes of the attitude object.
   What kinds of cookware are there?
2. Brand awareness.
   What brands of cookware are you familiar with?
3. Evaluation of attitude objects.
   Which brand is best, worst, and why?
4. Situational contexts/relevant others.
   How, when, and where do you use cookware?
5. Weights of situational contexts/relevant others.
   When giving cookware as a gift, what is important?
6. Evaluation of each attitude object in each situational context/relevant others.
   Which brands do you prefer as a gift, and why?
7. Attributes of the attitude object for each situational context.
   a. *Physical attributes.*
      When you think about cooking with aluminum pans, what features of the cookware come to mind?
   b. *Interpersonal.*
      Does anyone in your family care what type of cookware you use?
   c. *Affective.*
      Do you have any special feelings toward particular pots and pans?
8. Association among attributes.
   If a pot is heavy, will it be more or less likely to have even heat distribution?
9. Dimensions, levels, and range of attributes.
   When you say you want a heavy pot, what do you mean by "heavy"?
10. Threshold of satisfaction.
    How long does a pot have to last for you to consider it durable?
11. Beliefs and opinions of brands on attributes, dimensions, and threshold of satisfaction.
    Are Mirro aluminum pans durable enough for you to consider buying them?
12. Latitude of acceptance of beliefs and opinions.
    Would you believe it if I said that the Teflon(TM) coating on a pan will last longer than the pan itself?
13. Evaluation of attributes (salience).
    For which of these things which you say you want in your next set of cookware would you be willing to pay more?
14. Determination of values.
    How would you characterize someone who is a good cook?
15. Hierarchy of values.
    Would you rather be a good cook or have a successful business outside of the home?
16. Saliency of relationships between attributes and values.
    You say you want a pot with even heat distribution. What does that affect, your health, your reputation as a cook, or what?
17. Attribute salience and latitude of acceptance as related to values.
    How much do you think easy cleaning cookware can really affect your lifestyle?
18. Category importance as related to value system.
    How much time in an average day do you spend with cookware?

Source: Martin R. Lautman, "Focus Groups: Theory and Method," in *Advances in Consumer Research* 9, 1981, ed. Andrew Mitchell, pp. 55–56.

Focus groups are very flexible tools. One of their advantages is that they allow much greater probing than even relatively detailed questionnaires. Because they are flexible, they can take advantage of unexpected responses and probe areas previously thought unimportant. Also, people in the group may egg each other on so they will say things they never would say individually. Sensitive subjects, such as birth control, are often probed in focus group sessions. Moreover, a variety of interesting questions which are not suited to structured question format may be asked. In fact, the session is basically one big open-ended question. Finally, since the entire session is usually recorded, analysts can review the results several times before drawing any conclusions.

The role of the leader is to gently but firmly keep the discussion moving. This requires an empathetic attitude and efforts to keep all members of the group involved. The leader should be interested in the topic and have some, but not too much, information about it so a certain "freshness" is apparent. Possibly most important, the leader must be both prepared and flexible.

TABLE 4–3 A Six-Step Procedure for Conducting Group Discussions of New Product Concepts

I. *Problem/Need Identification.*
What problems/shortcomings/unmet needs have you experienced with existing products?
What new products in this area have caught your eye/would you like to see?

II. *Presentation of Product Concept(s).*
Statement of product concept.
Detailed discussion of product features/capabilities.

III. *Evaluation of Product Concept.*
Get global reactions first.
Solicit reactions feature by feature.
Ranking of most/least attractive features.

IV. *Determination of Price Points.*
Either suggest a price to the group, *or*
Have the group suggest an appropriate price.

V. *Extensions to the Product.*
Determine whether options could enhance the product.
Address specific strategic concerns.

VI. *Suggestions for Improving the Product.*
Summarize group reactions.

Source: E. F. McQuarrie and S. H. McIntyre, "Focus Groups and the Development of New Products by Technologically Driven Companies: Some Guidelines," *Journal of Product Innovation Management* (March 1986), p. 44.

Preparation includes an outline of topics to be covered and a general concept of the order in which they should be discussed. A useful outline of topics and sample questions from a focus group on cookware was provided by Lautman (1981) from ARBOR, Inc. (Table 4–2).

A somewhat less specific suggested outline for discussing new product concepts provided by McQuarrie and McIntyre (1986) is shown in Table 4–3. Flexibility means allowing the group discussion to find its own path through the topics and to accept and encourage unexpected (as opposed to totally nonsensical) comments. Hence, the focus group leader plays a role quite similar to that of a faculty member leading a case.

The problems with focus groups are also numerous. First, the process is heavily dependent on the moderator's ability to direct the discussion. A poor leader or group selection will make the results relatively useless. Second, bad group dynamics (one loud mouth, and the like) can greatly reduce the value of the results. Third, interpreting the results requires considerable skill. A corollary to this is the buyer of research who does not observe a focus group either in person or on tape may lose much of the value of the session. For purposes of idea generation, one study indicated separate interviews produced more ideas than a focus group (Fern, 1982). The study also suggested that two focus groups of four may be more productive than one of size eight. Finally, focus groups are not useful for projecting to total markets (Bellenger, Bernhardt, and Goldstucker, 1976).

On balance, then, focus groups have a valuable role to play in understanding the market. On the other hand, they are not useful for producing quantitative projections. For this reason, many researchers will use a focus group as a first step in a research strategy which later includes large-scale surveys and quantitative analysis.

OBSERVATIONS

Direct observation of behavior is a very important tool. Its major advantage is that in many circumstances it is the most accurate way to measure overt behavior. In some cases, observation is the only way to measure behavior due to either unwillingness (bank robbers are unlikely to recount their actions very accurately) or inability on the part of a consumer to report past behavior (ever asked a two-year-old something?). Its major disadvantages are *(a)* it cannot be used to measure thoughts, preferences, and so forth, and *(b)* it can be fairly costly. Actually, several types of observation methods exist. Some of the major choices to be made include scope of observation, degree of control over the setting, direct versus indirect measurement, observer (human versus mechanical), and obtrusiveness of observer (known versus hidden observer).

Scope of Observation

An observation can be highly structured if the key behavior is well established in advance. For example, in observing soap purchased at a given store, it is possible to observe only *(a)* brand purchased and *(b)* length of time to make the choice. Alternatively, an observation could include all aspects of behavior, including number of packages examined, number of people talked to, and so forth. The scope of the observation has a great deal to do with the problem definition. A vague problem definition and exploratory research (e.g., "let's see how people buy soap") tend to call for all inclusive observation, while a tight problem definition (e.g., "measure the relation between brand bought and time spent shopping") leads to much more structured and less extensive observations.

Degree of Control Over the Setting

In observing behavior, there is a choice between observing behavior in a natural setting (where observation is fairly difficult) and a more controlled situation (where observation and control of extraneous and desired influences is easier but behavior may be more artificial). Not surprisingly, controlled observation is usually both less expensive and less realistic.

Direct versus Indirect Measurement

Most observational methods involve directly measuring behavior. A variety of indirect methods have been employed. One example involved newspaper readership in New York City. Surveys consistently showed that the *New York Times* was the paper of choice even though the *Daily News* was clearly a large seller. Given the large social pressure to give the "right" answer (the *Times*), one enterprising researcher decided to check the garbage cans of a number of residents. In addition to some fairly unpleasant items, the researcher found a preponderance of the *Daily News*.

A related and interesting approach for measuring food consumption was based on a "census" of items found in household refuse (Rathje and Ritenbaugh, 1984). By examining items in a family's garbage, some conclusions concerning differences in consumption across national identity, ethnicity, region, income, and minority states were derived (Reilly and Wallendorf, 1987).

A more common indirect method for measuring food purchase behavior is a pantry audit. By literally going through a kitchen and recording what is on the shelves, an estimate of food shopping and consumption patterns can be made. It is only an estimate, however, since the items will be on the shelf because they were bought but not consumed, which tends to occur with rarely used or bad tasting foods at least as often as popular/commonly used ones.

A final example of indirect observation research is TV ratings, an arena in which Nielsen and AGB are competing suppliers. By attaching a recording device to TV sets, the programs that are on can be monitored. Whether they are being watched or slept through, however, is unknown. In fact, any audit is a form of indirect observation. Hence, almost all accounting data (sales records, inventories, and so on) involve observations and, except in the case of physical audits, usually indirect observations.

Observer (Human versus Mechanical)

The choice between human and mechanical observations usually depends on which is easier to utilize in a given situation. When choosing between human and mechanical observation, the accuracy of mechanical observation must be contrasted with the less accurate but often more insightful human observations. One form of human observation is to have a subject of observation also serve as an observer. This *participant observer* then records both his or her own behavior as well as that of other participants.

One of the most widely used types of mechanical observation is *optical scanning*. Here customer purchases are automatically recorded and keyed to the customer's account via a credit card. Products are coded in terms of the Universal Product Code (UPC), and information on price, quantity, etc. is gathered for each transaction. This allows extensive data to be collected by store, product type, brand, or customer. These data are now extensively used by packaged goods manufacturers.

Another basic type of mechanical response observation is *physiological measures*. An eye camera can be used to monitor what an individual is looking at. These have been used in studies of both shopping behavior and advertising response. A *pupilometer* is a device which attaches to a person's head that measures interest/attention by the amount of dilation in the pupil of the subject's eye. A *galvinometer* measures excitement by means of the electrical activity level in a subject's skin. For example, one toy company exposed 400 children to a collection of new toys and, based on galvinometer readings and other physical measures, selected a single toy to emphasize in a particular selling season. Obviously, the subject is acutely aware of such observation because of the equipment involved. Still, these "unnatural" measurement devices have in some cases accurately measured level of response to an ad.

Two less obtrusive measures are response latency and voice pitch analysis. *Response latency* measures how long a person takes to respond to a question. The length of time is often thought to be related to the difficulty of the decision. Voice pitch analysis measures the interest by monitoring the voice of a respondent.

Obtrusiveness of Observer (Known versus Hidden Observer)

The choice between hidden and revealed observers depends on how differently the researcher believes the subject will behave if it is known that the subject is being observed. One can imagine all kinds of modified behavior in which the subject attempts to appear more logical, and so forth, than he/she/it really is (Webb et al., 1966). In many cases, however, this source of bias is likely to be fairly small.

The question of obtrusiveness also raises myriad legal and ethical questions concerning protection of subjects. Many situations require that formal subject consent forms be signed by the subjects in advance. Moreover, whenever subjects are exposed to a manipulation (e.g., a mock-up ad) it is important to "debrief" the subjects at the end of the observation by explaining the purpose of the manipulation to them. The debriefing is especially crucial when one or more of the manipulations involve false information. The principles of consent and debriefing apply both to observational and experimental settings.

In summary, then, observation is really a broad category involving a variety of techniques. Examples are found in Table 4–4. It is important to

TABLE 4–4 Some Examples of Observational Methods

	Characteristics				
Method	*Scope (Structured versus Extensive)*	*Degree of Control (Natural versus Controlled)*	*Directness (Direct versus Indirect)*	*Observer (Human versus Mechanical)*	*Obtrusiveness (Known versus Hidden Observation)*
Hidden camera	Extensive	Either	Direct	Mechanical	Hidden
Store clerk with check list	Structured	Natural	Direct	Human	Known
Physiological measurement (galvinometer, etc.)	Structured	Controlled	Direct	Mechanical	Known
Pantry audit	Structured	Natural	Indirect	Human	Known
Nielsen TV ratings	Structured	Natural	Indirect	Mechanical	Known
Participant observer	Extensive (usually)	Either	Direct	Human	Either

remember that observations can be used as complements to surveys or other methods. In fact, most experiments involve both observations and surveys to ascertain the effect of the experiment.

SURVEYS

Surveys are one way of collecting data, and unfortunately in marketing research sometimes thought of as the only way. Several companies prepare massive (syndicated) surveys, usually annually, which collect data on a variety of topics, such as background (age, income, and so on), media exposure (magazines read, TV shows viewed), and product ownership. For a fee, a company can buy into such a survey. In addition, a company can add a few special questions of its own. The advantage is that by cooperating with others, the costs are shared and thus lower for each of the participants. The disadvantages are:

1. The timetable for the survey is rigid and may not match the decision-making process.
2. The number and type of questions a company may add are very limited.

Custom-designed surveys are much more flexible than syndicated surveys. Among their disadvantages are the requirements (both time and monetary) of sample selection and questionnaire design. Actually, these surveys can be conducted in a variety of ways including personal, mail, or phone interviews. These are discussed in detail in Chapter 6.

PANELS

Continuous Reporting Panels

Many companies maintain panels of individuals who agree to report all their purchases of a certain category of products, such as groceries and clothing. These panels allow tracking of brand, size, and quantity purchased over time. This allows both the continuous monitoring of shares by brand, size, and so forth, and the identification of which brands compete most closely. The problems with continuous reporting panels are unfortunately fairly severe (Boyd and Westfall, 1960; Sudman, 1964). Yet, in spite of these problems, panels are widely used and useful.

Panel Membership Bias. The panel recruitment process is one which produces a high level of nonparticipation. A 10 percent or smaller recruitment rate is typical. Reporting every bottle of catsup purchased by brand, size, store, price, whether it was on special, whether a coupon was used, and so forth, is an activity in which most people refuse to participate. While the people who are eventually included in the panel are typically matched to the general population in terms of obvious characteristics, such as age and income, there is a nagging worry that the same motivation which led someone to join the panel would cause him or her to behave differently from those "normal" people who refused.

False Reporting. The reporting forms are sufficiently complex that a variety of shortcuts may be appealing to the respondents. One obvious way to shorten the task is to simply fail to report some purchases. Alternatively, it is convenient to report multiple purchases of a single brand and size or to report more purchases of the brand immediately previously reported. Finally, there is the real problem of forgetting and either failing to report a purchase or reporting it incorrectly. Thus, reporting rates and accuracy vary (McKenzie, 1983).

Panel Aging and Dropouts. A problem all panels struggle with is aging. A panel with the right average age in 1980 will be on average about 10 years too old in 1990 if no one drops out. Hence, it is important to continually update the panel by adding members, both to keep the average age down and to replace respondents who for one reason or another (moving, loss of interest, death) depart from the panel.

Panel Conditioning. The mere fact that an individual is reporting purchases of a product is likely to make the person think more carefully about the product. Consequently, being on the panel may create an expert consumer whose behavior no longer is representative of consumers in general.

Getting the Data in Shape for Analysis. The problems involved in transforming the returned forms into computer-ready data are legion. As such, the chance for error is great.

Special-Purpose Panels

To avoid the aging, conditioning, and other problems with existing panels, as well as to collect data on subjects not covered by existing panels, it is possible to set up a special-purpose panel to gather data. The two main problems with this approach are:

Recruitment of panel members is expensive both in terms of effort and money.

The dropout rate may be a problem (Sobol, 1959). For example, in one study a special phone panel was established to monitor sales of a new car over an 18-month period in five measurement waves. In spite of the strong "guarantee" of the supplier that dropouts would be 5 percent or at most 10 percent per wave, the actual dropout rate was nearly 20 percent per wave. By wave 5, less than half the original panel members remained (Farley, Katz, and Lehmann, 1978). Since dropouts were, as expected, less interested in new cars, this dropout problem led to a biased sample in later waves which required some gyrations to overcome (or at least reduce).

Standby Panels

To ensure a large response rate, it is possible to utilize panels of people who have previously agreed to provide information on any subject. Background information, such as age and income, is maintained on these panel members. The most common form of the standby panel is the mail panel. These panels are often maintained in units of 1,000, each of which is intended to be representative of the total United States in terms of age, region of the country, and so on. Two major problems with this approach are the low recruitment rate and the underrepresentation of minority groups.

The Low Recruitment Rate. Typically fewer than 1 in 10 people will agree to serve on a standby panel. Those who do obviously are more interested in filling out questionnaires and, hence, are at least in one aspect atypical of the general population. They are also relatively literate. (Illiterates have problems with six-page mail questionnaires.)

The Underrepresentation of Minority Groups. Mail panels typically underrepresent minority groups, such as blacks and Spanish-speaking Americans. The minority members included tend to be older. Therefore, for some purposes, these panels are seriously (no pun intended) biased.

Scanner Panels

A relatively recent development is so-called scanner panels. These panels collect data by means of optical scanners, which record items purchased and prices paid at a checkout counter. These data are often augmented by advertising data (e.g., newspaper ads) and promotions (e.g., if a coupon was used). Panel members are identified by means of a credit card.

Scanner data thus contain a wealth of information. For example, they make it possible to track the effect of ads or promotions at the store level. Such tracking, however, is far from trivial. The basic unit of data is the individual transaction (e.g., a tube of toothpaste purchased by J. Doe on

March 15 for 87 cents). This unit is then typically stored on separate files relating to the store and the family. The resulting data files for even a single store or family are amazingly long. Moreover, data on advertising or family characteristics (age, income, and so forth) are typically stored on separate files. Hence, even attempting to study the impact of advertising on sales involves a tedious task of file manipulation.

Aside from the problem of handling the essentially infinite quanity of scanner data, some other problems have also been noted. First, the data are at the family rather than the individual level. Second, many influences on sales, such as TV advertising, point of purchase displays, and number of shelf facings, may not be included in the data set. Third, behavior of nonbuyers must be inferred (e.g., did they not buy the toothpaste at 87 cents because they failed to receive a coupon, were on vacation, and so on?). Fourth, store coverage by scanners is not complete and many purchases are not included in the database (e.g., purchases made for cash at a local deli). Fifth, certain customers refuse to join such a panel, leading to possible nonresponse bias.

In spite of these and other problems, however, scanner data provide a welcome addition to the market research arsenal. They are particularly useful for tracking the effects of price and promotions on sales. Moreover, as some of the current limitations are overcome, scanner data seem destined to be one of the best primary sources on frequently purchased goods. (Obviously, it is not likely to be a major data source for studying the process by which $10 billion construction projects are awarded.) A more detailed discussion of scanner data is included in Chapter 8.

EXPERIMENTS

An important source of information is experiments. These come in two basic types: laboratory and field.

Laboratory

Laboratory experiments are the epitome of tightly controlled experiments. Here, essentially all the stimuli the respondent is exposed to can be controlled. Therefore, the effect of a single variable (e.g., a particular ad) can be assessed. The disadvantage of a lab setting is its lack of realism and the resulting likelihood that lab results will differ from field results, usually in the form of being more dramatic. For this reason, absolute results are generally recalibrated according to the past correspondence between lab results and subsequent field results.

Field

The opposite of a lab experiment, a field experiment is the ultimate in realism but the worst in terms of control. To be effective, it is important to insure (*a*) that the controlled variable did, in fact, vary according to the design and (*b*) that other things which influence the results did not change concurrently (i.e., when the ads shown were changed, the prices did not also change).

In constructing these polar extreme types of experiments, it is important to realize that intermediate services are available. One of the best known is a controlled store test where "real" shoppers in a real store are exposed to an experiment (e.g., changes in shelf facings or prices). Such tests are designed to achieve most of the control of a lab experiment plus most of the realism of a field setting. Another important distinction is between controlled and natural experiments. In a controlled experiment, the subjects are assigned to a "treatment" by the researcher. If you were testing three prices, you could assign every third person to a particular price setting. By contrast, in a natural experiment, respondents are allowed to select (naturally) their own treatment. For example, if I were interested in assessing the effect of education on job choice, I could try to control the situation by assigning subjects to educational levels. This, however, would be both grossly expensive and morally questionable. Hence, an alternative is to simply observe how job choice and education correlate in a sample of individuals. The problem with this (natural) approach is that the education level is likely to be related to a set of variables, such as parents' education and income, attitude toward school, and IQ, which also influence job choice. Consequently, a natural experiment is cheap in terms of data collection but expensive in terms of the analysis required to deduce correctly the effect of the treatment variable on the criterion. (Survey data, the mainstay of current marketing research, is basically treated as a series of natural experiments when it is analyzed.)

MODELS / SIMULATIONS

At the polar extreme from focus groups are the collection of models which are formal/mathematical descriptions of a situation. These models are typically the result of analysis of some form of data plus a theory and are calibrated to answer "what if?" questions (e.g., "What if I increase price 10 percent?"). What is available to a potential user is typically a general description of the model plus the model's answer to a series of questions.

Actually models are at least as much users of data as sources of data. Typically, they require one of the other forms of input data (panel, special survey, and the like) for calibration. Only after these data are available and analyzed do the models become sources of information. For that reason, they are not discussed extensively here.

SUMMARY

This chapter has described several sources of information, with secondary data and qualitative methods getting relatively detailed treatment. Often, unless both secondary sources have been examined and some qualitative research has been performed, proceeding to collect more primary data is premature. The following two chapters provide more extensive discussion of two of the other methods of primary data collection: experiments and surveys. It is important to recognize, however, that these methods, while they compete for budget dollars, are complementary in terms of the information they provide and are often used in conjunction with each other.

PROBLEMS

1. Discuss the appropriateness of a continuous panel versus a revolving panel (new respondents each wave) for monitoring.
   a. Advertising awareness.
   b. Brand-switching patterns.
   c. Attitude toward a brand.
2. What were U.S. dishwasher sales in 1987? Compare several sources and explain the disparity.
3. Where would you go to find out information about the PVC business?
4. What would you do to estimate the growth rate of sales of microcomputers and microwave ovens in the United States?

BIBLIOGRAPHY

Agricultural Statistics. Washington, D.C.: Department of Agriculture, published annually.

Allard, Patsy Bailey. *Making Sense of Census '80: A Marketer's Guide*. New York: American Management Associations, 1983.

Annual Survey of Manufacturers. Washington, D.C.: Department of Commerce, Bureau of the Census, published annually.

Ayer Directory of Publications. Philadelphia: Ayer Press, published annually.

Barton, Roger, ed. *Handbook of Advertising Management*. New York: McGraw-Hill, 1970.

Bellenger, Danny N.; Kenneth L. Bernhardt; and Jac L. Goldstucker. *Qualitative Methods in Marketing*. Chicago: American Marketing Association, 1976.

Bonoma, Thomas V. "Case Research in Marketing: Opportunities, Problems, and a Process." *Journal of Marketing Research* 22 (May 1985), pp. 199–208.

Boyd, Harper W., Jr., and Ralph L. Westfall. *An Evaluation of Continuous Consumer Panels as a Source of Marketing Information*. Chicago: American Marketing Association, 1960.

Britt, Steuart H. *Marketing Manager's Handbook*. Chicago: Dartnell, 1973.

______, and Irwin A. Shapiro. "Where to Find Marketing Facts," *Harvard Business Review* 40 (September–October 1962), pp. 44–50 and 171–78.

Buell, Victor, ed. *Handbook of Modern Marketing*. New York: McGraw-Hill, 1970.

Business Statistics. Washington, D.C.: Department of Commerce, Bureau of the Census, published biannually.

Calder, Bobby J. "Focus Groups and the Nature of Qualitative Marketing Research." *Journal of Marketing Research* 14 (August 1977), pp. 353–64.

Census of Business. Washington, D.C.: Department of Commerce, Bureau of the Census, published annually.

Churchill, Gilbert A., Jr. *Marketing Research*. 4th ed. New York: Dryden Press, 1987.

Crop Production. Washington, D.C.: Department of Agriculture, published annually.

Crop Values. Washington, D.C.: Department of Agriculture, published annually.

Current Survey Statistics Available from the Bureau of the Census. Washington, D.C.: Department of Commerce, Bureau of the Census, 1975.

Daniells, Lorna M. "Note on Sources of External Data." HBS Case Services #9–580–107. Boston: Harvard Business School, 1980.

Digest of Educational Statistics. Washington, D.C.: Department of Health and Human Services, published annually.

Editor and Publisher Market Guide. New York; The Editor and Publisher Co., published annually.

Farley, John U.; Jerrold P. Katz; and Donald R. Lehmann. "Impact of Different Comparison Sets on Evaluation of a New Subcompact Car Brand." *Journal of Consumer Research* 5 (September 1978), 138–42.

Federal Reserve Bulletin. Washington, D.C.: Federal Reserve, published monthly.

Ferber, Robert, ed. *Handbook of Marketing Research*. New York: McGraw-Hill, 1974.

Fern, Edward F. "The Use of Focus Groups for Idea Generation: The Effects of Group Size, Acquaintanceship, and Moderator on Response Quantity and Quality." *Journal of Marketing Research* 19 (February 1982), pp. 1–13.

Fisk, Margaret, and Mary Wilson Pair, eds. *Encyclopedia of Associations*. 11th ed. Detroit: Gale Research, 1977.

Fries, James R. "Library Support for Industrial Marketing Research." *Industrial Marketing Management* 11 (1982), pp. 47–51.

Garry, Leon, ed. *Standard Periodical Directory*. 4th ed. New York: Oxbridge, 1973.

Goldman, Alfred E. "The Group Depth Interview." *Journal of Marketing* 46 (Fall 1982), pp. 61–68.

A Guide to Consumer Markets. New York: The Conference board, published annually.

Harvey, Joan, ed. *Statistics—Europe: Sources for Social, Economic, and Market Research*. 3rd ed. Beckenham, Kent, England: CBD Research Ltd., published monthly.

Havlena, William J. and Morris B. Holbrook. "The Varieties of Consumption Experience: Comparing Two Typologies of Emotion in Consumer Behavior." *Journal of Consumer Research* 13 (December 1986), pp. 394–404.

Hirschman, Elizabeth C. "Humanistic Inquiry in Marketing Research: Philosophy, Method, and Criteris." *Journal of Marketing Research* 23 (August 1986), pp. 237–49.

______, and Morris B. Holbrook. "Hedonic Consumption: Emerging Concepts, Methods, and Propositions." *Journal of Marketing* 46 (Summer 1982), pp. 92–101.

Hodgson, Richard S. *Direct Mail and Mail Order Handbook*. 3rd ed. Chicago: Dartnell, 1976.

Johansson, Johny K., and Ikujiro Nonaka. "Market Research the Japanese Way." *Harvard Business Review* 65 (May–June, 1987), pp. 16–22.

Langer, Judith. "The process of Insight: How Researchers Turn Qualitative Research into Marketing Insight." *Marketing Review* 43 (November 1987), pp. 11–15.

Lautman, Martin R. "Focus Groups: Theory and Method." In *Advances in Consumer Research*, ed. Andrew Mitchell. September, 1981, pp. 52–56.

McKenzie, John. "The Accuracy of Telephone Call Data Collected by Diary Methods." *Journal of Marketing Research* 20 (November 1983), pp. 417–27.

McQuarrie, Edward F., and Shelby H. McIntyre. "Focus Groups and the Development of New Products by Technologically Driven Companies: Some Guidelines." *Product Innovation Management* 3 (March 1986), pp. 40–47.

Mick, David Glen. "Consumer Research and Semiotics: Exploring the Mythology of Signs, Symbols, and Significance." *Journal of Consumer Research* 13 (September 1986), pp. 196–213.

Monthly Labor Review. Washington, D.C.: Department of Labor, published monthly.

Morton Reports. Merrick, New York: Morton Research, published annually.

Rand-McNally Commercial Atlas and Marketing Guide. Skokie, Ill.: Rand-McNally, published annually.

Rathje, William and C. K. Ritenbaugh. "The Household Refuse Analysis." *American Behavioral Scientist* 28 (September/October 1984), pp. 115–28.

Reilly, Michael D. and Melanie Wallendorf. "A Comparison of Group Differences in Food Consumption Using Household Refuse." *Journal of Consumer Research* 14 (September 1987), pp. 289–94.

Riso, Ovid, ed. *Sales Promotion Handbook*. 6th ed., Chicago: Dartnell, 1973.

Rook, Dennis W. "The Ritual Dimension of Consumer Behavior." *Journal of Consumer Research* 12 (December 1985), pp. 251–64.

Sales Management Survey of Buying Power. New York: Bill Brothers, published bimonthly.

Sobol, M. "Panel Mortality and Panel Bias." *Journal of the American Statistical Association* 54 (1959), pp. 52–68.

Standard Industrial Classification Manual. Washington, D.C.: Office of Statistical Standards, 1967.

Stansfied, Richard H. *Advertising Manager's Handbook*. Chicago: Dartnell, 1969.

Statistical Abstract of the United States. Washington, D.C.: U.S. Department of Commerce, Bureau of the Census, published annually.

Stewart, David W. *Secondary Research.* Beverly Hills, Calif.: Sage Publications, 1984.

Sudman, Seymour. "On the Accuracy of Recording of Consumer Panels." *Journal of Marketing Research* 2 (May 1964), pp. 14–20, and 2 (August 1964), pp. 69–88.

Survey of Current Business. Washington, D.C. Department of Commerce, Bureau of Economic Analysis, published monthly.

Thomas Register of American Manufacturers. New York: Thomas, Published annually, 11 volumes.

Trachtenberg, Jeffrey A., ed. "Listening, the Old-Fashioned Way." *Forbes* 140 (October 5, 1987), pp. 202–04.

United Nations Statistical Yearbook. New York: United Nations, published annually.

U.S. Bureau of the Census. "Census Bureau Programs and Products." *Factfinder for the Nation.* CFF no. 18 (September 1985), pp. 1–16.

U.S. Department of Commerce. *User's Guide to the* 1980 *Census of Population and Housing.* Washington, D.C.: U.S. Government Printing Office, 1982.

Vital Statistics of the United States. Washington, D.C.: Department of Health and Human Services, published annually.

Vital Statistics Report. Washington, D.C. Department of Health and Human Services, published monthly.

Wasserman, Paul; Betsy Ann Olive; Eleanor Allen; Charlotte Georgi; and James Woy, eds. *Encyclopedia of Business Information Sources.* 3rd ed. Detroit: Gale Research, 1976.

Wasson, Chester R. "Use and Appraisal of Existing Information." In *Handbook of Marketing Research*, ed. Robert Ferber. New York: McGraw-Hill, 1974, pp. 2–11 to 2–25.

Webb, Eugene J.; Donald T. Campbell; Richard D. Schwartz; and Lee Sechrest. *Unobtrusive Measures.* Skokie, Ill.: Rand-McNally, 1966.

Zajonc, Robert B. and Hazel Markus. "Affective and Cognitive Factors in Preferences." *Journal of Consumer Research* 9 (September 1982), pp. 123–31.

Part II

Collecting Information and Preparing for Analysis

Chapter 5

Causality and Experiments

The notion of causality is both subtle and crucial. When a manager cuts price 10 percent, there is usually an implicit assumption about how this will affect sales and profits. For example, it may be assumed that sales will increase 30 percent. This assumption is based on the events that a price change precipitates (causes) in the market. Such assumptions may be intuitive or based on actual experience (e.g., "That's what happened in Des Moines in 1978"). The purpose of this chapter is (1) to indicate how important a concept causality is, (2) to indicate that causality is difficult to uncover, and (3) to discuss experiments that are the best but far from an infallible tool for assessing certain kinds of causality.

BASIC CONCEPTS

The concept of causality implies that, if I change a particular variable (e.g., advertising), then another variable (e.g., sales) will change *as a result of my actions*. Hence, almost any marketing decision (and in fact any decision) is implicitly made by considering its "consequences." If managers can develop an understanding of the causal relations in a market, then they can make "optimal" decisions. Causal inference, therefore, is essential to effective decision making.

One way to make causal inferences is deductively. For example, one can use a strong theory about the way the world behaves (e.g., Einstein's theory of relativity) to predict the consequences of various actions. Much work in mathematics and physics falls into this category where causal inferences are deduced and then examined. When the inferences are proven false, then a new theory is required. Similarly, economists often deduce consequences of actions in the market based on their models.

A second way to draw causal inferences is to examine data in an attempt to see what they indicate about the world. Actually, a pure "inductive" process is never practiced, since even the most naive managers or researchers have some causal notions or theories. In fact, deciding whether data or theory should come first is similar to the proverbial debate about which came first—the chicken or the egg. The crucial fact is that theory (causal notions) leads to data collection, which in turn leads to revised theory in a never ending series.

A third way to draw causal inferences is intuitively. Experienced managers, through a process that contains elements of both deduction and induction and that is often not completely conscious, may be good at predicting the consequences of their actions. If such managers are available, they should be utilized. However, relying on this approach will have two unpleasant consequences. First, crucial mistakes will be made, and the more complex the situation, the greater the likelihood of a mistake. Second, how they draw conclusions will remain a black box both to them and to the rest of the company. Thus, when they leave, their knowledge leaves with them.

Causality can be understood on several levels. On the one hand, it is possible to construct an understanding of simple cause and effect relationships of the following type:

Here we understand that advertising (A) causes sales (S), but not how. While this level of understanding may be adequate for many simple decisions, it fails to consider more complex situations. For example, if our competitors' advertising and prices as well as our advertising change during a period of inflation and recession, what will happen to our sales? In this situation, one should consider both the simultaneous impact of advertising and prices as well as competitors' reactions. Put differently, incomplete causal understanding can be misleading and even dangerous.

On the other hand, it is possible to search for a complete model of the world. While this is an (the?) appropriate goal for academic research and a worthwhile pursuit for business, it is also an expensive and time-consuming task. Hence, most businesses make the decision to operate in a world of incomplete understanding and imperfect prediction of the consequences of their actions. While this is appropriate, especially in the short run, some people (including guess who?) feel that, in the long run, firms would benefit from a relatively more thorough attempt to explicitly examine the likely consequences of their actions.

ESTABLISHING CAUSALITY

As an example of the difficulty in deducing causality, consider the following scenario. In one of a company's eight sales districts (Cleveland), both the promotion budget and sales increased 20 percent, while in the other seven districts, promotion and sales were unchanged. A deduction one could (and, in some sense, would like to) draw is that increasing promotion 20 percent *caused* sales to increase 20 percent. Unfortunately, such a deduction is likely to be unwarranted for one of several reasons:

1. *Randomness.* To assume that the 20 percent change produced exactly a 20 percent increase ignores the essential randomness in the world. At the extreme, this may have been a fluke that would never recur. At the least, the conclusion that a 20 percent increase in promotion budget produces a 20 percent increase in sales ignores the need to hedge such a prediction. Put differently, given human knowledge, it is impossible to predict the consequences of an action with certainty.

2. *Other explanations.* It is possible that a major competitor withdrew from the market in Cleveland and that this, not promotion, caused sales to increase. Alternatively, it may be that top management targeted Cleveland for extra effort this year, including greater advertising support, more salespeople, and so on, and that this effort caused the increase in sales. Finally, it could be that a general economic upsurge in the Cleveland district caused both promotional budgets and sales to increase.

3. *Reverse causality.* The assumption made in drawing the promotion-causes-sales deduction is that promotion precedes sales. Given that many promotional budgets are set as a percent of sales, an equally plausible explanation of the facts is that such a promotional budgeting rule was followed by the company.

In attempting to establish causality, then, several steps are required. These are generally grouped into three major categories: demonstrating concurrent variation between two variables, establishing precedence, and eliminating alternative explanations.

1. *Concurrent variation.* A necessary but insufficient condition for establishing causality between two variables (A and B) is that the two move together in a consistent pattern (i.e., when A goes up, B goes up). Returning to the promotion-sales example, consider the following two situations representing the combination of promotion and sales across 200 districts:

		Sales	
		Up	*Down*
Case I:			
Promotion:	Up	80	20
	Down	20	80
Case II:			
Promotion:	Up	50	50
	Down	50	50

In case I, sales and promotion tend to move together, while in case II they are unrelated. Assuming that we are looking for a simple promotion-to-sales relationship, case I looks promising, while case II indicates that no simple causal relationship exists.

2. *Precedence.* Case I passed the concurrent variation test. The next issue is to determine which came first—promotion increases or sales increases. Clearly if sales increased first, it is not appropriate to say that promotion caused sales.

The notion of precedence is conceptually clear. Unfortunately, it is often difficult to determine which came first in nonexperimental settings. For example, if the effect of promotion on sales occurs within one week, if data on promotion are available monthly, and if data on sales are available bimonthly (e.g., from Nielsen), then it is very difficult to determine which change came first. For this reason, experiments are often promoted as the best hope for establishing causality.

3. *Elimination of alternative explanations.* A variety of alternative explanations may exist for a set of results—any one of which could cause one to alter the apparent causal inference from a set of data. Unless these can be ruled out, a causal relationship has not been conclusively established. Notice that it is almost always possible to come up with an essentially infinite number of alternative explanations, although not all may be particularly believable. Hence, causality can rarely be established with absolute certainty. The best we can hope for, therefore, is to establish causality beyond reasonable doubt.

EXPERIMENTS

To make decisions concerning price, advertising, and so forth, a manager is concerned with how these factors influence sales and profits. In other words, the manager wants to know what will happen to sales if the price is increased 10 cents a package. The obvious way to get the answer is to raise the price 10 cents and see what happens. This straightforward experimental approach has two problems. First, most experiments have unforseen problems that make direct causal interpretation difficult. Second, causality and certainty are not synonyms. Even if I know that a price increase will cause sales to drop, the amount of the decrease will not be known with certainty. Put differently, the best one can hope for is an estimate of the effect of price on sales with a fairly narrow range of uncertainty.

In designing experiments, concerns about the validity (usefulness) of the experiment are traditionally grouped into two categories. Internal validity refers to the experiment producing a "clean" result, which rules out competing explanations for the results. By contrast, external validity refers to the extent to which the results of an experiment are generalizable. A perpetual conflict exists between these two goals. Concern about internal validity leads to strict controls in a laboratory setting, which may not bear much resemblance to the real world, while realistic (natural) situations have numerous competing explanations for their results. The craft of market research, therefore, involves balancing these two concerns.

Internal Validity

Interpretation of an experiment can be clouded by several factors, including:

Noncomparability of Groups (Selection). In many field or natural experiments, the subjects are assigned to groups after the treatment occurs. In such cases, it is not unusual for the subjects who "selected" the treatment (e.g., read *The Wall Street Journal*) to differ from those who were not exposed to the treatment in some unmeasured way (e.g., interest in reading, desire/need to keep current on topics, etc.) that could affect the results.

Lost Subjects (Mortality). Over the course of an experiment, subjects inevitably drop out (e.g., individuals can get tired, move; businesses can fold or get new management teams who are less hospitable to the research). Dropout rates of 20 percent are not uncommon in survey research between waves of a study, and single studies often have termination rates of 10 to 30 percent, especially for long surveys. If dropouts differ from the retained subjects (which they often do), then the results are affected.

Exogeneous Occurrences (History). During many experiments (especially field experiments), an event occurs outside the control of the researcher (e.g., an oil embargo, a strike, a new product introduction). This event influences the measured results and makes it hard to estimate the treatment effect. In test markets, it is not uncommon for competitors to increase advertising or reduce price, thus making interpretation of the results difficult.

Changes over Time (Maturation). Over the course of an experiment, the subjects change. Aside from the obvious fact that respondents age over a period, they can also become more expert consumers, tired, or better off financially.

Effect of the Experiment (Testing / Conditioning). The fact that an experiment is being conducted often has an important effect on the subjects. Even prior measurement can, by alerting the subjects to the topic of the study, cause them to change their behavior. Hence, even a measurement can be a factor that influences results.

Instrument Variability. Any change in the measuring instrument (e.g., changing the number of scale points on a questionnaire, changing the inventory method from FIFO (first in, first out) to LIFO (last in, first out) in measuring profits) can produce a change in the results due to the instrument, rather than the treatment. Consequently, it is advisable to keep the measuring device as constant as possible.

Luck. In any test situation there is an element of luck involved. To do well, one generally benefits from good luck. Hence, if a person scores well on a test (e.g., an aided recall test), chances are he or she was lucky as well as smart. Consequently, the test score probably overstates true ability and, hence, is not an accurate measure. (Similarly, someone with a low test score is likely to be better than the score indicates.) This means care must be taken in interpreting the results of tests of knowledge or skill.

External Validity

Many of the threats to internal validity (e.g., noncomparability of groups or exogenous events) are reduced through the use of a strictly controlled environment. This makes tremendous sense in many physical science studies where, for example, identically sized marbles can be subjected to various repeated tests in a closed environment. Unfortunately, people cannot be transferred to a laboratory without recognizing the change in settings and, consequently, potentially altering their behavior. External validity is the extent to which experimental results can be generalized to apply to other settings.

Part of the problem of laboratory experiments is that there are limits to which human subjects may be submitted. For example, assume that I were interested in determining the impact of smoking on individuals. Since smokers and nonsmokers are rarely perfectly matched, a dedicated researcher (albeit a slightly demented one) concerned with internal validity might propose an experiment in which some people were forced to smoke and others were prevented from doing so. Aside from the problems in conducting such an experiment logistically, there are certain ethical issues raised by this design. Consequently, a more likely design is to compare actual smokers and nonsmokers. Unfortunately, smokers and nonsmokers may differ on both obvious (e.g. physical) and subtle (e.g., personality) dimensions. It is possible to draw what are known as matched cohorts by pairing smokers with nonsmokers who are similar in age, lifestyle, and so on. Unfortunately, producing such a sample is difficult; and while it is a reasonable compromise between internal and external validity, it still may have some of both types of limitations. The point, therefore, is that any single experiment involves a balancing of internal and external validity concerns.

If a certain finding or area of investigation is particularly crucial, then a series of experiments is typically used. Such studies should be different in nature, ranging from those with strong internal validity (e.g., lab experiments) to those with great external validity (e.g., field experiments). Only when a result holds up across such a broad range of situations is the cautious researcher willing to claim that a causal relationship has been demonstrated.

Another issue is how well the results measured in an experiment will persist over time. To illustrate, a promotion often increases sales in the period in which the promotion takes place by cannibalizing the next period's sales. If an experiment is run for only one period, longer-term impact (which is typically crucial to decisions) must be either guessed or ignored. Obviously, running an experiment longer increases both costs and the likelihood that internal validity will be compromised. Still, the issue of what will happen over time is an area that is frequently ignored in both design and interpretation of experiments—occasionally with disastrous consequences.

DESIGN: MANAGERIAL ISSUES

To run an experiment, it is important to have one or more causal schemes in mind. In general, the following types of variables should be considered:

1. General conditions (e.g., economic, regulatory).
2. Competitive actions.
3. Your own marketing mix.
4. Characteristics of the sample (e.g., people or markets).

In designing an experiment, carefully consider all factors that might influence results and then classify them as:

1. Those that will be ignored.
2. Those that will be controlled for (i.e., each treatment group will be matched in terms of these variables).
3. Those that will be monitored to see if they were important after the fact.
4. Those that will be manipulated in the design.

Variables that are ignored can be taken care of by a randomization process, whereby subjects are randomly assigned to treatments. This process generally (but not necessarily) produces treatment groups that are equal in terms of these variables. Random assignment is also implicitly assumed by many of the statistical procedures used to evaluate the results. When a variable is considered sufficiently crucial to the design that the researcher is not willing to risk unequal groups in terms of that variable, then assignments are made in order to "balance" the groups in terms of that variable. When a variable is considered a possible key influence, it should be measured (as well as controlled for in some situations). Finally, some key variables become the basis for the actual experimental manipulation.

Selection of Dependent (Criterion) Variables. Selection of one or more variables that measure the impact of the experiment is a more difficult task than it first appears to be. Assuming a business application, the appropriate criterion for any decision is value of the firm's stock or at least profits. Unfortunately, if Maytag tries a different cooperative advertising program for dishwashers in Kansas City, the impact is unlikely to be found in stock price or profit statements. On the other hand, one could choose awareness of the ad as the criterion measure. Unfortunately, awareness does not guarantee either a positive reaction mentally or any increase in sales at the expense of competitors. Hence, the choice of a dependent variable is a trade-off between measuring what is likely to change as a result of the experiment and what is likely to matter if it does vary.

Controllable versus Uncontrollable Variables. Many people assume (somewhat egotistically) that the major causes of consequences of interest should be within their control. They spend most of their time worrying about how their actions affect the consequences of interest and are typically frustrated by their limited impact. This is true of public policy-makers as well as business executives who are typically frustrated about their relative impotence when introducing rules (e.g., unit pricing) in markets. The point here is that other forces (e.g., general economic trends) may be more powerful than marketing mix variables (e.g., ad copy). Any causal understanding of the world should, therefore, include uncontrollable as well as controllable variables.

Aggregation. Most studies ignore the issue of aggregation. The most common approach to causality is to assume that the same event or action should, at least on the average, produce the same consequence. This is often false, as the Lehmann family's reaction to brussels sprouts indicates. Assume that such a typical American family of four is served this delicate vegetable at dinner. The "cause" is constant; the consequences quite different (while the wife enjoys the treat, the other members alternate between sulking, dropping items on the floor, and questioning the sanity of the cook).

Aggregation deserves special consideration because it tends to obscure important relationships. For example, assume that feeding bulk food to weight lifters is beneficial, while feeding bulk food to white-collar workers is detrimental. If a researcher feeds bulk food to a sample made up of 50 percent weight lifters and 50 percent white-collar workers, then half would be better off and half would be worse off. In other words, on average, bulk food would have no impact on people. This would lead to an incorrect and in fact harmful medical conclusion: Consumption of bulk food has no impact on health. The point here, therefore, is that the nature of the sample points (people, sales districts, etc.) must be considered in searching for causal relationships. Notice also that balancing treatment groups in terms of key variables (e.g., percent of weight lifters) does not prevent aggregation from obscuring the true causal relationships. All balancing does is prevent the variable from being a cause of *average* differences.

DESIGN: BASIC NOTIONS

The logic underlying a simple experiment is fairly straightforward. Assume that a company is considering changing advertising strategy from copy A to copy B. It could do the following:

1. Expose subjects to copy B.
2. Measure attitude toward the product after exposure.

This seems logical except for one point. Attitude after exposure needs to be compared with something. An attitude after exposure of 4 on a 5-point scale may sound good; but if the attitude before exposure was 4.5, it may indicate an impending disaster. The basic choices for standards of comparison are:

1. Attitude before exposure to copy B.
2. Attitude after exposure to copy A.

Comparing attitude after exposure to copy B with attitude after exposure to copy A gives an indication of whether copy A or copy B is better. Hence, we could design the following two treatments to test whether copy A or copy B is more effective:

	Treatment	
	1	*2*
Premeasure of attitude	x	x
See copy A	x	
See copy B		x
Postmeasure of attitude	x	x

Assume the results (a bigger number indicates more favorable attitude) were as follows:

	Treatment	
	1	*2*
Premeasure	10	10
Postmeasure	15	13

We can thus see that copy B appears effective in an absolute sense but not as effective as copy A in a relative sense.

Alternatively, we might have been concerned about the possible effect of the premeasure of the results. Then we could have designed the following four treatments:

	Treatment			
	1	*2*	*3*	*4*
Premeasure of attitude	x(10)	x(10)		
See copy A	x		x	
See copy B		x		x
Postmeasure of attitude	x(15)	x(13)	x(14)	x(15)

The reason for including treatments 3 and 4 is the possibility that the premeasure could influence the results by heightening awareness of the product and, hence, either receptivity or resistance to the ads. By measuring the effect of the copy both with and without premeasures, the difference between the results gives an estimate of the effect of the premeasure.

If, as before, one only looks at treatments 1 and 2, it appears that copy A (15) is more effective than copy B (13). Looking at treatments 3 and 4, on the other hand, it appears that copy B (15) is more effective than copy A (14). In this case, the premeasure seems to have improved the effect of copy A by one (15 − 14), while the premeasure reduced the effect of copy B by two (13 − 15). However, in removing the possible effect of the premeasure in treatments 3 and 4, we have also removed the check that indicated that the groups exposed to treatments 3 and 4 had the same initial attitudes. To put it bluntly, we're not sure which ad is better.

If you are now somewhat confused as to the effect of copy A versus copy B, good. The seemingly simple problem of determining which ad is better is actually considerably harder to solve than it appears at first. While using experiments is an obvious approach, the choice of (*a*) which experiment to run and (*b*) how to interpret the results can be fairly difficult.

At this point, three things should be apparent. First, the design of an experiment depends heavily on logic and is essentially the process of deciding which factors (variables) could influence the results so that the effect of each one can be separately isolated by either manipulation or control. Second, the number of factors that could possibly influence the results is enormous. Therefore, choosing the most important variables for designing treatments and controlling and monitoring other variables that could influence results is crucial. Finally, one must be very careful in interpreting the results, since the differences may not be statistically significant. For this reason, interpretation of the results of an experiment almost always involves a statistical analysis—usually analysis of variance (see Chapter 12).

FORMAL EXPERIMENTAL DESIGNS

In the previous section, the basic notion of an experiment was introduced. In this section, some examples of experimental designs will be shown. Before proceeding, however, it is useful to adopt the following definitions:

Factor: A variable that is explicitly manipulated as a part of the experiment (e.g., price, advertising copy).

Levels: The values a factor is allowed to take on (e.g., prices of $100, $200, and $300; advertising copy A or B).

Treatment: The combined levels of the factors to which an individual is exposed (e.g., price of $200 and advertising copy A).

Control group: Subjects who are exposed to no treatment.

Measurement: The recording of a response of the respondent by any means (observation, survey, etc.).

Variation in the results of an experiment can be due to several factors:

1. *Treatment effects.* These are the effects of interest, since the treatments typically vary the decision variables (price, advertising copy). While in controlled situations exposure to a treatment is usually forced, it is still often useful to use a "manipulation check" to make sure subjects were aware of the treatment (Perdue and Summers, 1986).

2. *Experimental effects.* These include the impact of a measurement on a subject's subsequent behavior, as well as the impact of being in the experiment. These are unintended/nuisance effects, which need to be measured so they can be removed.

3. *Other variable effects.* These are the effects of ignored variables. They are assumed to be zero but, in the case of field experiments, often appear. While these variables can sometimes be measured after the fact, their impact is often so large that it obscures the impact of the treatments.

4. *Randomness.* Not everyone, or even one person on every occasion, responds the same way to a treatment. Hence, a part of the response is essentially random and, for small sample sizes, the average responses (i.e., to an ad) can be unstable, leading an inferior ad to outperform a superior one. This effect on the average response is reduced by increasing the sample size in the experiment.

The trick in interpreting the results of an experiment, and, therefore, in designing it, is to separate these effects. In the next section, we describe several simple designs and show how they can be used to estimate the treatment effect and, in some cases, to isolate some of the experimental effects.

Single-Factor Designs. These designs, which vary a single treatment variable, differ in the amount of attention they pay to the various problems and, hence, the precision with which they assess the impact of the treatment.

After-only without control group. This, the simplest design, selects a single group of subjects, exposes them to a treatment (X), and then takes a measurement (O). For example, a group of purchasing agents might be sent to a training program and then their performance measured. Since there is no premeasure or control group, it is impossible to tell if performance improved or deproved. Hence, this design is essentially worthless. Graphically, this can be described as:

Group 1 $\quad X \quad O$

Before-after without control group. This adds a premeasure to the after-only design:

Group 1 $\quad O_1 \quad X \quad O_2$

Unfortunately, it does not make it possible to separate the effect of the premeasure (the measurement effect) from the treatment effect.

After-only with a control group. To measure the impact of a treatment without the confounding effect of a premeasure, two groups are needed: one exposed to the treatment and one which is not.

Group 1	X	O_1
Group 2		O_2

This design is often used post hoc when exposure to a treatment (e.g., an ad) is monitored after the fact. The effect of the treatment is given by $O_1 - O_2$. However, this design makes the untestable assumption that measurements would have been equal in the two groups before the study.

Before-after with one control group.

Group 1	O_1	X	O_2
Group 2	O_3		O_4

The advantage of a premeasure is it allows for slightly unequal groups in terms of key variables, since the difference (change) in the key variable is used to estimate the effect of a treatment. Here, the effect of the treatment is given by $(O_2 - O_1) - (O_4 - O_3)$. The control group is used to estimate the maturation and testing effects.

Four-group, six-study.

Group 1 (experimental)	O_1	X	O_2
Group 2 (control)	O_3		O_4
Group 3 (experimental)		X	O_5
Group 4 (control)			O_6

The so-called four-group, six-study design is used when an interaction effect between the premeasure and the treatment is expected (e.g., when asking opinion about a topic causes a subject to begin thinking about the topic and, thus, to respond differently to information on the subject). The prior level of the variable of interest is estimated as the average of the two premeasures: $\frac{1}{2}(O_1 + O_3)$.

Consequently, the four groups yield estimates of the impact of the experimental treatment (E), premeasurement (M), the interaction between the premeasure and the treatment (I), and uncontrolled variables (U) as follows:

$$\begin{array}{ll} \text{Group 1} & O_2 - O_1 = M + E + I + U \\ \text{Group 2} & O_4 - O_3 = M + U \\ \text{Group 3} & O_5 - \tfrac{1}{2}(O_1 + O_3) = E + U \\ \text{Group 4} & O_6 - \tfrac{1}{2}(O_1 + O_3) = U \end{array}$$

By solving these four equations in four unknowns, we can estimate each of the separate effects. For example, we can estimate the experimental effect based on groups 3 and 4 as $(O_5 - O_6)$. This design costs twice what an after-only or before-after with a control group costs, since it requires four groups instead of two. If one can assume the premeasure has no major interaction with the treatment, then the simpler design is used. Put differently, this design is elegant and thorough but rarely used.

Multiple-Factor Designs. Designs involving the monitoring of two or more factors are very common. The basic idea of such experiments is to simultaneously assess the effects of varying levels on several factors.

Factorial design. The most complete information can always be obtained by means of a full factorial design. A full factorial design requires exposing two or more subjects to each of the various possible combinations of the factors. The results allow estimation of the effect of each level for each factor, as well as the interaction (synergy) between each combination of factor levels. Consider for a moment a problem involving in-store testing of four advertising strategies (A, B, C, D), three packages (I, II, III), and three colors (red, green, orange). There are $4 \times 3 \times 3 = 36$ combinations possible (see Table 5–1). To implement a full factorial design, I need at least 36 stores. To estimate interactions (e.g., the unique effect of putting package design III and red color together), 72 stores (2 per possible treatment) are needed. Factorial designs are thus essentially two things:

1. The best in terms of information attainable since all possible combinations are examined.

2. The most expensive to implement.

Finding 72 stores which are both comparable and willing to participate in an experiment is often impossible; and even if it were possible, it is a highly unmanageable experiment. Hence, researchers tend to use less than full factorial designs. These designs, such as the so-called fractional factorial designs (Holland and Cravens, 1973; Green, 1974), require substantially less data than a full factorial design.

There are a massive number of nonfull factorial designs which are commonly used. All of these designs involve a "trick": in order to simplify

TABLE 5–1 A Three-Factor Factorial Design Example: All Possible Treatments

Advertising Strategy	*Package Design*	*Colors*
A	I	Red
A	I	Green
A	I	Orange
A	II	Red
A	II	Green
A	II	Orange
A	III	Red
A	III	Green
A	III	Orange
B	I	Red
B	I	Green
B	I	Orange
B	II	Red
B	II	Green
B	II	Orange
B	III	Red
B	III	Green
B	III	Orange
C	I	Red
C	I	Green
C	I	Orange
C	II	Red
C	II	Green
C	II	Orange
C	III	Red
C	III	Green
C	III	Orange
D	I	Red
D	I	Green
D	I	Orange
D	II	Red
D	II	Green
D	II	Orange
D	III	Red
D	III	Green
D	III	Orange

the problem, we assume something about the way the influencing variables affect the dependent variable. Some of the most common are as follows:

1. *Independent factor testing.* In this method, we assume the factors (influencing variables) all affect the dependent variable separately. We can separately use four stores to check on the effect of advertising, three stores to check packaging, and three stores to check color, for a total of 10 instead of 72 stores.

2. *Orthogonal designs.* If it is possible to assume that certain interactions do not occur (e.g., advertising and color do not interact), subsets of the factorial array can often be used to estimate the direct effects of the influencing variables. Such designs are available in table form (Addleman, 1962) and are discussed in conjunction with conjoint measurement in Chapter 15.

3. *"Logical" designs.* In many cases, it is relatively easy to eliminate several combinations as either infeasible technically (e.g., a machine which is inexpensive, has high output, and produces high-quality products), unappealing intuitively (plain packaging with a high fashion appeal item), or infeasible politically (e.g., company policy is to produce high-quality products; the boss likes TV advertising, etc.). Therefore, we can reduce many apparent factorial problems to testing of a small number of feasible combinations.

4. *Latin square.* Latin square designs apply when two factors are involved. For example, in studying three package designs, we may wish to use actual store testing. We may also feel that store sales change over time due to seasonal demand variation. Since recruiting stores is very difficult, we attempt to use as few as possible. The Latin square "trick" is twofold. First, assume that there is no interaction between the factors (often a reasonable assumption) and that there is no carryover effect; that is, sales in one period do not influence sales in the next. Then use only three stores over three time periods by cycling each package through each store (Table 5–2). This allows estimation of both the time effect and the package design effect. A major problem with Latin square designs when one factor is time is the no-carry-

TABLE 5–2 Latin Square Design

	Store		
Time	*1*	*2*	*3*
1	A	B	C
2	B	C	A
3	C	A	B

where

A = package design A
B = package design B
C = package design C

over assumption, which is clearly inappropriate for any product that either can be stockpiled (e.g., canned fruit) or satisfies a demand for a long time period (e.g., a car).

Summary. Developing an ability to design successful experiments requires a combination of logic, perseverance, and experience (plus a nontrivial amount of luck). Cookbook approaches are useful only in formulating a basic design. Still, in designing an experiment, there are a variety of considerations, including the following:

Always have a control group or result to serve as a baseline, since absolute results are usually meaningless.

Choose a criterion variable which is both measurable and translatable to market results. The variable chosen to be measured during an experiment has to be both readily measurable and relevant. Awareness may be measurable but not closely related to market results; actual sales in stores are impractical to measure. For this reason, such intermediate measures as attitude are often used.

Calibrate before the experiment, so the translation from the experimental criterion variable (e.g., attitude) to the likely market result (e.g., share) is well established.

Be careful not to assume that the result of a one-shot treatment (e.g., price, ad copy) will be repeated with multiple exposures. Competitive reaction and boredom will both tend to affect results if a marketing program is continued over time. On the other hand, several exposures to certain advertisements may be necessary before the advertisement has an impact.

If you want to measure the effect of a particular factor or variable, make sure that it (a) varies (if I only expose subjects to regular cigarettes, I can't assess the effect of filters on preference) *and (b) varies in such a way that its variation is not perfectly related to the variation of other factors*. If all low-price products were also late entries in the market, it is impossible to know whether their share is a function of late entry or price.

Be aware that the experiment itself may influence behavior by, for example, heightening awareness on the part of respondents. Even the time of day at which the experiment occurs may influence the results. (Post-lunch studies about food will differ from prelunch studies, etc.)

LABORATORY EXPERIMENTS

Most people's notion of experiments comes from the natural sciences, where laboratories are used to tightly control conditions. In lab experiments, we can control the angle at which a marble hits a wall to find out the angle of incidence equals the angle of reflection. Lab experiments are also commonly used in dealing with animals, and many psychologists are especially fond of rats. Unfortunately, consumers and businesses are both more likely to realize they are being observed and to refuse to participate than a marble or a rat. (Only on New Year's Eve do most people get sufficiently interested in cheese to crawl through a maze to get it.) In fact, lab experiments are difficult to use for a number of reasons, including the following:

"Normal" people may refuse to participate, leaving the sample stocked with "weirdos."

Those people who participate may be more likely to game-play than respond normally.

There may be such a tremendous number of variables of interest that a manageable design for separating all their effects is impossible. Assume you believed there were eight key variables, each with three possible levels. This would produce $3^8 = 6{,}561$ possible combinations and thus, 6,561 potential treatments. Unless simplifying assumptions can be made so that less than full factorial designs are employed, this is an essentially hopeless situation.

Lab conditions may be sufficiently different from the real world that laboratory results do not accurately reflect real-world results. Often this is a difference of degree, not kind, however. For example, in a lab setting everyone may see the test ad, while if the same ad ran on television, only 20 percent of viewers might see it with the other 80 percent busy sleeping, talking, reading, getting a snack, or going to the bathroom. Hence, it is especially crucial in the case of lab experiments to calibrate the results, so a given lab result can be translated into a useful prediction of market results.

An Example. An example of a laboratory experiment concerning soft drink preference (Bass, Pessemier, and Lehmann, 1972) is instructive. This experiment involved 264 students and secretaries (your basic convenience sample) who participated in a study over a three-week period. Part of the study involved filling out questionnaires at four points during the three-week period. The other basic part of the experiment consisted of subjects selecting soft drinks on 12 occasions. All soft drinks were in 12-ounce cans and served cold. The eight soft drinks themselves were selected to reflect two dimensions: flavor and calories (Figure 5–1). As part of the experiment, subjects were denied the opportunity to purchase Coke in the fifth occasion. The purpose of this was to see if those who had bought Coke in the

FIGURE 5–1 Brands in Soft Drink Experiment

Calories	*Flavor*	
	Cola	*Lemon-Lime*
Nondiet	Coke Pepsi	7up Sprite
Diet	Tab Diet Pepsi	Like Fresca

TABLE 5–3 Percent Switching from Coke to Each Brand

	Coke	*7up*	*Tab*	*Like*	*Pepsi*	*Sprite*	*Diet Pepsi*	*Fresca*	*Sample (n)*
Average switching in periods 1–2 2–3, 3–4	48	16	2	6	15	6	2	5	239
Period 4–5 switching	x	22	2	3	53	13	3	5	64

previous period would switch to the most similar brand, Pepsi. The results are in Table 5–3. The obvious conclusion from this is that the majority of individuals did indeed switch to Pepsi when Coke was out of stock.

FIELD EXPERIMENTS

Field experiments are the opposite of lab experiments on the realism scale. By moving the experiment to the real world, many of the problems based on the artificial nature of lab experiments are reduced. As a corollary, field experiments tend to be concerned with aggregate and objective data (such as sales) rather than individual and subjective data (such as attitudes).

In solving the artificiality problem, field experiments pay a heavy price. One of the major detriments is cost in terms of money, time, and aggravation. Field experiments, such as test markets in two cities, run budgets of $700,000 routinely and require a minimum of six months to complete.

The other major problem with field experiments is the lack of control. I can show an ad on TV but I can't control who watches it. Similarly, I can cut price 5 cents but can't control competitive activity. It would be hard to tell the effect of a price cut if simultaneously one competitor introduced a new product, a second dropped an old product, a third ran a major coupon special, and a fourth doubled advertising. Such events often happen without planning, but companies are likely to do anything possible to confuse test markets in order to deny useful information to their competitors.

NATURAL EXPERIMENTS

The standard view of an experiment is the situation in which a researcher assigns subjects to treatments in either a random or systematic manner. While this is possible in lab experiments, it is difficult in field settings. (How do I convince Mr. Smith of 123 Maple Street that he must watch channel 7 at 7:30 Monday night?) The concept of a natural experiment is to allow subjects to choose which treatment they receive. For example, some people will have been exposed to ads and some not. To measure the effect of an ad, we simply observe (after the fact) the difference in behavior between those who happened to see the ad and those who did not see it. Put differently, performing a natural experiment is treating data as though they were the output of an experiment.

The advantage of a natural experiment is that the artificial nature of a controlled experiment is circumvented. The disadvantage is that interpretation becomes a serious problem. Often the characteristic which led the subject to select a particular treatment is related to the criterion variable. Put differently, an important covariate may exist. For example, those who saw an ad may have been exposed to the ad because they sought it out and, thus, their likelihood of buying the product after the ad is greater not because of the effect of the ad but because of greater prior interest. Still, post hoc experimentation is a very useful tool.

An Example. To see how a natural experiment works, consider the issue of which media, TV or magazine, is more effective in increasing perceived knowledge of a new small car. It is possible to design either a lab or field experiment and control advertising exposure to examine the effect of advertising exposure on perceived knowledge. Such experiments, however, tend to be either unrealistic or expensive.

An alternative approach is to examine the perceived knowledge of subjects based on their actual exposure. In this case, subjects were asked their perceived knowledge (on a 10-point scale) of a new car both before and after the presentation of a major introductory campaign. The subjects were also asked to report which magazines they read and which television shows they viewed. By using the actual media plan, a potential advertising exposure measure was established (Lehmann, 1977). While this measures potential rather than actual exposure (I may read a magazine and skip the ads), this objective measure seemed preferable to self-reported advertising exposure, which can be expected to be both inaccurate and contaminated

TABLE 5–4 Average Change in Perceived Knowledge

Magazine Advertising Exposure	*TV Advertising Exposure*		
	Low	*Medium*	*High*
Low	1.68 (72)	1.32 (74)	1.90 (61)
Medium	1.19 (66)	1.50 (78)	1.61 (65)
High	1.89 (58)	2.30 (84)	2.70 (64)

Source: Donald R. Lehmann, "Responses to Advertising a New Car," *Journal of Advertising Research* 17 (August 1977), p. 25.

by attitudes. Based on the advertising exposure measures, 622 subjects were divided into nine categories. Next, the average change in perceived knowledge was calculated for each of the nine possible combinations of TV and magazine advertising exposure. The average changes and number of subjects in each cell are shown in Table 5–4.

Ignoring issues of statistical significance and "fancy" analytical procedures, these results seem to indicate three interesting findings:

1. More exposure generally means a larger increase in perceived knowledge. The exception to this is the low-low group.

2. Both TV and magazine advertising seem to contribute (at approximately equal levels) to increased knowledge. Since the budget was split about 50:50, this suggests (albeit weakly) that both media were about equally effective.

3. Even low-exposure people become noticeably more knowledgeable, presumably due to word-of-mouth discussion, and so forth.

A major problem exists with these results. The problem (common to all natural experiments) is that other variables are uncontrolled. It is possible that, for example, all high-income people are in the high magazine–low TV exposure cell. Hence, the results in this cell could be as much or more attributable to the effect of income (and its covariates, such as education) as to advertising exposure. This problem of uncontrolled variables which are related to the measured/key variables—often called *covariates*—makes simple analysis of the results dangerous. Dealing with covariates requires analytical procedures (such as the brilliantly named analysis of covariance, which is essentially multiple reggression) beyond the scope of this chapter. It is interesting to note, however, that, in this case, employing "sophisticated" analytical procedures to control for the effect of these covariates did not change the findings.

SUMMARY

Volumes can and have been written on the design and interpretation of experiments. The major point of this chapter is that experimental design is basically logic and common sense. Variables which don't matter should be ignored. Those variables which matter but are not the focus of the study should be controlled for (by making the groups equal) and/or measured so their impact can be assessed. The variables that are the focus of the study should be so manipulated that they vary and that their variation is not confounded with other variables (e.g., a premeasurement).

This chapter has attempted to focus attention on the logical issues involved in deducing causality and designing experiments. Interpretation has been discussed in only general terms. Specific statistical analysis of results is typically accomplished by means of analysis of variance (ANOVA), which will be discussed in a later chapter.

PROBLEMS

1. Assume I ran an experiment and got the following results:

	Treatment				
	1	*2*	*3*	*4*	*5*
Premeasure	x(10)		x(11)	x(9)	x(10)
Exposure to ad			x		x
Exposure to cents off coupon	x	x			x
Postmeasure	x(14)	x(13)	x(13)	x(11)	x(16)

   a. Estimate the effects of the ad and the coupon.
   b. What assumptions did you make in (*a*)?
   c. Change one of your assumptions and see if the results change.
2. The market research department of brand A ran an experiment involving a promotion and got the following results:

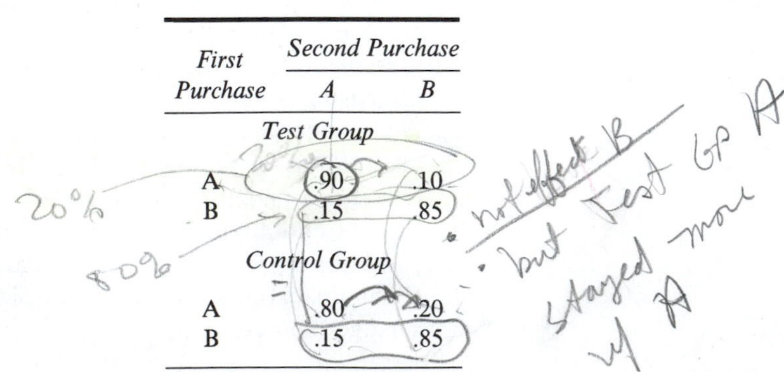

First Purchase	*Second Purchase*	
	A	*B*
Test Group		
A	.90	.10
B	.15	.85
Control Group		
A	.80	.20
B	.15	.85

Assuming brand A has a 20 percent share currently, interpret the results.

3. Write down a model of how you think people go about buying beer.
4. Get a group of friends altogether. Have them discuss beer purchasing. Summarize the discussion.
5. The sales levels in each of the two weeks following distribution of cents-off redeemable coupons were as follows:

	Sales after Distribution	
Coupon	*1st Week*	*2nd Week*
5¢ off one package	20	0
10¢ off on purchase of second package	50	10
10¢ off one package	40	40
20¢ off one package	90	70

The coupon distributions were made several months apart to allow the effects of previous coupons to die out before the next coupon was distributed. What can you conclude about the difference in sales due to the coupons?

6. In the Yuk market, there are two major brands: Awful and Bad. Currently, their shares are 40 percent and 30 percent, respectively. Traditionally, the percentage of people who repeatedly purchase these brands from one period to the next has been 80 percent and 70 percent, respectively. Also, 80 percent of the users of minor brands in one period purchase a minor brand in the following period. If a minor brand purchaser in a previous period does not buy a minor brand, he or she is equally likely to purchase Awful and Bad. Similarly, purchasers of Awful, who are not repeat purchasers, are equally likely to purchase Bad or a minor brand. However, purchasers of Bad that don't repeat purchase are twice as likely to buy Awful as any of the minor brands. What will be the market shares next period?
7. Assume you have 100 samples of a particular product which you wish to measure the ignition point of given different air temperature and humidity conditions. How would you proceed?
8. You have been assigned to find out which of three advertising campaigns, which of three package designs, and which of four names are best for a particular new detergent. How would you proceed, given:
   a. A budget of $5,000 and one month.
   b. A budget of $30,000 and three months.
   c. A budget of $500,000 and one year.

BIBLIOGRAPHY

Addleman, Sidney. "Orthogonal Main-Effects Plans for Asymmetrical Factorial Experiments." *Technometrics* 4 (February 1962), pp. 21–46.

Banks, Seymour. *Experimentation in Marketing*. New York: McGraw-Hill, 1965.

Bass, Frank M. "The Theory of Stochastic Preference and Brand Switching." *Journal of Marketing Research* 11 (February 1974), pp. 1–20.

______; Edgar A. Pessemier; and Donald R. Lehmann. "An Experimental Study of Relationships between Attitudes, Brand Preference, and Choice." *Behavioral Science* 17 (November 1972), pp. 523–41.

Campbell, Donald T., and Julian C. Stanley. *Experimental Designs for Research*. Skokie, Ill.: Rand-McNally, 1966.

Claycamp, Henry J., and Lucien E. Liddy. "Prediction of New Product Performance: An Analytical Approach." *Journal of Marketing Research* 4 (November 1969), pp. 414–20.

Green, Paul E. "On the Design of Choice Experiments Involving Multifactor Alternatives." *Journal of Consumer Research* 1 (September 1974), pp. 61–68.

Holland, Charles W., and David W. Cravens. "Fractional Factorial Experimental Designs in Marketing Research." *Journal of Marketing Research* 10 (August 1973), pp. 270–76.

Kalwani, Manohar U., and Donald G. Morrison. "A Parsimonious Description of the Hendry System." *Management Science* 23 (January 1977), pp. 467–77.

Kerlinger, Fred N. *Foundations of Behavioral Research*. 2nd ed. New York: Holt, Rinehart & Winston, 1973.

Lehmann, Donald R. "Responses to Advertising a New Car." *Journal of Advertising Research* 17 (August 1977), pp. 23–32.

Lynch, John G., Jr. "On the External Validity of Experiments in Consumer Research." *Journal of Consumer Research* 9 (December 1982), pp. 225–39.

Perdue, Barbara C., and John O. Summers. "Checking the Success of Manipulations in Marketing Experiments." *Journal of Marketing Research* 23 (November 1986), pp. 317–26.

Sellitz, Claire. *Research Methods in Social Relations*. New York: Holt, Rinehart & Winston, 1959.

Webb, Eugene J.; Donald T. Campbell; Richard D. Schwartz; and Lee Sechrest. *Unobtrusive Measures*. Skokie, Ill.: Rand-McNally, 1966.

Chapter 6

Survey Design

Surveys are the mainstays of marketing research. Even when such other methods as experiments are used, a survey is often also employed. One reason for this is that surveys are relatively easy and cheap to administer. They are also the only known way to get measures of thoughts and attitudes. The disadvantage with surveys is that reported behaviors are often inaccurate. In spite of occasional (make that constant) problems, however, surveys remain an integral part of research.

This chapter proceeds by describing some of the choices and problems involved in developing a questionnaire. Next, choice of survey method is discussed. Finally, some issues of pretesting and control are addressed.

The best way to learn about surveys and their problems is to become involved in them. Especially useful is assuming the role of a personal interviewer so problems such as refusal to cooperate, don't know responses, and bad respondents become real. Filling out a few questionnaires will also help hone your skills.

Before beginning to design a survey, the problem should be well defined. Moreover information needs and more specific research objectives should be delineated. If a survey appears to be an appropriate part of the research project, two related tasks must be performed: the survey instrument must be designed and a method of administering it (e.g., telephone) selected. This chapter proceeds to discuss these two issues. Specifically, the chapter proceeds through the steps listed in Figure 6–1, beginning by considering types of information needed and specific examples. A more technical discussion of scale design, as well as a general discussion of types of errors which affect research usefulness, appears in the following chapter.

FIGURE 6–1 Stages in Survey Design

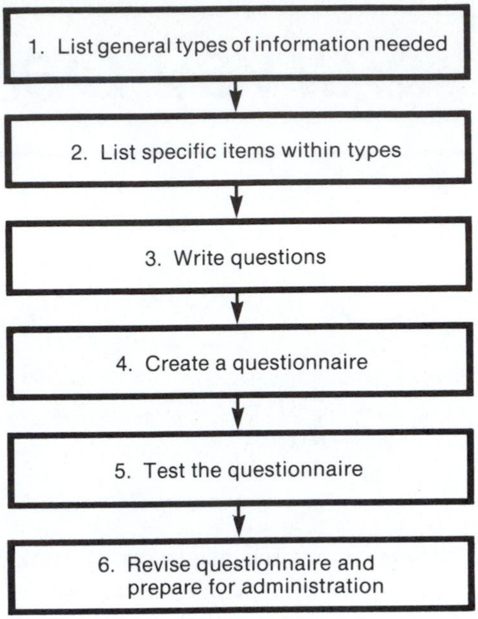

1. List general types of information needed
2. List specific items within types
3. Write questions
4. Create a questionnaire
5. Test the questionnaire
6. Revise questionnaire and prepare for administration

CONTENT

There is a danger that too little information will be collected. This is especially true when the final version of the questionnaire is frozen before pilot tests or respondent interviews. On the other hand, it is very common to end up with an unwieldy document, especially if the "wouldn't it be nice to know" mentality dominates questionnaire construction. Another sure way to generate a massive, incoherent questionnaire is to allow everyone in the neighborhood to put in a few questions. This questionnaire-by-committee approach may solve many individuals' data needs for no apparent additional cost (the something-for-nothing syndrome), but chances are the results will be sufficiently cumbersome or muddled that even the original sponsor of the research will be unsatisfied.

The types of information which can be collected via surveys fall into four broad basic categories: general background, behavior, knowledge, and attitudes. These fall into two major categories: product category variables, which relate directly to the product category under consideration; and segmenting variables, which help in describing, locating, and effectively reaching present and potential users of a product category. Generally, segmenting variables are useful predictors of product usage rates, but poor predictors of brand choice (e.g., Hunt's Catsup versus Heinz Ketchup) or individual consumer behavior. This section proceeds by describing examples of the various types of questions which can be asked.

Segmenting Variables

Demographics. These are numerous but, for individual consumers, often include the following:

1. Age.
2. Sex.
3. Marital status.
4. Household size.
5. Number of children.
6. Region.
7. Degree of urbanization.

For research involving industrial products, data on the firm in terms of size (number of employees, size of plant) and type of business (often defined by SIC codes) are commonly sought. Many times data on the individual being surveyed are also collected.

Socioeconomics. These relate to the economic status of the individual or household:

1. Income.
2. Education.
3. Occupation.

For industrial products, data on sales, market share, and profits, as well as elements of the company's general strategy (e.g., the percent of sales spent on R & D), are frequently obtained.

Ownership. Ownership of related but different products is frequently obtained. For individuals, these include appliances, automobiles, and homes. For an industrial survey, this might include type of copying equipment, automation of the manufacturing process, or telecommunication devices on hand.

Media Exposure. Media exposure variables (e.g., TV and print) are often collected to increase the efficiency of advertising spending.

Personality. A variety of general personality variables have been applied in marketing studies for many years (Gottlieb, 1959; Robertson and Myers, 1969). The hope is to find an enduring general characteristic of a person which relates to many aspects of behavior. Generally these variables have been fairly weak predictors of consumer behavior. Massy, Frank, and Lodahl (1968) found background (demographic and socioeconomic) and personality variables together account for less than 10 percent of the variation in brand choice.

In his summary, Kassarjian (1971) reviews several basic psychological theories: Freudian, social theory, stimulus-response, trait and factor theories, and self-concept. Some general personality instruments which have been used in marketing research (typically of the trait or factor theory type) include the following:

Gordon Personal Profile, used by Tucker and Painter (1961) and Kernan (1968).

Edwards Personal Preference Scale, made famous in marketing by the 1960s controversy over whether you could tell a Ford owner from a Chevy owner (Evans and Roberts, 1963). (Answer: Not very well, unless of course you observe what car they drive.)

Thurstone's Temperament Scale used by Kamen (1964) and Westfall (1962).

California Personality Inventory, used for innovativeness and opinion leadership studies by Robertson and Myers (1969) and Bruce and Witt (1970), topics also investigated by King and Summers (1970) and Darden and Reynolds (1974). Also, considerable work has been done on self-concept in general (Birdwell, 1968; Grubb and Hupp, 1968) and self-confidence and risk taking in particular (Cox and Bauer, 1964; Barach, 1969; Venkatesan, 1968), as well as inner-outer directedness (Kassarjian and Kassarjian, 1966).

Some other scales which have been used include:

McClosky Personality Inventory.

Dunette Adjective Checklist.

Borgatta Personality Scale.

Strong Vocational Interest Bank.

Cattell's 16 Personality Factor Inventory.

In spite of all this effort, the predictive power of these general variables has been low, typically around 5 to 10 percent of the total variation available to be explained. Both Kassarjian (1971) and Jacoby (1971) point out that, given the purposes for which general personality scales were developed, the low predictive power for brand choice decisions is quite reasonable. Product class choice seems more promising as a subject for personality variable prediction (Alpert, 1972; Bither and Dolich, 1972; Greeno, Sommers, and Kernan, 1973). Still, personality variables are generally of little valu

TABLE 6–1 A Set of Lifestyle Variables

Activities	*Interests*	*Opinions*	*Demographics*
Work	Family	Themselves	Age
Hobbies	Home	Social issues	Education
Social events	Job	Politics	Income
Vacation	Community	Business	Occupation
Entertainment	Recreation	Economics	Family size
Club membership	Fashion	Education	Dwelling
Community	Food	Products	Geography
Shopping	Media	Future	City size
Sports	Achievements	Culture	Stage in the life cycle

Source: Joseph T. Plummer, "The Concept and Application of Life Style Segmentation," *Journal of Marketing*, January 1974, p. 34.

General Activities / Attitudes / Opinions / Interests. Generally known as lifestyle or psychographic measures, these variables are still general characteristics but logically more closely related to product choice than personality scales, such as dominance-compliance. Exactly where to draw the line between personality, lifestyle, and product-related variables is somewhat unclear. Nonetheless, most researchers agree that dominance-compliance is a personality trait, love of the outdoors a lifestyle (attitude) variable, and time spent playing tennis is a product-use variable (at least if the product I'm studying is a tennis racket). Hence, we will classify a lifestyle variable as something more general than a product-related variable and something more product oriented than a personality trait. Lifestyle variables come in two major types: activities and attitudes.

Activities. Measures of the actual involvement in various activities such as sports, crafts, watching TV, reading magazines, and so forth.

Attitudes. Opinions about life in general, institutions (e.g., credit, education, churches), particular issues (e.g., welfare programs), as well as activities (e.g., baking from scratch) and interests (e.g., reading). A list of lifestyle variables taken from Plummer appears as Table 6–1.

Tremendous effort has been involved in using lifestyle measures (see Wells, 1974; Plummer, 1974; Reynolds, 1973; Hustad and Pessemier, 1971). A major inventory of lifestyle questions is that used extensively by Market Facts, reported by Wells and Tigert (1971). Reliability of lifestyle measures has been investigated and found to be reasonably good (see Pessemier and Bruno, 1971; Villani and Lehmann, 1975). Moreover, several companies have used lifestyle segmentations as the basis for developing marketing strategy (e.g., White Stag used lifestyle analysis to reposition its entire clothing product line). Yet, here again the predictive results have often been disappointing in spite of some reported successes. One thing which is true (and not at all surprising) is that the closer the lifestyle variables are to product variables, the better they are as predictors. An excellent review of psychographics is provided by Wells (1974)—"must" reading if you are interested in using these variables.

Values. Recently, considerable interest in relating behavior to basic values of individuals has been evident. Early research focused on a categorization provided by Rokeach, but recently the VALS (values and lifestyles)

TABLE 6–2 The VALS Segments

Descriptor	*Percent of Population*	*Lifestyle*	*Buying Style*
Need driven:			
Survivors	4%	Struggling for survival; distrustful.	Price dominant; focused on basics.
Sustainers	7	Hopeful for improvement over time; concerned with security.	Price important; want warranty.
Outer directed:			
Belongers	38	Preservers of status quo; seek to be part of group.	Do not want to try something new; heritage brand buyer.
Emulators	10	Upwardly mobile; emulate rich and successful.	Conspicuous consumption; sacrifice comfort and utility for show.
Achievers	21	Materialistic, comfort-loving; oriented to fame and success.	Luxury and gift items; like "new and improved," but not radically changed, products.
Inner directed:			
I-am-me	3	Transition between outer and inner directed; very individualistic.	Impulsive; trendy products.
Experiential	5	Seek direct experience; intense personal relationship.	Process over product; interested in what product does for them, not what it says about them.
Societally conscious	12	Simple, natural living; socially responsible.	Discriminating; want true value and environmentally sound products.

Source: SRI International Values & Lifestyles (VALS) Program.

typology of the Stanford Research Institute has become more popular. This typology groups individuals into categories such as "belonger," "socially conscious," and "survivor."

The eight basic types of customers as defined by VALS are shown in Table 6–2. New York Telephone Company (predivestiture) used VALS to segment markets for its decorator sets and to help train sales personnel (Schiffman and Jones, 1983). Interestingly, the VALS variables seem to differ across regions of the United States (Whalen, 1983).

Another scale, the List of Values (LOV) Scale, has been promoted as superior to VALS (Kahle, Beatty, and Homer, 1986) for predicting various behaviors. The nine basic values in that scale are:

1. Self-respect.
2. Security.
3. A warm relationship with others.
4. A sense of accomplishment.
5. Self-fulfillment.
6. A sense of belonging.
7. Being well-respected.
8. Fun and enjoyment.
9. Excitement.

These values have also been shown to differ across regions of the United States (Kahle, 1986).

Product Category Variables

Product and Brand Usage. Typically, the key variable for marketing decisions is actual brand choice. Hence, considerable effort is devoted to measuring both product class and brand choice. Common variables include the following:

1. Usage rate of the product class as a whole.
2. Brand used/planned to use. This includes brand bought last time, time before last, and planned to buy next time.
3. Quantity purchased.
4. Time between purchases.

Determinants of Brand Choice. A number of variables have been hypothesized to be determinants (or antecedents) of choice. Some of the most widely used are:

1. Awareness of the product class in general and particular brands.
2. Awareness of advertising.
3. Knowledge/understanding of the brand.

4. Perception/rating of brands on specific attributes. (For example, in the case of toothpaste, ratings of Crest, Colgate, etc., on such attributes as decay prevention and tooth whitening.)
5. Importance of product attributes.
6. Satisfaction with present product.
7. Perceived risk in using the product.
8. Approach used to make the choice.

The last item mentioned, approach used, is generally overlooked. Still it is often important to understand whether a respondent is just learning about the product (extensive processing), actively comparing alternatives (limited processing), or simply following a rule for making choices (routinized behavior) (Howard, 1977).

Contextual / Situational Variables. A variety of contextual/situational variables influence product and brand choice (Belk, 1975). A purchase of a sofa may depend on where it will be used (basement versus formal living room), who will use it (kids versus guests), and amount of wear you expect it to suffer. These variables break into two basic types:

Usage situation. This includes place used, alternatives, time of day, social visibility, heaviness of usage, and so forth.

Influence of others (children, spouse, etc.) on the decision.

Intention. A very common element on both consumer and industrial surveys is measuring planned or intended behavior. Such data are unreliable at the individual level (i.e., many who say they will buy won't and vice versa), but on average, often provide a useful barometer of future prospects (Juster, 1966; McNeil, 1974). Recent studies of intentions data (Morrison, 1979; Kalwani and Silk, 1983) indicate transformations of the data which effectively discount intentions levels are important in interpreting responses to such questions. For example, on a five-point scale, the "top box" (most favorable) intention score is likely to be converted to actual behavior between 50 and 60 percent of the time and less favorable intentions much less frequently (Infosino, 1986; Mullet and Karson, 1985).

Summary

The list of potential variables to include in a survey is effectively endless. In designing a study of customers, however, it is possible to group most of these into the two main categories:

1. Descriptive variables.
   a. Who are:
      (1) The purchasers.
      (2) The users.

   b. What they do with it:
      (1) What they buy.
      (2) What they use it for.
   c. Where they buy it:
      (1) Information sources.
      (2) Shopping location.
      (3) Purchase location.
   d. How they buy it:
      (1) Amount.
      (2) Terms (e.g., credit).
   e. When they buy it:
      (1) Time of year.
      (2) Full price versus on deal.
2. Explanatory variables.
   a. Why buy product category:
      (1) Alternatives considered.
      (2) Needs met.
   b. Why buy brand:
      (1) Benefits sought.

By considering these variables in past, present, and (most importantly) future terms, a reasonably complete assessment of customers is possible.

WRITING QUESTIONS

This section discusses some of the major issues in designing questions.

Open- versus Closed-End Questions

Data can be gathered in either open- or closed-end forms. Consider the following examples;

In the case of the brand choice question, since the major brands are often well known, the reason for an open-ended question is unclear. Its only advantage is that users of off-brands might not feel as conspicuous as they would if they were relegated to the "other" (translation: they must be a weirdo) category. On the other hand, for many product categories the number of people in the "other" category should be negligible and both the respondent (because it's easier to check a space than write a word) and the analyst (because the data are precoded) will find the closed-end format better.

Open end: What brand of toothpaste do you use most often? ____________

Closed end: Please indicate which brand of toothpaste you use most often:

Aim __________
Colgate __________
Crest __________
Other (please specify) __________

Open end: Why do you choose a particular brand of toothpaste? __________

Closed end: Please indicate the importance of the following attributes in selecting a toothpaste:

	Very Unimportant				*Very Important*
Decay prevention	1	2	3	4	5
Price	1	2	3	4	5
Tooth whitening	1	2	3	4	5

In the case of the question relating to reason for brand choice, the closed-end question requires more careful consideration. To be successful, we must first assume that the decision rests on attributes and their relative importances. Second, we must assume that the relevant attributes are known and included in the questionnaire. For many product categories this is a fairly believable assumption, but it does require the researcher to have either knowledge of the product or past research data. It also is important to notice that the open-end question is not without problems, since such incisive answers as "to put on my toothbrush" and "for brushing my teeth" are likely responses.

A serious general problem with open-ended questions is that the extent of the response depends on the glibness and interest of the respondent. Hence, the open-end answers are the result of opinionated, glib respondents and may not be representative of the total population. (This is especially true of political surveys.) Also, open-end questions do not produce direct comparisons between competing attributes (i.e., the relative importance of two attributes), and the relative importance must be inferred from the percent of the time each of the attributes is mentioned. While generalizations are dangerous, it is usually true that open-end questions should be restricted to the following:

1. Exploratory studies from which closed-end questions will be formed.
2. Pilot tests where they can be used to pick up missing relevant data by allowing the respondent to report them.
3. Small sample studies of especially articulate respondents or respondents who are being surveyed by special interviewers.

4. As a final catchall question to pick up any ideas the respondent holds or provide the respondent a chance to voice his or her opinion on a subject of interest. (Many people will put up with a certain amount of pain and suffering if they have the feeling that somehow their opinions will be listened to.)
5. As the first question(s) in situations where the response could be biased by responses to the closed-end questions.

An example of the value of an open-end question occurred in a study of soft drink preference. After ranking eight soft drinks on a set of prespecified attributes, respondents were asked to list other attributes which were important to their choice. Several respondents listed "after taste" (which they apparently distinguished from the included variable "flavor") and "packaging" (which, since all soft drinks were served cold in 12-ounce pop-top cans, suggested that some people got their jollies by looking at the designs on the cans—possibly a result of spending the summer in West Lafayette). Since this was a multiwave study, these attributes were included in a subsequent wave of data collection.

Direct versus Indirect

In asking a question, the researcher must decide whether to ask the question directly or indirectly. The indirect method assumes that an individual will not accurately respond to a direct question because of:

Inability to understand the question if it is asked directly (e.g., would you characterize your decision style as sophisticated or routinized?).

Inability to answer the question (e.g., you might not know how long you spend eating each day).

Unwillingness to provide the accurate response because of social pressure (e.g., nutrition is important, etc.). A favorite gambit for avoiding this problem is a projective technique where, instead of asking directly, the question is phrased in terms of the person's reference group, such as "my neighbors." The assumption here is that you are more willing to expose undesirable traits if they are not personally attributed to you. The disadvantage is that you assume neighbors are similar (how many of your neighbors do you exactly match?), which guarantees some error in the results.

The direct method, on the other hand, assumes that the respondent can and will try to respond accurately. While indirect methods may be necessary for complex social issues or unstructured problems, most of the questions in marketing research are sufficiently straightforward that direct questions will do most of the time. The indirect method is also somewhat condescending, since it assumes that (*a*) the respondent isn't too bright or honest and (*b*) the respondent can be easily tricked. Actually, most normal respondents will try to respond honestly if given that opportunity, but may be offended by "tricks." Incidentally, the best respondents tend to be those who have normal profiles (high school or college graduates with a job, etc.) or grammar school students (whose interest in filling out questionnaires is remarkable). Experts (especially MBAs or market researchers) are typically poor respondents, since they spend time evaluating the questionnaire, making helpful suggestions, and trying to figure out what tricks have been employed, not to mention protesting the format.

Aided versus Unaided

Another issue is whether the responses should be aided or unaided. This is really a variation of the open- versus closed-end question theme which deals with how much information to give the respondent. A common example of this problem is the question of whether to measure aided or unaided advertising recall. Several levels of "aidedness" can be envisioned:

1. Have you heard anything lately?
2. Have you heard any ads lately?
3. Have you heard any motor oil ads lately?
4. Have you heard any ads for Mobil lately?
5. What is Mobil 1's main advantage?
6. Who claims their oil will add to your gas mileage?

Depending on what you want the percentage who are aware of Mobil 1's claim that it adds to gas mileage to be, you can use the first two (likely response less than 1 percent), the third (probably about 10 percent), or the specified aided versions 4 through 6, where the recall may be more than half. Which you use depends on what you want: top of the mind recall or to know if someone has stored the message in memory. For most studies, it is not the absolute value but the changes over time which matter, so the real problem is to keep using the same scale over time.

Phraseology

Choosing a set of words to convey a construct is at best a difficult task. Words are imprecise, and most individuals' knowledge of their meanings even fuzzier. By being overly detailed, you run the risk of creating fatigue and boredom. Also, many individuals typically try to answer questions without looking at the directions (just like putting together a tool or a toy without using the directions, it seems so much easier that way). On the other hand, vague phrasing can create problems in interpreting the response. For example, I could respond affirmatively to "Do you like Rolls-Royce?" either because I like it but have no intention of buying it given my cash position, or to indicate I am considering buying it. Hence, the solution is to be "just right" in terms of detail.

Two procedures are very important in getting good wording for a question. First, give up on the notion that the first draft of a questionnaire is the final one. During tests, continually see if respondents (*a*) answered, (*b*) answered with some reasonable dispersion, and (*c*) seemed to understand the question. Second, the translation practices used in going from one language to another can be employed in a modified fashion. (In translating questions from one language to another, it is advisable to have one person translate the question from the first language to the second and a second translator translate the translated question back to the original language. Only when the retranslated question matches the original is the question used.) Here, a researcher writes a question and a respondent then assesses what the researcher really wanted to know. Only when the researcher's problem matches the data the respondent thinks he or she is supposed to give is the question accepted. Some general tips include the following:

Be direct. Don't ask, "May I know your age?" since the correct answer is yes or no. Ask, "What is your age?"

Avoid slang and fancy/polysyllabic wording. For example, use "like" instead of "appreciate."

When rating products, specify their use/purpose. Rating products without use/situation specification can be very hard for the respondent and misleading to the researcher.

Ask questions that can reasonably be answered. Don't ask typical respondents questions which would be difficult for a Ph.D., or ask for excessive detail (e.g., number of glasses of water drunk in the last month).

Use unambiguous wording. "Do you appreciate the ad?" could be interpreted to mean you like it or understand it, two different issues.

Ask simple, not compound, questions. Don't ask, "Have you stopped eating candy?" Unless they started, the grammatically correct answer is "no"; although, given current literacy, the answer may not reflect this.

Don't ask slanted questions. Don't make the correct answer obvious (e.g., don't ask, "You do care about health, don't you?").

Borrow someone else's questions. Why start from scratch if a proven alternative already exists?

Response Format

Response format determination has three main aspects: multiple measures, scale type, and provision for don't knows and refusals. A more detailed discussion appears in the next chapter.

Multiple Measures. A fundamental issue is whether a single scale or multiple items will be used to measure a construct. The advantage to the multiple item approach is that it increases the reliability of the measure of the construct. Using multiple items may help cancel out some errors which are idiosyncratic to a particular item. One disadvantage is that the presentation of multiple measures may either irritate the respondent (who then could retaliate by giving poor-quality responses) or convince the respondent that the survey is a consistency test and bias the responses accordingly. The main disadvantage is that it takes time and space for multiple measures, which means either extending the questionnaire with the effect of increasing both cost and respondent fatigue or eliminating other items from the survey. In most marketing research studies where the focus is on group, rather than on individual behavior, the choice between a few reliable measures and many relatively unreliable measures is usually resolved in favor of many unreliable measures. One reason for this is that, if respondents are assumed to be homogeneous, then average values can be calculated, and the averaging process creates a reliable statistic. However, for key constructs, multiple measures should be used if practical.

Scale Type. The scale type (nominal, ordinal, interval, ratio) used depends on (*a*) the analysis desired and (*b*) the amount of effort obtainable from the respondents. Most questions should be gathered on interval scales when at all possible. One interesting point concerns the choice between rankings (i.e., "please rank the following brands with 1 being your most preferred...") and ratings (i.e., "please indicate how well you like each of the following scales by circling a 1 if you strongly dislike it, a 6 if you strongly like it, or somewhere in between depending on how well you like the brand."). Rankings (ordinally scaled) are usually harder to obtain than ratings and produce more refusals, bad data (i.e., incomplete rankings), and so forth. The reason for choosing a ranking over a rating is to prevent ties. Hence, if it is important to know what *the* first choice brand is, rankings may be required. Otherwise, ratings will usually suffice. The next chapter discusses specific question format in more detail.

Provision for Don't Knows and Refusals. The don't know/refusal response presents a difficult problem. In some cases it is a legitimate answer (e.g., "Do you know what the term *compact* means in numerical topology?"). In other cases, it is a convenient cop-out to avoid answering taxing or unpleasant questions. For example, I might wish to get a person's perception of a brand even though he or she had never used it to either assess its image or see if there were a reason for the nonuse. In general, experienced/involved respondents produce fewer don't know responses, and don't knows increase as the number of scale points increase (Leigh and Martin, 1987).

A key decision, therefore, is whether to formally provide the respondent with the don't know response or not. (You can be sure some respondents will leave questions blank anyway.) If the "don't know" response is meaningful data, it should usually be used as a response category even though some respondents will use it as an easy out. If "don't know" is an unusual response, however, providing a don't know response will generally reduce the quality of the data (e.g., Malhotra, 1986). In any event, provision for don't knows needs to be made in the coding phase of analysis.

General Suggestions

Ask simple, not complex questions. A question such as:

Do you own a summer house and a snowmobile?
Neither ____________
Summer house only ____________
Snowmobile only ____________
Both ____________

is generally inferior to:

Which of the following do you own:

Summer house	_____ Own	________ Do not own
Snowmobile	_____ Own	________ Do not own

Use nontechnical language. Too many studies go to the field in a form which is useful to engineering but meaningless to customers. For example, in one study concerning a major purchase item, a group of nontechnically trained respondents were exposed to product features developed and named by the R&D group. While the terms used were precise (e.g., response time in milliseconds, frame buffer), the typical respondent simply didn't know (or much care) what the technical features were and, hence, the responses were of limited value.

Group questions of similar types together. It is possible to ask questions in the following manner:

	Dislike Very Much					*Like Very Much*
How well do you like yogurt?	1	2	3	4	5	6
	Very Infre-quently					*Very Fre-quently*
How often do you watch TV?	1	2	3	4	5	6

However, it is often more efficient to get this information by combining the questions into a series of agree-disagree questions:

Please indicate your degree of agreement with the following statements:

	Disagree Strongly					*Agree Strongly*
I like yogurt	1	2	3	4	5	6
I watch TV frequently	1	2	3	4	5	6

Use mutually exclusive and exhaustive categories for multichoice questions. On the technical level, this means the following scale is bad:

1–10, 10–20, 20–30, . . .

while this scale is good:

0–9, 10–19, 20–29, . . .

On the more general level, it means you should take care to (*a*) specify all reasonable responses and (*b*) make it clear when only one answer is desired.

When appropriate, use objective, rather than subjective, scales for key constructs. It is possible to measure TV viewing on subjective scales, such as "none" to "a great deal" or on agree-disagree scales. As long as TV viewing is not a key question, this is probably good enough. If a question is central, however, a quantitative scale is better:

How much TV do you watch on a typical weekday night?

____	____	____	____	____	____
None	Less than $\frac{1}{2}$ hour	$\frac{1}{2}$–1 hour	1–2 hours	2–3 hours	More than 3 hours

While this scale requires the researcher to know a priori something about typical amounts of TV viewing, the scale may actually be easier for the respondent to use than a vague agree-disagree type question.

Use balanced scales. Unbalanced scales are generally undesirable, since they give clear indication to the respondent which end of the scale is expected to attract the majority of the responses. This is especially true of rating scales which have such categories as "poor," "satisfactory," "good," "very good," and "excellent." However, when the construct to be measured is importance or desirability, a scale such as "extremely important," "very important," "quite important," "somewhat important," "not very important," and "not at all important" may produce better information than a perfectly balanced scale, since most respondents tend to list all attributes of a product as important.

Rate brands attribute by attribute. It is possible to rate all the brands on one attribute at a time or a single brand on all the attributes. The former approach is better in that it reduces a respondent's tendency to "halo" ratings by responding only to overall feeling about the brand, rather than the particular attribute in question. Hence, this is bad:

Please rate Crest on the following attributes:

	Very Poor				*Very Good*
Decay prevention	____	____	____	____	____
Price	____	____	____	____	____
Tooth whitening	____	____	____	____	____

While this is better:

Please rate the following brands in terms of decay prevention:

	Very Poor				*Very Good*
Aim	____	____	____	____	____
Crest	____	____	____	____	____
Colgate	____	____	____	____	____

Nothing, however, can be done to totally eliminate halo effects in ratings. Also, respondents often use their assumptions about relations between attributes (e.g., price and quality) in answering questions. To illustrate, if they know a brand is high in price they may rate (and believe) it is high in quality (Bettman, John, and Scott, 1986). Hence, ratings on an attribute frequently contain elements of both overall attitude and ratings on other attributes.

Be careful of the order in which a set of alternatives are presented. Since items in the first position tend to get a disproportionate number of mentions due to heightened visibility, it is often useful to put a weak alternative in this position to force respondents to look further in the list when the responses are of the multiple-choice type. Some people like to randomly order lists, and others use alphabetical order. If the question asks the respondent to rate a series of alternatives on some criteria, the first alternative serves as a reference point. For this reason, some people try to put a neutral/typical alternative first on the assumption it will be rated in the middle of the scale and, hence, leave room for both more positive and negative responses. While the order bias cannot be removed on an individual question, it is possible to reduce its effect on average responses by rotating the order of the responses. This could be done for three brands (A, B, and C) by giving each third of the sample a different format:

Format 1	*Format 2*	*Format 3*
A	B	C
B	C	A
C	A	B

Don't worry too much about the physical format for scaled questions. A variety of response formats can be used for scale questions. Some of the most popular are:

	Very Sad				Very Happy
Please circle the answer which best describes your feelings.	1	2	3	4	5
Please check the answer which best describes your feelings.	_____	_____	_____	_____	_____
	□	□	□	□	□
	○	○	○	○	○

Other scales have also been used. (Many researchers have used 3- to 7-point "smile" scales with pictures ranging from a sad to a happy face when questioning children.) Fortunately, the choice of format is usually more a matter of aesthetic opinion than practical importance.

On the other hand, for self-administered questions the format can impact on the responses. Obviously, the question should be pleasing to the eye (which means well reproduced with adequate blank space and large type face) and easily filled out (which means response categories should line up in columns). The example in Figure 6–2 from Dillman (1978) illustrates several less-than-desirable formats.

Try to get relative ratings. Absolute ratings of brands are interesting (i.e., brand X is good; averaging 4 on a five-point scale) but often disguise information. (If competitive brands Y and Z rate 4.5 and 4.7, 4.0 is pretty bad, while if the other brands rate 3.5 and 3.7, brand X is in good shape.)

Beware recall data. Individuals' ability to recall data is limited (otherwise we would all have had straight As). When the question concerns an important event (e.g., marriage date), at least most people can accurately recall the information. For low-salience items, by contrast, recall is subject to very severe limitations, including "telescoping" (thinking something happened more recently than it actually did). Recalling, for example, the last five brands of soft drink you purchased or the last five customers who entered your store is a difficult task. For this reason, many researchers prefer a "critical incidence" approach, where people are asked to recall a single incidence or, better still, are asked to check their last MasterCard or Visa slip or monthly bill to see what they purchased.

In asking for usage data, a choice must be made between asking for usage rate (e.g., times per month) and recency data (e.g., when did you last

FIGURE 6–2 Unacceptable Formats of Commonly Asked Survey Questions

Q–22 Your sex:___ Male___ Female
Q–23 Your present marital status:___ Never Married___ Married ___ Separated___ Widowed
Q–24 Number of children you have in each age group:___ Under five years___ 5–13___ 14–18___ 19–25 and over
Q–25 Your present age:________
Q–26 Do you own (or are you buying) your own home?___ No___ Yes
Q–27 Did you serve in the armed forces?___ No___ Yes (Year entered___, Year discharged___)
Q–28 Are you presently:___ Employed___ Unemployed___ Retired ___ Full-time homemaker
Q–29 Please describe the usual occupation of the principal wage earner in your household, including title, kind of work, and kind of company or business. (If retired, describe the usual occupation before retirement.)
Q–30 What was your approximate net family income, from all sources, before taxes, in 1970?

Less than $3,000___	10,000 to 12,999___	20,000 to 24,999___
3,000 to 4,999___	13,000 to 15,999___	25,000 to 29,999___
5,000 to 6,999___	16,000 to 19,999___	Over $30,000___
7,000 to 9,999___		

Q–31 What is the highest level of education that you have completed?

No formal education___	___ Some college
Some grade school___	___ Completed college . . . major___
Completed grade school___	___ Some graduate work
Some high school___	A graduate degree . . . degree and major___
Completed high school___	

Q–32 What is your religious preference?___ Protestant denomination ___ Jewish___ Catholic___ Other___ Specify___ None
Q–33 How frequently did you attend religious services in a place of worship during the past year:___ Regularly___ Occasionally___ Only on special days___ Not at all
Q–34 Which do you consider yourself to be?___ Republican___ Democrat ___ Independent___ Other___ Specify
Q–35 Which of these best describes your usual stand on political issues? ___ Conservative___ Liberal___ Middle of the road___ Radical

Source: D. Dillman, *Mail and Telephone Surveys*, p. 134. Copyright © 1978 by John Wiley & Sons, Inc., Reprinted by permission of John Wiley & Sons., Inc.

__________?). A study involving questions about dining out showed that the way respondents answer varies with the two most prevalent approaches: actual counting (enumeration) of occurrences and direct estimation (Blair and Burton, 1987). Actual counting was most frequent for low-incidence individuals, and when shorter time frames were used. Another study suggested that recency data are better than usage rate data for low-usage, low-salience events (Buchanan and Morrison, 1987). The moral of this is that even the seemingly trivial choice between asking how often something was done and how recently it was done can impact the results.

Don't automatically assume literacy. Most of the world is in some sense functionally illiterate (including a substantial fraction in the United States) and most do not speak English (again including a sizable fraction in the United States). Try to ask questions which are simple and in the appropriate language. Also, be aware that, in self-administered surveys, eyesight and lack of literacy will adversely affect quality of response as well as response rate.

Key informants may misinform. It is often convenient to ask one person to provide data about others (e.g., family members or others in a firm). Unfortunately, they are not always accurate, especially in giving nonfactual information.

Make it fun or at least nonawful. Respondents will produce better data if they find the task fun (as opposed to overly cute).

QUESTION SEQUENCE

The order in which questions are placed is often very important. The early questions set the tone of the survey by creating the mental set the respondent uses to produce answers. This is true in terms of both content and interest. For example, a series of early questions on symphony orchestra music might serve to (*a*) lead the consumer to assume that the subject matter was music preference and, thus, answer accordingly or (*b*) increase (or decrease) the subject's interest and, consequently, the likelihood the respondent will complete the questionnaire. In fact, maintaining interest is one of the largest problems in many surveys. While some topics are inherently more interesting than others, proper format (including plenty of white space) and sequencing can do a lot to maintain the respondent's concentration. Some issues include placement of hard questions, placement of sensitive or experimental questions, variety of format, and branching.

Placement of Hard Questions. Many surveys have two or three key questions which are particularly difficult (e.g., preference rankings from 1 to 20 of 20 TV shows or suppliers). When these questions are placed at the very beginning of a study, they may convince a subject that the study is overly difficult and, hence, lead to a refusal to participate. On the other hand, placing these questions last will confront tired respondents with a difficult task, leading to either refusals or poor-quality data. The best solution is often to put them fairly early but interspersed with easy questions. Hence, many surveys will begin with a simple "warm-up" question or two (the marketing research equivalent of "What color is the White House?"), then go to the real questions.

Placement of Sensitive Questions. There is no place to hide questions which people don't want to answer (including income). Typically, however, a survey will still have some value without these responses. Therefore, it is often advisable to put these questions toward the end to avoid contaminating the other responses.

Variety of Format. To keep respondents alert, it is useful to vary the format somewhat throughout the questionnaire. Thus, when gathering data on a large number of variables of the same type (e.g., 150 lifestyle measures), some people choose to break up the section into parts (e.g., three parts of 50 each) and intersperse the parts with other questions. It is not clear, however, that this type of variety markedly improves data quality.

FIGURE 6–3 Flow Diagram of Question Branching

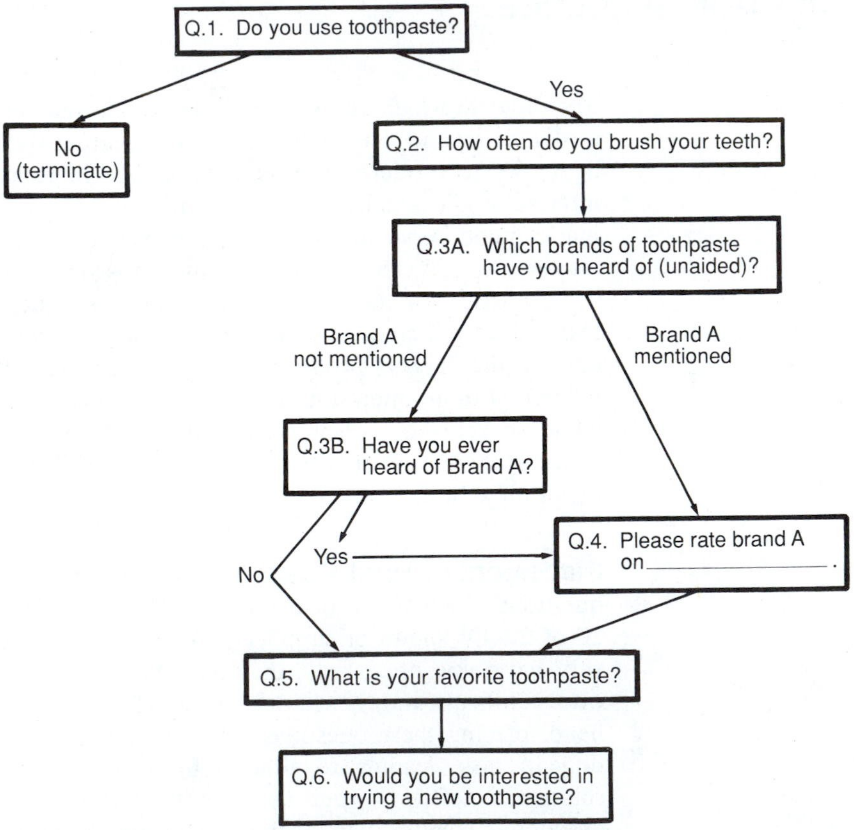

Branching. In many questionnaires, the questions to be asked depend on the answer to previous questions. One piece of advice is not to branch unless absolutely necessary, especially in self-administered surveys. When branching is used, the branch should immediately follow the answer on which the branch is based.

If branching is needed, it is useful to first set up a diagram to summarize the flow, such as Figure 6–3. Translating this into questionnaire form, we get Figure 6–4. As can be seen from this example, even simple branching instructions can be hard to follow. Some become so elaborate that they can quickly get out of hand, although computer-controlled interviews can handle them quite well.

FIGURE 6–4

1. Do you use toothpaste?
   _____Yes (go to question 2)
   _____No (terminate)

2. How often do you brush your teeth?

____	____	____	____	____
Rarely	Weekly	A few times a week	Daily	More than once per day

3*a*. What brands of toothpaste have you heard of?
   ____
   ____
   ____

3*b*. If brand A is not mentioned, have you heard of brand A?
   _______Yes (go to question 4)
   _______No (go to question 5)

4. Please rate brand A in terms of its sex appeal.

Very Ordinary				*Very Sexy*
1	2	3	4	5

5. What is your favorite toothpaste?
   Aim______________________
   Colgate______________________
   Crest______________________
   Ultra Bright______________________
   Other (please specify)______________________

6. Would you be interested in trying a new toothpaste?

Very Uninterested				*Very Interested*
1	2	3	4	5

A related issue is whether you can ask someone to rate a product which he or she has not actually used. Some people believe in branching around such questions to avoid burdening the respondent. An alternative approach is to ask everyone to rate a product whether they have heard of it or not. The rationale for this is they have perceptions of the brand which may explain their nonuse (e.g., I can rate bank robbing as risky without doing it). Since I can also ask (preferably later to cut down on refusals) whether the product has been used, I have the option of looking at only those people who use the product anyway. This strong-arm approach may produce additional information while avoiding branching instructions and is typically preferable if the respondents can reasonably be expected to have some knowledge of or attitude toward the product in question.

Pretest and Revision

The stage in the research process which is most likely to be squeezed out due to cost/time pressures is the pretest. This is unfortunate, since a pretest is also the stage in which fundamental problems in a survey can be corrected. There are an incredible number of disasters around which a pretest of 50 to 100 "real" subjects would have prevented. Pretests allow checking to see (*a*) whether there are a disproportionate number of nonresponses to particular questions, (*b*) whether the questions discriminate (respondents give different answers), and (*c*) whether the respondents seem to understand the questions.

Pretests can also be used to convert open-ended questions to categories for the final study. There is also no shame in using multiple pretests, especially if convenience samples are used at most of the stages. A questionnaire which does not change between initial drafting and field execution is probably one which has not been carefully examined.

Coding the Questionnaire

Have a clear coding scheme for inputting the data for analysis before collecting them. A discussion of coding and editing issues appears in Chapter 10.

TYPE OF SURVEY

This section focuses on alternative methods of collecting survey data from individuals. The choice of how to collect survey data is typically viewed as the choice between the big three: personal, mail, and phone interviews.

Here, eight major methods will be discussed:

1. Personal (in home) interviews.
2. Telephone interviews.
3. Mail surveys.
4. Drop-off, callback.
5. Panels.
6. Group interviews.
7. Location interviews.
8. Computer-directed interviews.

Personal Interviews

The view of marketing research in the general public is likely to consist of a mental picture of an interviewer asking questions of an individual and recording the responses on a clipboard (Figure 6–5). Indeed, the personal interview is a major tool of marketing research. Like all the survey approaches, it has both advantages and disadvantages.

Advantages

Relatively complex presentations can be shown to subjects in conjunction with questioning (e.g., samples of different packages, mock-ups of a new machine).

FIGURE 6–5

Higher completion rates are likely, since the interviewer can urge the respondent to finish ("Just one more minute, please").

Depending on what answer a respondent gives to a particular question, the interviewer can then branch to the next appropriate question. Branching instructions are often quite complex. For example, "If it's Tuesday and the person answered "2" to question 31, go to question 34. If not, ..." While complex branching could theoretically be done with other designs, in practice only telephone surveys also do this as "standard practice."

Respondents can be asked to give responses other than the multiple-choice type. For example, respondents could be asked to sort cards containing the names of different brands into piles based on some criterion.

The presence of the interviewer can help convince the respondent to answer questions he or she might otherwise leave blank. Alternatively, the interviewer may be able to deduce the answer to questions, such as annual income based on cues, such as the size of the house and type of furniture.

The interviewer can also observe the respondent and record the observations as data.

Disadvantages

The presence of the interviewer may influence the responses. This influence may be the result of the interviewer's opinions showing or the respondent giving those answers which he or she perceives will meet with approval from another human being.

Since the interviewer often is required to interpret the response and assign it to a predesignated category, there is a serious potential problem of errors in interpretation caused either because of the selective perception of the interviewer based on personal opinions or expectations of the likely response, or simply random error in recording the answer.

There is a strong possibility of interviewer cheating. The firms which offer personal interviewing services generally bid on a potential job based on the number of completed interviews. Once they get a job, there is a very obvious incentive to get the interviews completed as quickly as possible. This incentive is likely to be transferred from the project director to the interviewers, often very directly by means of a pay schedule which is based on the number of completed interviews. Hence, it is very common for interviewers to "help out" a respondent by filling in some answers without asking the questions, and not uncommon for an interviewer to dummy up an entire questionnaire. For example, they might play-act: "If I lived at 1182 Maple Avenue, how would I respond?" Besides dealing with a reputable firm or, more drastically, doing the interviewing yourself, the only alternative is to check up on the interviewers. Calling back 20 percent of the respondents and asking four to five questions to see if the responses match is a common practice. Unfortunately, even this process is inexact, since the demographics may be relatively easily guessed by the interviewer and attitudes are subject to change over time. The shrewd interviewer who asks the objective questions and a few of the subjective ones and then fills out the rest is especially difficult to catch. Since the respondent may be reluctant to "rat" on the interviewer, even asking what the interviewer did may fail to uncover the cheating. In short, interviewer cheating is a difficult problem to control.

"Completion time" is fairly long. It takes several weeks for a typical personal interview study to be completed.

Costs. Personal interviews are, in general, the most expensive way to collect data from individual respondents. Costs can range from about $10 per completed interview for relatively short questionnaires (those requiring about five minutes to complete) with simple instructions and sample designs (e.g., any warm body) to $500 or more for longer questionnaires (requiring 45 minutes to one hour to complete) and "hard-to-get" respondents, such as executives or ghetto dwellers. For a half-hour questionnaire (six to eight pages) and a sample consisting of typical consumers, the cost tends to be about $50 to $80 per completed interview.

Response Rate. The response rate to personal interviews obviously depends on many factors, including the sample chosen, the length of the questionnaires, the number of callbacks, the reward offered, and the competence of the interviewer. Nonetheless, typical response rates run between 50 and 80 percent.

Telephone Interviews

Phone interviewing is essentially a low-cost form of personal interviewing, which has gained in popularity and now, by some measures, accounts for about 40 percent of all surveys. As such, it shares many of the pros and cons of personal interviewing.

Advantages

Like personal interviews, phone interviews may follow fairly elaborate branching patterns.

The phone interviewer may help prod the respondent to answer questions.

Some individuals are more likely to answer a phone than to let a stranger enter their house, especially in high-crime areas and in the evening when interviewing of people who work during the day is normally done.

It can be completed quickly. Phone interviews on a topic can be ready for analysis faster than personal interviews, sometimes within 24 hours.

It can be done from a single location. By using WATS lines, all the interviewing can be conducted from a central location, simultaneously increasing control and reducing travel time.

Interviewer bias is reduced somewhat, since the interviewer is not physically present.

Disadvantages

The questions must be asked without any visual props, such as actual packages or pictures of products.

People may well respond differently to phone interviews than they do to personal interviews or, in fact, than they actually feel. In general, a person responding to a phone interview will probably concentrate less than when responding to a personal interview.

The responses are limited, in that complex response scales (such as a constant sum scale) are not practically usable. Also, it is rare for a phone interview to exceed 30 to 45 minutes in duration, and much shorter ones are the norm.

As in the case of personal interviews, there is the opportunity for the interviewer to exert influence either overtly or subconsciously, misperceive the answer given, or outright cheat.

Unless the person you are trying to contact has a phone, you can't get him or her. This is an especially serious problem when phone books are the source of the sample, since, in areas like southern California, up to 30 percent of the phones are unlisted. Fortunately, studies have shown that, for many responses, nonlisted phone owners are very similar to listed phone owners. However, unlisted phones are most common among the young or the very old, the poor or the very rich. The use of a technique called *random digit dialing* which, as the name implies, dials numbers randomly and then includes the person answering the phone in the sample, circumvents the problem of only listed phone owners being available. Random digit dialing does have the disadvantage of generating a lot of worthless responses (numbers not in service, businesses, and other people outside the target population). Also, those with unlisted numbers may not respond even if you call them. After all, they have their numbers unlisted to keep from getting nuisance calls. In fact, some people have been known to complain bitterly to the phone company, which they believe has given out their number. Nothing, however, helps with the problem of reaching individuals without phones, and about 10 percent of households are without phones (Tyebjee, 1979). Since, for most products, people without phones account for a very small share of the business, this is fortunately more of a theoretical than a practical problem.

People may hang up. This fact gives the respondent greater control than in the case of a personal interview. This can lead to, for example, fewer mentions of brands used; in one case, 2.5 for phone versus 4.8 for personal interviews (Telser, 1976). It also can lead to premature termination of an interview. Even when the interview is completed, distractions (TV, children, etc.) may detract from the quality of the responses.

Costs. Compared to personal interviews, phone interviews are relatively inexpensive. Although costs vary depending on the length of the interview, and so forth, costs for a completed interview tend to run between $10 and $50. A 1987 bid for a ten-minute, 25-question phone survey of 200 executives was $6,000—about $30 per completed interview.

This low cost is partly due to the existence of WATS (Wide Area Telephone Service, in case you've been wondering) lines, which allow unlimited calling from a particular area to another area for a fixed monthly charge. Hence, WATS lines allow interviewers in a central location to do interviewing essentially anywhere. Phone interviews also eliminate the costs associated with travel between interviews, which is a part of personal interviewing costs.

The current trend is toward the use of computer-controlled telephone interviewing. This provides for easy (once programmed) branching. In fact, since the data are input during the interview, branching can be based on an analysis of responses to previous questions.

Response Rate. The response rate of phone surveys is usually slightly below that of personal interviews, ranging from 40 to 75 percent.

Mail Surveys

The third of the big-three methods of obtaining responses from individuals is the mail survey. This method, which is self-administered, provides a clear contrast with both personal and phone surveys (see Figure 6–6).

Advantages

The respondent is allowed to work at his or her own pace in completing the questions.

No interviewer is present to bias or misinterpret the responses.

FIGURE 6–6 A Comparison of Three Survey Methods

Characteristic	*Personal*	*Mail*	*Phone*
Usable length	Good	Fair	Poor to fair
Suitability for complex questions	Good	Poor	Fair
Minimization of process bias	Poor	Good	Fair
Cost per completed interview	High	Low	Low to moderate
Speed	Moderate	Slow	Fast

With adequate instructions, fairly complicated scales (e.g., 10 points) can be used to gather responses.

By receiving the responses directly, the possibility of interviewer cheating is essentially eliminated. (If you allow a firm to collect the responses for you, they could potentially "doctor" them to improve the response rate.)

Disadvantages

There is no one present to prod the respondent to complete the questions. This leads to greater numbers of partially completed questions and also to a higher rate of discontinuance in the middle of the survey (or, for that matter, before the start).

No one is available to help interpret instructions or questions. This can lead to both confusion and frustration on the part of the respondent. One partial solution is to provide an 800 telephone number for respondents with questions to call.

There is a nontrivial chance the survey will be treated as another piece of junk mail and appropriately filed (discarded). Alternatively, someone else in the household or firm may complete the survey.

Since most mail lists are at least one to two years old, many people on the list will have moved and, hence, many of the respondents will be unreachable. Unlike the case in personal and phone interviews, however, this will not be immediately obvious.

Most mail surveys are left open three to four weeks, although the bulk of responses come in during the first two weeks. This means that mail surveys may take longer to complete than phone or personal interviews if the latter are fully expedited.

Respondents tend to be slightly more up-scale (higher income, education, etc.) than nonrespondents.

Branching instructions are not generally recommended. Respondents follow directions about as well as parents follow instructions for putting together toys on Christmas Eve.

Don't know / blank responses are more frequent. The largest fraction of don't know responses typically occurs on self-administered questionnaires (e.g., mail) with personal interviews producing possibly slightly fewer than telephone surveys.

Costs. The cost of mail surveys is similar to or somewhat smaller than that of phone surveys (e.g., $10 per completed interview). An example of the cost basis for a single mailout is approximately as follows:

Stamp	$ .25
Envelope	.15
Return envelope and stamp	.35
Cover letter	.15
Questionnaire (6 pages)	.25
Name label	.10
Total	$1.25

While labor increases this cost, the cost base is still very low when compared to a personal interview. As in the case of phone surveys, very short (10 questions or fewer) surveys are even less expensive.

Response Rate. The response rate of mail surveys varies widely and is currently the subject of considerable research. The lower bound can be close to zero if too much is asked of the respondent. For example, direct-mail solicitations typically get 1 percent or smaller responses. On the other hand, some interesting surveys with artful cover letters have received 50 to 60 percent responses. Somewhere in the middle of these two extremes lies the most likely result. To illustrate, one survey which was six pages long, focusing on durable goods ownership plus demographics, and containing no other incentive than a cover letter penned by yet another fictitious research director, produced a response rate of 20 percent out of 100,000 mailed questionnaires.

Drop-off Callback

A procedure designed to include the best aspects of several methods, drop-off callback involves dropping off a questionnaire (usually after asking the respondent a few initial questions) and then returning to pick it up sometime later. This strategy allows the respondent to complete the questionnaire on his or her own time and yet has the advantage of an interviewer to build initial commitment and "check up" on the responses.

This technique has been used extensively for super-long questionnaires, which often run over 100 pages and take several hours to complete (Pessemier, DeBruicker, and Hustad, 1971; Lovelock et al., 1976).

Panels

One way to collect data is to utilize a group of individuals who have already agreed to participate. This approach includes both using commercially available panels and instituting and maintaining your own panel. There are really three major types of panels. The first is the diary panel, in which members agree to record their purchases of a variety of products in terms of brand, price, size, and so forth. M.R.C.A. and N.P.D. maintain well-known panels of this type. A second type of panel is one in which individuals' behavior is monitored by some device which does not require panel member participation. Nielsen's audiometer, which records data on television viewing among participating households for the famous Nielsen TV ratings, is the prime example of this type. Monitored panels could be totally unobtrusive by basing them on credit card receipts, utility bills, and so forth. The third type of panel is simply a list of a set of individuals who agree to answer questionnaires. The mail panels of Market Facts, National Family Opinion (NFO), and Home Testing Institute (HTI) are examples of the third type of panel. While the particulars of the panels obviously are important, some general comments about panel usage are appropriate.

Advantages

The response rate among panel members is extremely high. Even for mail panels, the response rate to four- to six-page questionnaires is usually 70 to 80 percent.

For established panels, a great deal of other information, such as demographics, is already available on each of the respondents.

Using a panel is "easy," since the sample design issue is already taken care of.

Disadvantages

At least in one aspect, panel members are clearly not typical individuals. Recruitment is difficult, with typically 10 percent or fewer of the individuals agreeing to participate. Hence, panel members tend to be "questionnaire freaks."

Panels have a tendency to age. Consequently, as time passes, either the average age increases or the panel must be "rolled over" by the addition of younger panel members.

Most mail panels, including those designed to represent all segments of the population, tend to underrepresent both minority groups and low-education levels. (Someone who can't read will hardly be likely to fill out six-page questionnaires.)

Being in a panel tends to "condition" respondents. Someone who has filled out three questionnaires about a product or seen the name of an unfamiliar product may tend to behave differently by, for example, spending more time considering the product or trying the unfamiliar product as a result of being made aware of it. Therefore, care must be taken that panel members' responses have not been conditioned by prior questionnaires or information collection.

Costs. Costs vary greatly depending on the panel in question. Six-page questionnaires sent to standby mail panels tend to cost about $15 to $20 per completed interview. Ongoing panels generally require a yearly subscription—at a price from $50,000 to $200,000.

Response Rate. The response rates of panels are very high, ranging from 70 to 80 percent for the mail panels to close to 100 percent for mechanical observation panels, such as Nielsen.

Group Interviews

Group interviews are widely used in marketing research. They are essentially a combination of "cheap" personal interviews and self-administered questionnaires. A leader administers a questionnaire to a group of individuals at one time in a single location. This technique can be very economical, especially when used with church or community groups.

Location Interviews

One of the least-expensive ways to collect survey data is to station an interviewer in a central ("high traffic") location. The interviewer then "accosts" unsuspecting individuals and attempts to convince them to participate in the study. One of the most common forms of this type of study is shopping center or mall intercept interviews, which now account for close to 20 percent of consumer surveys.

In such studies, the interviewer may conduct the interview on the spot as a personal interview. Alternatively, the interviewer will lead the respondent to a separate area where the respondent may be treated to either a self-administered, personal, or group interview. Usually, the separate area will contain some type of demonstration, either of a product or of advertising. Not surprisingly, only people who are not very busy or who are intrigued by marketing research tend to be included in shopping mall studies.

Computer-Assisted Interviewing

Computer-assisted (-directed) interviewing has grown tremendously in popularity. A large fraction of WATS phone interviewing is now computer-directed, which allows for consistent questioning, complex branching, randomizing of question order, automatic consistency checks, automated callback procedures, and almost immediate conversion of responses into analysis. In-person computer-directed questionnaires seem to generate considerable interest and high levels of respondent cooperation. There is also some question about how people with certain backgrounds respond to being "interrogated" by a machine. Still this seems destined to be an increasingly common form of data collection.

Combination of Methods

The methods of collecting survey data described to this point are not necessarily mutually exclusive. For example, one could use a phone-screening questionnaire followed by a personal interview with a self-administered questionnaire left behind to be mailed in later. In fact, combinations of methods are often the most effective way to collect data. For example, it is possible to provide an 800 phone number with a mail survey so they can call if they have any questions.

With VCR penetration having passed 50 percent of U.S. households, another method for gathering data is to send to respondents both a VCR tape and a mail questionnaire. The tape allows for product descriptions and advertisements to be presented, with reactions then collected with self-administered surveys (or a follow-up phone survey). While VCR owners are different from nonowners in at least one way, this approach seems likely to gain in popularity.

FIELDING THE SURVEY

When a survey is finally deemed acceptable, it then must be fielded. Although the process is typically handled by a supplier, a few points are worth making. First, the survey should have a short but pleasing introduction, which indicates the name of the firm collecting the data (e.g., XYZ Research Corporation). In general, however, it is not advisable (and sometimes disastrous) to make known the identity of the firm that wishes to use the survey (e.g., the IRS). Similarly, a simple closing including thanks is appropriate. Finally, a well-defined sampling plan (to be discussed in Chapter 9) is needed.

Quality control while the study is in the field is very important. Interviewers are motivated to get completed interviews and will tend to help respondents by either suggesting answers or by simply filling in sections of the survey to ease the burden on the respondent. To control this, checking is required. Typically, this is done by recontacting 15 to 20 percent of the sample and asking (*a*) if they were in fact interviewed and (*b*) some questions to which the answers should not have changed. By comparing answers to these questions between the original and follow-up surveys, grossly disparate response patterns can be seen, which can be used to eliminate both the respondent and the interviewer.

EXAMPLES

Examples of surveys can be misleading, since there is no such thing as a typical survey. Nonetheless, Appendixes 6–A to 6–C present three examples worth studying: a personal interviewer's guide for a typical commercial survey, a nutritional survey, and an ownership and values survey. Note the difference in format between the personal interview and the self-administered surveys.

Typical Commercial Survey

Appendix 6–A presents a survey which represents the typical format of a commercial study done by personal interviewing about a product category with several different brands (Katz, 1974). With the exception of the income categories, it is a good model/starting point for such a study. The purpose of each of the product-related questions is to measure the following:

1. Unaided recall of brands.
2. Unaided advertising recall of brands.

3–5. Purchase.

6. Aided recall.
7. Opinion/attitude.
8. Ever tried.
9. If repeat purchase.
10. Advertising recall.
11. Copy point recall (unaided).
12. Copy point recall (aided).
13. Brand ratings on attributes.

14–16. Size and style used.

The classification questions measure:

1–3. Price change perceptions.
4. TV viewing.
5. Age.
6. Household size.
7. Income.

Nutritional Survey

Appendix 6–B presents the questionnaire which serves as a basis for discussion throughout much of the rest of this book. It was administered to a mail panel and is more structured than the personal interview survey of Appendix 6–A. (It also is academic, rather than commercial, in purpose, and hence less tightly focused.) The questions were as follows:

Section I:
1– 8 Food shopping habits.
9–10 Food attribute importance.
11–14 Personal food consumption.
15 Change in household consumption.

Section II:
Nutritional information sources and perceived needs.

Section III:
Background (over and above already collected demographics).

Section IV:
Lifestyle.

Section V:
Knowledge and perception of foods.

As an aside, it is useful to remember that this questionnaire, imperfect as it is, went through five revisions, including a field pretest. The pretest found a serious problem in the wording of the final three questions, which caused 20 percent of the sample to refuse to answer the section. Consequently, the wording of question 2, section V, was changed from "Please indicate which of the nine functions of the body listed below are aided by consuming whole milk, beef, tomatoes, and enriched bread by putting a check in the appropriate box" to "For each of the nine body functions listed down the side of the page, please indicate which of the four foods contribute *importantly* to the function. *Check as many or as few* of the foods as you think apply to each function." This seemingly small change greatly reduced non-response and, hence, again demonstrated the value of a pretest. As a further aside, the last three questions were added (*a*) to replicate questions on a study done for the FDA and (*b*) to serve as input for the use of multidimensional scaling algorithms. Since the scaling procedures basically recovered the four basic food groups, the value of these questions is debatable after the fact.

Ownership and Values Survey

The focus of this study[1] was the relation between ownership of major products and services and basic values of customers. Thirty products which were considered to be optional purchases (e.g., VCR, piano, vacation home) were included. For each product, three separate pieces of information were sought:

1. Current ownership (question 1*a*).
2. Intention to buy (question 1*b*).
3. Importance of having (question 2).

The ownership question allowed for multiple items since, for example, the first color TV may almost always be purchased before a compact disc player and, hence, not really compete; but the second color TV and a compact disc player might compete for dollars in a person's budget. Intention was asked over a two-year period as a compromise between "too short" a period (e.g., one month) and too long a period (e.g., 10 years). The 100-point scale was used, rather than a 6- or 7-point scale, in the hope of getting responses which could be interpreted as probabilities of purchase. The question about importance of owning was assumed to be a good way to get at basic values and, unlike ownership data, to be minimally contaminated by gifts. (However, if having a product leads one to appreciate it, the two are clearly related.)

To measure basic values, several scales were considered. The basic two scales which were chosen were the LOV (List of Values) scale and the VALS typology. Questions pertaining to the nine LOV scales are the first nine responses in question 3 (self-respect, security, . . . , excitement). The VALS typology, even with its short form, still requires several pages in a questionnaire (Mitchell, 1983). Given page constraints, an attempt was made to provide a basic description of each of the eight basic types and then to have respondents rate how well each description described themselves (question 4). The remaining items in question 3 were other values culled from a number of sources which seemed worth investigating.

---

[1]The study was developed by a market research class to serve as the common core of course projects in a marketing research class. Each team focused on a particular product or service and collected 50 observations, which included the common core questions plus those that pertained to their particular product. This allowed each group to have a large sample to analyze and to profile those who owned and intended to buy their product.

In addition to the product-based and value-based questions, a number of demographic questions ("background") were also included. The survey appears in Appendix 6–C. This self-administered study, like the nutritional survey, is used as a basis for discussion in this book.

SUMMARY

Survey design is a craft which requires balancing various sources of error and costs. It is important to recognize that many sources of error are beyond the control of the researcher, such as the respondent's lack of interest in the subject and resulting lack of care in filling out the survey. Survey execution requires effort and care. In short, survey design and execution is an area where additional effort improves results. The desire to "get on with it," so data can be analyzed and decisions made is understandable but, unless held in check, is often counterproductive.

This chapter has focused on a six-step process for developing a survey: listing general types of information needed, listing specific information items, writing questions, creating a questionnaire, testing the questionnaire, and revising the questionnaire. It has also discussed different means for administering a questionnaire: personal interviewing, phone interviewing, mail, drop-off, panels, group interviews, location interviews, and computer-directed interviews (common for phone surveys). Those desiring more detail should consult other sources, such as Sudman and Bradburn (1982). The next chapter discusses measurement issues that relate to writing questions in greater detail.

PROBLEMS

1. Evaluate the questionnaire in Appendix 6–A.
2. Evaluate the questionnaire in Appendix 6–B.
3. Evaluate the questionnaire in Appendix 6–C.
4. Assume you were designing a phone survey to find out how consumers choose a new appliance.
   a. Design the flow of the questionnaire (similar to Figure 6–4).
   b. Would you have a screening question?
   c. If your client were General Electric, how would the survey change?
   d. If your client were White-Westinghouse, how would the survey change?
5. Which type of survey (personal, phone, mail) would you use to get:
   a. Opinions about political issues.
   b. Ratings of a new product.
   c. Ratings of a new product concept.
   d. Priority rankings of 15 goals.
6. List 10 things that you could do *wrong* in a survey.

BIBLIOGRAPHY

Alpert, Mark I. "Personality and the Determinants of Product Choice." *Journal of Marketing Research* 9 (February 1972), pp. 89–92.

Bailar, Barbara; Leroy Bailey; and Joyce Stevens. "Measures of Interviewer Bias and Variance." *Journal of Marketing Research* 14 (August 1977), pp. 337–43.

Barach, Jeffrey A. "Advertising Effectiveness and Risk in the Consumer Decision Process." *Journal of Marketing Research* 6 (August 1969), pp. 314–20.

Beckwith, Neil E., and Donald R. Lehmann. "The Importance of Differential Weights in Multiple Attribute Models of Consumer Attitude." *Journal of Marketing Research* 10 (May 1973), pp. 141–45.

_____. "The Importance of Hal Effects in Multi-Attribute Attitude Models." *Journal of Marketing Research* 12 (August 1975), pp. 265–75.

Belk, Russell; W. "Situational Variables and Consumer Behavior." *Journal of Consumer Research* 2 (December 1975), pp. 157–64.

Bettman, James R.; Deborah Roedder John; and Carol A. Scott. "Covariation Assessment by Consumers." *Journal of Consumer Research* 13 (December 1986), pp. 316–26.

Birdwell, Al E. "A Study of the Influence of Image Congruence on Consumer Choice." *Journal of Business* 41 (January 1968), pp. 76–88.

Bither, Steward W., and Ira J. Dolich. "Personality as a Determinant Factor in Store Choice." *Proceedings*, Third Annual Conference, Association for Consumer Research, 1972, pp. 9–19.

Blair, Edward, and Scot Burton. "Cognitive Processes Used by Survey Respondents to Answer Behavioral Frequency Questions." *Journal of Consumer Research* 14 (September 1987), pp. 280–88.

Blair, Ed.; Seymour Sudman; Normal M. Bradburn; and Carol Stocking. "How to Ask Questions about Drinking and Sex: Response Effects in Measuring Consumer Behavior." *Journal of Marketing Research* 14 (August 1977), pp. 316–21.

Blankenship, A. B. *Professional Telephone Surveys*. New York: McGraw-Hill, 1977.

Bogart, Leo. "No Opinion, Don't Know, and Maybe No Answer." *Public Opinion Quarterly* 31 (Fall 1967), p. 332.

Bruce, Grady D., and Robert E. Witt. "Personality Correlates of Innovative Buying Behavior." *Journal of Marketing Research* 7 (May 1970), pp. 259–60.

Buchanan, Bruce, and Donald G. Morrison. "Sampling Properties of Rate Questions with Implications for Survey Research." *Marketing Science* 6 (Summer 1987), pp. 286–98.

Cahalan, Don. "Correlates of Respondent Accuracy in Denver Validity Survey." *Public Opinion Quarterly* 32 (Winter 1968–69), pp. 607–21.

Cannell, Charles F.; Lois Oksengerg; and Joan M. Converse. "Striving for Response Accuracy: Experiments in New Interviewing Techniques." *Journal of Marketing Research* 14 (August 1977), pp. 306–15.

Cox, Donald F., and Raymond A. Bauer. "Self-Confidence and Persuasibility in Women." *Public Opinion Quarterly* 28 (Fall 1964), pp. 453–66.

Darden, William R., and Fred D. Reynolds. "Backward Profiling of Male Innovators." *Journal of Marketing Research* 11 (February 1974), pp. 79–85.

Dillman, Don A. *Mail and Telephone Surveys*. New York: John Wiley & Sons, 1978.

Erdos, Paul. *Professional Mail Surveys*. New York: McGraw-Hill, 1970.

Evans, Franklin B. "Ford versus Chevrolet: Park Forest Revisited." *Journal of Business* 41 (October 1968), pp. 445–59.

______. "Psychological and Objective Factors in the Prediction of Brand Choice." *Journal of Business* 32 (October 1959), pp. 340–69.

Evans, Franklin B. and Harry V. Roberts, "Fords, Chevrolets, and the Problem of Discrimination." *Journal of Business* 36 (April 1963), pp. 242–49.

Ferber, Robert. *The Reliability of Consumer Reports of Financial Assets and Debts*. Urbana, Ill.: Bureau of Economic and Business Research, University of Illinois, 1966.

Fouss, James H., and Elaine Solomon. "Salespeople as Researchers: Help or Hazard?" *Journal of Marketing* 44 (Summer 1980), pp. 36–39.

Frankel, Martin R., and Lester R. Frankel. "Some Recent Developments in Sample Survey Design." *Journal of Marketing Research* 14 (August 1977), pp. 280–93.

Gottlieb, Morris J. "Segmentation by Personality Types." In *Advancing Marketing Efficiency*, ed., Lynne H. Stockman. Chicago: American Marketing Association, 1959, pp. 148–58.

Greeno, Daniel W.; Montrose S. Sommers; and Jerome B. Kernan. "Personality and Implicit Behavior Patterns." *Journal of Marketing Research* 10 (February 1973), pp. 63–69.

Grubb, Edward L., and Gregg Hupp. "Perception of Self, Generalized Stereotypes, and Brand Selection." *Journal of Marketing Research* 5 (February 1968), pp. 58–63.

Hagburg, Eugene C. "Validity of Questionnaire Data: Reported and Observed Attendance in an Adult Education Program." *Public Opinion Quarterly* 32 (Fall 1968), p. 453.

Herriot, Roger A. "Collecting Income Data on Sample Surveys: Evidence from Split-Panel Studies." *Journal of Marketing Research* 14 (August 1977), pp. 322–29.

Howard, John A. *Consumer Behavior: Application of Theory*. New York: McGraw-Hill, 1977.

Hustad, Thomas P., and Edgar A. Pessemier. "Segmenting Consumer Markets with Activity and Attitude Measures." Institute Paper no. 298. Lafayette, Ind.: Krannert Graduate School of Industrial Administration, Purdue University, 1971.

Infosino, William J. "Forecasting New Product Sales from Likelihood of Purchase Ratings." *Marketing Science* 5 (Fall 1986), pp. 372–84.

Jacoby, Jacob. *Handbook of Questionnaire Construction*. Cambridge, Mass.: Ballinger Publishing, 1976.

______. "Personality and Innovation Proneness." *Journal of Marketing Research* 8 (May 1971), pp. 244–47.

Juster, F. T. "Consumer Buying Intentions and Purchase Probability: An Experiment in Survey Design." *Journal of the American Statistical Association* 61 (September 1966), pp. 658–96.

Kahle, Lynn R. "The Nine Nations of North America and the Value Basis of Geographic Segmentation." *Journal of Marketing* 50 (April 1986), pp. 37–47.

Kahle, Lynn R.; Sharon E. Beatty; and Pamela Homer. "Alternative Measurement Approaches to Consumer Values: The List of Values (LOV) and Values and Life Style (VALS)." *Journal of Consumer Research* 13 (December 1986), pp. 405–09.

Kalwani, Manohar U., and Alvin J. Silk. "On the Reliability and Predictive Validity of Purchase Intention Measures." *Marketing Science* 1 (Summer 1983), pp. 243–86.

Kamen, Joseph M. "Personality and Food Preferences." *Journal of Advertising Research* 4 (September 1964), pp. 29–32.

Kassarjian, Harold H. "Personality and Consumer Behavior: A Review." *Journal of Marketing Research* 8 (November 1971), pp. 409–19.

Kassarjian, Harold H., and Waltraud M. Kassarjian. "Personality Correlates of Inner- and Other-Direction." *Journal of Social Psychology* 70 (June 1966), pp. 281–85.

Katz, Jerrold P. "An Examination of Sample Survey Research in Marketing in the Context of a Buyer Behavior Model." Ph.D. dissertation. Columbia University, 1974.

Kernan, Jerome, "Choice Criteria, Decision Behavior, and Personality." *Journal of Marketing Research* 5 (May 1968), pp. 155–64.

King, Charles W., and John O. Summers. "Overlap of Opinion Leadership Across Consumer Product Categories." *Journal of Marketing Research* 7 (February 1970), pp. 43–50.

Krugman, Herbert E. "The Impact of Television Advertising: Learning without Involvement." *The Public Opinion Quarterly* 29 (Fall 1965), pp. 349–56.

Kuehn, Alfred A. "Demonstration of a Relationship between Psychological Factors and Brand Choice." *Journal of Business* 36 (April 1963), pp. 237–41.

Leigh, James H., and Claude R. Martin, Jr. "'Don't Know' Item Nonresponse in a Telephone Survey: Effects of Question Form and Respondent Characteristics." *Journal of Marketing Research* 24 (November 1987), pp. 418–24.

Lovelock, Christopher H.; Ronald Stiff; David Cullwick, and Ira M. Kaufman. "An Evaluation of the Effectiveness of Drop-Off Questionnaire Delivery." *Journal of Marketing Research* 13 (November 1976), pp. 358–64.

McKenzie, J. R., "An Investigation into Interviewer Effects in Market Research." *Journal of Marketing Research* 14 (August 1977), pp. 330–36.

MacLachlan, James; John Czepiel; and Priscilla LaBarbera. "Implementation of Response Latency Measures." *Journal of Marketing Research* 16 (November 1979), pp. 573–77.

McNeil, J. "Federal Programs to Measure Consumer Purchase Expectations, 1946–73: A Post-Mortem." *Journal of Consumer Research* 1 (December 1974), pp. 1–10.

Malhotra, Naresh K. "An Approach to the Measurement of Consumer Preferences Using Limited Information." *Journal of Marketing Research* 23 (February 1986), pp. 33–40.

Massy, William F.; Ronald E. Frank; and Thomas M. Lodahl. *Purchasing Behavior and Personal Attributes*. Philadelphia: University of Pennsylvania Press, 1968.

Mitchell, Arnold. *The Nine American Life Styles*. New York: Warner, 1983.

Morrison, Donald G. "Purchase Intentions and Purchase Behavior." *Journal of Marketing* 43 (Spring 1979), pp. 65–74.

Mullet, Gary M. and Marvin J. Karson. "Analysis of Purchase Intent Scales Weighted by Probability of Actual Purchase." *Journal of Marketing Research* 22 (February 1985), pp. 93–96.

Payne, Stanley L. *The Art of Asking Questions*. Princeton, N.J.: Princeton University Press, 1951.

Pessemier, Edgar A., and A. Bruno. "An Empirical Investigation of the Reliability and Stability of Selected Activity and Attitude Measures." *Proceedings*, Annual Conference, Association for Consumer Research, 1971, pp. 389–403.

Pessemier, Edgar; Stewart Debruicker; and Thomas Hustad. "The 1970 Purdue Consumer Behavior Research Project." Lafayette, Ind.: Purdue University, 1971.

Plummer, Joseph T. "The Concept and Application of Life Style Segmentation." *Journal of Marketing* 38 (January 1974), pp. 33–37.

Pressley, Milton M., ed. *Mail Survey Response: A Critically Annotated Bibliography*. Greensboro, N.C.: Faber, 1976.

Pressley, Milton M. and William L. Tullar. "A Factor Interactive Investigation of Mail Survey Response Rates from a Commercial Population." *Journal of Marketing Research* 14 (February 1977), pp. 108–11.

Reynolds, Fred D. *Psychographics: A Conceptual Orientation*, Research Monograph no. 6. Athans, Ga.: College of Business Administration, University of Georgia, 1973.

Robertson, Thomas S., and James H. Myers. "Personality Correlates of Opinion Leadership and Innovative Buying Behavior." *Journal of Marketing Research* 6 (May 1969), pp. 164–68.

Schiffman, Leon G., and Michael D. Jones. "New York Telephone's Use of VALS," *Marketing Review* 38 (December–January 1983), pp. 25–29.

Schuman, Howard, and Stanley Presser. *Questions and Answers in Attitude Surveys*. New York: Academic Press, 1981.

Spaeth, Mary A. "Recent Publications on Survey Research Techniques." *Journal of Marketing Research* 14 (August 1977), pp. 403–09.

Sudman, Seymour, and Norman M. Bradburn. *Asking Questions*. San Francisco: Jossey-Bass, 1982.

Telser, Eugene. "Data Exorcises Bias in Phone vs. Personal Interview Debate, but If You Can't Do It Right, Don't Do It At All." *Marketing News* 9 (September 10, 1976), pp. 6–7.

Torgerson, Warren S. *Theory and Methods of Scaling*. New York: John Wiley & Sons, 1958.

Tucker, William T., and John Painter. "Personality and Product Use." *Journal of Applied Psychology* 45 (October 1961), pp. 325–29.

Tyebjee, Tyzoon T. "Telephone Survey Methods: The State of the Art." *Journal of Marketing* 43 (Summer 1979), pp. 68–78.

______. "Response Latency: A New Measure for Scaling Brand Preference." *Journal of Marketing Research* 16 (February 1979), pp. 96–101.

Venkatesan, M. "Personality and Persuasibility in Consumer Decision Making." *Journal of Advertising Research* 8 (March 1968), pp. 39–45.

Villani, Kathryn E. A., and Donald R. Lehmann. "An Examination of the Stability of AIO Measures." *Proceedings*, Fall Conference American Marketing Association, 1975, pp. 484–88.

Walsh, T. C. "Selected Results from the 1972–73 Diary Surveys. *Journal of Marketing Research* 14 (August 1977), pp. 344–52.

Wells, William D. "Psychographics: A Critical Review." *Journal of Marketing Research* 12 (May 1975), pp. 196–213.

______. *Life Style and Psychographics*. Chicago: American Marketing Association, 1974.

Wells, William D., and Douglas J. Tigert, "Activities, Interests, and Opinions." *Journal of Advertising Research* 2 (August 1971), pp. 27–35.

Westfall, Ralph. "Psychological Factors in Predicting Product Choice." *Journal of Marketing* 26 (April 1962), pp. 34–40.

Whalen, Bernie. "Ad Agency Cross-Tabs VALS with 'Nine Nations'; Results 'Unnerving.'" *Marketing News* 16 (January 21, 1983), p. 20.

Wright, Peter. "Consumer Choice Strategies: Simplifying Optimizing," *Journal of Marketing Research* 12 (February 1975), pp. 60–67.

Appendix 6–A

Commercial Personal Interview Survey*

*Printed with permission of Professor Jerrold P. Katz, Simmons College, Boston, Massachusetts.

DO NOT WRITE IN THIS SPACE

Study #	(1–3)	X05
Respondent #	(4–7)	
Area Code	(8–9)	
Questre. Type	10–5	
Card #	11–1	

Interviewer's Name ______________

City ______________ State ______________

Date ______________

Respondent's Name ______________

Address ______________

City, State ______________ Zip Code ______________

Telephone # ______________

(Area Code_____)

1. First, when you think of product 1 what brands come to mind? Any others? (CIRCLE BELOW BY ORDER OF MENTION)

2. What brands of product 1 have you seen or heard advertised recently? Any others? (CIRCLE BELOW BY ORDER OF MENTION)

3. The last time you bought product 1 what brand did you buy? (CIRCLE BELOW)

4. What other brands have you bought in the last two months? (CIRCLE BELOW)

5. And what brand do you buy most often? (CIRCLE BELOW)

INTERVIEWER: CIRCLE UNDER Q.6 "YES", EACH BRAND MENTIONED IN Q.1 THROUGH Q.5 THEN ASK Q.6 FOR EACH BRAND NOT YET CIRCLED "YES".

6. Have you ever heard of__________product 1? (CIRCLE BELOW)

ASK Q.7 AND Q.8 FOR EACH BRAND CIRCLED UNDER Q.6 "YES".

7. Everything considered, what is your overall opinion of__________? Would you say it is one of the Best, Very Good, Good, Fair or Poor? (CIRCLE BELOW)

8. Have you ever tried________product 1 (CIRCLE BELOW)

11-3	Q.1 Come to mind			Q.2 Advertised		Q. 3,4,5 – Brand buying Q.3	Q.4	Q.5	Q.6 Heard Of		Q.7 Overall Opinion						Q.8
	1st	2nd	Others	1st	Others	Last	Others	Most	Yes	No	One of The Best	Very Good	Good	Fair	Poor	No Opinion	Tried
Brand E	12-1	14-1	16-1	18-1	20-1	22-1	24-1	26-1	28-1	30-1	32-1	-2	-3	-4	-5	X	45-1
Brand F	-2	-2	-2	-2	-2	-2	-2	-2	-2	-2	33-1	-2	-3	-4	-5	X	-2
Brand B1	-3	-3	-3	-3	-3	-3	-3	-3	-3	-3	34-1	-2	-3	-4	-5	X	-3
Brand B2	-4	-4	-4	-4	-4	-4	-4	-4	-4	-4	35-1	-2	-3	-4	-5	X	-4
Brand B3	-5	-5	-5	-5	-5	-5	-5	-5	-5	-5	36-1	-2	-3	-4	-5	X	-5
Brand G	-6	-6	-6	-6	-6	-6	-6	-6	-6	-6	37-1	-2	-3	-4	-5	X	-6
Brand A	-7	-7	-7	-7	-7	-7	-7	-7	-7	-7	38-1	-2	-3	-4	-5	X	-7
Brand R	-8	-8	-8	-8	-8	-8	-8	-8	-8	-8	39-1	-2	-3	-4	-5	X	-8
Brand P	-9	-9	-9	-9	-9	-9	-9	-9	-9	-9	40-1	-2	-3	-4	-5	X	-9
Brand H	-0	-0	-0	-0	-0	-0	-0	-0	-0	-0	41-1	-2	-3	-4	-5	X	-0
Brand I	13-1	15-1	17-1	19-1	21-1	23-1	25-1	27-1	29-1	31-1	42-1	-2	-3	-4	-5	X	47-1
Brand U	-2	-2	-2	-2	-2	-2	-2	-2	-2	-2	43-1	-2	-3	-4	-5	X	-2
Other	-3	-3	-3	-3	-3	-3	-3	-3	-3	-3		44-45					

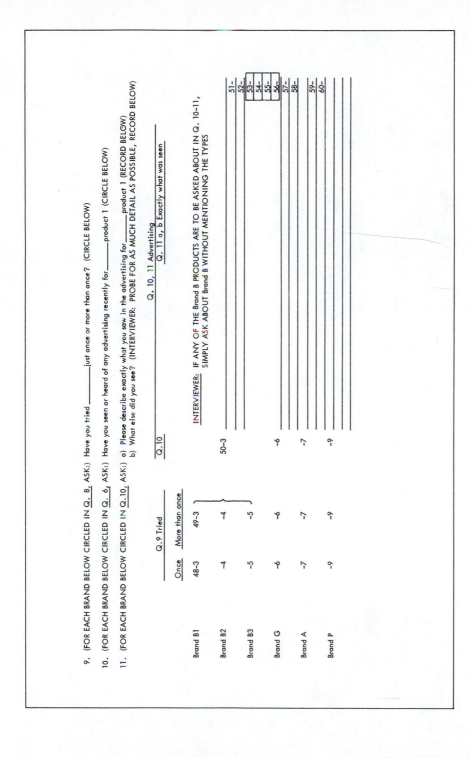

9. (FOR EACH BRAND BELOW CIRCLED IN Q. 8, ASK:) Have you tried ________ just once or more than once? (CIRCLE BELOW)

10. (FOR EACH BRAND BELOW CIRCLED IN Q. 6, ASK:) Have you seen or heard of any advertising recently for ______ product 1 (CIRCLE BELOW)

11. (FOR EACH BRAND BELOW CIRCLED IN Q. 10, ASK:) a) Please describe exactly what you saw in the advertising for ______ product 1 (RECORD BELOW)
b) What else did you see? (INTERVIEWER: PROBE FOR AS MUCH DETAIL AS POSSIBLE, RECORD BELOW)

INTERVIEWER: IF ANY OF THE Brand B PRODUCTS ARE TO BE ASKED ABOUT IN Q. 10–11, SIMPLY ASK ABOUT Brand B WITHOUT MENTIONING THE TYPES

	Q.9 Tried		Q. 10, 11 Advertising	
	Once	More than once	Q.10	Q. 11 a, b Exactly what was seen
Brand B1	48–3	49–3		
Brand B2	–4	–4	50–3 (Brands B1–B3 bracketed)	______ 51– ______ 52–
Brand B3	–5	–5		53– 54– 55– 56–
Brand G	–6	–6	–6	______ 57– ______ 58–
Brand A	–7	–7	–7	______ 59– ______ 60–
Brand P	–9	–9	–9	______

12. Different brands of product 1 say and show different things in their advertising. I'm going to read you some of these things, and I'd like you to tell me which brand's advertising I am describing. (DO NOT READ BRANDS – CIRCLE OR WRITE IN BRANDS MENTIONED BY RESPONDENT)

11 - 2
12 - x
13 - x

		Brand B	Brand G	Brand A	Brand P	Other (SPECIFY EXACTLY)	Don't Know
a.	Advertising Copy 1	14-3	-6	-7	-9	______ 15-	X
b.	Advertising Copy 2	16-3	-6	-7	-9	______ 17-	X
c.	Advertising Copy 3	18-3	-6	-7	-9	______ 19-	X
d.	Advertising Copy 4	20-3	-6	-7	-9	______ 21-	X
e.	Advertising Copy 5	22-3	-6	-7	-9	______ 23-	X
f.	Advertising Copy 6	24-3	-6	-7	-9	______ 25-	X
g.	Advertising Copy 7	26-3	-6	-7	-9	______ 27-	X
h.	Advertising Copy 8	28-3	-6	-7	-9	______ 29-	X
i.	Advertising Copy 9	30-3	-6	-7	-9	______ 31-	X

ASK Q.13 FOR EACH BRAND LISTED BELOW THAT WAS CIRCLED IN Q.6.

13. Now, I'd like your opinion of a few brands of product 1 on some of their specific features. For example, would you say that __________ product 1 is one of the best, very good, fair or poor on Attribute 1? (CIRCLE BELOW AND REPEAT EACH FEATURE FOR EACH BRAND CIRCLED IN Q.6)

ATTRIBUTE ONE		One of the best	Very good	Good	Fair	Poor	Have no opinion
	Brand E	36–1	2	3	4	5	X
	Brand F	6	7	8	9	0	Y
	Brand B	37–1	2	3	4	5	X
	Brand A	6	7	8	9	0	Y
	Brand P	38–1	2	3	4	5	X
	Brand H	6	7	8	9	0	Y
	Brand I	39–1	2	3	4	5	X
ATTRIBUTE TWO							
	Brand E	40–1	2	3	4	5	X
	Brand F	6	7	8	9	0	Y
	Brand B	41–1	2	3	4	5	X
	Brand A	6	7	8	9	0	Y
	Brand P	42–1	2	3	4	5	X
	Brand H	6	7	8	9	0	Y
	Brand I	43–1	2	3	4	5	X
ATTRIBUTE THREE							
	Brand E	44–1	2	3	4	5	X
	Brand F	6	7	8	9	0	Y
	Brand B	45–1	2	3	4	5	X
	Brand A	6	7	8	9	0	Y
	Brand P	46–1	2	3	4	5	X
	Brand H	6	7	8	9	0	Y
	Brand I	47–1	2	3	4	5	X

14. As you probably know there are size 1 and size 2 units of product 1. About how many size 1 units did your family use last month?

RECORD # UNITS____________(64–65) IF NONE, CIRCLE: Y

15. About how many size 2 units of product 1 did your family use last month?

RECORD # UNITS____________(66–67) IF NONE, CIRCLE: Y

16. For the next few questions, please tell us how often you buy different kinds of product 1. Your answer should be either frequently, occasionally, seldom or never. For example, how often do you buy..........(CIRCLE)

		Frequently	Occasionally	Seldom	Never
a.	Kind 1	68–1	69–1	70–1	71–1
b.	Kind 2	-2	-2	-2	-2
c.	Kind 3	-3	-3	-3	-3
d.	Kind 4	-4	-4	-4	-4
e.	Product 1 on special price, coupon, cents-off, or on some other special deal	-5	-5	-5	-5

CLASSIFICATION

1. Please think for a moment about your purchase of product 1 in the past six months. In general, do you seem to be buying....(CIRCLE BELOW)

2. And what about your purchase of product 2 in the past six months? In general, do you seem to be buying....(CIRCLE BELOW)

		Q.1 Product 1	Q.2 Product 2
	More expensive brands	72-1	73-1
	Less expensive brands or	2	2
	The same priced brands that you have always bought	3	3
(DO NOT READ)	Don't know	X	X

3. Generally speaking, in the next six months do you expect the price of products such as product 1, product 2, etc. ....(CIRCLE BELOW)

Go up some	74-1	Don't know (DO NOT READ)	X
Go down some or	(2)		
Remain the same	3		

4. In terms of a typical seven-day week, how much television do you watch at different times of the day and night? For example, during the day before 5 pm, do you watch a lot of TV, or none at all? Now in the evening.....(REPEAT FOR EACH OF THE THREE REMAINING TIME PERIODS - CIRCLE BELOW)

11-1
CONT'D

	A Lot	A Little	None	(DO NOT READ) Don't Know	
During the day before 5 PM	63-1	64-1	65-1	-9	
Between 5 and 7:30 PM	-2	-2	-2	-0	66-X
Between 7:30 and 11 PM	-3	-3	-3	-X	
After 11 PM	-4	-4	-4	-Y	

5. Which of these age groups are you in? (CIRCLE NUMBER UNDER THE GROUP)

	Under 25	25 - 34	35 - 44	45 - 54	Over 54
67	-1	-2	-3	-4	-5

6. How many members of your family are living at home now, including yourself? (CIRCLE)

68	-1	-2	-3	-4	-5	-6+

7. And to help us tabulate your answers, what is your total family income per year before taxes? (CIRCLE NUMBER TO LEFT OF GROUP)

69-1	Under $3,000	-4	$7,500 - $10,000	
-2	$3,000 - $5,000	-5	$10,000 - $15,000	70-
-3	$5,000 - $7,500	-6	Over $15,000	71-

Appendix 6–B

Nutritional Questionnaire

SECTION I - FOOD AND SHOPPING HABITS

1. Please check to indicate what portion of the food shopping for your household you do personally . . . .

- ☐ None of it
- ☐ Less than half of it
- ☐ About half of it
- ☐ Most of it
- ☐ All of it

2. About how many times PER WEEK do you shop for food? . . . .

- ☐ Less than once a week
- ☐ Once a week
- ☐ 2 - 4 times a week
- ☐ 5 or more times a week

3. a) Do you prepare a shopping list before you go to the store?

☐ YES - Continue ☐ NO - Skip to Question 4

b) About what portion of the items that are purchased at the grocery store or supermarket are on your shopping list? . . . .

- ☐ None of them
- ☐ Some of them
- ☐ About half of them
- ☐ More than half
- ☐ Almost all of them

4. Approximately how much money is spent on food for your household in an average week? . . . .

- ☐ Under $15
- ☐ $15 - $29
- ☐ $30 - $44
- ☐ $45 - $60
- ☐ Over $60

5. Approximately how much different is the amount you now spend on food each week as compared to one year ago at this time? . . . .

- ☐ Spend at least $10 less than last year
- ☐ $5 - $10 less than last year
- ☐ About the same as last year
- ☐ $5 - $10 more than last year
- ☐ Over $10 more than last year

6. When you buy staple products (i.e. canned soup, ketchup, etc.), how many brands and sizes do you usually consider? (CHECK ONLY ONE) . . . .

- ☐ Only 1 or 2
- ☐ Many brands, one size
- ☐ Many sizes, one brand
- ☐ Many brands and sizes

7. Which one of the following best describes the way you shop for food? (CHECK ONLY ONE)

- ☐ I actively seek information about food in terms of nutritional value, price, etc.
- ☐ I sometimes try new foods because of new information, but generally buy the same foods
- ☐ The food I buy is almost always the same, and I spend very little time thinking about it

8. Have you, or any members of your immediate family, ever used food stamps?

- ☐ Never
- ☐ Used to, but do not use them now
- ☐ We are presently using them

National Family Opinion, Inc.

50739

9. When deciding which foods to serve, how important are the following considerations? Indicate the degree of importance for each either by checking under the heading that describes your feelings, or by checking a box in between the headings that describe your feelings if your feelings fall somewhere between the headings.

	VERY IMPORTANT		SOMEWHAT IMPORTANT		NOT VERY IMPORTANT
Variety	☐	☐	☐	☐	☐
Taste	☐	☐	☐	☐	☐
Other family members' preferences	☐	☐	☐	☐	☐
Diet restrictions	☐	☐	☐	☐	☐
Price	☐	☐	☐	☐	☐
Availability at stores where you normally shop	☐	☐	☐	☐	☐
Ease of preparation	☐	☐	☐	☐	☐
Habit (past eating patterns)	☐	☐	☐	☐	☐
Advertised specials	☐	☐	☐	☐	☐
Nutritional value	☐	☐	☐	☐	☐

10. When you are deciding which brand of a particular food to purchase in the store, how much attention do you pay to the following?

	Pay a Great Deal Of Attention	Pay Some Attention	Pay Little or No Attention
Brand name	☐	☐	☐
Number of servings	☐	☐	☐
Net weight or volume	☐	☐	☐
Total price	☐	☐	☐
Amount of ingredients	☐	☐	☐
Unit price	☐	☐	☐
List of ingredients	☐	☐	☐
Nutritional value	☐	☐	☐
Recipes	☐	☐	☐
Food additives and preservatives	☐	☐	☐
Date of manufacture or expiration	☐	☐	☐

11. Please check below to indicate how many times per week you, personally, eat each of the following meals.

	Never	1 - 2	3 - 4	5 - 6	Everyday
Breakfast	☐	☐	☐	☐	☐
Lunch	☐	☐	☐	☐	☐
Dinner	☐	☐	☐	☐	☐

12. How many snacks do you, personally, have in a typical day?

- None.......................... ☐
- One.......................... ☐
- Two.......................... ☐
- Three or more................ ☐

50739

13. How much food do you can yourself?

☐ None ☐ A small amount ☐ A large amount

14. How often do you personally consume each of the following?

	Never	A Few Times A Year	1 - 2 Times A Month	Weekly	Several Times A Week	Once A Day	More than Once A Day
Canned fruit.................	1 ☐	2 ☐	3 ☐	4 ☐	5 ☐	6 ☐	7 ☐
Fresh fruit..................	☐	☐	☐	☐	☐	☐	☐
Bread........................	☐	☐	☐	☐	☐	☐	☐
Rice.........................	1 ☐	2 ☐	3 ☐	4 ☐	5 ☐	6 ☐	7 ☐
Butter.......................	1 ☐	2 ☐	3 ☐	4 ☐	5 ☐	6 ☐	7 ☐
Margarine....................	☐	☐	☐	☐	☐	☐	☐
Cheese.......................	☐	☐	☐	☐	☐	☐	☐
Ice cream....................	1 ☐	2 ☐	3 ☐	4 ☐	5 ☐	6 ☐	7 ☐
Whole milk...................	1 ☐	2 ☐	3 ☐	4 ☐	5 ☐	6 ☐	7 ☐
Skim milk or low fat milk....	☐	☐	☐	☐	☐	☐	☐
Snack foods (potato chips, pretzels, etc.)..........	☐	☐	☐	☐	☐	☐	☐
Desserts.....................	1 ☐	2 ☐	3 ☐	4 ☐	5 ☐	6 ☐	7 ☐
Alcoholic beverages (beer, wine, liquor)............	1 ☐	2 ☐	3 ☐	4 ☐	5 ☐	6 ☐	7 ☐
Soft drinks..................	☐	☐	☐	☐	☐	☐	☐
Fish.........................	☐	☐	☐	☐	☐	☐	☐
Cold cereal..................	1 ☐	2 ☐	3 ☐	4 ☐	5 ☐	6 ☐	7 ☐
Frozen vegetables............	1 ☐	2 ☐	3 ☐	4 ☐	5 ☐	6 ☐	7 ☐
Fresh vegetables.............	☐	☐	☐	☐	☐	☐	☐
Canned vegetables............	☐	☐	☐	☐	☐	☐	☐
Poultry......................	1 ☐	2 ☐	3 ☐	4 ☐	5 ☐	6 ☐	7 ☐
Beef (hamburger or stew meat)	1 ☐	2 ☐	3 ☐	4 ☐	5 ☐	6 ☐	7 ☐
Beef (steak or roast)........	☐	☐	☐	☐	☐	☐	☐
Pork.........................	☐	☐	☐	☐	☐	☐	☐
Tuna fish....................	1 ☐	2 ☐	3 ☐	4 ☐	5 ☐	6 ☐	7 ☐
Frozen dinners...............	1 ☐	2 ☐	3 ☐	4 ☐	5 ☐	6 ☐	7 ☐
Hot dogs.....................	☐	☐	☐	☐	☐	☐	☐
Coffee or tea................	☐	☐	☐	☐	☐	☐	☐
Pasta (pizza, spaghetti, etc.)	1 ☐	2 ☐	3 ☐	4 ☐	5 ☐	6 ☐	7 ☐
Food at "fast food" restaurant (i.e. McDonald's, etc.)....................	1 ☐	2 ☐	3 ☐	4 ☐	5 ☐	6 ☐	7 ☐
Food at regular restaurants..	1 ☐	2 ☐	3 ☐	4 ☐	5 ☐	6 ☐	7 ☐

National Family Opinion, Inc. 50739

15. How has the amount your household consumes of each of the following food categories changed in the past year?

	Much Less	Somewhat Less	About The Same	Somewhat More	Much More
Canned fruit	☐	☐	☐	☐	☐
Fresh fruit	☐	☐	☐	☐	☐
Bread	☐	☐	☐	☐	☐
Rice	☐	☐	☐	☐	☐
Butter	☐	☐	☐	☐	☐
Margarine	☐	☐	☐	☐	☐
Cheese	☐	☐	☐	☐	☐
Ice cream	☐	☐	☐	☐	☐
Whole milk	☐	☐	☐	☐	☐
Skim milk or low fat milk	☐	☐	☐	☐	☐
Snack foods (potato chips, pretzels, etc.)	☐	☐	☐	☐	☐
Desserts	☐	☐	☐	☐	☐
Alcoholic beverages (beer, wine, liquor)	☐	☐	☐	☐	☐
Soft drinks	☐	☐	☐	☐	☐
Fish	☐	☐	☐	☐	☐
Cold cereal	☐	☐	☐	☐	☐
Frozen vegetables	☐	☐	☐	☐	☐
Fresh vegetables	☐	☐	☐	☐	☐
Canned vegetables	☐	☐	☐	☐	☐
Poultry	☐	☐	☐	☐	☐
Beef (hamburger or stew meat)	☐	☐	☐	☐	☐
Beef (steak or roast)	☐	☐	☐	☐	☐
Pork	☐	☐	☐	☐	☐
Tuna fish	☐	☐	☐	☐	☐
Frozen dinners	☐	☐	☐	☐	☐
Hot dogs	☐	☐	☐	☐	☐
Coffee or tea	☐	☐	☐	☐	☐
Pasta (pizza, spaghetti, etc.)	☐	☐	☐	☐	☐
Food at "fast food" restaurants (i.e. McDonald's, etc.)	☐	☐	☐	☐	☐
Food at regular restaurants	☐	☐	☐	☐	☐

SECTION II - NUTRITIONAL INFORMATION

1. How much information about nutrition have you gained from each of the following sources?

	None	Very Little	Some	Quite A Bit	A Tremendous Amount
Books	☐	☐	☐	☐	☐
Magazines	☐	☐	☐	☐	☐
Labels on the packages food comes in	☐	☐	☐	☐	☐
Your mother	☐	☐	☐	☐	☐
Other family members	☐	☐	☐	☐	☐
Friends	☐	☐	☐	☐	☐
Doctors	☐	☐	☐	☐	☐
TV programs	☐	☐	☐	☐	☐
TV advertisements	☐	☐	☐	☐	☐
Newspapers	☐	☐	☐	☐	☐
Your own experience	☐	☐	☐	☐	☐
Courses in school	☐	☐	☐	☐	☐

2. In the past year, have you read book(s) about any of the following? . . . .

	NO	YES
Dieting	☐	☐
Nutrition	☐	☐
Cooking	☐	☐

3. Assume the Federal Government were about to launch a major nutrition education campaign aimed at adults. Which of the following forms would you prefer the campaign to take?

1 ☐ Column in the newspapers
2 ☐ TV special
3 ☐ Special edition of a prominent magazine
4 ☐ Government brochure
5 ☐ Extension courses
6 ☐ Workshops
7 ☐ Public Service TV announcements
8 ☐ Information on packages
9 ☐ Information in TV advertisements
11 ☐ Don't Care

4. If a service were to become available which provided specific information about the nutritional value of the brands offered in your local supermarkets, how much would you be willing to pay per week to subscribe to it?

1 ☐ Nothing
2 ☐ 10¢ - 19¢
3 ☐ 20¢ - 49¢
4 ☐ 50¢ - 99¢
5 ☐ $1 - $2
6 ☐ Over $2

5. Have you ever had a formal nutrition course in any of the following? . . . .

	NO	YES
High School	☐	☐
College	☐	☐
Adult Education/Workshop	☐	☐

SECTION III - BACKGROUND INFORMATION

1. Please indicate if any members of your household are on any of the following special diets:

CHECK HERE IF NO MEMBERS OF YOUR HOUSEHOLD ARE ON A DIET ☐

	Self-imposed	Doctor's Orders
Low cholesterol	1 ☐	1 ☐
Low fat/calorie	2 ☐	2 ☐
Diabetic	3 ☐	3 ☐
Low salt	4 ☐	4 ☐
Vegetarian	5 ☐	5 ☐
Low triglyceride	6 ☐	6 ☐

2. How often do you smoke?

☐ Never
☐ Occasionally
☐ Regularly, but light (less than 1 pack of cigarettes each day)
☐ Regularly (one pack of cigarettes a day)
☐ Heavily (more than 1 pack each day or equivalent)

3. Which of the following types of vitamin pills do you personally take?

1 ☐ None
2 ☐ Multiple
3 ☐ Vitamin C
4 ☐ Vitamin G
5 ☐ Vitamin B-12 Complex
6 ☐ Vitamin A
7 ☐ Iron

National Family Opinion, Inc.

50739

4. How much time do you spend watching TV on an average day? . . . .

☐ None
☐ Less than 1 hour
☐ 1 - 2 hours
☐ 3 - 4 hours
☐ Over 4 hours

5. How has <u>your family income</u> changed in the last year? . . .

☐ Gone down a lot
☐ Gone down a little
☐ Stayed about the same
☐ Gone up a little
☐ Gone up a lot

6. How has your household size changed in the past year? . . .

☐ Decreased by two or more
☐ Decreased by one
☐ Stayed the same
☐ Increased by one
☐ Increased by two or more

SECTION IV - GENERAL ATTITUDE INFORMATION

Please indicate how much you agree or disagree with each of the following statements by checking a box under the heading that best describes your feelings.

	STRONGLY AGREE	SOMEWHAT AGREE	NEITHER AGREE NOR DISAGREE	SOMEWHAT DISAGREE	STRONGLY DISAGREE
People need to eat meat to be healthy.........	☐	☐	☐	☐	☐
A high level of consumption is necessary to maintain a high standard of living........	☐	☐	☐	☐	☐
I am personally more conscientious in conserving energy than I was 3 years ago.....	☐	☐	☐	☐	☐
The government should be more active in giving information about nutrition to consumers..	☐	☐	☐	☐	☐
I expect things to get better for my family next year................................	☐	☐	☐	☐	☐
I feel the need for more information about nutrition................................	☐	☐	☐	☐	☐
All people would have better diets if there were fewer mouths to feed................	☐	☐	☐	☐	☐
All cold cereals are about the same nutritionally............................	☐	☐	☐	☐	☐
Health is more important than money...........	☐	☐	☐	☐	☐
I get more exercise than the average person...	☐	☐	☐	☐	☐
We entertain at home more than the average family..................................	☐	☐	☐	☐	☐
I am healthier than the average American......	☐	☐	☐	☐	☐
I consider myself better informed about nutrition than the average American.......	☐	☐	☐	☐	☐
National brands of food are a better buy than local brands........................	☐	☐	☐	☐	☐
Life is going well for me....................	☐	☐	☐	☐	☐
Prices of food are so high that my nutrition is suffering............................	☐	☐	☐	☐	☐
Television advertising has an adverse effect on diets because it encourages people to eat "junk" foods.........................	☐	☐	☐	☐	☐
I am heavier than I should be................	☐	☐	☐	☐	☐
I would be willing to eat less if the food were sent to the poor <u>in the United States</u>	☐	☐	☐	☐	☐

SECTION IV - GENERAL ATTITUDE INFORMATION (Continued) Please continue to indicate how much you agree or disagree with each of the following statements by checking a box under the heading that best describes your feelings.

	STRONGLY AGREE	SOMEWHAT AGREE	NEITHER AGREE NOR DISAGREE	SOMEWHAT DISAGREE	STRONGLY DISAGREE
America has a responsibility to share our agricultural abundance with hungry people in poor countries as well as home in the United States..............................	☐	☐	☐	☐	☐
The United States Government should pass laws which would encourage and reward the farmer for full scale production..................	☐	☐	☐	☐	☐
The children in our household have a large influence on what we eat....................	☐	☐	☐	☐	☐
Filling out this questionnaire has made me think about things which will change the types of foods I buy........................	☐	☐	☐	☐	☐

SECTION V - FOOD OPINIONS This final section deals with food opinions. I am asking questions about how you feel about certain types of foods. It would be quite unusual for a person to know the correct answers to every one of these questions. However, your feelings are very important to me, and I would like you to answer every question even if you have to guess.

1. Please answer the following questions by checking TRUE, FALSE, or DON'T KNOW.

	True	False	Don't Know
Hamburger contains substantially more protein per ounce than do soy beans...	☐	☐	☐
Pasta is high in cholesterol....................................	☐	☐	☐
Poultry are more efficient than cattle as producers of protein...	☐	☐	☐
A large amount of one vitamin is sufficient to overcome deficiencies of other vitamins..............................	☐	☐	☐
Beans and rice together are a low-protein meal..................	☐	☐	☐
Eating a variety of foods from the supermarket will ensure a balanced diet......................................	☐	☐	☐
The cost of the vitamins needed to meet 100% of the minimum daily requirements is less than 10¢ per day..........	☐	☐	☐
Food coloring additives create hyperactivity in children.........	☐	☐	☐
Sugar causes cavities in children...............................	☐	☐	☐
Whole wheat bread is healthier than enriched white bread.........	☐	☐	☐

2. For each of the nine body functions listed down the side of the page, please indicate which of the four foods contribute importantly to the function. Check as many or as few of the foods that you think apply to each function.

	Whole Milk	Beef	Tomatoes	Enriched Bread
Eyes are aided by:..........................	1 ☐	2 ☐	3 ☐	4 ☐
Teeth and bones are aided by:................	☐	☐	☐	☐
Muscle tissue is aided by:.................	1 ☐	2 ☐	3 ☐	4 ☐
Repair of body tissues is aided by:.........	1 ☐	2 ☐	3 ☐	4 ☐
Blood cells are aided by:...................	☐	☐	☐	☐
Fighting infection is aided by:............	1 ☐	2 ☐	3 ☐	4 ☐
Nervous system is aided by:................	1 ☐	2 ☐	3 ☐	4 ☐
Skin is aided by:..........................	☐	☐	☐	☐
Proper growth of children is aided by:......	1 ☐	2 ☐	3 ☐	4 ☐

3. For each of the nutrients listed down the side of the page, check as many or as few of the four foods (whole milk, beef, tomatoes, enriched bread) that you think contain a lot of the nutrients.

	Whole Milk	Beef	Tomatoes	Enriched Bread
There is a lot of Vitamin A in:..................	1 ☐	1 ☐	1 ☐	1 ☐
There is a lot of Thiamin (Vitamin B_1) in:........	2 ☐	2 ☐	2 ☐	2 ☐
There is a lot of Riboflavin (Vitamin B_2) in:.....	3 ☐	3 ☐	3 ☐	3 ☐
There is a lot of Niacin in:....................	4 ☐	4 ☐	4 ☐	4 ☐
There is a lot of Vitamin C in:..................	5 ☐	5 ☐	5 ☐	5 ☐
There is a lot of Vitamin D in:..................	6 ☐	6 ☐	6 ☐	6 ☐
There is a lot of Protein in:....................	7 ☐	7 ☐	7 ☐	7 ☐
There are a lot of Carbohydrates in:.............	8 ☐	8 ☐	8 ☐	8 ☐
There is a lot of Fat in:........................	9 ☐	9 ☐	9 ☐	9 ☐
There are a lot of Calories in:..................	10 ☐	10 ☐	10 ☐	10 ☐
There is a lot of Iron in:.......................	11 ☐	11 ☐	11 ☐	11 ☐
There is a lot of Calcium in:....................	12 ☐	12 ☐	12 ☐	12 ☐

4. And finally, I would like you to match certain foods with others. Check as many or as few of the four (4) foods (whole milk, beef, tomatoes, enriched bread) that you think have a lot of the same benefits to the body as each of the 14 foods listed down the side of the page.

	Whole Milk	Beef	Tomatoes	Enriched Bread
Oatmeal provides a lot of the same benefits as:.......	1 ☐	2 ☐	3 ☐	4 ☐
Fish provides a lot of the same benefits as:..........	☐	☐	☐	☐
Rice provides a lot of the same benefits as:..........	☐	☐	☐	☐
Navy beans provide a lot of the same benefits as:....	1 ☐	2 ☐	3 ☐	4 ☐
Chicken provides a lot of the same benefits as:.......	1 ☐	2 ☐	3 ☐	4 ☐
Potatoes provide a lot of the same benefits as:.......	☐	☐	☐	☐
Eggs provide a lot of the same benefits as:...........	☐	☐	☐	☐
Macaroni provides a lot of the same benefits as:......	1 ☐	2 ☐	3 ☐	4 ☐
Pork and Lamb provide a lot of the same benefits as:..	1 ☐	2 ☐	3 ☐	4 ☐
String beans provide a lot of the same benefits as:...	☐	☐	☐	☐
Carrots provide a lot of the same benefits as:........	☐	☐	☐	☐
Bananas provide a lot of the same benefits as:........	1 ☐	2 ☐	3 ☐	4 ☐
Peanut butter provides a lot of the same benefits as:.	1 ☐	2 ☐	3 ☐	4 ☐
Cottage cheese provides a lot of the same benefits as:	1 ☐	2 ☐	3 ☐	4 ☐

National Family Opinion, Inc. 50739

Appendix 6–C

Ownership and Values Survey

Columbia University in the City of New York | New York, N.Y. 10027

GRADUATE SCHOOL OF BUSINESS **URIS HALL**

This survey is part of an academic research project at Columbia University Graduate School of Business. It will require about 20 minutes of your time to fill out, and concerns products and services you own and/or may want to acquire as well as some general background questions. The results will be treated anonymously and used only for statistical analysis.

While we cannot offer you a large incentive other than our sincere thanks for participation, we have arranged to enter you, along with the other participants, in a lottery. The winner of the lottery will receive a check for $500. If you wish to participate in the lottery, simply put your name and address on this sheet and return it with your survey. (The cover sheet will be detached to insure anonymity.)

Thank you in advance for your cooperation.

NAME________________________
ADDRESS________________________
____

PRODUCTS AND SERVICES

1. This question concerns products and services you may own and which you may plan to buy. For each product and service listed, please indicate:

a. How many you have *in your household*, and

b. How likely you are to buy one in the next 2 years.

Please write a number from 0 to 100 in the space provided (0 = definitely will not buy, 100 = definitely will buy). Please fill this out even for items which you already own.

	(a) *Number of Each Owned (fill in number)*	*(b)* *Likelihood of Buying in Next 2 Years (# between 0 and 100)*
Cable TV service	________	________
Piano	________	________
Microwave oven	________	________
Cat	________	________
Dog	________	________
Car	________	________
VCR	________	________
Sofa bed	________	________
Personal computer	________	________
Copying machine	________	________
Fur coat	________	________
Window air conditioner	________	________
Downhill skis	________	________
Cross-country skis	________	________
Weight-lifting equipment	________	________
Sailboat	________	________
Original artwork	________	________
Sports car	________	________
Dishwasher	________	________
Compact disc player	________	________
Phone answering machine	________	________
Color TV	________	________
Wide-screen TV	________	________
Vacation home	________	________
Van or camper	________	________
Food processor	________	________
Burglar alarm/home security system	________	________
35mm camera	________	________
Video recorder/camcorder	________	________
Exercise bike	________	________

2. This question concerns how important the following products and services are to you. If you had *nothing at all* and were starting from scratch to acquire possessions, how important would it be to acquire each of these products and services? Please indicate your answer by checking "Extremely Important" for those products to which you would give the highest priority, "Not important" for those to which you give the lowest priority, and somewhere in between for the others.

	Not Important					*Extremely Important*
Cable TV service	___	___	___	___	___	___
Piano	___	___	___	___	___	___
Microwave oven	___	___	___	___	___	___
Cat	___	___	___	___	___	___
Dog	___	___	___	___	___	___
Car	___	___	___	___	___	___
VCR	___	___	___	___	___	___
Sofa bed	___	___	___	___	___	___
Personal computer	___	___	___	___	___	___
Copying machine	___	___	___	___	___	___
Fur coat	___	___	___	___	___	___
Window air conditioner	___	___	___	___	___	___
Downhill skis	___	___	___	___	___	___
Cross-country skis	___	___	___	___	___	___
Weight-lifting equipment	___	___	___	___	___	___
Sailboat	___	___	___	___	___	___
Original artwork	___	___	___	___	___	___
Sports car	___	___	___	___	___	___
Dishwasher	___	___	___	___	___	___
Compact disc player	___	___	___	___	___	___
Phone answering machine	___	___	___	___	___	___
Color TV	___	___	___	___	___	___
Wide-screen TV	___	___	___	___	___	___
Vacation home	___	___	___	___	___	___
Van or camper	___	___	___	___	___	___
Food processor	___	___	___	___	___	___
Money market account	___	___	___	___	___	___
IRA	___	___	___	___	___	___
Life insurance policy	___	___	___	___	___	___
Burglar alarm/home security system	___	___	___	___	___	___
35mm camera	___	___	___	___	___	___
Video recorder/camcorder	___	___	___	___	___	___
Exercise bike	___	___	___	___	___	___

3. Please indicate how important the following are to you by checking the appropriate spaces. As in question 2, please spread your answers out to indicate the relative importances of the items.

	Not Important					*Extremely Important*
Self-respect	___	___	___	___	___	___
Security	___	___	___	___	___	___
Warm relationship with others	___	___	___	___	___	___
Sense of accomplishment	___	___	___	___	___	___
Self fulfillment	___	___	___	___	___	___
Sense of belonging	___	___	___	___	___	___
Being well-respected	___	___	___	___	___	___
Fun & enjoyment	___	___	___	___	___	___
Excitement	___	___	___	___	___	___
Physical fitness	___	___	___	___	___	___
Being in control	___	___	___	___	___	___
Knowledge	___	___	___	___	___	___
Convenience	___	___	___	___	___	___
Owning things	___	___	___	___	___	___
Beauty	___	___	___	___	___	___
Getting a good deal	___	___	___	___	___	___
Being practical	___	___	___	___	___	___
Travel	___	___	___	___	___	___
Variety	___	___	___	___	___	___
Success	___	___	___	___	___	___
Wealth	___	___	___	___	___	___
Fame	___	___	___	___	___	___
Being unique	___	___	___	___	___	___
Personal growth	___	___	___	___	___	___
Fairness	___	___	___	___	___	___
Simplicity	___	___	___	___	___	___

4. Please indicate how well each of the following statements describes you:

	Describes Me Very Poorly					*Describes Me Very Well*
I seek intense personal experiences	___	___	___	___	___	___
I am worried about financial security	___	___	___	___	___	___
Fame and success are important to me	___	___	___	___	___	___
I am struggling to survive	___	___	___	___	___	___
I am individualistic	___	___	___	___	___	___
I am concerned about social issues	___	___	___	___	___	___
I try to live like the rich and successful	___	___	___	___	___	___
I seek to be part of a group	___	___	___	___	___	___

BACKGROUND

5. Which of these best describes your occupation?

_____ Professional/technical
_____ Managerial
_____ Skilled worker
_____ Clerical/sales
_____ Farmer
_____ Student
_____ Homemaker
_____ Retired
_____ Unemployed
_____ Other (please specify) ______

6. What is your sex?

___ male ___ female

7. What is your marital status?

___ single ___ married ___ divorced, widowed, or separated ___ other

8. How many children do you have who are under 18 and living in your home?

___ 0 ___ 1 ___ 2 ___ 3 ___ 4 or more

9. What is your age?

_____ under 25 _____ 25–34 _____ 35–44 _____ 45–54 _____ 55–64 _____ 65 or over

10. What is the highest level of school you have completed?
___ Elementary school ___ Some high school ___ High school
___ Some college ___ College graduate ___ Graduate school

11. What type of dwelling do you live in?
___ Studio apartment ___ 1 bedroom apartment
___ 2 or more bedroom apartment ___ House

12. Do you own or rent your home? ___ own ___ rent

13. What is your total annual household income?
___ Under $15,000 ___ $15,000–24,999 ___ $25,000–34,999
___ $35,000–49,999 ___ $50,000–99,999 ___ $100,000 or over

14. How much of your household income did you save or invest last year?

_____ None _____ Less than $1,000 _____ $1,000–2,999 _____ $3,000–9,999 _____ $10,000 or more

15. What is your zip code?__________

Chapter 7

Measurement and Scaling

This chapter deals with general issues of measurement and specific issues of question and scale design in survey research in some detail. In discussing the topic, some of the fundamental concepts of social science research are relevant. While these concepts will be introduced, however, this book is positioned as an applied and analytically oriented book. Hence, those with strong interests in measurement should consult another source to fill out their study of measurement fundamentals. This chapter begins by describing the basic types of scales and what analyses can be performed on the different types of scales. Next, some fundamental concepts in measurement (e.g., validity, bias) are described, as are a series of data collection issues. Finally, a typology of errors which can occur in a study is presented.

SCALES AND SCALE TYPES

The notion of measurement assumes that there is something worth measuring. The "thing" to be measured (e.g., an attitude toward a supplier, favorite color, or sales) is referred to here as a *construct*. Many constructs are fairly complex (e.g., one's attitude toward Japanese restaurants selling liquor on Sundays includes feelings toward Japanese, restaurants, liquor, etc.) Nonetheless, in order to arrive at a bottom-line statement about such constructs, there is a strong tendency to convert/simplify these constructs into a single scale or series of scales, usually quantitative ones.

In many cases, the underlying construct may in fact be numerical (e.g., sales). In other cases, the construct is measured numerically because this proves to be a useful way to represent the construct. While quantification of some constructs, such as attitude, may lose some of the subtleties of the concept, the advantages of a quantitative representation for purposes of analysis and interpretation often outweigh the costs. One motivation for the quantification of a construct is the desire to convert a problem to a form where current computer technology and programs can deal with it. Therefore, for better or worse (and in general for better), constructs are converted to quantitative scales.

Several schemes for classifying data have been proposed, most notably by Coombs (1964) and Stevens (1946, 1952). In this book, the commonly used four-part classification will be followed: nominal (categorical), ordinal, interval, and ratio.

Nominal (Categorical)

The simplest scale type is a nominal scale. A nominal scale arbitrarily assigns a number to each response so its only value is as an identification number. The scale number has no meaning in and of itself. Some obvious examples of nominal scales include Social Security numbers and the numbers on basketball players' jerseys. Put differently, there is no obvious relation between the quantity of the construct being measured and the numerical value assigned to it (e.g., the picture in Figure 7–1A).

Ordinal

The next type of scale is an ordinal scale. In an ordinal scale, the higher the number, the more (or less) the construct exists. The absolute size of the number, however, has no meaning, nor do the differences between two scale values. Consider the most common form of an ordinal scale, a ranking. If the ranking is based on intelligence, we know that the subject ranked first is more intelligent (at least according to our ranking method) than the person ranked second, but we have no idea how much smarter he or she is. A graphical example of an ordinal scale is shown in Figure 7–1B.

Interval

An interval scale is a scale where differences (intervals) between scale values have meaning, but the absolute scale values are not meaningful. A good example of an interval scale is the fahrenheit temperature scale. The difference between 41 degrees and 42 degrees is the same as the difference between 8 degrees and 9 degrees. The origin (0 degrees), however, has no particular meaning. All we can say is that 0 degrees is colder than 1 degree

FIGURE 7–1

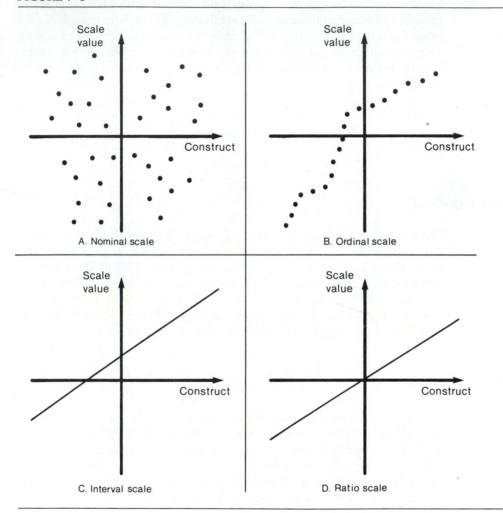

and warmer than −1 degree. Hence, 100 degrees is not twice as hot as 50 degrees. An interval scale can be represented as a straight line which does not pass through the origin (Figure 7–1C).

Ratio

A ratio scale, as the name implies, is one where the ratio between scale values is meaningful. A ratio scale is one where the 0 value indicates the absence of the construct; put differently, a ratio scale is an interval scale with a natural origin. A good example of this type of scale is money, where $100 is twice as much as $50. Graphically, a ratio scale would appear as a straight line through the origin (Figure 7–1D).

THE EFFECT OF SCALES ON ANALYSIS

The previous section discussed scale types in a fairly abstract way. One could appropriately wonder what difference scale types make. The answer is that scale types directly affect the type of analysis which can be usefully performed. Put differently, if you plan to do a particular type of analysis, you better have data which are appropriate.

Nominal Scales

Nominal scales are useful only for computing frequencies. Hence, for a scale which indicates color preference with 1 = blue, 2 = red, 3 = green, and 4 = yellow, it is possible to compute the percent of the people in a sample who like each of the four colors. Other calculations, such as the average value, are meaningless.

Ordinal Scales

In addition to computing frequencies, ordinal scales allow medians, percentiles, and a variety of other order statistics to be utilized.

Interval Scales

While the first two scale types are called nonmetric, interval and ratio scales are called metric. The presence of an interval scale allows computation of means and standard deviations, the use of parametric statistical tests, and the computation of product-moment correlations between two intervally scaled variables. This in turn allows the application of such "fancy" techniques as regression, discriminant, and factor analysis. In short, interval scales are highly desirable, in that they allow the use of most of the analytical tools common to statistics and marketing research.

Ratio Scales

Ratio scales allow, in addition to the analysis permitted by interval scales, some specialized calculations, such as a geometric mean or the coefficient of variation. They are also meaningful when multiplied together, something which is desirable in certain models.

The practical significance of scale type is fairly clear. Higher order scales can be subjected to more analytical procedures and, hence, are easier to analyze. On the other hand, getting a higher order scale often requires more effort on the part of the subject. Consequently, choosing a scale type involves a trade-off between putting the burden on the respondent and putting the burden on the analyst. While no general solution is apparent, an interval scale is usually the chosen alternative in applied marketing research. It also is important to understand that some constructs are inherently only nominally scaled (e.g., eye color) and attempts to get them measured on higher order scales (e.g., degree of blueness) may be foolish. A more complete discussion of the relation of scale type to analysis appears in Chapter 11.

EXAMPLES

This section will provide some examples of scales used in marketing research in general and surveys in particular. The coverage is intended to be useful but not necessarily complete. Nonetheless, the vast majority of types of questions used in market research studies are discussed here, and this section should provide guidance for writing questions.

Nominal Scales

Multiple Choice. One of the most obvious ways to get a nominally scaled measure of a construct is to get a respondent to check a single answer from a set of alternatives. This type question (known to students as multiple guess) is of the following general form:

Which of the following terms best describes inizlots?

_______ A Riboflavit.

_______ B Ordils and humspiels.

_______ C Octiviniginianus.

_______ D All of the above.

_______ E B on alternate Tuesdays.

_______ F None of the above.

For quantification purposes, one would typically assign a 1 to the first answer (riboflavit), a 2 to the second (ordils and humspiels), and so forth so the "none of the above" response would be coded as a 6. These numbers would only indicate which response category was chosen, not how much of the construct was present. Some marketing research examples of multiple-choice questions are:

Region: Where do you live?

______	______	______	______
East (= 1)	Midwest (= 2)	South (= 3)	West (= 4)

(Notice this is a poor question because the regions are not clearly defined for the respondent.)

Marital status: What is your marital status?

______	______	______	______
Single (= 1)	Married (= 2)	Divorced, separated (= 3)	Widowed (= 4)

Occupation: What is your occupation?

______	______	
Lawyer (= 1)	Teacher (= 2)	. . .

Brand choice: Which brand of soft drink did you last buy?

______	______	______	______
Coke (= 1)	7up (= 2)	Pepsi (= 3)	Other (= 4)

The categories used may be either supplied in advance to the respondent (aided) or coded after the respondent gives a verbal/written answer (unaided). In general, the aided/structured approach is easier for both the respondent and the analyst.

Yes-No (Binary). Measures which have only two possible values are typically nominal scales. Some examples are:

Ownership: Do you own a color TV?

___ Yes (= 1)	___ No (= 2)

Awareness: Have you heard of new Znarts cereal?

___ Yes (= 1)	___ No (= 2)

Trait association (adjective checklist): Please indicate which of the following descriptions apply to these products. Check as many descriptions as you feel apply to each product.

	Descriptions			
Product	*Necessary*	*Fun*	*Useless*	*Good Investment*
Color TV	___	___	___	___
Snowmobile	___	___	___	___
Life insurance	___	___	___	___

Notice that the trait association question is presented in matrix (table) format to save space. One could repeat the traits for each product (or products for each trait). Questions like this trait association question are often called a "pick any of *n*" scale, since the respondent is free to check any of the *n* (here 4) descriptors (necessary, fun, useless, good investment). Frequently researchers attempt to get a fixed number (K) of responses toward each object—the so-called "pick K of n" data. In the previous case, the respondent could be given the following instruction: for each product, please indicate the 2 traits which best describe it (pick 2 of 4).

Ordinal Scales

Forced Ranking. The most obvious ordinal scale is a forced ranking:

An interesting application of ranking data involves the ranking of durable goods in priority order for purchase. These data are used to evaluate the appeal of new durables and to assess the value of existing ones (Hauser and Urban, 1986).

> Please rank the following five brands in terms of your preference by marking a 1 next to your most preferred brand, a 2 next to your second most preferred brand, and so forth:
>
> Coke____________
> Pepsi____________
> 7up____________
> Dr Pepper____________
> Slice____________

Paired Comparison. Paired comparisons are essentially a means of generating an ordinal scale without asking the respondent to consider all the alternatives simultaneously. Rather, respondents only choose the more preferred (or heavier or prettier, or any other characteristic you wish to measure) of two alternatives at a time. Converting the previous question involving five soft drinks into a paired comparison framework, there are 10 pairs:

Coke, Pepsi
Coke, 7up
Coke, Dr Pepper
Coke, Slice
Pepsi, 7up
Pepsi, Dr Pepper
Pepsi, Slice
7up, Dr Pepper
7up, Slice
Dr Pepper, Slice

The derived scale value for each brand is simply the number of times that the brand was preferred in comparisons involving it. The advantage of this method is that each individual decision made is as simple as possible. The method also allows for intransitivity (i.e., preferring Coke to Pepsi, Pepsi to Dr Pepper, and Dr Pepper to Coke), which is an advantage in uncovering choice processes but a disadvantage in that it sometimes raises questions about data quality which we may prefer to have hidden. The major disadvantage with paired comparisons is that they become quite cumbersome with many alternatives. If there are 15 alternatives, there are 105 paired comparisons required, quite a lot of trouble to get an ordinal scale.

Because of their cumbersome nature, complete paired comparisons are rarely used except in pilot studies or laboratory situations.[1]

Semantic Scale. A semantic scale obtains responses to a stimulus in terms of semantic categories. For example, we could ask:

Do you like yogurt?

______	______	______	______	______
Dislike tremendously (= 1)	Dislike (= 2)	Neutral (= 3)	Like (= 4)	Like tremendously (= 5)

Respondents are instructed to check the category which best describes their feelings. Since they choose the category on the basis of the words (semantics) attached to it, this is a semantic differential scale. The scale is ordinal but not interval. For example, it is not clear what is the relation between the difference between like and neutral and the difference between dislike and dislike extremely (Myers and Warner, 1968; Dickson and Albaum, 1977).

A modification of the semantic scale is the Stapel scale, which uses a single key word (e.g., like) and gets people to rate an object (e.g., yogurt) on a scale from, for example, "does not apply" to "applies." This makes the derivation of opposites unnecessary and can also uncover complex attitudes (e.g., one could like yogurt and also dislike its consistency, so both like and dislike could be associated with it). In practice, however, there appears to be no important difference between the two scales (Hawkins, Albaum, and Best, 1974).

Picture Scales. An alternative to a semantic scale is a graphical scale. Such scales are particularly useful for children and those populations where literacy is low. For example, a so-called smile scale with faces ranging from sad to happy is often used with children to derive attitudes.

Picture scales can also be utilized even when an interviewer or physical questionnaire is not present. Phone surveys are typically limited in the number of scale points that can be used in response to a question. However,

[1]A modification of this approach, called *triads*, where respondents pick the most and least favored alternative from triples has also been used. Since it only works for certain numbers of alternatives and saves space but not respondent effort, this approach is almost never used in marketing research.

asking respondents to use the phone dial/push buttons as a 1-to-9 scale, a clock as a 1-to-12 scale, or a thermometer permits finer distinctions to be obtained.

Summated (Likert). A Likert scale is an extension of a semantic scale in two ways. Rather than measure a construct by a single item, a series of items are used to measure the construct and a summed score is calculated. Second, the scales are traditionally calibrated so a neutral response is coded "0." (This difference is, however, unimportant.) For example, attitude toward yogurt might be assessed by several questions:

Do you like the taste of yogurt?

	X			
Dislike strongly (−2)	Dislike (−1)	Neutral (0)	Like (+1)	Like strongly (+2)

Is yogurt a healthful food?

		X		
Extremely not healthful (−2)	Not healthful (−1)	Neutral (0)	Healthful (+1)	Extremely healthful (+2)

Do you feel your friends like yogurt?

X				
Dislike strongly (−2)	Dislike (−1)	Neutral (0)	Like (+1)	Like strongly (+2)

In this case, the summed score would be $-1 + 0 + (-2) = -3$, which indicates a negative attitude toward yogurt.

Others. There are a variety of other ordinal scales. One is the Guttman scale, which is really designed to order statements but is rarely used in marketing research. Another is the Q-sort technique, which is designed to cluster either respondents or alternatives. This works in several steps:

1. A set of items to be sorted is chosen. (Traditionally about 100 items have been used.)

2. Subjects are required to sort the items (usually represented by cards) into piles (traditionally 11), which represent degrees on a scale, such as aesthetic beauty, value for the money, and so on.
3. The results are used to indicate similarity among either subjects (by seeing how closely subjects agree on the sorting results) or items (by seeing which items are consistently sorted into the same pile).

Unfortunately this technique is so unwieldy that it, too, is almost never used in large-scale marketing research. It is sometimes used in small sample studies, usually as a basis for structuring a large-scale study.

Interval Scales

Equal Appearing Interval. Thurstone (1959) proposed that an interval scale measure of an overall attitude could be constructed by a series of steps: (*a*) At least 100 statements related to the overall attitude are chosen. (*b*) A set of judges rate the statements in terms of their favorability from 1 to 11. (*c*) The 10 to 20 statements which get the most consistent ratings are selected, and they are assigned the median value from the 1 to 11 scale given them by the judges. (*d*) Subjects indicate which of the statements they agree with. (*e*) Attitude scores are created as the sum of the scale values in (*c*) for the statements that the subject checked. Given the difficulty in applying this technique, it is almost never used.

Bipolar Adjective. The bipolar adjective scale is a revision of the semantic scale with the express hope that the subjects will respond to it by giving intervally scaled data. Rather than attaching a description to each of the response categories, only the two extreme categories are labeled:

Dislike Tremendously					*Like Tremendously*
1	2	3	4	5	6

Since the scale points are equally far apart both physically and numerically, it can be assumed that the responses will be intervally scaled. Two points are worth making here. The first is that many people find this argument wanting and argue that at best the scale is somewhere in between an interval and an ordinal scale. Second, when respondents are asked to rate on both bipolar adjective and semantic scales, the results are typically almost identical. In fact, both types are commonly referred to as semantic differential scales (Osgood, Suci, and Tannenbaum, 1957). Hence, for practical purposes, either scale is equally useful if intervally scaled data are needed.

Agree-Disagree Scale. A variant of the bipolar adjective scale which is frequently used is an agree-disagree scale. For example, in order to obtain a subject's opinion of yogurt, we could ask the subject to indicate his or her agreement with the statement, "I like yogurt" on an agree-disagree scale:

Disagree Strongly					*Agree Strongly*
1	2	3	4	5	6

There is a minor logical problem with interpreting responses on the disagree end of this scale. In the case of "I like yogurt", I could disagree because (*a*) I am strongly neutral or (*b*) I dislike yogurt. However, most respondents seem to interpret a "1" as indicating strong dislike and, thus, the scale has proved to be quite useful.

Continuous Scales. It is also possible to get people to respond on a continuous scale:

Very bad ______________________________ *Very good*

and then actually measure (usually with an optical scanner) the exact position on the scale. This is generally agreed to be an intervally scaled measure. However, since results using these continuous scales are essentially identical to bipolar adjective scales, they are almost never worth using. Continuous scales have recently grown in popularity in studies where subjects use a cursor or a "mouse" to give responses on a computer.

Another continuous measurement device is the attitude pollimeter, which involves filling in a circle with two colors in proportion to the degree of positive or negative attitude toward a statement (Lampert, 1979).

Equal Width Interval. Another way to generate intervally scaled data is to ask respondents to indicate into which category they fall when the categories are quantitative groupings of equal size. The following scale is only ordinal:

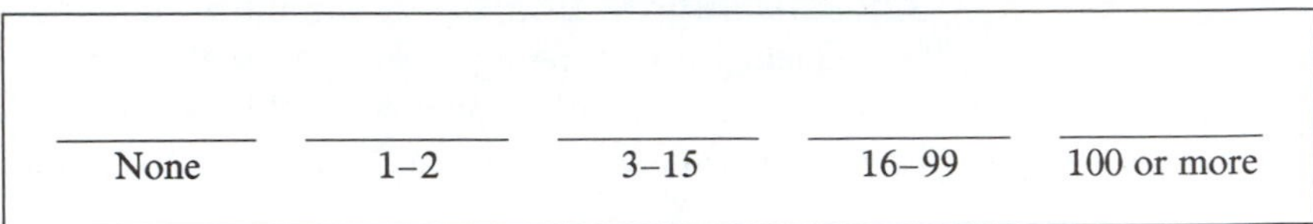

while this scale is "good" (intervally scaled):

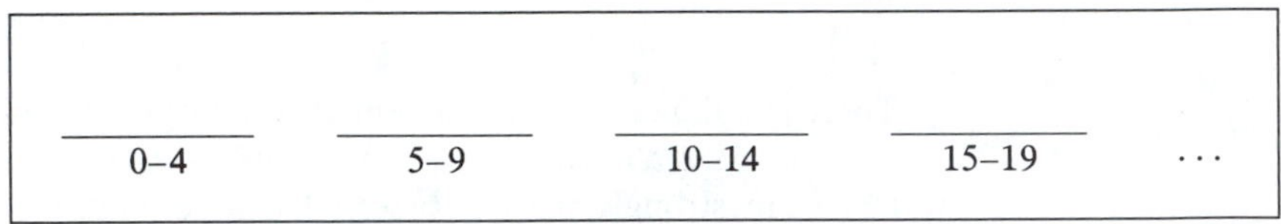

While the practical difference is small, the second approach to grouping responses has a slight advantage and no obvious cost associated with it if likely responses are fairly evenly distributed. When the vast majority of responses are likely to be 0 or 1 to 2, however, the unequal-sized categories are more useful.

At this point three questions usually arise. The first is how many scale points to use. The number depends on the ability of respondents to make discriminations on the construct. The finer the discriminations the respondent makes, the more scale points are appropriate. For individual level analysis, six or more scale points are usually sufficient to account for respondents' discriminatory abilities (Lehmann and Hulbert, 1972). Obviously, for aggregate analysis, even fewer are needed. Therefore, most scales should use between four scale points (for phone surveys, intercept interviews, low commitment situations) and eight (for committed and knowledgeable respondents).

The second major question is whether there should be an odd or even number of scale points. Arguments can be made on either side of the issue. Proponents of odd numbers argue that the presence of a neutral point allows respondents who are neutral to quickly and easily indicate so. Proponents of even numbers argue that the neutral vote is a cop-out, that the respondent is really leaning one way or the other, and that using an even number forces the respondent to reveal which way he or she is leaning. While, in general, this author prefers even numbers, the differences in results between well-done studies using, for example, five and six scale points are essentially unnoticeable.

A third question has to do with whether a scale should be balanced or not. Consider these examples of balanced and unbalanced scales:

How do you rate the writing style of this book?

____	____	____	____	____
Poor	Average	Good	Very good	Excellent
____	____	____	____	____
Very Poor	Poor	Neutral	Good	Very good

In the first case, the responses are stacked toward the positive. While this may be beneficial to the ego, it probably biases the results unfairly since the midpoint of the scale is "good," and many respondents will consider the position and not the semantic cues. On the other hand, balanced scales often produce highly skewed results so that almost all the responses fall in one half of the scale. This typically happens when subjects rate the importance of a list of attributes. Almost no respondents are willing to say that an attribute is unimportant. Hence, an unbalanced scale is occasionally used to increase dispersion of the responses. Unless there is a particular reason, however, balanced scales are typically employed.

Law of Comparative Judgment. Paired comparison judgments can be converted into intervally scaled data by means of Thurstone's law of comparative judgment. Two basic assumptions are required: (*a*) a group of respondents are homogeneous (in agreement) with respect to their ratings of the alternatives and (*b*) individuals are uncertain about their feelings toward each alternative and respond with some random component toward it. Based on these and some interesting manipulations, an interval scale is obtained. This technique is interesting (see Appendix 7–A) but very infrequently used in marketing research.

Dollar Metric (Graded Paired Comparison). An interesting way to generate an interval scale is an extension of the paired comparison method known as the dollar metric (Pessemier, 1963). This method works by getting paired comparison judgments of both which brand is preferred and the amount (in dollars) by which it is preferred. Returning to the example involving the five brands of soft drinks, the responses could be as follows:

Which Brand Do You Prefer?	*How Much Extra Would You Be Willing To Pay To Get Your More-Preferred Brand?*
Coke, Pepsi	2¢
Coke, 7up	8¢
Coke, Dr Pepper	5¢
Coke, Slice	12¢
Pepsi, 7up	6¢
Pepsi, Dr Pepper	3¢
Pepsi, Slice	10¢
7up, Dr Pepper	3¢
7up, Slice	4¢
Dr Pepper, Slice	7¢

By summing the values when a brand is being compared, a preference scale can be generated. Here we have:

$$\text{Coke}: 2 + 8 + 5 + 12 = 27$$

$$\text{Pepsi}: -2 + 6 + 3 + 10 = 17$$

$$\text{7up}: -8 + (-6) + (-3) + 4 = -13$$

$$\text{Dr Pepper}: -5 + (-3) + 3 + 7 = 2$$

$$\text{Slice}: -12 + (-10) + (-4) + (-7) = -33$$

Thus, we have an intervally scaled measure of preference. For a variety of reasons, this does not directly represent the actual strength of preference between brands. It is possible, however, to transform this scale into a predicted market share for each brand.[2]

[2] This is done by first converting the dollar metric scale to a 0 to 1 adjusted scale where Coke becomes a 1, Slice a 0, and the rest of the brands in between. The formula for this is:

$$\frac{\$\ \text{Metric scale value}_i + |\text{Smallest scale value}|}{\text{Range of scale values}} = \frac{\text{Scale value} + 33}{60}$$

Ratio Scales

Direct Quantification. The simplest way to obtain ratio scaled data is to ask directly for quantification of a construct which is ratio scaled. For example:

How many dress shirts do you own?________ How old are you?________

The problem with this approach is that the respondent probably doesn't know (i.e., how many dress shirts do you own) or want to reveal (e.g., age) what the exact answer is. Instead of upgrading from an intervally to ratio scaled answer, you may end up with no answer at all. Consequently, direct quantification tends to be used only in pilot/small-scale surveys or for very high salient items which are not considered socially sensitive (e.g., number of VCRs owned).

One fairly common example of direct quantification is the so-called willingness-to-pay scale (c.f., Cameron and James, 1987). These are often used to assess a new product and, when used directly, produce ratio scaled data. In many instances, however, categories (intervals) are provided to make the response task easier.

Constant Sum Scale. A very popular device in marketing research is the so-called constant sum scale. Respondents are given a number of points (if the process is conducted in person, chips or other physical objects are often used) and told to divide them among alternatives according to some criteria (e.g., preference, importance, aesthetic appeal). Since respondents are told to allocate chips in a ratio manner (if you like brand A twice as much as brand B, assign it twice as many chips, etc.), then the results are presumably ratio scaled.

The predicted share is given by:

$$\text{Predicted share}_i = \frac{(\text{Adjusted score}_i)^K}{\text{Sum of } (\text{adjusted score}_j)^K \text{ for all } j \text{ brands}}$$

The K value is a constant (usually between 2 and 6) determined by trial and error, so the predicted share matches the actual share as closely as possible. The effect of K is to increase the predicted share of the first-choice brand and to reduce the predicted shares of the less-preferred brands.

For example, I might ask for 10 points to be allocated among three brands:

A	2
B	3
C	5
	10

At least two problems exist with this approach. First, respondents may mess up the allocation by not using 10 points, necessitating recalculation by the analyst. Hence, some time is often required to teach the approach to respondents. Secondly, determining the appropriate number of points/chips to use requires trading off between rounding error if too few are used and fatigue/frustration/refusal problems if too many are used. Still, the approach is quite useful.

Constant Sum Paired Comparison. By combining a constant sum scale and paired comparison methods, we get a constant sum paired comparison. This allows for ratio scaled paired comparison judgment.

Delphi Procedure. The Delphi procedure is a modification of the constant sum scale designed to produce agreement among judges. For a more thorough discussion, see Appendix 7–B.

Reference Alternative. Sometimes called *fractionation* or *magnitude scaling*, this approach seeks a ratio scale by having respondents compare alternatives to a reference alternative. Respondents are instructed to indicate how alternatives compare to the reference alternative on some criterion, such as preference, by putting down a number half as large if the alternative is half as preferred, and so on:

Reference alternative X = 100
Alternative A ______
Alternative B ______
Alternative C ______

A respondent might then assign 50 to A, 250 to B, and 130 to C. In essence, this is a paired-comparison type method where respondents only consider two alternatives at once. Unfortunately, choice of the reference alternative has been found to influence the results, necessitating rotating the reference alternative to remove this effect. Since this approach is somewhat more cumbersome vis-à-vis a constant sum scale, the constant sum scale is typically used in place of the reference alternative approach.

Specialized Measurement Scales

As was suggested earlier, one of the best ways to generate a scale is to borrow one from past work. A number have become established (e.g., VALS and LOV, as discussed in Chapter 6), although most use several items to measure a single construct. These vary considerably in content. As a sample, consider the following:

1. Customer orientation of salespeople (Saxe and Weitz, 1982; Michaels and Day, 1985).
2. Opinion leadership (Childers, 1986).
3. Consumer ethnocentrism (Shimp and Sharma, 1987).
4. Consumer response to advertising (Wells, 1964; Leavitt, 1970; Zinhan and Fornell, 1985).
5. Basic human values (Rokeach, 1973; Munson and McIntyre, 1979).

The moral of this, then, is if you want to measure something, see if it has already been measured (hopefully successfully) and then borrow from past researchers, and modify as necessary.

PRACTICAL CONSIDERATIONS

Having completed a discussion of different scaling approaches, it is interesting to consider how crucial the choice of method is. One study (Haley and Case, 1979) compared 13 disparate measures of response to a brand (Figure 7–2). Their main findings were:

1. All 13 are highly correlated.
2. Awareness and brand choice are somewhat different from the other measures.
3. Acceptability, 6-point adjective, agreement, quality, 10-point numerical, thermometer, and Stapel tend to produce predominantly favorable readings (Figure 7–3).

FIGURE 7–2 Scales Tested

Scale	*Structure*	*Subject*	*Scores**	
1. Acceptability	7-point verbal balanced	Brand acceptability	Extremely acceptable (7) Quite acceptable (6) Slightly acceptable (5) Neither one nor the other (4) Slightly unacceptable (3) Quite unacceptable (2) Extremely unacceptable (1)	
2. Purchase probability	11-point numerical and verbal	Chance of buying brand next time product is purchased	100 absolutely certain 90 80 strong possibility 70 60 50 40 30 20 slight possibility 10 0 absolutely no chance	100 in 100 90 in 100 80 in 100 70 in 100 60 in 100 50 in 100 40 in 100 30 in 100 20 in 100 10 in 100 0 in 100
3. Six-point adjective	6-point verbal unbalanced	Brand opinion	Excellent (7) Very good (6) Good (5) Fair (4) Not so good (2) Poor (1) "Don't know" permitted (3)	
4. Paired comparison	51 value positions, constant sum	Brand liking	Possible range of brand scores: 0 to 50. Sum of six brand scores: 150. (Each of the 15 brand pairs compared and rated by dividing 10 points between the two brands in that pair. A brand's score is the sum of points received in the five pairs where that brand appeared.)	
5. Brand choice	3-point	Brand choice if purchased tomorrow	First choice (2) Second choice (1) No mention (0)	
6. Ten-point numerical	10-point numerical	Brand opinion	1 poor 2 . . . 9 10 excellent	
7. Thermometer	11-point numerical and verbal	Brand liking opinion	100 90 excellent 80 like very much 70 like quite well 60 like fairly well 50 indifferent 40 not like very well 30 not so good	

FIGURE 7–2 (concluded)

Scale	Structure	Subject	Scores*
			20 not like at all 10 terrible 0 Where numbers represent degrees on a thermometer
8. Verbal purchase intent	5-point verbal unbalanced	Chance of buying brand next time product is purchased	Definitely will buy (5) Very likely will buy (4) Probably will buy (3) Might or might not buy (2) Definitely will not buy (1)
9. Agreement with strongly positive statement	5-point verbal	Brand opinion	Agree completely (5) Agree somewhat (4) Don't know (3) Disagree somewhat (2) Disagree completely (1) (Statement saying that brand "would be considered one of the best" was read for each brand.)
10. Constant sum	11 value positions, constant sum	Brand liking	Possible range of brand scores: 0 to 10. Sum of six brand scores: 10. (Respondent divided 10 pennies among brands, giving more to brands she liked.)
11. Quality	7-point verbal balanced	Brand quality	Extremely high quality (7) Quite high quality (6) Slightly high quality (5) Neither one nor the other (4) Slightly low quality (3) Quite low quality (2) Extremely low quality (1)
12. Stapel scale	11-point numerical	Brand opinion	−5 poor −4 . . . 0 . . . 4 5 excellent
13. Awareness	5-point	Awareness of brand names	Top of mind (4). Second unaided mention (3). Other unaided mention (2). Aided recall (1). Never heard of (0)

*Scores assigned to verbal scales are indicated in parentheses.

Source: Russell I. Haley and Peter B. Case, "Testing Thirteen Attitude Scales for Agreement and Brand Discrimination," *Journal of Marketing* 43 (Fall 1979), p. 22.

FIGURE 7–3

Response Distributions with Many Favorable Ratings

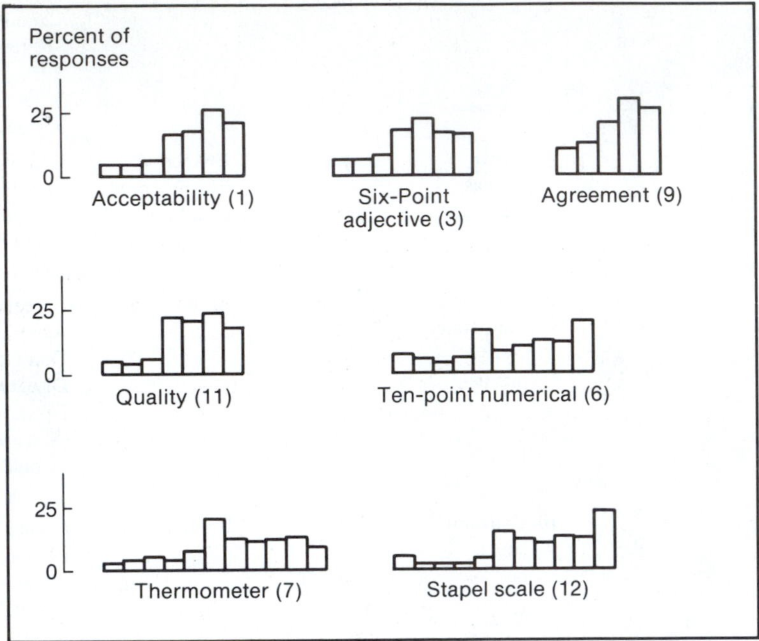

Balanced Response Distributions

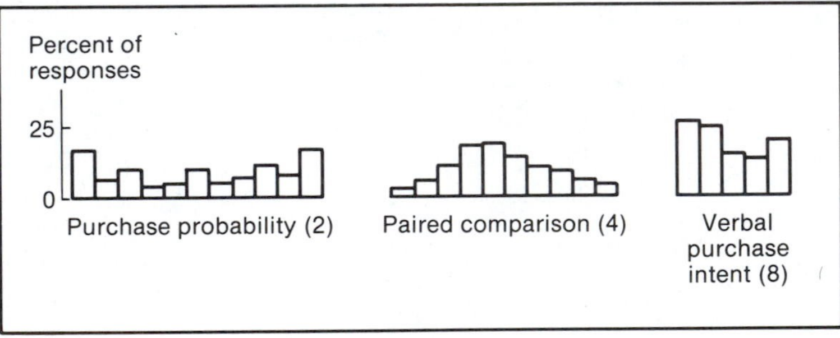

Response Distributions with Few Favorable Ratings

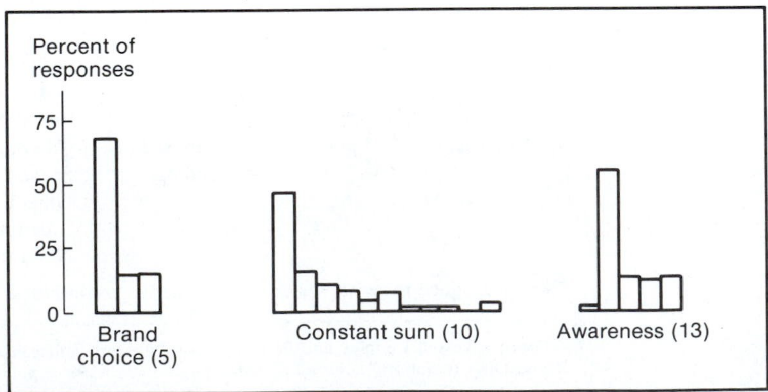

Source: Russell I. Haley and Peter B. Case, "Testing Thirteen Attitude Scales for Agreement and Brand Discrimination," *Journal of Marketing* 43 (Fall 1979), p. 24.

FIGURE 7–4 Brand Share by Rating Scale Point

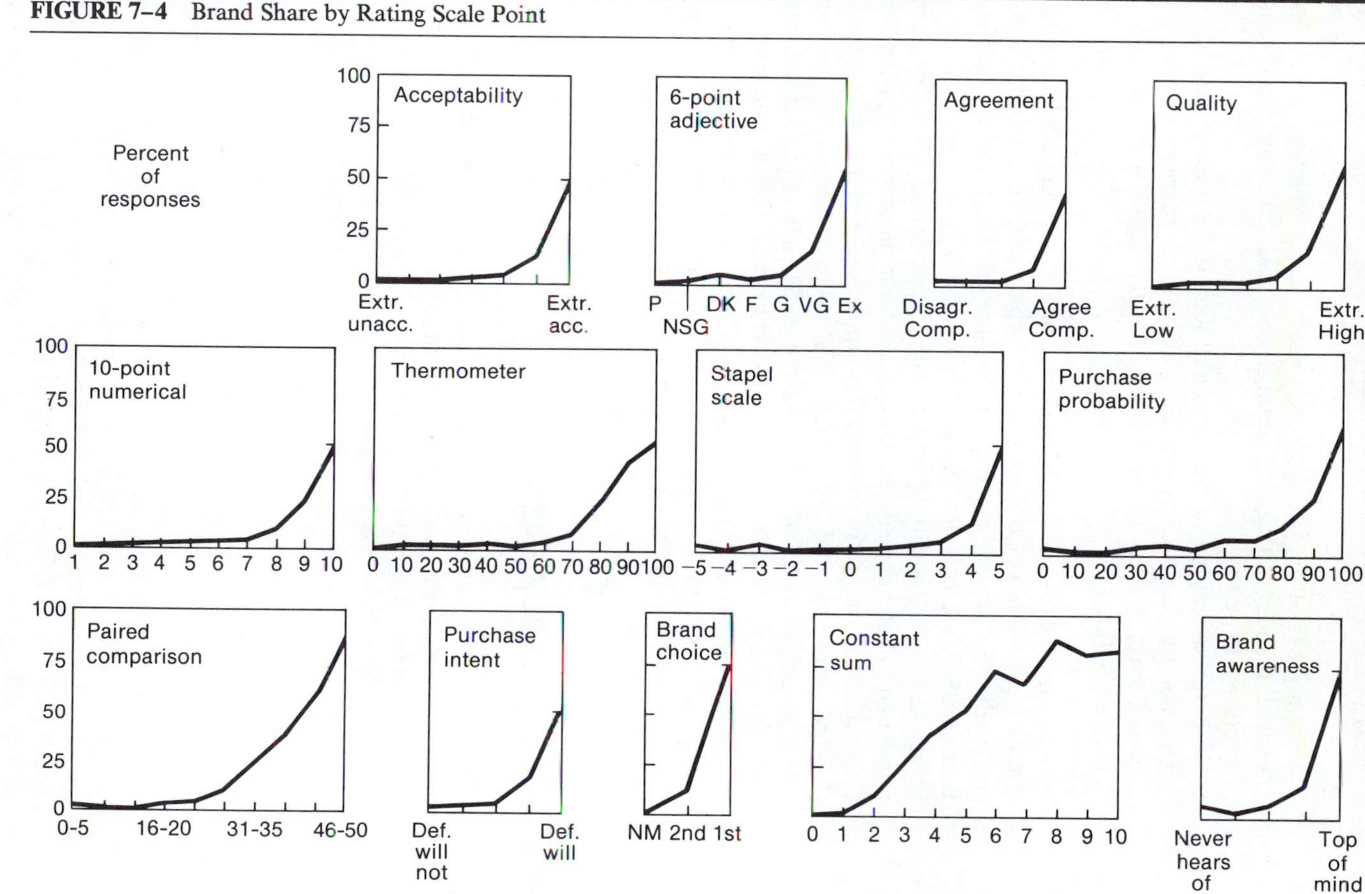

Source: Russell I. Haley and Peter B. Case, "Testing Thirteen Attitude Scales for Agreement and Brand Discrimination," *Journal of Marketing* 43 (Fall 1979), p. 30.

4. For purposes of predicting market share, scales which restrict the number of brands getting top ratings (such as constant sum) tend to discriminate better.
5. With the exception of the constant sum scale, ratings less than the midpoint were associated with essentially a zero share and even top-category ratings tended to be related to only about a 50 percent share (Figure 7–4).

In terms of choice of scale wording, one study suggests semantic differential is preferable to Likert scales, which are, in turn, preferable to single-adjective scales in terms of measure reliability (Ofir, Reddy, and Bechtel, 1987). A broader range of alternatives were compared for their ability to measure attribute importances: open-ended elicitation, acquisition-based information, direct ratings, conjoint measurement (discussed in Chapter 15), a subjective probability approach, and paired comparisons (Jaccard, Brinberg, and Ackerman, 1986). Here, the correlations among scales, though positive, were fairly low (e.g., .2), indicating that the methods had considerable impact on the results. Thus, while tending to give similar directional indications (e.g., from attitude to choice), various scales are sufficiently different that they are not interchangeable. Consequently, it appears that consistency in use of a scale is at least as important as the specific scale used.

BASIC CONCEPTS OF MEASUREMENT

There is a long tradition in measurement, especially in the psychological literature (see Torgerson, 1958; Thurstone, 1959). From this literature come two major terms which relate to measurement: *reliability* and *validity*. From statistics come the terms *biased*, *efficient*, and *consistent*. While these terms themselves have no great value, the ideas they represent are quite important.

Reliability

A measure is said to be reliable if it consistently obtains the same result. Hence, a scale which measured a weight and got 90.10 pounds, 89.95 pounds, 90.06 pounds, and 89.98 pounds in four trials would be quite reliable (the spread/range is only .15 pounds) even if the true weight were 100 pounds. Conversely, a second scale which produced weights of 95 pounds, 103 pounds, 92 pounds, and 109 pounds would be less reliable than the first even if in the sense of being closer to the true value it was better. Reliability, thus, is synonymous with repetitive consistency.

Two basic operational approaches exist to measuring reliability: test-retest and alternative forms.

Test-Retest. By applying the same measure to the same subjects at two different points in time, we can compare the two measures and see how closely they match and what the test-retest reliability is. This is a common approach in such areas as educational testing. In marketing, one generally expects a correlation in the range of .5 to .7. Using test-retest reliability as an indicator of true reliability makes some fairly strong assumptions. First, it assumes that the measurement process has no effect on the subject. Second, it assumes the subject's opinion/behavior has remained constant over the time period between the two measures. Since at least one of these assumptions is likely to be violated, test-retest comparisons are imperfect measures of reliability.[3]

Alternative Form. The alternative form approach to measuring reliability assumes that equivalent measuring devices (forms) are available. By applying two or more equivalent forms to the same subjects and checking the consistency of the results, a measure of reliability can be obtained. Unfortunately, this measure depends at least as much on the degree of equivalency of the alternative forms as on the true reliability of the measure. Still, some researchers have found this measure superior to test-retest or split half sample procedures (Parameswaran et al., 1979).

Validity

The term *valid* is essentially synonymous with the word *good*. In fact, the term is loosely used in conversation as a synonym by many people. This is unfortunate, since it causes purists to be unbearably uncomfortable and occasionally leads to important misunderstandings. Actually there are a

[3] It is also true that test-retest measures are heavily influenced by the heterogeneity of the sample. Reliability is often written as:

$$\frac{\text{Variance (true score)}}{\text{Variance (true score)} + \text{Variance (error)}}$$

Therefore, it is possible to increase reliability by either decreasing error or increasing the variance of the true score. For example, I can increase most measures of test-retest reliability of attitude toward yogurt by either producing a measure which produces very consistent responses over time (reducing the error) or by using a sample with big differences in attitudes toward yogurt (increasing the variability of the true score).

variety of subclasses of validity. The most common types of validity are construct validity, content validity, convergent validity, and predictive validity.

Construct Validity. Construct validity refers to the ability of a measure to both represent the underlying construct (concept) and to relate to other constructs in an expected way. This is a fairly amorphous term and really says that a measure has construct validity if it behaves according to existing theory. Given the relative paucity of good theory in marketing, this type of validity rarely receives much attention in applied marketing research. A construct should also possess what is known as *discriminant validity*, which means the construct should be sufficiently distinct from other constructs to justify its existence (see, for example, Peter, 1981).

Content Validity. Content validity refers to the logical appropriateness of the measure used. For example, one might argue that observing how much a person eats of a vegetable on his or her plate is a measure of the person's liking of the vegetable. This has logical appeal (often called *face validity*), and, hence, the measure would appear to have content validity. (Actually, the amount eaten might depend on how hungry the person was or some other variable.) Content validity also refers to the inclusiveness in the measure of all relevant aspects of the construct. A content valid measure of your opinion of this book should include your opinion of its topic, style, format, and so on. In order to achieve content validity, constructs often must be measured by more than one item.

Convergent Validity. A measure has convergent validity if it follows the same pattern as other measures of the same construct. For example, three different measures of attitude would be said to have convergent validity if they were highly correlated with each other, and if the construct they are measuring is said to be unidimensional. When a construct does not achieve convergent validity, either the measures are poor or the construct is multidimensional. A related concept is *concurrent validity*, which occurs when a measure is highly correlated with known values of the underlying construct. One method of examining simultaneous convergent and discriminant validity is through a multitrait-multimethod matrix (Campbell and Fiske, 1959; see Appendix 7–C.)

Efforts to assess convergent and discriminant validity and more generally to separate trait (construct), method (e.g., scale type), and error variation in responses have employed increasingly sophisticated procedures. These procedures require relatively complex analytical methods, are currently mainly employed by academic researchers (Anderson and Gerbing, 1982; Widaman, 1985; Peter and Churchill, 1986; Rentz, 1987; Cote and Buckley, 1987; and Kumar and Dillon, 1987), and are beyond the scope of this section.

Predictive Validity. Predictive validity is the most pragmatic form of validity. In the narrow sense of the term, the predictive validity of a measure is the ability of the measure to relate to other measures in a known/predicted way. Taken in its loosest form, predictive validity is synonymous with predictive usefulness/accuracy. In the extreme, predictive accuracy is the engineering (as opposed to scientific) view, which says if a measure is useful in prediction then use it, regardless of whether we can explain why it works. To take an extreme example, assume I predicted sales of a new product by multiplying the number of letters in the name by the weight of a package. Assume somehow this turned out to be predictive of sales. While the measure has no construct or content validity, it works and is predictively valid. Most people smirk at this point and argue they would never use such a foolish measure. Consider the following: Would you use it if it worked 10 times in a row? How about 100 times? The point is that, at some stage, the predictive accuracy of a measure will outweigh the prior theories and can, in fact, lead to the development of new theories. (If this were not true, it would imply we already perfectly understood the world, which is both scary and untrue.)

Unbiased/Biased

The term *biased* as used in marketing research has nothing to do with holding offensive personal opinions or prejudices. The term *bias* is borrowed from statistics, and a biased measurement is one where we expect the measured result to be different from the true value of the construct/variable. A person who consistently underestimates how long a task will take gives biased estimates. Similarly, the "reliable" scale of the previous section which kept measuring the 100-pound weight at about 90 pounds would also be called biased. Actually, a biased measure can be very useful if the extent of the bias can be assessed. For example, if the temperature control on an oven consistently registers 50 degrees warmer than the actual oven temperature, it is fairly simple to adjust the control to achieve the desired temperature. Similarly, panels may be biased in that they overreport purchases of a certain brand; but if one looks at purchases of the brand over time, then the result can be very useful for signaling changes in sales.

Efficient

Another term borrowed from statistics, a procedure is said to be *efficient* if it gets the maximum possible information from a given sample size. In measurement terms, a simple scale may be just as accurate a measuring device as a more elaborate setup and, thus, would be chosen because of its superior efficiency.

Consistent

The third major statistical term relevant here, *consistency*, refers to the ability of a statistic to tend toward the true value of the construct/variable as more data are gathered. In measurement terms, a measure would be consistent if averaging repeated measures produced a result which approached the true value as the number of measures averaged increased.

So What?

The terms and issues just discussed are important to someone who decides to specialize in measurement theory and methods. To the applied researcher or manager, however, the terms often are either foreboding or used merely as advertising slogans. For example, "We have a valid study which . . . ." Therefore, it is useful to translate these concepts into some action suggestions. At least six suggestions are relevant:

1. Select only those variables to measure which make logical sense in the context of the problem being studied.
2. Use measures which seem logically appropriate to the construct/variable to be measured.
3. Use measures which are fairly stable over time.
4. Use variables which produce similar results over related measurement methods. (If the response obtained depends heavily on the measurement method employed, chances are the information being collected is a response to the measurement method and not the construct.)
5. Use measures which are as easily usable by researcher and respondent as possible.
6. Use measures which prove to be useful in a pragmatic way (i.e., if a variable proves to be a good predictor of a key variable, use it; if a variable doesn't seem to be related to any other variables, save your effort and don't measure it.)

OTHER ISSUES

Individual versus Group–Level Study

Most of the measurement and scale discussion presented here is directed at accurately estimating an individual's scale value. In marketing, one typically is interested in group/average behavior for decision purposes (at least in consumer marketing). One advantage of this is that averaging out results tends to cover up problems in scale type. Averages are intervally scaled even if the original scale is binary. Moreover, if you're lucky, averages reduce some measurement and response style problems as well.

There are, however, two disadvantages to grouping respondents/data points. The first is that the respondents are implicitly assumed to be homogeneous, a sometimes fallacious assumption. For example, if some people like tea hot and some cold, the average preferred temperature for tea would be lukewarm. While this suggests an interesting marketing strategy ("Try Blahz, the room temperature tea"), the strategy is likely to be a disaster. Hence, making sure that only homogeneous data points are grouped is an important (but difficult) task.

The second disadvantage deals with the operational problem of comparing responses of different people on nonobjective questions, such as attitudes. Consider the following two respondents:

	Very Bad							*Very Good*
			Respondent 1					
A	1	2	3	④	5	6	7	8
B	1	2	3	4	5	⑥	7	8
C	1	2	3	4	5	6	7	⑧
D	1	2	3	4	5	⑥	7	8
E	1	2	3	④	5	6	7	8
F	1	2	3	4	5	6	7	⑧
			Respondent 2					
A	1	②	3	4	5	6	7	8
B	1	2	③	4	5	6	7	8
C	1	2	3	④	5	6	7	8
D	1	2	③	4	5	6	7	8
E	1	②	3	4	5	6	7	8
F	1	2	3	④	5	6	7	8

In considering the response to A, there are at least three pieces of information in the "4" given by respondent 1: the absolute value of the response (indicating a slightly negative attitude), the position relative to a typical response (lower, indicating a negative attitude), and the difference between "4" and a typical response (two scale points). If we believe that only relative responses matter, we could *normalize* the data to obtain only relative responses. Alternatively, if we believe both the typical response and the amount of spread a respondent uses in answering is not meaningful, we can *standardize* the data to remove both effects (see Appendix 7–D). If we standardized the answers of both respondents, we would argue that both respondents view the six alternatives identically. Without any adjustment, respondent 1 appears to be favorable toward all but A and E, while respondent 2 thinks all the alternatives are bad. What you believe about the meaning of a response thus has a lot to say about how data are grouped and analyzed.

Direct versus Indirect Probing

Another issue involves whether information should be gathered directly or in a more circuitous manner. The simplest way to gather data is the obtrusive, direct method, where the subject is aware of being studied and is directly asked the question at hand. This method works quite well most of the time.

The straightforward approach runs into trouble, however, when respondents either have a reason to hide their feelings (as in the case of certain antisocial attitudes) or can't really express their feelings accurately. In these cases, indirect methods are often employed. Here, rather than asking persons what they personally do or think, the subject may be asked how friends or neighbors think or behave. The assumptions underlying this approach are that (*a*) neighbors behave the same way and (*b*) I will be more honest in revealing my neighbors' behavior patterns than my own. Another indirect method is the projective technique. Here a subject is given a vague task and the response then is used to deduce the subject's feelings. This technique takes many forms, including sentence completion (e.g., "people who eat Znarts are ____________"), scenario/cartoon interpretation known as TATs (thematic apperception test), and word association (e.g., "What word do you associate with Znarts?"). Possibly the best-known projective technique is the Rorschach Inkblot Test. Interesting as these techniques are, however, they are used almost exclusively in small-scale or pilot studies in marketing research. Anyone interested in using projective techniques should consult another source, such as Kassarjian (1974).

Soft (Survey) versus Hard (Observed) Data

The distinction between survey and hard data appears to be quite great. Yet, on closer inspection, there are more similarities than most people notice. First, much so-called hard data is estimated/projected/fudged. (Do you really believe anyone knows exactly how many dishwashers were sold in the United States last year?) Also, with the exception of mechanical recording devices (which are far from foolproof themselves), a person gathers data either by interpreting written reports (e.g., audits) or by actually asking a question. Hence, these data are subject to many of the same sources of error (misinterpretation, expectation, etc.) as survey data.

A more meaningful distinction is between objective data (for which a right answer exists and is directly measurable) and subjective data (for which the right answer, if it exists, is not precisely measurable). For example, the number of cars I own is objective data, while my attitude toward public education is subjective. In measuring an objective variable, both survey and hard methods are applicable. For example, to measure how many cars I own, one could (*a*) ask me, (*b*) check the motor vehicle registration list, or (*c*) observe how many cars are parked at my house at night. The survey method may produce a wrong answer if I decide to hide the true number of cars owned for whatever reason. On the other hand, checking the auto registration lists may fail because (*a*) you have registered a car in another state or not at all, or (*b*) the auditor makes a mistake. Similarly, observing how many cars are at home at night may (*a*) spot a neighbor's cars, or (*b*) fail to spot a car which is in a body shop for repairs.

Subjective constructs, such as attitudes, are generally thought to be measurable mainly through questions. While observed behavior is often indicative of attitude ("actions speak louder than words" or, as economists argue, "revealed preference" is an/the appropriate measure of attitude), the only way to directly assess attitude is through questions. However, when attitudes are either poorly formed or likely to be "hidden" by the respondents (e.g., what do you say when your professor asks how the course is going?), actual behavior may be a better measure of attitude than response to a question.

Share Data

One of the key measures used by marketers is market share. Yet calculations of share are very imprecise. The biggest problem in defining share is in answering the question, "Share of what?" For example, should you compute Sugar Pops' share of presweetened cereals, ready-to-eat cereals, or cereals in general? Second, you must decide, "Share on what basis—dollars, unit sales, net weight, or number of servings?" Even having settled on a market definition and a measurement basis, the share measures are subject to all the sources of error that any other objective variable faces. In short, share measures are rarely as objective and accurate as their numbers (e.g., 32.7 percent) seem to indicate.

AN ERROR TYPOLOGY

Having discussed measurement methods and problems, it is useful to lay out some of the major sources of error which affect research. These sources of error, here divided into five major categories, go far beyond measurement

FIGURE 7–5 Sources of Errors

General Source	Type
I. Researcher/user	Myopia (wrong question)
	Inappropriate analysis
	Misinterpretation:
	Mistaken
	Researcher expectation
	Communication
II. Sample	Frame (wrong target population)
	Process (biased method)
	Response (biased respondents)
III. Measurement process	Conditioning
	Process bias
	Recording:
	Interpretation (mistaken)
	Carelessness
	Fudging
IV. Instrument	Individual scale item:
	Rounding
	Truncating
	Ambiguity
	Test instrument:
	Evoked set
	Positional (order)
V. Respondent	Response style:
	Consistency/inconsistency
	Boasting/humility
	Agreement (yea saying)
	Acquiescence
	Lying
	Extremism/caution
	Socially desirable
	Response:
	Mistakes
	Uncertainty
	Inarticulation

issues (Hulbert and Lehmann, 1975). Their purpose, therefore, is to put measurement issues "in their place" (see Figure 7–5).

Researcher

The following variety of errors in marketing research are directly traceable to the researcher: myopia, inappropriate analysis, misinterpretation, and communication.

Myopia. Research results can be reduced in value if the wrong questions are asked. This is usually a manifestation of poor problem definition and research objective specification.

Inappropriate Analysis. There are two major ways a researcher can err in performing analysis. The first is an error of omission: failing to perform what would be a meaningful analysis. The second is an error of commission: performing an analysis for which the data are not suited.

Misinterpretation. The two kinds of misinterpretation errors are quite different. A mistaken interpretation can be the result of poor training, inability to understand the results of the analysis performed because of a technical deficiency, or just a bad day (even we brilliant researchers occasionally make an error in judgment due to time pressure, fatigue, carelessness, poor eyesight, etc.). On the other hand, misinterpretation may be the result of *researcher expectation*. When one has a strong prior feeling about the results of a study for either logical or emotional reasons, it is usually possible to find some result which supports this prior feeling. Hence, the interpretation may be unduly influenced by prior opinions.

Communication. Even the most competent researcher has a serious problem in communicating results. Often the users of research are unable to correctly perceive the results because of technical deficiencies, strong prior opinions, or a general distrust of or dislike for research. Also, the technically competent researcher is frequently unable to translate results into a form which is understandable by intelligent, decision-oriented managers.

Sample

Since most data collection is partial in nature, the selection of who to analyze can greatly influence the results. There are at least three basic types of sampling error: frame, process, and response.

Frame. In studying a particular problem, an early decision must be made concerning who are the relevant subjects/respondents. For example, in studying the market for TV video games, one could target on male heads of households. Since others in the family, especially children, influence this decision, the target population would be defined too narrowly. Alternatively, it is possible to design the target population so broadly that the "frame" includes many irrelevant people. Matching the sampling frame to the appropriate population is very important, and erring by having too narrow a frame is especially disastrous.

Process. Once the frame is chosen, a process must be chosen for selecting respondents. If, for example, a list is chosen as the source of respondents, it can be too broad and include people not in the target population. (The National Association of Retired Persons has been trying to get me to join since I was 29 which, unless they know something I don't, is just a bit too premature.) This is wasteful but not necessarily destructive. On the other hand, the process may be so narrow that it excludes important segments of the target population.

Response. Even with a good frame and process, the sample may be unrepresentative because many people fail to respond to research inquiries. Response rates are rarely above 70 percent and sometimes as low as 10 percent or less. If the nonrespondents have different characteristics than respondents, then the results can be badly distorted. One general tendency is for both old people and poor people to respond less than other groups. Also, people with strong opinions about the subject in question are more likely to respond. An example of this is a survey about school priorities undertaken in New Jersey in the late 1970s. Under both court and legislative mandates to find out what localities want in a "thorough and efficient" education, many districts mailed questionnaires to all residents in their towns. With response rates of 10 percent or less in many localities, it is hard to argue convincingly that the results are projectable to the community at large. This nonresponse problem is typically greatest when either recruitment for extended tasks (e.g., panel membership) or mail surveys are used.

Measurement Process

The measurement process itself is an important determinant of responses and, therefore, a potential source of error. Some of the major characteristics of the measurement process are conditioning, process bias, and recording.

Conditioning. Data collection processes are outside stimuli which can condition/affect responses. By exposing a subject to a topic, the subject's attention will be drawn to the topic, and consequently the subject may behave differently. This is an especially serious concern when the subject is questioned several times.

Process Bias. Respondents often are motivated by the data collection process as a "game" and respond to beat the game. The best-known example of this problem is interviewer bias, where the presence of the interviewer leads the respondents to respond to please (or occasionally, to irritate or surprise) the interviewer. An example of this is that, when the interviewer is identified as working for a particular company, the respondent often tends to give answers favorable to the company in order to please the interviewer. Also the physical surroundings (e.g., a bright, cheerful, air-conditioned room) can affect the respondent's overall attitude and, hence, responses.

Recording. The process of recording a response is subject to many possible sources of error. The most obvious error of this type, mistaken interpretation, is usually associated with an interviewer misinterpreting a verbal response. This error can also occur when gremlins infest mechanical recording devices. A related form of error is due to simple carelessness, where the interviewer or recording device records the wrong answer due to sloppiness. A third type of recording problem is fudging. Here, answers are recorded without measurement to speed up the data collection or to make life easier for the respondent and interviewer. Given crafty interviewers, this source of error is quite hard to detect.

Instrument

The particulars of the questions/measures themselves have a strong influence on responses. Two basic sources of these problems exist: the individual question/scale and the test instrument.

The Individual Question/Scale. One problem with questions is that the response categories given often *truncate* responses. Multiple-choice questions tend to limit the respondents' consideration to the listed alternatives even if an "all other" category is included. (Filling out an "other" response is more trouble than checking one of the listed alternatives and also may connote that the respondent is somehow different/weird.) In quantitatively scaled questions (e.g., rate how well you like brussels sprouts on a six-point scale from 1 = dislike somewhat to 6 = like somewhat), especially strong feelings cannot be expressed and, hence, are truncated. (On the brussels sprouts scale, my true feelings are about −8; but, being a good subject, I would circle a 1.)

Another major scale problem is *rounding error*. Given a multiple-choice question, a respondent will tend to choose the answer which is closest to his or her true response. The classic example is a numerical scale. For example, if I truly feel about brussels sprouts 3.4 on a six-point scale, I would round off my response to the closest digit (3) and the rounding error would be .4. Similarly, if I were asked, "Are you going to vote in the next election?" and I were 60 percent sure I would, I would have to round my response to "yes" (100 percent certain) or "no" (no chance at all of voting).

A final type of problem is *ambiguity*. Ambiguity can occur because the underlying construct to be measured and the question are not perfectly congruent. For example, in order to measure attitude toward the environment one might ask, "Should pollution control standards on automobiles be relaxed?" An affirmative answer would presumably indicate a relatively low environmental concern. Unfortunately, it could also indicate a great concern for jobs or for increasing the use of coal to conserve petroleum reserves. Hence, the match between the construct and the question is imperfect. Another source of ambiguity is confusion about the meaning of the particular combination of words used to define the question. Both gross lack of understanding due to poor vocabulary skills on the part of either the question writer or the respondent or more subtle different nuances in meanings resulting from different cultural backgrounds can lead the respondent to answer a different question than the researcher wished answered.

The Test Instrument. The instrument (questionnaire) itself has an effect on the response. The items discussed bring to mind an *evoked set* of thoughts and standards of comparison which the respondent uses to determine his response. For example, if one designed a questionnaire concerning such leisure time activities as bridge, chess, backgammon, cribbage, and football; football would on an exertion or risk of injury scale probably be rated at the maximum. If, on the other hand, football were being compared with rugby, sword fighting, and motorcycle racing; it probably would be rated more moderately in terms of exertion or injury risk. In short, the responses depend on the bases of comparison which the test instrument (questionnaire) establishes.

The *position* (*order*) of items is also important. This is true at both the macro level (question order) and micro level (order of responses within question). At the micro level, the response category in the first possible position tends to get an inordinate number of responses simply because it is convenient to use. At the macro level, the position of an item in the test affects both the attentiveness of the respondent (one tends to be pretty casual about answering the 141st lifestyle question) and the frame-of-reference which the previous questions have imparted.

Respondent

Ultimate control over the quality of data is in the hands of the subject/respondent. This control is exercised in two major ways: response style and the response.

Response Style. The way a respondent approaches the data collection process influences the responses obtained. Responses may be as much the result of the respondent's response style as his or her true feelings/behavior. A variety of such styles may exist, including the following:

Consistency/inconsistency. Many respondents give answers to questions under the assumption that their answers to the questions should be what they perceive to be consistent, even if their feelings or behavior is not (i.e., if I have previously indicated that I am in favor of equal rights, I "should," to be consistent, also indicate support of such programs as the ERA). Similarly, some respondents give inconsistent responses to appear interesting to the researcher.

Boasting/humility. Respondents may overstate their position (e.g., income, possessions) in order to appear superior. There also is the tendency in some individuals to state that "I can do anything better than you!" Alternatively, some humble souls may understate their accomplishments out of some form of humility. (An excellent example of this is available to anyone who plays golf and attempts to subjectively establish a handicap with three other players.)

Agreement. Some respondents have a tendency to be yea-sayers, responding positively to most questions. (Do you like to swim? *Yes*. Do you like to sit on the beach? *Yes*. Do you like to stay home? *Yes*.)

Lying. Respondents sometimes knowingly falsify data. While some may be pathological liars, most probably lie out of self-interest. One need only observe a few individuals filling out tax returns to notice this tendency. Also, respondents will give answers they think are "right" in order to get a possible reward—a free product, a trip, and so on.

In the extreme, fear of responding honestly can lead to no response at all if the question asked is sufficiently sensitive. One way to reduce the unwillingness to answer sensitive questions is to guarantee respondent anonymity. To guarantee anonymity, administering questionnaires in a group setting (obviously without identifying the respondents) is a useful approach. When a one-on-one interview is used, one helpful technique is a *randomization procedure*. For example, by having two questions (where A is sensitive and B is not) with the same answer scale (e.g., Yes-No), an interviewer can ask the respondent to *secretly* flip a coin and then answer A if the coin is heads and B if the coin is tails:

	Yes	*No*
A. Do you beat your spouse?	☐	☐
B. Are you left handed?	☐	☐

The respondent then reports the answer *without* indicating which question was answered. If the nonsensitive question B has a known distribution (e.g., the percent of left-handed people in the population), then the overall fraction of Yes and No responses can be used to derive the fraction of Yes responses to the sensitive question. For example, if the fraction of Yes responses to the question is 40 percent and we know 25 percent of the people are left-handed, then by solving:

$$25\left(\tfrac{1}{2}\right) + X\left(\tfrac{1}{2}\right) = 40$$

we can see that 55 percent of the people beat their spouses. The disadvantages of this ingenious approach are twofold. First, it is relatively time-consuming. Second, it does not make it possible to determine which respondents perform the sensitive behavior. If in the previous example my objective was to see if spouse-beating were related to demographic or psychographic measures (e.g., "I get frustrated when people aren't on time"), I'm out of luck.

Extremism/caution. Some respondents tend to use extreme responses on scaled questions (i.e., 1s and 5s on a 1-to-5 scale), while others may use more moderate (i.e., 2s and 4s) responses. The tendency toward caution is generally correlated with cynical or highly educated people who do not believe in absolutes.

Socially desirable. Many respondents feel uncomfortable admitting to unusual behavior or attitudes. As a consequence, their answers reflect as much what they perceive to be the desirable answer as they do their own true responses. For example, in a jury selection process, prospective jurors were asked if they liked to read. Not surprisingly, 90 percent said they did, although one suspects a smaller percentage were actually avid readers. Sudman and Bradburn (1982) report socially desirable behavior, such as voting, is overstated by about 25 percent in person, 23 percent on the telephone, and 22 percent by a mail survey. Moreover, socially desirable response bias tends to be greater in nonobjective questions (Gruber and Lehmann, 1983).

Response. The respondent is the source of the following three other errors:

Inarticulation. In responding to a question (especially an open-ended one), a respondent may be unable or unwilling to accurately articulate a response.

Mistakes. Even sincere respondents can make errors by marking the wrong response carelessly, especially if they are not committed to the task. Also, for many questions, there is a strong tendency to give a particular answer because, for example, a brand has become synonymous with the product category. (What soft drink did you last have? Coke. What kind of facial tissue do you use? Kleenex.)

Uncertainty. All the above sources of error are theoretically controllable. Yet even perfect control of these (the impossible dream of researchers) would not guarantee perfect data. Individuals are often not sure exactly what their true feelings are or actual behavior has been. This underlying source of measurement error is irreducible.

Controlling Errors

A general comment about control of errors is in order. Setting aside for the moment researcher and sampling errors, we can view the measured response as a sum of the true response plus the possible errors:

$$\text{Measured value} = \text{True value} + \text{Measurement errors}$$
$$+ \text{Instrument errors} + \text{Respondent errors}$$

While it would be nice and convenient to assume that all the sources of error will cancel out, this approach is pure Polyanna. In order to make the measured value closer to the true value, there are a variety of fairly obvious methods available, such as precise wording, which should reduce ambiguity errors and possible general fatigue by making the task easier.

Still, three points remain:

1. Reducing one type of error will often increase another (e.g., increasing scale points reduces rounding error but increases respondent burden and, hence, respondent errors).
2. Some random error remains no matter what you do.
3. As an individual progresses through a test situation (experiment, questionnaire, etc.), the experience will change him or her by both conditioning and fatigue.

The purpose of these three points is not to discourage efforts to reduce error but, rather, to indicate that error reduction is a vexing, complex problem. Fortunately, if one is concerned with relative, rather than absolute, values, many of these sources of error will tend to cancel out. Also, unless, for example, response style and the true value being measured are correlated, average responses will not be affected. Thus, by focusing on average and relative values, many of the measurement problems become less serious.

SUMMARY

Having read (or at least turned the pages of) this chapter, someone may pose the question, "Can a few simple notions be taken from this chapter?" Put more crudely, "What good is all this?" This section is an attempt to respond to that question.

Measurement Theory

A variety of concepts have been advanced which are desirable characteristics of measurement. Though the terms are formidable, the concepts are largely intuitive. Good measures are ones which produce consistent (reliable) estimates of the constructs and which are useful in terms of relating to other measures.

Scale Types

There are four basic scale types: nominal (categorical), ordinal, interval, and ratio. Whenever possible, intervally scaled data should be obtained, since they allow the more powerful statistical tools (e.g., regression analysis) to be applied. It is possible to use nonmetric data in calculations, such as correlations and means. The problem is that some error is introduced by using nonintervally scaled data, such as rankings, in these calculations which we have classified as "inappropriate analysis." As long as the data are ordinally scaled (monotonic), these calculations are, in general, not so badly distorted that they need be abandoned. While the results of such calculations are not appropriate for fine tuning, they certainly are useful for getting a general notion about the results.

One final point is that the respondent controls the quality and scale of the data. A respondent can respond on a continuous scale as though it were ordinal or an interval scale even if the scale appears to be only ordinal. Thus, respondent committment is at least as important as the scale in determining the quality of data (Hauser and Shugan, 1980).

Typical Scales

In spite of the variety of scales available, a surprisingly small number form the mainstay of market research data. The following are the most commonly used:

Nominal (categorical):

1. Multiple choice (e.g., region, occupation, brand chosen).
2. Yes-no (e.g., ownership, awareness).

Ordinal:
Forced ranking (e.g., brand preference).

Ordinal-interval:
Semantic differential/bipolar adjective (e.g., attitudes, opinions).

Ratio:
1. Direct quantification (e.g., number of people in household).
2. Constant sum scale.

Sources of Error

There are a vast number of sources of error which *cannot* be simultaneously reduced. Many of these sources of error depend on researcher, sample, or respondent and are beyond the control of the measurement process, which is not the major source of error in most studies. Put differently, worrying about measurement errors is productive only when problem definition and sample composition are well established.

PROBLEMS

1. How would you determine:
   a. How important nutrition was to consumers in their choice of food?
   b. What process consumers follow in selecting a brand of gasoline for their cars?
   c. How many pairs of slacks a sample of consumers own?
   d. What consumers feel is the effect of television advertising on children?
2. Write a dollar metric question to assess preference for brands of washing machines.
3. Assume you had to predict the likely winner of the next presidential election based on a single poll two weeks before the election. A good sample has already agreed to participate.

   Assume you are to ask two questions: Will you vote? and Who will you vote for? Describe:
   a. The exact form of the response scale.
   b. Exactly (mathematically) how you would go about making your prediction.
4. List the major control variables a survey/question designer has at his or her disposal (e.g., number of scale points).
5. Suggest how the control variables in your answer to problem 4 relate to the sources of error in Figure 7–5.

BIBLIOGRAPHY

Anderson, James C., and David W. Gerbing. "Some Methods for Respecifying Measurement Models to Obtain Unidimensional Construct Measurement." *Journal of Marketing Research* 19 (November 1982), pp. 453–60.

Anderson, James C.; David W. Gerbing; and John E. Hunter. "On the Assessment of Unidimensional Measurement: Internal and External Consistency, and Overall Consistency Criteria." *Journal of Marketing Research* 24 (November 1987), pp. 432–37.

Burns, Alvin C., and Mary Carolyn Harrison. "A Test of the Reliability of Psychographics." *Journal of Marketing Research* 16 (February 1979), pp. 32–38.

Cameron, Trudy A., and Michelle D. James. "Estimating Willingness to Pay from Survey Data: An Alternative Pre-Test-Market Evaluation Procedure." *Journal of Marketing Research* 24 (November 1987), pp. 389–95.

Campbell, Donald T., and Donald W. Fiske. "Convergent and Discriminant Validation by the Multitrait-Multimethod Matrix." *Psychological Bulletin* 56 (1959), pp. 81–105.

Childers, Terry L. "Assessment of the Psychometric Properties of an Opinion Leadership Scale." *Journal of Marketing Research* 23 (May 1986), pp. 184–88.

Coombs, Clyde H. *A Theory of Data*. New York: John Wiley & Sons, 1964.

Cote, Joseph A., and M. Ronald Buckley. "Estimating Trait, Method, and Error Variance: Generalizing Across 70 Construct Validation Studies." *Journal of Marketing Research* 24 (*August* 1987), *pp.* 315–18.

Dickson, John, and Gerald Albaum. "A Method for Developing Tailormade Semantic Differentials for Specific Marketing Content Areas." *Journal of Marketing Research* 14 (February 1977), pp. 87–91.

Gruber, Robert E., and Donald R. Lehmann. "The Effect of Omitting Response Tendency Variables from Regression Models." In *Research Methods and Causal Modeling in Marketing*, ed. W. R. Darden, K. B. Monroe, and W. R. Dillon. Chicago: American Marketing Association, 1983, pp. 131–36.

Haley, Russell I., and Peter B. Case. "Testing Thirteen Attitude Scales for Agreement and Brand Discrimination." *Journal of Marketing* 43 (Fall 1979), pp. 20–32.

Hauser, John R., and Steven M. Shugan. "Intensity Measures of Consumer Preference." *Operations Research* 28 (March–April 1980), pp. 278–320.

Hauser, John R., and Glen L. Urban. "The Value Priority Hypotheses for Consumer Budget Plans." *Journal of Consumer Research* 12 (March 1986), pp. 446–62.

Hawkins, Del I.; Gerald Albaum; and Roger Best. "Stapel Scale or Semantic Differential in Marketing Research." *Journal of Marketing Research* 11 (August 1974), pp. 318–22.

Heeler, Roger M.; Chike Okechuku; and Stan Reid. "Attribute Importance: Contrasting Measurements." *Journal of Marketing Research* 16 (February 1979), pp. 60–63.

Hulbert, James, and Donald R. Lehmann. "Reducing Error in Question and Scale Design: A Conceptual Framework." *Decision Sciences* 6 (January 1975), pp. 166–73.

Jaccard, James; David Brinberg; and Lee J. Ackerman. "Assessing Attribute Importance: A Comparison of Six Methods." *Journal of Consumer Research* 12 (March 1986), pp. 463–68.

Kassarjian, Harold H. (1974). "Projective Methods." In *Handbook of Marketing Research*, ed. Robert Ferber. New York: McGraw-Hill, 1974, pp. 3–85 to 3–100.

Kumar, Ajith, and William R. Dillon. "Some Further Remarks on Measurement-Structure Interaction and the Unidimensionality of Constructs." *Journal of Marketing Research* 24 (November 1987), pp. 438–44.

______. "The Interaction of Measurement and Structure in Simultaneous Equation Models with Unobservable Variables." *Journal of Marketing Research* 24 (February 1987), pp. 98–105.

Lampert, Schlomo I. "The Attitude Pollimeter: A New Attitude Scaling Device." *Journal of Marketing Research* 16 (November 1979), pp. 578–82.

Leavitt, C. "A Multidimensional Set of Rating Scales for Television Commercials." *Journal of Applied Psychology* 54 (1970), pp. 427–29.

Lehmann, Donald R., and James Hulbert. "Are Three-Point Scales Always Good Enough?" *Journal of Marketing Research* 9 (November 1972), pp. 444–46.

Michaels, Ronald E., and Ralph L. Day. "Measuring Customer Orientation of Salespeople: A Replication with Industrial Buyers." *Journal of Marketing Research* 22 (November 1985), pp. 443–46.

Munson, J. Michael, and Shelby H. McIntyre. "Developing Practical Procedures for the Measurement of Personal Values in Cross-Cultural Marketing." *Journal of Marketing Research* 16 (February 1979), pp. 48–52.

Myers, James H., and W. Gregory Warner. "Semantic Properties of Selected Evaluation Adjectives." *Journal of Marketing Research* 4 (November 1968), pp. 409–13.

Ofir, Chezy; Srinivas K. Reddy; and Gordon G. Bechtel. "Are Semantic Response Scales Equivalent?" *Multivariate Behavioral Research* 22 (January 1987), pp. 21–38.

Osgood, C.; G. Suci; and P. Tannenbaum. *The Measurement of Meaning*. Urbana: University of Illinois Press, 1957.

Parameswaran, Ravi; Barnett A. Greenberg; Danny N. Bellenger; and Dan H. Robertson. "Measuring Reliability: A Comparison of Alternative Techniques." *Journal of Marketing Research* 16 (February 1979), pp. 18–25.

Pessemier, Edgar A. *Experimental Methods of Analyzing Demand for Branded Consumer Goods with Applications to Problems in Marketing Strategy*. Bulletin no. 39. Pullman: Washington State University Bureau of Economic and Business Research, June 1963.

Peter, J. Paul. "Construct Validity: A Review of Basic Issues and Marketing Practices." *Journal of Marketing Research* 18 (May 1981), pp. 133–45.

______. "Reliability: A Review of Psychometric Basics and Recent Marketing Practices." *Journal of Marketing Research* 16 (February 1979), pp. 6–17.

Peter, J. Paul, and Gilbert A. Churchill, Jr. "Relationships among Research Design Choices and Psychometric Properties of Rating Scales: A Meta-Analysis." *Journal of Marketing Research* 23 (February 1986), pp. 1–10.

Rentz, Joseph O. "Generalizability Theory: A Comprehensive Method for Assessing and Improving the Dependability of Marketing Measures." *Journal of Marketing Research* 24 (February 1987), pp. 19–28.

Robinson, John P., and Philip R. Shaver. *Measures of Social Psychological Attitudes*. Rev. ed. Ann Arbor: Institute of Social Research, University of Michigan, 1973.

Rokeach, Milton J. *The Nature of Human Values*. New York: Free Press, 1973.

Saxe, Robert, and Barton A. Weitz. "The SOCO Scale: A Measure of the Customer Orientation of Salespeople." *Journal of Marketing Research* 19 (August 1982), pp. 343–51.

Sewall, Murphy A. "Relative Information Contributions of Consumer Purchase Intentions and Management Judgment as Explanators of Sales." *Journal of Marketing Research* 18 (May 1981), pp. 249–53.

Shimp, Terence A., and Subhash Sharma. "Consumer Ethnocentrism: Construction and Validation of the CETSCALE." *Journal of Marketing Research* 24 (August 1987), pp. 280–89.

Stevens, S. S. "Mathematics, Measurement, and Psychophysics." In *Handbook of Experimental Psychology*, ed. S. S. Stevens. New York: John Wiley & Sons, 1962.

______. "On the Theory of Scales of Measurement." *Science* 103 (June 17, 1946), pp. 677–80.

Sudman, Seymour, and Norman M. Bradburn. *Asking Questions*. San Francisco: Jossey-Bass, 1982.

Thorndike, Robert L., ed. *Educational Measurement*. Washington, D.C.: American Council on Education, 1971.

Thurstone, L. L. *The Measurement of Value*. Chicago, University of Chicago Press, 1959.

Torgerson, W. S. *Theory and Methods of Scaling*. New York: John Wiley & Sons, 1958.

Wells, W. D. "EQ, Son of EQ, and the Reaction Profile." *Journal of Marketing* 28 (1964), pp. 45–52.

Widaman, Keith F. "Hierarchically Nested Covariance Structure Models for Multitrait-Multimethod Data." *Applied Psychological Measurement* 9 (March 1985), pp. 1–26.

Wind, Yoram, and David Lerner. "On the Measurement of Purchase Data: Surveys versus Purchase Diaries." *Journal of Marketing Research* 16 (February 1979), pp. 39–47.

Zinkhan, George M., and Claes Fornell. "A Test of Two Consumer Response Scales in Advertising." *Journal of Marketing Research* 22 (November 1985), pp. 447–52.

Appendix 7–A

Law of Comparative Judgment

The law of comparative judgment requires that several subjects (or one subject at several points in time) perform paired comparisons on a set of alternatives.

Consider the following example:

Number of times column item preferred to row item (n = 200)

	A	*B*	*C*	*D*
A	—	40	80	130
B	160	—	140	180
C	120	60	—	150
D	70	20	50	—

We next compute the percent of time each alternative is preferred to each other alternative. (Note that 50 has been put on the diagonal. This is unnecessary but traditional and has no effect on the result.)

FIGURE 7A–1

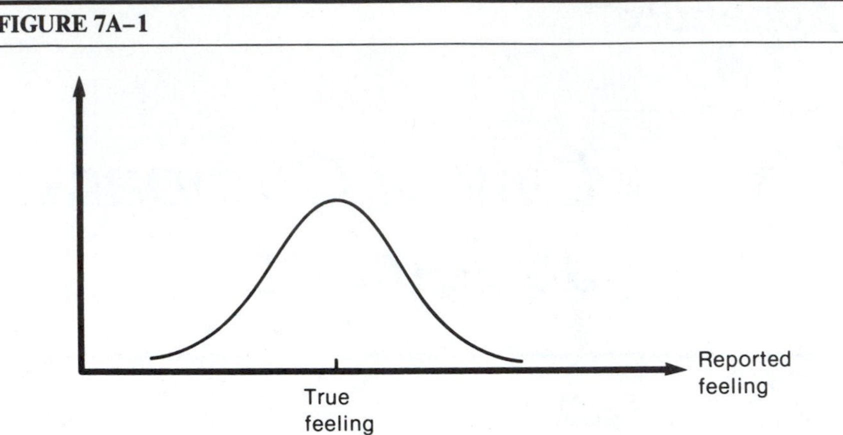

Percent of time column item preferred to row item

	A	*B*	*C*	*D*
A	50	20	40	65
B	80	50	70	90
C	60	30	50	75
D	35	10	25	50
Total	225	110	185	280

We can see that D is most preferred followed by A, C, and B (D > A > C > B). To convert this to an interval scale, we will assume the following:

1. Respondents have the same preferences on some underlying interval scale.

2. Respondents are equally uncertain about the alternatives and draw their preference feelings from a normal distribution (Figure 7A–1). Since preferences are stochastic, it is possible that a respondent will say B is preferred to A when, in fact, A is truly preferred to B. The number of times this occurs is an indication of how far apart the alternatives are on the underlying scale. The trick of the law of comparative judgment is to deduce the underlying scale from the preference data.

Consider the preference distribution for A and B (Figure 7A–2). The percent of the time A is preferred to B depends on (*a*) the difference in

FIGURE 7A–2

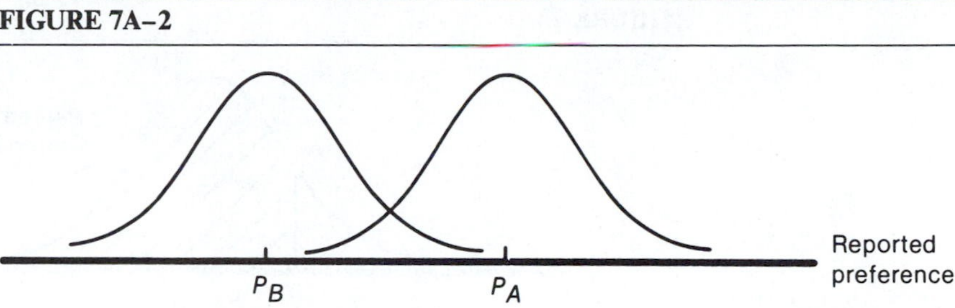

their preferences $P_A - P_B$ and (*b*) the amount of uncertainty in their preferences. Since the reported feelings toward A and B are assumed to be normally distributed and independent, the difference between them will also be normally distributed with mean $P_A - P_B$ and

$$\text{Standard deviation} = \sqrt{S_A^2 + S_B^2} = S\sqrt{2}$$

since we assume S_A and S_B are equal (Figure 7A–3). If we knew P_A, P_B, and S, we could get the percent of the time that A should be preferred to B from the standard normal table. Here we reverse that procedure, taking the percent of the time A is preferred to B to the table and deducing how far apart A and B are in standard deviations. For example, since A is preferred to B 80 percent of the time, we estimate A is .84 standard deviations above B on the preference scale. Similarly, we fill in an entire table of estimates of the number of standard deviations between pairs of alternatives:

Standard deviations apart

	A	*B*	*C*	*D*
A	0	−.84	−.25	.39
B	.84	0	.52	1.28
C	.25	−.52	0	.67
D	−.39	−1.28	−.67	0
Total	.70	−2.64	−.40	2.34

FIGURE 7A–3

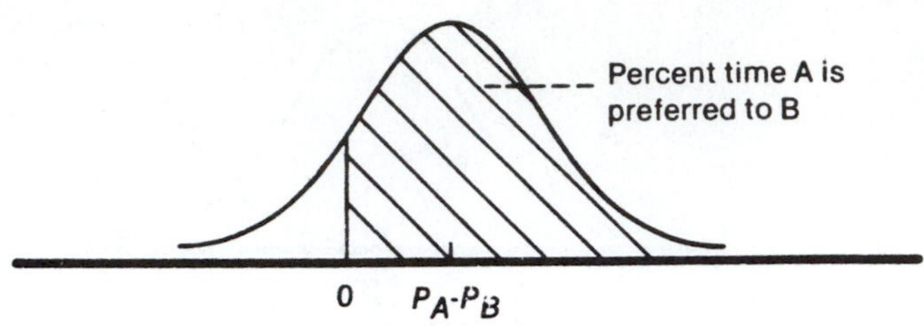

Since the column sums are measured in units (standard deviations) of the underlying preference distribution, the totals form an interval scale. (Actually a normalized interval scale, since the scale values sum to zero.)

This clever approach is perhaps most useful because of its two major assumptions. The formalized homogeneity assumption, which is used in many calculations but usually hidden or ignored, is bothersome, as it should be. The random response notion is basic to the concept of measurement. Hence, even if the technique is not used, its two major assumptions require attention in analysis of any type of survey data.

Appendix 7–B

The Delphi Procedure

The Delphi procedure is designed to produce a consensus ratio-scaled evaluation of alternatives among a set of judgments. It is most commonly used in evaluating budget priorities. To see how it works, consider the following example:

Assume three trustees were assigned to allocate funds ($100) to four projects. At step 1, each would be asked to allocate the $100 among the four projects:

	Trustee		
Project	*A*	*B*	*C*
I	40	20	15
II	10	30	50
III	20	15	10
IV	30	35	25
	100	100	100

Someone then collates the responses from the three trustees and computes the average allocation for each project. Each trustee is then given a copy of both the original allocation and the average, and asked to modify the original allocation. For example, Trustee A would receive a form, such as:

Project	*Original Allocation*	*Average Allocation*	*New Allocation*
I	40	25	
II	10	30	
III	20	15	
IV	30	30	
	100	100	100

By repeating the process several times, presumably agreement (or at least near agreement) can be reached. The big advantage of this technique is that it can be used for individuals who are distant geographically or who have difficulty discussing allocations amicably. It also downplays the importance of slick verbal presentations in obtaining allocations. On the other hand, several problems exist. First, participants must be sufficiently committed that they respond honestly but not so fanatical that they refuse to budge (having participated in three such studies, I found that the game could be brought to a conclusion by adopting the mean as my response by wave 3). Second, shrewd respondents can influence results by a modified "bullet-vote" technique, where they inflate the allocation to their pet project and reduce it to their main competitors, thereby biasing the averages and hopefully, from their point of view, the final solution. Finally, there is the implicit assumption that either the average is right (very democratic but often false) or that agreement is an end in itself (which it can become, given especially strident arguments). Consequently, the technique is very specialized and not useful for most marketing research purposes.

Appendix 7–C

Multitrait-Multimethod Matrix

The basic notion of a multitrait-multimethod matrix is that the correlations (or whatever measure of association is appropriate, given the scales used) among multiple measures of the same trait should be the largest correlations in the matrix. For example, if five measures (e.g., 6-point bipolar adjective scales) measure two traits, then the largest correlations between the measures should be among pairs of measures of the same trait. This incorporates notions of convergent (alternate forms) and discriminant validity. Continuing with a hypothetical example, assume the two traits are educational ability and "ability to pay":

Trait	*Measure*
A. Educational ability	1. Years of school
	2. SAT score
	3. Self-reported aptitude
B. Ability to pay	1. Salary
	2. Investments

Hence, one would, under the model I in Figure 7C–1, expect the correlations between years of school and SAT score and salary and investments to be higher than the correlation between SAT score and investments, which should be close to zero. If educational ability and ability to pay are related

FIGURE 7C–1

I. Three Independent Traits

II. Three Related Traits

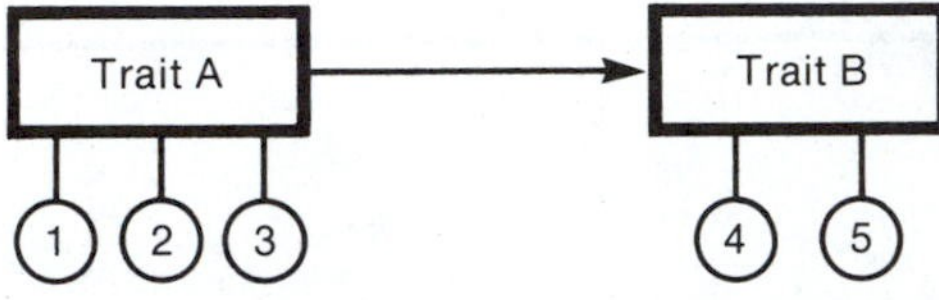

III. Three Related Traits with a Measurement (Method) Effect

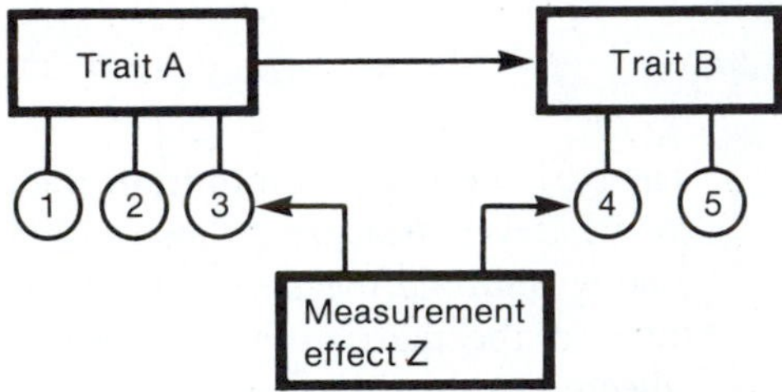

(model II, Figure 7C–1), then the correlation between SAT score and investments should be larger but still not as large as between, say, SAT score and self-reported aptitude. Also, a common measurement bias or method effect will generally increase correlations. For example, if ego boosting leads some people to overstate *both* educational aptitude and income (model III, Figure 7C–1), then measures 3 and 4 will be more

FIGURE 7C–2 Multitrait-Multimethod Correlation Matrix

Trait	*Measurement Method*	*Measure*	*Measure* 1	2	3	4	5
A	X	1	1	Big	Big	Small	Small
A	Y	2		1	Big	Small	Small
A	Z	3			1	Moderate	Small
B	Z	4				1	Big
B	W	5					1

highly correlated. Consequently, the relative sizes of the correlations between the five measures should be as in Figure 7C–2.

If this "relative size" tendency is not borne out in data, one of two things must be true. First, the data themselves may be atypical. Second, the original definition of the traits or their measures may be in error. Obviously if the second is true, the constructs, at least as operationalized, are invalid.

Appendix 7–D

Normalizing and Standardizing

NORMALIZING

Normalizing is the process of removing the mean (average) from a series of responses:

$$\text{Normalized } X = \text{Original } X - \text{Mean } X$$

$$\text{or } X_N = X - \overline{X}$$

Example:
Given:

X
4
6
8
6
4
8

Thus, $X = 6$, and we get:

$X_N = X - \overline{X}$
−2
0
+2
0
−2
+2

STANDARDIZING

Standardizing is the process of making the mean 0 and the standard deviation 1 for a series of responses:

$$\text{Standardized } X = \frac{\text{Original } X - \text{Mean } X}{\text{Standard deviation of } X}$$

$$\text{or } X_S = \frac{X - \overline{X}}{S_X}$$

Example:
Given:

X
4
6
8
6
4
8

$$\overline{X} = 6$$

and

$$S = \sqrt{16/5} = \sqrt{3.2} = 1.79$$

Thus,

X_S
−1.12
0
+1.12
0
−1.12
+1.12

APPLICATIONS

There are two basic applications of normalizing and standardizing. One is by variable across people to indicate which people are relatively high or low on the variable. The other is by person across response. This approach obtains, on the individual level, the relative responses to a series of questions, and removes the tendency of individuals to generally give either high or low responses. It is also possible to double standardize by standardizing first by person across variables and then across people by variable. The purpose of all these transformations is to convert data to a form which is more useful for comparative purposes. The danger is that both normalizing and standardizing cause the loss of information (the absolute values of the variables) which may be useful. Hence, decisions concerning normalizing or standardizing should be made only if (*a*) a firm grasp of the problem and (*b*) an assumption about the meaning of the absolute level of a response are available.

Chapter 8

Major Research Suppliers

Even in the largest companies, data collection is rarely carried out by company personnel. Rather, the company will subcontract the work to suppliers. Hence, most marketing research work involves dealing with suppliers. It is important to remember, however, that the responsibility for the study and a good part of the burden of design and interpretation should rest with the company, not the supplier.

This section is designed to acquaint readers with some of the major issues in supplier selection and monitoring. It has been described (probably accurately) as both boring and useful. This chapter begins by briefly discussing supplier selection and quality control. Then some of the services offered by the larger research firms are highlighted. The chapter then concludes with a brief summary.

THE SUPPLIER BUSINESS

For many years the supplier business was pretty much a cottage industry. A large number of small firms existed with particular product or regional specialties. Recently, however, consolidation into full-service companies has increased, as has the merging, acquiring, and diversifying common to much of U.S. business. For example, in 1986, Control Data sold 40 percent of Burke to Time, Inc., which combined it with SAMI (Selling Area Markets, Inc.), a warehouse withdrawal auditing firm. SAMI/Burke then formed a joint venture with Arbitron (a TV ratings supplier owned by Control Data) called ScanAmerica to combine TV viewing measurements with product purchase data. Then, in late 1987, Time, Inc., announced plans to sell

SAMI/Burke back to Control Data. Control Data's decision was reportedly influenced by Dun & Bradstreet's proposed acquisition of IRI. Since Dun & Bradstreet already owned Nielsen, which in turn was involved in a joint venture with NPD, Dun & Bradstreet would have controlled most of the consumer household purchase tracking business. As it turned out, the Dun & Bradstreet–IRI merger plans were dropped because of objections by the Federal Trade Commission on antitrust grounds. The point of this discussion is to suggest that the research business has emerged as an industry where consolidation and economies of scale seem to be increasing.

SELECTING A SUPPLIER

Probably the key decision a company researcher makes is which suppliers to employ. A variety of considerations are relevant for this decision.

Reputation of the Supplier. The supplier's reputation is important for lending credibility to the results. Even if firm XYZ, Inc., can do a better job, a study by Gallup or Nielsen will have more clout with the average person. This is important when the study is designed to have impact on someone who is not knowledgeable about marketing research suppliers and practices.

Technical Competence of the Supplier. The technical competence of a supplier should always be assessed. Many suppliers who are good at basic studies do not possess the personnel or computer capability to do complex analyses. Those who profess to possess such capabilities may have one technician who is supposed to oversee all "fancy" analysis, or even an outside consultant who serves as a hired gun on technical matters.

Experience of the Supplier. General experience is very important in doing good marketing research. Often overlooked, however, is experience in a particular type of research. It is generally advisable to avoid paying a supplier's development costs to learn about a new type of analysis if an experienced alternative supplier is available.

Costs. The instinct to cut costs is essentially sound. A little price shopping is desirable. After a point, however, cost cutting may be false economy. Suppliers are in business to make a profit and can only be squeezed so far before they lower the quality of the results by hidden methods, such as cutting the number of callbacks or time spent on the project, or obvious methods, such as cutting sample size or pretests.

TABLE 8–1 Some Criteria for Evaluating Suppliers

Design
Product knowledge
Experience with type of study
Skill of the account person
Technical backup staff
Sampling Selection
Basic design
Nonresponse follow-up procedures
Procedure for checking responses
Supervision of Data Collection
Level of personal involvement
Procedures
Data Processing
Procedures for coding
Editing and cleaning of responses
Basic reports
More complex analyses
Interpretation and Follow-Up
Interpretation skills
Follow-up work
Overall Quality
Competence
Likely effort level
Specific Factors
Delivery time
Cost

Reliable Delivery Schedule. Most suppliers require approximately the same amount of time for a given project. Still, checking to make sure the supplier consistently delivers on time is advisable.

Project Director. The person who will be project director is the key to the success of a project. An experienced director with sufficient time, interest, and knowledge is a quantum improvement over an inexperienced, harrassed, or uninterested one.

Since no one supplier is always dominant on all these criteria, a reasonable approach is to compare a few (e.g., three) viable alternative suppliers in terms of their abilities à la Table 8–1. While all of the elements in the table are important, two often are especially so: the skill of the person handling your account (job) and the likely effort level expended on your behalf. Put most crudely, consider both competence and how badly they want your business.

The Research Proposal and Job Specifications

Before going to outside suppliers, it is important to carefully specify what the task of the supplier is. In general, the more detail the better. Specifically, all of the following should be addressed:

1. Sampling requirements, including screening criteria and callback procedures, as well as size.
2. Data collection method. If it is a questionnaire, this includes content by type (e.g., demographics) and rough idea of the number of each type of question.
3. Pilot testing: size, method, and number required.
4. Data coding and editing procedures.
5. Analysis to be performed, including basic tabs and multivariate procedures.
6. Ownership of results and their "final resting place"—that is, who gets to keep the data and analysis.
7. Reports required in terms of content.
8. Time schedule for each of the above.
9. Price (preferably broken down by component) and contingencies (e.g., ± 15 percent).
10. Work schedule.
11. Payment schedule.

Also, you may wish to obtain a confidentiality agreement so the supplier agrees not to work with your major competitor for *X* months.

QUALITY CONTROL

There are two basic methods of employing suppliers. One is to request bids on a project. This requires either (*a*) well-defined specs, which might be prematurely drawn, or (*b*) loosely defined specs, which can lead to widely disparate proposals and, hence, comparisons of very different approaches to a problem. The other approach is to deal over time with a small number of suppliers (e.g., two to four). This strategy has the advantage of economies of scale, in the sense that the time spent by the supplier in understanding the company's business is greatly reduced, especially if the supplier assigns a permanent account representative to the client. Also, dealing consistently with a given supplier makes comparability of results across studies somewhat easier. The disadvantage of this approach is that new ideas/approaches may be overlooked and that research may become stereotyped. This approach also may raise costs by making the supplier take his business for granted. In any event, a price quote should be obtained before work begins so neither party (company or supplier) faces an unpleasant surprise later on.

FIGURE 8–1 Product Focus and Major Services of the Top 15 Research Companies, 1986 (Honomichl, 1986)

Company (parent)	*Product Focus*	*Special Services*
1. A. C. Nielsen (Dun & Bradstreet)	Grocery, health & beauty aids, drugs TV viewing	Retail audits Scanner data TV viewing panels & meters
2. IMS	Pharmaceuticals	Audits of drug stores, hospitals, medical labs, and nursing homes
3. SAMI/Burke (Control Data)	Packaged goods TV commercial measurement	Warehouse audits Scanner data Copy testing New-product testing
4. AGB	Appliances, packaged goods, TV viewing	Diary panels TV viewing meters Mail panels Phone interviews (NFO)
5. Arbitron (Control Data)	Media usage	Radio-TV audience measurement
6. Information Resources, Inc. (IRI)	Packaged goods	Scanner data Market modeling
7. GFK	TV viewing Packaged goods Industrial	TV meters Diary panel Mail panel Store audits
8. MRB Group (J. Walter Thompson)	Media research (via Simmons) Advertising research	Product and media survey
9. Research International (Ogilvy Group)	Packaged goods	Research for Unilever
10. Infratest Forsching KG	Advertising research Media research Automobile Industrial Health care Financial	Media analysis
11. MARC	Packaged goods	Phone surveys Diary panel
12. Video research (Dentsu, Toshibo, 20 others)	Radio, TV Audience measurement	Mail panels Meters

FIGURE 8–1 (*concluded*)

Company (parent)	*Product Focus*	*Special Services*
13. Market Facts	Packaged goods	Mail panels Mall interviews Phone interviews
14. NPD	Packaged goods Toys, restaurants, apparel	Scanner panel Mail panels
15. Maritz Market Research	Packaged goods	Surveys Central location

Checking up on suppliers is advisable. Without being a complete stickler, it is advisable to monitor what is going on by such activities as spending a day in the field and keeping in contact with the supplier during the course of the study. This both helps ensure attention to the project and tends to give insights into what happened which are unavailable from the summary report.

At this point, a few words can be said about academic suppliers. With the exception of those who have genuine businesses established, academics are typically understaffed. Consequently, they are relatively poor at meeting deadlines and giving polished presentations. On the other hand, they are witty, have low overhead, and occasionally have novel ideas. If one can put up with their occasional lapses into academic jargon, they are often useful in helping specify research design or analytical procedures. Basically, they are complementary to, rather than replacements for, "real" suppliers. (This commercial was brought to you by your local chapter of the Hire/Employ Local Professors Association.)

The rest of this chapter exposes readers to the real data sources—suppliers. The number of suppliers is enormous. What this chapter does, therefore, is to concentrate on the major sources, especially those which apply to consumer packaged goods (Figure 8–1). The reasons for this focus are (*a*) research suppliers have concentrated on packaged goods, and their services are extensively developed, and (*b*) the information on them is widely available. Also, by examining the services offered by these suppliers, an understanding can be reached of the kinds of services that are perceived as valuable.

It is important to understand that this chapter is not an endorsement or advertisement. Many excellent suppliers are not discussed here. Moreover, the information is presented largely as it is given to prospective clients by the suppliers themselves. Therefore, editorializing is minimized. Suffice it to say that there are enough war stories around that, before using one of these services, it makes sense to talk to some past users.

PARTICULAR SERVICES

There are two basic ways to organize the remainder of this chapter: by company or by type of service. While organization by type of service has some advantages, it goes against the trend toward full-service research organizations that provide a broad range of services. (Quite frankly, it also would require some critical comparisons, which the author would prefer to avoid.) Therefore, this chapter will proceed by describing the services of the 25 largest U.S. research firms (Honomichl, 1987) plus a selection of others. (A census is impossible, which a quick perusal of the Green Book, an international directory of market research companies and services published annually by the New York chapter of the American Marketing Association, will demonstrate.)

1. A. C. NIELSEN

The largest research supplier (and a subsidiary of Dun & Bradstreet), Nielsen's specialty is syndicated services, meaning it signs up clients in advance for a period (i.e., one year) and provides a service to a number of clients simultaneously. Nielsen offers numerous services, some of which are described in this section.

Retail Audits

By far the biggest part of the Nielsen portfolio was its auditing service, covering food, drug, mass merchandise, and alcoholic beverage outlets. Scanner panel data have now largely replaced audit data in food and drug outlets. Still, the audit data continue to be used in some areas (e.g., to measure snack items in gas stations and mom-and-pop stores, as well as alcoholic beverage sales in liquor stores). Moreover, since the auditing service was responsible for Nielsen's position as the largest research supplier, and the method is still applicable to areas where scanner data are inadequate, a brief discussion of the auditing system is presented here.

The heart of the system was in-store audits. Every two months, an auditor (there were over 500 of them) arrived at each store in the sample and recorded:

Beginning inventory.

Ending inventory.

Purchases.

Price at date of audit plus special prices (if any).

Distribution (if stocked and levels).

Deals (factory packs).

Local advertising.

Displays.

Total sales (all products).

In addition, major media advertising (newspaper, magazines, network TV, and spot TV) was also monitored. For each brand, sales were estimated, as shown in Figure 8–2.

The audit period actually ran over several weeks. Auditing began about two weeks before the end of the bimonthly period and continued two weeks after the next one started. Hence, the auditing cycle looked like the following:

February–March Period								
	First (Prior) Audit				*Second (Post) Audit*			
	Jan. 10,	*Jan. 11,*	*...,*	*Feb. 12*	*Mar. 10,*	*Mar. 11,*	*...,*	*Apr. 12*
Store group 1	*x*				*x*			
Store group 2		*x*				*x*		
Store group 3			⋱				⋱	
⋮								
Store group n				*x*				*x*

Sales in the February–March bimonthly period were thus a "smoothed" average of sales January 10–March 10, January 11–March 11, and so forth, through February 12–April 12. This average was an annoying problem in certain modeling endeavors, especially in estimating the effectiveness of advertising and promotion (Shoemaker and Pringle, 1980).

The sample used for the audit was a set panel of stores. Stores were recruited and induced to participate based on (*a*) an appeal for cooperation in the spirit of learning, (*b*) information provided to the stores about trends in business, and (*c*) monetary compensation (an above the table payment).

Until 1976, 1,600 stores were included in the grocery index. These stores were grouped into five categories and selected disproportionately to reflect the sales volume accounted for by five store types, rather than just their number—see Figure 8–3. In early 1976, the sample of stores was changed (*a*) to reflect changes in the market and (*b*) to cut cost. The new sample of 1,300 stores (fewer stores means less cost) differed mainly in that A & P stores were now included, and many ma-and-pa stores were eliminated. For a single two-month period, both the old and new stores were monitored. This was supposed to provide a means of assurance that the sample change

FIGURE 8–2 Principles of Nielsen Retail Index Auditing
("Alpha" Brand of Spot Remover—3 Ounces in Super X Market)

	For June–July	
	Packages	*Value*
Inventory:		
May 30	114	
July 30	93	
Change	21	
Purchases:		
From manufacturer (1 order)	12	$ 3.72
From wholesalers (4 orders)	48	15.00
Total	60	$18.72
Consumer sales:		
Packages	81	
Price, per package		$ 0.39
Dollars, total		31.59
Adv. 1 2 3 4 5		
6 7 8 9		
Display X		Selling price, 39¢
		Special price, 35¢

Source: A. C. Nielsen Company, *Nielsen Retail Index Services*, 1975. Reprinted with permission.

FIGURE 8–3 Disproportionate Sampling Concept

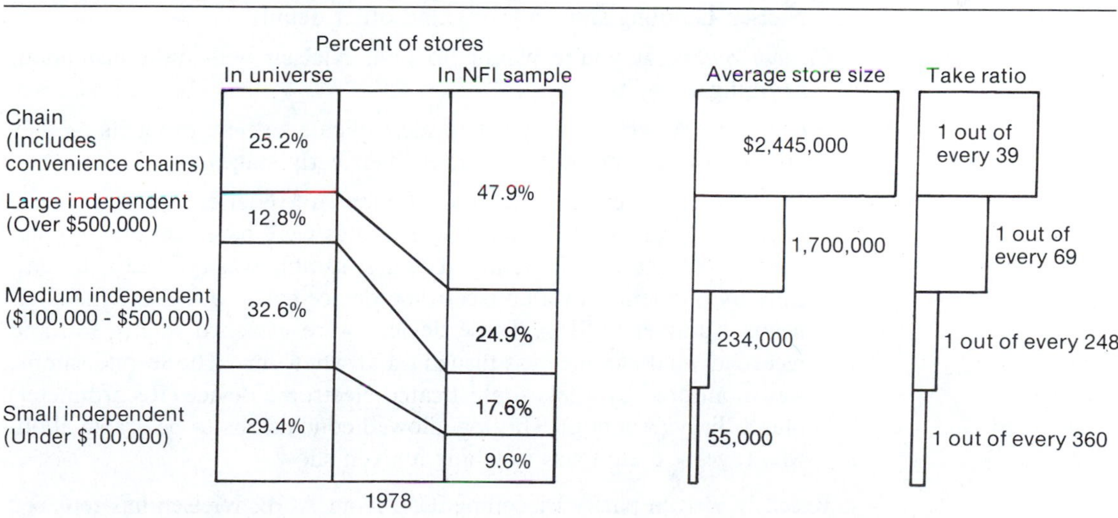

Source: "Management with the Nielsen Retail Index System," Northbrook, Ill.: A. C. Nielsen Company, 1980, p. 11.

did not affect the results. For most brands, the national results were in fact stable (i.e., the share in the old sample was 29.1 versus 28.9 in the new sample). For some brands, however, national shares changed by three or four points. Since a difference of this size means a lot in terms of profits (and jobs retained or lost), a big question arose about which share was correct.

ScanTrack

Partly as a reaction to the threat to its auditing business posed by scanner data, Nielsen entered the scanner panel business in a major way. Currently over 3,000 stores with scanners are included in the sample, and separate reports are available for over 40 major markets (Atlanta, Boston, Chicago, and so on). Not surprisingly, the stores tend to be larger in size (not many country stores have scanners) and, hence, underrepresent sales at small outlets. As mentioned earlier, scanner data are now the main source for retail sales measurement in the food and drugstore industries.

Other Services

ERIM is a service which allows for over-the-air commercial testing by merging TV viewing data with local scanner sales data in Sioux Falls, South Dakota, and Springfield, Missouri.

Data Markets serves seven smaller cities (Boise, Charleston, Green Bay, Peoria, Portland, Savannah, and Tucson) where tests can be run with Nielsen handling store stocking and other details.

Custom audits. If you're willing to pay, Nielsen will audit just about anything.

Intelligence. A service designed to alert clients to new products as they are introduced and how they do in their early stages.

Media research. Perhaps the most famous of Nielsen services is the Nielsen ratings of TV shows. These ratings were based on two samples which were queried differently. The first sample was queried automatically by phone lines via an electronic device called a Storage Instantaneous Audimeter (SIA). These devices were attached to the TV, and recorded what channel was turned on at what time. The second sample was monitored by a less-sophisticated electronic device (Recordimeter) plus a diary (Audilog). This log allowed conclusions to be drawn about who (age, sex, etc.) was watching a given show.

Recently, driven partly by competition from AGB, Nielsen has replaced diary panels with people meters, which record individual family members' viewing behavior.

Nielsen Clearing House. More of a marketing than a marketing research service, Nielsen offers to do the work on redeeming store coupons by collecting redeemed coupons and simultaneously paying retailers and billing manufacturers, as well as reporting on the results.

Majers. An acquisition of Nielsen, Majers measures retail advertising support by product category, retailer, and market.

2. IMS

IMS is the major supplier of research to the pharmaceutical industry, and it does a large portion of its business in other countries than the United States. Its main services include:

Pharmaceutical Market Studies. The purchases of a sample of 840 pharmacies, proprietary stores, and discount houses are audited and reported monthly. (This sample also provides data on toiletries and beauty aids.) Similarly, the purchases of 350 hospitals are audited. In addition, pharmaceutical warehouse withdrawal data are also collected.

Prescription Audit (NPA). Based on a panel of computerized pharmacies, data on prescription volume, price, dosage information, etc., are collected weekly and reported biweekly, monthly, or quarterly.

National Disease and Therapeutic Index (NDTI). Based on 2,100 physicians who report case histories over a 48-hour period four times a year, reports on drug use, diagnosis, etc., are prepared.

The New Product Digest. A monthly report on use during the first three months of introduction of new drugs based on surveys of 360 office-based physicians.

National Mail Audit. A panel-based report of pharmaceutical mail received by a panel of 300.

National Journal Audit. A monthly audit of advertising in 350 medical journals.

National Detailing Audit. Monthly reports of 2,800 office-based physicians on the personal selling activities of pharmaceutical sales representatives.

Audatrex. A sample of 1,000 physicians who provide copies of each prescription they write. A subpanel of 300 physicians (called Medilink) also furnishes qualitative information on heart-related disorders and musculoskeletal ailments (who said only researchers used big words?).

IMS also monitors government contract awards and does custom research.

3. SAMI / Burke

Burke is probably the largest custom research supplier in the United States. It is also well known for its advertising copy testing, and "Burke Scores" (day-after recall measures) are a widely used measure of commercial effectiveness. Specialized parts of Burke include:

The Test Marketing Group, which does controlled store tests as well as sales and distribution studies.

BASES, a new product sales forecasting system that converts attitudinal measures into sales projections.

Burke International Research.

Consulting and Analytical Services, which provides assistance in the design and analysis of studies.

The Burke Institute, which offers training programs in various elements of the research process.

SAMI specializes in syndicated research, and its main products are warehouse withdrawal surveys of food and drugstores and mass merchandisers. The food store data cover 54 markets, which account for 88.1 percent of total food sales in the United States (see Figure 8–4). Warehouse withdrawals are monitored every four weeks. Results are then reported to the owners of the warehouses (food operators) and to individual manufacturers. Food operators receive reports every 12 weeks, while manufacturers may get reports every 4 weeks. Food operators' cooperation is solicited by promising (a) information and (b) cash.

The operators include chains, wholesalers, health and beauty aid rack operators, and frozen food warehousers. For example, in 1975 the participating food operators in the Cincinnati/Dayton/Columbus area were the following:

A & P
Big Bear
Columbus Merchandise
Creasey
Fisher Foods
Kroger
Liberal Markets
March
Redi-Frog
Scot Lad
Super Food Services
Super-Value
White Villa

Typically, the operators included account for over 80 percent of the volume in the area. Hence, one problem is obvious with SAMI (or Nielsen or any other auditing service, for that matter): if a product tends to do better (or worse) in the nonincluded areas or with the nonincluded operators, the SAMI report will be misleading at least as an absolute measure.

FIGURE 8–4 SAMI Market Area

SAMI MARKET AREA

	POPULATION		HOUSEHOLDS		FOOD STORE SALES	EFFECTIVE BUYING INCOME
	Total Population (000's)	% of U.S.*	Total Households (000's)	% of U.S.*	% of U.S.*	Per Household ($)
Albany/Schenectady/Troy	1,885.0	.78	695.7	.78	.93	34,783
Atlanta	3,778.9	1.56	1,376.2	1.54	1.50	33,623
Baltimore/Washington	7,862.4	3.25	2,898.3	3.25	3.35	39,245
Birmingham/Montgomery/Huntsville	2,966.5	1.23	1,092.5	1.23	0.97	26,213
Boston/Providence	6,943.5	2.87	2,573.8	2.89	3.43	38,950
Buffalo/Rochester	2,979.9	1.23	1,092.2	1.23	1.29	34,077
Charleston/Huntington	1,723.6	0.71	627.9	0.70	0.61	24,689
Charleston/Savannah	1,152.2	0.48	396.2	0.44	0.46	27,924
Charlotte	2,423.8	1.00	894.4	1.00	1.00	28,970
Chicago	8,922.8	3.69	3,214.5	3.61	3.07	37,711
Cincinnati/Dayton/Columbus	5,529.9	2.29	2,057.7	2.31	2.12	31,248
Cleveland	4,371.7	1.81	1,633.7	1.83	1.76	32,226
Dallas/Fort Worth	4,670.3	1.93	1,743.7	1.96	2.14	34,767
Denver	2,865.6	1.19	1,126.2	1.26	1.38	34,310
Detroit	5,348.9	2.21	1,946.4	2.18	2.03	35,145
El Paso/Albuquerque/Lubbock	2,997.4	1.24	1,038.9	1.17	1.26	29,164
Grand Rapids/Kalamazoo	2,371.7	0.98	856.2	0.96	0.80	32,437
Green Bay	1,498.5	0.62	550.4	0.62	0.48	28,975
Greenville/Spartanburg/Asheville	1,417.0	0.59	531.5	0.60	0.56	26,447
Hartford/New Haven/Springfield	2,691.5	1.11	992.3	1.11	1.35	39,329
Houston	4,213.5	1.74	1,523.3	1.71	2.00	36,331
Indianapolis	2,676.2	1.11	978.9	1.10	1.02	31,823
Jacksonville/Orlando/Tampa	6,660.5	2.76	2,671.6	3.00	2.77	28,780
Kansas City	2,255.2	0.93	848.2	0.95	0.98	34,135
Los Angeles/San Diego	16,467.5	6.82	5,966.3	6.69	6.96	38,279
Louisville/Lexington	2,238.0	0.93	801.2	0.90	0.82	28,183
Memphis/Little Rock	3,316.1	1.37	1,195.5	1.34	1.28	26,250
Miami	4,226.8	1.75	1,703.7	1.91	1.83	33,145
Milwaukee	2,445.1	1.01	918.2	1.03	0.91	33,976
Minneapolis/St. Paul	3,362.0	1.39	1,242.1	1.39	1.38	35,725
Nashville/Knoxville	3,292.0	1.36	1,216.5	1.36	1.34	27,404
New Orleans	3,825.0	1.58	1,342.9	1.51	1.69	29,029
New York	18,054.3	7.47	6,771.9	7.60	7.94	40,893
Norfolk/Richmond	3,094.7	1.28	1,081.2	1.21	1.18	32,360
Oklahoma City/Tulsa	2,974.6	1.23	1,126.8	1.26	1.27	29,275
Omaha/Des Moines	2,411.1	1.00	923.2	1.04	1.00	32,234
Peoria/Springfield	1,473.2	0.61	554.9	0.62	0.53	33,069
Philadelphia	7,600.8	3.15	2,811.2	3.15	3.30	35,093
Phoenix/Tucson	3,275.2	1.36	1,257.6	1.41	1.48	29,969
Pittsburgh	4,081.4	1.69	1,552.2	1.74	1.53	29,278
Portland, Me./Concord	1,461.6	0.61	545.4	0.61	0.83	30,032
Portland, Oregon	2,876.8	1.19	1,107.5	1.24	1.07	29,080
Quad Cities	1,297.3	0.54	486.7	0.55	0.47	31,090
Raleigh/Greensboro/Winston-Salem	2,997.2	1.24	1,095.0	1.23	1.15	29,630
Salt Lake City/Boise	2,404.9	1.00	768.8	0.86	0.90	29,335
San Antonio/Corpus Christi	3,706.9	1.53	1,227.4	1.38	1.63	29,404
San Francisco	9,887.4	4.09	3,727.6	4.18	4.47	38,753
Scranton/Wilkes Barre	1,022.7	0.42	386.2	0.43	0.41	27,039
Seattle/Tacoma	3,129.9	1.30	1,232.9	1.38	1.40	33,997
Shreveport/Jackson	2,876.7	1.19	1,019.1	1.14	1.03	25,373
Spokane/Yakima	1,359.4	0.56	508.7	0.57	0.57	28,035
St. Louis	3,057.9	1.27	1,112.1	1.25	1.29	33,637
Syracuse	2,349.9	0.97	839.2	0.94	0.98	32,860
Wichita	1,006.2	0.42	387.3	0.43	0.44	33,481
TOTAL	**211,779.1**	**87.66**	**78,270.0**	**87.80**	**88.33**	**33,975**
CONTERMINOUS U.S.*	**241,582.4**	**99.33**	**89,142.3**	**99.41**	**99.26**	**33,202**
TOTAL U.S.	**243,211.7**	**100.0**	**89,670.4**	**100.00**	**100.00**	**33,252**

SOURCE: MARKET STATISTICS 1987 SURVEY OF BUYING POWER
* Conterminous U.S. (Excludes Alaska and Hawaii)
NOTE: Details may not add to totals due to rounding.

SAMI
Time & Life Bldg., Rockefeller Center, New York, N.Y. 10020 (212) 522-5800
541 North Fairbanks Court, Chicago, Illinois 60611 (312) 329-7259
501 Santa Monica Boulevard, Santa Monica, California 90401 (213) 451-8033

The product categories monitored by SAMI fall into four major categories:

1. *Dry grocery—food.* Over 200 product categories including pancake mix, croutons, and canned shrimp are included.
2. *Refrigerated and frozen foods.* About 80 categories including frozen pies, butter, and refrigerated pastries are monitored.
3. *Dry grocery—nonfood.* About 75 categories from housecleaning compounds (e.g., scouring pads) and household supplies (e.g., cellophane tape, furniture polish, and insect repellents) to laundry supplies (e.g., liquid bleach), paper products (e.g., paper towels, aluminum foil), and soaps (e.g., bath additives, dishwater detergents) are available.
4. *Health and beauty aids.* The major categories include baby needs, deodorants, first aids, hair care needs, oral hygiene, proprietory remedies, shaving needs, and skin care aids. The 50 specific categories include roll-on deodorants, antacids, and suntan lotions.

Reports are made available to both food operators and manufacturers. The basic reports are:

Basic Reports, prepared every four weeks, report on an item-by-item basis sales by sizes, flavors, and so on (Figure 8–5).

SAMI Charts present trend data in a graphical format.

Executive Review is a trend report, which compares current to past sales (Figure 8–6). A more detailed Brand Trend Report is also available.

Market Résumé reports changes in market activity of all brands.

Rank Reports rank items by volume.

Other reports include:

Category Size and Trend Reports, which track volume by category.

Million Dollar Brand Report, which reports all brands with over $1 million in volume.

Manufacturer Rank Reports rank total dollar volume of manufacturers totaled across all brands.

In addition to these reports, a service called SARDI (*SA*MI *R*etail *D*istribution *I*ndex) is available. SARDI is based on the assumption that, if a retail store makes a withdrawal of a product from a central warehouse during a given time period (usually four weeks), then the retail store stocks/distributes the products. By arranging with each food operator to provide store-by-store withdrawal data for a sample of retail stores (over 6,000 in total), an index of distribution is obtained.

SAMI also provides scanner panel data via SAMSCAN, which monitors 500 product categories. The data are matched to SAMI markets and were in about 38 markets with about 2,300 stores at the end of 1987. SAMSCAN

FIGURE 8–5 SAMI Basic Report

Manufacturer Noncontract	*Category Coffee: Regular*	*Page 0701–001*
Contract No.	*Issue Number: 202*	*Units Dollar Volume*
Market Area	*Current 4 wk. Period: 02/06/82–03/05/82*	*Case Volume*
		Period Covered: 03/07/81–03/05/82

	Item Size	*Pack per Case*	*Avg Shelf Price*	*Measured Case Volume 4 Weeks*	*Measured Case Volume 52 Weeks*	*Measured Dollar Sales 4 Weeks*	*Measured Dollar Sales 52 Weeks*	*Dollar Share of Brand 4 Weeks*	*Dollar Share of Brand 52 Weeks*	*Dollar Share of Category 4 Weeks*	*Dollar Share of Category 52 Weeks*	*F.O. Shipping 4 Weeks*	*NE WIN Drop (D) Item in Market Period Ending*
Coffee: Regular				39,379	477,378	2,388M	27,571M			100.000%	100.000%		
BRAND A				2,559	31,246	224,047	2,561M	100.000%	100.000%	9.384%	9.287%	5	
A P DCF	1 lb	24	3.661	253	3,645	22,232	300,556	9.923%	11.738%	0.931%	1.090%	5	
A P DCF	2 lb	12	7.280	313	4,586	27,344	373,441	12.205%	14.584%	1.145%	1.354%	5	
AUTO DRIP DCF	1 lb	24	3.661	584	5,731	51,313	475,319	22.903%	18.563%	2.149%	1.724%	5	
AUTO DRIP DCF	2 lb	12	7.280	907	10,184	79,236	831,157	35.366%	32.459%	3.319%	3.015%	5	
ELEC PERK DCF	1 lb	24	3.660	141	2,198	12,385	181,572	5.528%	7.091%	0.519%	0.659%	*	
ELEC PERK DCF	2 lb	12	7.280	361	4,902	31,537	398,568	14.076%	15.565%	1.321%	1.446%	5	
BRAND B					13		846	100.000%	100.000%	0.000%	0.003%	0	
ELEC PERK 10S	12 oz	24	0.000		13		846	0.000%	100.000%	0.000%	0.003%	0	0501D
BRAND C				1,754	22,971	109,698	1,333M	100.000%	100.000%	4.594%	4.835%	5	
REGULAR	1 lb	24	2.680	55	1,294	3,538	77,036	3.225%	5.778%	0.148%	0.279%	*	
REGULAR	2 lb	12	5.349	42	736	2,696	44,202	2.458%	3.315%	0.113%	0.160%	*	
AUTO DRIP	1 lb	24	2.686	440	5,666	28,360	338,095	25.853%	25.360%	1.188%	1.226%	5	
AUTO DRIP	2 lb	12	5.160	640	9,249	39,629	527,806	36.126%	39.589%	1.660%	1.914%	4	
AUTO DRIP	3 lb	8	7.660	395	3,561	24,206	206,358	22.066%	15.478%	1.014%	0.748%	*	
ELEC PERK	2 lb	12	5.160	182	2,428	11,269	137,665	10.273%	10.326%	0.472%	0.499%	*	
ELEC PERK	3 lb	8	0.000		37		2,039	0.000%	0.153%	0.000%	0.007%	0	0501D
BRAND D				1,490	19,116	130,469	1,568M	100.000%	100.000%	5.464%	5.687%	5	
REGULAR	1 lb	24	3.661	233	3,248	20,470	268,424	15.690%	17.121%	0.857%	0.974%	5	
REGULAR	2 lb	12	7.280	275	3,325	24,024	270,898	18.414%	17.278%	1.006%	0.983%	*	
DRIP-MATIC	1 lb	24	3.660	384	4,708	33,734	389,729	25.856%	24.858%	1.413%	1.414%	5	
DRIP-MATIC	2 lb	12	7.280	598	7,132	52,241	581,377	40.041%	37.081%	2.188%	2.109%	5	
ELEC PERK	1 lb	24	0.000		213		17,861	0.000%	1.139%	0.000%	0.065%	0	1211D
ELEC PERK	2 lb	12	0.000		490		39,560	0.000%	2.523%	0.000%	0.143%	0	1211D
BRAND E				1,860	7,120	130,245	493,542	100.000%	100.000%	5.455%	1.790%	5	
REGULAR	1 lb	24	2.940	467	1,686	32,955	117,679	25.302%	23.844%	1.380%	0.427%	5	
REGULAR	2 lb	12	5.760	73	411	5,046	27,717	3.874%	5.616%	0.211%	0.101%	*	1113N
DRIP	1 lb	24	2.940	668	2,460	47,134	172,082	36.189%	34.867%	1.974%	0.624%	*	
DRIP	2 lb	12	5.760	114	576	7,880	38,924	6.050%	7.887%	0.330%	0.141%	*	1113N
AUTO DRIP	1 lb	24	2.940	30	103	2,117	7,240	1.625%	1.467%	0.089%	0.026%	*	1211N
AUTO DRIP	2 lb	12	5.760	293	791	20,252	54,096	15.549%	10.961%	0.848%	0.196%	*	1016N
ELECTRAMATIC	1 lb	24	0.000		640		44,857	0.000%	9.089%	0.000%	0.163%	0	0205D

Note: M = 000 W = 000,000

* = 3 or less food operators shipping

Source: "How to Use SAMI for Making More Effective Presentation" New York: Selling Areas-Marketing, Inc., 1983. Reprinted with permission.

FIGURE 8–6 SAMI Participant Executive Review

Market: *Issue:* 4 Week Period Covered:
12 Week Period Covered:
15 Week Period Covered:

		Total Measured Market			*Participant*					
		Volume			*Volume*			*Share of Market Dollars and 12-Pack Cases*		
		4 weeks	*12 weeks*	*52 weeks*	*4 weeks*	*12 weeks*	*52 weeks*	*4 weeks*	*12 weeks*	*52 weeks*
GRAND TOTAL	DOL	105W	307W	1,284W	18618M	53846M	208W	17.8%	17.6%	16.2%
	CAS	8,166M	24012M	102W	1,484M	4,402M	17268M	16.7%	18.9%	16.8%
DRY GROCERIES	DOL	73681M	216W	908W	12612M	36510M	139W	17.1%	16.9%	15.4%
	CAS	4,335M	12729M	54050M	752448	2,216M	8,621M	17.8%	17.6%	15.9%
BABY FOOD	DOL	1,704M	5,080M	20905M	224223	664514	2,677M	13.2%	13.1%	12.8%
	CAS	129470	381771	1,643M	19,266	55,765	236415	15.2%	14.6%	14.2%
CEREAL BABY FOOD	DOL	47,785	145326	589431	6,014	17,898	69,451	12.6%	12.3%	11.8%
	CAS	5,038	15,557	64,062	711	2,181	8,609	15.7%	15.9%	15.0%
JUICE BABY FOOD	DOL	145100	413503	1,846M	20,101	55,364	238704	13.9%	13.4%	12.9%
	CAS	17,590	50,644	236369	2,784	7,708	34,512	16.2%	15.6%	14.8%
FORMULA BABY FOOD	DOL	1,077M	3,260M	13066M	139253	429197	1,693M	12.9%	13.2%	13.0%
	CAS	51,670	155854	653604	7,503	23,131	97,468	14.5%	14.5%	14.1%
STRAINED BABY FOOD	DOL	282930	826938	3,566M	40,689	112216	480024	14.4%	13.6%	13.5%
	CAS	39,123	114408	496118	6,207	17,117	73,778	15.9%	15.0%	14.9%
JUNIOR BABY FOOD	DOL	141139	406843	1,728M	16,323	45,529	180296	11.6%	11.2%	10.4%
	CAS	14,977	42,429	180349	1,846	5,118	20,244	13.0%	12.5%	11.7%
MISC BABY FOOD	DOL	9,564	27,710	109772	1,843	4,310	14,979	19.3%	15.6%	13.6%
	CAS	1,072	2,879	12,256	215	510	1,804	20.1%	15.1%	13.9%
BAKING MIXES	DOL	1,513M	3,675M	15097M	268754	589811	2,067M	17.8%	16.0%	13.7%
	CAS	103068	236810	972446	18,506	39,445	137082	18.5%	16.0%	13.9%
DESSERT BAKING MIXES	DOL	969591	2,100M	8,759M	190094	371004	1,246M	19.6%	17.7%	14.2%
	CAS	67,850	140664	574428	13,876	25,843	84,745	21.0%	18.9%	15.2%
PRIVATE LABEL/GENERIC	DOL	56,908	176105	642258	14,105	36,280	139025	24.8%	20.6%	21.6%
	CAS	4,870	15,281	55,138	1,032	2,753	10,602	27.3%	22.1%	22.8%
PVT LABEL $ SHR OF PART								7.4%	9.8%	11.2%
PVT LBL $ AND 12-PACK	DOL	5.9%	8.4%	7.3%						
CASE SHARE OF MARKET	CAS	7.9%	11.5%	11.5%						
GENERIC	DOL	14,245	33,229	113557	7,734	15,867	47,471	54.3%	47.8%	41.8%
	CAS	998	2,304	7,864	467	896	2,563	58.0%	50.0%	43.3%
GENERIC $ SHR OF PART								4.1%	4.3%	3.8%
GENERIC $ AND 12-PACK	DOL	1.5%	1.6%	1.3%						
CASE SHARE OF MARKET	CAS	2.3%	2.5%	2.5%						
PIECRUST MIX	DOL	37,911	111775	649621	5,924	16,304	95,127	14.0%	14.6%	14.6%
	CAS	2,305	6,567	37,306	323	974	5,516	13.9%	14.7%	14.6%
BISCUIT MIX	DOL	202064	606132	2,168M	33,523	82,785	283192	16.6%	13.7%	13.1%
	CAS	7,830	23,100	89,944	1,304	3,624	13,583	27.4%	13.4%	13.8%

Note: M = 000 W = 000,000

Source: How to Use SAMI for Making More Effective Sales Presentations," New York: Selling Areas-Marketing, Inc., 1983. Reprinted with permission.

also has a consumer panel of 12,500 households in five small cities: Portland, Maine; Evansville, Indiana; Orlando, Florida; Quad Cities, Iowa/Illinois; and Boise, Idaho.

4. ARBITRON (CONTROL DATA)

A subsidiary of Control Data, Arbitron specializes in measuring media (radio and TV) audiences on a local basis. Data are collected on a regional basis and grouped, among other ways, according to a measure called ADI (area of dominant influence). The basis for this breakdown is areas where media (radio and TV stations) reach from the "center" of the area. Hence, a county is included in the area from which the majority of its radio or television programs are broadcast.

Data were once collected exclusively by diaries. The steps used in the radio diary panel are:

1. Preplacement letter (to listed numbers).
2. Placement phone call.
3. Diary mailed for each person in household, along with token ($1 per person) premium. (More is sent in minority households.)
4. Reminder call.
5. Letter containing additional dollar per household premium.

Initial contact is made by phone to homes with up to four callbacks (five attempts) to each listed number in the sample and nine callbacks to unlisted numbers. Premiums are not mentioned in gaining cooperation. Names of sample members are drawn from the list maintained by Metro-Mail of households with listed telephone numbers. This is then augmented with numbers which are not listed and which appear to be residential phone numbers.

The sample size varies, depending on the size of the market. Standard market samples vary from 550 to 4,000, while condensed market samples range from 250 to 400 (Arbitron, 1987).

For radio, every person age 12 or older is sent a diary. The diary covers one week, with a page for each day of the week (Figure 8–7).

A major use of these data is in evaluating advertising alternatives. In each area, audience by station is estimated in hourly blocks of time as well as in larger aggregations (e.g., 6 A.M. to noon). For each period, the following are calculated:

1. Average *number* of persons listening.
2. Average *rating* (average number/population of area).
3. Metro *share* (shares of listening audience).
4. *Cume persons* (number of persons who listen during at least some part of the time period, often called *Reach*).
5. *Cume ratings* (cume persons/population).

FIGURE 8–7 Arbitron Ratings Radio Diary

Please start recording your listening on the date shown on the front cover.

Thursday								
Time			**Station**			**Place**		
						Check One (✓)		
			Fill in station "call letters" (If you don't know them, fill in program name or dial setting)	Check One (✓)		At Home	Away From Home	
	From	To		AM	FM		In a Car	Some Other Place
Early Morning 5am to 10am								
Midday 10am to 3pm								
Late Afternoon 3pm to 7pm								
Night 7pm to 5am								
If you did not listen to the radio today please check here ☐								

Each time you listen to the radio, please be sure to use a new line, and write in the station "call letters."

Source: Arbitron Ratings/Radio, 1986.

FIGURE 8–8 ARB TV Diary

Leaving this portion of the page open will assist you in keeping the diary.

What TV stations (channels 2-83) can you receive clearly enough for viewing on this set? (Fill in below)

Channel Number	Station Call Letters	City	Channel Number	Station Call Letters	City

Accurate station identification is very important. Please use both the station call letters and channel number in your viewing entries.

MALE HEAD OF HOUSE	FIRST NAME ONLY:

FEMALE HEAD OF HOUSE	FIRST NAME ONLY:

OTHER FAMILY MEMBERS

NAMES

6:00 A.M.

WEDNESDAY

TIME	TV SET		STATION TUNED IN		NAME OF PROGRAM	AGE →								VISITORS	VISITORS	VISITORS
QUARTER HOURS	OFF	ON	CALL LETTERS	CHAN. NO.		SEX → M	F									
6:00- 6:14																
6:15- 6:29																
6:30- 6:44																
6:45- 6:59																
7:00- 7:14																
7:15- 7:29																
7:30- 7:44																
7:45- 7:59																
8:00- 8:14																
8:15- 8:29																
8:30- 8:44																
8:45- 8:59																
9:00- 9:14																
9:15- 9:29																
9:30- 9:44																
9:45- 9:59																
10:00-10:14																
10:15-10:29																
10:30-10:44																
10:45-10:59																
11:00-11:14																
11:15-11:29																

Source: Arbitron Television Research, *Diary of Television Viewing*, November 3, 1976.

These numbers are used to derive several key figures:

1. *Gross impressions* (Average number of persons × Number of spots of a given ad aired during the time period).
2. *Cost per thousand* (CPM = Cost/1,000 gross impressions).
3. *Gross rating points* (GRP = Average rating × Number of spots).
4. *Frequency* (gross impressions/cume persons).

The data are also used to rank stations and programs based on audiences. The makeup of station audiences is available in terms of age and sex.

The television diary data is essentially the same as the ratio data. Its diary is a bit more structured; but, other than that, the two services are basically twins. Television ratings based on diaries of one week in length are produced (see Figure 8–8).

In addition to the diary data, each ADI is used to generate a sample whose TVs are equipped with a meter. Data are received by Arbitron via telephone lines. (The sample includes households with unlisted phone numbers.) Households are replaced every five years. As in the sales monitoring business, mechanical recording devices seem to be replacing diary panels in TV audience measurement.

Arbitron also operates a scanner-based TV viewing and product sales monitoring system, ScanAmerica. This service uses a panel of households who agree to record both television viewing and product purchase data. ScanAmerica, which originated in Denver, combines people-meter measurement of television viewing for household members and a hand-held scanning wand-based self-measurement of household purchases. The wand is used by panelists in their homes, typically as bags are unpacked, to record all items purchased and the store where the purchase was made. People-meter usage is encouraged by an on-screen prompt, which reminds viewers to punch a button on a remote hand-held keypad. The data thus allow examination of purchase data versus show viewing at the individual level.

5. INFORMATION RESOURCES, INC. (IRI)

IRI was the pioneer in providing optical scanning-based research. Its original product, BehaviorScan, provided scanner tracking of sales in test market areas (initially Marion, Indiana, and Pittsfield, Massachusetts). A sample of 2,400 households per market is included in each panel. When they pay for their purchases, they show a special identification card so their purchases can be tracked. These households can be reached with split-cable TV, so different ones can be exposed to different ads. Local advertising and promotion, as well as in-store environment variables, are also monitored periodically.

In mid-1986, IRI introduced InfoScan, a general retail auditing service based on scanners which competed directly with Nielsen's auditing service. Monitoring over 800,000 UPC items in 2,400 stores and 70,000 households in 1987, the scanner panel method has become the dominant way to measure manufacturer, retailer, and consumer behavior in the packaged goods area, as Nielsen's rapid conversion to scanner-based reporting attests. Ironically, in 1979, IRI founders John Malec and Gerry Eskin (a professor, no less) were told by Nielsen that their concept for a new product was dumb (Kreisman, 1985).

In addition to these two major syndicated data services, IRI offers a number of other products. These include a number of decision-support systems (e.g., ASSESOR, designed to measure market potential based on new product concepts; PROMOTER, a model for analyzing the effect of promotions; and EXPRESS, a language for database management and analysis). IRI also has a full-service custom research operation (The Data Group, acquired in 1986) which specializes in computer-assisted telephone interviewing (CATI) and in-home computer interviewing. It also owns ABA Group, which provides merchandising systems to retailers.

6. MRB GROUP

The main components of MRB in the United States are the Simmons Market Research Bureau and Winona Research. While Winona is best known for phone interviewing, Simmons's major products derive from a massive once-a-year survey called the Study of Media and Markets.

The Study of Media and Markets involves a sample of 19,000 households. Respondents go through two interviews (four to six weeks apart) with an extensive questionnaire on over 800 products left with them to be filled out between the first and second interviews. The first interview gathers demographic data, newspaper reading data (by showing them yesterday's paper), and magazine reading (again, by showing the actual magazine). The second interview asks about newspaper and magazine readership as well as radio listening. Finally, a two-week diary of television viewing is mailed to the respondents and a second radio listening interview is conducted. The respondents also complete the VALS battery of questions, allowing comparison of results across VALS segments. (This study is conducted with great care; but having seen the questionnaire, it is not at all obvious that most of us would be willing to fill it out.) The study is mainly used for targeting certain groups and relating product-use data to media exposure. In addition, the results can be tied to other segments, such as Cluster-Plus, a system of 47 clusters based on block groups, census tracts, and ZIP codes demographic data developed by Donnelley Market Information Services.

7. MARC

MARC primarily does custom work. It has a linked network of 55 local mall and central location facilities and a major central location WATS phone survey center. MARC conducts multiclient surveys every two months

FIGURE 8–9 Sample NFO Special-Purpose Diary

''MARKET RESEARCH THROUGH REPRESENTATIVE HOUSEHOLDS''

National Family Opinion, Inc.

A

POST OFFICE BOX 474
TOLEDO, OHIO 43654

99900

Dear Homemaker,

Thank you for agreeing to help with our diary type study which will last for several months. Here is your first diary in this series, for the next two weeks:

MONDAY, FEBRUARY 10 through SUNDAY, FEBRUARY 23

During this two-week period, please record in your diary (on the inside pages) each time you, or any member of your family purchase any of the following:

COFFEE - both regular and instant. Please be sure to include all purchases made -- including decaffeinated coffees.

JAMS, JELLIES and PRESERVES.

LAUNDRY DETERGENTS -- (liquid, powder, flakes, tablets) -- all detergents bought for family laundry.

HERE ARE A FEW INSTRUCTIONS TO HELP YOU IN COMPLETING YOUR DIARY:

Each time you return from shopping, complete a line in the diary for each different type and brand bought. Only items EXACTLY ALIKE and bought at the SAME TIME should be reported on the same line in your diary.

Write in the DATE bought.

Write in SIZE, NUMBER BOUGHT and TOTAL PRICE paid.

Indicate if a SPECIAL OFFER was used.

Check to indicate the type of store where the purchase was made.

Near the end of the two-week reporting period, I'll be writing again. At that time I'll send you a postage-paid envelope for returning this diary, as well as the next diary in the series.

Thanks again for your help with this study!

Sincerely, Carol

MEMBER OF AMERICAN MARKETING ASSOCIATION TOLEDO CHAMBER OF COMMERCE

FIGURE 8–9 (concluded)

Monday, FEBRUARY 10 through Sunday, FEBRUARY 23

☐ NONE RECEIVED — COUPONS RECEIVED

DATE REC'D	FOR WHICH OF THE DIARY PRODUCTS? Please write in.	BRAND NAME:	HOW RECEIVED? ✓ OR WRITE IN: By Mail	From Ad	From Pkg.	From Friend	Other
			☐	☐	☐	☐	
			☐	☐	☐	☐	
			☐	☐	☐	☐	
			☐	☐	☐	☐	

☐ NONE RECEIVED — SAMPLES RECEIVED

DATE REC'D	FOR WHICH OF THE DIARY PRODUCTS? Please write in.	BRAND NAME:	HOW RECEIVED? ✓ OR WRITE IN: By Mail	From Ad	From Pkg.	From Friend	Left at Door	Other
			☐	☐	☐	☐	☐	
			☐	☐	☐	☐	☐	
			☐	☐	☐	☐	☐	
			☐	☐	☐	☐	☐	

☐ COFFEE (☐ NONE BOUGHT)

DATE BOUGHT	Copy complete BRAND NAME from package	TYPE: (✓) ONE		Is it Decaf-feinated?		IF INSTANT, does label say "freeze-dried"?		IF GROUND COFFEE, check (✓) to indicate TYPE OF GRIND					SIZE: # lbs. or # of oz.	NUMBER BOUGHT	HOW MUCH DID YOU PAY? Don't include taxes. TOTAL PRICE PAID	WAS THIS A SPECIAL PRICE OR OFFER?		IF YES, DESCRIBE OFFER:					TOTAL AMOUNT SAVED (if any)--value of special offer, cents off, value of coupon, etc.	WHERE BOUGHT?		
		Instant	Ground	YES	NO	YES	NO	Regular	Drip	Fine	Electric	Other				YES	NO	Coupon Used	Cents Off	Combination deal	Store Special	Other - describe		Supermarket	Independent Grocery	Other - describe
		☐	☐	☐	☐	☐	☐	☐	☐	☐	☐	☐				☐	☐	☐	☐	☐	☐		¢	☐	☐	
		☐	☐	☐	☐	☐	☐	☐	☐	☐	☐	☐				☐	☐	☐	☐	☐	☐		¢	☐	☐	
		☐	☐	☐	☐	☐	☐	☐	☐	☐	☐	☐				☐	☐	☐	☐	☐	☐		¢	☐	☐	
		☐	☐	☐	☐	☐	☐	☐	☐	☐	☐	☐				☐	☐	☐	☐	☐	☐		¢	☐	☐	
		☐	☐	☐	☐	☐	☐	☐	☐	☐	☐	☐				☐	☐	☐	☐	☐	☐		¢	☐	☐	

☐ JAM, JELLY, PRESERVES, FLAVORED REFRIGERATED SPREADS, MARMALADE, FRUIT BUTTER, etc. (☐ NONE BOUGHT)

DATE BOUGHT	Copy complete BRAND NAME from package	KIND OF PRODUCT (jam, jelly, preserves, flavored refrigerated spread, marmalade, fruit butter, etc.)	FLAVOR (copy from the label - such as "raisin cinnamon", "grape", "strawberry", "fruit-nut", etc.)	TYPE OF PACKAGE			SIZE: # lbs. or # of oz.	NUMBER BOUGHT	HOW MUCH DID YOU PAY? Don't include taxes. TOTAL PRICE PAID	WAS THIS A SPECIAL PRICE OR OFFER?		IF YES, DESCRIBE OFFER:					TOTAL AMOUNT SAVED (if any)--value of special offer, cents off, value of coupon, etc.	WHERE BOUGHT?		
				Jar	Tub	Other				YES	NO	Coupon Used	Cents Off	Combination deal	Store Special	Other - describe		Supermarket	Independent Grocery	Other - describe
				☐	☐	☐				☐	☐	☐	☐	☐	☐		¢	☐	☐	
				☐	☐	☐				☐	☐	☐	☐	☐	☐		¢	☐	☐	
				☐	☐	☐				☐	☐	☐	☐	☐	☐		¢	☐	☐	
				☐	☐	☐				☐	☐	☐	☐	☐	☐		¢	☐	☐	

☐ LAUNDRY DETERGENTS - liquid, powder, flakes, or tablets (☐ NONE BOUGHT)

DATE BOUGHT	Copy complete BRAND NAME from package	FORM:				Is it mainly for use in COLD water?		Does it have active ENZYME ingredients?		SIZE - in lbs., ounces, quarts, pints, etc.	NUMBER BOUGHT	HOW MUCH DID YOU PAY? Don't include taxes. TOTAL PRICE PAID	WAS THIS A SPECIAL PRICE OR OFFER?		IF YES, DESCRIBE OFFER:					TOTAL AMOUNT SAVED (if any)--value of special offer, cents off, value of coupon, etc.	WHERE BOUGHT?		
		Liquid	Powder or Flakes	Tablets or Packets	Other, specify:	YES	NO	YES	NO				YES	NO	Coupon Used	Cents Off	Combination deal	Store Special	Other - describe		Supermarket	Independent Grocery	Other - describe
		☐	☐	☐		☐	☐	☐	☐				☐	☐	☐	☐	☐	☐		¢	☐	☐	
		☐	☐	☐		☐	☐	☐	☐				☐	☐	☐	☐	☐	☐		¢	☐	☐	
		☐	☐	☐		☐	☐	☐	☐				☐	☐	☐	☐	☐	☐		¢	☐	☐	
		☐	☐	☐		☐	☐	☐	☐				☐	☐	☐	☐	☐	☐		¢	☐	☐	

Source: National Family Opinion, Inc., New York, 1975.

at a price of $15,425 for 50,000 households for a limited one "card" survey. MARC also maintains a national panel of over 300,000 households that can be surveyed by either mail or phone. A smaller panel, the so-called national neighborhood panel (sounds a bit contradictory, but it does convey something) of 75,000 households in 27 prime markets is available for central location testing (including focus groups), in-home personal interviews, product testing, and phone interviewing.

8. NFO (AGB)

NFO (National Family Opinion) is mainly known for its standby panel, which consists of over 375,000 households. Panel members are identifiable by various geo-demographic segments, such as Cluster Plus, Acorn (CACI), Prizm (Claritas), and Vision (National Decision Systems), and part of the panel is tied to the VALS segments.

In addition to one-shot surveys, NFO also constructs special-purpose panels. Recruitment is usually done by phone. Diaries are then sent by mail over the period of a test market. The dropout rate for the panel tends to run between 30 and 40 percent (an obvious source of potential bias). A sample format is shown in Figure 8–9. The data are typically analyzed in terms of (*a*) brand switching, (*b*) trial level tracking, and (*c*) repeat purchase level tracking, pretty much the standard approach.

Special samples are also maintained, including mothers of new babies (800), high school students (9,200), college students (11,800), and executives (10,000). NFO's TRAC division performs surveys of beverage consumption and major textile purchases (carpets and rugs) and a quarterly multiclient survey mailed to 80,000 households.

9. MARKET FACTS

Market Facts is best known for its Consumer Mail Panel of over 250,000 households in the United States and Canada. It also has a phone interviewing facility of over 100 stations, conducts shopping mall interviews, does personal interviewing, and provides qualitative research. It has a multiclient weekly phone survey (questions by Friday, answers by the following Wednesday) of 1,000 households. The cost per question per wave (week) is $950, with a discount for heavy users. In addition, Market Facts provides test marketing services, with emphasis on controlled store testing, product pickup, and store observation (price, point-of-purchase displays, facings, etc.) in drug, auto parts, liquor, camera, home/hardware, and grocery stores. Other services focus on store satisfaction studies and health care studies, as well as extensive model building and analysis (in the Decision Systems group). A separate group also concentrates on industrial, agribusiness, medical, and high technology clients.

10. NPD

Originally a major supplier of diary panel data (over 13,000 households per month), NPD now consists of six divisions:

NPD Packaged Goods, which focuses on scanner and diary panel monitoring (see Figure 8–10). Both a major scanner panel (MARKETRAX) and special-purpose diary panels are available.

HTI Custom Research, which maintains a standby panel of 200,000 and which is available for mail or phone surveys.

Special Industry Services for nonpackaged goods, including special studies of toys/games, apparel/textiles, sewing patterns, and books.

Marketing Models, which focuses on premarket sales forecasting using the ESP model.

NPD CREST, which tracks restaurant/food service industry data via a diary panel which reports meals eaten away from home.

Information Technologies, which sells data collection and analytical systems.

THE NEXT FIFTEEN IN SIZE

11. *Westat,* which does personal, phone, and mall survey research for federal agencies in areas including health, social services and housing, employment and training, education, energy, science and technology, military, and transportation. It also maintains a market research division, Crossley Surveys, which does custom research and analysis for private corporations.

12. *Maritz Marketing Research,* which does custom survey research, focus groups and custom audits, and has a system called MAPPS for new-product concept evaluation. Maritz does syndicated studies in the automotive and agricultural business and also has a group specializing in research on financial services.

13. *Elrick and Lavidge,* owned by Equifax, Inc., performs qualitative research mall interviews and phone interviews. It has a new packaged goods product evaluation procedure called COMP and also works on industrial products.

14. *Yankelovich, Skelly, and White/Clancy-Shulman* (Saatchi and Saatchi), performs both consumer and "business to business" research using surveys.

FIGURE 8–10 Diary Panel Format

CODES FOR SPECIAL OFFERS & PRICES

COUPON OFFERS
CODE
01 FROM STORE AD-NEWSPAPER/FLYER
02 FROM MANUFACTURERS NEWSPAPER AD
03 FROM PRIOR PURCHASE OF SAME ITEM
04 FROM PURCHASE OF OTHER PRODUCT
05 RECEIVED IN MAIL
06 FROM MAGAZINE
07 OTHER COUPON OFFER

NON-COUPON OFFERS
CODE
11 CENTS OFF – PRINTED ON PACKAGE
12 STORE SALE
13 MORE OF THE SAME FREE/BONUS SIZE
14 GIFT OR PREMIUM ATTACHED TO PACKAGE
15 DAMAGED OR OPEN CONTAINER
16 OTHER SPECIAL OFFER

NOTE: Extra space below Index. Free Gifts and Samples on Back Cover.

HOT CEREALS BREAKFAST TIPS

- Tell us about the special flavors and fruits included in the package, not those added at the table.
- If the purchase was made primarily for individual family members, be sure to write in the ages of family members. If item was purchased for general family use, check (✓) the appropriate box.
- Tell us whether cereal is instant, quick or regular. Read label.

HOT CEREALS

DATE of PURCHASE | BRAND | MANUFACTURER | HOW MANY OF EACH KIND DID YOU BUY? | TOTAL CASH PAID (do not include taxes) $ C | SPECIAL OFFER/SPECIAL PRICE?: NO (✓) here; SEE CODES ABOVE. ENTER BELOW ALL CODES THAT APPLY; TOTAL CENTS OFF (if any) | WHERE PURCHASED?: NAME of STORE or COMPANY; STORE TYPE: GROCERY OR FOOD; OTHER Write in | WEIGHT (SIZE) SHOWN ON LABEL: NUMBER OF OUNCES OR POUNDS PER CONTAINER | DOES PACKAGE SAY: Check (✓) One: INSTANT, QUICK, REGULAR | HOW PREPARED FOR EATING? Check (✓) One: PREPARED IN BOWL, ONLY ADD HOT LIQUID; COOK ON STOVE: REQUIRES 3 MINUTES OR LESS, REQUIRES 4 – 5 MINUTES, REQUIRES 6 MINUTES OR MORE | KIND (✓) One: OATS, WHEAT, FARINA, OTHER | DOES THE CEREAL INCLUDE ANY SPECIAL FRUITS, FLAVORS OR SPICES ALREADY IN THE CONTAINER?: IF YES, WRITE IN ALL FRUITS, FLAVORS OR SPICES (Copy from label); IF NO Check (✓) here | WHO EATS THIS CEREAL BRAND?: IS THIS CEREAL PURCHASED FOR SPECIFICALLY ONE FAMILY MEMBER? IF YES, write in age and sex; NO ✓; IF PURCHASED FOR MORE THAN ONE FAMILY MEMBER WRITE IN AGES OF ALL WHO USE: FEMALES AGE, MALES AGE | HOW WILL THIS PURCHASE BE USED? Check (✓) One: AS CEREAL, AS BAKING OR COOKING INGREDIENT, BOTH WAYS

READY-TO-EAT BREAKFAST CEREALS
(Including Bran and Wheat Germ)

WEIGHT (Size) SHOWN ON LABEL: NUMBER OF OUNCES OR POUNDS PER CONTAINER, Write In | DOES PACKAGE HAVE SEPARATE SERVING BOXES OR ENVELOPES? Check (✓): YES, NO | KIND SUCH AS: CORN FLAKES, WHEAT FLAKES, BRAN, ASSORTED PACKAGES, ETC. (Copy from label) | IS THERE A SPECIAL FLAVOR OR ARE FRUIT OR NUTS ADDED?: IF YES, WRITE IN FLAVOR OR TYPE OF FRUIT OR NUTS; IF NO (✓) Here | TYPE OF SPECIAL OFFER Check (✓) One: GIFT OR PREMIUM CAME WITH PACKAGE; GIFT OR PREMIUM OFFERED BUT MUST SEND FOR ITEM; COUPON INSIDE PACKAGE; MONEY BACK REFUND OFFER; NO GIFT OR PREMIUM OFFERED | DESCRIBE GIFT IN DETAIL Write In | WHO EATS THIS CEREAL BRAND?: ONE SPECIFIC FAMILY MEMBER? IF YES, write in age and sex; NO ✓; IF PURCHASED FOR MORE THAN ONE FAMILY MEMBER WRITE IN AGE OF ALL WHO USE: FEMALES AGE, MALES AGE

MEAL and SNACK BARS, SQUARES and WAFERS
(Include Breakfast Bars, Granola Bars, Diet Bars, etc.)

MEAL AND SNACK BARS, SQUARES, AND WAFERS DIARY TIPS:

- THESE ITEMS MAY RESEMBLE COOKIE, CANDY, OR CAKE – LIKE BARS OR WAFERS.
- THEY MAY BE EATEN IN PLACE OF (OR ALONG WITH) BREAKFAST OR OTHER MEALS, OR AS A BETWEEN MEAL SNACK.

WEIGHT: NUMBER OF OUNCES PER ITEM OR PACKAGE | NUMBER OF SERVINGS: NUMBER OF IDENTICAL MEALS OR ITEMS IN PACKAGE (FROM LABEL) Write In | KIND OF PRODUCT: SUCH AS BREAKFAST BAR, GRANOLA BAR, DIET BAR, GRANOLA WAFER, ETC. (FROM LABEL) Write In | FLAVOR: SUCH AS CHOCOLATE, PEANUT BUTTER, CINNAMON, RAISIN, CHERRY, ETC. (FROM LABEL) Write In | DOES ITEM HAVE COATING or FILLING?: (✓) IF NO; IF COATED: WHAT FLAVOR? Write In; IF FILLED: WHAT FLAVOR? Write In | PRIMARY EATERS (✓ All that apply): ADULTS-18 & OVER, TEENAGERS-13-17, CHILDREN-UNDER 13 | WHEN WILL YOU SERVE? (✓) all that apply: SNACK; MEAL: BREAKFAST, LUNCH, DINNER | IS IT EATEN PRIMARILY AS A DIET FOOD?: YES, NO

Source: Reprinted with permission of American Shoppers Panel, 1979.

FIGURE 8–10 (concluded)

CODES FOR SPECIAL OFFERS & PRICES

COUPON OFFERS CODE		NON-COUPON OFFERS CODE	
01	FROM STORE AD-NEWSPAPER/FLYER	11	CENTS OFF – PRINTED ON PACKAGE
02	FROM MANUFACTURERS NEWSPAPER AD	12	STORE SALE
03	FROM PRIOR PURCHASE OF SAME ITEM	13	MORE OF THE SAME FREE/BONUS SIZE
04	FROM PURCHASE OF OTHER PRODUCT	14	GIFT OR PREMIUM ATTACHED TO PACKAGE
05	RECEIVED IN MAIL	15	DAMAGED OR OPEN CONTAINER
06	FROM MAGAZINE	16	OTHER SPECIAL OFFER
07	OTHER COUPON OFFER		

COOKING & SALAD OIL, SOLID SHORTENING, LARD & AEROSOL SPRAYS

DATE of PURCHASE	BRAND AS SHOWN ON LABEL	HOW MANY OF EACH KIND DID YOU BUY?	TOTAL CASH PAID (do not include taxes) $	¢	SPECIAL OFFER/SPECIAL PRICE? NO (✓) here	SEE CODES ABOVE. ENTER BELOW ALL CODES THAT APPLY	TOTAL CENTS OFF (if any)	WHERE PURCHASED? NAME of STORE or COMPANY	STORE TYPE: GROCERY OR FOOD	OTHER Write in	WEIGHT (SIZE) SHOWN ON LABEL: NUMBER OF OUNCES, POUNDS, PINTS, OR QUARTS PER CONTAINER	IF SOLID, Check ✓ One: SOLID SHORTENING	LARD	IF OIL, WHAT TYPE IS IT? Read label and check ✓ all that apply: OLIVE	CORN	SUNFLOWER	BUTTERY FLAVOR	SOYBEAN	SAFFLOWER	PEANUT	BLEND	OTHER	CONTAINER TYPE Check (✓) One: BOTTLE	CAN	AEROSOL	OTHER

COFFEE
Ground, Instant, Freeze Dried, Other Types

WEIGHT Shown on Label: NUMBER OF POUNDS AND OUNCES PER CONTAINER	TYPE OF COFFEE (✓) One: GROUND	INSTANT	FREEZE DRIED	WHOLE BEAN	IF GROUND COFFEE TYPE OF GRIND (✓) One: REGULAR OR ALL PURPOSE	DRIP	FINE	ELECTRIC PERCOLATOR	AUTOMATIC DRIP	TYPE OF CONTAINER (✓) All That Apply: GLASS JAR	TIN	BAG	SPECIAL REUSABLE CONTAINER	OTHER	KIND OF COFFEE Check (✓) One: PURE COFFEE	COFFEE MIXED WITH OTHER PRODUCTS (CHICORY, ETC.)	DECAFFEINATED COFFEE	FLAVOR: IF SPECIAL FLAVOR SUCH AS: MOCHA, RUM, ETC. Write In

ENGLISH MUFFINS
Fresh, Refrigerated, or Frozen

STORE TYPE: GROCERY OR FOOD	THRIFT OR DAY OLD	OTHER Write in	WEIGHT (SIZE) Shown On Label: NUMBER OF OUNCES PER PACKAGE	FORM (✓) One: FRESH (On Grocery Shelf)	REFRIGERATED (In Dairy Case)	FROZEN (IN FROZEN FOOD CASE)	NUMBER OF MUFFINS PER PACKAGE	VARIETY/FLAVOR: COPY VARIETY/FLAVOR EXACTLY AS IT APPEARS ON THE PACKAGE, SUCH AS ONION, RAISIN, CINNAMON RAISIN, SOURDOUGH, ETC. If no Variety/Flavor is shown on package, write in "PLAIN"	WHO WILL EAT THIS? (✓) All that Apply: ADULT 18 OR OVER	TEENAGER 13-17	CHILDREN UNDER 13	WHEN IN WEEK WILL IT BE SERVED? (✓) One: WEEKDAY	WEEKEND	BOTH	WHEN WILL YOU SERVE THIS? Check (✓) All that Apply: BREAKFAST	LUNCH	DINNER	SNACK	WITH HAMBURGERS: OUTSIDE GRILL BARBECUE	INDOOR OVEN or TOASTER

NON DAIRY CREAMERS
Including Powdered, Frozen, Liquid and Refrigerated Liquid Creamers, etc.

STORE TYPE: GROCERY OR FOOD	OTHER Write In	WEIGHT: NUMBER OF OUNCES PER ITEM OR CONTAINER	FORM WHEN PURCHASED Check (✓) One or Write In: POWDERED	FROZEN LIQUID	REFRIGERATED LIQUID	OTHER Write In	WHERE WILL IT BE USED? Check (✓) One or Write In: HOME	WORK	SCHOOL	CAMPING/VACATION	OTHER Write In

15. *Walker Research* is known for both personal and mail survey work. It also does trials of drugs, cosmetics, foods, animal products, medical devices, and electronic products.

16. *Chilton Research* conducts election polling as well as custom research for business.

17. *ASI* (IDC Services) specializes in advertising research, in particular on-air commercial testing.

18. *Decision Center* does custom research and copy testing.

19. *Louis Harris and Associates* (Gannett Company) does a large amount of survey work for foundations and governmental agencies.

20. *Opinion Research Corporation* (Arthur D. Little) does custom surveys plus a biweekly survey in which multiple clients participate.

21. *Ehrhart-Babic* performs audits for controlled store tests and test markets plus a periodic National Retail Tracking Index audit of 8,000 stores.

22. *National Analysts* (Booz Allen and Hamilton) does survey research in financial services, information services, pharmaceuticals and medical equipment, utilities, and automotive markets.

23. *Harte-Hanks Marketing Services Group* specializes in media research and phone interviewing.

24. *Mediamark Research, Inc.,* (MRI) provides a syndicated service based on a survey of 20,000 households' use of 450 products and exposure to 250 media sources. A lifestyle segmentation scheme is also available.

25. *Data Development Corporation* specializes in custom research. It also does product and copy testing.

OTHER FIRMS

A sampling of other firms includes:

Starch INRA Hooper, which specializes in magazine readership studies (and also owns Roper, a survey research firm). Starch is best known for its Starch Message Report. This report attempts to measure the impact of ads in magazines and newspapers. Between 100 and 150 men and 100 and 150 women over age 18 are interviewed. Only individuals who have read at least some part of the magazine issue being studied are used as respondents. For each ad studied, respondents are classified in terms of:

1. Nonreader (does not remember reading the ad).
2. Noted reader (remembers reading the ad).
3. Associated reader (remembers the brand or advertiser).
4. Read most (read more than half the ad).

The data are summarized for each individual ad, and also each ad is compared with other ads in the same issue in terms of both raw readership scores and readership/cost ratios.

McCollum / Spielman, which specializes in TV commercial awareness and attitude studies.

J. D. Power, which specializes in car buyer and dealer surveys.

Survey Sampling, which, not surprisingly, specializes in sample design.

MRCA, which specializes in diary panel data. The Menu Census is MRCA's best-known service. Two thousand households are queried about what they typically eat and drink. The households report for a period of 14 days by filling in a daily menu diary, 500 doing so each quarter. The information includes the following:

1. Every food dish served at home plus time of day served.
2. Food eaten away from home.
3. Items added to a dish.
4. How item was served (main dish, dessert, etc.).
5. Who prepared the meal.
6. Who ate the meal.
7. Leftovers.
8. Cooking fats and oils used as frying agents; flour used for dusting.
9. Brand name of packaged products used and type (ready-to-eat, canned, etc.).
10. How the dish was cooked.
11. Recipes used.

In addition to actual food usage and preparation, other data collected include the following:

1. Diet status of household members.
2. Attitudes, interests, and opinions about homemaking, nutrition, etc.
3. Demographic data.

Dun & Bradstreet Business Marketing Services provides a variety of services to industrial markets. The most widely used is the Dun's Market Identifiers (DMI). This service is based on a data bank of over 4 million businesses in the United States and Canada. The companies are grouped according to four-digit SIC codes. For example, there were 7,130 truck rental and leasing firms (SIC code 7513), 2,919 metal door, sash and trim firms (SIC code 3442), and 27 firms mining bauxite and aluminum ore (SIC code 1051).

The main use of this service has been for industrial marketers to estimate market potentials. The data are also used to help define sales territories and to pinpoint particularly good prospects as well as to provide a mailing list of potential customers. For each firm 27 variables are available (Figure 8–11). A customer selects the type of business he or she is interested in (typically described by geographic

FIGURE 8–11 Dun & Bradstreet Basic Marketing Facts

Identification:

1. Name of establishment.
2. D-U-N-S number.
3. D-U-N-S number of headquarters.
4. D-U-N-S number of parent.

Classification:

5. Headquarters.
6. Branch.
7. Subsidiary.
8. Manufacturing or nonmanufacturing location.
9. Single or multiple location.

Location:

10. Street address.
11. Mailing address (if different).
12. Zip code.*
13. City.
14. Country code.
15. SMSA code.†
16. State (or province).
17. Telephone number.
18. Area code.

Products or services:

19. Primary line of business (SIC).
20. Up to five secondary SICs.

Size:

21. Sales volume.
22. Employees at this location.
23. Total employees.

Financial strength:

24. Net worth.‡
25. Credit rating.‡

Other:

26. Year the business started.
27. Chief executive (and title).

* First three digits of zip code denote sectional center.
† Standard metropolitan statistical area.
‡ Credit and net worth data available only to subscribers to the D & B Credit Service at an additional charge.

Source: Dun & Bradstreet, Inc., *Dun's Market Identifiers*, © 1976.

area or SIC code, or both, but sometimes by a variety of measures, such as sales volume or employment size). The customer then receives anything from the name of the businesses which pass the screen to a complete profile of each of the companies based on the 27 available variables, depending on how much he is willing to pay. The majority

FIGURE 8–12

PRODUCED EXCLUSIVELY FOR USE BY
THE ALLIANCE COMPANY

SALES VOLUME
6,500,000.

PRIMARY SIC NO DEFINITION
3552 TEXTILE MACHINERY

LOCATION OF HEADQUARTERS
OUTWAY, N. Y.

NAME & ADDRESS (MAIL ADDR. & TRADE STYLE BELOW LINE)
CASTLE CORP.
549 OLDHAM STREET
OUTWAY, N. Y. 10498

P. O. BOX 3537
OUTWAY, N. Y. 10498

EMPLOYEES HERE
60

SECONDARY SIC NO DEFINITION
3566 SPEED GEAR CHANGERS

PROSPECT'S COUNTY NAME
ERIE

EMPLOYEES TOTAL
110

TERTIARY SIC NO DEFINITION
3562 BALL & ROLLER BEARINGS

PROSPECT'S SMSA NAME
BUFFALO

CONTRACT NAME AND TITLE
R. T. DREWERY, PRESIDENT
FRANKLIN BELL V.P. PRODUCTION
MICHAEL W. WEINSTEIN V.P. FINANCE

TELEPHONE NUMBER
317-435-0041

PARENT NAME
THE OUTWAY COMPANY INC.

YR STARTED
1935

SUB
YES

HQ

PROSPECTS DUNS NO
01-050-0108

MFG
YES

INDUSTRY DYNAMICS

SALES PER EMPLOYEE (IN THOUSANDS)	% CHG # OF EST	% CHG # OF EMP (TOTAL)
$48	+10%	-3%

JOB NO
4321

SEQUENCE NO
00005

LINE OF BUSINESS
MFG IND. MACH

COMPANY AFFILIATION
B & J MACHINERY CORP.

'Does not apply to branches
R Indicates minimum of range
E estimated sales
DUN'S MARKET IDENTIFIERS'
DUN'S MARKETING SERVICES
PRINTED IN U S A

Source: Dun's Marketing Services, "Sales Prospecting Services." Reprinted with permission.

choose the "Sales Prospecting Service" which provides cards as in Figure 8–12.

Audits and Surveys provides, also not surprisingly, auditing and custom survey services.

While this list is by no means complete, it hopefully will give the reader a sense of the type of research available as well as the large number of suppliers. Besides, more complete coverage would have an unduly soporific effect on the author (and, no doubt, the few readers who have struggled to arrive at this point).

SUMMARY

This chapter has attempted to outline some of the major types of services available from suppliers. In using suppliers, it is important to note that performance should be carefully evaluated (Mayer, 1967). Numerous others exist and many are quite specialized. For example, if you sell sporting goods (e.g., jogging shoes), you might use SMART—an audit service focused on sporting good stores, pro shops, etc.

While most of the major suppliers are honest, they are under time and profit pressures, which suggest continued involvement (but not harassment) on the part of the client is generally advisable from a quality control as well as an information perspective. Also, in using suppliers, be careful to check out exactly what is going on—this chapter is not gospel and did not attempt to list the many criticisms each of the services has encountered.

One final point concerns the use of "other brands." A variety of small research shops exist. Some are very competent (e.g., Sawtooth Software, which specializes in computer-designed interviewing and conjoint analysis). The disadvantages of using a small operator are (*a*) they will have to do more subcontracting, (*b*) they usually do not have the same experience base as larger operators, and (*c*) the results are less impressive to the average reader of the report if he or she has never heard of the company. On the other hand, small companies often have novel approaches to problems which may be particularly useful.

In the future, the research business seems destined to move toward increased concentration as well as the use of higher tech methods of data collection (e.g., scanners). Also, the use of sophisticated analytical methods seems to be increasing. (Even marketing brochures of suppliers now casually mention sophisticated statistical procedures.) Finally, the next move for suppliers will be to provide hands-on decision-support programs in response to the information deluge facing managers. NPD has a brochure headlined by a quote from T. S. Eliot: "Where is the knowledge we have lost in the information?" The successful suppliers of the future will not only collect and analyze data but convert it to a form which adds to knowledge rather than overwhelms it.

PROBLEMS

1. Why do you think companies, including big ones like General Foods, hire suppliers rather than gathering and analyzing data themselves?
2. For each of the following problems, suggest the likely research approach(es) and at least two potential suppliers:
   a. Estimating the effect of a proposed TV advertising copy for shampoo.
   b. Estimating eventual sales of a new food product now in test market.
   c. Evaluating the appeal of various hypothetical product designs for a dishwasher.
   d. Understanding how consumers approach the decision to purchase a house.
   e. Studying the use of a new drug by physicians.
   f. Measuring the closeness of competition between two food products.
3. Interpret the following audit share data, assuming you were brand manager for Znarts:

		Brand Share by Store				
Total U.S.	*Brand*	*A & P*	*Grand Finast*	*Other Union*	*Chains*	*Others*
18%	Znarts	12%	18%	17%	21%	16%
25	A	19	28	32	25	28
18	B	21	18	15	20	16
28	C	31	30	26	24	28
4	Other	3	3	5	4	10
5	Private label	15	3	5	6	2
100%						

4. Assume you were monitoring sales in a region and found the following results concerning market share:

	Jan.–Feb. 1978	*Mar.–Apr. 1978*	*May–June 1978*	*July–Aug. 1978*	*Sept.–Oct. 1978*	*Nov.–Dec. 1978*	*Jan.–Feb. 1979*
Audit data	29%	29%	28%	30%	32%	31%	30%
Panel data	29	28	27	28	31	29	33

   a. Is anything happening?
   b. If so, what might be the explanation for the data?

5. Assume you switched suppliers for audit data and overlapped suppliers for one period. The estimated shares were as follows:

	Jan.– Feb. 1978	*Mar.– Apr. 1978*	*May– June 1978*	*July– Aug. 1978*	*Sept.– Oct. 1978*	*Nov.– Dec. 1978*	*Jan.– Feb. 1979*	*Mar.– Apr. 1979*	*Ma Jur 197*
Old supplier	29.2	28.7	26.9	27.3	28.3	27.9	28.1	27.0	—
New supplier	—	—	—	—	—	—	—	29.2	30.

   a. Are we better or worse off than we were one year ago in May–June (and by how much)?
   b. What do you expect to happen to share next period (July–August)?
   c. Suggest how you might estimate what sales in July–August 1978 would have been under the new supplier.

6. Which brand is doing better?

Brand	*Percent of Distribution ACV*	*Sales Units*
A	70%	18,000
B	90	23,000

7. Assume I wanted to know how much a new brand would cannibalize sales of an existing brand. What research methods might be employed?
8. Explain the calculations of reach, frequency, and gross rating points. How accurate do you think the calculations are and what does this accuracy depend on? Under what circumstances would each be the appropriate objective to maximize in setting a media advertising schedule?
9. Given the following breakdown on sterling silver flatware purchase by magazine readership (see table at top of p. 289), how would you go about constructing a magazine advertising schedule?
10. Assess the effect of the 80-cents-off coupon run by Wisk in the second four-week period of the following data compiled by AdTel from their panel:

	Period							
	1	*2*	*3*	*4*	*5*	*6*	*7*	*8*
Total share	4.7	6.4	16.5	10.6	5.4	4.6	4.5	5.8
Deal share	0.7	3.3	11.7	7.9	1.8	0.6	1.2	1.9
Nondeal share	4.0	3.1	4.8	2.7	3.6	4.0	3.3	3.9

AVERAGE ISSUE AUDIENCE
FLATWARE - PLACE SETTINGS PERSONALLY PURCHASED, AMOUNT SPENT AND PURPOSE OF PURCHASE IN LAST YEAR
TOTAL ADULTS

(IN THOUSANDS)

	U.S. TOTAL	AMERICAN BABY	AMERICAN HOME	BARRON'S	BETTER HOMES & GARDENS	BUSINESS WEEK	CAR AND DRIVER	COSMOPOLITAN	ESQUIRE	FAMILY CIRCLE	FAMILY WEEKLY	FIELD & STREAM	FORBES	FORTUNE	GIRL TALK	GLAMOUR
TOTAL	149056	1871	4446	1054	24743	3837	3180	9498	4634	20908	18451	10061	1773	1661	1320	7256
RATING	100.0	1.3	3.0	.7	16.6	2.6	2.1	6.4	3.1	14.0	12.4	6.7	1.2	1.1	.9	4.9
BOUGHT FLATWARE (STERLING, SILVER PLATE, STAINLESS) IN LAST YEAR	11233	**102	591	**39	2590	383	*261	956	544	2242	1648	682	174	154	**107	847
PCT COMP	7.5	5.5	13.3	3.7	10.5	10.0	8.2	10.1	11.7	10.7	8.9	6.8	9.8	9.3	8.1	11.7
INDEX	100	73	177	49	140	133	109	135	156	143	119	91	131	124	108	156
RATING	100.0	.9	5.3	.3	23.1	3.4	2.3	8.5	4.8	20.0	14.7	6.1	1.5	1.4	1.0	7.5
PLACE SETTINGS BOUGHT LESS THAN 8	4088	**50	*260	**9	1001	*95	**139	319	*219	765	654	*226	**54	*104	**39	324
PCT COMP	2.7	2.7	5.8	.9	4.0	2.5	3.4	3.4	4.7	3.7	3.5	2.2	3.0	6.3	3.0	4.5
INDEX	100	100	215	33	148	93	126	126	174	137	130	81	111	233	111	167
RATING	100.0	1.2	6.4	.2	24.5	2.3	2.7	7.8	5.4	18.7	16.0	5.5	1.3	2.5	1.0	7.9
8	5173	**33	*244	**17	1031	*204	**118	454	*227	926	644	345	**65	**36	**50	396
PCT COMP	3.5	1.8	5.5	1.6	4.2	5.3	3.7	4.8	4.9	4.4	3.5	3.4	3.7	2.2	3.8	5.5
INDEX	100	51	157	46	120	151	106	137	140	126	100	97	106	63	109	157
RATING	100.0	.6	4.7	.3	19.9	3.9	2.3	8.8	4.4	17.9	12.4	6.7	1.3	.7	1.0	7.7
9 OR MORE	1972	**18	**87	**13	557	**84	**33	*182	**98	551	*350	**112	**55	**15	**19	**127
PCT COMP	1.3	1.0	2.0	1.2	2.3	2.2	1.0	1.9	2.1	2.6	1.9	1.1	3.1	.9	1.4	1.8
INDEX	100	77	154	92	177	169	77	146	162	200	146	85	238	69	108	138
RATING	100.0	.9	4.4	.7	28.2	4.3	1.7	9.2	5.0	27.9	17.7	5.7	2.8	.8	1.0	6.4
AMOUNT SPENT LESS THAN $40	6889	**66	*288	**8	1427	*189	**191	560	349	1247	901	352	*106	*112	**48	469
PCT COMP	4.6	3.5	6.5	.8	5.8	4.9	6.0	5.9	7.5	6.0	4.9	3.5	6.0	6.7	3.6	6.5
INDEX	100	76	141	17	126	107	130	128	163	130	107	76	130	146	78	141
RATING	100.0	1.0	4.2	.1	20.7	2.7	2.8	8.1	5.1	18.1	13.1	5.1	1.5	1.6	.7	6.8
$40 OR MORE	4343	**36	*303	**31	1163	195	**69	396	*196	995	748	330	*69	*42	**59	378
PCT COMP	2.9	1.9	6.8	2.9	4.7	5.1	2.2	4.2	4.2	4.8	4.1	3.3	3.9	2.5	4.5	5.2
INDEX	100	66	234	100	162	176	76	145	145	166	141	114	134	86	155	179
RATING	100.0	.8	7.0	.7	26.8	4.5	1.6	9.1	4.5	22.9	17.2	7.6	1.6	1.0	1.4	8.7

Source: W. R. Simmons and Associates Research, *1976 / 77, The Study of Selective Markets and the Media Reaching Them,* New York © 1977.

11. Interpret the following data based on a two-year (July 1969–July 1971) AdTel study. The data show percent of Brand Buyers' Total Furniture Polish Volume accounted for by their favorite brand.

Favorite Brand	*Favorite Brand Share of Total Purchases*
Lemon Pledge	41.5%
Regular Pledge	34.4
Favor	34.1
Behold	32.7
Pride	31.1
Jubilee	30.2
Old English	28.8
Endust	22.9

Source: Reprinted with permission from AdTel, inc., New York.

12. Interpret these two tables taken from AdTel results. What other data sources could be used to collect such data?

Deal Loyalty

	Ajax	*Comet*	*Total Scouring Cleanser*
Brand buyers purchasing 50 percent or more of brand volume on deal	27.1%	17.1%	15.9%
Volume accounted for by buyers purchasing 50 percent or more of brand volume on deal	20.1	9.9	11.5
Brand buyers purchasing 80 percent or more of brand volume on deal	17.7	9.1	5.1
Volume accounted for by buyers purchasing 80 percent or more of brand volume on deal	10.6	3.4	2.9

Source: Reprinted with permission from AdTel, Inc., New York.

Combination Buying Patterns among Heavy/Light Brand Buyers of Scouring Cleanser (equivalent units bought during two-year period)

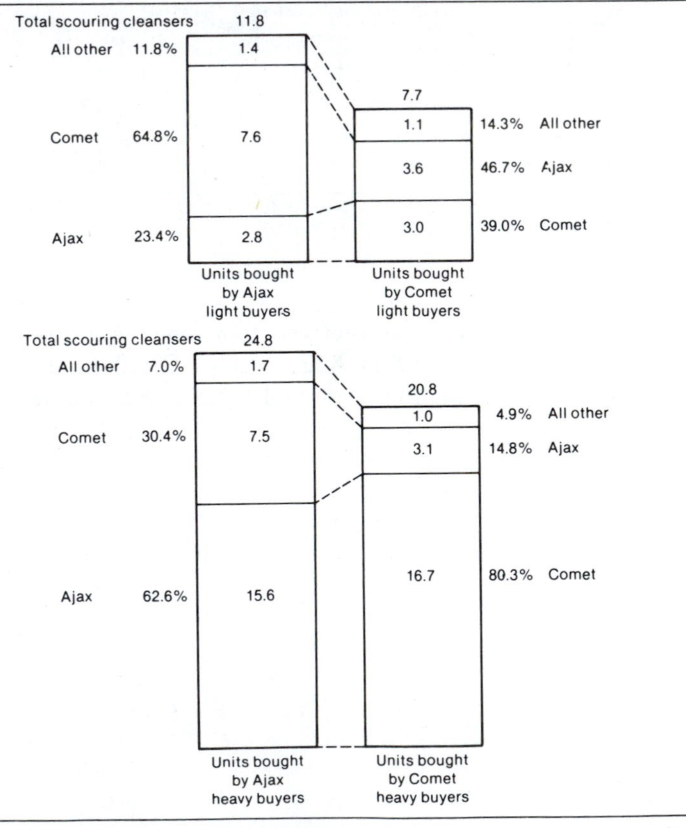

Source: Reprinted with permission from AdTel, Inc., New York.

13. Using scanner data in Kansas City, a company found its share was 14 percent and increasing. Audit data put share at 10 percent and constant. Diary panel indicated share was 9 percent and dropping. Company sales records indicated sales were 150 percent of the level reported by the diary panel. SAMI warehouse withdrawal showed a 12 percent share.
    a. Explain why these measures can differ.
    b. Suggest a logical (as opposed to methodological) explanation for the results.
14. What does this purchase record suggest this consumer is doing?

Actual Purchase Record—Margarine

N.CP. Family: #46141–Product Class: 34–Size: 00100

	Day of Purchase	*Type*	*Units*	*Deal*	*Price*	*Outlet*	*Weight*
Mazola	7–7	02	1	X	$.36	13	1.00
Mazola	8–4	02	1		.43	12	1.00
Imperial	8–8	00	1	X	.36	60	1.00
Gold O'Corn	8–9	02	1		.35	12	1.00
Gold O'Corn	9–19	02	1	X	.35	12	1.00
Nucoa	9–21	00	1		.30	12	1.00
Gold O'Corn	9–22	02	1	X	.35	01	1.00
Miracle	9–26	00	1		.35	12	1.00
Fleischmann's	9–28	02	1	X	.33	12	1.00
Fleischmann's	10–6	02	1	X	.35	12	1.00
Gold O'Corn	10–12	02	1		.35	60	1.00
Gold O'Corn	10–13	02	1		.35	12	1.00
Gold O'Corn	11–2	02	1		.35	12	1.00
Golden Glow	11–15	03	1	X	.35	12	1.00
Gold O'Corn	11–24	02	1		.35	60	1.00
Golden Glow	11–27	03	1	X	.35	12	1.00
Fleischmann's	12–7	02	1	X	.34	12	1.00
Gold O'Corn	12–15	02	1	X	.35	12	1.00
Fyne Spread	12–20	00	2		.35	12	2.00

Source: Market Research Corporation of America, *National Consumer Panel Diary*, p. 1.

BIBLIOGRAPHY

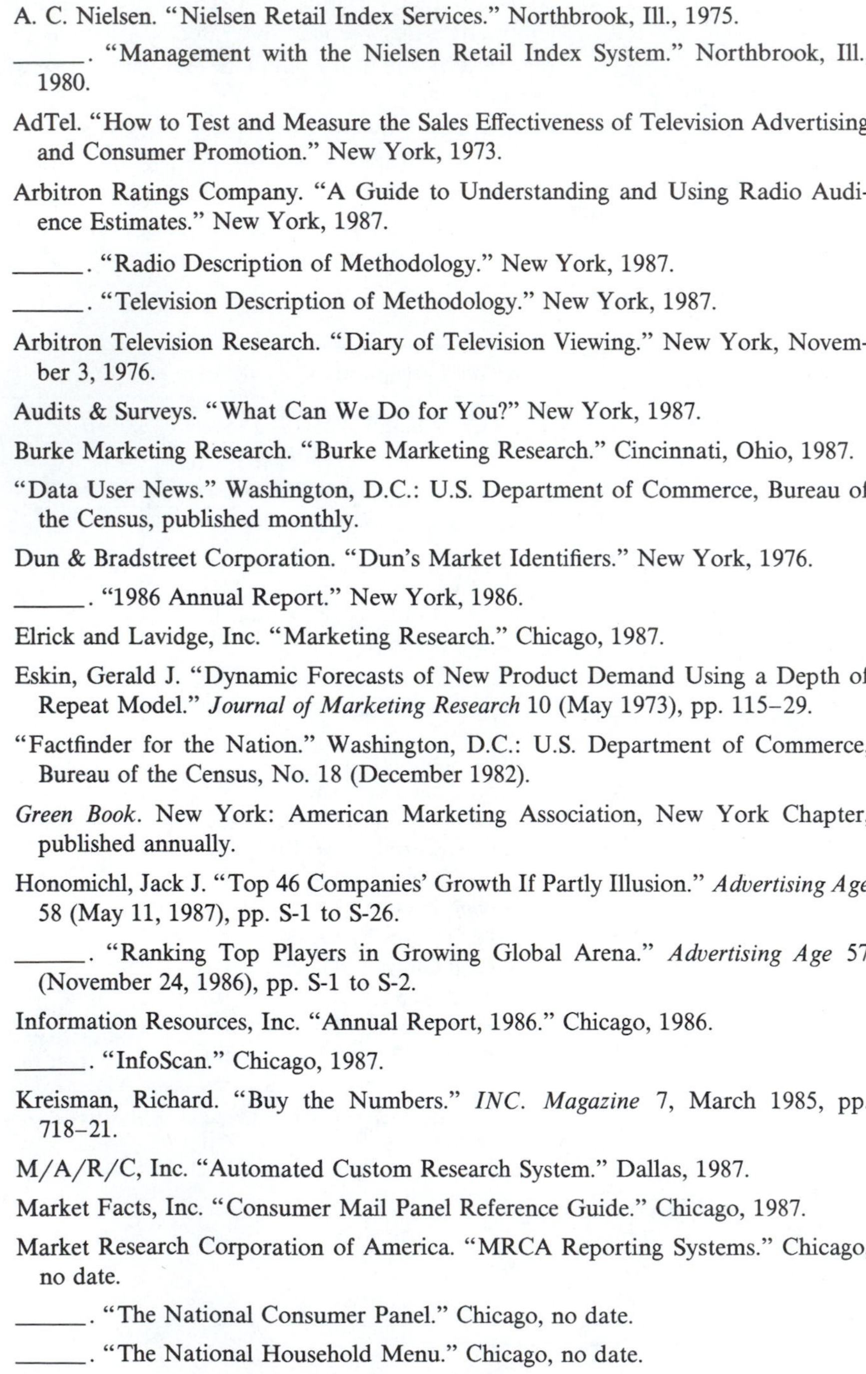

A. C. Nielsen. "Nielsen Retail Index Services." Northbrook, Ill., 1975.

______. "Management with the Nielsen Retail Index System." Northbrook, Ill., 1980.

AdTel. "How to Test and Measure the Sales Effectiveness of Television Advertising and Consumer Promotion." New York, 1973.

Arbitron Ratings Company. "A Guide to Understanding and Using Radio Audience Estimates." New York, 1987.

______. "Radio Description of Methodology." New York, 1987.

______. "Television Description of Methodology." New York, 1987.

Arbitron Television Research. "Diary of Television Viewing." New York, November 3, 1976.

Audits & Surveys. "What Can We Do for You?" New York, 1987.

Burke Marketing Research. "Burke Marketing Research." Cincinnati, Ohio, 1987.

"Data User News." Washington, D.C.: U.S. Department of Commerce, Bureau of the Census, published monthly.

Dun & Bradstreet Corporation. "Dun's Market Identifiers." New York, 1976.

______. "1986 Annual Report." New York, 1986.

Elrick and Lavidge, Inc. "Marketing Research." Chicago, 1987.

Eskin, Gerald J. "Dynamic Forecasts of New Product Demand Using a Depth of Repeat Model." *Journal of Marketing Research* 10 (May 1973), pp. 115–29.

"Factfinder for the Nation." Washington, D.C.: U.S. Department of Commerce, Bureau of the Census, No. 18 (December 1982).

Green Book. New York: American Marketing Association, New York Chapter, published annually.

Honomichl, Jack J. "Top 46 Companies' Growth If Partly Illusion." *Advertising Age* 58 (May 11, 1987), pp. S-1 to S-26.

______. "Ranking Top Players in Growing Global Arena." *Advertising Age* 57 (November 24, 1986), pp. S-1 to S-2.

Information Resources, Inc. "Annual Report, 1986." Chicago, 1986.

______. "InfoScan." Chicago, 1987.

Kreisman, Richard. "Buy the Numbers." *INC. Magazine* 7, March 1985, pp. 718–21.

M/A/R/C, Inc. "Automated Custom Research System." Dallas, 1987.

Market Facts, Inc. "Consumer Mail Panel Reference Guide." Chicago, 1987.

Market Research Corporation of America. "MRCA Reporting Systems." Chicago, no date.

______. "The National Consumer Panel." Chicago, no date.

______. "The National Household Menu." Chicago, no date.

Mayer, Charles S. "Evaluating the Quality of Market Research Contractors." *Journal of Marketing Research* 4 (May 1967), pp. 134–41.

Mediamark Research, Inc. "Mediamark Research." New York, 1987.

NFO Research, Inc. "The NFO Household Sample." New York, 1986–87.

NPD Group. "Tools for Knowledge." Port Washington, N.Y., 1986.

Nielsen Marketing Research. "1986 Nielsen Business Information Manual." New York, 1986.

SAMI/Burke, Inc. "SAMI Reports, 1985." New York, October, 1985.

______. "SAMI Warehouse Withdrawals." New York, 1987.

ScanAmerica. "Redefining the American Television Audience." New York, 1986.

Selling Areas-Marketing, Inc. "The Facts of SAMI, SARDI, and Market Segmentation." New York, 1985.

______. "How to Use SAMI for Making More Effective Sales Presentations." New York, 1983.

Shoemaker, Robert, and Lewis G. Pringle. "Possible Biases in Parameter Estimation with Store Audit Data." *Journal of Marketing Research* 17 (February 1980), pp. 91–96.

Simmons Market Research Bureau, Inc. "Study of Media & Markets." New York, 1987.

Starch INRA Hooper. "Starch Readership Report Scope, Method and Use." Mamaroneck, N.Y., 1987.

Westat, Inc. "Westat." Rockville, Md., 1987.

______. "Crossley Surveys." New York, 1987.

Chapter 9

Sampling in Marketing Research

Sampling is fundamental to most human behavior. When trying a new food, a person will typically eat one or two bites and then form an opinion. Similarly, a reader of this book will often sample several passages in order to make a decision about whether to continue reading. Yet somehow sampling in marketing research has achieved an aura of mystery and even science, due only in part to the quantitative formulations of the effects of employing various sampling procedures. While one approach to making sampling decisions is to call in a high priest (read Ph.D. in statistics), for most common situations a few basics plus some common sense will suffice. The purpose of this chapter is to introduce such basics. More detailed treatments are found in Hansen, Hurwitz, and Madow (1953); Deming (1960); Cochran (1977); Kish (1965); Sudman (1976); and Kalton (1983).

IS A SAMPLE REALLY NEEDED?

Often a researcher will be faced with a situation where someone has suggested that a sample should be taken. Before dashing out to begin interviews, however, a good researcher will do two things. First, the researcher will ask, "What is the problem?" Since the first response will often be something like, "To find out what people think of —," the question will then be repeated until the researcher is satisfied that the "real" problem has been found. For example, "A decision must be made about which of two package designs to use." At this point, the researcher should evaluate whether information gained by sampling anything will help solve the problem. Assuming the conclusion is that a sample would be useful, the researcher then will proceed to the second step—finding out if there is an easier way to solve the problem. While the odds are low that the exact information needed exists, the odds are not so low that information is available which would be "good enough" to at least solve part of the problem. There also may be an easier way than a formal sample to make the decision (e.g., ask someone who seems to have a good head for that type of decision). Only then should the researcher worry about what type of sample to take. (However, political realities within an organization being what they are, if the boss or company policy says "sample," the best response is often "How many?")

THE BASIC ISSUES OF SAMPLE DESIGN

The basic issues of sample design are really twofold. The first is that the sample should be representative of the population of interest in terms of the key responses. A sample does not have to be typical of the general population or even the part of the population under study in terms of other characteristics. While one would expect a sample which had the same average income, age, and so forth as the population of interest to be representative in terms of purchase behavior, it may not be. Conversely, a sample can be very different demographically and still be representative of some types of behavior. Obviously, a sample which is similar to the population under study is, in general, more likely to be representative in terms of key responses than one which is not.

The second basic issue of sampling has to do with nonresponse. Even the best designed sampling plans encounter nonresponse (the person/sample point designated by the sample plan cannot be located or refuses to cooperate) and partial nonresponse (the respondent does not provide complete response to all questions). In the real world, the handling of nonresponses often is much more important than the particular sampling plan chosen.

In order to cover the major aspects of sampling in a systematic way, the remainder of this chapter will proceed to address the following issues:

1. Who is the target population (frame)?
2. What method (process) will be used to elicit responses?
3. How many will be sampled?
4. How will the sampling points be selected?
5. What will be done about nonresponse?

WHO IS THE TARGET POPULATION?

The target population, or frame, is that part of the total population (universe) to which the study is directed. For example, for a company selling automobiles in the United States, the universe could be the entire

U.S. population plus foreign visitors, and the frame might be people aged 18 or over. Alternatively, the focus could be on relatively well-off individuals, and, hence, the target might be those with annual incomes above $50,000. Choice of a target population which is too large leads to the collection of data from people whose responses are meaningless. For example, car preferences of eight-year-olds, assuming they are relatively uninfluential in family auto purchase decisions, are irrelevant. On the other hand, choice of an overly narrow frame will tend to exclude potentially useful responses. For example, focusing on males aged 25 to 49 may cover the majority of a market but will undoubtedly exclude some important segments. The choice of a target population, then, requires balancing between including irrelevant sampling points and excluding relevant ones.

WHAT METHOD WILL BE USED?

Choice of method depends on the type of information desired and, importantly, on the available budget. For example, for a survey a choice must be made between the cost and speed of a phone survey versus the personalization and detail obtainable in personal interviews. Since the advantages of various methods were discussed in some detail in Chapter 4, they will not be discussed further here.

HOW MANY WILL BE SAMPLED?

The decision about how many to sample can be very complex. An entire branch of Bayesian statistics is devoted to this issue (Schlaifer, 1959). For the practical marketing researcher, however, four major considerations are paramount: statistical precision, credibility, company policy (generally accepted practice), and financial constraints.

Statistical Precision

The larger the sample size, the more confident the researcher can be that the results are representative of the things being measured. In general, the precision of a sample is related to the square root of the sample size. (By precision, we mean the level of uncertainty about the value of the construct being measured.) In other words, to double the precision of an estimate, the sample must be four times as large.

Once the sample is drawn, the level of precision is already determined. If the level of precision needed can be specified ahead of time, however, it is possible to determine the minimum required sample size. This sample size refers to the number of usable responses, not to the number of individuals in the target sample (e.g., if you expect a 50 percent response rate, the number in the target sample will be twice the number of usable responses needed, assuming equal response rates in all segments).

It is important to note that the formulas for precision given in this section strictly apply to probability samples only—that is, samples drawn where each member of the population has a known and equal probability of being selected. Also, it is important to recognize that most surveys have multiple items of interest, while the formulas that follow assume there is a single key item. Therefore, this section should be used to provide a general guideline, rather than an absolute answer, to the question of how many must be sampled in the cases where you are interested in measuring a numerical average (e.g., income) or a percent (e.g., the percent who buy a given brand).

Averages. Consider the problem of estimating average income of U.S. households from a sample. As you may recall from statistics (but undoubtedly do not; see Appendix 9–A), the average income generated by the sample ($\bar{x}$) is the best guess of the average income of U.S. households. However, the sample $\bar{x}$ may not exactly equal the population average due to idiosyncracies of the sample. The most accurate statement that can be made is that the true mean is within some range about $\bar{x}$. In order to quantify this range, two important facts are used:

1. The sample mean ($\bar{x}$) is approximately normally distributed.
2. The standard deviation of the sample mean is the standard deviation calculated in the sample divided by the square root of the sample size:

$$s_{\bar{x}} = \frac{s}{\sqrt{n}}$$

Using these two facts, it is possible to construct a range (known to statistics students as a *confidence interval*) into which the true mean will fall with a given level of certainty (known to statistics students as a *confidence level*). This range is given by:

$$\text{Range in which true mean falls} = \text{Sample mean} \pm z_{\alpha}\frac{s}{\sqrt{n}}$$

where z_{α} is a constant drawn from a standard normal table which depends on the level of confidence desired (Figure 9–1). For example, the commonly used 95 percent confidence interval (range in which we are 95 percent sure the true mean falls) is given by

$$\bar{x} \pm 1.96\frac{s}{\sqrt{n}}$$

FIGURE 9–1 Estimating the True Mean from a Sample Mean

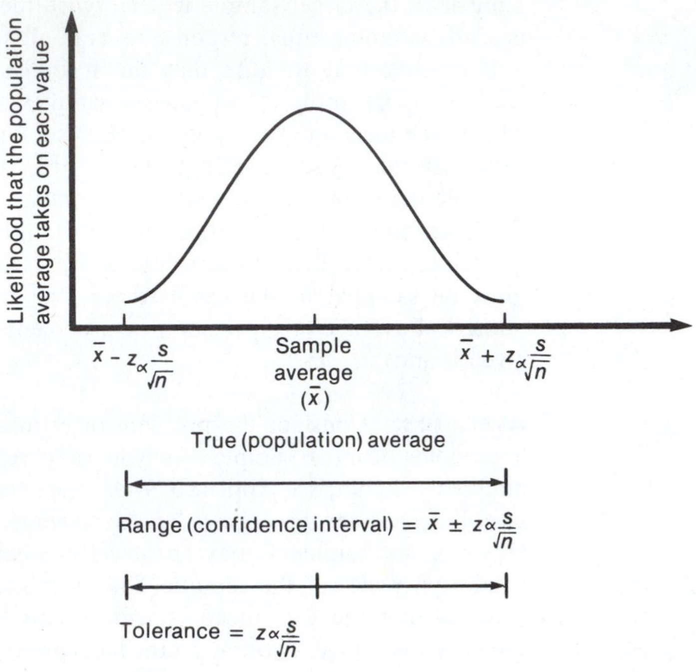

Hence, if we took a sample of 400 households in the United States and measured their average income as $32,172 and the standard deviation of their income as 6,216, the 95 percent confidence interval for true household average income in the United States would be:

$$32{,}172 \pm 1.96\left(\frac{6{,}216}{\sqrt{400}}\right) = 31{,}172 \pm 609$$

$$= \text{between } 31{,}563 \text{ and } 32{,}781$$

A slight variation on this formula can be used to determine necessary sample size in advance. First, decide on an acceptable confidence level. Second, estimate the standard deviation of income(s) in the target population. (In order to be conservative and guarantee the sample size is adequate, make sure this is a generous estimate.) This can be done either objectively (from a prior or special small sample) or subjectively (in other words, a guess). One useful method for estimating the standard deviation is to first estimate the range of the distribution and then divide by 6. Third, establish what is an acceptable "tolerance"—that is, how tightly/accurately you need to measure the variable of interest (e.g., if you need to measure income within $700, that means the tolerance is $700. Notice in Figure 9–1 that the tolerance is half the confidence interval.)

Once you know the confidence level, standard deviation, and tolerance, you can use the following formula:

$$\text{Tolerance} = z_\alpha \frac{s}{\sqrt{n}}$$

$$\text{or } n = \frac{z_\alpha^2 s^2}{(\text{Tolerance})^2} \tag{9.1}$$

For example, assuming s were 3,000, the tolerance acceptable were 100, and we wanted to be 95 percent sure that we would be within the tolerance, we then get:

$$n = \frac{(1.96)^2(3{,}000)^2}{(100)^2}$$

and

$$n = 3{,}457.44 \Rightarrow 3{,}458$$

(We can't sample fractional people, and 3,457 won't give quite enough precision.) Hence, if we sample 3,458 people, we can estimate the mean within ± 100.

In deciding on sample size, a researcher may be interested in relative precision. That is, the desire may be to estimate a quantity within a fixed percent (e.g., 10 percent) of the mean value. In such a case, the tolerance level acceptable would be set equal to 10 percent of the anticipated mean value. Assuming the mean was expected to be about 1,000, this leads to a tolerance level of (.10)(1,000) = 100.

Percents. Assume, for example, we wish to estimate the percent of our accounts who also buy from a major competitor. If we take a sample of our accounts and calculate the percent of them who also buy from the competitor (p), the percent is approximately normally distributed. The percent of our accounts who buy from the competitor can be estimated by a confidence interval:

$$p \pm z_\alpha \sqrt{\frac{p(1-p)}{n}}$$

For example, assume we sample 400 of our 30,000 accounts and find that 32 percent also buy from our competitor. The 95 percent confidence interval for the percent of all our accounts who buy from the competitor is given by:

$$\text{Range of true percent} = \text{Sample percent} \pm z_\alpha \sqrt{\frac{p(1-p)}{n}}$$

$$= 32 \pm 1.96\sqrt{\frac{(32)(68)}{400}}$$

$$= 32 \pm 4.6$$

so the range is from 27.4 percent to 36.6 percent.

As in the case of the mean, this formula can be modified to estimate the necessary sample size in advance. In this case, the required sample size can be derived from the following:

$$n = \frac{z_\alpha^2 p(100-p)}{(\text{Tolerance})^2} \tag{9.2}$$

Assuming we wanted to be accurate within 3 percent at the 95 percent confidence interval, this reduces to:

$$n = \frac{(1.96)^2 p(100-p)}{(3)^2}$$

If we have a prior notion of p, we then proceed to plug it in. If, for example, we thought p were about 10 percent, then we would get:

$$n = \frac{(1.96)^2(10)(90)}{3^2}$$

Therefore

$$n = 384.16 \Rightarrow 385$$

Alternatively, we could adopt the "conservative" procedure and assume p were 50 percent. (This produces the maximum sample size needed for a given tolerance. Actually, any p between .3 and .7 produces fairly similar results.) In this case, we would obtain:

$$n = \frac{(1.96)^2(50)(50)}{3^2}$$

Therefore

$$n = 1{,}067.1 \Rightarrow 1{,}068$$

Notice that this result produces the "magic" sample size of between 1,000 and 1,500, which is characteristic of most national samples. In fact, this size national sample is chosen with just such notions of precision in mind.

Finite Population Correction. Both of the previous procedures apply to a situation where the target population is essentially infinite. This is the case of most consumer goods studies. When the sample gets large in relation to the target population (over 10 percent of its size), however, these formulas will overestimate the required sample. Assuming sample points are expensive, the finite sample size correction factor should be employed. (The correction factor accounts for the fact that when the sample size n approaches the population size N, the uncertainty about the population average drops to zero.) This would convert the formula for sample size when you were interested in measuring an average to:

$$n' = \frac{z_\alpha^2 s^2}{(\text{Tolerance})^2}\left(\frac{N - n'}{N - 1}\right) \tag{9.3}$$

Notice in Formula 9.3 if N is much larger than n', then the $(N - n')/(N - 1)$ term approaches 1 and in effect drops out of the formula, leaving us with Formula 9.1. You may have also noticed that the desired sample size n' now appears on both sides of the equation. The formula to solve for n' now becomes:

$$n' = \frac{\left(\dfrac{z_\alpha^2 s^2}{\text{Tolerance}^2}\right)}{1 + \dfrac{1}{N}\left(\dfrac{z_\alpha^2 s^2}{(\text{Tolerance})^2} - 1\right)} \tag{9.4}$$

Alternatively, you can compute n without the correction factor using (9.1) and then convert to the (smaller) required number n' by:

$$n' = n\left(\frac{N}{N + n - 1}\right).$$

Again, however, unless the sample size is a substantial size of the population (e.g., above 10 percent), the more complex formula makes only a minor adjustment in the suggested sample size and, hence, is typically not used.

Planning for Subsamples. In many if not most studies, a major purpose is to compare various subgroups of the population (e.g., users of our product with users of competitive products). All the formulas for sample size given previously deal with precision at the aggregate level. Hence, while a sample of 1,000 to 1,500 will produce an estimate of a percent within 2 to 3 percentage points of a true value at the aggregate level, it will be much less accurate at the subgroup level. For example, assume there are nine groups in the population. Even if the groups are equal in size (which they rarely are), this leaves only about 150 responses per group, and consequently the 95 percent confidence interval for the fraction in the subgroup is about plus or minus 8 percent (e.g., 42% to 58%).

A sampling plan for studying mustard consumption might consider the following segments:

Family Size	*Income*		
	Under $20,000	*$20,000–$50,000*	*Over $50,000*
1–2			
3–4			
5 or more			

To accurately represent mustard consumption in each of the nine segments would require nine times as many observations as to represent mustard consumption in general. Since the costs of increasing a sample size ninefold are usually prohibitive, samples are generally allocated on a number affordable/number of segments basis. While this is reasonable, it is important to recognize that the ability to profile each of the segments is fairly weak. Put differently, for samples from big populations (e.g., U.S. households), it is usually desirable to have at least 50 to 100 observations per segment.

One useful approach for dealing with subgroups is to see whether they are, in fact, different. If certain groups are not different either importantly (i.e., the numbers are quite similar) or statistically, then the groups may be combined.

Credibility

Since the purpose of gathering data is to provide information someone else will use, it is important to have a credible sample size. Statistical issues aside, 100 is a sine qua non and 1,000 a magic cutoff among many users of research. Since marketing research is part marketing, a wise researcher takes this into account.

Company Policy (Generally Accepted Practice)

Many companies develop a sampling pattern over time which becomes a standard operating procedure. For example, for a new product 200 interviews are gathered in the Albany area during test marketing. While these policies (written or unwritten) usually have a logical basis, a different sample size may be better. Unless the sample is woefully inadequate, however, attempts to change the policy may prove more quixotic than useful (not to mention politically unwise, since your boss may have established the precedent).

Financial Constraints

When all the scientific talk subsides, someone always asks how much money is available for the study. If this is known, the easiest way to calculate the sample size is to take the budget (SP), subtract the fixed costs of the study (EN) plus any dinners, trips, or expenses we can charge to it (D) and then divide by the variable cost of a sample point or interview (IT). This leads to the very scientific formula:

$$n = \frac{SP - EN - D}{IT}$$

This formula is, in reality, every bit as important in determining sample size as those relating to the statistical precision of the results.

SELECTION OF SAMPLE POINTS

In deciding who to sample, one can turn to the supplier or to a firm which specializes in sampling, such as Survey Sampling, Inc. However, even if outside help is used, it is important to have some basic concept of the choices and issues involved. In deciding who will be sampled, the first step often is to see if some list or other organized breakdown (e.g., geographic) of the target population exists. If not, location sampling or random digit dialing are probably the only alternatives. In this section, we assume some list is available when it is required by the sampling procedure.

One commonly drawn distinction in sampling is between probabilistic and purposive samples. In probabilistic samples, each member of the target population has a fixed (often equal) probability of being a member of the target sample. Purposive samples, on the other hand, place greater importance on some segments of the target population and, consequently, are drawn to "overrepresent" these important segments. Some of the major sampling approaches include simple random sampling, *n*th name (systematic) sampling, stratified sampling, universal sampling (census), quota sampling, convenience/location sampling, cluster sampling, and sequential and replicated sampling.

Simple Random Sampling

The best known and most "democratic" form of selecting the sample points to be contacted is random. This method basically assures every individual in the target population an equal chance of being drawn. This is done by using a random number table to generate *n* (the desired number to sample) random numbers between 1 and the number of names on the list. The individuals with numbers corresponding to the random numbers then become the target sample. This method is equivalent to the classic lottery where names are placed in a hat and drawn out randomly.

Random samples have many nice properties. They are not, however, the most efficient (either logically or in a statistical estimation sense) procedure for many situations. For example, a random sample of 20 could contain all nonsmokers, with the resulting average opinions about the dangers of cigarettes seriously distorted. While such inhospitable results are relatively rare, they do occur (especially in small samples). For that reason, some of the subsequent procedures which guarantee the correct proportion of smokers and nonsmokers are sometimes more efficient in representing the target population (i.e., get a closer estimate of the true population value for a given sample size). In spite of this, however, random is a word close to motherhood and apple pie in the ears of many laypersons. One reason for this is that most of the statistical formulas used assume a random sample was taken. For that reason, random samples are often taken (or other sampling plans described as random) to gain credibility for the study. In fact, some researchers have been known to keep drawing random samples until the sample drawn looks good in terms of its characteristics. The resulting sample, however, is obviously neither very efficient in a practical sense nor truly random in a statistical sense.

Consider the data presented in Table 9–1, which represent the 50 states in the United States, with data drawn mainly from the 1974 *Statistical Abstract of the United States*. (The interested reader will note these figures are no longer accurate; but, since they are used in later examples, they are retained so the author doesn't have to redo all his calculations.) To draw a random sample of the states, we could use the first two columns of Appendix A (pp. 861-62). If the number is 00 or 01, we will choose Alabama, if the number is 02 or 03, Alaska, and so forth. The random

TABLE 9–1 Data on the 50 States

	Inc.	*Pop.*	*Popch.*	*Urb.*	*Tax*	*South*	*Govt.*	*Col.*	*Min.*	*For.*	*Mfg.*	*Farm*
1. Alabama	4.6	3.6	0.9	62	383	1	236	136	765	21.8	5.8	1,384
2. Alaska	8.8	0.4	2.9	44	611	0	41	14	448	119.1	0.2	5
3. Arizona	5.3	2.2	4.3	74	582	0	155	132	1,562	18.6	2.4	1,232
4. Arkansas	4.4	2.1	1.8	38	384	1	120	56	407	18.3	3.2	2,547
5. California	6.6	21.2	1.1	93	762	0	1,549	1,312	2,797	42.4	30.7	8,212
6. Colorado	5.8	2.5	2.6	81	587	0	206	130	750	22.5	2.7	2,051
7. Connecticut	6.9	3.1	0.4	89	689	0	171	150	35	2.2	7.9	200
8. Delaware	6.8	0.6	1.1	68	679	0	40	29	5	0.4	1.4	257
9. Florida	5.5	8.4	4.0	84	520	1	511	277	1,044	17.9	6.5	2,029
10. Georgia	5.0	4.9	1.4	57	477	1	352	152	363	25.5	8.6	2,225
11. Hawaii	6.4	0.9	2.2	81	765	0	73	37	42	2.0	0.5	226
12. Idaho	5.0	0.8	2.7	17	479	0	59	34	209	21.6	1.0	1,425
13. Illinois	6.8	11.1	0.1	81	699	0	699	468	1,149	3.8	29.4	6,256
14. Indiana	5.6	5.3	0.4	66	547	0	314	199	441	3.9	16.4	3,250
15. Iowa	5.9	2.9	0.3	37	590	0	186	104	177	2.5	5.6	7,698
16. Kansas	6.0	2.3	0.2	43	573	0	169	111	889	1.3	3.4	4,362
17. Kentucky	4.7	3.4	1.0	47	441	1	197	108	2,563	12.0	6.5	1,587
18. Louisiana	4.7	3.8	0.8	63	496	1	243	141	8,147	15.4	4.8	1,258
19. Maine	4.8	1.1	1.2	24	597	0	68	34	36	17.7	1.6	466
20. Maryland	6.4	4.1	0.8	85	674	1	279	167	173	3.0	5.3	620
21. Massachusetts	6.2	5.8	0.5	87	767	0	377	343	62	3.5	11.7	195
22. Michigan	6.2	9.2	0.6	82	679	0	612	383	1,040	19.3	27.2	1,691
23. Minnesota	5.8	3.9	0.6	63	696	0	263	165	1,026	19.0	6.7	4,754
24. Mississippi	4.0	2.3	1.1	26	425	1	151	78	391	16.9	3.5	1,614
25. Missouri	5.4	4.8	0.3	64	501	0	310	192	691	14.9	9.1	2,849
26. Montana	5.4	0.7	1.4	24	587	0	60	28	575	22.8	0.5	1,154
27. Nebraska	6.2	1.5	0.8	44	543	0	123	64	99	1.0	2.0	4,028
28. Nevada	6.5	0.6	3.7	80	738	0	44	20	258	7.7	0.2	141
29. New Hampshire	5.2	0.8	2.0	36	483	0	55	32	14	5.1	1.5	74
30. New Jersey	6.6	7.3	0.4	93	683	0	453	263	141	2.5	17.8	342
31. New Mexico	4.5	1.1	2.3	34	484	0	97	50	1,942	18.3	0.4	733
32. New York	6.6	18.1	−0.1	89	952	0	1,320	962	441	17.4	33.6	1,525
33. North Carolina	4.8	5.5	1.3	45	461	1	311	182	156	20.6	12.6	2,575
34. North Dakota	5.9	0.6	0.5	12	517	0	60	26	159	0.4	0.3	2,417
35. Ohio	5.9	10.8	0.2	80	497	0	632	370	1,108	6.5	31.2	2,668
36. Oklahoma	5.0	2.7	1.1	56	428	1	206	128	2,124	9.3	2.6	1,994
37. Oregon	5.6	2.3	1.7	61	570	0	173	110	104	30.4	4.3	1,119
38. Pennsylvania	5.9	11.8	0.0	81	615	0	687	423	2,375	17.8	26.8	1,500
39. Rhode Island	5.9	0.9	−0.5	91	606	0	60	59	6	0.4	1.9	25
40. South Carolina	4.5	2.8	1.6	48	422	1	182	110	105	12.5	5.9	907
41. South Dakota	5.0	0.7	0.5	14	519	0	54	27	103	1.7	0.4	1,937
42. Tennessee	4.8	4.2	1.2	63	424	1	265	164	396	13.1	8.8	1,134
43. Texas	5.4	12.2	1.7	78	467	1	779	507	9,999	24.1	17.7	5,968
44. Utah	4.8	1.2	2.5	79	472	0	111	75	952	15.3	1.2	330
45. Vermont	4.9	0.5	1.1	00	661	0	36	28	35	4.4	0.7	218
46. Virginia	5.7	5.0	1.3	66	510	1	352	205	1,058	16.4	6.9	1,031
47. Washington	6.2	3.5	0.7	71	622	0	273	164	144	23.1	5.7	1,766
48. West Virginia	4.8	1.8	0.6	37	450	1	108	67	2,403	12.2	2.9	153
49. Wisconsin	5.6	4.6	0.8	60	696	0	291	180	115	14.9	10.8	2,552
50. Wyoming	5.9	0.4	2.3	00	590	0	33	18	1,437	10.1	0.2	360
Average	5.6	4.2	1.2	58	572	0.3	283	184	1,029	15.1	8.1	1,901

(*continued*)

TABLE 9–1 (*concluded*)

Key to variable names:
Inc.: Average personal income in thousands.
Pop.: Population in millions.
Popch.: Percent change in population over the last 5 years.
Urb.: Percent of population living in metropolitan areas.
Tax: State and local taxes per capita.
South: 1 if yes, 0 if no.
Govt.: Government employees in thousands.
Col.: College enrollment in thousands.
Min.: Mineral production in millions of dollars.
For.: Forest acreage in millions.
Mfg.: Value added by manufacturers in billions of dollars.
Farm: Farm cash receipts in millions of dollars.

numbers and the states selected along with their income and population data will be:

Set	*Random Number*	*State*	*Income*	*Population*
1	56	New Hampshire	5.2	0.8
	83	Tennessee	4.8	4.2
	55	Nevada	6.5	0.6
	47	Mississippi	4.0	2.3
	84	Texas	5.4	12.2
2	08	California	6.6	21.2
	36	Maine	4.8	1.1
	05	Arizona	5.3	2.2
	26	Indiana	5.6	5.3
	42	Michigan	6.2	9.2
3	95	West Virginia	4.8	1.8
	95	(West Virginia)		
	66	North Dakota	5.9	0.6
	17	Florida	5.5	8.4
	03	Alaska	8.8	0.4
	21	Hawaii	6.4	0.9

Notice that, in some sense, even the sample of size 15 does not represent the United States well since *none* of the major northeastern states (New York, Pennsylvania, Connecticut, Massachusetts) are included. Breaking the sample into three sets of five states makes this difference even more noticeable, with set 3 (West Virginia, North Dakota, Florida, Alaska, and Hawaii) especially suspect. In terms of average income and population, the three sets of five differ noticeably both among themselves and from the U.S. average:

	Average Income	*Average Population*
Set 1	5.18	4.02
Set 2	5.70	7.80
Set 3	6.28	2.42
15 states	5.72	4.75
50 states	5.62	4.24

Also, the major differences occur in population due to its relatively greater variability across the states. The point, therefore, is that while, *on average*, random samples will represent a population well, particular random samples and especially small random samples may not represent the general population well at all.

*n*th Name (Systematic) Sampling

An *n*th name sample is, in effect, a poor person's random sample. The procedure generates target sample points by picking an arbitrary starting point and then picking every *n*th person in succession from a list. For example, if I wished to draw a target sample of 30 from a target population of 1,200, I might arbitrarily select the 11th individual (a number between 1 and 40) as a starting point and then individuals 51, 91, 131, . . . , 1,171 as my 30 target sample points.

The major problem with *n*th name procedures occurs if there is a cycle in the data which is related to the interval between respondents. Especially obvious would be an *n*th name sample of daily sales of a particular store. If I took a seventh name sample, I would hit the same day of the week every time. If the day were Sunday and blue laws closed the store on Sundays, this would be especially unfortunate. While such cycles are obvious, occasionally a more subtle relation does appear. Assuming no cyclical problems, however, *n*th name samples turn out to be more efficient (give a more reliable estimate of some variable) than random samples when the underlying list used is logically ordered (e.g., from smallest to largest or by geographic area).

The major advantage of *n*th name sampling is its ease vis-à-vis random sampling. First, a set of random numbers does not have to be generated. Second, these random numbers do not have to be matched with individual respondents. Since some lists contain over 50 million households on computer tapes, matching is inefficient unless the random numbers are arranged in order, and even then the length of time to scan the tapes and pull off the names and addresses or phone numbers of the designated individuals is longer than in an *n*th name sample. For this reason, most consumer mail surveys are based on *n*th name designs.

Returning to the example of the 50 states, one *n*th name sample is states 2, 12, 22, 32, and 42, which turn out to be Alaska, Idaho, Michigan, New York, and Tennessee. While not a perfect sample, it seems to be as useful as any of the three pure random samples in the previous section.

Stratified Sampling

For many studies, the target population can be divided into segments with different characteristics. In this case the information about the segments (strata) can be used to design the sampling plan. Specifically, separate sampling plans can be drawn for each of the stratum. This guarantees that each stratum will be adequately represented, something which random sampling does not. (It is possible, albeit unlikely, for a random sample to fail to contain adequate representation of a particular segment of the population.)

In the example involving states, we might classify states into "big industrial" versus "other" strata. Then drawing randomly from each stratum, we could guarantee representation of each type, something random set 3 failed to provide.

Assuming different samples are drawn from each of k strata, the mean and standard deviation of a variable in the entire target population can then be estimated as follows:

Let N_i = size of the ith stratum
n_i = sample size in the ith stratum
N = size of the total target population
n = total sample size
w_i = weight of the estimate of the ith stratum = $\dfrac{N_i}{N}$
k = number of stratum
s_i = standard deviation in the ith stratum
$\bar{x}_i$ = mean in the ith stratum

Then

$$\bar{x} = \sum_{i=1}^{k} w_i \bar{x}_i \tag{9.5}$$

and

$$s_{\bar{x}} = \sqrt{\sum_{i=1}^{k} w_i^2 s_{\bar{x}_i}^2} = \sqrt{\sum_{i=1}^{k} w_i^2 \frac{s_i^2}{n_i}} \tag{9.6}$$

For proportions, the formulas become

$$p = \sum_{i=1}^{k} w_i p_i \tag{9.7}$$

and

$$s_p = \sqrt{\sum_{i=1}^{k} w_i^2 \frac{p_i(1 - p_i)}{n_i}} \tag{9.8}$$

Stratified sampling actually encompasses two approaches: proportionate (where the number sampled in each stratum is proportional to the size of the stratum) and disproportionate (where the number sampled is based on something other than the sample size).

Proportionate Stratified Sampling. For proportionate stratified sampling, the sample size of each stratum (n_i) is given by the proportion of the population that falls into that stratum (N_i/N). The formula for the standard deviation of the estimate of the mean (Formula 9.6) can be rewritten as:

$$s_{\bar{x}} = \sqrt{\sum \left(\frac{N_i}{N}\right)^2 \frac{s_i^2}{n_i}}$$

And since $n_i = \frac{N_i}{N} \cdot n$

$$s_{\bar{x}} = \sqrt{\frac{\sum w_i s_i^2}{n}}$$

Consider the hypothetical situation (Table 9–2) where beer consumers were divided into four segments (strata) on the basis of demographics. A proportionate sample would be drawn with sample size in each stratum proportional to the size of the sample:

$$n_i = \frac{N_i}{N} \cdot n$$

Hence, a proportionate sample of size 200 would consist of 80, 60, 40, and 20 people, respectively, from the four strata.

Now assume a proportionate sample of 200 were drawn from the target population and the results in Table 9–2 were obtained. Thus, my estimate of overall average beer consumption would be:

$$\begin{aligned}\bar{x} &= .4(20) + (.3)(10) + (.2)(15) + (.1)(6)\\ &= 8 + 3 + 3 + .6\\ &= 14.6\end{aligned}$$

TABLE 9–2 An Example of Proportionate Stratified Sampling

Stratum	*Size of Stratum*	*Stratum Sample Size* $\left(= \frac{N_i}{N} \cdot n\right)$	*Average Beer Consumption*	*Standard Deviation of Beer Consumption*
1	8,000	80	20	4
2	6,000	60	10	4
3	4,000	40	15	5
4	2,000	20	6	2
	20,000	200		

Similarly, using the general Formula 9.6:

$$s_{\bar{x}.} = \sqrt{(.4)^2\frac{4^2}{80} + (.3)^2\frac{4^2}{60} + (.2)^2\frac{5^2}{40} + (.1)^2\frac{2^2}{20}}$$

$$= \sqrt{.032 + .024 + .025 + .002}$$

$$= \sqrt{.083} = .288$$

Alternatively, the shortcut Formula 9.9 gives:

$$s_{\bar{x}} = \sqrt{\frac{.4(4)^2 + .3(4)^2 + .2(5)^2 + .1(2)^2}{200}}$$

$$= \sqrt{\frac{6.4 + 4.8 + 5.0 + .4}{200}}$$

$$= .288$$

Disproportionate Sampling. A proportionate sample is designed to give each individual in the target population an equal chance of being included. Disproportionate samples, on the other hand, are "undemocratic" since some strata are deemed more important than others. A disproportionately large part of the sample is then obtained from these important strata.

The reasons for disproportionate sampling are multiple. One obvious reason is that certain segments of the population may be considered key for marketing strategy, and a researcher will want a relatively large number of sample points in these segments, while at the same time other strata may be sufficiently important potentially that they cannot be totally ignored.

Another reason for disproportionate sampling is that the costs of sampling across strata may be quite different. Therefore, a fixed budget dictates both logically and statistically that a relatively large proportion of the sample be drawn from the relatively cheap-to-question strata.

There also is a statistical reason for sampling disproportionately. If the goal is to produce the most reliable estimate possible, the optimal sample size drawn from each stratum depends on both the size of the stratum and the variance within the stratum. Taking an extreme example, assume one segment exists with average consumption of 3 and standard deviation of 4 and another exists with average consumption of 320 and standard deviation of 0. Here a single observation from the second stratum will produce all the information available from the stratum (the mean of 320) and all other sample points in this stratum will be redundant. In this case, all of the sample except one should be drawn from the first segment if the goal is to produce the minimum variance (most reliable) estimate of the overall mean. (Notice here that it is the uncertainty/standard deviation and not the mean which determines sample allocation.)

The formula for optimal sampling to minimize total variance of the estimate of an average is:

$$n_i = \frac{w_i s_i}{\sum_{i=1}^{k} w_i s_i} \cdot n \tag{9.10}$$

and the resulting standard error of the mean:

$$s_{\bar{x}} = \sqrt{\frac{\left(\sum_{i=1}^{k} w_i s_i\right)^2}{n}} \tag{9.11}$$

(The interested reader can prove this is a special case of the general formula, 9.6).

Returning to our beer (example, that is), we can find the optimal sample allocations as follows:

$$n_1 = \frac{.4(4)}{.4(4) + .3(4) + .2(5) + .1(2)} \cdot 200$$

$$= \frac{1.6}{4.0} \cdot 200$$

$$= 80$$

Similarly we can see:

$$n_2 = 60$$

$$n_3 = 50$$

$$n_4 = 10$$

It is important to notice that this procedure requires knowing the standard deviations in each stratum in advance. Since the true standard deviations are never deducible, we substitute either subjective estimates of the sample or the results of a prior study.

Assuming we now proceeded to take another survey of size 200 according to the disproportionate approach, the results might be as follows:

Strata Size	*Size of Sample*	*Mean*	*Standard Deviation*
8,000	80	20	4
6,000	60	10	4
4,000	50	15	5
2,000	10	6	2

Average beer consumption would then be, as before:

$$\bar{x} = .4(20) + (.3)(10) + (.2)(15) + (.1)(6)$$

$$= 14.6$$

The standard deviation would be:

$$s_{\bar{x}} = \sqrt{\frac{[4(4) + .3(4) + .2(5) + .1(2)]^2}{200}}$$

$$= \sqrt{\frac{4^2}{200}} = \sqrt{.08}$$

$$= .283$$

In this case, the standard deviation is only slightly (less than 2 percent) smaller under the disproportionate sampling plan, a surprisingly typical result. In fact, unless the standard deviations of the strata are very different, disproportionate sampling does very little to the variance estimate. For example, if 50 were sampled from each of the four strata, the standard deviation of the mean would be (assuming the estimates of the mean and standard deviations were unchanged):

$$s_{\bar{x}} = \sqrt{(.4)^2\frac{4^2}{50} + .3^2\frac{4^2}{50} + .2^2\frac{5^2}{50} + .1^2\frac{2^2}{50}}$$

$$s_{\bar{x}} = \sqrt{\frac{5.04}{50}} + \sqrt{.1008}$$

$$= .317$$

The point, therefore, is that, for most marketing surveys, sampling disproportionately to get the most reliable estimates is not very useful. Since it is both troublesome and a source of headaches for certain types of analysis, such "scientific" sampling is rarely employed purely to reduce overall variance in estimates. The major reason for using a stratified sample, therefore, is to ensure adequate representation of key subgroups of the target population.

Stratified samples often are applied to situations where more than one variable serves as a basis for stratification. For example, I might be interested in a consumer product which appealed primarily to middle-aged, high-income consumers. Given a budget which allowed for a sample of 2,000, a stratified sampling plan might look like Table 9–3.

If one were interested in estimating percents via a stratified sample, then the equivalent to Formula 9.10 would be found by replacing s_i with $p_i(1 - p_i)$. Notice here you would tend to allocate sample points to strata with the most uncertainty about the percents, those with p_is close to 50 percent.

Often we are more interested in estimating the total market than in estimating market share. In such cases, one often estimates the average consumption in various strata and then estimates total consumption as the

TABLE 9–3 Stratified Sampling Plan

	Age Group			
Income Level	*Under 30*	*30–50*	*51 and Over*	
Under $20,000	50	50	50	
$20,000–$29,999	50	200	100	
$30,000–$49,999	100	400	100	
$50,000 and over	200	500	200	
				2,000

sum over strata of the number of members in each stratum times the estimated average consumption in each stratum:

$$\text{Total market} = \sum_{\substack{\text{all}\\ \text{strata}}} (\text{Number members of stratum}) \cdot (\text{Average in stratum}) \tag{9.12}$$

The estimated standard deviation for the total market is then (assuming the number in each stratum is known):

$$\text{Standard deviation of total market} = Ns_{\bar{x}} \tag{9.13}$$

As mentioned before, these formulas are only usable if good estimates of standard deviations are available. In attempting to estimate standard deviations subjectively prior to data collection, one can take advantage of the fact that the standard deviations often are proportional to the mean. Since most managers feel more comfortable (and are better at) estimating means than standard deviations, it is possible to get subjective estimates of the means and then to use the means in place of the standard deviations in the formulas for optimal sample allocation in stratified sampling. Alternatively, one can ask for an estimate of the range of values in a stratum and (assuming the item being measured is approximately normally distributed in each stratum) use the range in place of the standard deviation to allocate sample points.

Pragmatically, however, these formulas often give unappealing results (e.g., sampling only three in some strata). Since an implicit goal in most research is to estimate within strata as well as for the population as a whole, the numbers tend to be adjusted, anyway. Consequently, a reasonable approach is to assign more sample points to strata which (*a*) have more members and (*b*) are likely to have a larger average amount of the behavior of interest, while still guaranteeing a "reasonable" sample size in each stratum (e.g., Table 9–3). While doing this subjectively does not guarantee a plan which is optimal statistically, it tends to produce a pretty good plan in terms of statistical efficiency. Moreover, the plan tends to be seen as more reasonable by users of the research.

Universal Sampling (Census)

In most consumer surveys, it is obviously overly expensive to survey all possible customers. In industrial surveys, on the other hand, there may be only 30 to 40 important customers. In these situations, sampling all the important customers is both logically and statistically desirable. It is important to note, however, that a true census is almost never obtained.

Quota Sampling

A quota sample is based on the preconceived notion that certain individual characteristics must be adequately represented if the sample is to be projectable. It is essentially a compromise between a stratified and a convenience sample. For example, a firm may want the opinions of at least 30 housewives between the ages of 40 and 55. Hence, a quota sample may be generated by having the interviewer collect data from the first 30 women who fall into that category who agree to participate. Such a procedure obviously does not make the quota sample as good as a random sample; but it does guarantee that, in terms of some obvious characteristics, the sample will represent the target population. Whether such a sample is a "good enough" approximation to a more elaborate design is an open question. The fact that quota samples are widely used indicates that, for at least some purposes, some relatively intelligent researchers think they are. One of the major uses of quota samples is in maintaining panels. NPD concentrates on variables which relate to expenditures, including household income, household size, employment/occupation/education, as well as market area in balancing its panel.

Convenience / Location Sampling

The cheapest form of sample design is referred to as a *convenience sample*. This translates to using any warm body that is available. It is very popular in academic research (remember reading about samples of 56 college sophomores?) but also has a useful place in "real" research. While their projectability is very questionable, convenience samples are extremely useful for hypothesis generation and initial pilot testing of surveys.

A relatively useful form of convenience sample is a central location study, such as a mall intercept survey. These take advantage of central locations where large numbers of the target population arrive (e.g., shopping malls, trade shows, conventions). Shopping mall studies have become a mainstay of research and are second only to phone surveys in usage rate. By balancing respondents based on demographics or other characteristics (typically with a quota system), these produce reasonable samples at a reasonable cost. In comparing mall intercept with phone interview responses, Bush and Hair (1985) found no difference in the completeness of response (e.g., number of brands mentioned) or in lifestyle responses. By contrast, phone respondents tended to report more socially desirable behaviors (newspaper subscription, voting). Refusals to participate were also higher for the phone survey (37.1 versus 26.5 percent). Not surprisingly, mall respondents tend to visit more stores on a shopping trip. Still, for many purposes, central location sampling is quite useful. (They do not pick up stay-at-homes, however, and hence, for such purposes as assessing direct marketing programs, are not very helpful.)

Cluster Samples

Cluster samples are exactly what the name implies, samples gathered in clusters. The basic motivation for cluster sampling is cost reduction. In the case of personal interviews, giving each interviewer a series of addresses leads to a large amount of travel time, even when an elaborate scheduling mechanism is employed. To cut this travel time (or to draw a sample when no list is available), a common approach is to draw samples in clusters. This means that areas (e.g., blocks), are selected and then interviewers are instructed to get several interviews from the same block. This type of cluster sampling is commonly known as *area sampling*. Cluster samples can also be drawn from lists. An example of this is sampling people whose names begin with a set of randomly selected letters.

Returning to the 50 states example, we could first choose five states in which to sample (e.g., Alaska, Idaho, Michigan, New York, and Tennessee). We could then proceed to choose sample points within each of the states by either taking a census (which would lead some to call this a one-stage cluster sample) or select respondents within each state based on any of the methods discussed here, such as random, *n*th name, convenience, etc. (called a *two-stage cluster sample*). We could also choose a second level of cluster within each of the first-level clusters (e.g., counties within states) and then proceed. In fact, many cluster sampling plans have several stages, such as:

1. Pick states.
2. Pick counties or MSAs within states.
3. Pick census tracts, block groups, or ZIP codes within counties or MSAs.
4. Choose respondents randomly within census tract, etc.

Notice that cluster samples differ from stratified samples, in that in cluster sampling many/most of the strata (e.g., states) are left out of the sampling plan. However, it is quite common to select clusters and then use stratified sampling (e.g., based on income) within each cluster.

Sequential and Replicated Sampling

The sampling plans discussed to this point all assume a single sample is taken. Two alternative approaches are possible.

One is to take several smaller samples simultaneously. Such replicated samples (e.g., 10 samples of 100) have some advantages over a single sample of equal size. They are, however, rarely used in marketing research.

The other alternative sampling approach is sequential. In this method, a small sample is drawn and the results analyzed. If the results are sufficiently clear, a decision is made and the rest of the sample is not drawn. If not, another sample is drawn subsequently. This approach offers potential economy by possibly reducing sample size. (Some of this economy is lost if any economies of scale exist in data collection.) On the other hand, this approach takes longer in calendar time than a one-shot study. Given the usual time pressure and fear of competitive reaction most market researchers face, sequential sampling is also rarely employed.

Sources of Sampling Points

Many of the sample designs require a list of the target population. While this may seem to be a simple requirement, finding a good list is rarely a trivial task. Lists are notorious for containing outdated information. Given the large fraction of people (and businesses) who move each year, this is partially inevitable. Add in copying mistakes, list inflation (the longer the list, the higher price it commands), duplicate names, and less-than-annual updates, and the portion of usable names on many lists drops to 50 percent.

There are several major sources for consumer lists. Telephone directories are a major source. Magazine subscriptions form a well-known basis, as do organization membership lists and credit cards. Professional associations are another common source of lists. Lists are available for just about anything, however, including everyone from agricultural agents to zoologists. Lists of industrial concerns are also legion. Often based on trade association memberships, these lists cover almost every imaginable business. Lists are also available for associations, such as PTAs.

A major focal point for such lists is the Direct Marketing Association. A variety of companies compile "lists of lists" (catalogs). SRDS offers over 55,000 lists of both businesses and consumers. Professional Mailing Lists offers such interesting lists as High School Bowling Coaches (n = 1,400) and Wholesale Confectionery Businesses (n = 4,100). American Business Lists provides lists of 14 million businesses compiled from the Yellow Pages, broken down by SIC code. Zellner's 1988 catalog offers such exciting lists as Abattoirs and Slaughterhouses, Meat Packers (n = 5,700), a list of 21,900 morticians, and a list of 99,000 trial lawyers, all for $40 per 1,000 names.

In keeping track of households, the obvious "best" source is the U.S. census. Since these data are generally unavailable, some number of years out of date, and, according to some, not all that reliable, anyway, especially in rural and ghetto areas, alternatives have been produced.

Several firms have mailing lists of over 50 million households. In addition to addresses, the most recent census data available are so coded into each household that median income and age of the neighborhood, among other variables, are available as a basis for selectively pulling samples. For example, Burke's CMAS (Custom Market Area Sampling) uses a file of 52 million listed telephone residences and draws samples based on geographic and census data at a cost of about 6 cents per mailing label. Reuben H. Donnelley (cousin of R. A. Donnelley of Yellow Pages fame and son of Dun & Bradstreet) maintains a list based on merging a list based on telephone books with the auto registration lists of the various states. (States sell these lists to help defray costs of registration.) Not surprisingly, these lists are more widely used for direct-mail solicitation than for research.

When no list of members of the sampling frame exists, sampling is more difficult. Often the "special population" of interest is geographically clustered in certain segments (e.g., ethnic groups, employees of certain industries, purchasers of products with limited distribution). If a proportion p of the general population falls in a special population (e.g., 10 percent) then, to get a sample from the special population of size n, one can survey n/p people. Such a procedure is inefficient, however, since in many segments very few members of the population of special interest may exist. For that reason, one may want to screen segments and then concentrate sampling on the segments where the population of special interest is located (Sudman, 1985).

For extremely rare populations, sampling is often done via a "snowballing" procedure. Here members of the population are asked to provide the names of other members (referrals), who are then included in the study. Such procedures work when members of the target population know each other and when a quota or cluster, as opposed to a random sample, will suffice.

Screening Questions

Many interviews begin by screening the respondents. The basis of screening may be visual (e.g., age, make of car, whether they just bought a particular product) or verbal (asking a screening question, such as "Do you smoke?"). Screening questions are used to avoid interviewing individuals not in the target population. Only those subjects who "qualify" are then presented with the full survey. Assuming the objective is to interview respondents with incomes over $40,000, a screening questionnaire is typically used. Such a questionnaire may include two or three general questions as a warmup to the key income question. In form, the questions used (in phone survey format) might be:

> Hello, my name is J. R. Sincere from the ZYX Market Research Corporation. I would like to ask you a few questions about your opinion of the economy. Would you please help me?
>
> Before we begin, I need to ask you a few questions to help us classify your responses. Your answers are confidential, and will be used only for tabulation purposes.

S1: How old are you?

______ under 30 ______ 31–40 ______ 41–50 ______ 51–60 ______ over 60

S2: How many people live in your household?____________

S3: What is your total annual household income?

______ under 20,000 ______ 20,000–39,999 ______ 40,000–59,999 ______ 60,000 and over

If the answer to question 3 is 1 or 2, terminate interview. If the answer to question 3 is 3 or 4, continue.

One interesting way to obtain a sample of purchase data is the purchase intercept technique (McIntyre and Bender, 1986). In this method, subjects were observed making a purchase and then immediately interviewed about the current shopping trip. This allows for data collection when the consumer is most likely to be aware of what he or she bought and why (although for low-involvement goods, recall is still pretty limited even 60 seconds after product selection). One study found that only 28 percent of people queried by phone identified the brand bought "most often" as the one which their purchase diaries reported as most often bought (Wind and Lerner, 1979). Hence, using behavior as a screen has some notable advantages.

THE PROBLEM OF NONRESPONSE

Even the best-planned samples of researchers and statisticians generate many nonrespondents. A major issue, therefore, is what bias does this nonresponse bring into the sample? Put differently, how much of the result is attributable to which sample points responded? Obviously, the lower the response rate, the more nervous one tends to become about the representativeness of the sample. While doubling sample size may make the results seem more believable, it does nothing to reduce response bias. Actually, the response bias has two major parts; noncoverage and nonresponse.

Response Bias

Noncoverage. Most methods of obtaining samples have an inherent noncoverage element. Personal interviews are not useful for surveying people in remote areas due to cost and in areas where door-to-door interviews are banned by local ordinance. Mail questionnaires will not be filled out by illiterates or when the occupant moves. Phone questionnaires can only contact those with phones, excluding about 10 percent of U.S. homes.

If phone books are used as the source of names, only those with listed numbers are covered. Since over 40 percent of the phones are unlisted in 13 of the top 100 metropolitan areas (topped by Las Vegas and including 10 in California), this can be a severe problem.

Nonresponse. The nonresponse bias is another problem. This bias can occur when a target subject cannot be found. In addition to those who are *unable to respond*, there are those people who are *not at home*. A classic example of a question which would be biased by the not-at-home problem is, "What do you do during the evening?" Taking an evening survey would yield a disproportionately high "stay at home" response since those who don't stay at home are nonrespondents. A final category of nonresponse is *refusals*. A person may refuse to participate because of fear for personal safety (would you open the door at night for a stranger with a clipboard?), desire to protect privacy, lack of interest in the subject, time pressure, or a general dislike for marketing research or business. Insomuch as any of these nonrespondents would have responded differently to the questions asked, the results are biased. In fact, respondents to mail surveys tend to be somewhat more upscale: younger, richer, and better educated than the total population. Similarly phone surveys initially obtain older, poorer, less-educated, female, rural respondents (Nelson, 1982).

Given the risk of nonresponse bias, the obvious solution is to minimize the nonresponse rate. A plethora of devices are used to increase the response rate. To understand how they work, consider the following typology of potential respondents:

1. Happy to respond (15 percent).
2. Willing to be convinced to respond with modest effort (50 percent).
3. Can be bought at a high price (15 percent).
4. No way to make them respond (10 percent).
5. Not even covered by the process (10 percent).

Looking at this typology, we see that category 1 is pretty much guaranteed. (It is possible to destroy even these respondents, however, with an especially arduous and confusing questionnaire or experiment.) On the other hand, people in categories 4 and 5 are practically unattainable. Given limited budgets, category 3 is usually conceded as well. That means the effort is usually placed on category 2 people. It also means that response rates tend to run from a low of 10 to 20 percent to a high of around 80 percent of the population of interest.

Measurement and reporting of response rate is important for interpreting the results of a study. Still, the calculation of response rate is not always simple. Table 9–4 is taken from a filing with the FCC by MCI to establish cellular mobile phone service in Pittsburgh, Pennsylvania. Households with incomes above a certain minimum were the target population. Phone interviews were done by random digit dialing and the disposition of those

TABLE 9–4 Sample Disposition (Pittsburgh SMSA)

Households:	
a. Completed interviews	796
b. Ineligibles	1,490
c. Eligible refusals	63
d. Undetermined refusals	365
e. Eligible callbacks	257
f. Undetermined callbacks	63
g. Language barriers, ill, etc.	21
h. No answer, busy	621
Nonhouseholds:	
i. Businesses, institutions, etc.	241
j. Nonworking numbers	1,153
Total	5,070

Incidence of eligible households:

$$P_e = (a + c + e)/(a + c + e + b) = 1{,}116/2{,}606 = .428$$

Response rate:

$$RR = \frac{a}{P_e[d + f + (.4)(h)] + a + c + e} = 796/1{,}405 = .57$$

Note: In the response rate formula above, .4 is multiplied by the number of households in the no answer/busy category because the experience of previous surveys has shown that, on the average, only 40 percent of the no answer/busy numbers are actually households.

calls used to give a response rate estimate of 57 percent. However, different approaches are also used. Wiseman and McDonald (1980) surveyed 40 leading marketing and public opinion research firms leading to 29 different formulas for measuring response rate for a given set of results (Table 9–5). Consequently, one is well advised to see how reported response rates are actually calculated.

Determinants of Response Rate

A variety of factors influence the response rate. The effects of those factors under the control of the researcher have been studied extensively, especially in mail surveys (Kanuk and Berenson, 1975; Linsky, 1975; Houston and Ford, 1976; Yu and Cooper, 1983). These factors include interest, length, opening gambit, incentives/bribery, format, advance notice, and callback/follow-up.

Interest. The greater the interest, the lower the portion of nonrespondents. In fact, interest is probably the major determinant of response rate. Unfortunately, interest is largely inherent in the topic (most people would

TABLE 9–5 Response Rate Calculations

The data in these tables are based on the following example, which appeared in the questionnaire with the requests indicated.

For the survey outcomes described below, please indicate the numbers that you would include in the numerator and denominator when calculating response, contact, and completion rate.

Source of Sample: Telephone Directories

Category	*Frequency*
Total numbers dialed	4,175
Disconnected/nonworking number	426
No answer, busy, not at home	1,757
Interviewer reject (language barrier, hard of hearing, etc.)	187
Household refusal	153
Respondent refusal	711
Ineligible respondent	366
Termination by respondent	74
Completed interviews	501

A: *Response Rate Calculations for Telephone-Directory Sample*

Most frequently used definitions:	*Value*	*Freq.*
$\frac{\text{Household refusals + Rejects + Ineligibles + Terminations + Refusals + Completed interviews}}{\text{Total numbers dialed}}$	48%	3
$\frac{\text{Rejects + Ineligibles + Terminations + Refusals + Completed interviews}}{\text{Total numbers dialed}}$	44%	3
$\frac{\text{Completed Interviews}}{\text{Total numbers dialed}}$	12%	3
Sample statistics:		
Mean	35%	
Median	30%	
Minimum	12%	
Maximum	90%	
Standard deviation	19	
Number of different definitions reported	29	

B: *Contact Rate Calculations for Telephone-Directory Sample*

Most frequently used definitions:	*Value*	*Freq.*
$\frac{\text{Household refusals + Rejects + Ineligibles + Terminations + Refusals + Completed interviews}}{\text{Total numbers dialed}}$	48%	20

TABLE 9–5 (*concluded*)

Definition	Value	Freq.
$\frac{\text{Rejects + Ineligibles + Terminations + Refusals + Completed interviews}}{\text{Total numbers dialed}}$	44%	11
$\frac{\text{Household refusals + Rejects + Ineligibles + Terminations + Refusals + Completed interviews}}{\text{Total numbers dialed—(Disconnected/nonworking)}}$	53%	7
Sample statistics:		
Mean	46%	
Median	48%	
Minimum	23%	
Maximum	53%	
Standard deviation	6	
Number of different definitions reported	12	

C: *Completion Rate Calculations for Telephone-Directory Sample*

Most frequently used definitions:	*Value*	*Freq.*
$\frac{\text{Completed interviews}}{\text{Total numbers dialed}}$	12	13
$\frac{\text{Completed interviews}}{\text{Household refusals + Rejects + Ineligibles + Terminations + Refusals + Completed interviews}}$	25%	11
$\frac{\text{Completed interviews}}{\text{Rejects + Ineligibles + Terminations + Refusals + Completed interviews}}$	27%	7
Sample statistics:		
Mean	22%	
Median	25%	
Minimum	12%	
Maximum	61%	
Stand deviation	10	
Number of different definitions reported	13	

Note: A comparison of the most frequently used definitions given in A and B for response and contact rate illustrates the confusion that exists among practitioners with these two terms. The first two definitions listed in both examples are identical. In a survey, the response rate should always be less than or equal to the contact rate, because the former rate takes into account refusals and terminations as well as those not contacted.

Source: Frederick Wiseman and Philip McDonald, "Movement Begins toward Much Needed Response Rate Standards," *Marketing News* 13, January 11, 1980, p. 4.

rather answer a questionnaire about food or sports than about caskets). Nonetheless, tedious surveys dampen enthusiasm, and clever design (use of white space, pictures, etc.) may increase interest.

Length. The longer the interview, questionnaire, or experiment appears to be, the less likely someone is to begin it. The longer it takes to complete, the better chance there is the respondent will either terminate the survey or leave large numbers of questions unanswered. (These partial nonresponses pose a particularly difficult problem for complex forms of data analysis, such as regression analysis.) Length also noticeably increases fatigue. While an amazing number of questions can be asked, typically, a small number will suffice. Still, response rates are remarkably constant for 8- to 20-page questionnaires. The cost of length, then, is more likely to be in lowered respondent quality than lowered response rate.

Opening Gambit. The opening, which invites the individual to participate, is very important. Aside from the appearance of the interviewer or questionnaire (or the sound of the interviewer's voice in the case of phone interviews), the first two or three sentences must grab the prospective respondent much like the beginning of an ad. Appeals of many types are useful, including mercy ("I'm a poor college student..."), self-interest ("your opinion will count"), or duty ("you should express your views"). Guarantees of anonymity are useful in persuading reluctant individuals to participate, as are the "right" credentials for the interviewer or survey company. Use of the person's name to get a personal touch tends to increase the response rate. In mail surveys, better responses are obtained by using a personalized letter, a return envelope with postage paid, and classy format. Other variables, such as the color of the questionnaire, seem to have little effect.

Incentives / Bribery. The most blatant (and expensive) way to increase sample size is to buy respondents. This is commonly done by a monetary inducement. Sometimes this inducement is offered in advance to shame the individual into responding. A typical bribe in mail surveys is to include a small amount of money (the source of my current collection of Susan B. Anthony dollars) when the questionnaire is mailed. This is designed to increase both commitment and response rate, and, even though it is usually a pittance on a per hour basis, it often helps. One problem with bribery is that the respondents may be more likely to give responses they think you want to hear, rather than true answers.

While modest monetary inducements help with some respondents, they do very little for those who can only be bought for a high monetary price. On the other hand, "end around" strategies may prove more successful than monetary rewards. For example, aesthetic appeals (stamps, pictures, etc.) may induce some to participate when money would fail. Similarly, offering to give a small sum to a favorite charity or church is often a successful inducement. In addition, some phenomenal successes have been achieved with gimmick rewards (who could refuse a Mickey Mouse ring or a yo-yo?) In general, however, incentives are not overly effective. In a study involving a survey about durable goods, three versions were sent to groups of 400 each: version one had just a cover letter, version two some mint coins (monetary), and version three some very appealing-looking stamps (aesthetic). Alas, when the results came back, there was essentially no difference in the response rates, and certainly not enough to justify anything except the plain cover letter approach. Another way to provide an incentive is to indicate that those who participate will be included in a lottery with a prize (e.g., color TV, $500). The lottery inducements seem to be quite useful.

Format. Using adequate white space on a mail survey or breaks in a personal interview helps keep the respondent fresh. Essentially, the format must make it easy (both in appearance and in fact) for the respondent to respond.

Advance Notice. To secure cooperation, it is common to give advance notice (by phone, postcard, or letter) of the impending study. This is often useful in increasing both response rate and quality.

Callback / Follow-up. Many individuals in the sample may not be home when the company makes the first attempt to contact a potential respondent. If no subsequent attempt is made to reach the individual, response rates to personal interviewing may dip below 50 percent. If, on the other hand, elaborate callback plans involving six to eight callbacks at different times of the day and week (or follow-up plans, in the case of a mail study) are employed, response rates may reach 80 percent. Two or three callbacks is fairly standard.

Overall. In getting a higher response rate, the cost per completed interview usually increases. This higher response rate is obtained not by magic but by work: more follow-ups, and so forth. The obvious question is, "Where does the trade-off between response rate and the cost/sample size occur?" The answer to this depends on the purpose of the study.

If the researcher is interested in studying the process/psychological phenomena on an individual level, biased samples may suffice. (How else could we publish articles based on 149 college sophomores in course X, etc.?) Similarly the relations among variables as measured by correlations may not be sensitive to modestly biased samples. When a study is interested in estimating levels (e.g., average income), however, nonresponse bias becomes a serious problem. (I would prefer a sample of 500 and a 60 percent response rate to a sample of 800 and a 35 percent response rate *ceteris paribus* for estimating certain facts and opinions.)

The Problem of Dropouts

In any study where the respondents are contacted repeatedly, a certain percentage drop out between waves. This percentage ranges from less than 5 percent in specially designed panels or experiments to 25 percent in some multiwave phone surveys. Since dropouts are typically different in some way from respondents (at least in terms of interest in the study), this makes subsequent analysis difficult. The two basic approaches are to use only those individuals who respond to all waves and waste the other responses or use all the responses and run the risk of measuring the differences between people, rather than changes over time.

Weighting to Account for Nonresponse

There are two basic sources of bias in the final sample. The first is noncoverage by the process of the target population, and the second is the nonrespondents being different in some important way from the respondents. The problem is that, to assess the bias, the characteristics of nonrespondents must be known.

One way to treat the nonresponse bias is to logically (subjectively) adjust the results. Consider, for example, a mail survey which attempted to find a number of people who would be interested in buying a new product. There was a 30 percent response rate, and, of the respondents, 40 percent said they would buy the product. One estimate for the percent of the population who would be interested in buying (which, incidentally, would greatly overstate actual buying) would thus be 40 percent. On the other hand, we could assume that the other 70 percent did not return the survey because they were not interested in the product. In that case, the appropriate estimate would be 40 percent × 30 percent = 12 percent. Actually, the number would probably lie somewhere in between 12 percent and 40 percent, but the 12 percent is likely to be a more accurate estimate than the 40 percent.

One interesting approach for dealing with a nonresponse problem was developed by Politz and Simmons (Politz and Simmons, 1949; Ackoff, 1953). This procedure is designed to estimate results without callbacks and to overcome the not-at-home bias. The procedure accomplishes this by asking respondents to classify themselves in terms of how often they are home (and available to be questioned). Assume, for example, that respondents classified themselves according to three categories: at home 80 percent of the time, 50 percent of the time, and 20 percent of the time. If we call at random, we would expect to get 80 percent of group 1, 50 percent of group 2, and 20 percent of group 3, and hence, overrepresent group 1 respondents. This overrepresentation is corrected by weighting each respondent in the group by the inverse of their likelihood of being home. (That is, weight each group 1 respondent by $1/.8 = 1.25$, each group 2 respondent by $1/.5 = 2$, and each group 3 respondent by $1/.2 = 5$.) This corrects the sample by removing the at-home bias in the original sample. Unfortunately, the accuracy depends on the (somewhat unreliable) self-reported probabilities of being home. While evidence conflicts somewhat, a recent study (Ward, Russick, and Rudelius, 1985) suggested that the costs of and problems with this weighting method may outweigh its benefits.

Another approach to nonresponse is to do a follow-up study on nonrespondents. Hopefully, nonrespondents reached on the second try will be similar to respondents. If the nonrespondents are somehow different, however, the problem is which result to believe. Consider another example, this one a mail survey of 100,000 which had a 20 percent response rate. A subsequent phone follow-up study of 1,500 initial nonrespondents revealed a pattern of slight differences based on 1,000 respondents (a 67 percent response rate). The weights given to the two samples can vary greatly, depending on whether you think the 1,000 respondents to the follow-up represent (*a*) the 70 percent of the individuals who did not respond, (*b*) 67 percent of the 70 percent, or (*c*) just themselves. Assuming the original 20,000 were given weights of 1 each, the respective weights given to the follow-up respondents would be (*a*) 70, (*b*) 46.66, and (*c*) 1. Since the first alternative essentially means the first study was largely worthless, this is very unappealing. In fact, because of the problems in deciding on appropriate weights and the problems of incorporating unequal weights into subsequent analysis, the nonresponse bias is often ignored. Fortunately, as long as the bias is small, this is an acceptable alternative. Still the problem of potential nonresponse bias and how to deal with it makes increasing the response rate a very important goal.

Item Nonresponse

A serious problem in many studies is the tendency of certain data to be missing (e.g., some people refuse to fill out income questions). The nonresponse to particular items makes interpretation of results difficult. When item nonresponse is truly random, it poses no major problems. When nonresponse occurs disproportionately in one category (e.g., high income), however, serious problems arise in estimating the population values based on the sample. A more complete discussion of the handling of this problem occurs in Chapter 10, on coding and editing data.

SAMPLE DESIGN EXAMPLES

Random Digit Dialing

Random digit dialing is often done via a computer-controlled probability sampling system. One example is MARC's TELNO, which is based on a county stratification and uses only working telephone prefixes, increasing "valid" numbers from 35 percent to 70 percent. A working record of individual numbers called with a 3-call-back maximum is shown in Table 9–6. A summary of the results of a callback analysis appears in Table 9–7.

The Literary Digest Poll

One of the classic examples of an unfortunate choice of sample involved the 1936 U.S. presidential election. Prior to the election, *The Literary Digest*, then among the most prestigious magazines in the country, predicted that Alf Landon would beat Franklin Roosevelt. Since FDR beat Landon in a landslide (for you trivia buffs, Landon carried only Maine and Vermont), this prediction seriously damaged the magazine's reputation.

The seeds of the diastrous prediction were sewn in the sampling plan. In the first phase, the magazine mailed cards to 10 million subscribers and asked those who would be willing to participate to return the card along with a phone number. About 2.3 million responded. A random sample was then drawn from those who agreed to participate. The problem was that the sample was biased. The popular version of this story suggests the problem was noncoverage based on the assumption that both subscribers to *The Literary Digest* and those who had telephones tended to be Republicans. Another explanation is that those who responded to the initial request were more committed/interested in the election and those who were interested were Republicans (Bryson, 1976). Whichever is true, it is clear that a response bias affected the results.

The Nutrition Study

The nutrition study previously referred to required that a sample be drawn. Given a budget of about $9,000, this made personal interviews too costly to get a "reasonable" sample size (800 to 1,000). On the other hand, phone interviews were deemed inappropriate because of the length of the survey (it takes about 30 minutes to complete). That left, in order to get broad geographic and demographic coverage, mail.

The choice then boiled down to a choice between a special mail-out and use of a mail panel. The mail panel has inherent bias in its makeup. In the

TABLE 9–6 Callback Analysis

Mon., Mar. 17, 1986, 1:24 p.m.
Shave Cream

Total Numbers in Sample	*Total Numbers Finished*	*Total Numbers Used*	*Total Interviews Completed*	*Total Number of Dialings*	*Average Dialings per Interview*
4232	2357	2890	400	4807	12.02

Dialing Summary

Call Results	*First Call*	*1st Callback*	*2nd Callback*	*3rd Callback*	*4th Callback*	*Total*
Completed	251 (8.7)	92 (8.7)	41 (7.0)	16 (5.9)	0 (.0)	400 (8.3)
Busy	66 (2.3)	30 (2.8)	22 (3.8)	15 (5.5)	0 (.0)	133 (2.8)
No answer	1070 (37.0)	597 (56.3)	364 (62.2)	177 (65.1)	0 (.0)	2208 (45.9)
Disconnect	600 (20.8)	34 (3.2)	7 (1.2)	4 (1.5)	0 (.0)	645 (13.4)
Business	116 (4.0)	55 (5.2)	22 (3.8)	6 (2.2)	0 (.0)	199 (4.1)
Resp. not at home	161 (5.6)	87 (8.2)	53 (9.1)	20 (7.4)	0 (.0)	321 (6.7)
No eligible resp.	113 (3.9)	44 (4.2)	21 (3.6)	10 (3.7)	0 (.0)	188 (3.9)
Refusal	394 (13.6)	101 (9.5)	38 (6.5)	18 (6.6)	0 (.0)	551 (11.5)
Terminate	79 (2.7)	11 (1.0)	9 (1.5)	5 (1.8)	0 (.0)	104 (2.2)
Quota filled	0 (0.0)	0 (0.0)	0 (0.0)	0 (0.0)		58 (0.0)
Other	40 (1.4)	9 (0.8)	8 (1.4)	1 (0.4)	0 (.0)	58 (1.2)
Total	2890 (100.0)	1060 (100.0)	585 (100.0)	272 (100.0)	0 (.0)	4807 (100.0)

Final Disposition of Calls Summary

Call Result	*First Call*	*1st Callback*	*2nd Callback*	*3rd Callback*	*4th Callback*	*Total*
Completed	251 (13.7)	92 (19.4)	41 (13.1)	16 (5.9)	0 (.0)	400 (13.8)
Busy	10 (0.5)	6 (1.3)	4 (1.3)	15 (5.5)	0 (.0)	35 (1.2)
No answer	192 (10.5)	93 (19.6)	149 (47.6)	177 (65.1)	0 (.0)	611 (21.1)
Disconnect	600 (32.8)	34 (7.2)	7 (2.2)	4 (1.5)	0 (.0)	645 (22.3)
Business	116 (6.3)	55 (11.6)	22 (7.0)	6 (2.2)	0 (.0)	199 (6.9)
Resp. not at home	35 (1.9)	30 (6.3)	14 (4.5)	20 (7.4)	0 (.0)	99 (3.4)
No eligible resp.	113 (6.2)	44 (9.3)	21 (6.7)	10 (3.7)	0 (.0)	188 (6.5)
Refusal	394 (21.5)	101 (21.3)	38 (12.1)	18 (6.6)	0 (.0)	551 (19.1)
Terminate	79 (4.3)	11 (2.3)	9 (2.9)	5 (1.8)	0 (.0)	104 (3.6)
Quota filled	0 (0.0)	0 (0.0)	0 (0.0)	0 (0.0)	0 (.0)	0 (0.0)
Other	40 (2.2)	9 (1.9)	8 (2.6)	1 (0.4)	0 (.0)	58 (2.0)
Total	1830 (100.0)	475 (100.0)	313 (100.0)	272 (100.0)	0 (.0)	2890 (100.0)

case of this study, one would expect panel members to be relatively well-organized and systematic shoppers. A "blind" mailout, on the other hand, could be expected to get a relatively low response rate for this eight-page questionnaire. Nonetheless, a university cover letter and a good list could probably achieve as many respondents for the same cost. In this case, however, convenience in terms of both a panel having already collected socioeconomic variables (age, income, etc.) and not having the hassle

TABLE 9–7 Phone Interviewing Record

TELEPHONE HOUSEHOLD						CALL RESULTS						
SEQUENCE	STATE CODE	COUNTY CODE	AREA CODE	PREFIX	SUFFIX	COMPLETE	BUSY	NO ANSWER	DISCONNECT INVALID	BUSINESS NUMBER	NO ELIGIBLE RESPONDENT	REFUSED
80	26	161	313	475	7440			1,2			3	
81	26	125	313	477	4067				1			
82	26	115	313	567	2453		1	2,3,4				
83	26	099	313	725	1400			1,2				3
84	26	125	313	669	4638	1						
85	26	099	313	408	5644					1		
86	26	163	313	255	7478						1	
87	26	163	313	873	2933	4		1,2,3				
88	26	125	313	685	1204					1		
89	26	099	313	673	1510		1	2				
90	26	163	313	751	7792	1						
91	26	099	313	571	9603							1
92	26	099	313	758	5481			1,2,3,4				
93	26	151	313	791	5044	1						
94	26	161	313	622	8537		3	1,2			4	

involved in drawing a special sample (stuffing envelopes, etc.) favored the mail panel. As usual, convenience won out. The survey was mailed to an NFO panel of 1,000, which was designed to match national percentages of age, region, and income. An additional 200 surveys were mailed to the lowest income members of a second panel to increase representation of lower income groups. Four weeks after the initial mailing, 940 question-

TABLE 9–8 Demographic Characteristics of the Nutrition Study Sample (by percent)

	Sample	*U.S.*
Respondent's age:		
Under 30	19.7	23.8
30–39	17.4	20.7
40–49	18.6	20.7
50–59	19.7	18.6
60 and over	24.6	16.6
Household income:		
Under 6,000	32.9	19.3
6,000–9,999	16.9	19.9
10,000–14,999	21.5	25.5
15,000–19,999	13.9	16.7
20,000 and over	14.8	18.6
Family size:		
2	44.1	36.1
3	20.3	21.4
4	17.0	19.7
5 or more	19.6	22.8
Race:		
White	96.8	
Other	3.2	
Population density:		
Rural	18.9	15.3
2,500–49,999	11.4	11.3
50,000–499,999	19.0	18.4
500,000–1,999,999	23.3	24.6
2,000,000 and over	27.3	30.4
Education:		
Attended grade school	3.4	
Grade school graduate	4.5	
Attended high school	14.0	
High school graduate	42.1	
Attended college	19.7	
College graduate	13.4	
Graduate school	2.6	
No answer	0.2	

naires were returned. As is typically done, the sample was described in terms of some basic demographics (Table 9–8). The sampling plan did succeed in increasing low-income respondents but left the sample relatively old and rural. Similarly, blacks were badly underrepresented.

The Ownership and Values Survey

The ownership and values survey data were gathered by a cluster sampling procedure using multiple locations and an intercept method. While that may sound good, what it means is that each of the groups in my research class was required to find 50 "real" respondents. They effectively sampled the New York area and also some other locations (including 15 respondents from Hawaii—students do enjoy vacations). The resulting sample reasonably represents most major income and age categories (Table 9–9). Still, it would be best described as an upscale convenience sample.

TABLE 9–9 Demographic Characteristics of the Durable Ownership and Values Study (n = 796)

Age:	Under 25	15.2%
	25–34	40.6
	35–44	18.8
	45–54	14.2
	55–64	8.2
	65 or over	3.0
Sex:	Male	44.5%
	Female	55.5
Income:	Under $15,000	9.7%
	15,000–24,999	15.6
	25,000–34,999	15.6
	35,000–49,999	18.8
	50,000–99,999	29.8
	100,000 and over	10.2
Marital status:	Single	42.1%
	Married	47.2
	Other	10.7
Dwelling:	Studio apartment	4.9%
	1 BR apartment	18.0
	2 or more BR apt.	27.2
	House	49.9

SUMMARY

This chapter has outlined the most widely used means of obtaining a sample. In doing so, the advantages and disadvantages of each have been briefly discussed. For those who wish to really know about sampling, this chapter is only a sketchy introduction. Anyone who began this chapter hoping to find the "right" way should by now be disillusioned. There is no simple way to make sampling decisions. Cost, reliability of the results, and convenience all affect the choice of a sample design. Often a smaller, more costly sample may be preferred because of lower nonresponse bias or increased interviewer control. Similarly, the method of data collection used and the method of choosing sampling points are closely related. Worrying about statistical niceties will improve the quality of the results as well as making them more credible. Most serious errors in sample design, however, turn out to be errors in logic, not statistics.

PROBLEMS

1. Evaluate the quality of the sample in the nutrition study in Table 9–6.
2. Draw a random sample of 20 from a list of 83 potential respondents. (Hint: Use a table of random numbers.)
3. Assume that a customer's purchase probabilities of buying three brands (A, B, and C) are .7, .2, and .1, respectively.
   a. Using a table of random numbers, simulate 10 purchases.
   b. Simulate 10 more purchases.
   c. How representative are (*a*) and (*b*) of the customer's true purchase behavior?
4. Assume you were to take a sample of five customers for Junk, Inc. Which customers would you sample and why?

Capital District Customer List of Junk, Inc.

	Customer	*Location*	*Age*	*Business Annually*
1.	W. Rockhead	Albany, N.Y.	42	$110,000
2.	S. Blitz	Albany, N.Y.	24	32,000
3.		Albany, N.Y.	35	271,000
4.		Albany, N.Y.	57	14,000
5.		Albany, N.Y.	62	42,000
6.		Albany, N.Y.	21	5,000
7.		Albany, N.Y.	61	19,000
8.		Troy	35	41,000
9.		Troy	27	15,000

(*continued*)

Capital District Customer List of Junk, Inc. (concluded)

Customer	Location	Age	Business Annually
10.	Troy	51	7,000
11.	Troy	23	4,000
12.	Saratoga	34	37,000
13.	Saratoga	41	60,000
14.	Saratoga	42	15,000
15.	Schenectady	51	80,000
16.	Schenectady	41	14,000
17.	Schenectady	27	21,000
18.	Schenectady	35	87,000
19.	Schenectady	61	59,000
20.	Schenectady	58	8,000

5. Assume you had been retained to take a national sample of 1,000 to gauge opinions about food additives. Set up a plan to do personal interviewing.
   a. Use states as a starting point and draw 10 at random.
   b. Use states as a starting point and draw 10 randomly with the probability of inclusion proportional to their population.
   c. Set up a purposive plan for drawing states.
   d. Which of (*a*), (*b*), or (*c*) seems better?
   e. How would you go about sampling within states?
6. Assume you were going to set up a sample of 100 four-year colleges to monitor trends in undergraduate education. Which 100 would you choose?
   a. Assume cooperation is no problem.
   b. Develop a contingency procedure in the event of a refusal.
7. A mail survey produces a 43 percent response rate. Discuss potential nonresponse bias and what could be done to (*a*) assess it and (*b*) correct for it.
8. How many people in the United States must I sample to estimate preference in a two-way presidential race within 1 percent at the 95 percent confidence level?
9. Two years ago average consumption of fingles was 23 slops/slurp. The standard deviation of fingles consumption was .6. I feel that fingle consumption has about doubled and would like a new estimate on it. If I wish to be within .2 slops/slurp, how many people do I need to sample?
10. Assume you were in charge of setting up a panel to monitor introduction of a new breakfast food. How would you proceed? (Hint: Indicate

how you would select panel members and what characteristics you would control for to help insure its representativeness.)

11. Given the following situation:

Group (stratum)	Size	Standard Deviation of Bottles of Beer Consumed
A	2,000	4
B	4,000	1
C	6,000	4
D	8,000	3
E	2,000	2

a. How should I sample 600 people to minimize the variance of the estimate of average beer consumption?

b. If I sample and get the following results:

Group	Sample Size	Average Beer Consumption	Standard Deviation
A	100	5	4.5
B	100	1	.8
C	100	12	4.1
D	200	2	2.9
E	100	3	1.8

(1) What is your estimate of average beer consumption?

(2) What is your standard deviation of this estimate?

12. Two lists of names commonly used for obtaining samples are vehicle registration lists and telephone directory lists.

a. How would you draw a simple random sample from each list?

b. What statistical biases would you expect if your population of interest were all U.S. households?

c. What could you do to reduce these biases?

13. You wish to estimate the average consumption of caviar in the United States by interviewing a sample of 1,000 households drawn from the population of 100 million households. The research firm has proposed a stratified sample, which will "save you money." The firm said it would "oversample the high income and urban areas where the caviar consumption variance is larger." What does this mean? In what sense does it save you money? Why would the firm "oversample" these groups?

14. Recent studies by the Advertising Research Foundation have suggested that about 5 to 10 percent of field interviews are not actually conducted with the respondent, and that another 30 percent of the reported interviews contain substantial inaccuracies. What can be done to reduce the risk of such interviewer "cheating" or "bias"?
15. In assessing the market for a new consumer durable, your boss plans to do a national survey using personal interviews and a probability sample. Discuss the advisability of such a course of action and suggest some feasible alternatives.
16. In 1980, two mail surveys (one about donations, one about the school in general) were taken using alumni lists of a major business school. The response rates were as follows:

	Respondents	*Nonrespondents*
Donation survey:		
Donors	81	154
Nondonors	71	194
General Survey:		
Donors	89	71
Nondonors	89	231

Interpret.

BIBLIOGRAPHY

Ackoff, Russel L. *The Design of Social Research*. Chicago: University of Chicago Press, 1953.

American Business Lists, Inc. *Lists of 14 Million Businesses*. Omaha, Neb., published annually.

Armstrong, J. Scott, and Terry S. Overton. "Estimating Nonresponse Bias in Mail Surveys." *Journal of Marketing Research* 14 (August 1977), pp. 396–402.

Assael, Henry, and John Keon. "Nonsampling versus Sampling Errors in Survey Research." *Journal of Marketing* 46 (Spring 1982), pp. 114–23.

Blair, Edward. "Sampling Issues in Trade Area Maps Drawn from Shopper Surveys." *Journal of Marketing* 47 (Winter 1983), pp. 98–106.

Blair, Johnny, and Ronald Czaja. "Locating a Special Population Using Random Digit Dialing." *Public Opinion Quarterly* 46 (Winter 1982), pp. 585–90.

Brown, Stephen W., and Kenneth A. Coney. "Comments on 'Mail Survey Premiums and Response Bias'." *Journal of Marketing Research* 14 (August 1977), pp. 385–87.

Bryson, Maurice C. "The Literary Digest Poll: Making of a Statistical Myth." *The American Statistician* 30 (November 1976), pp. 184–85.

Bush, Alan J., and Joseph F. Hair, Jr. "An Assessment of the Mall Intercept as a Data Collection Method." *Journal of Marketing Research* 22 (May 1985), pp. 158–67.

Childers, Terry L., and O. C. Ferrell. "Response Rates and Perceived Questionnaire Length in Mail Surveys." *Journal of Marketing Research* 16 (August 1979), pp. 429–31.

Cochran, W. G. *Sampling Techniques*. 3rd ed. New York: John Wiley & Sons, 1977.

Deming, W. E. *Sampling Design in Business Research*. New York: John Wiley & Sons, 1960.

Dutka, Solomon. *Notes on Statistical Sampling for Surveys*. New York: Audits and Surveys, Inc., 1983.

Ferber, Robert. "Research by Convenience." *Journal of Consumer Research* 4 (June 1977), pp. 57–58.

Forsythe, John B. "Obtaining Cooperation in a Survey of Business Executives." *Journal of Marketing Research* 14 (August 1977), pp. 370–73.

Furse, David H., and David W. Stewart. "Monetary Incentives Versus Promised Contribution to Charity: New Evidence on Mail Survey Response." *Journal of Marketing Research* 19 (August 1982), pp. 375–80.

Gates, Roger, and Paul J. Solomon. "Research Using the Mall Intercept: State of the Art." *Journal of Advertising Research* 22 (September/October 1982), pp. 43–49.

Goodstadt, Michael S.; Linda Chung; Reena Kronitz; and Gaynoll Cook. "Mail Survey Response Rates: Their Manipulation and Impact." *Journal of Marketing Research* 14 (August 1977), pp. 391–95.

Grover, Robert M., and Robert L. Kahn. *Surveys by Telephone: A National Comparison with Personal Interviews*. New York: Academic Press, 1979.

Hansen, Morris H.; William N. Hurwitz; and William G. Madow. *Sample Survey Methods and Theory*. Vol. 1. New York: John Wiley & Sons, 1953.

Houston, Michael J., and Neil M. Ford. "Broadening the Scope of Methodological Research on Mail Surveys." *Journal of Marketing Research* 13 (November 1976), pp. 397–402.

Houston, Michael J., and John R. Nevin. "The Effects of Source and Appeal on Mail Survey Response Patterns." *Journal of Marketing Research* 14 (August 1977), pp. 374–78.

Kalton, Graham. "Introduction to Survey Sampling." Quantitative Applications in the Social Sciences Series. Beverly Hills: Sage Publications, 1983.

Kanuk, Leslie, and Conrad Berenson. "Mail Surveys and Response Rates: A Literature Review." *Journal of Marketing Research* 12 (November 1975), pp. 440–53.

Kish, Leslie. *Survey Sampling*. New York: John Wiley & Sons, 1965.

Landon, E. Laird, Jr., and Sharon K. Banks. "Relative Efficiency and Bias of Plus-One Telephone Sampling." *Journal of Marketing Research* 14 (August 1977), pp. 294–99.

Linsky, Arnold S. "Stimulating Responses to Mailed Questionnaires: A Review." *Public Opinion Quarterly* 39 (Spring 1975), pp. 82–101.

Lyons, William, and Robert F. Durant. "Interviewer Costs Associated with the Use of Random Digit Dialing in Large Area Samples." *Journal of Marketing* 44 (Summer 1980), pp. 65–69.

McGinnis, Michael A., and Charles J. Hollon. "Mail Survey Response Rate and Bias: The Effect of Home versus Work Address." *Journal of Marketing Research* 14 (August 1977), pp. 383–84.

McIntyre, Shelby H., and Sherry D. F. G. Bender. "The Purchase Intercept Technique (PIT) in Comparison to Telephone and Mail Surveys." *Journal of Retailing* 62 (Winter, 1986), pp. 364–83.

McKenzie, John. "The Accuracy of Telephone Call Data Collected by Diary Methods." *Journal of Marketing Research* 20 (November 1983), pp. 417–27.

National Business Lists, Inc. *Direct Mail List, Rates and Data*. Skokie, Ill.: Standard Rate and Data Service, Inc., published annually.

Nelson, James E. *The Practice of Marketing Research*. Boston: Kent Publishing, 1982.

O'Rourke, Diane, and Johnny Blair. "Improving Random Respondent Selection in Telephone Surveys." *Journal of Marketing Research* 20 (November 1983), pp. 428–32.

Pessemier, Edgar; Stewart DeBruicker; and Thomas Hustad. "The 1970 Purdue Consumer Behavior Research Project." Lafayette, Ind.: Purdue University, 1971.

Politz, Alfred, and Willard Simmons. "An Attempt to Get the Not-at-Homes into the Sample without Callbacks." *Journal of the American Statistical Association* 49 (March 1949), pp. 9–32.

Professional Mailing Lists. *The Direct Mail Marketing Guide*. New York, published annually.

Reingen, Peter H., and Jerome B. Kernan. "Compliance with an Interview Request: A Foot-in-the Door, Self-Perception Interpretation." *Journal of Marketing Research* 14 (August 1977), pp. 365–69.

Rich, Clyde L. "Is Random Digit Dialing Really Necessary?" *Journal of Marketing Research* 14 (August 1977), pp. 300–5.

Schlaifer, Robert. *Probability and Statistics for Business Decisions*. New York: McGraw-Hill, 1959.

Sudman, Seymour. *Applied Sampling*. New York: Academic Press, 1976.

______. "Efficient Screening Methods for the Sampling of Geographically Clustered Special Populations." *Journal of Marketing Research* 22 (February 1985), pp. 20–29.

Waksberg, Joseph. "Sampling Methods for Random Digit Dialing." *Journal of the American Statistical Association* 73 (March 1978), pp. 40–46.

Walker, Bruce J., and Richard K. Burdick. "Advance Correspondence and Error in Mail Surveys." *Journal of Marketing Research* 14 (August 1977), pp. 379–82.

Ward, James C.; Bertram Russick; and William Rudelius. "A Test of Reducing Callbacks and Not-At-Home Bias in Personal Interviews by Weighting At-Home Respondents."*Journal of Marketing Research* 22 (February 1985), pp. 66–73.

Whitmore, William J. "A Reply on 'Mail Survey Premiums and Response Bias.'" *Journal of Marketing Research* 14 (August 1977), pp. 388–90.

Wind, Yoram, and David Lerner. "On the Measurement of Purchase Data: Surveys versus Purchase Diaries." *Journal of Marketing Research* 16 (February 1979), pp. 39–47.

Wiseman, Frederick, and Philip McDonald. "Movement Begins toward Much Needed Response Rate Standards." *Marketing News* 13 (January 11, 1980), pp. 1, 4.

______. "Noncontact and Refusal Rates in Consumer Telephone Surveys." *Journal of Marketing Research* 16 (November 1979), pp. 478–84.

Wiseman, Frederick; Marianne Schafer; and Richard Schafer. "An Experimental Test of the Effects of a Monetary Incentive on Cooperation Rates and Data Collection Costs in Central-Location Interviewing." *Journal of Marketing Research* 20 (November 1983), pp. 439–42.

Wolfe, Lee M. "Characteristics of Persons With and Without Home Telephones." *Journal of Marketing Research* 16 (August 1979), pp. 421–25.

Yu, Julie, and Harris Cooper. "A Quantitative Review of Research Design Effects on Response Rates to Questionnaires." *Journal of Marketing Research* 20 (February 1983), pp. 36–44.

Zeller, Alvin B., Inc. *Catalog of Mailing Lists*. New York: published annually.

Appendix 9-A

Review of Probability and Statistics

The purpose of this appendix is to briefly summarize/review some basic concepts of probability and statistics.

PROBABILITY

Probability is a concept dealing with the likelihood (degree of certainty) that a series of events will occur. It is quantified on a scale from 0 (meaning the event definitely will not occur) to 1 (meaning the event definitely will occur).

Basic Concept

A basic method for determining the probability an event will occur is to calculate the ratio of the number of ways the event can occur to the number of things that can possibly happen (assuming all things that can happen are equally likely):

$$P(A) = \frac{N(A)}{N(S)} = \frac{\text{Number of ``favorable'' outcomes}}{\text{Number of possible outcomes}} \qquad (9A.1)$$

Hence, if I put five different names into a hat, the probability that I pull out a particular name is $\frac{1}{5}$. Similarly, if I draw a card from a standard deck of 52 cards, the probability the card is a heart is $\frac{13}{52} = \frac{1}{4}$.

Some Simple Formulas

In computing probabilities involving more than one result, the following three rules are particularly useful:

1. *Probability of either of two events occurring.*

$$P(\text{either } A \text{ or } B) = P(A) + P(B) - P(\text{both } A \text{ and } B)$$

or

$$P(A \cup B) = P(A) + P(B) - P(A \cap B) \qquad (9A.2)$$

For example, assume I were interested in the probability that a card drawn from a standard deck of 52 was either a heart or an ace. I could solve the problem brute force by counting the cards which satisfy the requirement (the 13 hearts plus the ace of spades, clubs, and diamonds for a total of 16) and getting the probability from Formula 9A.1:

$$P(\text{heart or ace}) = \frac{N(\text{hearts or aces})}{N(\text{cards})} = \frac{16}{52}$$

Alternatively, I could use equation (9A.2):

$$P(\text{heart or ace}) = P(\text{heart}) + P(\text{ace}) - P(\text{ace of hearts})$$

$$= \frac{13}{52} + \frac{4}{52} - \frac{1}{52} = \frac{16}{52}$$

The logic of equation (9A.2) can best be seen from Figure 9A–1, called a *Venn diagram*: If I simply add the areas of A and B, I will double-count the area in both A and B. In the previous example, this would count the ace of hearts twice. Hence, to get the area inside A or B, I add the area in A to the area in B and then subtract the overlap between A and B.

When $P(A \cap B)$ is 0, A and B have no overlap and are said to be mutually exclusive. An example of this is 10s and jacks. The $P(10 \cap \text{jack}) = 0$.

2. *Probability of two events both occurring.*

$$P(A \cap B) = P(A)[P(B|A)] \qquad (9A.3)$$

This is the basic method for calculating the probability of a sequence of events occurring. In words, it says that the probability of getting a Ph.D. is:

$$P(\text{Ph.D.}) = P(\text{finish high school})[P(\text{finish college}|\text{finished high school})][P(\text{finish Ph.D.}|\text{finish college})]$$

FIGURE 9A–1 Venn Diagram of Two Possible Events

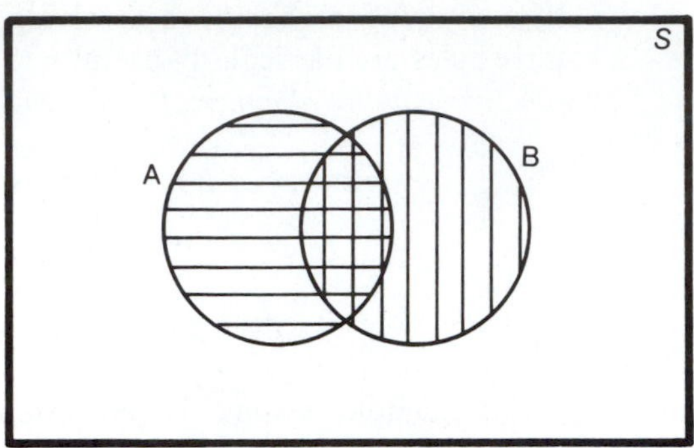

$P(B|A)$ means the probability B will occur, given that A has occurred. When $P(B|A) = P(B)$, then A and B are said to be independent. (Put differently, this means that knowing A occurred gives no information about whether B will occur.) Consider the following two examples:

$$P(\text{ace}|\text{heart})$$

$$P(\text{ace}|\text{“honor”—a 10, jack, queen, king, or ace})$$

In the first case, $P(\text{ace}|\text{heart}) = \frac{1}{13}$, since one of the 13 hearts is the ace. Here aces and hearts are independent. In the second case, however, $P(\text{ace}|\text{“honor”}) = \frac{4}{20} = \frac{1}{5} \neq \frac{1}{13}$, and, hence, aces and honors are clearly not independent.

3. *Conditional probability.* There is also a variation on (9A.3), known as conditional probability:

$$P(B|A) = \frac{P(A \cap B)}{P(A)} \tag{9A.4}$$

This is simply a rewrite of (9A.3). It says, for example, that:

$$P(\text{ace}|\text{heart}) = \frac{P(\text{ace} \cap \text{heart})}{P(\text{heart})} = \frac{\frac{1}{52}}{\frac{13}{52}} = \frac{1}{13}$$

Methods for Calculating the Number of Ways an Event Can Occur. In calculating the number of ways events can occur, the following formulas are sometimes useful. The formulas use two definitions:

$$\textit{Definition}: a! = (a)(a-1)(a-2)\cdots(2)(1) \tag{9A.5}$$

This is called "a factorial." For example, 5! = (5)(4)(3)(2)(1) = 120.

$$\textit{Definition}: \quad \binom{a}{b} = \frac{a!}{(a-b)!b!} \tag{9A.6}$$

For example,

$$\binom{5}{3} = \frac{5!}{2!3!} = \frac{(5)(4)(3)(2)(1)}{[(2)(1)][(3)(2)(1)]} = 10$$

Assume there are M possible outcomes. The question often arises: How many distinct ways can I draw a sample of size N? This problem depends on how I define distinct and how I draw the sample.

Case A. *Sample drawn with replacement, order matters:*

$$M^N \tag{9A.7}$$

In this approach, I draw an outcome from my "hat" with M outcomes in it, then replace the outcome. I also will agree that getting A, B on the first two draws is *not* the same as getting B, A (order matters). In this case, there are M possible outcomes on the first draw, M more on the second, and so forth, so the possible outcomes become:

$$(M)(M)(M)\cdots(M) = M^N$$

As an example, consider drawing three cards with replacement from a deck of 52. The number of possible outcomes is (52)(52)(52) = 52^3.

Case B. *Sample drawn without replacement, order matters:*

$$\frac{M!}{(M-N)!} \tag{9A.8}$$

In this case, I do not replace the item each time I draw an outcome. Hence, there are M possible choices for the first draw, $(M-1)$ possible choices for the second draw, $(M-2)$ possible choices for the third draw, and so forth. Hence, the number of possible draws is:

$$(M)(M-1)(M-2)\cdots(M-N+1) = \frac{M!}{(M-N)!}$$

This case is often called *permutations*. Now the number of ways I can draw three cards from a deck of 52 is (52)(51)(50) = 132,600.

Case C. *Sample drawn without replacement; order does not matter:*

$$\frac{M!}{(M-N)!N!} \tag{9A.9}$$

In this case, I assume that, not only do I not replace the drawn outcome in the "hat," but I also don't care in what order the cards come (the case in five-card draw poker).

To see the logic of this, consider the draw: $AH, 2D, 2C$. This is one of the (52)(51)(50) possible draws. However, $AH, 2D, 3C$ is (if order doesn't matter) indistinguishable from:

$$AH, 3C, 2D$$

$$3C, AH, 2D$$

$$3C, 2D, AH$$

$$2D, AH, 3C$$

$$2D, 3C, AH$$

Hence, there are six ways each of the possible outcomes can be rearranged. This means that we have overcounted by a factor of 6 and the "answer" should be:

$$\frac{(52)(51)(50)}{6} = \frac{52!}{49!(3!)} = \binom{52}{3}$$

This case is often called *combinations*.

Using these formats, we can generate two basic probability procedures. Assume there are g distinct outcomes in a population of size S:

Outcome	*Number of Events*	*Sample Result*
1	N_1	n_1
2	N_2	n_2
.	.	.
.	.	.
.	.	.
g	$\frac{N_g}{N}$	$\frac{n_g}{n}$

The probability of a sample result with N_1 outcomes of the first type, N_2 of the second type, and so forth, can be found from two formulas:

With replacement: Multinomial—

$$P(n_1, n_2, \ldots, n_g) = \frac{n!}{n_1!, n_2!, \ldots, n_g!} P_1^{n_1} P_2^{n_2} \cdots P_g^{n_g} \qquad (9A.10)$$

where

$$P_1 = \frac{N_1}{N}$$

$$P_2 = \frac{N_2}{N}$$

$$\vdots$$

$$P_g = \frac{N_g}{N}$$

Without replacement: Hypergeometric—

$$P(n_1, n_2, \ldots, n_g) = \frac{\binom{N_1}{n_1}\binom{N_2}{n_2}\cdots\binom{N_g}{n_g}}{\binom{N}{n}} \qquad (9A.11)$$

PROBABILITY DISTRIBUTION

A probability distribution indicates the relative likelihood of different possible outcomes. When there are a discrete (finite, manageable) number of possible outcomes (e.g., number of days it rains this week), the distribu-

FIGURE 9A–2 Discrete Probability Distribution

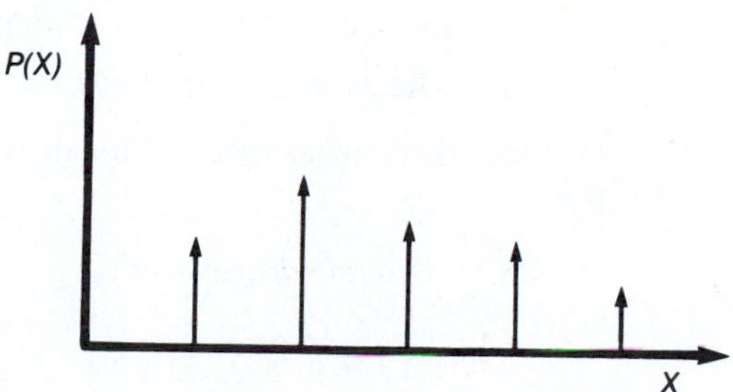

FIGURE 9A–3 Continuous Probability Distribution

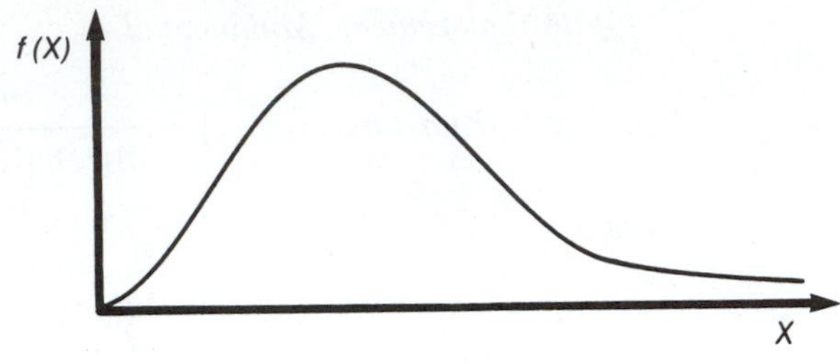

tion attaches a probability to each of the possible outcomes, as is indicated in Figure 9A–2. Here,

$$\sum_{\substack{\text{all}\\\text{outcomes}}} P(X) = 1$$

When the outcomes are continuous (e.g., the diameter of a part can be infinitely many sizes), the relative likelihood of different outcomes is given by a density function (Figure 9A–3). Here $_{-\infty}\int^{+\infty} f(X)\,dX = 1$. Also here, the probability of a particular result (e.g., $P(X) = 3.12471$) is 0.

SUMMARY STATISTICS

The most comprehensive information about possible occurrences is contained in the complete probability distribution or density function. Since these can be fairly unwieldy, however, measures are calculated which summarize the information contained in the distribution. The first group of measures concerns the notion of a "typical" response. Three measures are commonly calculated:

Mode: The most likely result.

Median: The result which lies exactly at the middle of the distribution (i.e., the score of the 49th student from a class of 99).

Mean: The average (expected) result.

Of these three measures, the mean is the most widely used. It is calculated by:

Discrete distribution	*Continuous distribution*	
$E(X) = \mu = \sum_{\substack{\text{all}\\X}} XP(X)$	$\mu = \int_{-\infty}^{+\infty} Xf(X)\,dX$	(9A.12)

FIGURE 9A–4 Skewness

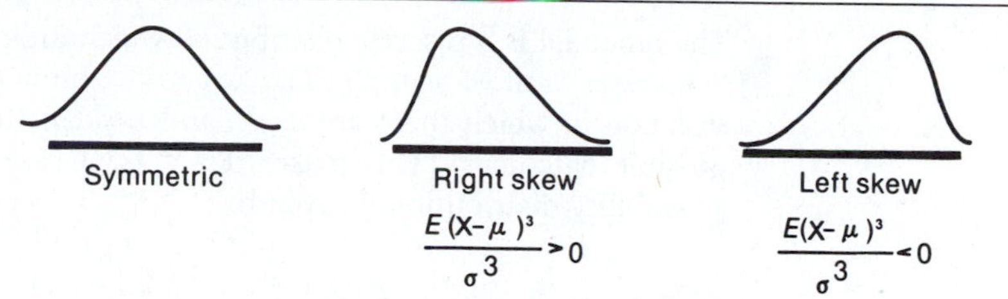

The second group of measures deals with the dispersion/"fatness" of the distribution. These measures indicate the uncertainty inherent in the outcome. The most typical measure is the variance (σ^2):

Discrete distribution *Continuous distribution*

$$E(X-\mu)^2 = \sigma^2 \qquad\qquad \sigma^2 = \int_{-\infty}^{+\infty} (X-\mu)^2 f(X)\,dx$$

$$= \sum_{\text{all } X}((X-\mu)^2 P(X)) \tag{9A.13}$$

$$= \Sigma X^2 P(X) - \mu^2$$

$$= E(X^2) - \mu^2$$

(N.B.: Variance $(a + bX) = b^2$ (variance X).) Actually, the square root of the variance, $\sigma = \sqrt{\sigma^2}$, is the most commonly used measure of dispersion. This is called the *standard deviation*.

Two other measures are occasionally calculated. These are as follows:

Skewness. $\dfrac{E(X-\mu)^3}{\sigma^3}$. If this equals zero, then the distribution is said to be symmetric (see Figure 9A–4).

Kurtosis. $\dfrac{E(X-\mu)^4}{\sigma^4}$. This is a measure of the height of the peak in a distribution, and is rarely used.

COMMONLY USED DISTRIBUTIONS

While an immense number of distributions exist, a small number turn out to be especially useful in marketing research. Some of these are the binomial, Poisson, normal (Gaussian), Student's t, chi-square, and F distributions.

Binomial

The binomial is a discrete distribution which indicates the probability of X "successes" out of n trials. The key to the binomial is that it represents a situation in which there are (a) n independent trials and (b) exactly two possible outcomes. (This makes it a special case of the multinomial.) Its probability distribution is given by:

$$P(X) = \binom{n}{X} p^X (1-p)^{n-X}$$

where p = probability of success on a given trial. Also:

$$\mu = np$$
$$\sigma = \sqrt{np(1-p)}$$

It turns out that the binomial can be approximated by other distributions:

1. For p close to 0 or 1, the binomial is similar to the Poisson.
2. For p close to .5 or for large n, the binomial is close to the normal.

Poisson

Another major discrete distribution is the Poisson. It is often viewed as the distribution of the number of successes in a given time period. Its density function is given by:

$$P(X) = \frac{\lambda^X e^{-\lambda}}{X!}$$

Its mean and standard deviation are:

$$\mu = \lambda$$
$$\sigma = \sqrt{\lambda}$$

For large λ, the poisson becomes approximately normal.

Normal (Gaussian)

The normal distribution is the standard bell-shaped symmetric curve which recurs in many situations. It is continuous, and its density function is given by:

$$f(X) = \frac{1}{\sqrt{2\pi}\,\sigma} e^{-\frac{1}{2}\left(\frac{X-\mu}{\sigma}\right)^2}$$

FIGURE 9A–5 Standard Normal Distribution

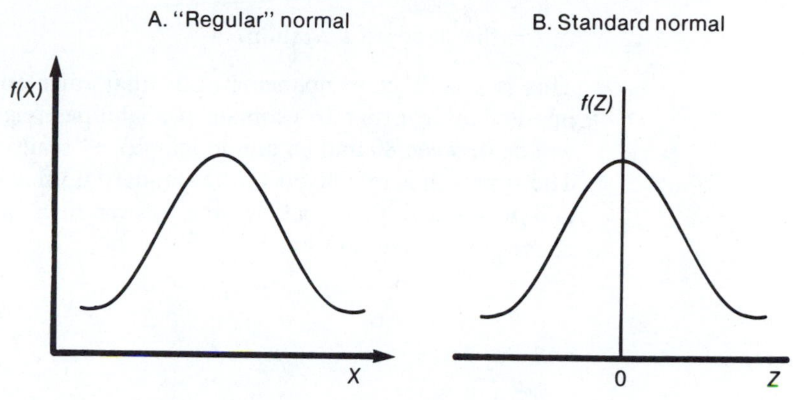

FIGURE 9A–6 Example of Conversion to Standard Normal

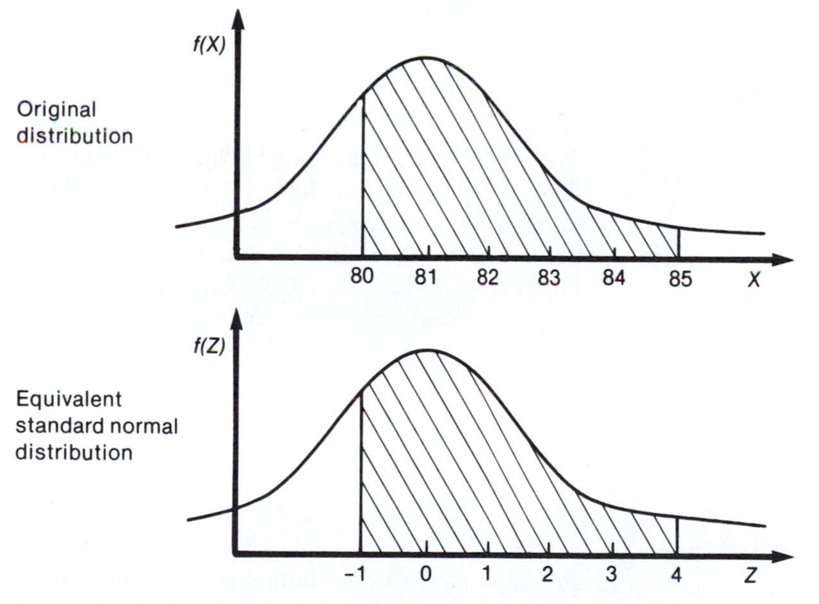

where

μ = the mean
σ = the standard deviation

This is such a mess mathematically that calculations of probabilities are impossible. In order to estimate probabilities (e.g., the probability a part will be between 80 and 85 mm in length), a "scale model" approach is used. The approach is to convert to the standard normal distribution where $\mu = 0$ and $\sigma = 1$ and then look up the answer in a table (Figure 9A–5). The conversion is achieved by:

$$Z = \frac{X - \mu}{\sigma}$$

For example, assume I were interested in obtaining the probability that a certain part were between 80 and 85 mm. If $\mu = 81$ and $\sigma = 1$, this means the shaded area in Figure 9A–6. Now from the table, the area from 0 to -1 standard deviation is about .34. Similarly, the area from 0 to $+4$ is about .5. Hence, the probability the part is between 80 and 85 mm is .5 + .34 = .84.

Student's *t*

The Student's *t* is another bell-shaped distribution which is slightly "fatter" than the normal. Its density function is also a "mess." (Since it was developed by the employee of an Irish brewery named Gosset, who used the pen name Student, its "sloppiness" is understandable.) Fortunately, the function is tabled so the density function is not used. The mean and standard deviation of the *t* distribution are given by:

$$\mu = 0$$

$$\sigma = \sqrt{\frac{v}{v - 2}}$$

For large v, the t distribution is approximately normal.[1]

[1] The t distribution is often expressed as the ratio of a standard normal to a chi-square: $t = \frac{X}{\sqrt{y/v}}$ where X is standard normal and y is chi-square with v degrees of freedom.

Chi-Square (χ^2)

The chi-square distribution is the distribution of a sum of squared independent standard normal variables.[2] Its density function is also unwieldy. Its mean and standard deviation are given by:

$$\mu = v$$

$$\sigma = \sqrt{2v}$$

For large v, the chi-square distribution is approximately normal.

F Distribution

The F distribution is the ratio of two chi-square variables.[3] Its density function is too messy to bother writing since it also is tabled. One interesting fact is that the F distribution has a fixed end point at 0 (no negative values are possible since it is made up of the ratio of squared numbers), a mean of 1, and a strong right skew (Figure 9A–7).

Other Distributions

The distributions just listed are the most commonly used for statistical testing in marketing research. Other distributions are used in special circumstances, especially stochastic modeling, including the negative binomial, exponential, gamma (of which both the exponential and chi-square are special cases), and the beta.

Estimates and Truth

The distributions just described were given in terms of their true parameters. Unfortunately, a researcher rarely knows the true parameters (μ, σ, etc.). We mortals then must estimate (guess) what the parameters are.

---

[2] $\chi^2 = \sum_{i=1}^{v} X_1^2$ where X_i is standard normal.

[3] $F = \dfrac{\frac{X_1}{v_1}}{\frac{X_2}{v_2}}$ where X_1 and X_2 are chi-square with v_1 and v_2 degrees of freedom, respectively.

FIGURE 9A–7

A. Chi-square distribution

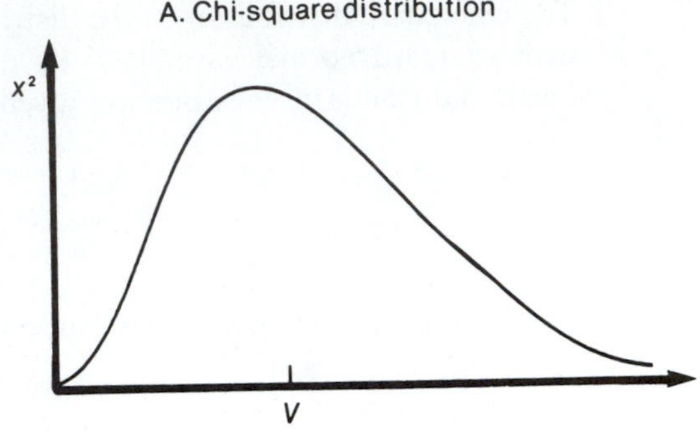

B. *F* distribution

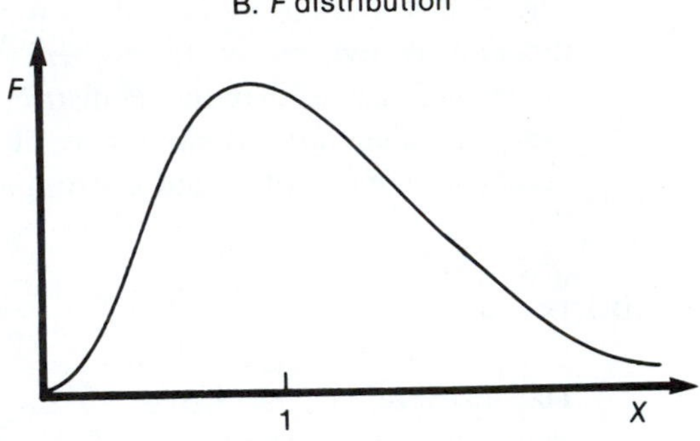

The estimates are typically given by the following:

	True Value	*Estimate*
Mean	μ	$\overline{X} = \frac{\Sigma X}{n}$
Variance	σ^2	$s^2 = s_X^2 = \frac{\Sigma(X - \overline{X})^2}{n - 1}$
Standard deviation (of population)	$\sigma = \sqrt{\sigma^2}$	$s = \sqrt{s^2}$
Standard deviation (of mean)	$\sigma_{\overline{X}} = \frac{\sigma}{\sqrt{n}}$	$s_{\overline{X}} = \frac{s}{\sqrt{n}}$
Proportion	θ	$p = \frac{\textit{Number of successes}}{n}$

FIGURE 9A–8 Confidence Interval

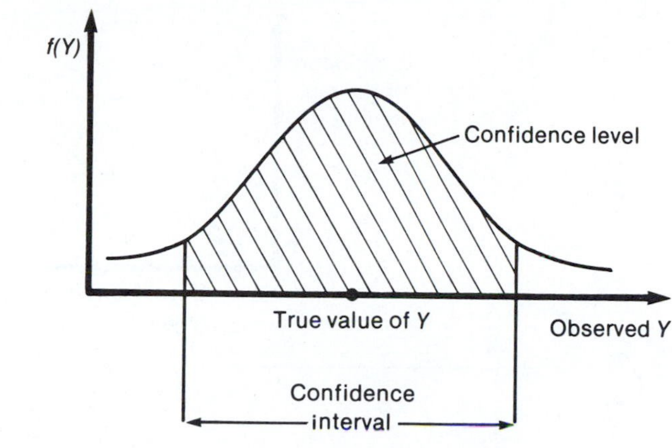

Notice that, by convention, Greek letters stand for true values and Arabic letters for approximations. (Everyone knows the ancient Greeks had truth, don't they?)

Confidence Interval

A confidence interval is a range into which we expect a value to fall. There are actually the following two types of confidence intervals:

1. Given true parameters (e.g., μ and σ), where will a measured value (e.g., $\overline{X}$) fall?

2. Given a measured value (e.g., $\overline{X}$ and s), in what range are the true values (e.g., μ) likely to be?

A confidence interval of the first type can be expressed graphically (Figure 9A–8). The confidence level $(1 - \alpha)$ is the probability that an event will fall in the confidence level. The significance level (α) is the probability an event will occur outside the confidence level.

Sampling Distributions

The key concept to determining statistical significance is that of a sampling distribution. A sampling distribution is the representation of the likelihood that a given value (e.g., an individual's weight, the mean diameter of a part, or the percent of a consumer sample who prefer a certain color) will occur.

FIGURE 9A–9 Sampling Distribution

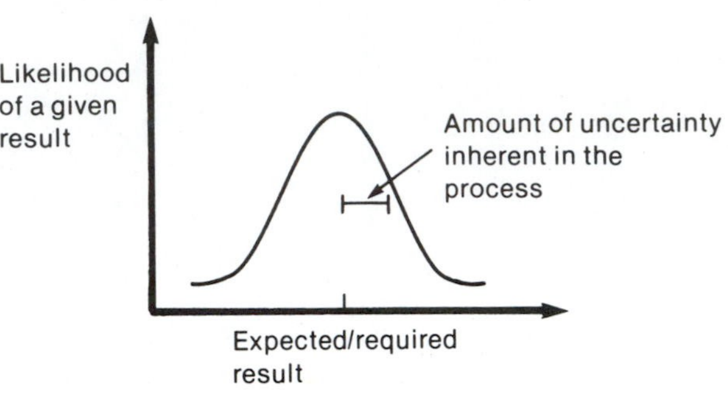

This likelihood could be based on past experience or, alternatively, a set of standards or specifications. The uncertainty in the results may be due to the measurement process and/or random differences among respondents. We can see this graphically in Figure 9A–9. The question which must be answered, then, is whether a particular sample result is "different." In answering this question we are really addressing the question, "Is the population from which the sample result was drawn different from the original population?" Consider the three situations in Figure 9A–10. In case A, the sample result is well outside the typical range of values and, hence, would be called significantly different. This implies that the population from which the sample was drawn is different from the original population in terms of this particular characteristic. In case B, the sample result is very close to the expected result and well within the range of typical values. Therefore, the result in case B is not significantly different. (Put differently, this result probably came from the same population of results as did the previous results.) In case C, the sample result is different

FIGURE 9A–10 Three Hypothetical Sample Results

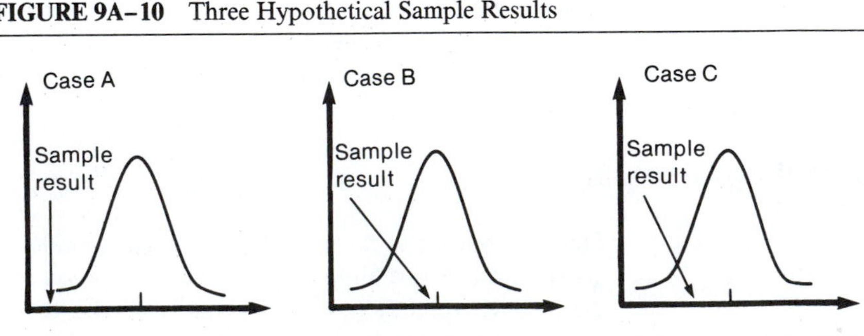

from the expected result but not so different as to be completely beyond the range of typical results. Hence, what will determine statistical significance is whether there is a reasonable likelihood that as "odd" a result would occur due to chance.

The reasonable chance cutoff (α level or Type I error) can be set at any level. In social science, however, the level is typically either .1, .05, or .01, and by far the most widely used cutoff is .05. In other words, if there is less than a 5 in 100 chance that the sample result or a more extreme result would come from the hypothesized process, then the sample result is declared significantly different.

The effect of sample size on statistical significance is very important. Consider again case C. If the sample result is based on a single observation, we would conclude it is not possible to label that person as significantly different from the original population. If it is the average of 10 observations, we are more likely to feel the population from which the sample is drawn is different from the original population. If the sample size were 2,000, we would almost certainly feel the second population is different from the first. While it is possible to subjectively take sample size into account, a more methodical way is available in two important cases: averages and proportions.

Sampling Distributions of an Average ($\overline{X}$)

Assume the value of a particular result has mean $\overline{X}$ and standard deviation s_X (usually just written as plain s). Then the mean and standard deviation of the sampling distribution (likely results) of the average of a sample of size n would be as follows:

$$\text{Mean of sample size } n = \overline{X}$$

$$\begin{array}{l}\text{Standard deviation of} \\ \quad\text{the mean of the} \\ \quad\text{sample of size } n\end{array} = s_{\overline{X}} = \frac{s}{\sqrt{n}}$$

What this means is that the sampling distribution becomes tighter as sample size increases (Figure 9A–11). Consequently, the result which is not significant as an isolated instance may become significant if it occurs repeatedly.

A useful result is that the mean ($\overline{X}$) follows the normal distribution, even if the underlying distribution of X is not normal (courtesy of the central limit theorem). What this means is that we can use the normal distribution to check for statistical significance. It is also interesting to note that precision increases as the square root of sample size. In other words, to be

FIGURE 9A–11

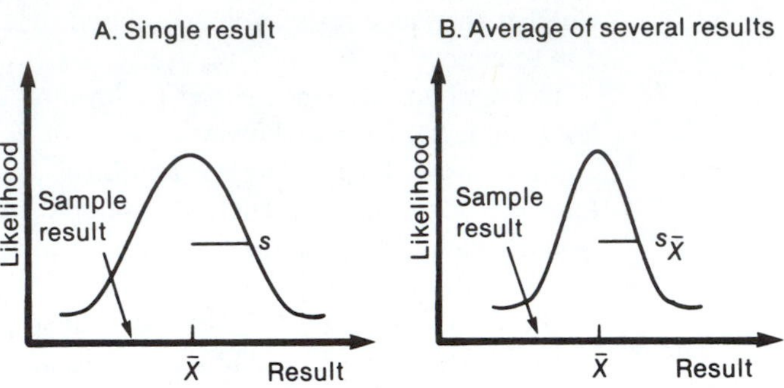

twice as confident of what the results are (cut the range in half), you need four times the sample size. (This has some real implications for the diminishing marginal utility of increasing sample size.)

Sampling Distribution of a Proportion

The sampling distribution of the proportion of respondents exhibiting a particular behavior (i.e., owning a color TV) is given by:

$$\text{Expected proportion} = p$$

$$\text{Standard deviation} = s_p = \sqrt{\frac{p(1-p)}{n}}$$

Notice that the closer p is to 50 percent, the greater the standard deviation. Since this distribution is also approximately normally distributed for n greater than 30, we can get the notion of how accurate proportions are. If we wish to get a range into which 95 percent of actual results are likely to fall (commonly known as the 95 percent confidence level), we get $P \pm 1.96S_p$. If we think p is .50 and take a sample of 100, this becomes:

$$.50 \pm 1.96\sqrt{\frac{(.5)(.5)}{100}} = .50 \pm .10 = .40 \text{ to } .60$$

In other words, we are 95 percent sure that the results would be between 40 and 60 percent. This is a very broad range and brings forth an important point: proportions are very imprecise measures and apparently big differences are often not significant.

Hypothesis Testing

Hypothesis testing is the process of determining whether a result is or is not statistically significantly different from an expected result. As such, it is the applied use of the notion of statistical inference. Numerous hypotheses can be tested. For marketing research, however, a few basic tests cover the majority of the situations encountered. These commonly used tests are introduced in this book when the problems to which they apply are discussed.

Chapter 10

Coding and Editing Responses

When the results of a study come in, there is an understandable desire to get to the interpretation phase as quickly as possible. There are, however, two basic stages between data collection and interpretation. The most interesting of these is the analysis phase. However, before analysis can begin, the data must be converted into a form suitable for analysis. The conversion of the data from "raw" form—typically questionnaires—to a form which facilitates analysis is the subject of this chapter. The problem of converting secondary data to a form ready for analysis is a much simpler but still important task. The steps include inspection, preparing a data file, editing, coding, inputting data, and dealing with missing responses.

SIMPLE INSPECTION

When the number of observations is small, it is possible to do the analysis by hand (assuming no fancy analyses are desired and that there are a fairly small number of variables). Pilot studies of size 20 and industrial marketing studies of 25 purchasing agents may be analyzed without resorting to computers. Here, a combination of scanning the results and a simple question-by-question tabulation is often sufficient.

PREPARING A DATA FILE

Assuming (*a*) there are a reasonably large number of respondents, (*b*) there are a large number of responses, or (*c*) there is a desire to get more than simple tabulations of the responses, the practical way to proceed is to prepare the data for computer analysis. By far the most popular way to do this is to create a data file or tape. Recently, it has become popular to input data directly into computer memories (e.g., by using WATS interviewing via CRT terminals).

Traditionally, the basic unit of data storage was the computer card; essentially, a table of 80 columns (the number of columns on many computer screens is also 80). Each of the 80 columns on a line could contain a separate piece of information. For example, column 8 might be the response to a question about how well I like yogurt, column 9 a question about what type of car I own, and so forth. Groups of columns can also be used to store information (e.g., age might be in columns 19 and 20). Whenever more data exist for a respondent than can be fitted onto a single line, a second line is used. Alternatively, it is possible to specify a "record length" of other than 80 and, hence, to put all the data for one person (observation) on a single record.

To keep track of individual respondents, it is desirable to keep a set of columns for identification purposes. For example, we could use columns 1 through 4 for an ID number. Assuming there is more than one line per respondent, column 5 might be used to indicate line number (actually, any column will do, and many suppliers tend to use column 80 to indicate line number).

Data are usually stored in a person-by-person fashion. Assuming we had a sample of four people with three lines per person, the data file might look like Figure 10–1.

FIGURE 10–1 Data File

	Column					
	ID				*Line No.*	*Data*
Line	*1*	*2*	*3*	*4*	*5*	*6 · · · 80*
1	0	0	0	1	1	
2	0	0	0	1	2	
3	0	0	0	1	3	
4	0	0	0	2	1	
5	0	0	0	2	2	
6	0	0	0	2	3	
7	0	0	0	3	1	
8	0	0	0	3	2	
9	0	0	0	3	3	
10	0	0	0	4	1	
11	0	0	0	4	2	
12	0	0	0	4	3	

In the "old days," tabulation analysis was performed by mechanical card sorters, which physically sorted the cards based on the code in one column. Currently, most of the analysis is done by "canned" (already written) computer programs.

EDITING

Rough Screening

The first thing that is typically done when a survey is completed is to do a rough screening job on the returned questionnaires. This essentially consists of looking for grossly "bad" respondents with illegible, incomplete, or inconsistent responses.

Illegible Responses. This is a common problem for poorly supervised personal interviews and questionnaires with a large number of open-ended responses.

Incomplete Responses. Many returned questionnaires will have a large percentage of nonresponses to individual questions.

Inconsistent Responses. Sometimes, a casual glance will indicate the respondent is not very believable (e.g., income > $50,000, age < 15, loves sports, never participates in sports, etc.). Alternatively, the respondent may have given the same response to a large number of consecutive questions, indicating a certain lack of interest.

Dealing with Bad Data

Since there are inevitably some "bad" respondents, a question which immediately arises is what to do with them. The decision concerning what to do with bad respondents is heavily dependent on how many good respondents there are. When there are a large number of good respondents both in an absolute sense and relative to the number of bad respondents, it may be possible to ignore the bad ones. When, on the other hand, data points are expensive and many are needed for purposes of analysis and projectability, then some way must be found to "fix up" the bad responses. Three basic approaches are used in dealing with bad respondents: going back to get better information, using the data as they are, and throwing out bad respondents.

Fixing Up the Data. Assuming the individuals in question can be identified, it is possible to go back and try to get the respondent to "correct" his or her responses. This is obviously fairly expensive in the case of a large-scale national survey. If (*a*) the percentage of bad respondents is small (less than 20 percent), (*b*) the bad respondents are not different in obvious ways (e.g., income, product usage, etc.) from good respondents, and (*c*) there is a reasonably large sample size (e.g., greater than 500), then it is probably better to avoid going back for more data. In the case of either lab experiments or industrial marketing surveys of a small number of key accounts, on the other hand, it is often relatively easy to go back to collect key pieces of missing data. It is important to realize, however, that data collected the second time may be different from the data at the time of the original survey, because of both changes over time and the different means of gathering the data (e.g., phone callbacks to mail survey respondents). As an alternative to remeasuring, we can attempt to "clean up" the bad/incomplete responses. Procedures for doing this are discussed later in this chapter.

Using the Data as They Are. It is possible to use the data exactly as they are received for basic analysis. This approach is commonly used by suppliers, not surprisingly so since they are typically committed to getting a certain number of respondents. Tabulations can keep track of the nonresponses as a separate category. Inconsistent responses might be assumed to average out over the sample. As long as only simple tabulations are performed, the results may not be too badly distorted. Whenever fancy analysis (e.g., regression) is to be performed, however, this approach leads to considerable problems. Some relatively complex procedures have been developed for dealing with incomplete data (Malhotra, 1987).

Throwing Out Bad Respondents. A third alternative is to discard the bad respondents. This is the easiest thing to do and a widely followed approach, given sufficient sample size to allow it. There are, however, three main drawbacks to this approach. First is that it is an extra step not typically performed by suppliers, which requires time and effort. Second, the bad respondents may, in fact, be very meaningful, in that they are, in essence, saying the topic of your survey is so uninteresting and irrelevant that they refuse to take the time to complete it. Finally, by deciding what a bad respondent is (especially an inconsistent one), the potential for researcher bias influencing the final results is high. Put differently, the bad respondents may be different from good respondents in terms of the variables being measured, and consequently excluding them may bias the results. While these problems discourage many researchers from discarding bad respondents, the key point to remember is that the purpose of information collection and analysis is to improve the odds of making a good decision. Hence, if the researcher believes the results will be more useful if bad respondents are removed, he or she can make the managerial decision to remove them as long as he or she carefully records and reports the procedure used.

CODING

The next step in preparing for analysis is to convert the responses into a coded form for inputting. Since open-ended questions require individual attention (theoretically, by multiple coders to ensure good results), most questions should generally be closed-end multiple-choice questions in a large-scale survey. Converting responses to a data file is essentially a two-step process: (*a*) converting the responses to code values on coding sheets (e.g., 80-column-wide sheets in which the appropriate codes are placed in the appropriate columns) and (*b*) inputting the data. To save time and money, it is usually possible to eliminate the first step by precoding the questionnaire so an operator can input data directly from the questionnaire. It is the desire to have precoded responses which pushes market researchers into the almost exclusive use of multiple choice questions.

Two standard approaches are used for coding. The first is to code possible responses from left to right beginning with "1." For example, if we asked the question:

	Definitely Not				*Definitely*
Is hard work good for you?	O	O	O	O	O

it would be coded 1 through 5, with a "1" representing a "definitely not" response and so forth. The second standard approach is to treat all nonresponses the same way. Some suppliers leave nonresponses blank, others punch a "9" or a ".". In many cases, it may be useful to code a nonresponse to a question separately from "don't know" responses. One more point is extremely important: Do not attempt to save space by "packing" data into a small number of columns. Let each piece of information have a separate column (in general, even if this requires extra lines per respondent).

Coding Questionnaires

To see how a questionnaire can be converted into a computer file, consider the example in Figure 10–2. In this case, the first five columns are devoted to an identification field—here, the respondent number "12345."

FIGURE 10–2 Sample Questionnaire

ID 1-5

1. Do you use toothpaste? ✓ ___ *Yes* ___ *No* 6

2. Please indicate your degree of agreement with the following statements by circling a 6 if you strongly agree, a 1 if you strongly disagree, or somewhere in between depending on your degree of agreement with the statement.

	Strongly Disagree					*Strongly Agree*	
Hard work is good for you.	1	2	③	4	5	6	7
I am very health-conscious.	1	②	3	4	5	6	8
I tend to be conservative in my dress.	1	2	3	④	5	6	9
I enjoy participating in vigorous exercise.	1	2	③	4	5	6	10
I am very family-centered.	1	2	③	4	5	6	11
My appearance is very important to me.	1	2	3	4	⑤	6	12
I use mouthwash often.	1	②	3	4	5	6	13
I enjoy meeting people.	1	2	3	④	5	6	14

3. Please rate each of the following brands of toothpaste by marking a 6 if you feel the brand is very good, a 1 if you feel the brand is very poor, or somewhere in between depending on how good you feel the brand is.

	Very Poor					*Very Good*	
Aim	1	2	③	4	5	6	15
Colgate	1	2	3	4	⑤	6	16
Crest	1	2	3	④	5	6	17
Macleans	1	②	3	4	5	6	18
UltraBright	1	②	3	4	5	6	19

4. Please rate the following brands in terms of their *breath freshening ability* by marking a 6 if you feel the brand is very good, a 1 if you feel the brand is very poor, or somewhere in between depending on how good you feel the brand is.

	Very Poor					*Very Good*	
Aim	1	2	3	④	5	6	20
Colgate	1	2	3	④	5	6	21
Crest	1	2	3	④	5	6	22
Macleans	1	2	3	4	⑤	6	23
UltraBright	1	2	3	4	⑤	6	24

FIGURE 10–2 (*continued*)

5. Please indicate how important each of the following features of toothpaste is to you by circling a 6 if the feature is very important, a 1 if the feature is very unimportant, or somewhere in between depending on how important the feature is to you.

	Very Unimportant					*Very Important*	
Breath freshening	1	2	(3)	4	5	6	25
Decay prevention	1	2	3	4	(5)	6	26
Taste	1	2	3	(4)	5	6	27
Price	1	2	(3)	4	5	6	28

6. How often do you brush your teeth?

____ Never ____ Rarely ____ Few times a day ✓ Daily ____ Two times a day ____ More than two times a day 29

7. Who makes the purchase decision concerning which brand of toothpaste your household uses?

Male head of household ✓ 30

Female head of household ✓ 31

Children ____ 32

8. What brand of toothpaste did your household last purchase? *CREST* 33

9. How old would you like to be?

____ Under 20 ✓ 21–35 ____ 36–50 ____ Over 50 34

10. What is the highest level of education you have completed?

____ 6th grade ____ High school ✓ College ____ Graduate school 35

11. What is your total annual household income?

____ Under $5,000 ____ $5,000–$9,999 ____ $10,000–$14,999 ____ $15,000–$19,999 ✓ Over $20,000 36

12. What is your occupation?

✓ White-collar ____ Blue-collar ____ Homemaker ____ Student ____ Other 37

13. How many people live in your household? 4 37

FIGURE 10–2 (*concluded*)

14. What is your sex?

    ✓ Male ___ Female — 39

15. What is your marital status?

    ___ Single ✓ Married ___ Divorced, widowed, or separated ___ Other — 40

16. Do you own a:

    House? ___ Yes ✓ No — 41

    Car? ✓ Yes ___ No — 42

    Snowmobile? ✓ Yes ___ No — 43

    Color TV? ___ Yes ✓ No — 44

    CB Radio? ✓ Yes ___ No — 45

17. How old are you? 27 — 46–47

Note: The numbers down the right side of the questionnaire indicate the column in which the particular piece of data will be placed.

Column 6 will be coded "1," since the first category was indicated on question 1.

Question 2 will occupy columns 7 through 14. Each separate piece of information gets its own column. In this case, the blanks checked indicate values "3, 2, 4, 3, 3, 5, 2," and "4."

Question 3 occupies columns 15 through 19 with numbers "3, 5, 4, 2, 2."

Question 4 occupies columns 20 through 24 with numbers "4, 4, 4, 5, 5."

Question 5 occupies columns 25 through 28 with values "3, 5, 4," and "3."

Question 6 is coded into column 29 with a "4," since *Daily* is the fourth category.

Question 7 takes up three separate columns (30 through 32), since it would be possible and logical to check more than one response (as this respondent did). While we could (and would if we were old-time coders) indicate this by punching both a "1" and a "2" in column 30 (called *multiple punching*), this would play havoc with many of the analysis routines to be used later. Therefore, we use three separate columns and indicate "1," "1," blank. (If we had asked which person has the most influence, then only one answer would have been appropriate and the data could have been coded in column 30 as a "1"—male head of household, "2"—female head of household, or "3"—children.)

Question 8 is an open-ended question, which must be manually coded. Actually, it could have been precoded by including the major brands and an "all other—please specify" category. Assuming our code were "1" = Aim, "2" = Colgate, "3" = Crest, "4" = Macleans, "5" = UltraBright, and "6" = all others, we would place a "3" in column 33.

Question 9 will produce a "2" in column 34.

Question 10 will produce a "3" in column 35.

Question 11 will generate a "5" for column 36.

Column 37 will be a "1" to represent the "white-collar" response to question 12.

Question 13 will place a "4" in column 38. Notice here that a response of 10 or more is unaccoaunted for. Hence, we must either collapse 10 into another value, such as 9, or save two columns (38–39) for the response.

Question 14 implies a "1" for column 39.

Question 15 implies a "2" for column 40.

Question 16 fills columns 41 through 45 with "2, 1, 1, 2," and "1." Notice again that, rather than collapse the information into a single column, each durable ownership response occupies a separate column.

Question 17 fills columns 46 and 47 with 27. If someone is over 100, we would punch a 99 and congratulate that person and ask for his or her secret of success. If someone is 8, we would place the 8 in column 47, a process known as *right justifying*. The reason for this is that the computer will read a __8 as 8, and an 8__ as 80.

One other point worth mentioning is that it is highly desirable to use fixed field codes. This means that (*a*) the number of lines for each observation is the same and (*b*) the same piece of data appears in the same column for all observations. Failure to do this is disastrous for most analytical procedures. The tendency to use uneven record lengths comes from questions where the respondent lists several items (e.g., family members, cars owned, credit cards carried). Since to use fixed record lengths the code will be determined by those with the largest number of responses, there will be a large amount of blank space on the cards of those respondents with few responses. Here, the puritan ethic of not wasting space will lead to the wrong decision. The cost of the blank space is usually far smaller than the cost of uneven record length. For example, in response to a question concerning car ownership, we might leave room for four cars, which will cover over 99 percent of the responses. (While we could include the one person with 13 cars, this is such an unusual observation that, in general, it is not worth the trouble of keeping track of all 13.)

Actually, assuming you plan to use certain computer algorithms for analysis, you can also input data by leaving a blank space between consecutive pieces of data. (This also allows you to use nonfixed-length formats, so we could input 9, 90, or 109 for age. Unfortunately, this also makes it harder to check for errors, since the data no longer line up neatly in columns on a computer screen or in printed output.) Still, since this is closer to typing for people familiar with typing or word processing systems, it is often useful for the person who only occasionally inputs data.

Coding Secondary Data

The conversion of secondary data into computer form is fairly simple. Assume I collected data on annual dishwasher sales in units and GNP:

Year	*Dishwasher Sales (units)*	*GNP ($ billion)*
1960	555,321	503.7
1965	1,260,462	684.9
1970	2,116,119	977.1
1972	3,199,201	1,155.2
1973	3,701,982	1,289.1

The ID field would be year, probably in columns 1 through 4. Since plenty of space is available, we could skip some space before beginning dishwasher sales in some column, such as 11. Clearly, we could input seven columns' worth of data for dishwasher sales. However, the accuracy of the last three columns, as well as their value, given only five data points, is very questionable. It seems more reasonable to only include the data in thousands of units. Since the maximum number of columns needed is 4 (for 3,702, the largest number), we assign columns 11 through 14 for dishwasher sales (remembering they are now measured in thousands of units sold).

In punching GNP, it is possible to input the data as is. However, it is unnecessary to input the decimal point, since (*a*) we could interpret the

FIGURE 10–3 Coded Dishwasher Sales Data

	Column																		
Line	*1*	*2*	*3*	*4*	*5*	*6*	*7*	*8*	*9*	*10*	*11*	*12*	*13*	*14*	*15*	*16*	*17*	*18*	*19*
1	1	9	6	0								5	5	5		5	0	3	7
2	1	9	6	5							1	2	6	0		6	8	4	9
3	1	9	7	0							2	1	1	6		9	7	7	1
4	1	9	7	2							3	1	9	9	1	1	5	5	2
5	1	9	7	3							3	7	0	2	1	2	8	9	1

results just as well in units of hundreds of millions as units of billions and (*b*) we can tell the computer where the decimal point belongs and have it replaced during analysis. (For Fortran fans, use F 5.1). Since 12891 is the largest number, we can use five columns (15 through 19) to represent GNP. The resulting data would then be input, as is shown in Figure 10–3.

DATA INPUT

The task of inputting data, formerly called *punching data* in the card era, is straightforward and essentially the same as typing. An experienced operator can turn out 80 to 100 lines or the equivalent per hour at a cost of about 15 cents per line from a supplier. Because operators occasionally make errors, it is usually desirable to check their work. The standard way to do this is to "verify" the work. This is done by a second operator. The operator essentially repunches the data from the original questionnaire. If the result matches the original operator's input, nothing happens. If the input does not match, then the observation is put aside for reentry.[1]

One point of caution: If you are inputting data yourself, be sure to save the data frequently. Otherwise, hours of work can be destroyed by a power failure or the accidental striking of a wrong key. Also, never rely on a single data set. Data sets have a habit of becoming mutilated. Typically, large data sets are stored on magentic tape or disks. The minimum safety margin is two copies (e.g., a tape and a disk copy) stored in different places.

The increasing use of WATS phone interviewing and the advent of microcomputers has made it possible for either the interviewer or the subjects themselves to directly create a data file. Such files are not constrained to the traditional 80-column format. More important, the key punching step in the data preparation stage is avoided.

Direct data entry, however, has some inherent problems. Care must still be taken to verify answers, since careless recording can produce nonsensical results. Also, care must be taken to design input routines to allow a mistaken entry to be fixed before it becomes part of a data file. For each answer, it is often desirable to give the respondent or the interviewer, or both, a printed (on the screen) summary of a response and then have the respondent verify (in which case, the next question is given) or contradict the response (in which case, the question is repeated). Also, this form of data entry tends to preclude marginal notes made by interviewers, which

---

[1] This used to be done by a machine called a *verifier*. Instead of punching holes in the cards, however, the verifier shot a beam of light at the card. If the light went through (meaning there was a hole in the correct space), the card proceeded to the next column. If the light did not go through, the card remained in the same position. The verifier then tried again. If the light still failed to go through, the card was marked and returned to be repunched. This verification process essentially doubled both the time and cost of punching.

have on occasion been useful in interpreting results. Still, direct entry is increasing in popularity, mainly as a result of the increased usage of WATS and computer-controlled interviewing.

CODE BOOK

The data delivered by a supplier are accompanied by a code book giving a column-by-column explanation of the relation between the codes and the responses to the questions. These can be quite extensive, as the code book from the nutrition study turned out to be. That 8-page questionnaire produced a 30-page code book, which is presented in abbreviated form in Appendix 10–A. Notice that, since this study was performed in the mid-1970s, data lines are referred to as cards. Also, typically included in a code book will be information on how to access the data (where it is physically stored if it is in card form, and what instructions access it if it is stored on tape or disk).

CLEANING THE DATA: MISSING RESPONSES

The problem of missing data is widespread. For example, a nationwide mail panel study (Horowitz and Golob, 1979) showed that, while 60 percent of the 1,565 respondents had fewer than 1 percent of their responses blank, about 10 percent had at least 5 percent missing data.

Cleaning the data for final analysis has several steps. First, a column-by-column count of the responses is made. Typical results are shown in Figure 10–4, taken from card 1 of the nutrition study. These results give indications of illegal entries and, also, an initial glimpse at the results.

The other stage of cleaning the data consists of deciding what to do with isolated missing responses. These are questions which an otherwise good respondent left blank. There are five major choices:

Leaving them blank. This is fine for tabs and cross-tabs but is a problem for many programs, such as regression, that treat blanks as zeros.

Substitute a neutral value. Typically, this approach involves substituting a value, usually the mean response to the question, for the missing response. This approach keeps the mean constant and also tends to have a relatively small effect on calculations such as correlations. Good as this may sound, putting a 3.5 (the mean for the missing question *across all respondents*) on the card of a respondent who mainly indicated 1s and 2s seems questionable.

Assign the value the individual "would have used" if he or she had answered the question. This approach suggests that, by looking at the individual's pattern of responses to other questions, we can logically deduce an appropriate answer to the missing question. Since this method (*a*) requires considerable effort and (*b*) risks considerable researcher bias,

FIGURE 10–4 Sample Basic Tabs from Nutrition Study

					Card 1								
COLUMN	TOTAL CODED	-12-	-11-	-0-	-1-	-2-	-3-	-4-	-5-	-6-	-7-	-8-	-9-
061	940				645	67	1	227					
062	940	3	234	135	39	109	59	41	135	113	50	3	19
063	940			407	362	171							
064	940			93	188	71	122	131	119	138	55	67	44
065	940				784	107	49						
066	940			8	758	168	6						
067	940		57	10	504	299	60	8	1	1			
068	940		478	206	226	20	8		1	1			
069	940			1	910	28	1						
070	940			367	109	59	49	77	123	102	31	23	
071	940			349	99	39	64	90	73	60	65	52	49
072	940			545	20	21	10	2	296	20	9	9	8
073	940				246	694							
074	940				53	156	186	88	142	67	96	41	111
075	940				178	107	179	219	257				
076	940				185	164	175	185	231				
077	940				309	159	202	131	139				
078	940					415	191	160	107	42	19	4	2
079	940			940									
080	940				940								

it is not very popular. Still, it is an approach which may be useful for some situations.

Assume they were "don't know" or "not applicable" responses. A nonresponse may mean the question does not apply (n.a.). For example, a survey may branch so that only owners of trucks fill out certain questions, meaning that nontruck owners will leave several questions blank. Alternatively, it may be that the respondent genuinely doesn't know (d.k.) the answer. (Do you know who advertised "Brings the taste to light"?)

Pairwise deletion. Another way to deal with missing data is to utilize all available data for each calculation. For a correlation coefficient, all observations with data on both variables are used, and any with missing observations on either of the variables are deleted. This procedure works well when (*a*) there is a large sample size and relatively few missing observations and (*b*) the variables are not highly related. However, it can produce unappealing results (such as an estimated correlation matrix which is "impossible"—i.e., not positive definite for linear algebra fans) for small sample sizes. Also, when the variables are highly interrelated, assuming missing data are random can distort relations. Hence, this method must be used with care.

A major problem in deciding how to "fill in" missing data is to determine whether the data missing are random or related to other variables. For example, assume income data are omitted by 10 percent of a sample. First, one must consider whether income omission is random or predominant in a particular income group (e.g., high). If high-income people have a disproportionate tendency to refuse to give income data, then randomly assigning income or putting in the average based on those who answered will produce a biased estimate of average income as well as lead to misestimation of relations between income and other variables. Second, income may be related to other variables, such as education. If the missing data follow the same relation between education and income as the obtained data (often a good assumption), then assigning a value for income without considering education will distort/bias relationships even if the mean is not affected.

To see the impact of various "data-fixing" procedures, consider the example in Figure 10–5, where income is assumed to be either $10,000 or $30,000 per year and education level either 12 years (high school) or 16 years (college). First consider case B. Here, the mean income is $20,000, as in the complete data. Substituting the mean or randomly assigning a value will not influence the mean, nor, since income and education are independent, will it change this relationship (case B′). In case C, however, missing income data come from the high-income category. The mean of the available data is $18,889, and, therefore, substitution of the mean will cause an underestimate of the true mean. However, since income and education are independent, the relationship (or, in this case, perfect independence between the two) will be maintained by random assignment (case C′).

If, on the other hand, income and education are positively related, as in case D (a seemingly just notion), things are worse. Notice again that, in the case of randomly missing data (case E), substitution of the mean income ($20,000) would not affect the average-income calculations. However, random assignment of income values to the missing data points will "depress" the relationship between income and education (case E′). When the data are omitted in high-income categories (case F), the mean is again $18,889 in existing data, and hence is biased downward. If data are assigned without

FIGURE 10–5 Missing Data Patterns: Hypothetical Examples

Income and education independent:

	Education	Income $10,000	Income $30,000	No Data
A. Complete data	12 years	50	50	—
	16 years	50	50	—
B. Randomly missing data (income only)	12 years	45	45	10
	16 years	45	45	10
B′. Randomly assigning missing data	12 years	50	50	—
	16 years	50	50	—
C. High income data missing	12 years	50	40	10
	16 years	50	40	10
C′. Randomly assigning missing data	12 years	56	44	—
	16 years	56	44	—

Income and education related:

	Education	Income $10,000	Income $30,000	No Data
D. Complete data	12 years	80	20	—
	16 years	20	80	—
E. "Randomly" missing data	12 years	72	18	10
	16 years	18	72	10
E′. Randomly assigning missing data	12 years	77	23	—
	16 years	23	77	—
F. High education causing missing income data	12 years	80	20	0
	16 years	16	64	20
F′. Randomly assigning high income missing data*	12 years	82	20	—
	16 years	27	73	—

* In proportion to 96 versus 84, the observed split on income.

regard to the relationship between income and education, then both the mean of income and the relationship between income and education are affected. It is also worth noting that, in case F, deleting observations with missing data on income will lead to an understatement of not just average income but average education as well.

One way to fill in missing data is to predict the value of the missing observation based on available data. For example, if we assume Income = $B_0 + B_1$ (Education), we can fill in missing income data if education data are available. This is done by (a) estimating B_0 and B_1 from observations where both income and education are available and (b) putting education into the resulting formula. In Figure 10–5 (case F), one would predict that 80 percent 64/(64 + 16) of the 20 nonresponses to income would have an income of $30,000 and 20 percent would have an income of $10,000. By randomly assigning people in those proportions, we would recreate case D, the complete data.

This "bootstrapping" approach is useful if the income-education relationship is the same in respondents as nonrespondents. It is possible that some Ph.D.s are ashamed to admit to poverty status, and this explains why they fail to give income data. If this is the reason for the nonresponse, this procedure will overestimate income for nonrespondents. The approach also requires a significant relationship between income and education (otherwise the equation will essentially predict the average income value for all education levels). For these reasons, this approach is rarely used.

The main point made here, therefore, is that the treatment of missing data can affect results—especially when variables are related. Hence, the moral of the story is to (*a*) keep item nonresponse to a minimum and (*b*) consider the implications of using various data-fixing procedures before employing them.

SUMMARY

Unless the data are converted accurately to a usable form, subsequent analysis will be both difficult and misleading. The secret is simply to be careful in establishing procedures for coding the data. Several key points need reiterating:

Keep an identification field that indicates both person and line number (if more than one). The ID field allows you to go back to the questionnaire if the data are incorrectly input, or to the respondent if further information is needed.

Code the data in a disaggregated form. Do not pack data in a few columns, as this is a false economy.

Don't multiple-punch. Multiple punches (inputting more than one piece of data in a column) are disastrous for most computer routines. In fact, some people strive valiantly to keep the number of possible responses to nine or fewer to reduce the tendency to multipunch. Also, take care to force suppliers into not multipunching, since, left to their own devices, some still multipunch as a carryover from the card era.

Keep fixed record lengths. Saving space is a false economy.

Keep backup data sets. Those who keep a single data set deserve the frustration of seeing it mangled.

Spend some time cleaning the data. This means both throwing out hopelessly bad respondents and seeing if nonresponses can be converted to responses.

Be lucky. Those who aren't careful almost always get burned, but it helps to be lucky to avoid trouble.

PROBLEMS

1. Assume you wished to build a model relating GNP, Housing Starts, the Dow-Jones average, the Consumer Price Index, and automotive sales in the United States on a yearly basis from 1972 to 1988. Set up the code sheets for your data set.
2. How would you interpret nonresponse to each of the following questions below?

Do you own an air conditioner?	____ Yes			____ No		
How many children do you have?	________					
	Dislike Very Much					*Like Very Much*
How well do you like peas?	1	2	3	4	5	6
What is the largest selling brand of shampoo?	____________					

3. Set up a coding scheme for the questionnaire above.

BIBLIOGRAPHY

Horowitz, Abraham D., and Thomas F. Golob. "Survey Data Reliability Effects on Results of Consumer Preference Analyses." In *Advances in Consumer Research*. Vol. 6., ed. William L. Wilkie. Ann Arbor: Association for Consumer Research, 1979, pp. 532–38.

Malhotra, Naresh K. "Analyzing Marketing Research Data with Incomplete Information on the Dependent Variable." *Journal of Marketing Research* 24 (February 1987), pp. 74–84.

Pessemier, Edgar A. "Data Quality in Marketing Information Systems." In *Control of Error in Market Research Data*, ed. John U. Farley and John A. Howard. Lexington, Mass.: Lexington Books, 1975, pp. 109–44.

Siedl, Philip S. "Coding." In *Handbook of Marketing Research*, ed. Robert Ferber. New York: McGraw-Hill, 1974, pp. 2–178 to 2–199.

Appendix 10–A

Nutrition Study Codebook

CARD 1: NFO Standard Family Background Codes*

Column	*Code*
1–6	Application number (identification)
7–8	State Codes—NFO standard codes
9–11	County codes—NFO standard codes
12–14	City codes—NFO codes
15	Live within city limits: 1—Inside city limits 2—Outside city limits
16	NFO use
17	Marital status: 1—Now married 2—Never married 3—Divorced 4—Widowed 5—Separated 0—No answer

Source: National Family Opinion, Inc., New York.

CARD 1 *(continued)*

Column	*Code*
18–19	Year married:
	Last two digits of year punched actual
	00—No answer
20–22	Homemaker:
20	Month of birth
	1—January
	2—February
	3—March
	4—April
	5—May
	6—June
	7—July
	8—August
	9—September
	0—October
	X—November
	+ —December
21–22	Year of birth (last two digits of year punched actual)
23–25	Husband:
23	Month of birth (see codes for column 20)
24–25	Year of birth (see codes for columns 21 & 22)
	X—Living away from home (service)
	Blank—No husband
26–53	Other family members:
26	Month of birth (see codes for column 20)
27–28	Year of birth (see codes for columns 21 and 22)
29	Sex
	1—Male
	2—Female
54–56	NFO use
57	Homemaker's education:
	1—Attended grade school
	2—Graduated from grade school
	3—Attended high school
	4—Graduated from high school
	5—Attended college
	6—Graduated from college
	7—Masters
	8—Doctors
	0—No answer
58	Husband's education:
	1—Attended grade school
	2—Graduated from grade school
	3—Attended high school
	4—Graduated from high school
	5—Attended college
	6—Graduated from college
	7—Masters
	8—Doctors
	0—No answer
	X—No husband

CARD 1 *(continued)*

Column	*Code*
59	Homemaker's employment: 1—Full time 2—Part time 3—Not employed 4—No answer
60	Husband's employment: 1—Full time 2—Part time 3—Not employed 0—No answer X—No husband
61	Principal wage earner: 1—Husband 2—Homemaker 3—Other 4—No wage earner (income derived from source other than employment)
62	Occupation: 0—Professional, technical, and kindred workers 1—Farmers and farm managers 2—Managers, officials, and proprietors (except farm) 3—Clerical and kindred workers 4—Sales workers 5—Craftsmen, foremen, and kindred workers 6—Operative and kindred workers 7—Service workers (including private household) 8—Farm laborers and foremen 9—Laborers (except farm and mine) X—Retired, students, disabled, unemployment, and armed forces +—No answer
63-64	Annual family income: 03—Under $3,000 04—$3,000-$3,999 05—$4,000-$4,999 06—$5,000-$5,999 07—$6,000-$6,999 08—$7,000-$7,999 09—$8,000-$8,999 10—$9,999-$9,999 11—$10,000-$10,999 12—$11,000-$11,999 13—$12,000-$12,999 14—$13,000-$13,999 15—$14,000-$14,999 16—$15,000-$15,999 17—$16,000-$16,999 18—$17,000-$17,999 19—$18,000-$18,999 20—$19,000-$19,999 21—$20,000-$24,999 22—$25,000-$29,999 23—$30,000-$35,000 24—Over $35,000

CARD 1 *(continued)*

Column	*Code*
65	Type of residence: 1—House 2—Apartment 3—Other 0—No answer
66	Home ownership: 1—Own 2—Rent 3—Live with relatives (in their home) 4—Other 0—No answer
67	Car ownership: 1—1 car 2—2 cars 3—3 cars 4—4 cars 5—5 cars 6—6 cars 7—7 cars 8—8 cars 9—9 cars X—None 0—No answer
68	Truck ownership: (see codes for car ownership)
69	Homemaker's race: 1—White 2—Negro or black 3—Oriental 4—Other 0—No answer
70-72	Metropolitan area NFO code
73	NFO use
74	Geographic divisions: 1—New England 2—Middle Atlantic 3—East North Central 4—West North Central 5—South Atlantic 6—East South Central 7—West South Central 8—Mountain 9—Pacific
75	Population densities: 1—Rural 2—Cities, 2,500-49,999 Metropolitan areas: 3—50,000-499,999 4—500,000-1,999,999 5—2,000,000 and over

CARD 1 *(concluded)*

Column	*Code*
76	Homemaker's age coded: 1—Under 30 years 2—30 through 39 years 3—40 through 49 years 4—50 through 59 years 5—60 years and over
77	Income coded: 1—Under \$6,000 2—\$6,000-\$9,999 3—\$10,000-\$14,999 4—\$15,000-\$19,999 5—\$20,000 and over
78	Size of family 2—2 members 3—3 members 4—4 members 5—5 members 6—6 members 7—7 members 8—8 members 9—9 or more members
79	NFO panel number
80	Card No. 1

	APPLICATION	STATE	COUNTY	CITY	IN-OUT	NFO USE	MARITAL	YEAR MARRIED	HMK MONTH	HMK YEAR	HUS MONTH	HUS YEAR	OFM 1 MONTH	OFM 1 YEAR	OFM 1 SEX	OFM 2 MONTH	OFM 2 YEAR	OFM 2 SEX	OFM 3 MONTH	OFM 3 YEAR	OFM 3 SEX	OFM 4 MONTH	OFM 4 YEAR
Columns	1 2 3 4 5 6	7 8	9 10 11	12 13 14	15	16	17	18 19	20	21 22	23	24 25	26	27 28	29	30	31 32	33	34	35 36	37	38	39 40

	SEX	OFM 5 MONTH	OFM 5 YEAR	OFM 5 SEX	OFM 6 MONTH	OFM 6 YEAR	OFM 6 SEX	OFM 7 MONTH	OFM 7 YEAR	OFM 7 SEX	NFO USE	HMK. EDUC.	HUS. EDUC.	HMK. EMPL.	HUS. EMPL.	PRIN. WAGE E	OCCUPATION	ANNUAL FAMILY INCOME	TYPE RES.	HOME OWN	CARS OWNED	TRUCKS OWNED	HMK. RACE	METRO AREA	NFO USE	CLASS GEO.	CLASS POP.	CLASS AGE	CLASS INCOME	FAMILY SIZE	PANEL NUMBER
Columns	41	42	43 44	45	46	47 48	49	50	51 52	53	54 55 56	57	58	59	60	61	62	63 64	65	66	67	68	69	70 71 72	73	74	75	76	77	78	79 80

CARD 2

Column	*Code*	
1–6	Application number	
7–8	Coded income	
		Section I—Food and shopping habits
9	Q. 1	Portion of household food shopping done personally: 1. None of it. 2. Less than half of it. 3. About half of it. 4. Most of it. 5. All of it. 0. No answer.

CARD 2 *(continued)*

Column	*Code*	
10	Q. 2	Number of times per week shop for food: 1. Less than once a week. 2. Once a week. 3. 2–4 times a week. 4. 5 or more times a week. 0. No answer.
11	Q. 3*a*	Shopping list prepared before going to the store: 1. Yes. 2. No.
12	Q. 3*b*	What portion of items purchased at store are on shopping list? 1. None of them. 2. Some of them. 3. About half of them. 4. More than half. 5. Almost all of them. 0. No answer.
13	Q. 4	Approximately how much money is spent on food in average week? 1. Under $15. 2. $15–$29. 3. $30–$44. 4. $45–$60. 5. Over $60. 0. No answer.
14	Q. 5	Approximately how much different is the amount spent now on food each week compared to one year ago? 1. Spend at least $10 less than last year. 2. $5–$10 less than last year. 3. About the same as last year. 4. $5–$10 more than last year. 0. No answer.
15	Q. 6	When buying staple products, how many brands and sizes do you usually consider? 1. Only 1 or 2. 2. Many brands, one size. 3. Many sizes, one brand. 4. Many brands and sizes. 0. No answer.
16	Q. 7	Which best describes the way you shop for food? 1. I actively seek information about food in terms of nutritional value, price, etc. 2. I sometimes try new foods because of new information, but generally buy the same foods. 3. The food I buy is almost always the same, and I spend very little time thinking about it. 0. No answer.
17	Q. 8	Have you or any members of your immediate family ever used food stamps? 1. Never. 2. Use to, but do not use them now. 3. We are presently using them. 0. No answer.

CARD 2 *(concluded)*

Column	*Code*	
18–27	Q. 9	How important are the following considerations when deciding which foods to serve? 1. Very important 2. 3. Somewhat important. 4. 5. Not very important. 0. No answer.
28–38	Q. 10	When deciding which brand to buy, how much attention do you pay to the following? 1. Pay a great deal of attention. 2. Pay some attention. 3. Pay little or no attention. 0. No answer.
39–41	Q. 11	Number of times per week you, personally, eat the following meals. 1. Never. 2. 1-2. 3. 3–4. 4. 5–6. 5. Every day. 0. No answer.
42	Q. 12	Number of snacks you, personally, have in a typical day. 1. None. 2. One. 3. Two. 4. Three or more. 0. No answer.
43	Q. 13	How much food do you can yourself? 1. None. 2. A small amount. 3. A large amount. 0. No answer.
44–73	Q. 14	How often do you personally consume each of the following? 1. Never. 2. A few times a year. 3. One to two times a month. 4. Weekly. 5. Several times a week. 6. Once a day. 7. More than once a day. 0. No answer.
74–78	Q. 15	How has the amount your household consumed of each of the following changed in the past year? 1. Much less. 2. Somewhat less. 3. About the same. 4. Somewhat more. 5. Much more. 0. No answer.
79	BLANK	
80	Card No. 2.	

CARD 3

Column	*Code*	
1–6	Application number	
		Section I—Food and shopping habits (continued)
7–31	Q. 15	How has the amount your household consumed of each of the following changed in the past year? 1. Much less. 2. Somewhat less. 3. About the same. 4. Somewhat more. 5. Much more. 0. No answer.
		Section II—Nutritional information
32–43	Q. 1	Degree of information gained from listed sources. 1. None. 2. Very little. 3. Some. 4. Quite a bit. 5. A tremendous amount. 0. No answer.
44–46	Q. 2	In the past year, have you read any books about any of the following?
44		Dieting: 1. No. 2. Yes. 0. No answer.
45		Nutrition: 1. No. 2. Yes. 0. No answer.
46		Cooking: 1. No. 2. Yes. 0. No answer.
47–56	Q. 3	If government launched a major nutrition education campaign aimed at adults, which form would you prefer?
47		0. No answer. 1. Column in newspaper.
48		1. TV special.
49		1. Special edition of a prominent magazine.
50		1. Government brochure.
51		1. Extension courses.
52		1. Workshops.
53		1. Public service TV announcements.
54		1. Information on packages.
55		1. Information in TV advertisements.
56		1. Don't care.
57	Q. 4	Amount willing to pay to subscribe to a service providing information about nutritional value of brands offered in local supermarkets. 1. Nothing. 2. 10¢–19¢. 3. 20¢–49¢.

CARD 3 *(concluded)*

Column	*Code*	
		4. 50¢–99¢.
		5. $1–$2.
		6. Over $2.
		0. No answer.
58	Q. 5	Any formal nutrition course in any of the following?
		High school:
		1. No.
		2. Yes.
		0. No answer.
59		College:
		1. No.
		2. Yes.
		0. No answer.
60		Adult education/workshops:
		1. No.
		2. Yes.
		0. No answer.
		Section III—Background information
61–72	Q. 1	Any members of household on any special diet?
61–66		Self-imposed:
		0. No answer.
		+. No members of household on a diet.
		1. Low cholesterol.
62		1. Low fat/calorie.
63		1. Diabetic.
64		1. Low salt.
65		1. Vegetarian.
66		1. Low triglyceride.
67–72		Doctor's orders:
67		0. No answer.
		1. Low cholesterol.
68		1. Low fat/calorie.
69		1. Diabetic.
70		1. Low salt.
71		1. Vegetarian.
72		1. Low triglyceride.
73	Q. 2	How often do you smoke?
		1. Never.
		2. Occasionally.
		3. Regularly, but light (less than one pack of cigarettes each day).
		4. Regularly (one pack of cigarettes a day).
		5. Heavily (more than one pack each day or equivalent).
		0. No answer.
74–79	Blank	
80	Card 3	

CARD 4

Column	*Code*	
1–6	Application number	
		Section III—Background information (continued)
		Section IV—General attitude information
		Section V—Food opinions
7–13	Q. 3	Which of following vitamin pills do you personally take?
7		0. No answer.
		1. None.
8		1. Multiple.
9		1. Vitamin C.
10		1. Vitamin G.
11		1. Vitamin B-12 complex.
12		1. Vitamin A.
13		1. Iron.
14	Q. 4	Amount of time spent watching TV on average day—
		1. None.
		2. Less than 1 hour.
		3. 1-2 hours.
		4. 3-4 hours.
		5. Over 4 hours.
		0. No answer.
15	Q. 5	How has your family income changed in the last year?
		1. Gone down a lot.
		2. Gone down a little.
		3. Stayed about the same.
		4. Gone up a little.
		5. Gone up a lot.
		0. No answer.
16	Q. 6	How has your household size changed in the past year?
		1. Decreased by two or more.
		2. Decreased by one.
		3. Stayed the same.
		4. Increased by one.
		5. Increased by two or more.
		0. No answer.
17–39		*Section IV—General attitude information*
	Indicate how much you agree or disagree with the following statements.	
		1. Strongly agree.
		2. Somewhat agree.
		3. Neither agree nor disagree.
		4. Somewhat disagree.
		5. Strongly disagree.
		0. No answer.
40–77		*Section V—Food opinions*
40–49	Q. 1	Opinions about certain types of food:
		1. True.
		2. False.
		3. Don't know.
		0. No answer.

CARD 4 *(concluded)*

Column	*Code*	
50–77	Q. 2	Which foods contribute importantly to listed functions?
50–53		Eyes are aided by:
		1—Whole milk.
		0—No answer.
51		1—Beef.
52		1—Tomatoes.
53		1—Enriched bread.
54–57		Teeth and bones are aided by:
		Code same as columns 50–53
58–61		Muscle tissue is aided by:
		Code same as columns 50–53
62–65		Repair of body tissues is aided by:
		Code same as columns 50–53
66–69		Blood cells are aided by:
		Code same as columns 50–53
70–73		Fighting infection is aided by:
		Code same as columns 50–53
74–77		Nervous system is aided by:
		Code same as columns 50–53
78–79		BLANK
80		Card No. 4

CARD 5

Column	*Code*	
1–6	Application number	
		Section V—Food opinions (continued)
7–14	Q. 2	Which foods contribute importantly to listed functions?
7–10		Skin is aided by:
		1—Whole milk.
		0—No answer.
8		1—Beef.
9		1—Tomatoes.
10		1—Enriched bread.
11–14		Proper growth of children is aided by:
		Code same as columns 7–10
15–62	Q. 3	Nutrients contained in listed items:
15–26		Whole milk:
15		1—There is a lot of vitamin A in—
		0—No answer.
16		1—There is a lot of thiamin (vitamin B) in—
17		1—There is a lot of riboflavin (vitamin B2) in—
18		1—There is a lot of niacin in—
19		1—There is a lot of vitamin C in—
20		1—There is a lot of vitamin D in—
21		1—There is a lot of protein in—
22		1—There is a lot of carbohydrates in—
23		1—There is a lot of fat in—
24		1—There is a lot of calories in—
25		1—There is a lot of iron in—
26		1—There is a lot of calcium in—

CARD 5 *(concluded)*

Column	
27–38	Beef: Code same as columns 15–26
39–50	Tomatoes: Code same as columns 15–26
51–62	Enriched bread: Code same as colmns 15–26
63–79	BLANK
80	Card No. 5

CARD 6

Column	*Code*	
1–6	Application number	
		Section V—Food opinions (continued)
7–62	Q. 4	Listed foods that you think have a lot of the same benefits to the body: 1st col. 1. Whole milk 0. No answer 2d col. 1. Beef 0. No answer 3d col. 1. Tomatoes 0. No answer 4th col. 1. Enriched bread 0. No answer
7–10		Oatmeal provides a lot of the same benefits as—
11–14		Fish provides a lot of the same benefits as—
15–18		Rice provides a lot of the same benefits as—
19–22		Navy beans
23–26		Chicken
27–30		Potatoes
31–34		Eggs
35–38		Macaroni
39–42		Pork and lamb
43–46		String beans
47–50		Carrots
51–54		Bananas
55–58		Peanut butter
59–62		Cottage cheese
63–79		BLANK
80		Card No. 6

Part 3

Analytical Methods

This section presents a number of methods for analyzing data. It proceeds from the simple (e.g., tabulations) to the relatively more complex (e.g., geometric mapping.) All of the techniques are useful, but one can get most of the information from a study using basic methods, such as those discussed in Chapter 11 and in the first part of Chapter 12. The purpose of this is to indicate why multivariate procedures are important and what they are. This brief discussion will hopefully provide a useful road map of Chapters 13–16. It will also provide a good after-the-fact summary. For those of you who decide to skip those chapters, at least you'll have some idea what you're missing.

WHY USE MULTIVARIATE PROCEDURES?

The use of multivariate procedures has become increasingly widespread in marketing research. The reasons for this increased use are numerous, including the following:

1. Multivariate procedures can assess complex interrelationships among variables more efficiently than simpler procedures such as cross-tabs. This is especially important when a key variable (e.g., sales) is assumed to depend on several other variables simultaneously.

2. Given the large data sets available, multivariate procedures are useful for simplifying them. This simplification often leads to the development of a model which captures much of the information contained in the full data set in a more parsimonious way (e.g., a data set containing a key

variable, such as sales, and 107 possible influences on sales can often be reduced to a model which has sales related to 5 to 10 variables).

3. Multivariate procedures often uncover relations which simpler procedures, such as two-way cross-tabs, overlook. Conversely, multivariate procedures sometimes indicate that apparently important correlations or cross-tabs are illusory.

4. Multivariate procedures are easy and relatively cheap to use given canned computer programs. (This has led to considerable misuse as well as use.) Also more researchers and managers have at least been exposed to such methods.

5. Some people attribute users of multivariate procedures special technical competence (which may or may not be true) as well as greater general competence in making decisions (rarely true). This leads some researchers to use multivariate procedures to increase their perceived credibility.

There are, then, at least five reasons for the increased use of multivariate procedures. While the fourth (increased availability) may be the most important reason, the first three reasons (advantages vis-à-vis simpler procedures) are good enough to outweigh the fifth (false scientification), so that multivariate procedures are a net positive addition to the researcher's tool kit.

A TYPOLOGY

There are innumerable ways to distinguish between types of analyses. Two of the best known appear in Sheth (1971) and Kinnear and Taylor (1971). Most such typologies place considerable importance on the form of the data in terms of its scale properties (nominal, ordinal, interval, or ratio). While the type of data available has an important role to play in determining what technique to use, its role is secondary to first deciding what the technique does. (It is also important to point out that the type of data available can be chosen during the design phase of a study, and, hence, overconcern about the scale issue is unwarranted.) By contrast, this typology focuses on the strength of preconception held by the researcher. As such, it is related to the type of study typology (exploratory, descriptive, causal) previously discussed.

The typology discussed here assumes that analysis ranges from simple perusal of the data to careful model testing and refinement. For the sake of simplicity, most analytical methods can be classified into four categories: descriptive, relationship portrayal, structure derivation, and effect assessment.

Descriptive

Descriptive procedures make no assumptions about the data; they merely describe data. The major example of this type is tabulation, which simply reports the percentage of the time each answer was recorded. Other examples include medians and percentiles (if the data are ordinal) and means (if the data are intervally scaled). Most of the univariate procedures used in exploratory studies fit this category.

Relationship Portrayal

These procedures examine variables (usually one pair at a time) to see if they are related. No prior notion about the nature of the relationship is required. The major example of this type of analysis is cross-tabs. If the general nature of the relationship is known, more "powerful" procedures such as Spearman's rank correlation coefficient (if the relationship is ordinal) or the product-moment correlation (if the relationship is linear) become useful. Such procedures are often used in descriptive studies, especially to uncover which variables are related to two or three key variables.

Structure Derivation

These procedures assume that data were generated according to some underlying but unknown structure; they attempt to deduce the structure from the data and, hence, to simplify it. For example, cluster analysis assumes that the observations came from groups and attempts to rediscover the groups. Factor analysis is a special case of cluster analysis which attempts to group either variables (based on the correlations between variables across people) or people (based on the correlation of people in terms of their values on the variables across variables). Multidimensional scaling assumes that similarity or preference data were generated by a geometric model of the stimuli and tries to deduce the underlying geometric model.

Effect Assessment

These procedures assume that there is a particular kind of relationship in the data. They assume that one variable (called the *dependent* or *criterion variable*) depends on a number of other variables (called *independent* or *predictor* variables) in a particular mathematical way. They then proceed to

FIGURE III–1 Typology of Analytical Procedures

General Category	*Specific Type*	*Data Scale Requirements*
Descriptive	Tabulations	Categorical (nominal)
	Medians, percentiles	Ordinal
	Mean	Interval
Relationship portrayal	Cross tabulation	Categorical
	Rank correlation	Ordinal
	Product moment correlation	Interval
Structure derivation	Cluster analysis	Different procedures for each type
	Factor analysis	Interval
	Multidimensional scaling	Ordinal
Effect assessment	ANOVA	Dependent-interval Independent-categorical
	AID	Dependent-interval Independent-categorical
	Regression analysis	Dependent-interval Independent-interval
	Discriminant analysis	Dependent-categorical Independent-interval
	Conjoint	Dependent-ordinal Independent-categorical

assess/estimate the strength of the dependence of the criterion variables on the predictor variable. The appropriate method of this type to use depends on the scale type of the independent and dependent variables. Examples of this type of analysis include ANOVA, regression analysis, and discriminant analysis. The advantage of these techniques is that when the researcher correctly identifies (*a*) the critical variables and (*b*) the way they relate to each other, these techniques produce far more information than simpler techniques. Their disadvantage is that, if the researcher incorrectly identifies the variables or the form of the relationship, the results may be misleading

A summary of the major types of analytical procedures appears in Figure III–1. Generally, all the techniques in a given category are substitutes for each other and complements to the techniques in the other categories. Put differently, an analysis plan which includes tabulations, factor analysis, and regression may be reasonable while one which attempts to study the relationship of sales to a collection of other variables by means of ANOVA, AID, regression analysis, and discriminant analysis is relatively inefficient.

SUMMARY

On balance, multivariate procedures provide a useful competitive advantage for the researcher who knows how to use them. Three caveats are in order. First, proper use of them requires a reasonable amount of understanding and experience. Second, because many of the techniques are related, there is a diminishing marginal utility of multivariate techniques. Put differently, there is no reason to try every conceivable analytical procedure on a given study—pick the most appropriate one or two. Finally, communication of the results often causes considerable problems. The "uninitiated" may respond with either unabashed (and unjustified) approval or open distrust (often motivated by insecurity). To make the results really useful, every attempt should be made to convert them to a simple form so that the implications can be seen and understood by nontechnicians.

A final point is that it is not necessary to have a deep understanding of the intricacies of all the procedures. Regression analysis has been in the past and will be for the foreseeable future the most widely used "fancy" marketing research technique. In fact, its versatility allows a researcher who understands it, plus the basis analytical procedures, to handle almost any situation. The moral of this is, if you have to pick one of these techniques to learn, pick regression. It is also true that understanding regression makes learning other multivariate procedures much easier.

Chapter
11

Basic Analysis

Having carefully coded and punched up a set of data, the analyst now must decide how best to interpret it. This chapter will proceed by first describing the basic types of analyses that are appropriate for various types of data (nominal, ordinal, interval, and ratio). Next, examples of the basic procedures are described. Before beginning, however, it is useful to visualize the structure of data. Imagine a sheet of paper on which each column represents a different variable and each row a different observation:

		Variable				
		1	2	3	...	k
	1					
	2					
Observation	3					
	⋮					
	n					

If data have been collected at several points in time, then each separate data collection would produce a different sheet of paper:

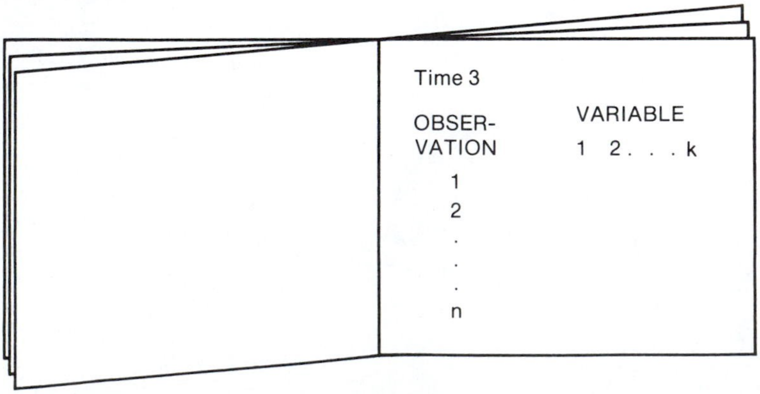

Time 3

OBSER-VATION	VARIABLE 1 2 . . . k
1	
2	
.	
.	
.	
n	

While it would be possible to present such a folder to a manager, in general it is not a good idea, since managers are busy and tend to prefer a somewhat more parsimonious summary. (Also, if there are, for example, 200 variables and 1,000 observations, each page in the notebook would be 9 feet wide and 28 feet long—a little difficult for the average analyst to carry.) Consequently, analysis can be viewed as the task of reducing the data to a more manageable and easily interpretable form. In this chapter, we focus on how to analyze a single time period of measurement (often known as a cross section). Moreover, we focus on two basic issues:

1. How can we describe the responses to a single variable?

2. How can we describe the relations among two variables?

SCALE TYPE AND ANALYSES

In analyzing data, it is important to understand the scale properties of the variable in question. These scales form a heirarchy so that any "higher-order" scale can use procedures for a lower-order scale, but not vice versa (Figure 11–1). For example, any analysis appropriate for nominally scaled data may also be applied to intervally scaled data. Hence, having higher-order data is very desirable.

Nominally scaled data, such as region of the country or preference for furniture style, are very limited in terms of their analysis. Logically, all one can do is report on the percent who live in each region or prefer each style—often called a *tabulation* or *frequency count*. One can also report which is

FIGURE 11–1 Scale Types and Analysis Methods

	Single Variable Description	*Measure of Relation Between Two Variables*
Nonmetric:		
Nominal	Frequency distribution Mode	Contingency table (cross-tab) and coefficient
Ordinal	Median	Nonparametric statistics: Spearman's R Kendall's Tau
Metric:		
Interval	Mean Standard deviation	Pearson product moment correlation
Ratio	Coefficient of variation ($S/\overline{X}$)	

the most common region or most preferred style, a statistic known as the mode.

In terms of relating two nominally scaled variables, the most appropriate method is to simply cross-tabulate the results:

Preferred Style of Furniture	*Region of the Country*				*Total by Style*
	East	*Midwest*	*South*	*West*	
Early American	90	5	5	0	100
Modern	5	5	10	80	100
Cheap (early grandmother)	5	90	85	20	200
Total by region	100	100	100	100	

In this hypothetical example, it appears obvious that Easterners like Early American, Westerners like Modern, and those in the Midwest and South prefer Cheap.

If one has ordinally scaled variables, then it is possible to describe each one in percentile terms. The most common example of this is standardized testing, where we find out such fascinating facts as B.J. is in the 92nd percentile in math (i.e., of 100 people taking the test, 91 did worse), the 58th percentile in vocabulary, and the 3rd percentile in music aptitude. (Hopefully, B.J. plans to be an engineer.) To relate two ordinally scaled variables, a number of so-called non-parametric measures of association are used, such as the Spearman rank correlation.

If a variable is metric (at least intervally scaled), then a number of other statistics become appropriate, such as the mean and standard deviation. Moreover, when examining the relationship between two intervally scaled variables, it is possible to use the Pearson product moment correlation. Since the mean, standard deviation, and correlation are required for many useful procedures (e.g., regression analysis), having intervally scaled data is a big plus.

When one has ratio scaled data, it is now possible to compute the coefficient of variation ($S/\overline{X}$), which is a measure of the variablity of a variable as a percent of its mean. Since this is not a widely used statistic, the advantage of going from an intervally scaled variable to a ratio scaled one is not overwhelming. The major advantage of ratio scaled data is that they allow one to multiply two variables (X and Y) together to form another (Z), whereas with two intervally scaled variables the coding of the variables (e.g., 1 to 5 versus -2 to $+2$) can affect the relative size of the product (Z). Consider the following example:

		Disagree				Agree
Person A:	Likes yogurts	✓				
	Likes diets	✓				
Person B:	Likes yogurt					✓
	Likes diets					✓
Person C:	Likes yogurt	✓				
	Likes diets					✓

If we code the two variables 1 to 5 and create the product of the two responses, we get 1, 25, and 5 for persons A, B, and C, respectively. If we code the variables -2 to $+2$, however, the products would be 4, 4, and -4, respectively. Notice that the ranking of people on the created variable has changed from B, C, A to B, A, C. Hence, the interpretation of the products depends on the arbitrary coding scheme followed.

Two important points are worth adding here. First, it is possible to violate the scale assumptions by, for example, computing averages from ordinal scales (e.g., ranking of five different package designs) or including ordinally scaled variables in regressions. Often, this produces useful insights. It does, however, violate the assumptions of the procedures themselves and affects significance tests on them. Therefore, to "get away" with "misusing" data, a combination of luck and experience is required.

A second point concerns use of a computer. Computer programs make no check to see if your data are properly scaled and will, for example, compute correlations between nominally scaled variables. Be careful interpreting results from situations where you "dump everything in to see what happens."

DESCRIBING A SINGLE VARIABLE

Simple Tabulation

The simplest way to analyze data is to tabulate the responses on a question-by-question basis. This form of analyzing the data (not so ingeniously called *tabulating*) is the most common form of analysis. The only calculation involved is that, after the number of respondents who chose each of the available answers is tabulated, the percentage of the time each

TABLE 11–1 Portion of Food Shopping Done

Response	*Frequency*	*Percent*
1. None	15	1.6
2. Less than half	34	3.6
3. About half	52	5.5
4. Most	295	31.4
5. All	538	57.2
6. No answer	6	.6
	940	99.9

response is given is calculated. For example, assume the following question was asked of 940 female heads of households:

What portion of the food spending for your household do you do personally?
_____ None of it.
_____ Less than half of it.
_____ About half of it.
_____ Most of it.
_____ All of it.

FIGURE 11–2 Bar Chart of Table 11–1 Responses

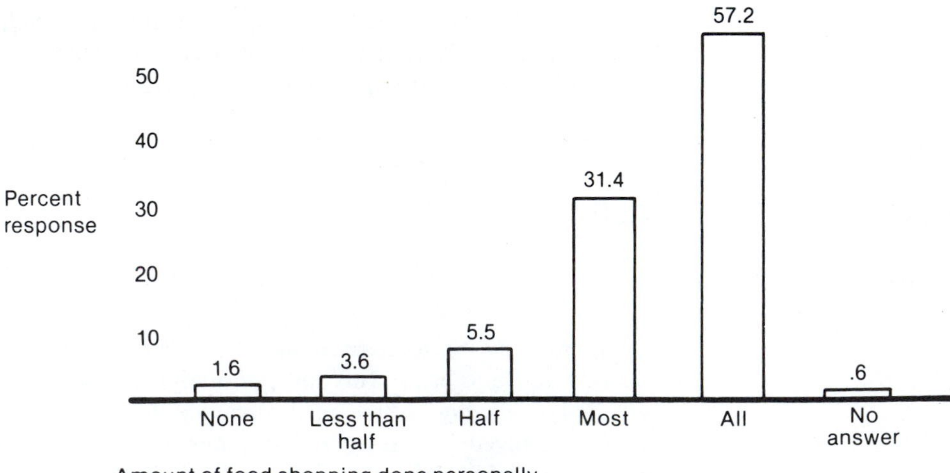

The tabulated results would be of the form of Table 11–1. It takes very little statistical analysis to see what this implies. Over half the sample are doing all the shopping, and almost another one third doing most of it. Thus, the vast majority of the sample are experienced food shoppers. To highlight such results, a common approach is to construct a bar chart to represent the results graphically (Figure 11–2).

It is also often the case that a particular response is the key one (i.e., the proportion of people who buy our brand). The percent who give that response is frequently more important than the entire distribution. This is especially true for questions such as purchase intention, where often only the most positive (top box) response is considered to be a useful measure of intention.

Simple Calculations

The other way to indicate the pattern of responses to a single question is to compute a statistic.

Mode. One common statistic is called the *mode*. This is the most frequently occurring response (in the case of Table 11–1, 5—all of it—is the most typical result).

Median. Another statistic commonly calculated is called the *median*. This is the score of the person who is exactly in the middle of the responses (in Table 11–1, this is also 5).

Mean. Another statistic which is often calculated is the *mean* (average) response. This is calculated by using the code value for each response and weighting by the frequency which the response is given.

Nonresponse Problem. A problem exists in calculating the mean, in that the no-response answers must be dealt with. Consider the response pattern of Table 11–2. A major problem in analyzing these results is the

TABLE 11–2 Sample Response Pattern

Response	*Code*	*Frequency*
None	1	425
1–2	2	61
3–4	3	11
5 or more	4	340
No answer	9	83

nonresponses. There are three major choices: do nothing with nonresponses, convert the no-answer response, and exclude no-answer responses.

Do nothing with nonresponses. If we do nothing, most computer programs will, by default, count nonresponses as whatever code they were given. In this case, that would mean the following:

Code	*Frequency*	*Code × Frequency*
1	425	425
2	61	122
3	11	33
4	340	1,360
9	83	747
	920	2,687

Hence, the mean $= \frac{2{,}687}{920} = 2.92$. Putting the 9s in implies that no answer means the person would have responded much more than 5. This is clearly ridiculous, and the mean of 2.92 is biased. However, if the number of nonresponses to all the questions is small (less than 1 to 2 percent), their effect on the mean will be slight enough so as to be unlikely to change any significant conclusions. Still, striving to prevent nonresponses is very desirable, in that it makes later gyrations to deal with them unnecessary.

Convert the no-answer response. Sometimes it is possible to logically assign no answers to a category. In this case, we might assume that nonresponses were some respondents' way of saying the question was irrelevant and really were responding "none." Thus, we could add them into the "none" category (code = 1). The results would then be:

Code	*Frequency*	*Code × Frequency*
1	508 (425 + 83)	508
2	61	122
3	11	33
4	340	1,360
	920	2,023

Here the mean $= \frac{2{,}023}{920} = 2.20.$

Exclude no-answer responses. It is possible to simply exclude no-answer respondents from each calculation. This is both easy, given current computer algorithms, and popular. One source of its popularity is that, in excluding these respondents, it appears that we are getting a "good" answer. Actually, the answer is good only if the nonresponses would, if we were able to convert them to responses, follow the same pattern as the responses. Since this is often not the case, converting no-answers may be better than ignoring them. The results of ignoring the nonresponses for our example would be as follows:

Code	*Frequency*	*Code × Frequency*
1	425	425
2	61	122
3	11	33
4	340	1,360
	837	1,940

$$\text{Mean} = \frac{1{,}940}{837} = 2.32.$$

Usefulness of Averages. Averages (means) are a popular measure. They are only useful, however, when the following conditions are met:

The data should be intervally scaled. If the codes (Table 11–2) had stood for favorite color (1 = blue, 2 = red, 3 = green, 4 = yellow), then the data say that blue and yellow are popular and red and green are not. Calculating an average of 2.3 could be misleading. (Both the mode—in this case, 1 = blue—and the median—in this case, 2 = red—would also be misleading.) When the data constitute an ordinal scale, it is also theoretically incorrect to compute an average. Nonetheless, since most ordinal scales are fairly close to interval scales in their composition, and since respondents may well respond to an ordinal scale as though it were an interval scale, calculation of averages on ordinal scales is a widely accepted practice in marketing research where the trade-off between simplification and theoretical correctness often leans toward simplification.

The data should have some central tendency. In other words, most responses should be clustered around the mean. In this example, a mean of 2.3 is misleading since almost the entire sample checked 1 or 4. The irrelevance of the mean can be seen by considering the temperature people prefer for tea. Most people either like tea hot or iced. Averaging the preferred temperatures produces room temperature, which represents no one's preference very well.

Sensitivity of the mean. It is also interesting to note how insensitive the mean is to fairly large changes in the response distribution. In the previous example, when we added the nonrespondents (10 percent of the original sample) to the extreme of the distribution (code = 1), the mean only changed from 2.32 obtained by excluding them to 2.2 found by including them. Given the importance of top box responses (e.g., "definitely will buy the product" responses), the average is a fairly insensitive measuring device and small changes in it may be very important managerially.

Standard Deviation

To assess the accuracy of the mean in representing responses, a measure of central tendency is needed. Consider the following three (hypothetical) response distributions:

Code	*A*	*B*	*C*
1	400	100	600
2	300	800	0
3	200	100	200
4	100	0	200

In each case, the mean response is 2. Yet obviously, the distributions are very different. In fact, only in case B does the mean represent a typical response well, and in case C, the mean response of 2 was given by none of the 1,000 respondents. By graphing the three distributions (Figure 11–3), we see that a major difference is spread (width) of the response patterns about the mean. The difference in spread is sometimes easier to see in a

FIGURE 11–3 Three Distributions with Equal Means

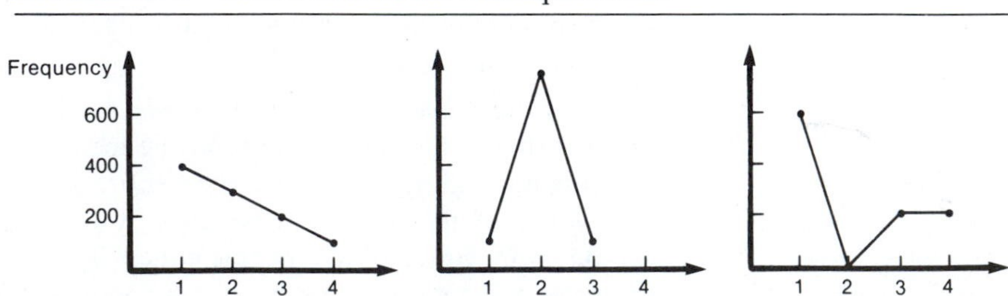

FIGURE 11–4 Two Response Distributions

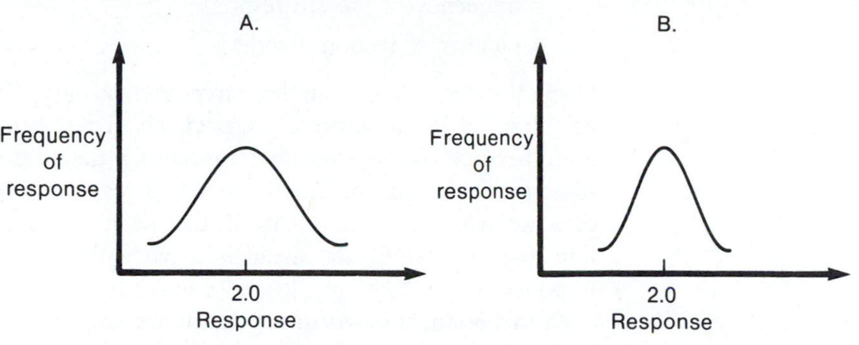

continuous case (Figure 11–4). Here, both cases have means of 2; but, in case A, there is more spread about the mean than in case B.

To have an index which captures this spread, most people use the standard deviation. It is estimated as follows:

$$s_x = s = \sqrt{\frac{\sum\limits_{\substack{\text{all}\\ \text{observations}}} (X - \bar{X})^2}{\text{Number of observations} - 1}} \cdot \sqrt{\frac{N-n}{N-1}}$$

$$= \sqrt{\frac{\sum\limits_{i=1}^{n} (X_i - \bar{X})^2}{n-1}} \cdot \sqrt{\frac{N-n}{N-1}}$$

When the sample size n is small in relation to the population size (which it typically is), the $\frac{N-n}{N-1}$ term (the finite population correction factor) is close to 1 and the formula reduces to:

$$s = \sqrt{\frac{\sum\limits_{i=1}^{n} (X_i - \bar{X})^2}{n-1}}$$

When data are grouped into categories (as they usually are in survey data), this formula reduces to:

$$s = \sqrt{\frac{\sum\limits_{j=1}^{c} f_i(X_i - \bar{X})^2}{n-1}}$$

where

f_i = frequency of the ith response.
c = number of response codes.

Using this formula on the three hypothetical sets of data, we find standard deviations of 1, .45, and 1.27, respectively. These values indicate the relative usefulness of the average in representing the responses. The smaller the standard deviation, the closer the actual responses are to the mean. In this case, we again see that, in case B, the mean is a relatively good representation and, in case C, the mean is a particularly terrible representation of responses.

At this point, it is worth noting (as the careful reader no doubt has) that case C is different from the other two in that it is bimodal—that is, the most likely results are either high or low, but not near the mean of 2. The easiest way to recognize this is to observe the frequency distribution. Since computing frequencies or even looking at them is somewhat tedious, however, it is useful to use the standard deviation as a tip-off/signal to look at responses more closely. Specifically, when the standard deviation becomes large in relation to the range of the variable (in case C, 1.43 versus 3; 4 minus 1; or almost half the range), then, by looking at the frequency distribution, we may uncover bimodal responses. On the other hand, when the standard deviation is small in relation to the range (in case B, .45 versus 3), then most of the information about responses is likely to be "captured" by the mean.

To give an example of the calculation of a standard deviation, we return to the example in Table 11–2. Assuming nonresponses were excluded (and, therefore, the mean was 2.32), we get the following:

Code	*Frequency* (f_i)	$(X_i - \bar{X})^2$	$f_i(X_i - \bar{X})^2$
1	425	1.74	739.50
2	61	.10	6.10
3	11	.46	5.06
4	340	2.82	959.62
	837		1,710.28

Thus,

$$s = \sqrt{\frac{1,710.28}{836}} = 1.43$$

COMPARING RESPONSES TO TWO OR MORE QUESTIONS

Until now, this chapter has been devoted to analyzing questions one at a time. This section, by contrast, discusses techniques for comparing the responses to several questions if the data are intervally scaled.

Consider, for example, ratings of a series of attributes in terms of their importance in decision making. Typically, most of the attributes will be rated as important. The key issue, however, is to uncover which are the most important attributes. Hence, we must look at responses across attributes to see which are the most important.

Plotting

The simplest way to do this is to plot the mean responses in a profile chart. Consider the example of Table 11–3, taken from question 9 in the nutrition study which rated importance of attributes of food on a five-point scale from 1 (very important) to 5 (very unimportant). We can construct a plot of these results to highlight them (Figure 11–5). It is obvious from this plot that taste is the key attribute, with other family members' preferences, price, and nutritional value all closely bunched as next most important. (Given the socially correct answer favors nutrition, my guess is that it is, in fact, the fourth most important attribute.)

Ranking

Another way to analyze the results is simply to rank the attributes by the mean response. In this case, we find the results are the following:

1. Taste.
2. Nutritional value.
3. Other family members' preferences.
4. Price.
5. Variety.
6. Availability.
7. Advertised specials.
8. Ease of preparation.
9. Habit.
10. Diet restrictions.

This ranking has several shortcomings. First, there is undoubtedly no statistical significance in some of the differences, such as between 3 and 4, and 8 and 9. Presentation of rankings (and to a lesser extent, the profile chart) tends to downplay this point. Second, the attribute "diet restrictions" intuitively is not the tenth most important. This is because it is essentially a binary attribute; either you have a diet restriction or you do not. Therefore, for those who think it is very important (26.7 percent), it may well be the most important attribute. Since we are ranking average importance, however, it appears unimportant and we could falsely conclude that it can be ignored.

TABLE 11–3 Importance of Attribute in Choosing Food

Attribute	*Mean Importance (1 = very important, 5 = very unimportant)*
Variety	2.02
Taste	1.24
Other family members' preferences	1.71
Diet restrictions	2.98
Price	1.74
Availability	2.16
Ease of preparation	2.78
Habit	2.82
Advertised specials	2.26
Nutritional value	1.66

FIGURE 11–5 Food Attribute Importances

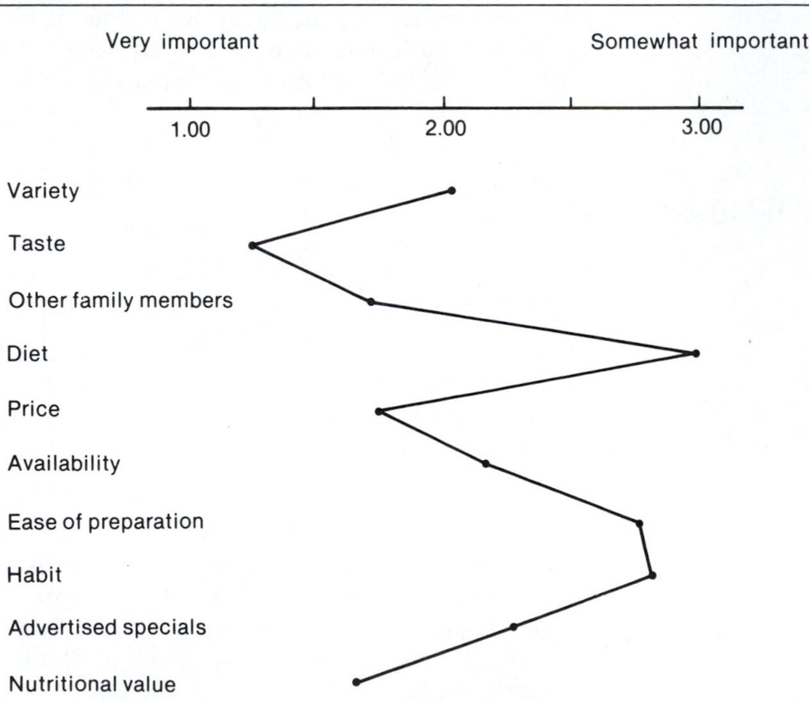

Indexing

A final approach for indicating relative scores is to recalibrate the scale. This approach is related to the issues of normalizing and standardizing discussed in Chapter 7. We can do this by first finding the typical average important score for an attribute by taking the average of the average importance scores:

2.02
1.24
1.71
2.98
1.74
2.16
2.78
2.82
2.26
1.66
21.37

$$\text{Average} = \frac{21.37}{10} = 2.14$$

We then can recompute averages in terms of either differences from this average value or as an index of the ratio of the average on the particular attribute to the overall average (Table 11–4). The advantage of these indexes is that they highlight extreme cases and quickly indicate relatively important and unimportant attributes.

TABLE 11–4 Attribute Importance Indexes

Attribute	*Difference Index*	*Ratio Index*
Variety	−.12 (2.02 − 2.14)	.94 (2.02/2.14)
Taste	−.90	.58
Other family members' preferences	−.43	.80
Diet restrictions	.84	1.39
Price	−.40	.81
Availability	.02	1.01
Ease of preparation	.64	1.30
Habit	.68	1.32
Advertised specials	.12	1.06
Nutritional value	−.48	.78

BASIC ANALYSIS EXAMPLES

Typically, analysis by a supplier is simply a series of tabulations. If a more elaborate form of presentation is desired, one would expect to see some interpretation interspersed with a question-by-question reporting of basic analyses. While there is no typical format, the report of the nutrition study in Appendix 11–B may provide, in addition to some interesting results, a basic format for preparation of such reports.

A more detailed example of the use of basic analyses can be found in a study of purchasing agents. Lehmann and O'Shaughnessy (1974) reported an attempt to assess which product attributes are most important for different types of products. Forty-five purchasing agents were asked to rate the importance of 17 product attributes for the following four situations:

Type I: Routine order product.

Type II: Procedural problem products (where the principal user must be taught to use the product).

Type III: Performance problem products (where there is some question about whether the product will perform adequately).

Type IV: Political problem products (where there is an extremely large capital outlay or several departments are involved in the decision, or both).

Importances were rated on six-point bipolar adjective scales from 1 = very unimportant to 6 = very important. Ignoring the real question of representativeness given a sample size of 45 (26 in the United States and 19 in the United Kingdom), the average results were computed (Table 11–5).

Looking at the averages leads to several interesting conclusions. First, almost all the attributes are rated in the important half of the scale for all product types. (This is a typical result for importance questions, since individuals seem averse to indicating anything is unimportant.) Second, as expected, the more complex problems produced higher importance ratings on all the attributes. In terms of seeing which were the most important attributes, however, the means alone are not easily interpretable. Hence, the attributes were ranked in terms of average importance for each of the four product types. The results here are quite interesting if not surprising. Reliability of delivery is always one of the most important attributes—not surprising given the criticism a purchasing agent has to endure when deliveries are late. For the routine order product, price, flexibility, and reputation also rank high. For the procedural problem product, technical service, ease of use, and training offered rank highest. For the performance problem product, flexibility, technical service, and reliability data are the other most important attributes. The unexpected results were those dealing with the political problem product. Here, the high importance attributed to price and reliability data was contrary to prior expectations. One explana-

TABLE 11–5 Average Attribute Importance for the Four Product Types

	Product Type							
	I		*II*		*III*		*IV*	
Attribute	*Mean*	*Rank*	*Mean*	*Rank*	*Mean*	*Rank*	*Mean*	*Rank*
1. Reputation	4.84*	4	5.33	7	5.29	5	5.53	2
	(1.09)		(.80)		(.82)		(.69)	
2. Financing	4.51	9	4.07	16	3.91	16	4.91	13
	(1.39)		(1.29)		(1.31)		(1.24)	
3. Flexibility	5.07	3	5.40	5	5.42	2	5.51	5
	(1.12)		(.62)		(.62)		(.59)	
4. Past experience	4.71	6	4.93	13	5.07	9	5.04	10
	(.94)		(.86)		(.69)		(.93)	
5. Technical service	4.36	12	5.53	1	5.38	3	5.40	7
	(1.28)		(.66)		(.89)		(.62)	
6. Confidence in	3.96	14	4.73	15	4.42	15	4.58	16
salespersons	(1.35)		(1.23)		(1.20)		(1.20)	
7. Convenience in	3.80	15	3.73	17	3.71	17	4.08	17
ordering	(1.32)		(1.29)		(1.34)		(1.24)	
8. Reliability data	4.47	11	5.16	11	5.33	4	5.53	3
	(1.24)		(1.07)		(.67)		(.59)	
9. Price	5.60	2	5.29	8	5.18	8	5.56	1
	(.62)		(.70)		(.94)		(.69)	
10. Technical	4.73	5	5.22	9	5.27	6	5.42	6
specifications	(1.25)		(.67)		(.69)		(.72)	
11. Ease of use	4.51	10	5.53	2	5.24	7	5.18	8
	(1.29)		(.59)		(.80)		(.83)	
12. Preference of user	4.00	13	4.76	14	4.53	13	4.84	14
	(1.19)		(1.11)		(1.14)		(.90)	
13. Training offered	3.22	16	5.42	3	4.73	12	5.00	11
	(1.18)		(.87)		(1.19)		(.83)	
14. Training required	3.22	17	5.11	12	4.44	14	4.69	15
	(1.22)		(1.23)		(1.22)		(1.02)	
15. Reliability of	5.64	1	5.42	4	5.44	1	5.53	4
delivery	(.53)		(.72)		(.66)		(.69)	
16. Maintenance	4.60	8	5.20	10	4.82	11	5.00	12
	(1.05)		(.69)		(.96)		(.74)	
17. Sales service	4.64	7	5.36	6	5.07	10	5.09	9
	(1.25)		(.77)		(.84)		(.70)	
Product type mean	4.46		5.07		4.90		5.11	

* Mean (standard deviation).

Source: Donald R. Lehmann and John O'Shaughnessy, "Differences in Attribute Importance for Different Industrial Products." Reprinted from *Journal of Marketing*, published by the American Marketing Association, 38 (April 1974), p. 39.

TABLE 11–6 Significance of Differences in Mean Importance across Product Types

		*Adjusted Average Importance**				
Attribute	*Significance† Raw*	*I*	*II*	*III*	*IV*	*Adjusted Significance‡*
Reputation	.01	.38	.26	.39	.42	—
Financing	.01	.05	−1.00	−.99	−.20	.01
Flexibility	—	.61	.33	.52	.40	—
Past experience	—	.25	−.13	.17	−.07	—
Technical service	.01	−.10	.46	.48	.29	.01
Confidence in salespersons	.05	−.50	−.34	−.48	−.53	—
Convenience in ordering	—	−.60	−1.34	−1.19	−1.03	—
Reliability data	.01	.01	.09	.43	.42	—
Price	.05	1.14	.22	.28	.45	.01
Technical specifications	.01	.27	.15	.37	.31	—
Ease of use	.01	.05	.46	.34	.07	—
Preference of user	.01	−.46	−.31	−.37	−.27	—
Training offered	.01	−1.24	.35	−.17	−.11	.01
Training required	.01	−1.24	.04	−.46	−.42	.01
Reliability of delivery	—	1.18	.35	.54	.42	.01
Maintenance	.05	.14	.13	−.18	−.11	—
Sales service	.01	.18	.29	.17	−.02	—

* For each product type, the mean product importance across the 17 attributes was subtracted from the importance for each of the 17 attributes.
† Significance of difference among product types based on raw average importance.
‡ Significance of difference among product types based on adjusted average importance.

Source: Donald R. Lehman and John O'Shaughnessy, "Differences in Attribute Importance for Different Industrial Products." Reprinted from *Journal of Marketing*, published by the American Marketing Association, 38 (April 1974), p. 40.

tion for this result is that purchasing agents aren't involved in such decisions, and, hence, the results are not meaningful. Alternatively, it may be that political problems are so amorphous and difficult that decision makers search for something they can evaluate, and look to such concrete attributes as price and reliability data to make, or at least justify (especially if something goes wrong), the appropriateness of their choice.

Another way to look at the data is to recalibrate the importance scale by subtracting the mean importance for the product type from the average importance for each attribute. For example, the recalibrated score for the attribute reputation for Type I products is 4.84 − 4.46 = .38. This gives a quick partitioning of the attributes into relatively more important (positive values) and relatively less important attributes (Table 11–6).

It is possible to compare the average importance of each of the attributes across the four product types. When significance tests are performed (see

Chapter 12 for an explanation of how the tests are done), the original attribute ratings are found to change significantly at the .05 significance level in 13 of the 17 attributes and in 10 of the 17 attributes at the .01 significance level. This establishes beyond reasonable doubt the fact that the ratings did change. However, we know that much of the change is due to the increasing importance credited to all attributes as the product becomes more complex. To see if relative importance changes, we need to test for significant changes in the adjusted scores. Six of the 17 attributes change significantly across the four product types. Two of these are price and reliability of delivery, which are by far the most important for Type I and about equally important for the other three product types. The other significant changes were for training offered and required (highest for Type II products), financing (highest for Type I products), and technical service (highest for Type II and III products). These significant results are all perfectly reasonable. (Notice that the seemingly counterintuitive result previously discussed for Type IV products is not significant when the results are viewed in this way.)

Two important points need to be made. First, it often takes some manipulation of data to get the form best suited for interpretation. Second, it is very desirable to check for statistical significance before interpreting results. This avoids the difficult and often misleading task of inventing explanations for what could well be chance results.

RELATIONS BETWEEN VARIABLES: CROSS-TABS

Two Variables

The question of how the response to one question relates to that of another question is crucial to most research. For example, I might like to see how heaviness of usage of a product category, region of the country, and household income relate to each of the questions in a survey. This is commonly done by specifying usage, region, and income as what are known as *banner points*. As the survey results are tabulated question by question, each question is tabulated and percentaged both in total and by each banner point. A typical page of the output might look like Table 11–7. From this table, one would probably conclude that most people are pretty neutral toward Znarts, that heavy users of the product category (which also includes such well-known brands as Whafles, Splibles, and Snuzzles) are somewhat more favorable toward it but not wildly so, that the brand is strongest in the Midwest and East, and that the brand appeals to high-income consumers.

In drawing conclusions from such pages, the key element of analysis is the cross-tabulation between two variables. For example, assume we had

TABLE 11–7 Tabulation by Banner Points (question 17: Do you like Znarts?)

		Usage			*Region*				*Income*		
Response	*Total*	*Low*	*Medium*	*High*	*East*	*Midwest*	*South*	*West*	*Under $20,000*	*$20,000–$40,000*	*Over $40,000*
1 (yes)	10%	8%	11%	15%	12%	16%	4%	7%	6	11%	14%
2	20	15	18	26	25	23	15	18	15	22	24
3	40	38	42	37	38	37	42	43	45	41	31
4	20	31	19	14	14	15	25	24	22	14	20
5 (no)	8	3	9	6	7	5	13	7	7	10	8
n.a.	2	4	1	2	4	4	1	1	5	2	3
Total	100%	100%	100%	100%	100%	100%	100%	100%	100%	100%	100%

Note: n.a. = not available.

TABLE 11–8 Purchase Level by Region

Region	Purchase Level 0–1	2–3	4 or more	Total
A	200	140	60	400
B	60	80	60	200
C	140	180	80	400
Total	400	400	200	1,000

the tabulation of purchase level versus region for a sample of 1,000 people shown in Table 11–8. This raw tabulation is interesting but, in general, not very telegraphic in conveying what is going on in the data. Hence, we need two things: a better way of highlighting results and a way to tell whether the results are meaningful or just a chance occurrence.

Highlighting Results

The most common way of highlighting results is to calculate conditional probabilities or, as they are often called, *contingencies*. We can compute a table of the conditional probability of region given purchase level. The purpose of this would be to isolate where heavy and light users of the product are located. This is done here by calculating the percent each entry is of the column total (often ingeniously called the *column percent*). For example, the probability that a person is from region B, given the person is a light (0–1) purchaser is $60/400 = 15$ percent. The complete contingency table is shown as Table 11–9. From this we can see that heavy users tend to be in region C and light users in region A.

We can also compute the row percents (the purchase level given region). This indicates which purchase levels are most prevalent in which regions. The percent of those people in region B who are light (0–1) purchasers is

TABLE 11–9 Column Percents (region, given purchase level)

Region	Purchase Level 0–1	2–3	4 or more
A	50%	35%	30%
B	15	20	30
C	35	45	40
	100%	100%	100%

TABLE 11–10 Row Percents (purchase level, given region)

	Purchase Level		
Region	*0–1*	*2–3*	*4 or more*
A	50%	35%	15%
B	30	40	30
C	35	45	20

60/200 = 30 percent. Similarly, we get Table 11–10. Here, we see that in region B, 30 percent are heavy purchasers, making region B the strongest market (at least in the past) for our product.

Checking for Statistical Significance

There are an incredible number of different ways to check a table for the presence of a significant relation between the variables (e.g., see Siegel, 1956). The most common, however, is a *chi-square* (χ^2) test. The χ^2 test has three basic steps:

1. It assumes as a basis of comparison that the two variables are not related (H_0: the two variables are independent).
2. It computes an index (χ^2 value) which measures how different the actual results are from what the results would have been if the variables had been independent.
3. The index is compared with a table value; and if the calculated index is bigger than the table value, then the assumption of independence is rejected (and therefore the two variables are related).

Computation of the Standard of Comparison. The standard of comparison assumes that the probability of being in each cell is independent of the two variables. Put differently, the probability of being in a particular cell is the product of the probability of being in that row and the probability of being in that column (these row and column probabilities are often called *the marginals*, presumably because they appear on the margin of the table).

Returning to the example in Table 11–8, we get the row and column probabilities as in Table 11–11. We can now calculate the expected number in each cell. For example, the probability of being from region B and having purchase level 0–1 is (Probability of being from region B) · (Probability of having purchase level 0–1) = (.4)(.2) = .08. The number of people expected in this cell is simply the probability of being in the cell times the total number of people in the table: .08(n) = .08(1,000) = 80.

TABLE 11–11 Relation of Purchase Level and Region

	Purchase Level				
Region	*0–1*	*2–3*	*4 or more*	*Total*	*Row Probability*
A	200	140	60	400	.4
B	60	80	60	200	.2
C	140	180	80	400	.4
Total	400	400	200	1,000	
Column probability	.4	.4	.2		1.0

TABLE 11–12 Expected Cell Sizes

	Purchase Level		
Region	*0–1*	*2–3*	*4 or More*
A	160	160	80
B	80	80	40
C	160	160	80

Hence, we can derive an expected table from:[1]

$$\text{Number expected in cell } i, j = (\text{Probability of being in row } i) \cdot (\text{Probability of being in row } j) \cdot (\text{Number of people in the table}) \quad (11.1)$$

Here, we get the expected numbers as in Table 11–12.

Building an Index. The index used measures the difference between the expected and actual number of observations in each cell of the table. The index is the sum of the squared differences between expected and observed numbers divided by the expected number in each cell (to keep the numbers

[1]For hand computational purposes, it is possible to use a short form of either (Probability of being in row i) (Number of people in column j) or (Number of people in row i) (Probability of being in column j). While mathematically identical, these formulas do not convey as clearly the role of the independence assumption in generating the expected values and, hence, were not used in the main presentation.

a manageable size) for all cells:

$$\text{Index} = \sum_{\text{all cells}} \frac{(\text{Observed number in cell } i, j - \text{Expected number in cell } i, j)^2}{\text{Expected number in cell } i, j}$$

$$= \sum_{i=1}^{r} \sum_{j=1}^{c} \frac{(f_{\text{obs}} - f_{\text{exp}})^2}{f_{\text{exp}}} \qquad (11.2)$$

where

r is the number of rows and c the number of columns. Obviously, the larger the index, the more different the observed and expected values are. In this case, by comparing Tables 11–8 and 11–12, we get:

$$\begin{aligned}\text{Index} &= \frac{(200-160)^2}{160} + \frac{(140-160)^2}{160} + \frac{(60-80)^2}{80} + \frac{(60-80)^2}{80} \\ &\quad + \frac{(80-80)^2}{80} + \frac{(69-40)^2}{40} + \frac{(140-160)^2}{160} \\ &\quad + \frac{(180-160)^2}{160} + \frac{(80-80)^2}{80} \\ &= 10 + 2.5 + 5 + 5 + 0 + 10 + 2.5 + 2.5 + 0 \\ &= 37.5\end{aligned}$$

Evaluating the Index. The standard of comparison for this index is the chi-square (χ^2) table. Specifically, the index is χ^2 with $(r-1)(c-1)$ degrees of freedom.[2] In this case, the χ^2 value has $(3-1)(3-1) = 4$ degrees of freedom.

[2] The degree of freedom notion is fairly subtle. The basic idea is that an observation is "free" if its value is unconstrained. Since in calculating the expected cell sizes we "rigged" the data so that the number in each row was equal to the actual number, there is one degree of freedom lost. (In other words, if you tell me all but one of the expected values, the other can be found.) Since this is true for each row and column, we are left with the following table without the bordering row and column in terms of free observations:

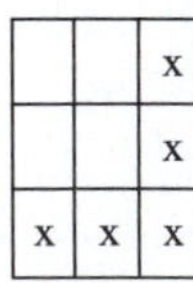

Hence, there are $(r-1)(c-1)$ "free" observations left. (If this brief explanation is unappealing, either (a) see a statistics book or (b) memorize $(r-1)(c-1)$, an inelegant but effective approach.)

Remembering the way the index was constructed, we are only willing to reject the independence assumption if the index is large. (Hence, it is almost universally accepted that a one-tail test is appropriate.) Therefore, for this case and the .05 significance level, we get from a table $\chi^2_{4,.05} = 9.49$. Since 37.5 is much larger than 9.49, we reject the independence hypothesis and conclude that region and purchase level are related. What this means, practically, is that the contingency table percentages are, in fact, worth studying.

Example

Income versus Food Expenditures. Returning again to the nutrition data, an interesting issue is what is the relation between household income and weekly food expenditures. To investigate this, data were categorized according to the scheme in Table 11–13. A cross-tab between food expenditures and income was then completed, using the SPSS computer program (see Appendix 11–C). The results appear in Table 11–14. Each cell contains four numbers:

1. *Count.* The number of people in the cell (i.e., 33 people had incomes under \$10,000 and spent less than \$15 per week on food).
2. *Row percent.* The percent of the people in the row who are in the column (i.e., 33/464 = 7.1 percent of the people with incomes under \$10,000 spent less than \$15 per week on food).
3. *Column percent.* The percent of the people in the column who are in the row (i.e., 33/39 = 84.9 percent of the people who spent less than \$15 per week on food had incomes under \$10,000).
4. *Total percent.* The percent of the total sample in the particular cell (i.e., 33/933 = 3.5 percent).

TABLE 11–13 Code Values for Food Survey

Code	*Meaning*
Weekly food expenditures:	
13	Less than \$15
23	\$15–\$29
38	\$30–\$44
53	\$45–\$59
70	\$60 or more
Income:	
1	Under 10,000
2	10,000–20,000
3	Over 20,000

FIGURE 11–14 Cross-Tabulation of Income versus Food Expenditures

	COUNT / ROW PCT / COL PCT / TOT PCT	Food Expenditures 13.	23.	38.	53.	70.	ROW TOTAL
Income	1.	33	226	149	45	11	464
		7.1	48.7	32.1	9.7	2.4	49.7
		84.6	70.2	47.8	23.1	16.9	
		3.5	24.2	16.0	4.8	1.2	
	2.	5	73	121	102	31	332
		1.5	22.0	36.4	30.7	9.3	35.6
		12.8	22.7	38.8	52.3	47.7	
		0.5	7.8	13.0	10.9	3.3	
	3.	1	23	42	48	23	137
		0.7	16.8	30.7	35.0	16.8	14.7
		2.6	7.1	13.5	24.6	35.4	
		0.1	2.5	4.5	5.1	2.5	
	COLUMN TOTAL	39	322	312	195	65	933
		4.2	34.5	33.4	20.9	7.0	100.0

While somewhat overwhelming, the table indicates that income and food expenditures are positively related (high income tends to go with high food expenditures and low income with low food expenditures). This is confirmed by the χ^2 statistic of 167.2, a huge value for $(5 - 1)(3 - 1) = 8$ degrees of freedom.[3] Notice, however, that the relationship between income and food expenditure does not "leap out" of the table. Since income and food expenditure are both ordinally (and close to intervally) scaled variables, more efficient means for describing the relationship may be appropriate.

You may notice that a variety of other statistics appear in computer output besides chi-square. These statistics are sometimes useful in specific situations. Nonetheless, most researchers and all managers can get along just fine without using them.

[3] A useful fact is that the mean of the chi-square is the number of degrees of freedom and, as the number of degrees of freedom increases, the test statistic becomes approximately normally distributed, with a standard deviation equal to the square root of two times the number of degrees of freedom. This fact makes it possible to quickly tell when something is clearly significant, as well as estimate significance if table values are not available.

Multiway Tables

In many cases, it is desirable to consider three or more variables simultaneously. In such instances, it is customary to break the data into multiple tables. For example, assume I wished to simultaneously study the effect of income and education on food expenditures. Hence, I might first remove the effect of income on expenditures by separating the sample into low- and high-income consumers and then doing a two-way cross-tab of education and expenditures for the two samples. The results would look something like the following:

	Low Income		*High Income*	
	Low Ed.	*High Ed.*	*Low Ed.*	*High Ed.*
Low expenditures				
High expenditures				

Often, three-way and higher tabulations reveal interesting results. Consider, for example, the study by Dr. Edwin Salzman and associates concerning the effect of aspirin on reducing blood clotting following major surgery for 95 patients (Lublin, 1977). In this case, aspirin appeared to be useful when the total sample was used. Breaking the sample by sex, however, revealed that aspirin seemed to be very useful for men ($\chi^2 = 7.62$) and not at all useful for women ($\chi^2 = .01$) (Table 11–15). Here, the simple two-way results were misleading.

TABLE 11–15 Relation between Aspirin Therapy and Blood Clots after Surgery

	Clot	*No Clot*
Total sample:		
Aspirin	11	33
Placebo	23	28
Men:		
Aspirin	4	19
Placebo	14	11
Women:		
Aspirin	7	14
Placebo	9	17

Source: Joann S. Lublin, "Aspirin Found to Cut Blood-Clotting Risks in Men, Not Women," *The Wall Stree Journal*, December 8, 1977. Adapted with permission.

Cross-Tabs: Pros and Cons

Cross-tabs are obviously a very useful tool. They have the following advantages:

1. They present results in a simple tabular form which is easy to communicate to management.
2. They work on nominal scale (categorical) data, something that most of the "fancy" analyses do not do.
3. They make no assumption about the form of the relationship. In the purchase level versus region example, the relationship between purchase level and region was not a simple monotonic one (i.e., as region gets "bigger," so does purchase level). While the χ^2 analysis uncovered this relation, analysis based on such measures as a correlation coefficient might not have. It is important to recognize, however, that 2×2 cross-tab tables will also hide nonlinear relationships. One classic example of this was a study by Cox (Buzzell, Cox, and Brown, 1969, pp. 174–75) on the relation between the persuadability of 121 shoppers and their self-confidence. The original 2×2 table made the two variables appear unrelated. When self-confidence was broken into three categories, however, the results changed (Table 11–16). Now we see a non-linear relationship between persuadability and self-confidence. (The relationship has an interesting implication for salespersons: Concentrate your efforts on those who have moderate self-confidence—those with high self-confidence can't be influenced and those with low self-confidence can't make up their minds.)

TABLE 11–16 Persuadability versus Self-Confidence

	Persuadability	
Self-Confidence	*Percent Persuaded*	*Percent Unpersuaded*
Original results:		
Low	47	53
High	45	55
Revised results:		
Very low	37	63
Moderately low	62	38
High	45	55

Source: Robert D. Buzzell, Donald F. Cox, and Rex V. Brown, *Marketing Research and Information Systems: Text and Cases* (New York: McGraw-Hill, 1969), pp. 174–75. © 1969 by McGraw-Hill Book Company. Used with permission.

In spite of these advantages, there are some problems in using cross-tabs:

1. *There should be at least five expected observations in each cell.* When less than five appear in a cell, the χ^2 value becomes unreliable.[4] Hence, it is often necessary to collapse categories together to get sufficient *expected*[5] size in each cell. For example, we might have to combine the "fairly strongly" and "strongly" categories to get sufficient representation in those cells.
2. *Cross-tabs are not an efficient way to search for results.* If there are 100 variables, there are 4,950 possible two-way cross-tabs to perform. Looking at all these is a huge chore, and generating them mainly creates a big pile of scrap paper. (It also is interesting to notice that you would expect at the .05 level to get .05(4950) = 248 "significant" results due to chance alone.) The portrayal of the results is also fairly cumbersome in that a table of conditional probabilities is more clumsy than a correlation coefficient.
3. *Cross-tabs burn up sample size.* An obvious extension of two-way cross-tabs is to sort the observations based on three or more variables at a time. Unfortunately, we soon find cells with few people in them. Assuming there are six categories for the first variable, four for the second, and five for the third, there are (6)(4)(5) cells or 120 different cells. Even with big sample sizes (e.g., 1,000), this is likely to leave small cell sizes. (How many green-eyed midwesterners bought Bufferin last time?) Consequently, the procedure tends to break down when complex relations are being studied.
4. *The size of the chi-square value depends on the number of degrees of freedom and, hence, is a poor index of association.* For example, a chi-square value of 42 would indicate no significant relationship if there were 48 degrees of freedom, and a value of 12 would show a significant relationship if there were only 2 degrees of freedom. Put differently, the chi-square value does not indicate the strength of the relationship between the two variables.[6]

In summary then, cross-tabs are an extremely useful tool. They are well suited to initial investigation of the relation between a few key variables

---

[4]Assume one cell had two observations and an expected size of .3 observations. This one cell would contribute $\frac{(2 - .3)^2}{.3} = 9.6$ to the total χ^2 value, which alone is enough to make it significant at the .05 level for 4 degrees of freedom.

[5]The reason the expected size is the key and not the observed is that the expected size is the denominator of the fraction.

[6]Since χ^2 depends on both the sample size n (the bigger the sample size, the bigger the χ^2 even for a constant relationship) and the number of categories, it is not a particularly useful measure of association. A variety of measures have been devised to overcome some of these

and the other variables. They are not particularly well suited to searching for relations in many-variable data sets. If results are uncovered, however, they often serve as a convenient format for conveying the results to "normal" people.

CORRELATION COEFFICIENTS

Probably the most popular method for quickly summarizing the degree of relation between two variables is a correlation coefficient. The essence of a correlation coefficient is that it is an index which ranges from +1 (the two variables are perfectly positively related—they both get larger together) to −1 (the two variables are perfectly negatively related; as one gets larger the other gets smaller).[7]

Pearson (Product-Moment) Correlation Coefficient

The most common correlation coefficient is the Pearson product-moment correlation (better known as r). This is the coefficient found in essentially all canned computer output. The computational formula for the correlation between two variables X_i and X_j is:

$$r = \frac{\sum_{i=1}^{n} (X_i - \bar{X}_i)(X_j - \bar{X}_j)}{\sqrt{\sum_{i=1}^{n} (X_i - \bar{X}_i)^2}\sqrt{\sum_{i=1}^{n} (X_j - \bar{X}_j)^2}}$$

$$= \frac{\sum_{i=1}^{n} (X_i - \bar{X}_i)(X_j - \bar{X}_j)}{n(s_{X_i})(s_{X_j})} \tag{11.3}$$

---

problems. Specifically, the contingency coefficient attempts to remove the effect of sample size:

$$C = \sqrt{\frac{\chi^2}{n + \chi^2}}$$

Unfortunately, this measure still depends on the number of rows and columns in the table. As a general rule, it is difficult to compare the level of association between two pairs of nominally scaled variables.

[7]By contrast, the size of the chi-square value depends on the number of degrees of freedom, and hence is a poor index of association.

FIGURE 11–6 Food Expenditure versus Income

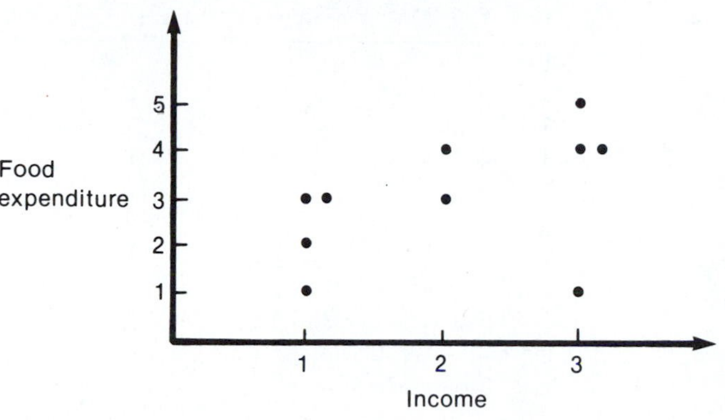

For example, assume we had the following 10 observations:

Person	X_i *(income)*	X_j *(food expenditures)*
1	1	2
2	3	4
3	3	1
4	3	4
5	1	3
6	2	3
7	1	1
8	1	3
9	3	5
10	2	4

When we plot these, as in Figure 11–6, there appears to be a positive relation between income and food expenditure. The computations would proceed as follows:

Find the means:

$$\Sigma X_i = 20, \therefore \overline{X}_i = 2$$

$$\Sigma X_j = 30, \therefore \overline{X}_j = 3.$$

TABLE 11–17 Calculations to Obtain a Correlation

X_i	X_j	$X_i - \bar{X}_i$	$X_j - \bar{X}_j$	$(X_i - \bar{X}_i)^2$	$(X_j - \bar{X}_j)^2$	$(X_i - \bar{X}_i) \cdot (X_j - \bar{X}_j)$
1	2	−1	−1	1	1	+1
3	4	+1	+1	1	1	+1
3	1	+1	−2	1	4	−2
3	4	+1	+1	1	1	+1
1	3	−1	0	1	0	0
2	3	0	0	0	0	0
1	1	−1	−2	1	4	+2
1	3	−1	0	1	0	0
3	5	+1	+2	1	4	+2
2	4	0	+1	0	1	0
				8	16	5

Compute the correlations using Equation 11.3 (see Table 11–17):

$$r = \frac{5}{\sqrt{8}\,\sqrt{16}} = .44$$

The correlation coefficient can be tested for statistical significance using the following statistic:

$$\frac{r\sqrt{n-2}}{\sqrt{1-r^2}}$$

This statistic is approximately distributed according to the t distribution with $n - 2$ degrees of freedom. The t distribution looks like the normal distribution but is somewhat "fatter" for a small number of degrees of freedom. When the degrees of freedom exceed 30, the t distribution is essentially the same as the normal distribution, and, hence, values from the normal table can be substituted for the t values.

In the previous example, which had a sample of size 10 and an $r = .44$, that means comparing a table value of $t_{.05,8} = 2.31$ with:

$$\frac{(.44)\sqrt{8}}{\sqrt{1-(.44)^2}}\ \frac{.44(2.83)}{.90} = 1.38$$

Since 1.38 is less than 2.31, the correlation is not significant. (In other words, the apparent relation may be due to chance and, hence, misleading.) Obviously, as the sample size gets bigger, the chance for a particular size correlation being significant increases. (In fact, a correlation of .001 is statistically significant, given a large enough sample size.) Also, the t

distribution is approximately normal for large (greater than 30) sample sizes. Hence, if we like to use the .05 significance level to quickly filter out important linear relations, for samples above 30 in size we can simply look for t values above 2 in absolute value.

Limitations. There are the following two major limitations on the value of a correlation coefficient:

Both Variables Are Assumed to Be Intervally Scaled and Continuous. Actually, for most purposes, this is an overly rigid assumption. Ordinally scaled data may be used if you recognize the resulting correlation will be biased downward slightly. Consider the following data:

X_1	X_2 *(rank)*
1	1
3	2
4	3
8	4
9	5

Obviously, the ordinal (rank) measure of X_1 is not an accurate reflection of the true value. Still, the correlation between the true and rank values of X_1 is high (r = .98), and, thus, the correlation between the ordinal measure of X_1 and anything that the true X_1 is correlated with will also tend to remain high. In short, the coefficient is very robust (stands up well) to modest violations of this assumption (Morrison, 1972).

The Relationship between the Variables is Linear. Consider the cases in Figure 11–7. In case A, there is a strong positive correlation (i.e., $r = +.9$). In case B, there is a negative relation ($r = -.6$), albeit weaker than case A. In case C, there is a clear relationship, but the simple correlation coefficient would be 0 ($r = 0$). This is because the correlation cannot detect severely

FIGURE 11–7 Sample Correlations

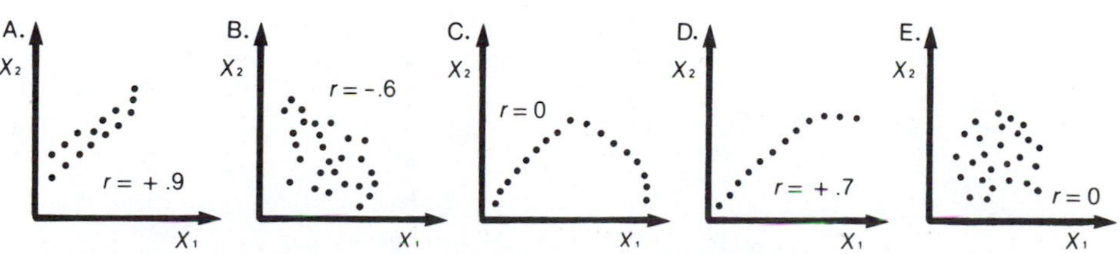

curvilinear (nonmonotonic) relations. In case D, we have a nonlinear relation; but since the relation is monotonic (as X_1 gets bigger so does X_2), the correlation will still be positive enough to indicate a substantial relationship ($r = +.7$). Case E gives an example where there is genuinely no relation between X_1 and X_2.

Correlation for Ranked (Ordinal) Data

When data are ordinally rather than intervally scaled, the following two choices appear:

Use the Product-Moment Correlation as an Approximation. While this would make a purist cringe, it is often a good approximation. Similarly, binary scales (e.g., yes-no) can be used to compute correlations which indicate whether the construct (e.g., the taking of aspirin) is related to another variable.

Use a Special Correlation which Takes the Ordinal Nature of the Data into Account. There are many such coefficients including the coefficient of concordance, the coefficient of consistency, and Kendall's tau. As an example of this type of correlation, Spearman's rank correlation coefficient computes the correlation between two sets of rankings using the following formula:

$$R = 1 - \frac{6 \sum_{i=1}^{n} d^2}{n^3 - n} \tag{11.4}$$

TABLE 11-18 Calculation of Spearman Rank Correlation Coefficient

First Person's Ranking	*Second Person's Ranking*	*Difference in Rankings (d)*	d^2
3	2	1	1
5	5	0	0
6	1	5	25
2	6	4	16
1	3	2	4
4	4	0	0
			46

$$R = 1 - \frac{6(46)}{6^3 - 6} = 1 - \frac{276}{210} = -.31$$

where

d = number of places that an object differs in the two rankings.

n = number of objects ranked.

An example of the use of this formula[8] appears in Table 11–18.

DATA ADJUSTMENT PROCEDURES

In analyzing a set of data, a variety of procedures are sometimes used. Two of the most common are recoding and weighting for unequal response rates.

Recoding

Data are often recoded. This is done for the following two major reasons:

To Produce More Simplified Results. For example, frequently examining the initial tabs indicates several responses (e.g., brand used last) receive a very small percentage of mentions. In such cases, it is often desirable to combine infrequently given responses into an "all other" category to simplify the analysis.

To Make the Top End of the Scale "Up." Data can be collected in many different ways. For example, importances can be collected on five-point scales with "5" representing very important or, alternatively, "5" representing very unimportant. This means that it is impossible to interpret a result (e.g., a score of 4) without knowing which end of the scale is "up." The problem is compounded when two variables are combined, as in a correlation coefficient. A numerical correlation may be positive, and the relation between the underlying constructs negative, or vice versa. For example, assume importance placed on money were coded 1 through 5 with a low number indicating great importance, and income was coded 1 through 6, with 6 being the highest category. If we assume that the importance of money would decrease as income increases, we would expect the basic concepts to be negatively related. Given this coding scheme, however, the correlation would be positive. Unless carefully interpreted, this positive number could lead to mistakenly concluding that the importance of money and income were positively related. To avoid such possible

---

[8]Interestingly, when there are no ties in the rankings, Formulas 11.3 and 11.4 will produce the same number.

confusion, it is often desirable to recode all variables so that a bigger code value means more of the variable.

Weighting for Unequal Response Rates

Given a sample which truly represents the frame, analysis can proceed directly. When the sample does not match the frame, however, the question arises of how to adjust the results. Consider again the nutrition example that consciously oversampled lower-income respondents:

Income	*Sample*	*United States*
Less than $10,000	49.7%	39.2%
$10,000–$19,999	35.6%	42.2%
$20,000 or more	14.7%	18.6%

In general, relationships among variables (e.g., correlations) are not affected by unequal sampling. The levels (means) of other variables, however, may be. In fact, for any variable which is related to income, a direct projection will be erroneous, although not necessarily greatly in error. The issue then becomes, "How can I weight responses to get a useful projection?" The procedure utilized is based on the stratified sampling formulas of Chapter 9. In this case, we can weight people in different income classes as follows:

Income	*Weight*
Less than $10,000	392/497 = .789
$10,000–$19,999	422/356 = 1.185
$20,000 or more	186/147 = 1.265

This weighting scheme will ensure that people in the less than $10,000 income category account for 39.2 percent of the responses, and so forth. (Actually, the weights should be calculated to more significant digits, but these are enough to demonstrate the process.) To show the effect of this weighting, assume that income was related to food expenditures, as in Table 11–19. Assume we coded the expenses as $13, $23, $38, $53, and $70, respectively, for the five categories (essentially substituting the category median). The estimated unweighted mean expenditures would then be $13(.042) + $23(.345) + $38(.334) + $53(.209) + $70(.070) = $0.55 + $7.94 + $12.69 + $11.08 + $4.90 = $37.16.

TABLE 11–19 Raw Cross-Tabs

	Expense per Week					
Income	*Under $15*	*$15–$29*	*$30–$44*	*$45–$60*	*Over $60*	*Total*
Under $10,000	33	226	149	45	11	464
$10,000–$19,999	5	73	121	102	31	332
$20,000 and over	1	23	42	48	23	137
Total	39	322	312	195	65	933
	4.2%	34.5%	33.4%	20.9%	7.0%	100%

TABLE 11–20 Weighted Cross-Tabs

	Expense per Week					
Income	*Under $15*	*$15–$29*	*$30–$44*	*$45–$60*	*Over $60*	*Total*
Under $10,000	26.0	178.3	117.6	35.5	8.7	366.1
$10,000–$19,999	5.9	86.5	143.4	120.9	36.7	393.4
$20,000 and over	1.3	29.1	53.1	60.7	29.1	173.3
Total	33.2	293.9	314.1	217.1	74.5	932.8
	3.5%	31.5%	33.7%	23.3%	8.0%	100%

Alternatively, we could reweight the data, producing Table 11–20. This implies a mean consumption of $13(.035) + $23(.315) + $38(.337) + $53(.233) + $70(.080) = $0.46 + $7.25 + $12.81 + $12.35 + $5.60 = $38.47. Hence, failure to weight the data would produce a noticeable but small (about 3.5 percent) error in the estimate of consumption expenditures. Obviously, had the sample been closer to the actual U.S. income distribution, this error would have been reduced.

The weighting problem can be further complicated if the sample is off in terms of two or more variables. In this case, the weights must be developed to account for two or more characteristics (e.g., income and age) which are disproportionately represented simultaneously. In such a case, use (*a*) common sense and (*b*) a consultant.

Given the need to weight, a mundane question arises about how to do it. The dominant solution is to use a canned (prewritten) program which allows unequal weights. If such a program is unavailable, the alternatives are the following:

Write your own routine (a tedious solution).

Adjust your sample. This can be done by reducing the sample to match the cell which is the most underrepresented. Assume, for example, we have the following results:

Income Group	*Original Sample Size*	*Sample Percent*	*"Correct" Percent*
A	500	50	50
B	400	40	30
C	100	10	20

We can now adjust the sample to match income group C, the most underrepresented. Since group C should represent 20 percent of the population, we will take all 100 respondents in group C for our new sample. The resulting reduced sample, thus, will be as follows:

Income Group	*Original Sample Size*	*Reduced Sample Size*
A	500	250
B	400	150
C	100	100

The 250 people in group A will be chosen randomly from the original 500; similarly, the 150 in group B will be chosen from the 400 originals in group B.

As can be seen from this example, this procedure is fairly inefficient in that 500 responses, half the original sample, are unused. Because of this (and a penchant for big sample sizes), many researchers will blow up, rather than reduce, a sample. This is done by increasing the results to match the overrepresented cell. In this case, we would match group B as the most overrepresented group. The resulting "sample" would then be:

Income Group	*Original Sample Size*	*Blown-up Sample Size*
A	500	667
B	400	400
C	100	267
	1,000	1,334

The new group A would consist of the original 500 plus 167 of the original 500 reproduced at random. The 267 of group C would consist of two duplicate sets of the original 100 plus 67 of the 100 chosen at random. While this method will produce an unbiased estimate of the means of variables, the increased sample size is deceiving. Hence, while this method may "trick" computer programs into weighting responses, it may also trick researchers into thinking they have a better sample than they really do.

The weighting of unequal responses is, thus, a nontrivial problem. It also makes statistical interpretation of the results much more difficult. The dominant solution is to get a good sample. Failing that, the researcher must choose between somewhat biased results and the prospect of some gyrations to overcome the unfortunate sampling result.

One final point is worth mentioning. Weighting can be used to cover up for a poor job of sampling. In the previous example, income group C was underrepresented. Once the data were weighted, however, this fact is not obvious. Therefore, make sure you know what weighting scheme was employed and that the weights are not grossly different (e.g., weight in one stratum = 1 and weight in another stratum = 40). If the weights are grossly different *and* this is not by design, as in the case of a disproportionate stratified sample, then additional sampling may be required. Put differently, some suppliers in effect cover up their inability to obtain respondents in hard-to-reach segments of the population by weighting the data.

SUMMARY

This chapter has presented a variety of ways for analyzing data: tabulations, means, cross-tabulations, and correlations. All these methods are standard procedures in the market research business, but the most standard is cross-tabs. As the book proceeds to more complicated analyses, remember that in most studies the majority of the results can be deduced from or at least reported in the form of such mundane but understandable procedures.

It is also worth emphasizing that cross-tabs and correlations are not causal. Cross-tabulation and the associated χ^2 statistic and correlations make no assumptions about how two variables are related. For example, we might find occupation and preference for type of painting are related. This does not say that occupation causes preference or that preference causes occupation. In fact, it may be that a third variable (e.g., education) affects both income and preference for type of painting. Thus, the relationships uncovered by a chi-square or a correlation are just that: observed association, which is why these methods can be thought of as means for relationship portrayal. In the next chapters we discuss methods which are designed to assess the impact (effect) of one variable on another.

PROBLEMS

1. A judge admonishes the jury: "I want you to be absolutely certain before you return a guilty verdict." What will the outcome be?
2. Given:

x	8	1	4	2	3	6	5	7
y	7	2	3.5	1	3.5	8	5	6

What is:
a. The Pearson correlation.
b. The Spearman rank correlation.

3. How can I test to see if two nominally scaled variables are related?
4. I sample 800 people to determine their cereal preferences. The results of the study are as follows:

	Brand			
Preference	*He-Man*	*Supa-Sweet*	*Little Crispies*	*Slush Puppies*
Like	90	100	90	120
Dislike	110	100	110	80

Are preferences and brands related?

5. In order to ascertain preferences for three new package designs, prototypes of each of the packages were shown to some people who then classified them as superior, average, or inferior. Interpret these results:

	Rating			
Design	*Inferior*	*Average*	*Superior*	*Total*
1	60	80	60	200
2	160	140	100	400
3	80	80	40	200
Total	300	300	200	800

6. Interpret the following tabulation of 2,500 responses:

Number of Contracts by School	*Contributions to Alumni Fund*			
	None	*Small*	*Large*	*Total*
1	150	150	200	500
2–3	350	200	450	1,000
4 or more	500	150	350	1,000

7. In estimating the demand for a new household appliance, the following table was compiled:

	Definitely Would Buy					
	Version A ($400)		*Version B ($200)*		*Version C ($200)*	
	No.	*%*	*No.*	*%*	*No.*	*%*
Under 25	211	23.8	964	17.2	240	13.3
25–34	253	28.5	1,916	34.2	606	33.5
35–44	34	3.8	906	16.2	166	9.2
45–54	279	31.1	1,324	23.6	615	34.0
55 and over	115	13.0	490	8.7	181	10.0

Interpret.

8. Are region and sales significantly related?

	Region		
Brand	*A*	*B*	*C*
1	40	50	60
2	20	40	90
3	30	60	150

9. In a blind test, 100 respondents tested our brand of detergent and rated its bleach content as follows:

16%	too little bleach
12	almost enough
36	just right
20	slightly too much
16	too much bleach
100%	

Another 200 respondents tested our main competitor's detergent and rated its bleach content as follows:

8%	too little bleach
12	almost enough
60	just right
12	slightly too much
8	too much bleach
100%	

Should we get concerned about the bleach level in our detergent since only 36 percent of the respondents rated ours "just right"?

10. The sale of beer to relatively few heavy users accounts for a large portion of the sales volume of Suds brand beer. The brand manager of Suds would like to expand the distribution but does not know which city should be selected to expand or "roll out" into. Three cities are being considered; Bluelaw, Wasdry, and Spilltown. The affluence of the citizens varies greatly between the towns. A survey of 200 Suds purchasers indicated that 70 percent of the purchasers were light users, and 50 percent had high incomes, as shown in the following table of percentages:

	High Income	*Low Income*
Heavy user	20%	10%
Light user	30%	40%

If the usage rate and income are not related, then the Suds brand manager will try to expand into Spilltown; but if they are related, then the manager will select the town with a favorable income distribution. What advice would you give the Suds brand manager?

11. A sample of 200 persons revealed that 55 percent of the sampled people who shop regularly in our chain of supermarkets usually buy our private brand of coffee. However, 63.3 percent of the sampled people who shop regularly in competing supermarkets usually buy the private label coffee in those stores. The sample included 80 persons who regularly shop in our stores and 120 persons who regularly shop in competing stores. We make more money on private brand coffee than on other coffee. The difference between 55 percent and 63.3 percent seems like a lot, especially when you consider all of our millions of customers. Does the sample indicate that our private brand coffee sales are significantly lower than competitors', or shouldn't we worry?

12. The sales of baby food to elderly people accounts for a significant portion of the sales volume. A canner has developed a line of "adult"

mushy, easily digestible foods and tried selling the new products to older customers in a store in Retirement Village. Sampling 50 shoppers in the store, the canner found that 20 percent had no money worries, 20 percent get along OK, and 60 percent are financially insecure. Also, 30 percent of the shoppers indicated that they had tried the new brand, as shown in the following table of percentages:

	Tried	*Did Not Try*
No money worries	12%	8%
Get along OK	2%	18%
Financially insecure	16%	44%

If trial and income are not related, then the food canner feels the distribution of the product can be increased quickly. However, if they are related, then perhaps the effect of income should be studied before distribution is expanded. What advice would you give the food canner?

13. A prestigious East Coast research house conducted a national telephone survey. The firm had been hired partly because of its sophisticated sampling capability. The final report indicated the following number of interviews in each geographic area, compared to the 1970 census breakdown for the same areas.

	Sample Size	*U.S. Percent of Population*
Northeast	125	24.4%
South	171	30.4
Northcentral	155	27.6
West	145	17.6
	597	100%

Is the geographic distribution of interviews consistent with the firm's contract to obtain a simple random sample of the U.S. population with telephones? What weighting of observations would you use in computing statistics from these interviews?

14. Four different BLUGOS price promotions have been advertised in successive Wednesday night newspapers. The sales (cases) of BLUGOS during the following three days were recorded each week:

Promotion	*Sales*
16¢ off, no coupon	105
18¢ off, no coupon	95
20¢ off, 5¢ coupon	113
25¢ off, 8¢ coupon	89

How much time should you spend understanding this data and determining the implications for our BLUGOS promotions?

15. Given the following situation where the population is divided into two strata:

Stratum	*Stratum Size (million)*	*Sample Size*	*Average Consumption*
A	20	900	48
B	80	100	3

What is your best estimate for overall average consumption?

16. Consider again the nutrition study described in Table 9–5 in Chapter 9. If income and family size were the two main determinants of weekly food expenditures, how would you weight the sample to produce an accurate representation of average food expenditures?

17. A distribution of the responses to a survey of 681 users of the product class is displayed below for the following measures;

    Preferred brand (A–D).
    Income level (under or over $18,000 for family).
    City (E–H).
    Marital status (M, S, O).

Respondents in City E or F	*Respondents in City G or H*
Low income—married;	Low income—married;
45 prefer A; 7, B; 8, C; 8, D	40 prefer A; 11, B; 13, C; 11, D
Low income—single:	Low income—single:
50 prefer A; 9, B; 8, C; 7, D	35 prefer A; 13, B; 11, C; 11, D
Low income—other:	Low income—other:
23 prefer A; 4, B; 4, C; 3, D	28 prefer A; 5, B; 5, C; 7, D
High income—married;	High income—married;
16 prefer A; 13, B; 12, C; 16, D	30 prefer A; 12, B; 13, C; 14, D
High income—single:	High income—single:
17 prefer A; 15, B; 13, C; 12, D	28 prefer A; 15, B; 13, C; 11, D
High income—other:	High income—other:
9 prefer A; 7, B; 7, C; 8, D	17 prefer A; 5, B; 6, C; 7, D

Use contingency tables to evaluate the difference in effect between advertising theme "value" (which has been played for years in cities E and F) and theme "style" (which has been played for years in cities G and H).

18. Over the past year, a manufacturer has increased advertising by 50 percent in city B. To assess the effectiveness of this move, the manufacturer has surveyed 300 people in city B and 300 people in city A, where the advertising has remained at the lower level.

    The respondents have been broken down by income and marital status:

Respondents in City A	*Respondents in City B*
Married—low income:	Married—low income:
39 preferred our brand	19 preferred our brand
20 preferred their brand	40 preferred their brand
Married—high income:	Married—high income:
48 preferred our brand	94 preferred our brand
92 preferred their brand	47 preferred their brand
Single—low income:	Single—low income:
21 preferred our brand	46 preferred our brand
10 preferred their brand	23 preferred their brand
Single—high income:	Single—high income:
22 preferred our brand	11 preferred our brand
48 preferred their brand	20 preferred their brand

    Interpret.

19. Rentz, Reynolds, and Stout (1983) assembled the following data on the percent of people who consume soft drinks on a typical day, based on surveys taken at four points in time:

	Survey Date			
Age	*1950*	*1960*	*1969*	*1979*
8–19	52.9	62.6	73.2	81.0
20–29	45.2	60.7	76.0	75.8
30–39	33.9	46.6	67.7	71.4
40–49	28.2	40.8	58.6	67.8
50 and over	18.1	28.8	50.0	51.6

    How do you interpret this?

BIBLIOGRAPHY

Buzzell, Robert D.; Donald F. Cox; and Rex V. Brown. *Marketing Research and Information Systems: Text and Cases*. New York: McGraw-Hill, 1969.

Dillon, William R. "Analyzing Large Multiway Contingency Tables: A Simple Method for Selecting Variables." *Journal of Marketing* 43 (Fall 1979), pp. 92–102.

Ehrenberg, A. S. C. *Data Reduction*. New York: John Wiley & Sons, 1978.

Hartwig, Frederick, and Brian E. Dearing. "Exploratory Data Analysis." Beverly Hills, Calif.: Sage University Paper Series on Quantitative Applications in the Social Sciences, 07-016, Sage Publications, 1979.

Kinnear, Thomas C., and James R. Taylor. "Multivariate Methods in Marketing Research: A Further Attempt at Classification." *Journal of Marketing* 35 (October 1971), pp. 56–58.

Lehmann, Donald R., and John O' Shaughnessy. "Difference in Attribute Importance for Different Industrial Products." *Journal of Marketing* 38 (April 1974), pp. 36–42.

Lublin, Joann S. "Aspirin Found to Cut Blood-Clotting Risks in Men, Not Women." *The Wall Street Journal*, December 8, 1977.

Magidson, Jay. "Some Common Pitfalls in Causal Analysis of Categorical Data." *Journal of Marketing Research* 19 (November 1982), pp. 461–71.

Morrison, Donald G. "Regression with Discrete Random Variables: The Effect on R^2." *Journal of Marketing Research* 9 (August 1972), pp. 338–40.

Olsson, Ulf. "Measuring Correlation in Ordered two-Way Contingency Tables." *Journal of Marketing Research* 17 (August 1980), pp. 391–94.

Rentz, Joseph O.; Fred D. Reynolds; and Roy G. Stout. "Analyzing Changing Consumption Patterns with Cohort Analysis." *Journal of Marketing Research* 20 (February 1983), pp. 12–20.

Sawyer, Alan G., and J. Paul Peter. "The Significance of Statistical Significance Tests in Marketing Research." *Journal of Marketing Research* 20 (May 1983), pp. 122–33.

Sheth, Jagdish N. "The Multivariate Revolution in Marketing Research." *Journal of Marketing* 34 (January 1971), pp. 13–19.

Shields, William S., and Roger M. Heeler. "Analysis of Contingency Tables with Sparse Values." *Journal of Marketing Research* 16 (August 1979), pp. 382–86.

Siegel, Sidney. *Nonparametric Statistics*. New York: McGraw-Hill, 1956.

Tukey, J. W. *Exploratory Data Analysis*. Reading, Mass.: Addison-Wesley, 1977.

Appendix 11–A

Basic Analysis of Nutritional Habits Survey

BASIC RESULTS

This section reports the simple question-by-question tabulations of the questionnaire on a percentage basis. The responses are unweighted, and, hence, the results are not directly projectable to the entire population of the United States. The decision to leave the data unweighted was based on the fact that a national census was impossible with these data since only households with two or more members which included a female (wife, etc.) were included. All averages are based on those respondents who answered the particular question being analyzed with nonresponses excluded.

Section I—Shopping Habits

1. Portion of shopping done by the respondent:

	Percent
No answer	.6
None of it	1.6
Less than half	3.6
About half	5.5
Most of it	31.4
All of it	57.2

Interpretation: The respondents are, as expected, the principal food shoppers for their households.

2. Number of times they shop for food each week:

	Percent
No answer	.5
Less than once	12.8
Once a week	49.1
2–4 times a week	35.7
5 or more times a week	1.8

Interpretation: Most of this sample shop for food about once a week.

3. Portion of the items purchased which are on a shopping list:

	Percent
No answer	.7
None (no list)	19.0
Some	3.3
About half	5.1
More than half	14.0
Almost all	57.8

Interpretation: While most people prepare a fairly complete list before shopping, almost 20 percent go to the store with no list at all.

4. Amount of money spent on food per week:

	Percent
No answer	.7
Under $15	4.1
$15–$29	34.3
$30–$44	33.2
$45–$60	20.7
Over $60	6.9

Interpretation: A "typical" family spends $35–$40 per week on food.

5. Change in weekly spending from last year:

	Percent
No answer	.9
Spend at least $10 less than last year	2.6
$5–$10 less than last year	3.6
About the same as last year	13.2
$5–$10 more than last year	48.7
Over $10 more than last year	31.1

Interpretation: The typical household is spending $5–$10 more per week for food this year than last. This implies an increase of about 20 percent.

6. Number of brands and sizes considered in buying staple products (soup, ketchup, etc.):

	Percent
No answer	.3
Only 1 or 2	49.5
Many brands, one size	8.6
Many sizes, one brand	3.3
Many brands and sizes	38.3

Interpretation: This question was intended to find out the number of people who actively shop for a product versus the number who have previously decided which alternative to select. Interestingly, about half the people have predetermined choices and, hence, are presumably very insensitive to new offerings, point of purchase materials, and specials.

7. Approach to food shopping:

	Percent
No answer	1.0
I actively seek information about food in terms of nutritional value, price, etc.	29.0
I sometimes try new foods because of new information, but generally buy the same foods	53.1
The food I buy is almost always the same, and I spend very little time thinking about it	16.9

Interpretation: This question was intended to find out how many people actively seek information about food. The 29 percent who say they do is probably biased upward since it is in some sense the "right" answer. The fact that 70 percent are not very interested in new information suggests that attempts to change behavior through "rational" appeals will not be easy, as food manufacturers can no doubt attest.

Section I *(continued)*

8. Use of food stamps by the immediate family:

	Percent
No answer	.1
Never used	87.9
Used to, but do not use them now	6.9
We are presently using them	5.1

Interpretation: Food stamp usage has occurred among 12 percent of the sample with 5.1 percent currently using them.

9. Importance of attributes in the decision about which food to serve:

Attribute	*No Answer*	*Very Important*				*Not very Important*	*Average Importance*	*Rank of Average Importance*
Variety	4.5%	38.8%	21.0%	32.2%	2.0%	1.5%	2.02	5
Taste	3.9	79.1	11.7	4.7	.2	.3	1.24	1
Other family members' preferences	5.2	51.5	23.5	16.8	1.6	1.4	1.71	3
Diet restrictions	6.8	26.7	10.5	21.1	7.6	27.3	2.98	10
Price	3.6	54.6	16.8	22.2	1.2	1.6	1.74	4
Availability at stores where you normally shop	6.1	35.4	21.6	28.9	2.9	5.1	2.16	6
Ease of preparation	5.9	18.4	17.6	36.6	9.5	12.1	2.78	8
Habit (past eating patterns)	7.9	13.0	20.3	40.1	10.5	8.2	2.82	9
Advertised specials	4.0	38.2	18.9	23.8	6.2	8.8	2.26	7
Nutritional value	3.2	55.5	21.9	16.6	2.0	.7	1.66	2

Interpretation: The importance of diet restrictions divides the sample in thirds: 27 percent find them very important, 46 percent somewhat important, and 27 percent find them completely unimportant. In terms of relative importance, taste is by far the most important variable. Nutrition is maintained to edge out price and other family members' preferences as second most important, although this is an obvious "right" answer, and hence, the stated importance of nutrition is inflated. Overall, it appears that taste and price dominate food selection decisions.

10. Attention paid to different product features.

		Amount of Attention Paid				
	No Answer	*Great Deal*	*Some*	*Little or None*	*Average*	*Rank*
Brand name	2.8%	38.5%	51.2%	7.6%	1.68	7
Number of servings	4.5	43.2	40.2	12.1	1.68	6
Net weight or volume	3.8	48.1	36.0	12.1	1.63	5
Total price	2.0	80.6	15.2	2.1	1.20	1
Amount of ingredients	4.9	39.6	40.3	15.2	1.74	8
Unit price	4.8	51.5	32.7	11.1	1.58	4
List of ingredients	4.7	33.4	46.3	15.6	1.81	9
Nutritional value	3.7	50.0	39.1	7.1	1.56	3
Recipes	4.8	13.9	41.8	39.5	2.27	11
Food additives and preservatives	3.7	31.3	37.2	27.8	1.96	10
Date of manufacture or expiration	2.8	65.5	26.4	5.3	1.38	2

Interpretation: Total price is by far the most salient characteristic of the purchase event. Freshness comes second with nutritional value third and unit price a close fourth. Recipes seem to be largely overlooked as are food additives and preservatives, possibly because few people (experts included) know what they really do.

Section I *(continued)*

11. Number of times per week the respondent eats different meals:

	No Answer	*Never*	*1–2*	*3–4*	*5–6*	*Everyday*
Breakfast	1.7%	10.1%	13.9%	8.9%	6.0%	59.4%
Lunch	2.4	1.6	7.3	12.4	11.3	64.9
Dinner	1.7	.3	1.3	1.6	6.1	89.0

Interpretation: One third of the population eats breakfast irregularly. Surprisingly, lunch is more often consumed than breakfast. Not surprisingly, dinner is almost universally eaten at least six days a week.

12. Number of snacks consumed per day:

	Percent
No answer	1.5
None	18.0
One	44.6
Two	27.9
Three or more	8.1

Interpretation: Less than 20 percent of the sample avoids snacks. On the other hand, only 8.1 percent and the author admit to three or more snacks per day.

13. Amount of food canned:

	Percent
No answer	2.0
None	39.7
Small amount	36.3
Large amount	22.0

Interpretation: About 60 percent of the sample indicated that they can food. This seems very high and suggests that this may have been a bad question.

14. Frequency of consumption of different foods:

	No Answer	*Never*	*A Few Times a Year*	*1–2 Times a Month*	*Weekly*	*Several Times a Week*	*Once a Day*	*More than Once a Day*	*Mean*	*Rank*
Canned fruit	2.1%	1.2%	18.5%	34.1%	20.2%	20.3%	2.9%	.6%	3.52	16
Fresh fruit	2.0	.7	4.1	12.7	22.4	30.3	19.0	8.6	4.73	4
Bread	2.0	.5	.9	2.2	6.0	18.4	36.3	33.7	5.90	2
Rice	1.9	5.3	19.8	45.3	22.2	4.8	.1	.5	3.04	23
Butter	5.4	30.3	17.7	6.9	4.0	9.0	12.3	14.3	3.40	20
Margarine	4.0	4.8	3.0	2.7	8.6	19.1	23.1	34.7	5.53	3
Cheese	3.3	1.4	2.2	12.7	25.4	44.6	7.8	2.7	4.48	5
Ice cream	1.8	3.4	15.6	35.4	21.9	18.9	2.3	.5	3.47	17
Whole milk	4.3	27.0	9.5	8.4	5.7	10.4	17.1	17.6	3.88	11
Skim milk or low fat milk	6.2	34.3	10.5	6.1	4.8	10.6	13.2	14.4	3.47	18
Snack foods (potato chips, pretzels, etc.)	2.6	9.4	15.5	28.4	20.7	18.0	3.8	1.6	3.41	19
Desserts	2.9	1.5	6.0	18.3	21.9	28.9	16.0	4.6	4.41	7
Alcoholic beverages (beer, wine, liquor)	1.9	35.4	21.4	16.5	10.0	8.6	5.2	1.0	2.54	29
Soft drinks	2.4	9.8	13.3	21.6	16.6	19.4	8.4	8.5	3.84	13
Fish	1.9	4.4	17.7	41.9	28.7	5.1	.2	.1	3.14	22
Cold cereal	2.0	12.6	13.9	19.9	15.6	22.9	12.1	1.0	3.64	15
Frozen vegetables	1.9	4.5	10.0	20.1	21.8	32.8	8.2	.7	3.98	10
Fresh vegetables	2.1	1.5	5.7	14.5	22.9	38.7	11.3	3.3	4.42	6
Canned vegetables	2.3	2.7	5.3	13.6	23.4	41.2	10.1	1.4	4.34	9
Poultry	1.5	.5	3.7	32.3	52.3	8.5	.9	.2	3.69	14
Beef (hamburger or stew meat)	1.2	.5	.4	7.3	47.4	40.6	2.1	.3	4.37	8
Beef (steak or roast)	3.0	1.0	3.9	24.5	48.0	18.6	1.0	.1	3.85	12
Pork	3.2	6.8	21.1	39.6	23.2	5.0	1.2	.0	3.02	24
Tuna fish	2.1	8.1	21.0	40.3	20.4	7.8	.3	.0	3.00	25
Frozen dinners	1.7	35.2	39.3	18.1	4.4	1.4	.0	.0	1.96	30
Hot dogs	2.6	7.6	24.6	40.9	19.9	3.4	.3	.9	2.91	26
Coffee or tea	3.2	4.7	1.6	2.1	2.8	5.5	14.9	65.2	6.19	1
Pasta (pizza, spaghetti, etc.)	2.4	6.5	13.2	43.1	28.9	5.9	.0	.0	3.15	21
Food at "fast food" restaurant (i.e. McDonald's, etc.)	2.3	12.8	35.1	35.2	12.0	2.1	.3	.1	2.56	28
Food at regular restaurants	1.8	7.7	42.8	31.0	14.1	2.3	.3	.0	2.61	27

Interpretation: Coffee and tea are the most widely consumed food followed closely by bread. Frozen dinners are the least frequently consumed followed by alcoholic beverages and food eaten at restaurants. Overall, "junk" food is rated as relatively little consumed although here again this is obviously the socially accepted response. Interestingly, margarine is consumed more frequently than butter and skim milk as often as whole milk.

Section I *(concluded)*

15. Change in consumption of different foods in the past year:

	No Answer	*Much Less*	*Somewhat Less*	*About the Same*	*Somewhat More*	*Much More*	*Mean*	*Rank*
Canned fruit	1.5%	8.9%	15.4%	64.8%	7.2%	2.1%	2.78	18
Fresh fruit	1.7	3.2	9.5	57.9	22.3	5.4	3.18	3
Bread	1.8	2.8	11.5	66.0	13.7	4.3	3.05	8
Rice	2.3	8.4	14.4	64.3	9.5	1.2	2.80	16
Butter	7.1	24.0	13.6	47.3	6.3	1.6	2.44	28
Margarine	2.4	3.9	7.3	66.2	15.7	4.4	3.10	7
Cheese	2.1	1.8	7.4	59.6	24.3	4.8	3.23	1
Ice cream	2.8	7.6	21.3	53.7	12.0	2.7	2.80	15
Whole milk	4.4	15.6	13.5	51.9	9.4	5.2	2.74	20
Skim milk or low fat milk	8.7	16.7	7.2	45.2	16.0	6.2	2.87	13
Snack foods (potato chips, pretzels, etc.)	3.1	16.5	24.6	46.6	7.4	1.8	2.52	26
Desserts	3.4	9.9	26.0	53.7	5.6	1.4	2.61	23
Alcoholic beverages (beer, wine, liquor)	9.5	21.1	11.5	53.0	4.7	.3	2.47	27
Soft drinks	3.2	13.6	18.8	50.3	11.6	2.4	2.70	22
Fish	2.9	5.9	14.8	63.6	11.4	1.5	2.88	12
Cold cereal	2.8	6.4	12.8	59.4	15.9	2.9	2.96	9
Frozen vegetables	1.9	5.5	11.8	68.5	10.6	1.6	2.91	11
Fresh vegetables	1.9	2.3	6.9	69.6	16.6	2.7	3.11	6
Canned vegetables	1.9	4.7	10.9	72.0	9.0	1.5	2.92	10
Poultry	1.8	2.3	8.1	67.2	17.6	3.0	3.11	5
Beef (hamburger or stew meat)	1.3	1.6	5.0	65.3	22.6	4.3	3.23	2
Beef (steak or roast)	2.4	7.2	19.7	59.5	9.3	1.9	2.78	17
Pork	3.6	20.6	26.8	44.4	3.2	1.4	2.36	29
Tuna fish	3.6	11.0	14.4	59.4	10.5	1.2	2.76	19
Frozen dinners	5.1	25.6	17.3	46.7	4.9	.3	2.34	30
Hot dogs	2.8	11.1	19.1	54.4	11.2	1.5	2.72	21
Coffee or tea	3.0	3.3	5.6	68.1	13.8	6.1	3.14	4
Pasta (pizza, spaghetti, etc.)	3.5	9.5	13.1	61.3	11.2	1.5	2.82	14
Food at "fast food" restaurants (i.e., McDonald's, etc.)	3.6	18.0	17.6	49.9	9.5	1.5	2.57	24
Food at regular restaurants	2.7	19.9	17.9	47.4	10.1	2.0	2.55	25

Interpretation: Frozen dinner consumption decreased the most followed by pork, butter, and alcoholic beverages. Cheese consumption increased the most followed by beef, fresh fruit, and coffee or tea. On balance, people seem to have cut back on food consumption of most items with 22 of the 30 products showing decreased average consumption.

Section II—Nutritional Information Sources

1. Amount of information gained from various sources:

	No Answer	*None*	*Very Little*	*Some*	*Quite a Bit*	*A Tremendous Amount*	*Mean*	*Rank*
Books	3.7%	20.6%	21.0%	35.3%	14.9%	4.5%	2.60	5
Magazines	3.2	8.7	12.6	44.9	26.3	4.4	3.05	3
Labels on the packages food comes in	3.7	5.7	16.5	43.6	26.4	4.0	3.07	2
Your mother	7.3	38.7	16.4	21.8	12.0	3.7	2.20	10
Other family members	6.0	34.7	23.8	26.7	7.2	1.6	2.12	11
Friends	5.5	22.4	26.5	36.8	8.1	.6	2.34	8
Doctors	5.0	29.6	22.4	28.8	11.2	3.0	2.32	9
TV programs	4.9	19.6	25.0	38.8	10.3	1.4	2.46	7
TV advertisements	4.8	17.8	27.1	39.1	10.1	1.1	2.47	6
Newspapers	5.2	12.9	20.7	44.1	15.5	1.5	2.71	4
Your own experience	4.1	4.3	6.2	35.4	39.3	10.7	3.48	1
Courses in school	5.4	50.9	9.1	16.1	11.1	7.4	2.10	12

Interpretation: Personal experience is by far the most important source of nutritional information with labels on packages and magazines next most important. The importance of school courses, other family members, doctors, and friends is rated very low. Whether this reflects unavailability or lack of expertise is not clear.

2. Books read in the past year:

	No Answer	*No*	*Yes*
Dieting	5.5%	51.7%	42.8%
Nutrition	8.0	58.7	33.3
Cooking	4.1	35.2	60.6

Interpretation: People read more to make gourmet treats or to solve a specific problem than to learn about nutrition in general. Still, one third of the sample claim to have read a book about nutrition this year.

Section II *(concluded)*

3. Preferred sources of information from a federal government campaign:

	Percent	*Rank*
Column in the newspapers	39.1	2
TV special	36.1	3
Special edition of a prominent magazine	15.9	7
Government brochure	19.8	6
Extension courses	11.1	9
Workshops	9.9	10
Public service TV announcements	25.0	4
Information on packages	39.8	1
Information in TV advertisements	22.1	5
Don't care	11.3	8

Interpretation: No source of information is favored by a majority. Information on packages edges out column in newspaper and TV special as most preferred. Workshops and extension courses inspire only about 10 percent of the sample's interest. The author's favorite, a government brochure, finished a dismal sixth.

4. Amount willing to pay per week for a service providing nutritional information about available brands:

	Percent
No answer	3.3
Nothing	48.2
10¢–19¢	25.3
20¢–49¢	17.1
50¢–99¢	5.3
$1–$2	.7
Over $2	.0

Interpretation: Half the sample is unwilling to pay anything to find out nutritional information about available brands, and only 6 percent is willing to pay over 50 cents per week. If this is not an artifact of the question, it suggests that consumers would not support such a service in the free market.

5. Formal courses in nutrition:

	No Answer	*No*	*Yes*
High school	6.1%	62.2%	31.7%
College	17.3	71.9	10.7
Adult education/workshop	18.5	74.6	6.9

Interpretation: Very few of this sample have taken a formal nutrition course.

Section III—Background

1. Diets any member of the household is on:

Diet	*Self-Imposed*	*Doctor's Orders*	*Total*
Low cholesterol	7.3%	13.1%	20.4%
Low fat/calorie	17.0	11.3	28.3
Diabetic	1.5	9.6	11.1
Low salt	5.0	13.0	18.0
Vegetarian	1.3	.3	1.6
Low triglyceride	1.0	1.7	2.7

Interpretation: A substantial fraction of the households sampled have a member on one diet or another with self-imposed low fat/calorie most prevalent followed by doctor-imposed low cholesterol, low salt, low fat/calorie, and diabetic. Very few low triglyceride and vegetarian diets were in evidence.

2. Smoking frequency:

	Percent
No answer	1.2
Never	70.2
Occasionally	5.0
Regularly, but light (less than one pack of cigarettes each day	8.6
Regularly (one pack of cigarettes a day)	9.1
Heavily (more than one pack each day or equivalent)	5.9

Interpretation: Over two thirds of this sample were nonsmokers with 15 percent heavy smokers.

3. Vitamin pills taken personally:

	Percent
No answer	1.9
None	48.9
Multiple	29.7
Vitamin C	17.3
Vitamin G	.0
Vitamin B-12 complex	8.9
Vitamin A	3.7
Iron	15.7

Interpretation: Half the sample take no vitamins at all. The most prominent vitamin is multiple followed by vitamin C and iron. Surprisingly, no one claimed to be taking vitamin G which indicated the sample was still awake at this point in the questionnaire.

Section III *(concluded)*

4. Time spent watching TV per day:

	Percent
No answer	.7
None	3.0
Less than 1 hour	10.0
1–2 hours	33.6
3–4 hours	35.4
Over 4 hours	17.2

Interpretation: The typical respondent watches 2–3 hours of TV daily and only 3 percent abstain entirely.

5. Change in family income:

	Percent
No answer	.9
Gone down a lot	11.4
Gone down a little	11.6
Stayed about the same	30.7
Gone up a little	41.4
Gone up a lot	4.1

Interpretation: Most people's incomes have stayed the same or increased slightly. On the other hand; 11.4 percent have experienced a large drop in income compared to only 4.1 percent who experienced a large increase.

6. Change in family size:

	Percent
No answer	1.4
Decreased by two or more	2.4
Decreased by one	9.7
Stayed the same	77.6
Increased by one	8.0
Increased by two or more	1.0

Interpretation: More of these families decreased in size than increased, a result of their age and tendency to enter the "empty nest" stage of the life cycle. Over three fourths, however, remained unchanged.

Section IV—General Attitudes

	No Answer	*Strongly Agree*	*Some-what Agree*	*Neither Agree nor Disagree*	*Some-what Disagree*	*Strongly Disagree*	*Average Response*	*Rank*
People need to eat meat to be healthy	1.0%	23.8%	38.2%	17.6%	13.7%	5.7%	2.39	8
A high level of consumption is necessary to maintain a high standard of living	2.6	3.0	11.0	17.9	29.1	36.5	3.87	23
I am personally more conscientious in conserving energy than I was 3 years ago	1.8	55.0	33.6	6.3	2.2	1.1	1.58	2
The government should be more active in giving information about nutrition to consumers	1.6	32.6	36.4	22.9	4.3	2.3	2.06	4
I expect things to get better for my family next year	1.5	16.6	34.5	34.4	10.4	2.7	2.47	9
I feel the need for more information about nutrition	1.6	20.1	37.0	32.1	6.3	2.9	2.34	7
All people would have better diets if there were fewer mouths to feed	2.3	7.9	14.8	25.5	23.6	25.9	3.46	20
All cold cereals are about the same nutritionally	2.3	7.7	24.5	19.9	26.5	19.0	3.25	18
Health is more important than money	1.3	83.6	11.1	2.6	.4	1.1	1.22	1
I get more exercise than the average person	1.7	12.2	25.4	33.0	20.6	7.0	2.85	13
We entertain at home more than the average family	2.8	2.7	9.9	23.6	29.5	31.6	3.80	22
I am healthier than the average American	2.8	7.3	23.6	43.0	15.6	7.7	2.93	15
I consider myself better informed about nutrition than the average American	1.5	5.6	21.4	43.6	18.4	9.5	3.05	17

Section IV *(concluded)*

National brands of food are a better buy than local brands	1.6	3.7	12.2	27.1	37.0	18.3	3.55	21
Life is going well for me	2.2	31.5	37.2	19.3	6.9	2.9	2.10	6
Prices of food are so high that my nutrition is suffering	1.8	7.2	21.1	26.2	24.1	19.6	3.28	19
Television advertising has an adverse effect on diets because it encourages people to eat "junk" foods	1.3	35.9	33.3	16.8	10.1	2.7	2.09	5
I am heavier than I should be	1.3	30.6	25.7	11.0	12.0	19.4	2.63	11
I would be willing to eat less if the food were sent to the poor *in the United States*	1.0	21.2	26.3	33.9	8.6	9.0	2.58	10
America has a responsibility to share our agricultural abundance with hungry people in poor countries as well as home in the United States	1.5	13.5	40.0	16.9	17.9	10.2	2.71	12
The U.S. government should pass laws which would encourage and reward the farmer for full-scale production	1.4	38.5	32.8	18.6	6.1	2.7	2.00	3
The children in our household have a large influence on what we eat	8.6	10.2	26.8	26.7	15.0	12.7	2.92	14
Filling out this questionnaire has made me think about things which will change the types of foods I buy	1.2	6.1	25.7	43.5	12.7	10.9	2.96	16

Interpretation: The respondents believe health is more important than money, that they are more conscientious in conserving energy, and that government should encourage full-scale farm production. They *do not believe* a high level of consumption is necessary to maintain a high standard of living, that they entertain at home more than the average family, that national brands are a better buy than local brands, that people would be better off if there were fewer mouths to feed, or that high food prices are hurting them nutritionally. The most surprising result is the lack of enthusiasm for the potential benefits of population control. The moderate support for more information was expected.

Section V—Food Perceptions

1. Knowledge questions:

	No Answer	*True*	*False*	*Don't Know*
Hamburger contains substantially more protein per ounce than do soy beans	1.4%	13.8%	[54.7]%	30.1%
Pasta is high in cholesterol	1.7	31.8	[31.0]	35.5
Poultry are more efficient than cattle as producers of protein	1.8	[37.4]	35.4	25.3
A large amount of one vitamin is sufficient to overcome deficiencies of other vitamins	1.4	2.2	[85.2]	11.2
Beans and rice together are a low-protein meal	1.7	17.7	[59.6]	21.1
Eating a variety of foods from the supermarket will ensure a balanced diet	1.5	32.1	58.0	8.4
The cost of the vitamins needed to meet 100 percent of the minimum daily requirements is less than 10 cents per day	1.4	[38.1]	16.7	43.8
Food coloring additives create hyperactivity in children	1.9	[25.1]	33.3	39.7
Sugar causes cavities in children	1.6	[73.8]	15.5	9.0
Whole wheat bread is healthier than enriched white bread	.9	[69.6]	17.0	12.6

Interpretation: Many respondents have a reasonable knowledge of nutrition but a disconcertingly large fraction are unsure or even worse, incorrect in their opinions. For four of the questions, less than half the sample knew the correct answer ("correct" answers are in brackets).

2. Which foods aid which functions:

	Whole Milk	*Beef*	*Tomatoes*	*Enriched Bread*
Eyes	49.4%	31.3%	37.0%	22.6%
Teeth and bones	[96.3]	33.3	13.4	27.4
Muscle tissue	46.1	[80.2]	14.5	32.4
Repair of body tissues	[57.9]	[65.6]	25.5	31.9
Blood cells	37.4	[76.8]	26.1	21.3
Fighting infection	47.7	41.1	45.9	25.7
Nervous system	[56.7]	44.3	26.4	36.3
Skin	[70.3]	36.6	37.0	27.7
Proper growth of children	[93.3]	[69.1]	49.8	[67.3]

Interpretation: As expected, whole milk is thought to be a "super" food. Beef is also very highly regarded by the sample; especially for muscle and blood. Interestingly, enriched bread is perceived to be more related to proper growth of children than tomatoes which seem to be perceived of as relatively nonbeneficial (answers above 50 percent are in brackets).

Section V *(continued)*

3. Which foods contain a lot of different nutrients?

	Whole Milk	*Beef*	*Tomatoes*	*Enriched Bread*
Vitamin A	[58.8]%	16.9%	31.5%	25.3%
Thiamin (vitamin B_1)	28.4	31.6	13.0	48.8
Riboflavin (vitamin B_2)	31.3	32.3	10.5	44.5
Niacin	22.7	23.4	15.5	45.2
Vitamin C	19.8	4.6	[76.0]	9.6
Vitamin D	[63.4]	11.8	11.2	13.7
Protein	41.7	[81.9]	3.4	22.0
Carbohydrates	28.4	14.0	9.9	[72.7]
Fat	[71.4]	49.1	.7	27.9
Calories	[56.9]	38.6	3.7	[73.9]
Iron	26.3	[64.0]	21.4	23.6
Calcium	[91.0]	6.1	4.9	18.7

Interpretation: More than half the sample felt whole milk had a lot of vitamin D, fat, calories, and calcium and over 40 percent listed protein. For beef, protein and iron were the main characteristics followed by fat. Tomatoes are perceived to mainly have vitamin C, while enriched bread is associated with carbohydrates and calories followed by vitamins A, B_1 and B_2 (answers above 50 percent are in brackets).

4. Foods similar in benefits to the body:

	Whole Milk	*Beef*	*Tomatoes*	*Enriched Bread*
Oatmeal	22.6%	14.6%	2.2%	[75.6]%
Fish	21.3	[76.1]	6.3	7.6
Rice	11.1	12.1	3.4	[78.8]
Navy beans	10.9	[59.1]	8.3	37.8
Chicken	14.6	[82.4]	3.0	11.2
Potatoes	11.0	6.6	14.4	[77.1]
Eggs	44.4	[61.0]	2.9	11.4

Macaroni	9.6	6.9	1.3	[83.3]
Pork and lamb	11.4	[82.9]	2.8	6.7
String beans	7.3	9.2	[73.5]	6.3
Carrots	17.9	5.9	[72.4]	6.3
Bananas	24.8	11.1	43.2	24.5
Peanut butter	26.0	[73.8]	4.0	19.9
Cottage cheese	[76.7]	36.3	4.8	10.7

Interpretation: People seem to group foods based on the four basic food groups (answers above 50 percent are in brackets).

Accuracy of Nutritional Knowledge

In order to get some overall indication of the accuracy of people's nutritional knowledge, a summed score was developed based on some of the answers to Section V, question 1 (the true-false questions). Specifically, a summed score was developed as follows:

	Answer		
	True	*False*	*Don't Know*
Hamburger contains substantially more protein per ounce than do soy beans	−.25	+1	0
Pasta is high in cholesterol	−.25	+1	0
Poultry are more efficient than cattle as producers of protein	+1	−.25	0
A large amount of one vitamin is sufficient to overcome deficiencies of other vitamins	−.25	+1	0
Beans and rice together are a low protein meal	−.25	+1	0
The cost of the vitamins needed to meet 100% of the minimum daily requirements is less than 10¢ per day	+1	−.25	0
Sugar causes cavities in children	+1	−.25	0

Section V *(concluded)*

The distribution of this "Nutritional Knowledge Score" was as follows:

Score	*Absolute Frequency*	*Adjusted Frequency*	*Cumulative Frequency*
−1.25	1	.1%	.1%
−1.00	1	.1	.2
−.75	2	.2	.4
−.50	4	.4	.9
−.25	10	1.1	1.9
.0	17	1.8	3.7
.25	6	.6	4.4
.50	10	1.1	5.4
.75	17	1.8	7.2
1.00	27	2.9	10.1
1.25	25	2.7	12.8
1.50	32	3.4	16.2
1.75	36	3.8	20.0
2.00	33	3.5	23.5
2.25	37	3.9	27.4
2.50	57	6.1	33.5
2.75	51	5.4	38.9
3.00	22	2.3	41.3
3.25	29	3.1	44.4
3.50	81	8.6	53.0
3.75	83	8.8	61.8
4.00	34	3.6	65.4
4.50	49	5.2	70.6
4.75	88	9.4	80.0
5.00	41	4.4	84.4
5.75	55	5.9	90.2
6.00	50	5.3	95.5
7.00	42	5.4	100.0
Total	940	100.0	

Interpretation: The average score was 3.465, and the standard deviation, 1.786. Nutritional knowledge varies widely across the sample with very few people extremely knowledgeable in an objective sense. Put differently, a substantial fraction of the sample is misinformed about nutrition.

Appendix 11–B

Sample Cross-Tab Output

```
STATISTICAL PACKAGE FOR THE SOCIAL SCIENCES SPSSH - VERSION 6.00                    10/05/76          PAGE     1

          SPACE ALLOCATION FOR THIS RUN..

              TOTAL AMOUNT REQUESTED                                  80000 BYTES


              DEFAULT TRANSPACE ALLOCATION                            10000 BYTES


                  MAX NO OF TRANSFORMATIONS PERMITTED           100
                  MAX NO OF RECODE VALUES                       400
                  MAX NO OF ARITHM.OR LOG.OPERATIONS            800

              RESULTING WORKSPACE ALLOCATION                          70000 BYTES

                     FILE NAME         LEHNLTRI
                     VARIABLE LIST     INCOME,FAMSIZE,EXPENSE
                     INPUT MEDIUM      DISK
                     N OF CASES        UNKNOWN
                     INPUT FORMAT      FIXED(76X,2F1.0/12X,F1.0////)

                     ACCORDING TO YOUR INPUT FORMAT, VARIABLES ARE TO BE READ AS FOLLOWS

                     VARIABLE  FORMAT  RECORD     COLUMNS

                     INCOME     F 1. 0        1     77-  77
                     FAMSIZE    F 1. 0        1     78-  78
                     EXPENSE    F 1. 0        2     13-  13

THE INPUT FORMAT PROVIDES FOR   3 VARIABLES.    3 WILL BE READ
IT PROVIDES FOR  6 RECORDS ('CARDS') PER CASE.  A MAXIMUM OF   78 'COLUMNS' ARE USED ON A RECORD.

                     RECODE            FAMSIZE (2=1)(3,4=2)(5 THRU 9=3)/
                                       INCOME  (1,2=1)(3,4=2)(5=3)/
                                       EXPENSE (1=12.5)(2=22.5)(3=37.5)
                                       (4=52.5)(5=70)
                     MISSING VALUES EXPENSE (0)
                     READ INPUT DATA

AFTER READING    540 CASES FROM SUBFILE LEHNLTRI,  END OF FILE WAS ENCOUNTERED ON LOGICAL UNIT # 8
```

```
STATISTICAL PACKAGE FOR THE SOCIAL SCIENCES SPSSH - VERSION 6.00          10/05/76        PAGE    6

          DATA TRANSFORMATION DONE UP TO THIS POINT..

                 NO OF TRANSFORMATIONS                     0
                 NO OF RECODE VALUES                       0
                 NO OF ARITHM. OR LOG. OPERATIONS          0
          THE AMOUNT OF TRANSPACE REQUIRED IS              0 BYTES


                    CROSSTABS       TABLES= INCOME BY EXPENSE
                    STATISTICS      ALL

 ***** GIVEN WORKSPACE ALLOWS FOR   4374 CELLS AND    2 DIMENSIONS FOR CROSSTAB PROBLEM *****
```

```
STATISTICAL PACKAGE FOR THE SOCIAL SCIENCES SPSSH - VERSION 6.00                  10/05/76        PAGE    7

FILE    LEHNLTRI (CREATION DATE = 10/05/76)

* * * * * * * * * * * * * * * * *   C R O S S T A B U L A T I O N   O F   * * * * * * * * * * * * * * * * * *
   INCOME                                                        BY  EXPENSE
* * * * * * * * * * * * * * * * * * * * * * * * * * * * * * * * * * * * * * * * * * * * * * * * *  PAGE  1 OF  1

                    EXPENSE
           COUNT  I
          ROW PCT I                                                    ROW
          COL PCT I                                                    TOTAL
          TOT PCT I      13.I      23.I      38.I      53.I      70.I
INCOME    --------I--------I--------I--------I--------I--------I
              1.  I     33  I    226  I    149  I     45  I     11  I    464
                  I    7.1  I   48.7  I   32.1  I    9.7  I    2.4  I   49.7
                  I   84.6  I   70.2  I   47.8  I   23.1  I   16.9  I
                  I    3.5  I   24.2  I   16.0  I    4.8  I    1.2  I
                 -I--------I--------I--------I--------I--------I
              2.  I      5  I     73  I    121  I    102  I     31  I    332
                  I    1.5  I   22.0  I   36.4  I   30.7  I    9.3  I   35.6
                  I   12.8  I   22.7  I   38.8  I   52.3  I   47.7  I
                  I    0.5  I    7.8  I   13.0  I   10.9  I    3.3  I
                 -I--------I--------I--------I--------I--------I
              3.  I      1  I     23  I     42  I     48  I     23  I    137
                  I    0.7  I   16.8  I   30.7  I   35.0  I   16.8  I   14.7
                  I    2.6  I    7.1  I   13.5  I   24.6  I   35.4  I
                  I    0.1  I    2.5  I    4.5  I    5.1  I    2.5  I
                 -I--------I--------I--------I--------I--------I
           COLUMN       39       322       312       195        65       933
            TOTAL      4.2      34.5      33.4      20.9       7.0     100.0
CHI SQUARE =    167.23013 WITH    8 DEGREES OF FREEDOM    SIGNIFICANCE =  0.0
CRAMER'S V =      0.29937
CONTINGENCY COEFFICIENT =      0.38987
LAMBDA (ASYMMETRIC) =  0.16418 WITH INCOME    DEPENDENT.          =  0.11948 WITH EXPENSE  DEPENDENT.
LAMBDA (SYMMETRIC) =  0.13889
UNCERTAINTY COEFFICIENT (ASYMMETRIC) =  0.09331 WITH INCOME    DEPENDENT.          =  0.06745 WITH EXPENSE  DEPENDENT.
UNCERTAINTY COEFFICIENT (SYMMETRIC) =  0.07830
KENDALL'S TAU B =     0.36468  SIGNIFICANCE =  0.0
KENDALL'S TAU C =     0.36058  SIGNIFICANCE =  0.0
GAMMA =    0.53056
SOMERS'S D (ASYMMETRIC) =  0.33443 WITH INCOME    DEPENDENT.          =  0.39767 WITH EXPENSE  DEPENDENT.
SOMERS'S D (SYMMETRIC) =  0.36332
ETA =  0.40195 WITH INCOME    DEPENDENT.          =  0.41076 WITH EXPENSE  DEPENDENT.

NUMBER OF MISSING OBSERVATIONS =       7
```

Chapter 12

Comparing Differences in Key Variables

In the previous chapter, measures of association between two nominal variables (χ^2) and two intervally scaled variables (correlation) were discussed. Often, one is interested in the association between group membership (nominally scaled) and an intervally scaled "criterion" variable (e.g., attitude or sales). For example, one might be interested in the relationship between region of the country and per capita consumption of a particular product, or advertising copy seen and attitude toward a product. In these situations, moreover, one generally has a conception that the criterion (key) variable (e.g., sales, attitude) depends on/is caused by the nominal variable (e.g., region, advertising copy). This chapter, therefore, focuses on relating nominally scaled and intervally scaled variables, with the implicit notion that the nominally scaled "independent" variable in some sense causes the intervally scaled "dependent" variable. The chapter also covers the special case where the dependent variable is binary by introducing tests about proportions. Specifically, this chapter covers comparing two means and two proportions as well as analysis of variance.

THE NOTION OF STATISTICAL INFERENCE

This section briefly describes the concept of statistical inference. If you (*a*) already understand the concept, (*b*) are a purist, or (*c*) have a fetish for complete treatment of this subject, please skip the section and/or refer to a basic statistics book. The purpose of this section is to provide a brief intuitive feel for inference.

The basic motivation for statistical inference is to detect significant unusual behavior. The notion of statistical inference suggests that it is possible for two numbers to be different mathematically but not different significantly. For example, one person might weigh 180.23 pounds and another 180.12. While these weights are different, for most decisions (*a*) the difference is unimportant and (*b*) the difference is well within the range of accuracy of most measuring devices and probably insignificant statistically. Hence, it is useful to distinguish between three kinds of differences:

1. *Mathematical.* If numbers are not exactly the same, they are different. (In marketing research, two results are almost always different.)
2. *Important.* If the numerical difference would matter in a managerial sense, then the difference is important.
3. *Statistical significance.* If the difference is big enough to be unlikely to have occurred due to chance, then the difference is statistically significant.

In determining statistically significant differences, I must make a trade-off between two extremes:

Calling every difference, no matter how small, significant. For example, someone with a weight fetish might weigh herself at 8 P.M. after a huge pasta dinner and again at 8 P.M. the next night immediately after a fish dinner. If the weights were 181 and 179 pounds respectively, she could think she had lost 2 pounds. Alternatively, however, she could think (*a*) that fish is lighter than pasta, (*b*) that she exercised differently, or (*c*) that the accuracy of the scale given changes in temperature, humidity, and position of the scale in the bathroom is insufficient to call a 2-pound difference statistically significant. Calling a difference significant when it is not is traditionally called *Type I* or *α error*.

Requiring absolute proof that a difference is significant. Carrying the weight example further, it is possible to argue that any change might have been due to a fluke measurement. Hence it is possible that a weight change from 181 to 170 is not important or significant. (However, anyone with the 24-hour flu would strongly disagree.) Calling a difference insignificant when it is significant is called a *Type II* or *β error*.

The problem of detecting significant results involving trading off these two considerations arises in many contexts:

1. *Machine retooling.* A machine in the middle of an assembly line has to produce parts within a given tolerance. If the machine is to be retooled, the assembly line must be stopped. If the machine produces bad parts,

considerable repair costs are required. Based on a sample of parts from the machine, do I retool or not?

2. *Evaluating a taste testing result.* In a blind test between two versions of the same product (one less costly), 37 prefer version A and 43 version B. Is the difference significant or can I use the cheaper version without sacrificing sales?
3. *Judicial decisions.* In rendering a decision, a judge or jury must implicitly decide between two risks: putting an innocent person in jail or letting a guilty person go free.

Interestingly, most of the basic literature on statistics, the practices of marketing research, and the legal system in the United States focuses on the Type I (α) error. This places the burden of proof on the data to disconfirm a hypothesis. (In the previous examples, the hypotheses are that the machine is OK, the two products are equal, and the defendant is innocent.) While this makes sense when the hypothesis is strongly maintained, it is somewhat senseless if the hypothesis is arbitrary. Still, the use of statistical inference in this and subsequent chapters will maintain the tradition of focusing on Type I (α) errors, and, therefore, a result said to be statistically significant will generally be one that differs from a null hypothesis beyond "reasonable doubt." The astute reader may also notice that most null hypotheses will implicitly assume there is nothing interesting in the data (e.g., two means are equal, two variables are unrelated). Consequently, statistically significant results will tend to be those that are "interesting" in the sense that a relationship is uncovered in the data.

TESTS CONCERNING ONE SAMPLE, ONE VARIABLE

Concept

Assume that the average consumption of beer in bottles per month was collected from a sample of 289 consumers. Since these consumers were rugby players, it seemed interesting to examine the theory that rugby players are heavy consumers of beer. Assume the data were as follows:

"Typical" beer consumption = 59.8

Sample result: Average beer consumption = 76.2

Given this result, it seems pretty obvious that rugby players are indeed heavy beer consumers. This managerial result/conclusion requires nothing more than the eyeball comparison of the sample mean with the standard. Unfortunately, results are not always this clear-cut. For example, if the average beer consumption in the sample of 289 rugby players had been

61.1, rather than 76.2, it is unclear whether the extra 1.3 bottles are the result of a "true" difference between rugby players and the general population or merely the result of having chosen a particularly heavy drinking sample of rugby players. Similarly, if the sample size had been 9 instead of 289, we again become unsure about the meaningfulness of the difference. In both cases, obviously the *sample* of rugby players differs from the typical consumer. The issue, however, is whether rugby players in *general* differ.

Approach

Whether a difference in a mean is significant or not depends on three things:

1. The standard of comparison (μ).
2. The sample mean ($\bar{x}$).
3. The degree of uncertainty concerning how well the sample mean represents the mean of the population of interest (in the previous example, all rugby players).

We can build an index of significance as follows:

$$\text{Index} = \frac{\text{Sample mean} - \text{Standard}}{\text{Uncertainty}}$$

This index increases as the difference between the sample mean and the standard increases, and decreases as the uncertainty increases.

Drawing on our statistics training (or asking someone who knows what to do), we recall that the uncertainty of our estimate of the sample mean is quantified by its standard deviation, the standard error of $\bar{x}$:

$$s_{\bar{x}} = \frac{s}{\sqrt{n}}$$

Hence, the index becomes:

$$t_{n-1} = \frac{\bar{x} - \mu}{s/\sqrt{n}} \tag{12.1}$$

This is the well-known (if you've recently taken a statistics course) t statistic. It tests the null hypothesis:

H_0 = The mean of the population represented by the sample is equal to the standard ($\bar{x} = \mu$)

A large value for the index would reject the null hypothesis and, consequently, imply that the population represented by the sample differs from the standard in terms of average behavior. The values can be checked for significance against the values in a t table with $n - 1$ degrees of freedom. Whenever the index is larger than the appropriate table value, the null hypothesis is rejected. For large sample sizes, t is approximately normally distributed. Combining these two points, we can see that (using the .05 significance level as a crude screen), in general, t values above 2 will be significant and those less than 2 are usually not significant.

Examples

Example A. Applying this test to the beer consumption example, we get the following results. Given:

$$\mu = 59.8$$

$$\bar{x} = 76.2$$

$$n = 289$$

$$s = 34$$

Thus, the index becomes:

$$t = \frac{76.2 - 59.8}{\frac{34}{\sqrt{289}}} = \frac{16.4}{2} = 8.2 > 2$$

and the difference is, as we thought, significant. This means that rugby players consume more beer than typical consumers.

Example B. Now assume the sample mean had been 61.1, instead of 76.2. Given:

$$\mu = 59.8$$

$$\bar{x} = 61.1$$

$$n = 289$$

$$s = 34$$

The index would now be:

$$t = \frac{61.1 - 59.8}{\frac{34}{\sqrt{289}}} = \frac{1.3}{2} = .65 < 2$$

This is not significant. Hence, in this case, there is a reasonable chance that the difference between the sample mean and the standard is not representative of a "true" difference in average consumption between rugby players and the typical person.

Example C. Finally, assume we had a sample mean of 76.2, but only a sample size of 9. The results would now be as follows. Given:

$$\mu = 59.8$$
$$\bar{x} = 76.2$$
$$n = 9$$
$$s = 34$$

Therefore:

$$t = \frac{76.2 - 59.8}{\frac{34}{\sqrt{9}}} = \frac{16.4}{11.33} = 1.45 < 2$$

Hence, in this case, the difference is not significant. While this may seem surprising, given the large difference in mean values, what it says is there is a nontrivial chance that the difference is a fluke due to the small sample size. (A general corollary to this result is that given a large enough sample size, even the smallest numerical difference becomes significant.)[1]

TESTS CONCERNING ONE SAMPLE, ONE PERCENTAGE

Approach

When the key variable is a binary variable such as a yes-no question, the test just discussed is inappropriate. However, if the percent of respondents (p) who answer yes is calculated, this can often be compared to a standard (θ) as follows:

$$\text{Index} = \frac{\text{Sample percent} - \text{Standard}}{\text{Uncertainty}}$$

$$= \frac{p - \theta}{\sqrt{\frac{\theta(1-\theta)}{n}}} \tag{12.2}$$

[1]It should also be pointed out that for very small sample sizes, unknown standard deviations, and non-normally distributed variables, the t distribution is only an approximation of the true sampling distribution.

As n increases, this index[2] becomes approximately normally distributed. The bigger the n and the closer to .5 the p, the better the approximation. Nonetheless, to have an arbitrary cutoff, we will say when n is above 30 and p between .1 and .9, this index is approximately normally distributed.

Here the null hypothesis is that the percent answering yes in the population represented by the sample is the same as the standard: H_0: $p = \theta$. A big index value (> 2 for the .05 significance level) indicates the difference is significant.

Since in many cases we are only concerned about values that exceed (or fall short of) the standard, the test may be set up as a one-tail test as follows: H_0: $p \geq \theta$ or H_0: $p \leq \theta$ and, hence, an index value of greater than 1.64 (or less than -1.64) will be necessary to statistically reject the null hypothesis at the .05 significance level.

Examples

Example A. Given:

$$\begin{aligned} \text{Standard} \quad \theta &= 20\% \\ \text{Sample} \quad p &= 30\% \\ n &= 100 \end{aligned}$$

Question: Does the sample group differ from the standard? This indicates we should test H_0: $p = \theta$. The index (test statistic) becomes:

$$\frac{30 - 20}{\sqrt{\frac{(20)(80)}{100}}} = \frac{10}{\frac{40}{10}} = 2.5$$

Since $2.5 > 2$, the results in the sample group differ significantly from the standard.

Example B. Given:

$$\begin{aligned} \theta &= 20\% \\ p &= 28\% \\ n &= 100 \end{aligned}$$

---

[2]Some people use:

$$\frac{p - \theta}{\sqrt{\frac{p(1 - p)}{n}}}$$

For practical purposes, the two formulas are usually equivalent because of the insensitivity of $p(1 - p)$ to p.

Question: Are the results significantly greater in the sample group? (H_0: $p \leq \theta$)

Test statistic:

$$\frac{28 - 20}{\sqrt{\frac{(20)(80)}{100}}} = \frac{8}{\frac{40}{10}} = 2$$

Since $2 > 1.64$ (this is a one-tail test), H_0 is rejected and, therefore, we conclude that the percent in the sample group is greater than 20 percent.

TESTS CONCERNING TWO MEANS

Concept

In many circumstances, measurements may be taken on a key variable in samples of two different populations (e.g., experimental and control groups, users and nonusers, etc.). The obvious question which can be asked, therefore, is whether the two populations represented by the sample are significantly different in terms of some key variable.

Approach

We can, again, build an index of the significance as follows:

$$\text{Index} = \frac{\text{Difference in means}}{\text{Uncertainty about difference in means}}$$

Let:

$\bar{x}_1$ = mean in first sample.

n_1 = size of first sample.

s_1 = standard deviation of first sample.

Then we get:

$$\text{Index} = \frac{\bar{x}_1 - \bar{x}_2}{s_{\bar{x}_1 - \bar{x}_2}} \tag{12.3}$$

which is t distributed with $n_1 + n_2 - 2$ degrees of freedom. The null hypothesis is H_0: $\mu_1 = \mu_2$ (or, alternatively, $\mu_1 \geq \mu_2$ or $\mu_1 \leq \mu_2$ if we are doing a one-tail test).

The formula for $s_{\bar{x}_1 - \bar{x}_2}$ comes in two forms:

1. If we do not assume $s_1 = s_2$, we have:

$$s_{\bar{x}_1 - \bar{x}_2} = \sqrt{\frac{s_1^2}{n_1} + \frac{s_2^2}{n_2}} \tag{12.4}$$

2. If we make the assumption that $s_1 = s_2$, we get:

$$s_{\bar{x}_1 - \bar{x}_2} = \hat{s}\sqrt{\frac{1}{n_1} + \frac{1}{n_2}} \tag{12.5}$$

where:

$$\hat{s}^2 = \frac{(n_1 - 1)s_1^2 + (n_2 - 1)s_2^2}{n_1 + n_2 - 2}$$

The advantage of assuming $s_1 = s_2$ is that the test is slightly more powerful in that we become more likely to detect a significant difference between the two means if, in fact, one exists. Practically, however, the difference is minimal when, in fact, s_1 and s_2 are close in size.

Example

Given:

$$\bar{x}_1 = 20 \qquad \bar{x}_2 = 22$$
$$s_1^2 = 3.78 \qquad s_2^2 = 10.44$$
$$n_1 = 10 \qquad n_2 = 10$$

Question: Is the mean of the first group significantly less than that of the second?

$$(H_0: \mu_1 \geq \mu_2)$$

Test statistic:

$$\frac{20 - 22}{\sqrt{\frac{3.78}{10} + \frac{10.44}{10}}} = \frac{-2}{\sqrt{.378 + 1.044}}$$

$$= \frac{-2}{\sqrt{1.422}} = \frac{-2}{1.19}$$
$$= -1.68 > -1.73 = t_{18,.05}$$

Hence we cannot reject H_0 at the .05 significance level, which indicates that the mean of the first group is not significantly less than the mean of the second group.

MATCHED SAMPLE TESTS

The test presented in the previous section assumed the two samples were independent. Yet, in many cases, a measure will be taken twice on the same sample. For example, attitudes may be measured before and after exposure to an advertisement. Consider the data in Table 12–1. (As you may recognize, these are the data which generated the example in the previous section.) Also recall that treating the data as two independent samples led to the conclusion that their means are not different. The real question is whether the average change differed from zero. There are two basic approaches for examining the changes for statistical significance.

Sign Test

First, we can simply observe the number of positive changes and see if this is different from 50 percent. If there were no change, we would expect that half would increase and half decrease. This can be set up as a sign test:

$$\text{Test statistic} = \frac{\text{Percent of positive changes} - 50 \text{ percent}}{\sqrt{\dfrac{(50)(50)}{n}}} \qquad (12.6)$$

$$H_0\text{: percent of positive changes} = 50 \text{ percent}$$

TABLE 12–1

	Attitude		
Person	*Before*	*After*	*Change*
1	21	24	+3
2	19	23	+4
3	18	19	+1
4	22	18	−4
5	21	25	+4
6	16	17	+1
7	21	24	+3
8	22	22	—
9	21	26	+5
10	19	22	+3
	$\bar{x}$ = 20	22	20

If n is greater than 30, this statistic is approximately normally distributed. Since n is only 10 in Table 12–1, however, we would have to make use of a set of binomial tables. Since these tables indicate that there is a .057 chance of 8, 9, or 10 positive changes given a $p = .5$, we would (just barely) fail to reject the hypothesis of 50 percent at the .05 significance level and conclude the changes may be random.

Paired Difference Test

The second approach to testing for a significant change is to see if the average change is different from zero. The test statistic is:

$$\text{Index} = \frac{\text{Average change}}{\dfrac{s_{\text{change}}}{\sqrt{n}}} \tag{12.7}$$

In the example of Table 12–1, we get:

$$\text{Average change} = +2.0$$
$$\text{Standard deviation of change} = +2.62$$

(Here $\Sigma(\Delta - \bar{\Delta})^2 = \Sigma(\Delta - 2)^2 = (3 - 2)^2 + (4 - 2)^2 + \cdots + (3 - 2)^2 = 62$. Thus, $s_{\text{change}} = \sqrt{62/9} = 2.62$.)

$$\text{Index} = \frac{2}{\dfrac{2.62}{\sqrt{10}}} = 2.41$$

At the .05 level we can reject the null hypothesis, since the table value of t is $1.83 < 2.41$. Note this index is not very different from the index of the t test assuming independence of the two samples, but it is enough different to alter the results from nonsignificant to significant at the .05 level. The point, however, is that it is incorrect to treat matched samples as independent, and some significant changes may be lost if the incorrect procedure is applied.

TESTS CONCERNING TWO PERCENTAGES

Approach

Just as it is possible to test two means to see if they differ significantly, so is it possible to compare two percentages. The formula for this is:

$$\text{Index} = \frac{p_1 - p_2}{s_{p_1 - p_2}}$$

where

p_1, p_2 = percents having the characteristic in the first and second samples, respectively.

n_1, n_2 = sizes of the first and second samples, respectively.

$S_{p_1-p_2}$ = standard deviation of the difference in percents.

This index is approximately normally distributed for large sample sizes. A pooled estimate of the overall percent is derived by assuming the percents are equal in the two groups.

$$\pi = \frac{n_1 p_1 + n_2 p_2}{n_1 + n_2} \tag{12.8}$$

Thus:

$$s_{p_1-p_2} = \sqrt{\frac{\pi(100-\pi)}{n_1} + \frac{\pi(100-\pi)}{n_2}} = \sqrt{\frac{n_1+n_2}{n_1 n_2}}\sqrt{\pi(1-\pi)} \tag{12.9}$$

Example

Given:

First Sample	*Second Sample*
$n_1 = 100$	$n_2 = 150$
$p_1 = 20\%$	$p_2 = 30\%$

$$H_0: \theta_1 = \theta_2 \qquad \text{(no significant difference)}$$

Test statistic:

$$\text{Index} = \frac{20 - 30}{s_{p_1-p_2}}$$

Here,

$$\pi = \frac{2{,}000 + 4{,}500}{250} = 26\%$$

$$s_{p_1-p_2} = \sqrt{(26)(74)}\sqrt{\frac{250}{15{,}000}}$$

$$= 5.66\%$$

TABLE 12–2 Actual Data

	Response		
Sample	*Yes*	*No*	*Total*
1	20	80	100
2	45	105	150
Total	65	185	250

TABLE 12–3 Expected Data

	Response		
Sample	*Yes*	*No*	*Total*
1	26	74	100
2	39	111	150
Total	65	185	250

Therefore, the test statistic $= \dfrac{-10}{5.66\%} = -1.77 > -1.96$. (In effect, we are comparing absolute value of the index to 1.96.)

Thus, here an apparently large difference in percents is not significant. The reason for this is the remarkable unreliability of percents based on samples as large as 100 in size. One moral of this example is beware of being overly zealous in interpreting differences in percents; they may not be significant.

An alternative (and equivalent) test is available based on the χ^2 for a 2×2 contingency table. For the previous example, we can derive Table 12–2. The frequency expected table becomes that of Table 12–3. Hence we get:

$$
\begin{aligned}
\chi^2 &= \frac{(20-26)^2}{26} + \frac{(80-74)^2}{74} + \frac{(45-39)^2}{39} + \frac{(105-111)^2}{111} \\
&= \frac{36}{26} + \frac{36}{74} + \frac{36}{39} + \frac{36}{111} \\
&= 1.38 + .49 + .92 + .32 \\
&= 3.11
\end{aligned}
$$

Since the .05 "cutoff" for a significant χ^2 with one degree of freedom is 3.84, we again conclude that the difference is not significant.

TESTS CONCERNING SEVERAL MEANS: ANOVA

In some situations, multiple samples are available. For example, four groups of respondents may be exposed to four separate ads. To see if the four groups differ, three basic approaches are possible. First, all pairs (in this case six) of samples can be compared with the two-sample t tests. This is fairly cumbersome. (Also, given enough t tests, some are likely to appear significant due to chance; for example, 1 of 20 at the .05 significance level.) Therefore, many people prefer to examine the four samples simultaneously. The methodology for such examination is essentially an extension of the two-sample t test known as ANOVA—analysis of variance.

A third approach to simultaneously examining several means is to use dummy variable regression. In fact, it is the approach the author tends to favor. However, since there are those who prefer ANOVA, and because understanding ANOVA aids in the interpretation of regression-based analysis, the rest of this chapter will focus on ANOVA. A reader who plans to skip the detailed explanation should at least read the sections on motivation, procedure, and pictorial/managerial interpretation.

Motivation

The simplest form of ANOVA deals with the case where there are multiple samples, with each sample corresponding to a different level of a single control variable. For example, assume I measured the sales response in 12

TABLE 12–4 Sales as a Function of Package Color

	Package Color		
	A	*B*	*C*
	14	8	8
	10	14	6
	11	3	5
	9	7	1
Average sales . . .	11	8	5

FIGURE 12–1

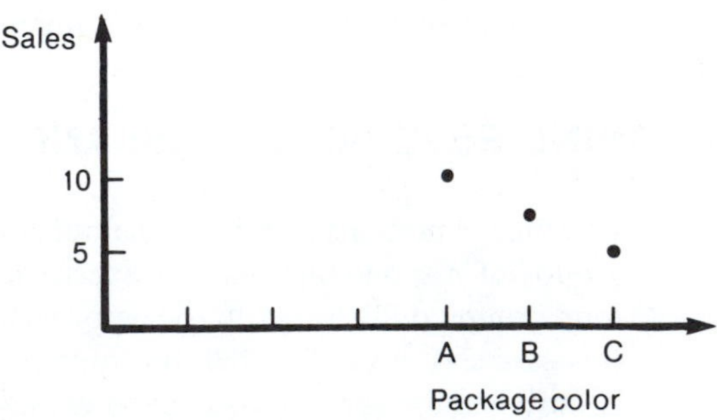

stores to three different package colors, with 4 stores using each of the three colors (Table 12–4).

Ignoring the crucial issue of whether the stores were comparable, we address the issue of whether the sales differed under the three colors. This can best be seen managerially by plotting the average sales versus color curve of Figure 12–1. Apparently, color A is the best. The question which might be asked, however, is whether these differences are statistically significant.

Procedure

Analysis of variance is logically quite simple. It consists of seeing whether the means of the several samples are far apart relative to our uncertainty as to what the means really are. Again we can construct an index:

$$\text{Index} = \frac{\text{Difference among means}}{\text{Uncertainty}}$$

For simple one-way ANOVA with only two groups (only one variable changes across the samples), the problem can be seen graphically (Figure 12–2). In case 1, the two samples clearly differ, in that all the x values for sample A are less than the x values for sample B. The same is true in case 2. Even though the means are close together, the results are sufficiently consistent to indicate a significant difference in means between the two samples. Case 3 shows a weak relationship; but in spite of the largest mean difference, substantial overlap exists due to the variability of the results within samples A and B. Case 4 shows so much overlap that we might well argue the difference in means is not significant. To capture the essence of this logic, the index[3] could well be:

$$\text{Index} = \frac{\bar{x}_A - \bar{x}_B}{s_{\bar{x}_A - \bar{x}_B}}$$

which was the two-sample t statistic discussed previously. To extend this to more than two samples, two changes are required. First, instead of measuring the difference between pairs of sample means, we measure the difference between each sample mean and the overall mean ($\bar{\bar{x}}$) (see Figure 12–3). Secondly, we use as a measure of uncertainty the pooled estimate of s_A and

[3]In keeping with the notation in the next chapter on regression analysis, the dependent (criterion) variable should be labeled as y and not x. However, since almost all other books use x as the notation for the dependent variable, this convention is observed here as well.

FIGURE 12–2

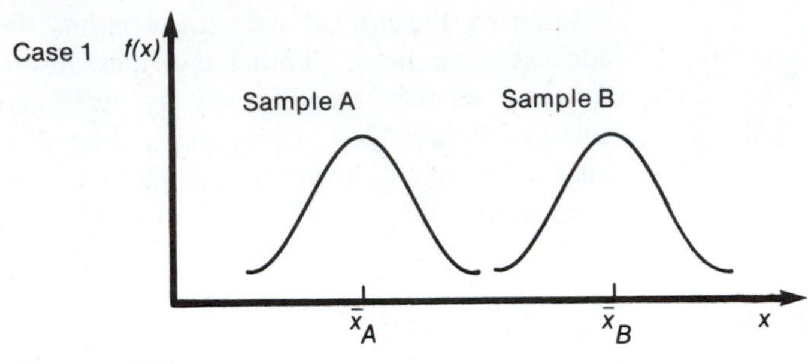
Case 1
f(x)
Sample A
Sample B
x̄A
x̄B
x

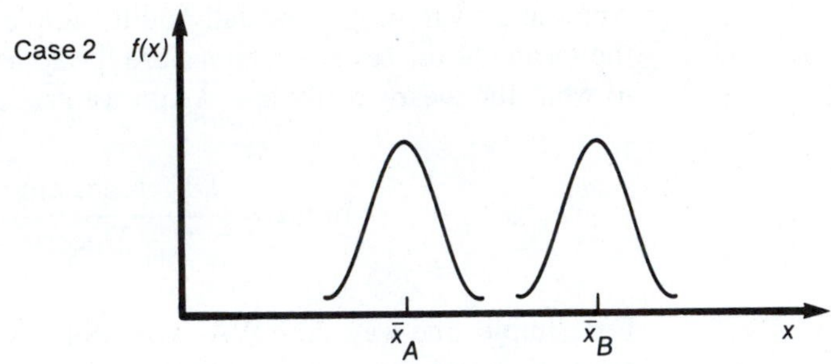
Case 2
f(x)
x̄A
x̄B
x

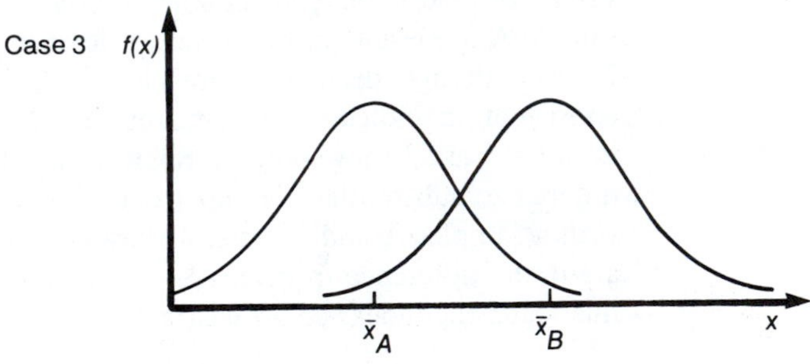
Case 3
f(x)
x̄A
x̄B
x

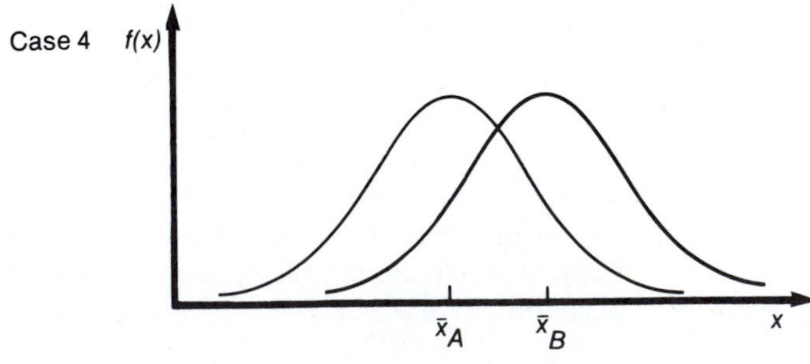
Case 4
f(x)
x̄A
x̄B
x

FIGURE 12–3

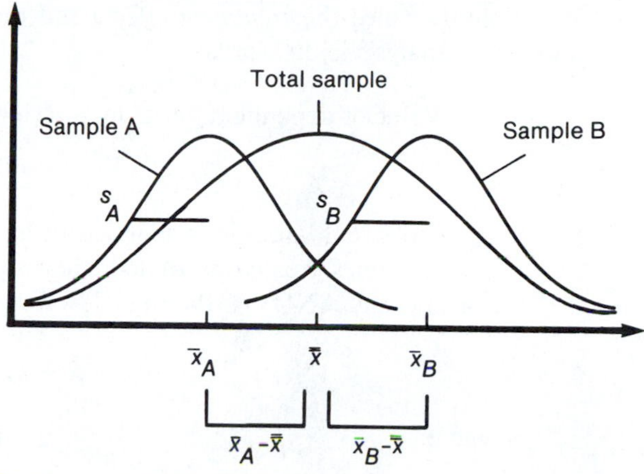

s_B. By squaring these differences and also the measure of uncertainty, we get:

$$\text{Index} = \frac{(\bar{x}_A - \bar{\bar{x}})^2 + (\bar{x}_B - \bar{\bar{x}})^2}{\hat{s}^2}$$

where $\bar{\bar{x}}$ is the overall mean across both samples. Since both numerator and denominator are variances (hence, the term *analysis of variance*), this index, when adjusted for degrees of freedom, follows the F distribution and can be checked for statistical significance by comparing it to values in an F table. When the value for the index is bigger than the table value, the difference in means is significant.

ONE-WAY ANOVA

Formulas

Mathematics often are so formidable that they inhibit understanding. Also, since practical applications of ANOVA generally are done on "canned" computer programs, knowledge of the algebra used is unnecessary to use the procedure for detecting significant influences. Nonetheless, in this case some derivations are very useful for explaining the "magic" formulas used. Hence, this section attempts to briefly delineate the formulas used for one-way ANOVA.

Each observation differs in value from the overall mean by some amount $(x - \bar{\bar{x}})$. Some of this difference may be attributable to the influence of another variable (i.e., color A, B, or C). The rest is essentially random/unexplained. The procedure followed in ANOVA attempts to partition the variance $(x - \bar{\bar{x}})^2$ in the dependent variable (e.g., sales) into two subsets: that attributable to the influence of another (independent) variable (commonly called the *treatment effect*) and the rest. The model which underlies this analysis is, in words:

$$\text{Value of dependent variable} = f(\text{levels of independent variables}) + \text{random element}$$

The dependent variable is assumed to be intervally scaled and the independent variables treated as though they were categorical (nominally scaled), For one-way ANOVA, the model becomes:

$$x_{jk} = \bar{\bar{x}} + C_j + e_{jk} \tag{12.10}$$

where:

x_{jk} = value of the dependent variable for the kth person in the jth sample (exposed to the jth level of the independent variable).

$\bar{\bar{x}}$ = overall mean.

C_j = treatment effect of the jth level of the independent variable $= \bar{x}_j - \bar{\bar{x}}$.

e_{jk} = random part of the kth observation in the jth sample.

Consider again our original example for one-way ANOVA with three colored packages (Table 12–4). In this case, the overall mean ($\bar{\bar{x}}$) is 8. The treatment effect of the first level (C_1) is $\bar{x}_1 - \bar{\bar{x}} = 11 - 8 = +3$. Similarly, C_2 and C_3 are 0 and -3, respectively. To see how the model works, consider the second observation in the color A sample:

$$x_{12} = \bar{\bar{x}} + C_1 + e_{12}$$

or

$$10 = 8 + 3 + e_{12}$$

Hence,

$$e_{12} = -1 \text{ to "balance" the books}$$

(Equivalently, $e_{12} = x_{12} - \bar{x}_1 = 10 - 11 = -1$.)

The statistical test for significant differences will thus be based on the relative size of the C_js and the e_{jk}s. The test is developed by taking the total variance in the x values and partitioning it into two parts: that due to the differences between group means and the overall mean (C_js) and that due to the "residual" error (e_{jk}s):

$$\text{Total variation} = \sum_{j=1}^{c} \sum_{k=1}^{n_j} \left(x_{jk} - \bar{\bar{x}}\right)^2 \tag{12.11}$$

where

c = number of categories of the independent variable (e.g., three colors).

n_j = number of observations of the dependent variable when exposed to level j of the independent variable.

x_{jk} = value of the dependent variable in the kth observation in the jth sample.

$\bar{\bar{x}}$ = overall mean.

This can be rewritten as the sum of two parts[4]:

"Between" sum of squares (treatment):

$$\sum_{j=1}^{c}\sum_{k=1}^{n_j}\left(\bar{x}_j-\bar{\bar{x}}\right)^2=\sum_{j=1}^{c}n_j\left(\bar{x}_j-\bar{\bar{x}}\right)^2 \qquad (12.12)$$

"Within" sum of squares (unexplained):

$$\sum_{j=1}^{c}\sum_{k=1}^{n_j}\left(x_{jk}-\bar{x}_j\right)^2 \qquad (12.13)$$

Two assumptions are necessary:

1. The variances in the separate samples are equal ($s_1^2 = s_2^2 = \cdots = s_c^2$).
2. The dependent variable (x) is normally distributed.

Statistical Test

The key issue in ANOVA is whether the differences in means between the groups are large in relation to the uncertainty/variability within the groups on the dependent variable. Consequently, we develop an index as follows:

$$\text{Index}=\frac{\sum_{j=1}^{c}n_j\left(\bar{x}_j-\bar{\bar{x}}\right)^2/(c-1)}{\sum_{j=1}^{c}\sum_{k=1}^{n_j}\left(x_{jk}-\bar{x}_j\right)^2/(n-c)} \qquad (12.14)$$

---

[4] This can be derived from

$$\Sigma\Sigma\left(x_{ijk}-\bar{\bar{x}}\right)^2=\Sigma\Sigma\left(x_{ijk}-\bar{x}_j+\bar{x}_j-\bar{\bar{x}}\right)^2$$

$$=\Sigma\Sigma\left(x_{ijk}-\bar{x}_j\right)^2+2\Sigma\Sigma\left(x_{ijk}-\bar{x}_j\right)\left(\bar{x}_j-\bar{\bar{x}}\right)+\Sigma\Sigma\left(\bar{x}_j-\bar{\bar{x}}\right)^2=\cdots$$

TABLE 12–5 One-Way ANOVA

Source	*Sum of Squares*	*Degrees of Freedom*	*Mean Square (SS / d.f.)*	*F*
Treatment (influencing variable)	$\sum_{j=1}^{c} n_j(\bar{x}_j - \bar{\bar{x}})^2$	$c - 1$	$\dfrac{\sum_{j=1}^{c} n_j(\bar{x}_j - \bar{\bar{x}})^2}{c-1} = A$	$\dfrac{A}{B}$
Unexplained	$\sum_{j=1}^{c}\sum_{k=1}^{n_j} (x_{jk} - \bar{x}_j)^2$	$n - c$	$\dfrac{\sum_{j=1}^{c}\sum_{k=1}^{n_j} (x_{jk} - \bar{x}_j)^2}{n-c} = B$	
Total	$\sum_{j=1}^{c}\sum_{k=1}^{n_j} (x_{jk} - \bar{\bar{x}})^2$	$n - 1$		

This index can be compared with the F table with $(c - 1)$ and $(n - c)$ degrees of freedom. The calculation steps for obtaining this statistic are often summarized in a table (Table 12–5). The null hypothesis is that all the treatment groups have equal means (H_0: $\bar{x}_1 = \bar{x}_2 = \cdots = \bar{x}_c$).

Numerical Example

Returning again to the packaging color example (Table 12–4), we have:

$$\text{Total sum of squares} = \sum_{j=1}^{3}\sum_{k=1}^{4} \left(x_{jk} - \bar{\bar{x}}\right)^2$$

$$= (14 - 8)^2 + (10 - 8)^2 + (11 - 8)^2 + (9 - 8)^2$$

$$+ (8 - 8)^2 + (14 - 8)^2 + (3 - 8)^2 + (7 - 8)^2$$

$$+ (8 - 8)^2 + (6 - 8)^2 + (5 - 8)^2 + (1 - 8)^2$$

$$= 174$$

$$\text{Treatment sum of squares} = \sum_{j=1}^{3}\sum_{k=1}^{4} \left(\bar{x}_j - \bar{\bar{x}}\right)^2$$

$$= \sum_{j=1}^{3} 4\left(\bar{x}_j - \bar{\bar{x}}\right)^2$$

$$= 4(11 - 8)^2 + 4(8 - 8)^2 + 4(5 - 8)^2$$

$$= 72$$

$$\text{Unexplained sum of squares} = \sum_{j=1}^{3}\sum_{k=1}^{4}(x_{jk} - \bar{x}_j)^2$$

$$= (14 - 11)^2 + (10 - 11)^2$$

$$+ (11 - 11)^2 + (9 - 11)^2$$

$$+ (8 - 8)^2 + (14 - 8)^2 + (3 - 8)^2$$

$$+ (7 - 8)^2 + (8 - 5)^2 + (6 - 5)^2$$

$$+ (5 - 5)^2 + (1 - 5)^2$$

$$= 102$$

(Alternatively: Unexplained sum of squares = Total sum of squares − Treatment sum of squares = 174 − 72 = 102.)

Interpretation

By using either the formulas just discussed or a canned computer program, we can construct an ANOVA table (Table 12–6). The key to interpretation is the test statistic F of 3.18. This statistic follows the F distribution with 2, 9 degrees of freedom. Going to the F table, we see that, at the .05 significance level, $F_{2,9} = 4.26$. Since $3.18 < 4.26$, we fail to reject the null hypothesis of equal mean response to the three package colors. In other words, the differences are not significant. The reason for this is that the variation within the three samples "swamps" the differences in means among the three samples. Note, for example, that this swamping can be seen by noticing that the range of observations in group B is from 3—lower than the smallest mean—to 14—higher than the largest mean. Consequently, the evidence is not sufficiently consistent to conclude that the means are different.

TABLE 12–6 ANOVA Table

Source	*Sum of Squares*	*Degrees of Freedom*	*Mean Square*	*F*
Treatment (colors)	72	2	36	3.18
Unexplained	102	9	11.33	
Total	174	11		

TWO-WAY ANOVA

The next logical extension of the ANOVA method is to the case where there are two influencing variables. For example, assume that, in addition to varying package color, we also changed advertising strategy, as in Table 12–7. This is a factorial design: all possible combinations ($2 \times 3 = 6$) of package color and advertising strategy are tested. There are also samples of size 2 in each of the six possible treatments. The possible treatments are often called *cells*. Having equal cell sizes is common to many experiments and is, in general, a desirable situation.

Examining the relative effects of the two variables is done by extending the one-variable procedure. We redefine the model as follows:

$$x_{ijk} = \bar{\bar{x}} + R_i + C_j + I_{ij} + e_{ijk} \tag{12.15}$$

where

x_{ijk} = kth observation in the sample with the ith level of the row variable and the jth level of the column variable.

R_i = average effect of the ith level of the row variable $= \bar{x}_i - \bar{\bar{x}}$.

C_j = average effect of the jth level of the column variable $= \bar{x}_j - \bar{\bar{x}}$.

I_{ij} = interaction effect of the ith level of the row variable interacting with the jth level of the column variable $= \bar{x}_{ij} - \bar{x}_i - \bar{x}_j + \bar{\bar{x}}$.

$\bar{x}_{ij}$ = mean of the dependent variable in the ith level of the row variable and the jth level of the column variable.

TABLE 12–7 Sales Results as a Function of Package Color and Advertising Strategy

	Package Color			*Average Sales for Each Advertising Strategy*	*Effect of Advertising Strategy*
	A	*B*	*C*		*(R_i)*
Advertising strategy I:	14 10	8 14	8 6	10	+2
Advertising strategy II:	11 9	3 7	5 1	6	−2
Average sales for each color	11	8	5		
Effect of color (C_j)	+3	0	−3		

TABLE 12–8 Average Responses ($\bar{x}_{ij}$)

Ad Type	Color: Red	Blue	Yellow	$\bar{x}_i$	R_i
Mood	7	11	3	7	.33
Factual	10	4	10	8	1.33
Scare	7	3	5	5	−1.67
$\bar{x}_j$	8	6	6	6.67	
C_j	1.33	−.67	−.67		

Conceptually, an interaction is the special effect due to putting two or more features in combination which cannot be predicted by knowing the effects of the two features separately. Hence, it is related to the notion of synergy and the discovery of particularly felicitous (or disastrous) combinations of factors in terms of their effect on the key (dependent) variable. Besides such obvious examples as nitro and glycerin, a variety of examples can be cited; but aesthetic items (music, paintings, etc.) are obvious examples of cases in which the whole is not the sum of the parts. For example, a blue color package combined with an advertising strategy using mood images and jazz music might be more effective than we would expect from the addition of a blue color and mood advertising effects. Put differently, red might be the best color and factual the best advertising strategy when studied separately; but the combination of blue and mood advertising might be better than the combinationof red and factual advertising, as in Table 12–8. The importance of the interaction term is that its significance indicates that there is a synergistic/nonadditive combination of the two variables which is particularly effective. If an interaction term is not significant, it means that optimum overall strategy may be obtained by separately choosing the best level of the two variables and then using them in combination. To estimate interactions, there must be at least two observations per cell.

Statistical Formulas: Unrelated Treatment Variables

The formulas for ANOVA, when the treatment variables are related, are much more complex. Therefore, since the purpose here is to understand ANOVA, we present the formulas for this special case. Dealing with related treatment variables is discussed in terms of an example.

The partitioning of the variance in the two-variable case with equal cell sizes can be viewed as a sequential process of continually pulling apart (decomposing) the "unexplained" variance into that part attributable to some variable and that part which is not. By first removing the variance attributable to the column variables as in one-way ANOVA, one can proceed to pull out the variance attributable to the row variables and then the variance attributable to the interactions as follows:

$$\text{Total variance: } \sum_{i=1}^{r}\sum_{j=1}^{c}\sum_{k=1}^{n_{ij}}\left(x_{ijk}-\bar{\bar{x}}\right)^2 \tag{12.16}$$

$$\text{Column variance: } \sum_{i=1}^{r}\sum_{j=1}^{c}\sum_{k=1}^{n_{ij}}\left(\bar{x}_j-\bar{\bar{x}}\right)^2 = \sum_{j=1}^{c} n_j\left(\bar{x}_j-\bar{\bar{x}}\right)^2 \tag{12.17}$$

$$\text{Row variance: } \sum_{i=1}^{r}\sum_{j=1}^{c}\sum_{k=1}^{n_{ij}}\left(\bar{x}_i-\bar{\bar{x}}\right)^2 = \sum_{i=1}^{r} n_i\left(\bar{x}-\bar{\bar{x}}\right)^2 \tag{12.18}$$

$$\text{Residual variance: } \sum_{i=1}^{r}\sum_{j=1}^{c}\sum_{k=1}^{n_{ij}}\left(x_{ijk}-\bar{x}_i-\bar{x}_j+\bar{\bar{x}}\right)^2 \tag{12.19}$$

$$\text{Interactions: } \sum_{i=1}^{r}\sum_{j=1}^{c}\sum_{k=1}^{n_{ij}}\left(\bar{x}_{ij}-\bar{x}_i-\bar{x}_j+\bar{\bar{x}}\right)^2$$

$$= \sum_{i=1}^{r}\sum_{j=1}^{c} n_{ij}\left(\bar{x}_{ij}-\bar{x}_i-\bar{x}_j+\bar{\bar{x}}\right)^2 \tag{12.20}$$

$$\text{Within variance: } \sum_{i=1}^{r}\sum_{j=1}^{c}\sum_{k=1}^{n_{ij}}\left(x_{ijk}-\bar{x}_{ij}\right)^2 \tag{12.21}$$

FIGURE 12–4 Variance Decomposition in Two-Way ANOVA

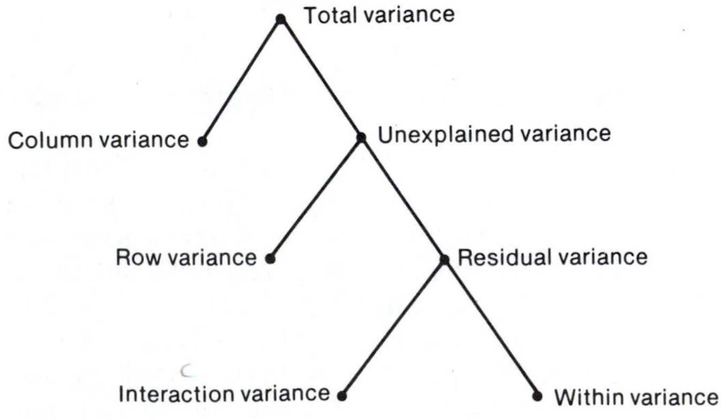

TABLE 12–9 Two-Way ANOVA without Interactions

Source	Sum of Squares	Degrees of Freedom	Mean Square	F
Column	$\sum_{j=1}^{c} n_j(\bar{x}_j - \bar{\bar{x}})^2 = ①$	$c - 1$	$\frac{①}{c-1} = A$	$\frac{A}{C}$
Row	$\sum_{i=1}^{r} n_i(\bar{x}_i - \bar{\bar{x}})^2 = ②$	$r - 1$	$\frac{②}{r-1} = B$	$\frac{B}{C}$
Residual	$\sum_{i=1}^{r} \sum_{j=1}^{c} \sum_{k=1}^{n_{ij}} (x_{ijk} - \bar{x}_i - \bar{x}_j + \bar{\bar{x}})^2 = ③$	$n - r - c + 1$	$\frac{③}{n-r-c+1} = C$	
Total	$\sum_{i=1}^{r} \sum_{j=1}^{c} \sum_{k=1}^{n_{ij}} (x_{ijk} - \bar{\bar{x}})^2$	$n - 1$		

where

c = number of categories in the column variable.

r = number of categories in the row variable.

n_{ij} = number of observations exposed to the ith level of the row variable and the jth level of the column variable.

This process can be viewed graphically in Figure 12–4. Notice that the within variance is the difference between the cell mean and the individual values in the cell. This is, in essence, the irreducible variance which is unexplained and unexplainable, given the two variables. (You may also notice that, unless there is more than one observation per cell, there is no way to calculate the within variance and, hence, no way to separate the interaction effect from within variance.) The other three variances (column, row, and interaction) divide up the explainable variance by assigning it to its "cause."

Examples

Two-Way ANOVA with No Interactions. The simplest form of two-way ANOVA assumes no interactions. Thus, the variance is partitioned into three parts (see Table 12–9):

Column variance: Equation 12.17.

Row variance: Equation 12.18.

Residual variance:[5] Equation 12.19.

---

[5] It is easier to compute the Residual variance as Total variance − Column variance − Row variance.

TABLE 12–10 Two-Way ANOVA without Interactions

Source	*Sum of Squares*	*Degrees of Freedom*	*Mean Square (SS / d.f.)*	*F*
Columns (colors)	72	2	36	5.33
Rows (advertising)	48	1	48	7.11
Residual	54	8	6.75	
Total	174	11		

To see how to apply these formulas, again return to the package color and advertising strategy example (Table 12–7). First, calculate the sums of squares:

$$\text{Column sum of squares} = 4(11 - 8)^2 + 4(8 - 8)^2 + 4(5 - 8)^2$$
$$= 72$$
$$\text{Row sum of squares} = 6(10 - 8)^2 + 6(6 - 8)^2$$
$$= 48$$
$$\text{Residual}^6 \text{ sum of squares} = 174 - 72 - 48 = 54$$

The resulting ANOVA table then becomes Table 12–10.

The test for column effects (H_0: all $\bar{x}_j$s are equal) is F with $c - 1$ and $n - r - c + 1$ degrees of freedom, and compares the column and residual variances. Similarly, the test for row effects (H_0: all $\bar{x}_i$s are equal) is F with $r - 1$ and $n - r - c + 1$ degrees of freedom, and compares the row and residual variances. Here, the test for the significance of the column effect at the .05 significance level is to compare 5.33 with $F_{2,8} = 4.46$. Since $5.33 > 4.46$, we reject the null hypothesis that the column means are equal. In other words, the package colors produce significantly different sales. Similarly, we can test the rows by comparing 7.11 with $F_{.05,1,8} = 5.32$. Since $7.11 > 5.32$, we conclude that advertising also significantly influences sales.

[6] To calculate the residuals directly, we first generate a table for $\bar{x}_i + \bar{x}_j - \bar{\bar{x}} = \bar{\bar{x}} + R_i + C_j$:

13	10	7
9	6	3

We then get the residual sum of squares as $= +(14 - 13)^2 + (10 - 13)^2 + (8 - 10)^2 + (14 - 10)^2 + (8 - 7)^2 + (6 - 7)^2 + (11 - 9)^2 + (9 - 9)^2 + (3 - 6)^2 + (7 - 6)^2 + (5 - 3)^2 + (1 - 3)^2 = 54$.

TABLE 12–11 Two-Way ANOVA with Interactions

Source	Sum of Squares	Degrees of Freedom	Mean Square	F
Column	$\sum_{j=1}^{c} n_j(\bar{x}_j - \bar{\bar{x}})^2 = ①$	$c - 1$	$\dfrac{①}{c-1} = A$	$\dfrac{A}{D}$
Row	$\sum_{i=1}^{r} n_i(\bar{x}_i - \bar{\bar{x}})^2 = ②$	$r - 1$	$\dfrac{②}{r-1} = B$	$\dfrac{B}{D}$
Interaction	$\sum_{i=1}^{r} \sum_{j=1}^{c} n_{ij}(\bar{x}_{ij} - \bar{x}_i - \bar{x}_j + \bar{\bar{x}})^2 = ③$	$rc - c - r + 1$	$\dfrac{③}{rc-c-r+1} = C$	$\dfrac{C}{D}$
Within	$\sum_{i=1}^{r} \sum_{j=1}^{c} \sum_{k=1}^{n_{ij}} (x_{ijk} - \bar{x}_{ij})^2 = ④$	$n - rc$	$\dfrac{④}{n-rc} = D$	

(Put differently, we can predict sales significantly more accurately from $\bar{\bar{x}} + C_j + R_i$ than we can from $\bar{\bar{x}}$ alone.)

It is interesting to note that the column effects now appear to be significant, whereas in the simple one-way analysis they were not. The explanation for this is that the row effects, which were not accounted for in the one-way ANOVA, inflated the unexplained variance sufficiently to mask the effect of package color.

Two-Way ANOVA with Interactions. The same data just analyzed can be examined for the presence of interactions (Table 12–11). The column, row, and total variance formulas are identical to those of the two-way without interaction formulas. The interaction and within formulas are those of (12.20) and (12.21):

$$\text{Interaction variance: } \sum_{i=1}^{r} \sum_{j=1}^{c} n_{ij}(\bar{x}_{ij} - \bar{x}_i - \bar{x}_j + \bar{\bar{x}})^2$$

$$\text{Within variance: } \sum_{i=1}^{r} \sum_{j=1}^{c} \sum_{k=1}^{n_{ij}} (x_{ijk} - \bar{x}_{ij})^2$$

Returning to our example, we calculate the interaction variance as follows:

First, produce a table of cell means ($\bar{x}_{ij}$s) as in Table 12–12. Second, produce the following $\bar{\bar{x}} + R_i + C_j = \bar{x}_i + \bar{x}_j - \bar{\bar{x}}$ table:

13	10	7
9	6	3

TABLE 12–12 Cell Means

	Color		
Ad Strategy	*A*	*B*	*C*
I	12	11	7
II	10	5	3

The differences between the values in the two tables are the interactions (I_{ij}s):

−1	1	0
1	−1	0

Hence, the interaction variance is given by:

$$2(-1)^2 + 2(1)^2 + 2(0)^2 + 2(1)^2 + 2(-1)^2 + 2(0)^2 = 8$$

To calculate the within variance, we compare the values of each observation with the cell means $\bar{x}_{ij}$:

$$\begin{aligned}\text{Within variance} &= (14 - 12)^2 + (10 - 12)^2 + (8 - 11)^2 \\ &\quad + (14 - 11)^2 + (8 - 7)^2 + (6 - 7)^2 \\ &\quad + (11 - 10)^2 + (9 - 10)^2 + (3 - 5)^2 \\ &\quad + (7 - 5)^2 + (5 - 3)^2 + (1 - 3)^2 \\ &= 46\end{aligned}$$

The resulting ANOVA table is shown as Table 12–13. The table values with which we compare the computed Fs are $F_{.05,2,6} = 5.14$ for both the column and interaction effects and $F_{.05,1,6} = 5.99$ for the row effects. This implies that only the row effects are significant. The column effects now appear to be insignificant (at the .05 significance level). While the "right" way to interpret this depends on the purpose of the analysis, it would be appropriate to return to the simple two-way without interaction analysis and conclude that both color and advertising influence sales and that they can be considered independently of each other.

TABLE 12–13 Two-Way ANOVA with Interactions

Source	*Sum of Squares*	*Degrees of Freedom*	*Mean Square*	*F*
Column	72	2	36	4.69
Row	48	1	48	6.26
Interaction	8	2	4	.52
Within	46	6	7.67	
Total	174	11		

A Pictorial / Managerial Interpretation

The awkward formulas and terminology of ANOVA often obscure what is going on. Remembering that the objective of any type of analysis is to make data clearer, it is useful to look at the example just completed in managerial terms. We can best do that by the inelegant but effective method of plotting the results. The mean sales for the different package designs and ads are shown in Figures 12–5 and 12–6. Let us first make two rather broad assumptions: that (*a*) all the colors are equally costly, as are the advertising strategies, and (*b*) the short-run experiment will be projectable both to the total market and over time. Faced with these results, any manager (or person with an IQ above that of a kumquat) would decide to use color A and advertising strategy I—exactly the correct decision. One need only

FIGURE 12–5 Column Effects

FIGURE 12–6 Row Effects

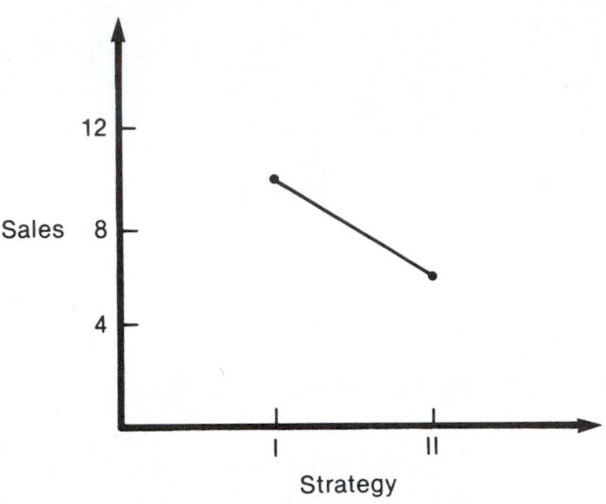

compute conditional means to draw this conclusion, and it is, in fact, the correct decision regardless of whether the differences are statistically significant or not. What checking for statistical significance does is provide a flag to indicate whether the best guess (e.g., color A) is really so much better than the other choices that it is worth arguing for.

The interaction concept is only slightly more involved. We recall that the average sales for each of the cells were those in Table 12–12. Faced with this, the manager would again select the combination of color A and advertising strategy I. Conceivably, however, a slight change could have made color B and advertising strategy I best, even though on average color A and advertising strategy I were best when color and advertising strategy were considered separately. The "flag" for this situation would be a significant interaction term in the analysis. In fact, all possible combinations of significant interactions and row or column variables are possible. These possible combinations can be displayed graphically (Figure 12–7).

The managerial value of ANOVA, then, is obtained by observing the average response to different combinations of the influencing variables. The statistical tests indicate whether the differences are real or illusory.

If statistically significant differences occur, then a cost benefit analysis is needed to determine whether the improved results of using the best mix are worth the cost. In practice, the mix which maximizes sales is rarely justified on a cost/benefit basis. Consequently, the key problem is to compare the costs and benefits (e.g., sales) of various combinations and choose the best one on a "net," rather than "gross" (i.e., unadjusted for cost), basis.

Referring back to the example of Table 12–4, it is clear that, in a gross sense, color A is best. If we assume sales generate profit according to the

FIGURE 12–7 Sales as a Function of Color and Advertising

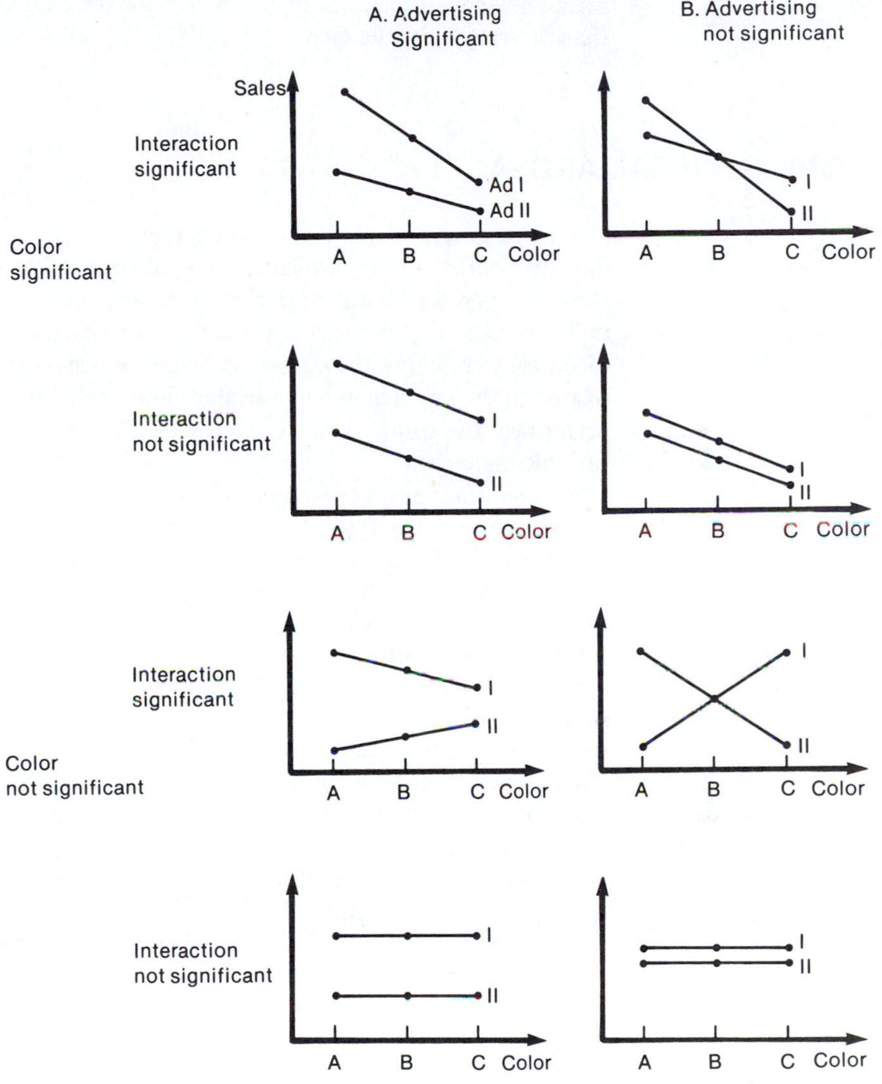

formula: Profit = 6(Sales) − 30, then the profits of the three colors are 36, 18, and 0. If the costs of using the three colors are 30, 5, and 10, however, then the net profits become 6, 13, and −10, indicating that color B is best. It is possible (and in the "real world" essential) to complicate this analysis by taking into account (*a*) the fact that the test area may be a small fraction (e.g., 1 percent) of the total market, and, therefore, the numbers need to be multiplied by a constant (e.g., 100) to convert to market level data, (*b*) the impact over time, properly discounted, and (*c*) competitive reaction. Thus, the choice of the best color depends on many factors other than statistical significance.

MORE GENERAL ANOVA

The more general case occurs when there are more than two influencing (independent) variables which all may affect the key (dependent) variable. Depending on how many variables there are and how many interactions are to be considered, the algebra may get extremely difficult. The concept, fortunately, remains the same: assessing which variables are significantly related to the key dependent variable. Practically, more general ANOVA is performed by using canned computer programs, typically via dummy variable regression.

An important source of variation in many results can be the subject of the observation itself (e.g., respondent, store). In some cases, it may be possible to perform an ANOVA "within subject," meaning, for example, using all the observations on a single respondent or store. More typically, however, the design will be "between subjects," where each respondent or store furnishes a single or at most a small number of observations. When dealing with between subject designs, it is often advisable to account for the subject (respondent, store) effect in the analysis by removing its average level. This can be done by estimating the subject effect (if there are multiple observations per subject) or by choosing variables that account for the differences across subjects (e.g., income or store size) and using those as covariates. Alternatively, a "repeated measures" design can be used when each subject gets each treatment. Here, the differences (contrasts) between the results of each of the other treatments and an (arbitrary) treatment is first calculated. These differences (which have the subject effect removed) are then analyzed.

ANALYSIS OF COVARIANCE

Rarely are all the variables of interest only nominally scaled (categorical). Analysis of covariance (ANCOVA) extends ANOVA to account for both continuous (intervally scaled) and categorical data. Frequently, the categorically scaled variables are manipulated in an experiment (e.g., advertising copy and color) and the intervally scaled ones are other measures which affect the dependent variable (e.g., store size or total sales).

Recalling the discussion in Chapter 5 concerning experimental design, we classified variables as:

1. Ignored.
2. Controlled for in the sample selection.
3. Monitored.
4. Manipulated.

Analysis of variance as we have discussed it in an experimental situation focuses on the impact of the fourth type, manipulated variables (e.g., package color), on the dependent variable. If we also wish to include intervally scaled monitored variables (e.g., average weekly store volume) in the analysis, these are often called *covariates*. Hence, analysis of covariance uses the following general scheme: Dependent variable = f(Experimental/manipulated variables, monitored/covariate variables). Special programs exist to perform ANCOVA, but one can satisfactorily handle most such situations using regression analysis.

MULTIPLE DEPENDENT VARIABLES

In some instances, more than one dependent variable may be important. For example, I might be concerned about the effect of different advertisements on the ratings of a product on several attributes. One way to handle this situation is to perform a separate ANOVA for each attribute. Alternatively, it is possible to simultaneously test the notion that all the attribute ratings remained constant. This second approach is beyond the scope of this book. Practically, it is carried out by using a canned computer program, such as MANOVA—multivariate analysis of variance.

A NUTRITION EXAMPLE

To see how ANOVA can be applied to nonexperimental data, consider again the nutritional study which has been mentioned throughout this book. In this case, assume we want to examine the effect of family size and household income on weekly food expenditures. The original data on 933 respondents (7 failed to answer all three questions) were coded as in Table 12–14. As you may notice, this categorization is somewhat unusual since both family size and income are variables which could be considered intervally scaled. Similarly, the use of median category values to represent food expenditure on an interval scale is not without error. Suffice it to say that such recoding is both pedagogically and practically useful, in this case mostly the former. The actual computer output on which this analysis is

TABLE 12–14 Coding Method

Family Size

Actual Number	*Category*
2	1
3 or 4	2
5 or more	3

Income

Actual Answer	*Category*
Under $10,000	1
$10,000–$20,000	2
Over $20,000	3

Food Expenditure

Answer	*Value*
Under $15	$12.50
$15–$29	22.50
$30–$44	37.50
$45–60	52.50
Over $60	70.00

based is found in Appendix 12–A. Notice that, in most statistical packages, the useful/managerial data on the averages in cells must be requested separately from the statistical analysis. (No pain, no gain?)

It is possible to look at the variables separately. Studying the effect of family size, we find that average expenditures vary by family size (Table 12–15). Obviously, this difference is very substantial. One-way ANOVA (Table 12–16) clearly confirms this. The F of 222.4 is very significant at any reasonable significance level. Food expenditures also vary by income category (Table 12–17). This difference, though not quite as massive as that due to family size, is still clearly significant (Table 12–18).

Since both of these variables are significant, an obvious extension of the analysis is to perform a two-way ANOVA with interactions. In this case,

TABLE 12–15 Family Size versus Expenditure

Family Size Category	*Number in Category*	*Average Expenditures*	*Effect*
1 (2)	411	$28.17	−$ 8.51
2 (3 or 4)	350	39.70	3.02
3 (5 or more)	172	50.86	14.18

TABLE 12–16 One-Way ANOVA for Family Size

Source	*d.f.*	*Sum of Squares*	*Mean Squares*	*F*
Between (family size)	2	67,535	33,767.5	222.4
Within (unexplained)	930	141,190	151.8	
Total	932	208,725		

TABLE 12–17 Income versus Expenditure

Income Category	*Number in Category*	*Average Expenditure*	*Effect*
1	464	$30.64	– $6.04
2	332	41.47	4.79
3	137	45.51	8.83

TABLE 12–18 One-Way ANOVA for Income

Source	*d.f.*	*Sum of Squares*	*Mean Squares*	*F*
Between (income)	2	35,217	17,608.5	94.4
Within (unexplained)	930	173,507	186.6	
Total	932	208,724		

however, we no longer have an equal number of observations per cell. Put differently, family size and income are related. Unlike the previous example, the sequential partitioning formulas for the variance no longer apply. Fortunately, someone programmed the computer with the correct formulas (we hope). The average expenditure pattern shows substantial variation between cells (Table 12–19). Again it is obvious that both income and family size affect food expenditures. The ANOVA results (Table 12–20) confirm this. Even without resorting to the F table, we can see that family size and income have significant effects on expenditures. Also clearly, the interactions are not significant.

Notice that the sum of squares attributed to family size and income separately is less than that attributed to both row and column effects. This is due to the unequal cell sizes which make part of the explained variance common to both variables. To understand where the 44,696.1 comes from, recall that income alone accounted for 35,217.0 in the one-way ANOVA.

TABLE 12–19 Average Food Expenditures

Family Size	*Income* 1	2	3
1	26.03	32.47	34.11
2	35.39	40.85	46.32
3	44.51	52.07	56.50

TABLE 12–20 Two-Way ANOVA with Interactions

Source	*Sum of Squares*	*d.f.*	*Mean Square*	*F*
Main effects (row and column)	79,913.4	4	19,978.3	143.7
Family size	44,696.1	2	22,348.1	160.8
Income	12,377.6	2	6,188.8	44.5
Interactions	355.5	4	88.9	0.6
Residual (within)	128,435.4	924	139.0	
Total	208,704.3	932		

FIGURE 12–8 Variance Partitioning: Food Expenditures

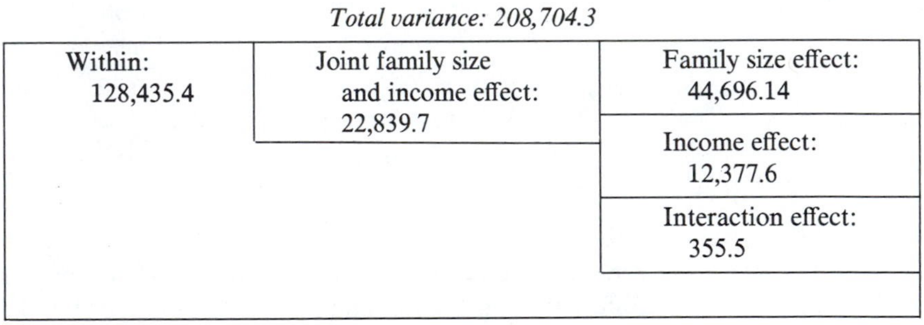

Total variance: 208,704.3

Within: 128,435.4	Joint family size and income effect: 22,839.7	Family size effect: 44,696.14
		Income effect: 12,377.6
		Interaction effect: 355.5

Hence, the marginal contribution of family size is 79,913.4 − 35,217.3 = 44,696.1. Similarly the marginal contribution of income is given by 79,913.4 − 67,535.0. The variance partitioning[7] can be seen in Figure 12–8.

[7]It is interesting to note that a large fraction of the variance in food expenditure is explained by the model. This fraction is:

$$\frac{79{,}913.4 + 355.5}{208{,}724.3} = 38.5 \text{ percent}$$

and is what will be subsequently called R squared (R^2) in the regression chapter.

SUMMARY

This chapter has discussed how to compare means and percentages. It also discussed analysis of variance. By contrast to the other procedures, analysis of variance can be a fairly messy technique. While the basic idea of looking at conditional means is very straightforward, assessing statistical significance using formulas based on interminable squaring of numbers is fairly foreboding. Fortunately, use of canned programs has made the algebraic manipulations a nonissue.

ANOVA's major strengths are the ability to uncover a lot of information from relatively few observations and the fact that the influencing variables need only be categorical. Useful as analysis of variance can be, it is possible for a manager and even a market researcher to survive and prosper knowing very little about it. There are two major reasons for this. The first is that the conditional means, the basis for managerial interpretation, can be calculated without knowing anything about ANOVA. The second is that the technique we will take up in the next chapter—regression analysis—can do essentially everything ANOVA does plus some.

PROBLEMS

1. MESS, a manufacturer of specialty steel products, traditionally held a 20 percent share of a market. After introductions of new products by both the company and a major competitor, the company called 100 potential customers and found 28 had purchased from MESS.
   a. Has anything significant happened?
   b. What could explain the change?
2. Using a random digit phone survey, a company surveyed potential customers in two regions. In region A, 46 of 100 were aware of the company, while in region B, 104 of 200 were aware of the company.
   a. Is the difference significant?
   b. What could explain the difference?
3. A large packaged goods manufacturer tried out a new package design in several stores. The results were as follows:

Store	*Sales with Old Design*	*Sales with New Design*
1	137	152
2	573	581
3	490	480
4	102	95
5	87	120
6	237	252
7	81	98
8	123	140

a. How should I interpret the change?
b. What besides package design might have caused a change?

4. In region A, managed by M.B. Alright, average sales were $11,200 per account, with a standard deviation of 3,400 based on a sample of 100 accounts. In region B, managed by I.M. Dropout, average sales were $12,100, with a standard deviation of 2,800 based on a sample of 64 accounts.
   a. Is there a difference?
   b. What could explain the difference?
5. A company claims to produce a product with an average weight of at least 2,100 kilograms. Having bought five products recently, a client finds they weigh 2,060, 2,090, 2,050, 2,060, and 2,040, respectively.
   a. Is there a reason to complain?
   b. Assume the client publicly claims the company is short weighting its products and sues. The company counter sues for libel. Who should win? Does the matter depend on who has the burden of proof?
6. Given the following test-market results for two stores in each cell (i.e., the two stores in Peoria exposed to strategy A sold 110 and 90 units, respectively).

	Display Strategy	
	A	*B*
Peoria, Ill.	110, 90	40, 80
Springfield, Mass.	140, 100	60, 100
Gainesville, Fla.	60, 80	40, 60

   What can I conclude about the display strategies?
7. Interpret the following results of a two-way ANOVA:

	d.f.	*F*
Advertising	1	1.31
Price	4	5.68
Interactions	4	7.26
Residual	10	

8. The All-Thumbs Hardware Store advertised outdoor grills, using three different advertising copy versions. The sales of their downtown store and suburban store following each ad are shown below.

Ads	*Downtown*	*Suburban*
"Smokey"	1	5
"Hot Dogs"	2	2
"Summer Evening"	3	5

Is the "Summer Evening" copy significantly better than the other advertising copy?

9. Smith's Department Store ran two advertisements, one featuring men's suits, the other featuring sports clothes. The two salespersons Al and Bob sold the following number of suits during each of the two weekends while each ad version ran:

Ads	*Al*	*Bob*
Men's suits	3, 5	5, 7
Sports clothes	2, 2	4, 4

(For example, during the two weekends when the men's suits version was playing, Al sold three suits one weekend and five on the other weekend.) Is there any real difference between the salespersons? Between the ad versions?

10. The DSNOB clothing store ran two different advertising campaigns: one an on-price promotion and the other an off-price promotion. Salespersons Jones and Smith both worked during the test period for both campaigns. During the two weekends when the off-price commercials were playing, Jones sold one men's suit each weekend. However, Smith sold four suits one of these weekends and six the other. Similarly, during the two weekends when the on-price ads were playing, Jones sold zero and two suits, while Smith sold one and one. What can you conclude about the campaigns? Does Smith really do unusually well with the off-price campaign, or could it have been just luck that Smith sold 10 suits on those two weekends?

11. Three different detergent brands were tested for whitening effectiveness at three different water temperatures using a full-factorial design. The measured whiteness of each of the three replications for each

combination of detergent and temperature was as follows:

Water Temperature	Detergent Brand		
	Jiff-O	*All-Temp*	*Hill Fresh*
45°F	47, 48, 52	50, 50, 53	54, 56, 58
95°F	48, 49, 47	45, 46, 44	49, 46, 49
145°F	56, 51, 52	49, 53, 51	47, 48, 52

a. What do you conclude about the whitening effectiveness of these detergents?

b. The present All-Temp advertising claim is "All-Temp washes equally well in hot or cold water." Could the claim be changed to "All-Temp washes equally well in any temperature water"?

12. The distributor of a perishable good ran an experiment to explore the differences between three advertising executions: Grabber, Holder, and Interest, and between three promotional deals denoted simply A, B, and C. The experiment was run in three test cities: Denver, Elmira, and Fort Wayne using a Latin square design. The test weeks were spaced about four weeks apart to lessen the order effects of previous promotions and deals. No other advertising or promotion was conducted in these cities during the three-month test. The number of cases sold during the week of the advertising and promotion plus the number sold in the following two weeks are shown below:

Advertising Copy	City		
	Denver	*Elmira*	*Fort Wayne*
Grabber	A 16	B 21	C 23
Holder	B 16	C 24	A 20
Interest	C 16	A 21	B 23

a. If you had to select one advertising copy and one promotional deal for national use, which would you select?

b. How confident are you that you have selected the correct choices?

13. An experiment was performed by a local retailer in which the price of an item was varied between 30 cents and 40 cents during eight weekly periods. During some of these periods an advertisement was also run. The sales of the product in each period are tabulated below:

	Week							
	1	*2*	*3*	*4*	*5*	*6*	*7*	*8*
Price	30	40	30	40	30	40	30	40
Ad run	Yes	No	Yes	No	No	Yes	No	Yes
Sales	7	7	4	5	1	13	8	11

What can you conclude about the sales response to the different prices?

14. The Hardsell Company tried two different sales pitches for its door-to-door salespersons. The old pitch was basically a demonstration. The new pitch is basically a verbal sales pitch. One of the salespersons, Smith, used the new pitch and the old pitch in two suburbs of Denver, which is a popular city for test marketing. Smith makes 200 calls each week. During the eight weeks Smith was selling in Denver, the following number of units in the two suburban areas known locally as Rockview and Plainview were sold:

	Rockview	*Plainview*
Demonstration	90, 100	70, 60
Verbal	80, 90	80, 70

(For example: Using the demonstration pitch in Rockview, Smith sold 90 units one week and 100 units another week.) What advice would you give Smith?

15. Assume you have just taken a job as assistant brand manager for General Products, Inc. Your first assignment is to help your boss decide which of three package designs and four advertising campaigns should be used next year for one of the company's major products. Your boss wants to do this by getting the opinions of a sample of 200 individuals from the panel which G.P.I. maintains.
    a. What alternatives (and their pros and cons) to the approach your boss has suggested should he or she be made aware of before making a decision?

b. Assume your boss decided to use the following test and got the following sales reports:

San Antonio, Tex.	*Albany, N.Y.*	*Muncie, Ind.*	*Portland, Ore.*
Package design 1	Package design 2	Package design 3	Package design 3
Ad campaign 1	Ad campaign 2	Ad campaign 3	Ad campaign 4
Sales:	Sales:	Sales:	Sales:
A & P 4	A & P 6	K mart 7	A & P 10
X-Mart 5	Grand Union 8	A & P 5	Fred's 11

(1) Is there any difference?

(2) Assume there is a statistical difference. How should I interpret it?

BIBLIOGRAPHY

Banks, Seymour. *Experimentation in Marketing*. New York: McGraw-Hill, 1965.

Cochran, W., and G. Cox. *Experimental Designs*. 2nd ed. New York: John Wiley & Sons, 1957.

Green, Paul E. "On the Design of Choice Experiments Involving Multifactor Alternatives." *Journal of Consumer Research* 1 (September 1974), pp. 61–68.

Hicks, Charles R. *Fundamental Concepts in the Design of Experiments*. New York: Holt, Rinehart & Winston, 1964.

Holland, Charles W., and David W. Cravens. "Fractional Factorial Experimental Designs in Marketing Research." *Journal of Marketing Research* 10 (August 1973), pp. 270–76.

Winer, B. J. *Statistical Principles in Experimental Design*. New York: McGraw-Hill, 1971.

Appendix 12–A

Sample ANOVA Output

```
STATISTICAL PACKAGE FOR THE SOCIAL SCIENCES SPSSH - VERSION 6.00             10/04/76        PAGE    1

        SPACE ALLOCATION FOR THIS RUN..

            TOTAL AMOUNT REQUESTED                                    80000 BYTES


            DEFAULT TRANSPACE ALLOCATION                              10000 BYTES

               MAX NO OF TRANSFORMATIONS PERMITTED              100
               MAX NO OF RECODE VALUES                          400
               MAX NO OF ARITHM.OR LOG.OPERATIONS               800

            RESULTING WORKSPACE ALLOCATION                            70000 BYTES

                  FILE NAME       LEHNUTRI
                  VARIABLE LIST   INCOME,FAMSIZE,EXPENSE
                  INPUT MEDIUM    DISK
                  N OF CASES      UNKNOWN
                  INPUT FORMAT    FIXED(76X,2F1.0/12X,F1.0////)

                 ACCORDING TO YOUR INPUT FORMAT, VARIABLES ARE TO BE READ AS FOLLOWS

                 VARIABLE   FORMAT   RECORD     COLUMNS

                 INCOME     F 1. 0        1      77-  77
                 FAMSIZE    F 1. 0        1      78-  78
                 EXPENSE    F 1. 0        2      13-  13

THE INPUT FORMAT PROVIDES FOR    3 VARIABLES.    3 WILL BE READ
IT PROVIDES FOR  6 RECORDS ('CARDS') PER CASE.  A MAXIMUM OF    78 'COLUMNS' ARE USED ON A RECORD.

                  RECODE             FAMSIZE (2=1)(3,4=2)(5 THRU 9=3)/
                                     INCOME (1,2=1)(3,4=2)(5=3)/
                                     EXPENSE (1=12.5)(2=22.5)(3=37.5)
                                     (4=52.5)(5=70)
                  MISSING VALUES EXPENSE (C)
                  READ INPUT DATA

AFTER READING    940 CASES FROM SUBFILE LEHNUTRI,  END OF FILE WAS ENCOUNTERED ON LOGICAL UNIT # 8
```

```
STATISTICAL PACKAGE FOR THE SOCIAL SCIENCES SPSSH - VERSION 6.00                10/04/76        PAGE    2

                 BREAKDOWN      TABLES=EXPENSE BY FAMSIZE BY INCOME/
                                EXPENSE BY FAMSIZE/EXPENSE BY INCOME

***** GIVEN WORKSPACE ALLOWS FOR  2915 CELLS AND    2 DIMENSIONS FOR SUBPROGRAM BREAKDOWN *****


STATISTICAL PACKAGE FOR THE SOCIAL SCIENCES SPSSH - VERSION 6.00                10/04/76        PAGE    3

FILE   LEHNUTRI (CREATION DATE = 10/04/76)

- - - - - - - - - - - - - - - - -   D E S C R I P T I O N   O F   S U B P O P U L A T I O N S   - - - - - - - - - - - - - - - -
CRITERION VARIABLE   EXPENSE
   BROKEN DOWN BY    FAMSIZE
               BY    INCOME
- - - - - - - - - - - - - - - - - - - - - - - - - - - - - - - - - - - - - - - - - - - - - - - - - - - - - - - - - - - - - - - -

VARIABLE                 CODE     VALUE LABEL            SUM          MEAN        STD DEV      VARIANCE        N

FOR ENTIRE POPULATION                                 34220.0000     36.6774      14.9651      223.9528     (  933)

FAMSIZE                   1.                          11577.500      28.169       10.274       105.557      (  411)
   INCOME                 1.                           7417.500      26.026        8.747        76.518      (  285)
   INCOME                 2.                           2727.500      32.470       11.774       138.630      (   84)
   INCOME                 3.                           1432.500      34.107       11.789       138.970      (   42)

FAMSIZE                   2.                          13895.000      39.700       13.572       184.186      (  350)
   INCOME                 1.                           4530.000      35.391       13.174       173.567      (  128)
   INCOME                 2.                           6822.500      40.853       12.923       167.001      (  167)
   INCOME                 3.                           2542.500      46.227       13.315       177.286      (   55)

FAMSIZE                   3.                           8747.500      50.858       14.024       196.666      (  172)
   INCOME                 1.                           2270.000      44.510       13.304       177.006      (   51)
   INCOME                 2.                           4217.500      52.068       13.612       185.281      (   81)
   INCOME                 3.                           2260.000      56.500       12.920       166.923      (   40)

  TOTAL CASES =      940
MISSING CASES =        7 OR    0.7 PCT.
```

```
STATISTICAL PACKAGE FOR THE SOCIAL SCIENCES SPSSH - VERSION 6.00            10/04/76        PAGE    4

FILE    LEHNUTRI (CREATION DATE = 10/04/76)

- - - - - - - - - - - - - - - - -  D E S C R I P T I O N   O F   S U B P O P U L A T I O N S  - - - - - - - - - - - - - - - - -
CRITERION VARIABLE    EXPENSE
    BROKEN DOWN BY    FAMSIZE
- - - - - - - - - - - - - - - - - - - - - - - - - - - - - - - - - - - - - - - - - - - - - - - - - - - - - - - - - - - - - - - - -

VARIABLE                  CODE      VALUE LABEL                SUM          MEAN        STD DEV       VARIANCE        N

FOR ENTIRE POPULATION                                      34220.0000      36.6774      14.9651      223.9539    (   933)

FAMSIZE                    1.                               11577.500       28.169       10.274       105.557    (   411)
FAMSIZE                    2.                               13895.000       39.700       13.572       184.186    (   350)
FAMSIZE                    3.                                8747.500       50.858       14.024       196.666    (   172)

  TOTAL CASES =        940
MISSING CASES =          7 OR    0.7 PCT.
```

```
STATISTICAL PACKAGE FOR THE SOCIAL SCIENCES SPSSH - VERSION 6.00            10/04/76        PAGE    5

FILE    LEHNUTRI (CREATION DATE = 10/04/76)

- - - - - - - - - - - - - - - - -  D E S C R I P T I O N   O F   S U B P O P U L A T I O N S  - - - - - - - - - - - - - - - - -
CRITERION VARIABLE    EXPENSE
    BROKEN DOWN BY    INCOME
- - - - - - - - - - - - - - - - - - - - - - - - - - - - - - - - - - - - - - - - - - - - - - - - - - - - - - - - - - - - - - - - -

VARIABLE                  CODE      VALUE LABEL                SUM          MEAN        STD DEV       VARIANCE        N

FOR ENTIRE POPULATION                                      34220.0000      36.6774      14.9651      223.9528    (   933)

INCOME                     1.                               14217.500       30.641       12.417       154.191    (   464)
INCOME                     2.                               13767.500       41.468       14.544       211.527    (   332)
INCOME                     3.                                6235.000       45.511       15.364       236.043    (   137)

  TOTAL CASES =        940
MISSING CASES =          7 OR    0.7 PCT.
```

```
STATISTICAL PACKAGE FOR THE SOCIAL SCIENCES SPSSH - VERSION 6.00          10/04/76        PAGE    6

        DATA TRANSFORMATION DONE UP TO THIS POINT..

             NO OF TRANSFORMATIONS                  0
             NO OF RECODE VALUES                    0
             NO OF ARITHM. OR LOG. OPERATIONS       0
        THE AMOUNT OF TRANSPACE REQUIRED IS         0 BYTES


               ONEWAY          EXPENSE BY FAMSIZE(1,3)/
                               RANGES=SCHEFFE(.10)/

***** ONEWAY PROBLEM REQUIRES     128 BYTES WORKSPACE *****


STATISTICAL PACKAGE FOR THE SOCIAL SCIENCES SPSSH - VERSION 6.00          10/04/76        PAGE    7

FILE    LEHNUTRI (CREATION DATE = 10/04/76)

- - - - - - - - - - - - - - - - - - - - - - - - - - - O N E W A Y - - - - - - - - - - - - - - - - - - - - - - - - - - -

     VARIABLE   EXPENSE

                                     ANALYSIS OF VARIANCE

            SOURCE              D.F.     SUM OF SQUARES    MEAN SQUARES        F RATIO     F PROB.

            BETWEEN GROUPS        2        67535.0000       33767.5000         222.422      0.000

            WITHIN GROUPS       930        141190.000          151.8172

            TOTAL               932        208725.000
```

```
STATISTICAL PACKAGE FOR THE SOCIAL SCIENCES SPSSH - VERSIUN 6.00          10/04/76       PAGE    8

FILE   LEHNUTRI (CREATICN CATE = 10/04/76)

- - - - - - - - - - - - - - - - - - - - - - - - - - - O N E W A Y - - - - - - - - - - - - - - - - - - - - - - - - - -

      VARIABLE  EXFENSE

MULTIPLE RANGE TEST

SCHEFFE PROCEDURE
RANGES FOR THE 0.100 LEVEL -

           3.02  3.02

  HOMOGENEOUS SUBSETS   (SUBSETS OF GRCUPS, NC PAIR CF WHICH HAVE MEANS THAT DIFFER BY MCRE THAN THE SHORTEST
                         SIGNIFICANT RANGE FOR A SUBSET OF THAT SIZE)

SUBSET  1

GROUP        GRP01
MEAN        28.1691
- - - - - - - - - - -

SUBSET  2

GROUP        GRP02
MEAN        39.7000
- - - - - - - - - - -

SUBSET  3

GROUP        GRP03
MEAN        5C.8575
- - - - - - - - - - -
```

```
STATISTICAL PACKAGE FOR THE SOCIAL SCIENCES SPSSH - VERSION 6.00          10/04/76      PAGE    9

            ONEWAY         EXPENSE BY INCOME(1,3)/
                           RANCES=SCHEFFE(.10)/

 ***** ONEWAY PROBLEM FEQUIRES    192 BYTES WORKSPACE *****


STATISTICAL PACKAGE FOR THE SOCIAL SCIENCES SPSSH - VERSION 6.00          10/04/76      PAGE   10
FILE   LEHNUTRI (CREATION CATE = 10/04/76)
- - - - - - - - - - - - - - - - - - - - - - - - - C N E W A Y - - - - - - - - - - - - - - - - - - - - - - - - -

    VARIABLE  EXPENSE
                                     ANALYSIS OF VARIANCE

          SOURCE            D.F.   SUM OF SQUARES   MEAN SQUARES      F RATIO   F PROB.

          BETWEEN GROUPS      2      35217.0000      17608.5          94.382    0.000

          WITHIN GROUPS     930     173507.000        186.5667

          TOTAL             932     208724.000
```

```
STATISTICAL PACKAGE FOR THE SOCIAL SCIENCES SPSSH - VERSIUN 6.00                10/04/76        PAGE  11
FILE   LEHNUTRI (CREATION CATE = 10/04/76)

- - - - - - - - - - - - - - - - - - - - - - - - - - O N E W A Y - - - - - - - - - - - - - - - - - - - - - - - - - -

      VARIABLE  EXPENSE

MULTIPLE RANGE TEST

SCHEFFE PROCEDURE
RANGES FOR THE 0.100 LEVEL -

           3.94  3.94  3.94  3.94

  HOMOGENEOUS SUBSETS    (SUBSETS OF GROUPS, NO PAIR OF WHICH HAVE MEANS THAT CIFFER BY MCRE THAN THE SHORTEST
                          SIGNIFICANT FANGE FOR A SLBSET OF THAT SIZE)

SUBSET  1

GROUP       GRP01
MEAN       30.6412
- - - - - - - - - - -

SUBSET  2

GROUP       GRP02
MEAN       41.4684
- - - - - - - - - - -

SUBSET  3

GROUP       GRP03
MEAN       45.5109
- - - - - - - - - - -
```

```
STATISTICAL PACKAGE FOR THE SOCIAL SCIENCES SPSSH - VERSION 6.00          10/04/76          PAGE   12


                  ANOVA           EXPENSE BY FAMSIZE (1,3) INCOME (1,3)

'ANOVA' PROBLEM REQUIRES   1995 BYTES OF SPACE.



STATISTICAL PACKAGE FOR THE SOCIAL SCIENCES SPSSH - VERSION 6.00          10/04/76          PAGE   13

FILE    LEHNUTRI (CREATION DATE = 10/04/76)

* * * * * * * * * * A N A L Y S I S   O F   V A R I A N C E * * * * * * * * * * *
              EXPENSE
           BY FAMSIZE
              INCOME
* * * * * * * * * * * * * * * * * * * * * * * * * * * * * * * * * * * * * * * *


                                      SUM OF                 MEAN            SIGNIF
SOURCE OF VARIATION                   SQUARES     DF        SQUARE       F     OF F

MAIN EFFECTS                        79913.375      4     19978.344 143.730   0.001
   FAMSIZE                          44696.141      2     22348.070 160.778   0.001
   INCOME                           12377.625      2      6188.812  44.524   0.001

2-WAY INTERACTIONS                    355.500      4        88.875   0.639   0.999
   FAMSIZE  INCOME                    355.470      4        88.867   0.639   0.999

RESIDUAL                           128435.375    924       138.999

TOTAL                              208704.250    932       223.932

   940 CASES WERE PROCESSED.
     7 CASES (  0.7 PCT) WERE MISSING.
```

Chapter 13

Regression Analysis

Of all the "fancy" multivariate procedures, regression analysis is by far the most widely used in marketing research. The basic purpose of regression analysis is to estimate the relationship between variables. While many people find it useful for forecasting, regression is not restricted to forecasting, and its applicability extends to problems such as market segmentation and model building.

To use regression, a researcher must specify which variable (e.g., sales) depends on which other variable(s) (e.g., GNP, price). The procedure then calculates estimates of the relationship between the independent variables (GNP, price, etc.) and the dependent variable (sales).

This chapter will proceed by first discussing the simple case of regression analysis where there is only one independent variable as a means of introducing and explaining the procedure. The more realistic case of more than one independent variable will be discussed next. After describing some of the problems which affect interpretation, applications of regression analysis to several situations will be described. Finally, the important distinction between correlation and causation will be addressed.

Before proceeding, one comment about the name *regression analysis* is appropriate. Like so many terms in our language, the term *regression analysis* bears no useful relationship to the technique. While the story of "how the technique got its name" is culturally interesting, suffice it to say that the title is a historical anachronism (Galton, 1889). Having saved you innumerable hours of frustration in attempting to understand the name of the technique, this chapter now turns to the real business of understanding regression analysis.

SIMPLE (TWO-VARIABLE) LINEAR REGRESSION ANALYSIS

Basic Concept

The simplest case of regression analysis is the situation where one variable is presumed to depend on only one other variable. For example, we may assume that sales depend solely on GNP. While this is not realistic, it serves as a useful example to introduce the method. In such a case, the researcher would gather data on sales and GNP for several different occasions. As a first means of analyzing the relationship, the data should be plotted (Figure 13–1). Simple observation of the data indicates that, as GNP increases, so do sales. To summarize the relationship, one would tend to draw a straight line through the data points (Figure 13–2). The line summarizes, in some average sense, the relationship between GNP and sales. Hence, we could express the relationship between GNP and sales mathematically as follows:

$$\text{Estimated sales} = B_0 + B_1\text{GNP}$$

The term B_0 is the constant or intercept. This might be interpreted literally as the predicted level of sales if GNP dropped to zero. However, since such a level of GNP has not recently been experienced, extrapolating to this level is foolish. (Also, if GNP goes to zero we'll all be dead, so who cares what sales would be?) The term B_1 is the slope of the line (soon to be called the *regression coefficient*) and is interpreted as the amount sales would increase

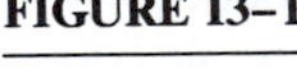

FIGURE 13–1

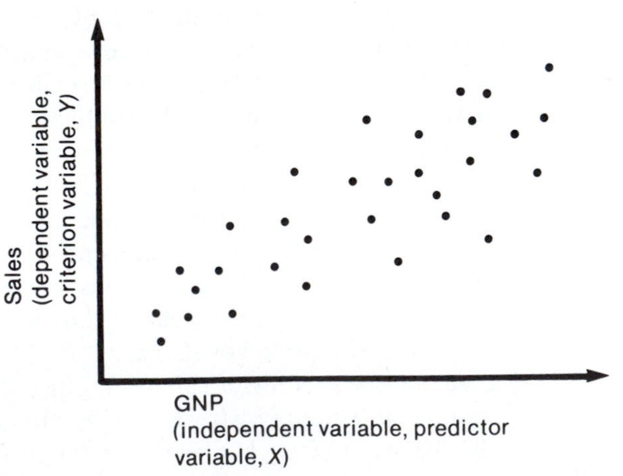

FIGURE 13–2

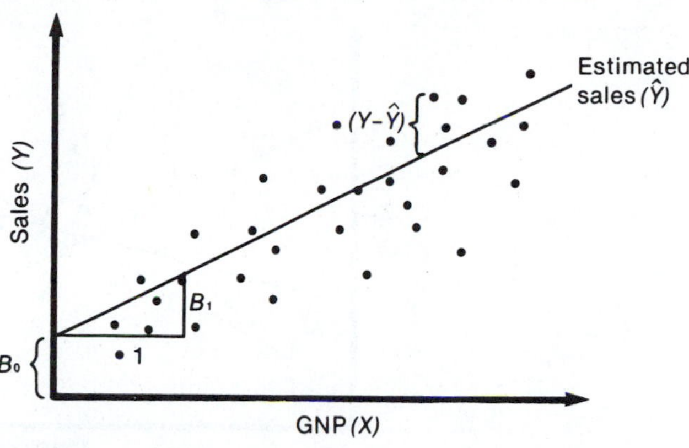

if GNP increased one (in whatever units the original data were measured, e.g., billions of dollars). The error in prediction, calculated as $Y - \hat{Y}$, is simply the difference between estimated and actual sales.

Estimation

A variety of other straight lines could also be drawn through the data (Figure 13–3), some (A and B) that obviously do not represent the data, and others (C and D) that seem to represent the data fairly well. A problem, therefore, is to decide which line best fits the data. The following procedures exist for deciding on the best line:

1. *Graphical eyeball: Pick the line that looks best.* This procedure is often useful. Unfortunately, it breaks down when there are either numerous data points or more than one independent variable.
2. *Find the line that optimizes some criterion measure of a good fit.* Two of these criteria include the following:
   a. The sum of the absolute differences between the predicted sales and actual sales ($\Sigma|Y - \hat{Y}|$).
   b. The sum of the squared differences between the predicted and actual sales values ($\Sigma(Y - \hat{Y})^2$).

The absolute differences, unfortunately, turn out to be relatively cumbersome mathematically. The generally accepted method is to minimize the sum of the squared errors (often called *least squares estimation*). One property of the squared differences is that they give slightly more weight to

FIGURE 13–3

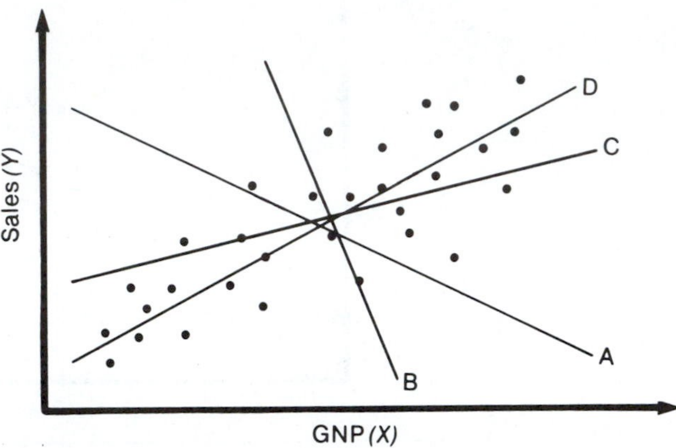

"far out" data points than does the absolute difference criterion. (In other words, the least squares criterion would favor a line which produced four differences of size two as opposed to a line which produced three of size one and one of size four.) Simple linear regression analysis calculates the coefficients of the line (B_0 and B_1) which minimize the sum of the squared differences between the actual value of the dependent variable and the value predicted by the line $\hat{Y} = B_0 + B_1X$.

Regression coefficients. To find the B_0 and B_1 which thus generate the "best" line, one need only plug into the two formulas (see Appendix 13–B for their derivation):

$$B_1 = \frac{\Sigma(X - \overline{X})(Y - \overline{Y})}{\Sigma(X - \overline{X})^2} = \frac{\Sigma XY - n\overline{X}\,\overline{Y}}{\Sigma X^2 - n\overline{X}^2} \tag{13.1}$$

and

$$B_0 = \overline{Y} - B\overline{X} \tag{13.2}$$

These formulas can be used manually. Much more desirable, however, is to utilize either a "canned" regression program on a computer or a calculator. Suffice it to say that hand calculations are rarely used for any problem with more than 8 to 10 data points. The following two measures are often also calculated:

The Standard Error of Estimate ($S_{Y.X}$). This is a measure of the typical deviation of the predictions from the actual values of the dependent variable (Y). It is analogous to the standard deviation (thus, the term *standard error*) and is calculated as:

$$S_{Y.X} = \sqrt{\frac{\Sigma(Y - \hat{Y})^2}{n - 2}} = \sqrt{\frac{\Sigma(Y - \overline{Y})^2 - B_1\Sigma(X - \overline{X})(Y - \overline{Y})}{n - 2}} \tag{13.3}$$

The Coefficient of Determination (r^2). While the standard error of estimate provides one measure of the accuracy of prediction, it is not particularly easy to interpret, much less compare across different analyses, because it depends on the units in which Y is measured. (Is a fit with a standard error of two cartons better or worse than one with a standard error of three dollars?) The correlation coefficient (r) measures the closeness of the relation between the predicted and actual values of the dependent variable. In regression, r^2, known as the *coefficient of determination*, is often used. Recall:

$$r = \frac{\Sigma(X - \overline{X})(Y - \overline{Y})}{\sqrt{\Sigma(X - \overline{X})^2}\sqrt{\Sigma(Y - \overline{Y})^2}} = \frac{\Sigma XY - n\overline{X}\overline{Y}}{ns_X s_Y} \tag{13.4}$$

We can also compute r^2 directly from:

$$r^2 = 1 - \frac{\Sigma(Y - \hat{Y})^2}{\Sigma(Y - \overline{Y})^2}$$

$$= 1 - \frac{\text{Unexplained variance in } Y}{\text{Total variance in } Y}$$

$$= \text{percent of the variance in } Y \text{ explained by } X.$$

A sample application of these formulas is shown in Appendix 13–A.

Interpretation

The previous section dealt with a description of the mechanics of how the regression coefficients are derived. The key issue for a user, however, is how to interpret the results. There are three major elements which are especially important outputs of a regression analysis: the regression coefficients, the standard error of estimate ($S_{Y.X}$), and the coefficient of determination.

The Regression Coefficients.

The constant or intercept, B_0, is interpreted as the value Y would take on if X were zero. Since many situations exist where the X values are unlikely to approach zero (e.g., a sales versus GNP equation), this interpretation is often either unnecessary or inappropriate.

The regression coefficient or slope, B_1, is interpreted as the amount Y would increase if X increased one unit. A negative regression coefficient means that, as X goes up, Y decreases in value. For example, in the equation:

$$\text{Sales} = B_0 + B_1 \text{ (price)}$$

we would expect B_1 to be negative. Hence, the slope is a measure of the marginal sensitivity of Y to changes in X. Consider, for example, the equation:

$$\text{Sales in cartons} = 2.5 + 2 \text{ (advertising in \$)}$$

Assuming for a moment that the relationship is causal, this implies that increasing advertising one dollar would increase sales by two cartons. The use of this would then suggest that if the marginal profit of two cartons of sales were greater than a dollar, then increasing advertising would increase profits in the short run. Conversely, if two cartons of sales produced less than one dollar of profit, then reducing advertising might improve profits.

The Standard Error of Estimate ($S_{Y.X}$). One of the uses of regression is as a predictive tool. Continuing the sales versus advertising example, a manager might ask, "What if advertising were set at \$10?" Using the equation, the forecast would be:

$$\text{Sales in cartons} = 2.5 + 2(10) = 22.5$$

This is the best guess available. In planning, however, it is necessary to know the range of likely outcomes as well as the most likely result to make production scheduling, etc., more efficient. Consider the three cases in Figure 13–4. In case A, the past data seem to fall exactly on the line. If the rather heroic assumption that nothing is changing in the market can be made, we would be fairly confident in the prediction of 22.5. Put differently, we would tend to hedge the prediction very little, using as the forecast $22.5 \pm .5$. In case B, the data fall less closely to the line and the prediction would be hedged to a greater extent, leading to a forecast of 22.5 ± 2. Case C shows a situation where the spread of data points about the line is much greater; hence, the forecast might be 22.5 ± 14. Since deciding on the range of a forecast by graphing the data is both tedious and inexact, an efficient procedure is to use the standard error of estimate as a measure of the likely accuracy of the prediction. To be 95 percent sure that actual sales fall within the range, this suggests predicting sales will be approximately

FIGURE 13–4

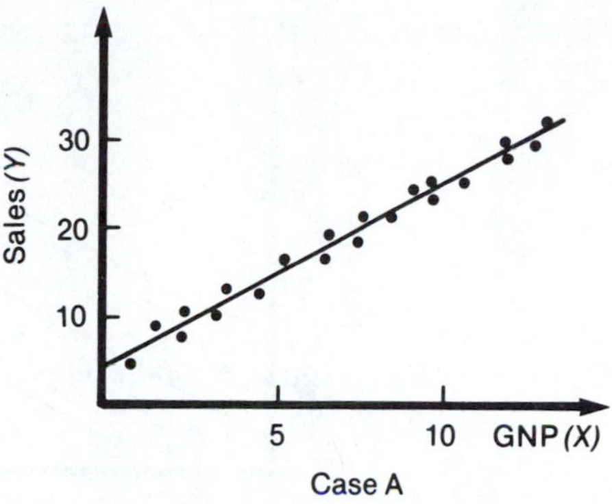

Case A

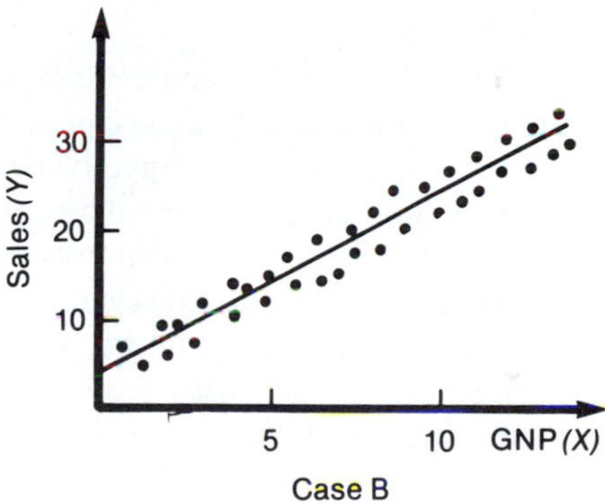

Case B

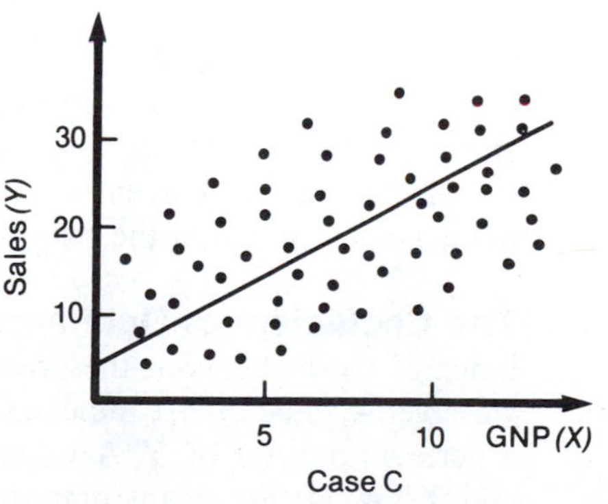

Case C

FIGURE 13–5

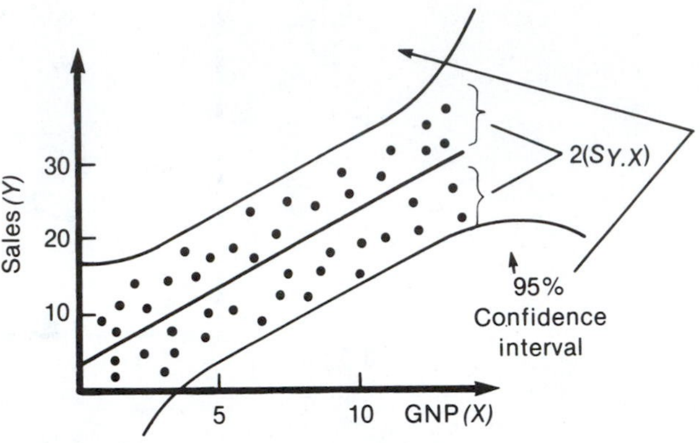

$22.5 \pm 2S_{Y.X}$. This could be represented graphically as Figure 13–5. As long as a reasonably large sample size were used and the advertising figures used were within the range of past experience, this would be a reasonable prediction. Should either the sample size (n) get small or the value of the dependent variable be well outside the range of past data (sometimes called the *relevant range*), however, then a forecaster would correctly feel more squeamish about his or her estimates and, consequently, want to give a larger range of possible outcomes. The formula which quantifies this squeamishness is:

$$\text{Forecast of } Y = \hat{Y} \pm t_{n-2,\alpha} S_{Y.X} \sqrt{1 + \frac{1}{n} + \frac{(X' - \bar{X})^2}{\Sigma(X - \bar{X})^2}} \tag{13.5}$$

where X' is the value of X for which the forecast is being generated. Since $t_{n-2,\alpha}$ is the number from the t distribution with $n - 2$ degrees of freedom at the $(1 - \alpha)$ confidence level, this reduces to approximately $\hat{Y} \pm 2S_{Y.X}$ (at the famous 95 percent confidence level) for large sample sizes and predictions well within the relevant range.

The Coefficient of Determination. The correlation coefficient is an index of the fit between the predicted and actual values of the dependent variable. A value of ± 1 indicates "perfect" correlation, meaning that X is a perfect predictor of Y. A value of 0 indicates no correlation between X and Y. (What this means practically is that X is useless as a predictor of Y.) A value between 0 and ± 1 indicates somewhere between no and perfect correlation.

The value of r^2, the coefficient of determination, is the percent of the variance in the values of Y accounted for (predictable by, explained by, associated with) the variance in X. Therefore, an r of .7 means an r^2 of .49 which, in turn, indicates that about half the variance in Y is accounted for by variance in X.

The size of the correlation is related to both the regression coefficient B_1 and the standard error. This relationship is summarized in Figure 13–6.

FIGURE 13–6

Plot of points	Regression coefficient	Standard error of estimate	Correlation
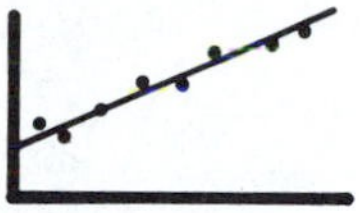	Positive	0	+ 1.0
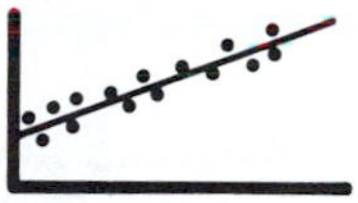	Positive	Small	.95
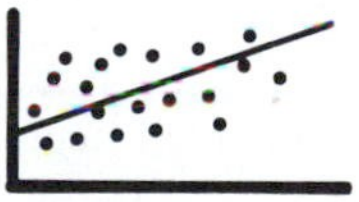	Positive	Large	.20
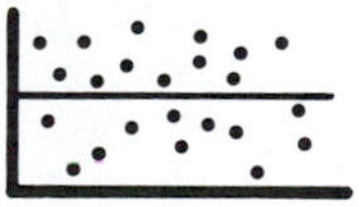	0	"Very" large (equal to the standard deviation of Y, sy)	0
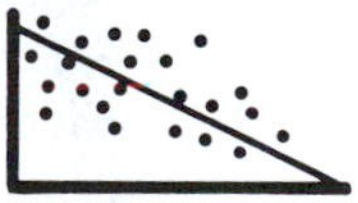	Negative	Large	-.20
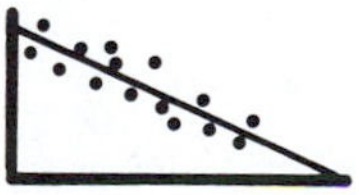	Negative	Small	-.95
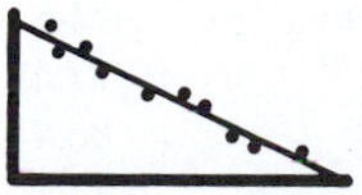	Negative	0	-1.0

Two Examples of Simple Linear Regression

Motor Vehicle Registrations. In the first example, we will consider the relationship between motor vehicle registrations and time between 1961 and 1968. The raw data, used as input, are as follows:

Year (X)	*U.S. Motor Vehicle Registrations (Y) (million)*
1	63.2
2	65.8
3	68.8
4	71.7
5	74.9
6	77.8
7	80.0
8	83.2

Plotting these data shows a very strong linear relation between time and motor vehicle registrations. Obviously, registrations are increasing at about

TABLE 13–1 Fuel Oil Regression

Variable	*Mean*	*Standard Deviation*
X	4.5	2.29
Y	73.2	6.58

Constant (B_0) = 60.3
Slope (B_1) = 2.87
Standard error ($S_{Y.X}$) = .21
Coefficient of determination (r^2) = .999

X	Y	*Estimated* $Y(\hat{Y})$	$Y - \hat{Y}$
1	63.2	63.1	.1
2	65.8	66.0	−.2
3	68.8	68.9	−.1
4	71.7	71.7	0
5	74.9	74.6	.3
6	77.8	77.4	.4
7	80.0	80.4	−.4
8	83.2	83.2	0

3 million a year, and in year 0 (in this case, equal to 1960), a shade over 60 million cars must have been registered. Performing the appropriate calculations leads to the results in Table 13–1. Hence, we conclude the following:

1. Motor vehicle registrations = 60.3 + 2.87 (number of years since 1960).
2. The relationship between time and motor vehicle registrations is very close ($r^2 = .999$, $S_{Y.X}$ is 200,000, compared to values of Y of about 70,000,000). Predicted 1969 registrations based on this model would then be:

$$60.3 + 2.87(9) \pm t_{6,.05}(.21)\sqrt{1 + \frac{1}{8} + \frac{(4.5)^2}{\Sigma(X - \bar{X})^2}} = 86.1 \pm .75$$

Since actual 1969 registrations turned out to be 86.4 million, this was a "good" prediction.

MBA Salaries. Now consider the relation between the salary an MBA received in 1972 and the number of years which had elapsed since he or she graduated. (Ancient history is used to prevent invidious comparisons.) Using a sample of over 4,000 graduates of the "big name" schools (and obviously a computer), the following results were obtained:

$$\text{Intercept} = \$19{,}650$$

$$\text{Slope} = \$630$$

$$r^2 = .184$$

$$S_{Y.X} = \$10{,}440$$

We therefore conclude a typical MBA's salary would be \$19,650 + \$630 (number of years since graduation). However, the relationship between years since graduation and salary, though significant, is subject to wide variation, as indicated by the r^2 of .184 and the standard error of estimate of \$10,440. This means that the forecast of the 1972 salary of an MBA 10 years after graduation would be:

$$19{,}650 + 630(10) \pm 2(10{,}440) = 25{,}950 \pm 20{,}880$$

To be 95 percent confident of including an individual's actual salary, a prediction would have to be between \$5,000 (Peace Corps, unemployment) and \$47,000 (corporate stardom).

Three factors contribute to this large uncertainty. The first is that the relation between salary and years since graduation is likely to be somewhat nonlinear. For example, the true relation might be that of Figure 13–7. Since most of the individuals in the sample had between 5 and 15 years

FIGURE 13–7

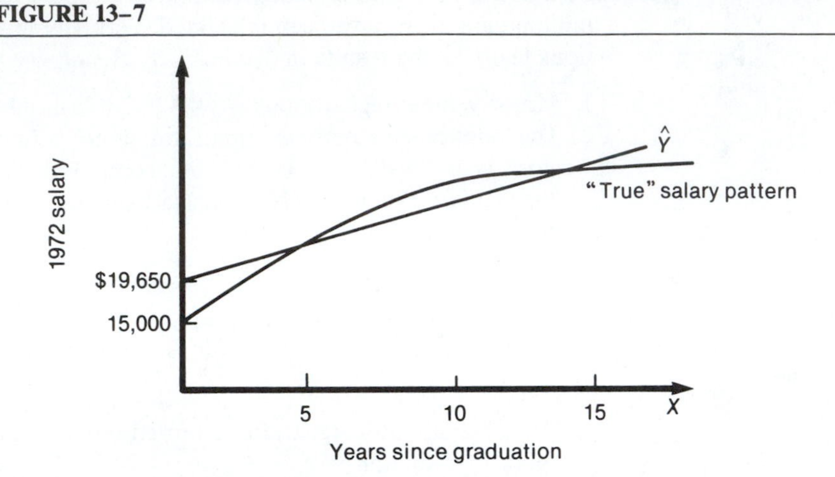

experience, this is really the only relevant range for the regression results. A nonlinear model would presumably improve the fit. It also would change the intercept to a lower figure than the implausible $19,650 (starting salaries for MBAs in 1972 were lower).

A second contributor to the low predictive value is the omission of other key variables. One would presume other variables such as school attended, major, and industry employed in would all affect salary. Inclusion of multiple variables will be discussed in another section.

The final explanation of the large variation of the predicted results is the possibility that salaries are uncertain. This uncertainty may stem from two sources. The first source is essentially noise in the data, consisting of such problems as the inaccuracy of the reported salary (how honest would you be in disclosing your salary?), the exclusion of bonuses and commissions from the salary measure of compensation, and any of a variety of coding and processing errors. The second source of uncertainty is essentially pure randomness, which stems from the fact that a large component of salary depends on unpredictable "luck."

MULTIPLE REGRESSION

Basic Concept

The basic concept of multiple regression is the same as that of simple regression: to find the relation between independent and dependent variables. In multiple regression, however, there are several independent variables. In other words, we might assume that sales depend not just on GNP but also on price, advertising, and distribution. The model is, assuming there are k independent variables:

$$Y = B_0 + B_1X_1 + B_2X_2 + \cdots + B_kX_k + \mu$$

Estimation

The estimation procedure developed for multiple regression is analogous to that for simple regression. The objective is to minimize the sum of the squared deviations between the actual and predicted values of the dependent variable. The regression coefficients are obtained from a mathematical formula which simultaneously estimates all the coefficients (see Appendix 13–B). In practice, the results are always found by using canned computer programs. In addition to the regression coefficients, the other two measures which are most useful are, as in the case of simple regression, the standard error of estimate and the coefficient of determination (R^2), which are direct extensions of the simple regression counterparts. The standard error of estimate is:

$$S_{Y.X} = \sqrt{\frac{\Sigma(Y - \hat{Y})^2}{n - k}}$$

and

$$R^2 = 1 - \frac{S^2_{Y.X}}{S^2_Y} = 1 - \frac{\text{Unexplained variance}}{\text{Total variance}} = \begin{array}{c}\text{Percent of the total variance}\\ \text{in } Y \text{ explained by } X\end{array}$$

At this point one might ask, "Why not run a series of simple regressions and use the coefficients from each of the separate regressions?" There are three reasons for not doing this:

1. It is difficult to decide what the intercept B_0 should be since each separate regression would produce a different intercept.
2. If some of the independent variables are strongly interrelated, then the estimates obtained from the simple regressions may be "bad." That is, the coefficients from the simple regressions may either over- or understate the effect of these independent variables on the dependent variable. This is due to what is called *omitted variable bias*, which will be discussed later.
3. It is inefficient. For example, 20 independent variables will require 20 separate regressions.

General Interpretation

Interpretation of the results of multiple regression is similar to interpretation of simple regression. The three major elements to consider are the regression coefficients, the standard error of estimate, and the coefficient of multiple determination (R^2).

The Regression Coefficients.

The constant, B_0, is the "baseline" value of Y, which is interpreted as the value Y would take on if all the independent variables were zero. As in the case of simple regression, this is rarely a meaningful interpretation, since in most marketing models the only way for all the independent variables to go to zero is for the world to end (which also tends to make the interpretation meaningless).

The regression coefficients (B_1 *through* B_k*).* A particular regression coefficient, B_i, is interpreted as the amount by which the dependent variable would change if the ith independent variable increased by one unit and all the other variables remained unchanged. In other words, a regression coefficient is the marginal influence of a single independent variable on the dependent variable. For example, if we obtained:

$$\text{Sales in cartons} = 1.2 + 1.3(\text{advertising } \$) - .2(\text{price in } \$) + .1(\text{GNP in billions of dollars})$$

then the effect of increasing advertising one dollar while holding price and GNP constant would be to increase sales by 1.3 cartons. In general, both the sign (indicating the direction of the effect) and the absolute size (indicating the magnitude of the effect) of a coefficient should be examined.

The Standard Error of Estimate. As in the case of simple regression, the standard error of estimate is used as a quantification of the amount a prediction must be hedged. Assuming that $S_{X.Y}$ was 15 in the previous example, the best estimate of sales given advertising of \$20, price of \$60, and GNP of \$1,000 billion, would be:

$$\begin{aligned}\text{Sales} &= 1.2 + 1.3(20) - .2(60) + .1(1{,}000)\\ &= 115.2\end{aligned}$$

The confidence interval for a prediction, assuming the values of the independent variables in the forecast were similar to those used to build the model, would be:

$$Y \pm t_{n-k-1,\,\alpha}(S_{Y.X}).$$

Assuming a large sample size, in this case the 95 percent confidence interval would be approximately:

$$115.2 \pm 2(15) = 115 \pm 30$$

The Coefficient of Determination (R^2). The coefficient of determination is interpreted as the percent of the variance in the dependent variable predicted by variation in all the independent variables. The coefficient of multiple correlation (R) is an index of the closeness of the relation between the dependent variable and the independent variables. It is calculated as the square root of the coefficient of determination, R^2. For the special case of only one independent variable, the multiple correlation coefficient is equal to the simple correlation coefficient.[1]

Statistical Interpretation

Interpretation of the results of regression is often aided by the following two types of statistical tests:

Tests on the Individual Coefficients (B_is). The individual coefficient estimates, the B_is, are obviously subject to error. Since the errors are usually assumed to be normally distributed, we can estimate the true value of a particular coefficient as:

$$\text{“True” value of } B_i = \text{Estimated value of } B_i \pm t_{n-k-1,\,\alpha}\begin{pmatrix}\text{standard}\\ \text{deviation}\\ \text{of } B_i\end{pmatrix}$$

One interesting question is whether the true B_i is really different from zero. (In other words, does the ith variable really influence the dependent variable?) This can be tested by either a t or F test (some computer outputs use each of these equivalent tests) as follows:

Hypothesis	*t Test Statistic*	*F Test Statistic*
The true value of the ith regression coefficient is zero ($B_i = 0$)	$\dfrac{B_i - 0}{S_{B_i}}$	$\left(\dfrac{B_i}{S_{B_i}}\right)^2$

[1]Since R^2 is based on the data used to construct the model, it only indirectly assesses the value of the model for predicting new observations. Therefore, especially when the sample size is small, many researchers will do some form of “cross-validation” (c.f., Cooil, Winer, and Rados, 1987), where a model is built on some of the data and then used to predict other observations (e.g., splitting the sample into halves; one for estimating the model and the other for assessing predictive power). Such procedures tend to favor simple models but are not used by most applied researchers.

Ignoring degrees of freedom and using the 95 percent confidence level, this means that, to be significant, the t ratio must be greater than about 2 and the F ratio greater than 4. (Actually, the t test statistic is t with $n - k - 1$ degrees of freedom, and the F test statistic is F with 1 and $n - k - 1$ degrees of freedom.) Failure to be significant indicates that, although the variable may be related to the dependent variable, the variable fails to marginally affect the dependent variable (and thus aid predictions) when the effects of the other independent variables are removed. What this means, practically, is that variables with nonsignificant coefficients may be eliminated from the equation without greatly harming predictions. Interpretation, on the other hand, may be more difficult as the variables are removed.

Test on the Coefficient of Determination (R^2). The tests on the individual coefficients address the question of whether a particular variable improves prediction. A test of R^2, on the other hand, addresses the question of whether the independent variables as a group are significantly related to the dependent variable. The test is based on an analysis of variance table (Table 13–2). The F test is:

$$\frac{\dfrac{\text{Explained sum of squares}}{k}}{\dfrac{\text{Unexplained sum of squares}}{n-k-1}} = \frac{\dfrac{\Sigma(Y-\bar{Y})^2 - \Sigma(Y-\hat{Y})^2}{k}}{\dfrac{\Sigma(Y-\hat{Y})^2}{n-k-1}}$$

where k is the number of independent variables. This can be shown to be equivalent to:

$$\frac{\dfrac{R^2}{k}}{\dfrac{1-R^2}{n-k-1}} \text{ which is } F_{k,\,n-k-1}$$

TABLE 13–2 Regression ANOVA Table

	SS	*d.f.*	*MSS*
Explained variation	$\Sigma(Y-\bar{Y})^2 - \Sigma(Y-\hat{Y})^2 = ESS$	k	ESS/k
Unexplained variation	$\Sigma(Y-\hat{Y})^2 = USS$	$n-k-1$	$USS/(n-k-1)$
Total variation in Y	$\Sigma(Y-\bar{Y})^2 = TSS$	$n-1$	

When the F test on R is insignificant, it means that the entire regression is essentially worthless (unless, of course, a negative finding is what the researcher wanted in the first place).[2]

NUTRITION SURVEY EXAMPLE

In analyzing the data from the nutrition study, one objective was to build a model which explained different levels of expenditures on food based on other variables. Food expenditures were regressed against 15 other variables:

1. Income (coded 1–6).
2. Age of respondent (in years).
3. Family size.
4. Number of brands and sizes shopped for (coded 1–4).
5. Habitual buying versus information seeking (coded 1–3).
6. Importance of variety (coded from 1 = very important to 5 = very unimportant).
7. Importance of taste.
8. Importance of other family members' preferences.
9. Importance of diet restrictions.
10. Importance of price.
11. Importance of availability.
12. Importance of ease of preparation.
13. Importance of habit.
14. Importance of specials.
15. Importance of nutritional value.

The weekly expenditure variable was recoded into dollar terms in the following manner:

Response	*Recode*
Under $15	$12.50
$15–$29	22.50
$30–$44	37.50
$45–$60	52.50
Over $60	70.00

[2] The more independent variables you have, the higher R^2 will be. Consequently, many researchers prefer to use a criterion which takes the number of independent variables into account. Hence, an adjusted R^2 is often used as follows:

$$\text{Adjusted } R^2 = 1 - (1 - \text{unadjusted } R^2)\left(\frac{n-1}{n-k-1}\right)$$

TABLE 13–3 Food Expenditure Variables

Variable	*Mean*	*Standard Deviation*
Food expenditures	37.52	15.12
Income (coded 1–6)	2.75	1.42
Age of respondent (in years)	43.70	16.54
Family size	3.29	1.38
Number of brands and sizes shopped for (coded 1–4)	2.34	1.42
Habitual buying versus information seeking (coded 1–3)	1.87	.65
Importance of variety (coded from 1 = very important to 5 = very unimportant)	2.04	.96
Importance of taste	1.24	.57
Importance of other family members' preferences	1.70	.90
Importance of diet restrictions	3.04	1.57
Importance of price	1.75	.96
Importance of availability	2.17	1.13
Importance of ease of preparation	2.75	1.22
Importance of habit	2.79	1.14
Importance of specials	2.26	1.25
Importance of nutritional value	1.67	.88

The 762 (of 940) individuals who provided usable responses to all 16 variables were then chosen for analysis. The means of all the variables are shown in Table 13–3. While looking at the means may seem trivial, it is a very good way to make certain that the data were input accurately. For example, had the mean of the diet importance variable been less than 1 or more than 5, the data would obviously have been input incorrectly. This check for reasonable means (or actual ones, if they are known) should always be made.

The independent variables were regressed against food expenditures. The results (Figure 13–8) were obtained from the SPSS program (Appendix 13–C). These results are interpreted in this section.

Overall Predictive Power

The R^2 is .43, a moderate value indicating that the independent variables help predictively but are not overly accurate in predicting individual food consumption expenditures. The test for the null hypothesis that all the

FIGURE 13–8 Regression Results for Predicting Food Expenditures

Variable	*Regression Coefficient*	*Beta*	*F*	*t*
Importance of nutrition	.47	.03	.76	.87
Income	2.89	.27	80.11	8.95
Age	.08	.09	8.85	2.97
Family size	5.86	.53	313.61	17.71
Brands shopped	.01	.00	.00	.00
Information sought	−1.09	−.05	2.43	1.56
Importance of variety	.02	.00	.00	.00
Importance of taste	−1.40	−.05	2.82	1.68
Importance of others' preferences	−.28	−.02	.32	.57
Importance of diet	−.46	−.05	2.65	1.63
Importance of price	.29	.02	.33	.57
Importance of availability	−.24	−.02	.35	.59
Importance of ease of preparation	.28	.02	.59	.77
Importance of habit	−1.07	−.08	7.18	2.68
Importance of specials	.49	.04	1.82	1.35

Constant	12.76
R squared	.43
Adjusted R^2	.42
Standard error	11.53

Analysis of Variance

	d.f.	*Sum of Squares*	*Mean Square*	*Overall F*
Regression	15	74,667.73	4,977.85	37.43
Residual	746	99,200.62	132.98	

regression coefficients are zero (and that the independent variables are worthless as predictors) is:

$$F = \frac{\dfrac{R^2}{\text{No. independent variables}}}{\dfrac{1 - R^2}{n - \text{No. independent variables} - 1}}$$

$$= \frac{4{,}978}{133} = 37.4$$

This compares with a "Table" $F_{15,746}$ of about 2.1 at the 1 percent significance level and indicates that the null hypothesis is convincingly rejected and thus that the independent variables definitely help in predicting food consumption expenditures.

The overall predictive power can also be seen in terms of the size of the standard error of estimate, \$11.53. This is obviously fairly large but noticeably smaller than the \$15.12 standard deviation of food consumption expenses. This also suggests that 95 percent of household weekly food consumption expenditures can be predicted within (1.96)(11.53) or about \$23.

Key Determinants

An obvious question is which of the independent variables are the most useful predictors of the dependent variable. The following three basic approaches are used.

The Absolute Size of the Regression Coefficients. The size of the regression coefficient indicates how much an increase of one unit of the independent variable would increase the dependent variable, assuming all the other independent variables remained unchanged. The results indicate that an increase of one in family size would increase weekly consumption expenditures by \$5.86, whereas movement to the next income category would increase expenditures by \$2.89 per week.

The Beta Coefficients. One problem with looking at the regression coefficients is that they depend on the scale of the variables. If income had been measured in dollars, the regression coefficient would have been much smaller. For this reason, many researchers (and especially those in psychology) prefer to use something called *beta coefficients*. These coefficients are the regression coefficients which would have been obtained if the regression had been performed on standardized (standard deviation equal to one) variables. Hence, a beta of .27 between income and expense indicates that, if an individual's income increased by one standard deviation (1.42 scale points), then food expenses would increase by .27 standard deviations. In general:

$$\text{Beta} = B\frac{\text{Standard deviation of independent variable}}{\text{Standard deviation of dependent variable}}$$

$$\left(\text{In this example, } .27 = 2.89\frac{1.42}{15.12}\right)$$

The Marginal Significance of the Variable. Each independent variable can be separately examined for the marginal contribution it makes to predicting the dependent variable. To do that we estimate how much variation in Y can be explained by each variable which is unexplained when the other independent variables are used alone. This is tested by an F

statistic (here the statistic is $F_{1,746}$). The bigger the F, the greater the significance. In this case, family size is the most significant ($F = 314$), with income also very significant and both age and habit significant at the 5 percent significance level.

ISSUES IN USING REGRESSION ANALYSIS

Users of multiple regression often encounter a variety of problems. While market researchers are rarely experts on these problems, because of their effect on interpretation it is important to be able to recognize when the problems occur, understand their effect on interpretation, and have a general idea of what to do next. (Calling in a statistician without a specific assignment often creates more problems than it solves.) This section is devoted to highlighting these problems.

Multicollinearity

One of the most common problems encountered in regression is the result of strong interrelations among the independent variables. This does not violate any assumptions (the independent variables do not have to be independent of each other) nor affect predictions. It does, however, make the estimates of the regression coefficients unreliable.

The logical importance of the problem caused by correlated independent variables can be seen by considering a flawed experiment. Assume I were testing two tire brands, Goodgrief and Fireside, and that I took two cars and placed Goodgrief tires on the front and Fireside tires on the back of each. Also assume I ran the cars and then found that the sets of front tires lasted 20,000 and 30,000 miles on the two cars and the back tires ran 12,000 and 14,000 miles, respectively. At first glance one might (mistakenly) assume Goodgrief tires were superior. However, since Goodgrief tires were never on the back and Fireside never on the front, it is impossible to logically separate the effect of brand from the effect of location on the car.

If we coded the data to run a regression, the data would be:

Y *(miles)*	D_1 *(1 if Goodgrief, 0 otherwise)*	D_2 *(1 if Front, 0 otherwise)*
20	1	1
30	1	1
12	0	0
14	0	0

In this case, D_1 and D_2 are perfectly collinear (and equal). Attempting to run a canned regression program to estimate $Y_1 = B_0 + B_1D_1 + B_2D_2$, will produce no results (albeit some funny language, such as "matrix singular," may appear).

Multicollinearity thus results from correlation among the independent variables. In its most severe case, it makes estimation impossible. In less severe cases, it damages the efficiency of the estimates. Put more bluntly, it makes one less certain what the individual regression coefficients are. Therefore, having independent variables which are not highly correlated is beneficial.

If we have two variables (X_1 and X_2), the level of correlation has a direct impact on the standard deviation of the regression coefficients. Consider the following four correlation matrices. Assume the correlation between X_1 and X_2 was 0, .1, .5, or .9. The relative sizes of the standard deviations of the coefficients of X_1 and X_2 become 1, 1.01, 1.33, and 5.26, respectively. Hence, for case D, a coefficient would have to be 5.26 times as large as in case A to appear as significant. Put differently, collinearity makes it difficult to find significant relations. (It also makes the coefficients themselves intercorrelated and thus less stable.) Thus collinearity can be a serious problem when correlations among the independent variables are large. (Notice *large* is an intentionally relative, rather than an absolute, term. Still, most people consider correlations above .7 as large.)

Detection. The most obvious way to detect collinearity is to check the simple correlations among the independent variables. When collinearity is the result of complex relations among several variables, this simple approach may fail to uncover the collinearity. Alternatively, in examining the results of a regression, large standard errors of the coefficients (leading to insignificant coefficients) are often a sign that serious collinearity may be present. Similarly, implausible coefficients may be a sign of collinearity. A number of other signals are used, including the ratio of the largest to the smallest eigenvalue in a principal components analysis of the independent variables (over 100 is considered fairly large). For a more thorough discussion of these, see Belsley, Kuh, and Walsh (1980), Judge et al. (1985), and Ofir and Khuri (1986).

Cure. One cure for collinearity is to reduce the variables to a set which are not collinear. This is best done on the basis of judgment, but many researchers employ factor analysis or stepwise regression as a means of deciding which variables to retain. Unfortunately, reducing the number of variables may lead to another problem; omitted variable bias.

A number of more elaborate procedures have been developed to deal with collinearity, such as ridge regression, which basically arbitrarily reduces the collinearity among the independent variables, which improves estimation efficiency at the cost of biasing the results (Hoerl and Kennard, 1970) and the equity estimator (Krishnamurthi and Rangaswamy, 1987). These procedures are beyond the scope of this discussion.

Autocorrelation

Autocorrelation occurs when the errors are correlated in a serial manner. Positive autocorrelation means that, if you encounter one positive error (the predicted value of the dependent variable is smaller than the actual value), you are likely to find the next error is also positive, and vice versa. This is a typical problem in time series data when a cycle has been ignored. It occurs occasionally in cross-sectional data when nonlinear relations exist.

FIGURE 13–9 Detection of Autocorrelation

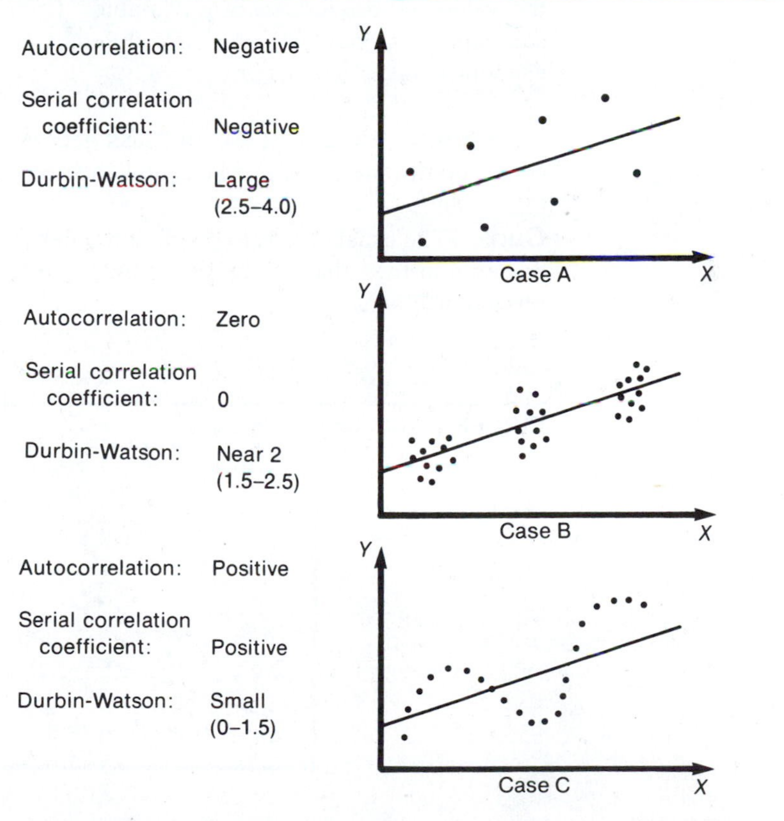

Detection. Autocorrelation may be detected by plotting the data or by means of the serial correlation coefficient or the Durbin-Watson statistic. These means of detection are related as can be seen by examining the three cases in Figure 13–9.

Cure. The cure for autocorrelation is to add some variable to remove the cycle (or nonlinearity) from the data. In time series data, this often involves either deseasonalizing data or using dummy variables to estimate the seasonal effect.

Heteroscedasticity

Heteroscedasticity, in addition to being the opposite of homoscedasticity and a terrific cocktail party term, is the situation where the error is related to the size of an independent variable (Figure 13–10). In this case, the larger the value of X, the larger the typical error in prediction. This problem usually occurs when there are orders of magnitude differences on the values of the independent variables. (Individuals studying output of companies or countries of vastly different sizes are especially likely to encounter this.)

Detection. The easiest way to detect heteroscedasticity is to calculate the correlation between the residuals and each of the independent variables.

Cure. The usual cure is to divide through by a variable which reduces the disparity in the values of the variables. For example, use income per capita instead of GNP.

FIGURE 13–10 Heteroscedasticity

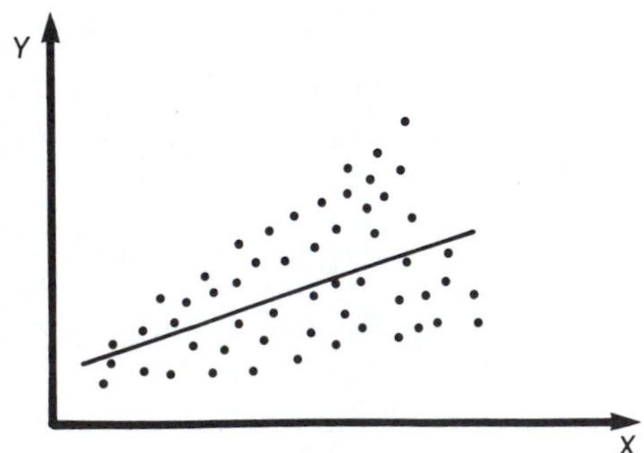

Omitted Variables (Specification)

One of the most serious problems occurs when variables that are related to both the dependent and at least one of the independent variables are omitted. While not always disastrous predictively, this will distort the coefficients and, hence, may lead to some inappropriate interpretations of the results.

To interpret regression coefficients, it is important that the regression model be logical and complete. If a model is underspecified, then overall predictive power of the model and the significance of the coefficients will be reduced. As bad as this is, it at least does not affect (bias) the coefficients of the included variable if the omitted variable is not related to the variables included in the model. For example, recall the ANOVA example in Chapter 12. The one-way ANOVA on package color was an underspecified model because the impact of advertising was not considered. However, since the design forced advertising strategy and package color to be unrelated, the one-way estimates of the impact of package color would be the same as the two-way estimates. Had advertising strategy and package color been related, however, the estimates would have been biased. The extent of the bias would have depended on how highly related advertising strategy and package color were.

Consider, for example, the following equation:

$$\text{Sales in units} = 2.1 + 3.2(\text{price})$$

An obvious implication of this is that increasing price would increase sales. While it is possible this is so, it is counterintuitive, and the result can be explained as the effect of an omitted variable. Assume sales really depends on quality and is slightly negatively price elastic. Also assume that the higher-priced products used in the study were higher in quality. In such a case, the positive price coefficient is really some weighted average of the positive quality effect and the negative price effect where the quality effect happened to be stronger.

Detection. Detection of this problem is often difficult. The major tip-off is implausible coefficients which cannot be explained on the basis of multicollinearity.

Cure. The cure is to find the omitted variable and include it in the equation. Unfortunately, this is not always easy and requires considerable judgment and knowledge of the situation being modeled. Even when the omitted variable can be identified, it may be difficult to find adequate measurements of it. While it is true that the inclusion of omitted variables tends to increase the problems of multicollinearity, this is usually not a good reason for leaving the variables out.

Measurement Error

The regression model implicitly assumes that the independent variables are measured without error. Since this is never true, the issue of the impact of such errors becomes relevant. If the measurement errors occur in the dependent variable and are uncorrelated and unbiased (the variable is not consistently under- or overmeasured), this leads to a lower R^2 and less significant coefficients. If measurement errors occur in the independent variables, then the coefficients themselves become biased. The solution to the situation is, obviously, to remove or at least minimize the measurement error. This is, unfortunately, a nontrivial task, especially when the cause of the error is not known and/or measured. The best suggestion is (*a*) try to reduce measurement error, and (*b*) if you can't *and* the coefficients themselves are crucial, consider using some so-called structural equation modeling approach (e.g., LISREL, soft modeling, PLS). Since these modeling procedures are beyond the scope of this book—except for Appendix 16–D—I would suggest (*a*).

Relevant Range

For a regression to be used predictively, it is important that the observation for which the forecast is to be made be similar to the observations used to build the model. Put simply, if you build a model of weight versus age on 3- to 7-year-olds, it will not give good predictions of the weight of 60-year-olds. Yet, in spite of the apparent obviousness of this, the concept of the relevant range often is ignored. Thus, a good rule is to ask yourself, "Does it make sense that this model apply here?" before using it.

The Use of Categorical Variables: Dummy Variables

A lot of data available to marketing researchers is categorical in nature (e.g., sex, occupation, region of the country). Since such variables are often presumed to be related to the dependent variables, it is obvious that it would be advantageous if such nominally scaled variables could be used in regressions. Four basic approaches are possible:

1. *Ignore the fact that the variables are categorical and run the analysis anyway:* Sales = $B_0 + B_1$ (advertising) + B_2 (region). This strategy is foolish (but may be used inadvertently by anyone who simply "throws the data in and lets the computer decide what's important"). Consider the variable region, where New England is coded 1, the West 2, Midwest 3, and South 4. It seems unlikely that the region variable would be related to anything and, even if it were, how would we interpret a significant coefficient?

FIGURE 13–11

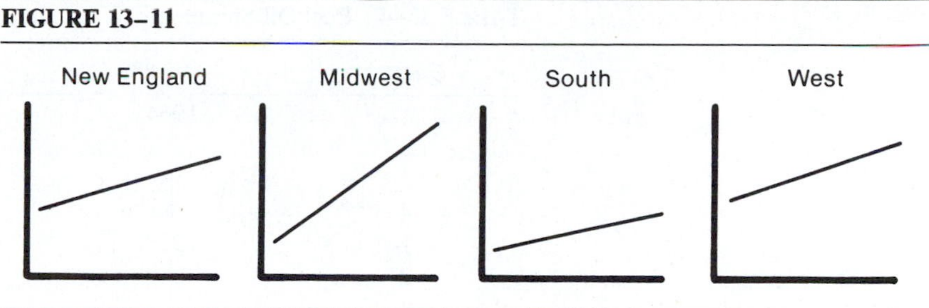

2. *Ignore the variable.* This is the easy way out but is not much better than the first approach.

3. *Use the variable as a means of segmenting the sample.* This would mean running a separate analysis for each region: Sales = $B_0 + B_1$ (advertising). Both the constant and the slope could vary across regions (Figure 13–11). This is the best method in terms of prediction and understanding. Unfortunately, it is also the most expensive in terms of sample requirements. If there are four regions, five occupations, and three marital statuses under consideration, the original sample must be divided into 4(5)(3) = 60 subsamples. Even given an original sample size of 1,000, this is likely to lead to inadequate sample rises in many of the 60 categories, not to mention a fairly unwieldy collection of results.

4. *Use dummy variables.* This procedure is somewhat of a compromise between strategies 2 and 3. One common assumption is that the effect of the other variables (e.g., advertising) is the same in all the regions but the constant differs from each of the regions.

Consider the following data on quarterly fuel oil shipments to the United Kingdom in 1964–66 (Table 13–4). In plotting this data, we see that there is, as expected, a very strong seasonal effect (Figure 13–12). Clearly, ignoring the seasonal effect would be a major error. (It would also produce significant autocorrelation.) Running four separate regressions is impractical because there would only be three observations per regression. It would be possible to deseasonalize the data before performing the regression using an adjustment factor for each quarter, such as:

$$\frac{\text{Average sales for the particular quarter}}{\text{Average sales for all quarters}}$$

Possibly the most appealing approach, however, is to employ dummy variables. This would consist of first creating (dummying up) a variable for

TABLE 13–4 Fuel Oil Shipments to the United Kingdom

Quarter	*Year*	*Sales*
1	1964	210
2		120
3		140
4		260
1	1965	220
2		125
3		145
4		270
1	1966	225
2		128
3		149
4		275

each of the four quarters (Table 13–5). The following equation would then be estimated by regression:

$$\text{Shipments} = B_0 + B_1\,(\text{time}) + B_2\,(\text{winter}) + B_3\,(\text{spring}) + B_4\,(\text{summer})$$

Note that one of the possible dummy variables must be left out so the computer program will run. If all the independent variables are included, they are perfectly multicollinear. In this case, it is impossible to invert a key matrix and the program will bomb. (Alternatively, we could drop the

FIGURE 13–12

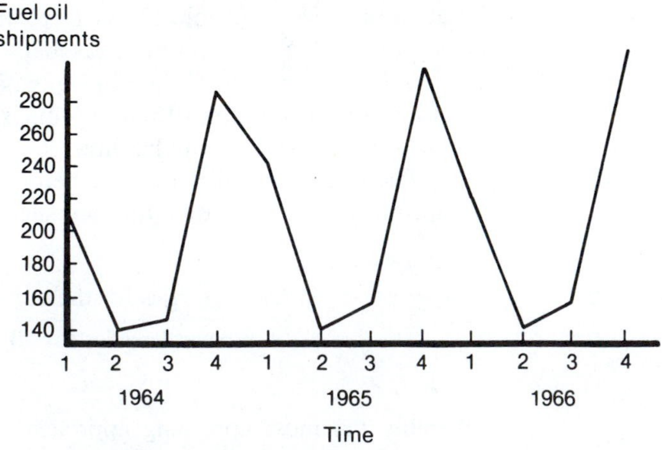

TABLE 13–5 Seasonal Dummy Variables

		Dummy Variables			
Shipments	*Time*	*Winter*	*Spring*	*Summer*	*Fall*
210	1	1	0	0	0
120	2	0	1	0	0
140	3	0	0	1	0
260	4	0	0	0	1
220	5	1	0	0	0
125	6	0	1	0	0
145	7	0	0	1	0
270	8	0	0	0	1
225	9	1	0	0	0
128	10	0	1	0	0
149	11	0	0	1	0
275	12	0	0	0	1

constant B_0 and retain all four dummy variables if that were an option of the computer program being used.) In general, if a categorical variable has c categories, $c - 1$ dummy variables must be employed. Here, fall was excluded. This does not affect the final predictions, which are independent of the variable deleted. The results were:

$$B_0 = 256.5$$

$$B_1 = 1.468$$

$$B_2 = -45.6$$

$$B_3 = -141.1$$

$$B_4 = -122.2$$

Predictions for each of the quarters are thus:

Winter:

$$\begin{aligned} \text{Shipments} &= B_0 + B_1(\text{time}) + B_2(1) + B_3(0) + B_4(0) \\ &= (B_0 + B_2) + B_1(\text{time}) \\ &= 210 + 1.468(\text{time}) \end{aligned}$$

Spring:

$$\begin{aligned} \text{Shipments} &= (B_0 + B_3) + B_1(\text{time}) \\ &= 115.5 + 1.468(\text{time}) \end{aligned}$$

Summer:

$$\text{Shipments} = (B_0 + B_4) + B_1(\text{time})$$
$$= 134.4 + 1.468(\text{time})$$

Fall:

$$\text{Shipments} = B_0 + B_1(\text{time})$$
$$= 256.6 + 1.468(\text{time})$$

The results are shown graphically as Figure 13–13. The coefficients of the dummy variables are interpreted as the difference in the average value of the dependent variable between the category of the dummy variable and the category of the variable which has no dummy. Here the coefficients of the dummy variables indicate the difference in average sales between each quarter and the fall quarter. For example, average shipments in the winter are 45.6 less than shipments in the fall. In essence, dummy variables perform analysis of variance. In fact, if all the variables are dummied, analysis of variance and regression are essentially equivalent. (Cultural digression: When some of the independent variables are dummies and some are intervally scaled, regression analysis is called *analysis of covariance*.)

If this model were used to predict shipments in the second quarter of 1968, the "best guess" prediction would then be:

$$\text{Predicted shipments} = 115.5 + 1.468(18) = 142$$

FIGURE 13–13

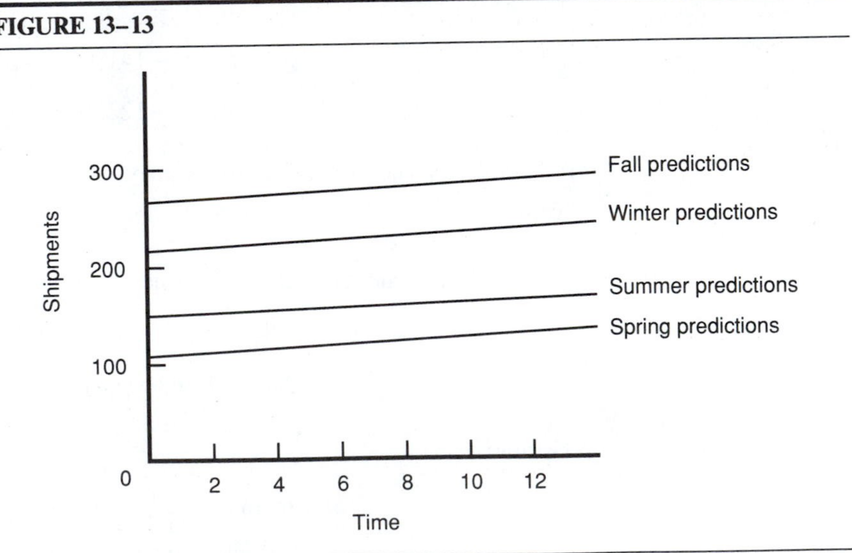

Dummy variables can be used to represent several independent variables (e.g., season and region). For *each* of the independent variables, one of its dummy variables must be left out of the equation to permit estimation.

By using dummy variable coding, it is possible to use a regression analysis program to perform analysis of variance. An example and discussion of this appears in Appendix 13–F.

Dummy variables can also be used to allow the effect of one independent variable on the dependent variable to change depending on the value of the dummy variable. For example, assume we were predicting sales based on advertising and whether a certain law had been passed. If we ran a regression:

$$\text{Sales} = B_0 + B_1(\text{Advertising}) + B_2(\text{Advertising})(\text{If law passed})$$

we would interpret B_1 as the effect of advertising before the law was passed and $B_1 + B_2$ as the effect of advertising on sales after the law was passed. Thus, dummy variables have many uses in regression analysis.

Stepwise Regression

When faced with a large number of potential independent variables, a researcher often wishes to let the computer select those variables which are in some sense best. The most popular approach is stepwise regression. This procedure begins by selecting the independent variable which is most correlated with the dependent variable, and then a regression is performed. Next, the variable which makes the greatest marginal improvement in prediction is added and a second regression run.

The basic criterion used by most of these programs is the correlation between each independent variable not in the equation and the portion of the variance in the dependent variable unexplained by variables in the equation, known as the *partial correlation*. Whichever independent variable has the largest partial correlation with the dependent variable is entered next. The procedure continues checking partial correlations, adding variables, and performing regressions until it (*a*) reaches a specified number of variables or (*b*) ceases to add variables which achieve a specified level of improvement in prediction.

Consider the following example based on a sample of 513 housewives taken in 1968. In order to attempt to profile Gleem toothpaste preferers, Gleem preference was regressed against seven other variables. The simple correlations among the variables are typical of the correlations among demographics, preferences, and importances (Table 13–6). Steps 1, 2, and 7 are summarized in Table 13–7. Examining these steps indicates that, in step 1, the procedure selected the variable which had the greatest (absolute) simple correlation with Gleem, importance of price. In the second step,

TABLE 13–6 Correlation Matrix

	Preference for Gleem	*Importance of Nutritional Value (orange juice)*	*Importance of Taste Flavor (tooth-paste)*	*Importance of Price (tooth-paste)*	*Cepacol Preference*	*Lavoris Preference*	*Like "Hawaii 5-0"*	*Own Residence*
Preference for Gleem	1.00	.12	.10	−.15	.13	.09	.09	−.08
Importance of nutritional value (orange juice)		1.00	.22	−.03	.02	.04	−.13	.10
Importance of taste/flavor (toothpaste)			1.00	.13	−.05	.02	−.09	.07
Importance of price (toothpaste)				1.00	−.08	−.05	−.03	−.03
Cepacol preference					1.00	−.28	−.04	.01
Lavoris preference						1.00	.04	.11
Like "Hawaii 5-O"							1.00	−.09
Own residence								1.00

TABLE 13–7 Stepwise Results

Variable		*Coefficient*	*F Ratio*
Step 1:			
Constant		3.52	
Importance of price (toothpaste)		−.11	5.9
	$R = .15$		
Step 2:			
Constant		3.31	
Importance of taste/flavor (toothpaste)		.11	4.0
Importance of price (toothpaste)		−.13	7.2
	$R = .19$		
Step 7:			
Constant		2.20	
Importance of nutritional value (orange juice)		.14	3.2
Importance of taste/flavor (toothpaste)		.11	3.7
Importance of price (toothpaste)		−.11	5.7
Cepacol preference		.14	7.2
Lavoris preference		.11	4.4
Like "Hawaii 5-O"		.08	2.8
Own residence		−.21	3.5
	$R = .3190$		

however, it found that the importance of taste was most helpful marginally, even though Cepacol preference had a larger simple correlation (.13 versus .10). The final step, which includes all the independent variables, indicates that, in spite of the model's relatively small overall predictive power ($R_2 = .1$), many of the variables are significantly related to Gleem preference (F ratios > 4). This is typical of segmentation type regression results that often uncover key correlates and tendencies but rarely predict individual consumer behavior well.

The advantages of stepwise regression are essentially twofold:

1. It produces a parsimonious model.
2. The resulting model tends to have relatively little multicollinearity among the independent variables.

Unfortunately, there are some important disadvantages to stepwise regression:

1. The results are notoriously unstable in split-half checks where each half of the data is analyzed separately. (The variables often enter differently in the two halves of the sample, thus making interpretation hazardous.)

2. The technique tends to increase the odds of omitting a key variable. For example, assume that the correlations between education and income with the dependent variable were .71 and .70, respectively. A stepwise procedure would then enter education first. If education and income were fairly highly correlated, however, income might never be brought in. Hence, an apparent interpretation of the results would be that education influenced the dependent variable but income did not, while income could be an important determinant.

3. Stepwise regression is inferior methodology if any prior model or theory exists. Most studies are more useful if a logical model is first constructed (how else do I know what variables to measure?) and then examined, rather than if the results depend on some search algorithm.

4. The statistical tests reported in the output are inaccurate, since the procedure selects variables which maximize those tests (McIntyre et al., 1983).

Hence, stepwise regression must be used with great care. While it may be an easy way to select variables, it is not clear that it is a good one.

Nonlinear Relations

In some situations, the relation between the independent and dependent variables will be nonlinear. In such situations, the researcher has a choice between two alternatives: using a search procedure for estimating the relationship or somehow utilizing the linear regression procedure to estimate the parameters of a nonlinear model. Practicality and laziness usually dictate the latter approach.

Using canned linear regression programs to generate nonlinear parameters basically involves "tricking" the computer. Consider the following data concerning registered small aircraft versus time (Figure 13–14). The decline appears to be of the logarithmic/exponential variety. By plotting the logarithms of the number of registered aircraft versus time, the plot appears to be much closer to linear (Figure 13–15). Mathematically, we are saying:

$$\text{Log(registered aircraft)} = a + b(\text{time})$$

By simply inputting the log of registered aircraft as the dependent variable and time as the independent variable, estimates of a and b are obtained.

This procedure can be extended to many other situations. For example, consider the situation where you believe:

$$Y = B_0 X_1^{B_1} X_2^{B_2}$$

FIGURE 13–14 Registered Small Aircraft (three seats and less) per Hundred Thousand Residents Plotted against Time

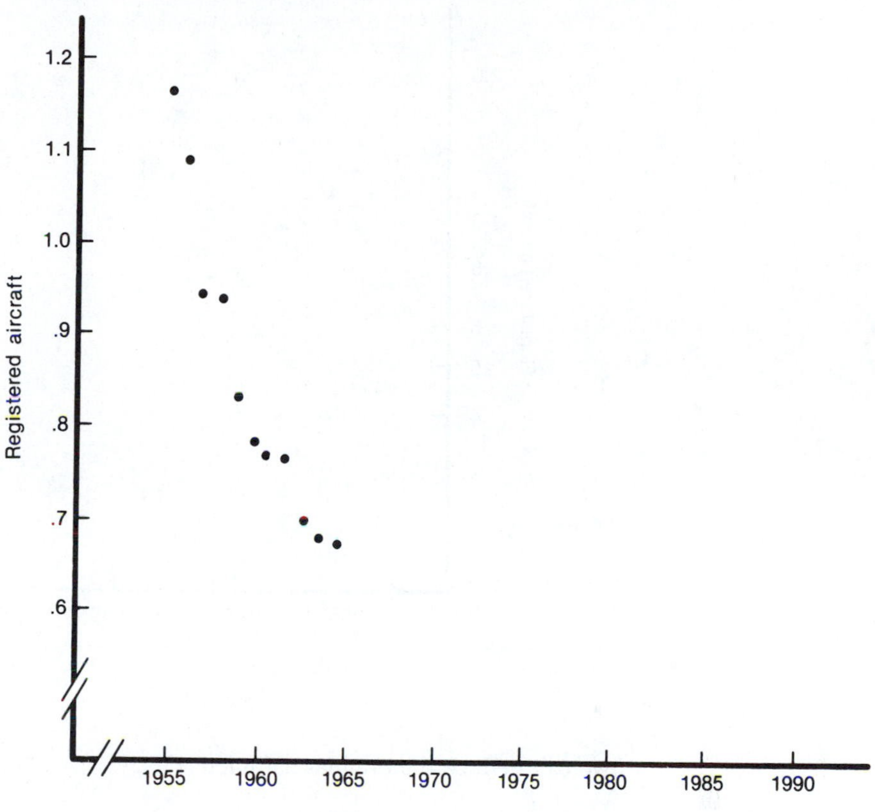

By taking logarithms of both sides, the model becomes

$$\log Y = \log B_0 + B_1 \log X_1 + B_2 \log X_2$$

By setting:

$$Y^* = \log Y$$

$$X_1^* = \log X_1$$

$$X_2^* = \log X_2$$

and running the linear regression:

$$Y^* = A_0 + A_1 X_1^* + A_2 X_2^*$$

FIGURE 13–15 Registered Small Aircraft (three seats and less) per Hundred Thousand Residents Plotted against Time–Logarithmic Scale

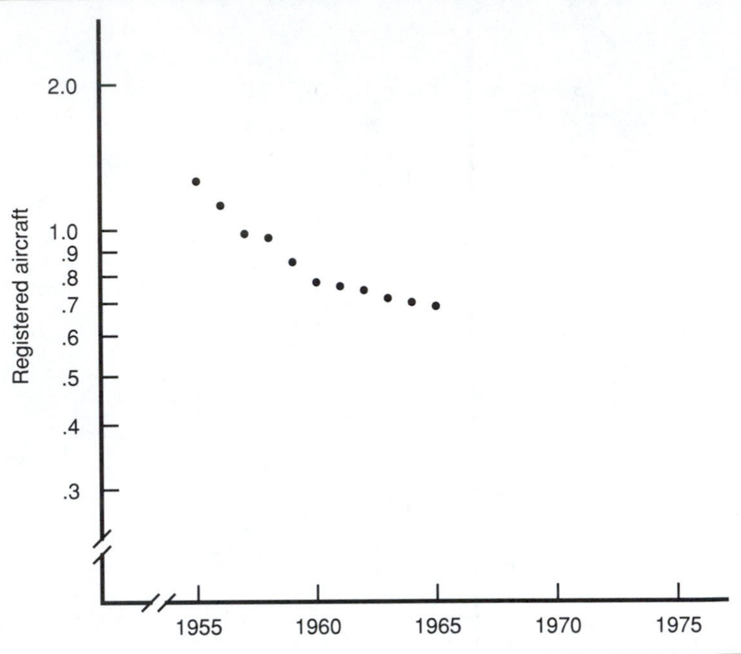

we can deduce the original parameters as:

$$B_0 = \log^{-1} A_0$$

$$B_1 = A_1$$

$$B_2 = A_2$$

Nonlinear forms involving a single variable are equally easy to handle. Consider $Y = B_0 + B_1X_1 + B_2X_1^2$. By submitting X_1 and X_1^2 as the two independent variables to a standard linear regression program, estimates of B_0, B_1, and B_2 can be directly obtained. There are two problems with the process of using linear regression programs to estimate nonlinear models. The first problem is that the estimates obtained are not exactly those which would have been obtained by a specially designed procedure and are, in some sense, inferior. Given the precision in most marketing data, however, this is unlikely to be a major problem. The second problem is that the procedure may be difficult to use under certain circumstances. For example, an equation involving X, X^2, and X^3 terms will be tremendously unstable due to high collinearity.

One final point worth making concerns why linear models are so widely used. The following three major reasons exist:

1. Canned programs do linear regression. This may be a bad normative reason but is a key descriptive explanation.

2. Linear models are usually good approximations of nonlinear models, especially over a small range. This is particularly true when there is noise in the data, as in the case of survey research.

3. There is one linear model for a set of variables but an infinite number of nonlinear ones. This makes trying to find an appropriate nonlinear model hazardous and time consuming.

Some good advice, therefore, is to always try a linear model unless:

a. The predictive power of the linear model is inadequate.

b. Some theory or simple results (e.g., data plots) exist, which suggest nonlinearity.

Dealing with Outliers

Since outliers can have a major effect on a regression, it is often useful to examine them to see if there is a reason for their unusual level of the dependent variable. One place to start looking for outliers is observations where the independent variables are extremely high or low (e.g., Alaska and forest acreage, as we shall see later). The most efficient means, however, is to look for observations where the actual and observed values of the dependent variable are very different (i.e., $|Y - \hat{Y}|$ is large). Once outliers are uncovered, there are three basic choices about what to do with them:

1. Remove them as unrepresentative (e.g., ice cream sales on a day with a 30-inch snowfall).

2. Learn from them and add a new variable to the model (e.g., bad weather).

3. Neutralize them. When one cannot explain a result, you may consider reducing its effect. In the extreme, this would entail deleting the observation entirely. A less extreme approach is to adjust the value of the dependent variable closer to its predicted value and then rerun the regression. For example, if $Y - \hat{Y}$ is 5 standard errors, revise Y so $Y - \hat{Y}$ is 2 standard errors and then rerun the regression. If this seems a bit like cheating, good—it is. Moreover, since this procedure is not only tedious but also only rarely improves results, it is not recommended for the casual user.

SOME USES OF REGRESSION ANALYSIS

Given the aggravation associated with understanding regression analysis, a reasonable question is whether the benefits outweigh the costs. Regression is an extremely useful tool for a variety of purposes. This section will delineate three major areas of applicability which highlight some of the benefits of regression.

Another example comes from the Durable Ownership and Values Study. Here we profile fur coat ownership in terms of some basic demographics. The sample of 796 claimed to own 293 fur coats (one person owned eight—an important outlier). The output generated by SAS using the PROC REG command appears as Figure 13–16. The results are typical of segmenting regressions: low R^2 (.07) and a few significant variables (age and income, both positively related). The LOV variables failed to be individually significant, due partly to collinearity among themselves. Interestingly, 8 of the 9 are positively related to ownership, suggesting people who rate values as important in general tend to own fur coats. An appropriate next step would be to factor analyze the LOV variables and use the factors in the regression. (The use of factor analysis to simplify regression will be discussed in the next chapter.)

Forecasting

Regression analysis is a widely used forecasting tool which is applied in two basic ways:

1. Using time as the key independent variable.
2. Using other variables (such as price and competitive advertising) as the independent variables.

In both cases, the objective is a good prediction which means a big R^2 and a small standard error of estimate. The coefficients themselves are used for generating predictions but are not important in their own right. Many time series regressions and regressions involving aggregate economic data produce R^2s over .99. A more detailed discussion of forecasting appears in Chapter 17.

Segmentation

Regression is often used to define segments of customers in terms of demographics, lifestyles, or general attitudes (Massy, Frank, and Lodahl, 1968; Frank, Massy, and Wind, 1972). This typically produces R^2 of .1 or smaller. If the goal were prediction of individual behavior, this would be poor. The goal of segmentation, however, is to find general tendencies, not to predict individual behavior. Since marketing strategy for frequently purchased products is directed at groups (e.g., high income), the basic goal

FIGURE 13–16 Cable TV Usage Regression

ANALYSIS OF VARIANCE

SOURCE	DF	SUM OF SQUARES	MEAN SQUARE	F VALUE	PROB>F
MODEL	14	24.58013536	1.75572395	2.881	0.0003
ERROR	746	454.64194	0.60943960		
C TOTAL	760	479.22208			

ROOT MSE	0.7806661	R-SQUARE	0.0513
DEP MEAN	0.6662286	ADJ R-SQ	0.0335
C.V.	117.1769		

PARAMETER ESTIMATES

VARIABLE	DF	PARAMETER ESTIMATE	STANDARD ERROR	T FOR H0: PARAMETER=0	PROB > |T|	STANDARDIZED ESTIMATE
INTERCEP	1	0.48174178	0.32749553	1.471	0.1417	0
SRESPCT	1	0.000154812	0.05141145	0.003	0.9976	0.000128088
SECURE	1	0.01811834	0.03393503	0.534	0.5936	0.02284821
WARMREL	1	-0.01390346	0.03704420	-0.375	0.7075	-0.01620320
ACCOMP	1	-0.06624131	0.04861312	-1.363	0.1734	-0.06719924
SLFFFIL	1	0.04809168	0.04301942	1.118	0.2640	0.05421671
BELONG	1	0.02296728	0.03151752	0.729	0.4664	0.03563310
WRESPCT	1	-0.000535298	0.03283062	-0.016	0.9870	-0.000716888
FUN	1	-0.06102127	0.03753099	-1.626	0.1044	-0.07625068
EXCITE	1	0.06037020	0.02782448	2.170	0.0303	0.09938459
KIDS	1	0.05218194	0.03077804	1.695	0.0904	0.06277274
AGE	1	0.01087498	0.02435732	0.446	0.6554	0.01753220
EDUC	1	-0.04503396	0.03098438	-1.453	0.1465	-0.05799037
INC	1	0.09159502	0.02418213	3.788	0.0002	0.17551139
SAVE	1	0.007121690	0.02653424	0.268	0.7885	0.01216146

FIGURE 13–16 (concluded) Fur Coat Ownership Regression

ANALYSIS OF VARIANCE

SOURCE	DF	SUM OF SQUARES	MEAN SQUARE	F VALUE	PROB>F
MODEL	14	35.41839909	2.52968565	4.195	0.0001
ERROR	746	449.92720	0.60311957		
C TOTAL	760	485.34560			

ROOT MSE	0.7766077	R-SQUARE	0.0730
DEP MEAN	0.3600526	ADJ R-SQ	0.0556
C.V.	215.6929		

PARAMETER ESTIMATES

VARIABLE	DF	PARAMETER ESTIMATE	STANDARD ERROR	T FOR H0: PARAMETER=0	PROB > |T|	STANDARDIZED ESTIMATE
INTERCEP	1	-0.99545138	0.32579301	-3.055	0.0023	0
SRESPCT	1	0.05770885	0.05114418	1.128	0.2595	0.04744480
SECURE	1	0.03467609	0.03375861	1.027	0.3047	0.04345171
WARMREL	1	0.01004801	0.03685162	0.273	0.7852	0.01163592
ACCOMP	1	-0.001620684	0.04836039	-0.034	0.9733	-0.001633717
SLFFIL	1	0.03342195	0.04279578	0.781	0.4351	0.03744017
BELONG	1	0.01915063	0.03135367	0.611	0.5415	0.02952363
WRESPCT	1	0.007189209	0.03265994	0.220	0.8258	0.009567093
FUN	1	0.000463430	0.03733588	0.012	0.9901	0.000575426
EXCITE	1	0.02360794	0.02767983	0.853	0.3940	0.03861867
KIDS	1	-0.04029092	0.03061804	-1.316	0.1886	-0.04816161
AGE	1	0.06508007	0.02423070	2.686	0.0074	0.10425552
EDUC	1	-0.03135994	0.03082330	-1.017	0.3093	-0.04012674
INC	1	0.06995727	0.02405642	2.908	0.0037	0.13320151
SAVE	1	0.03942686	0.02639630	1.494	0.1357	0.06690179

FIGURE 13–17

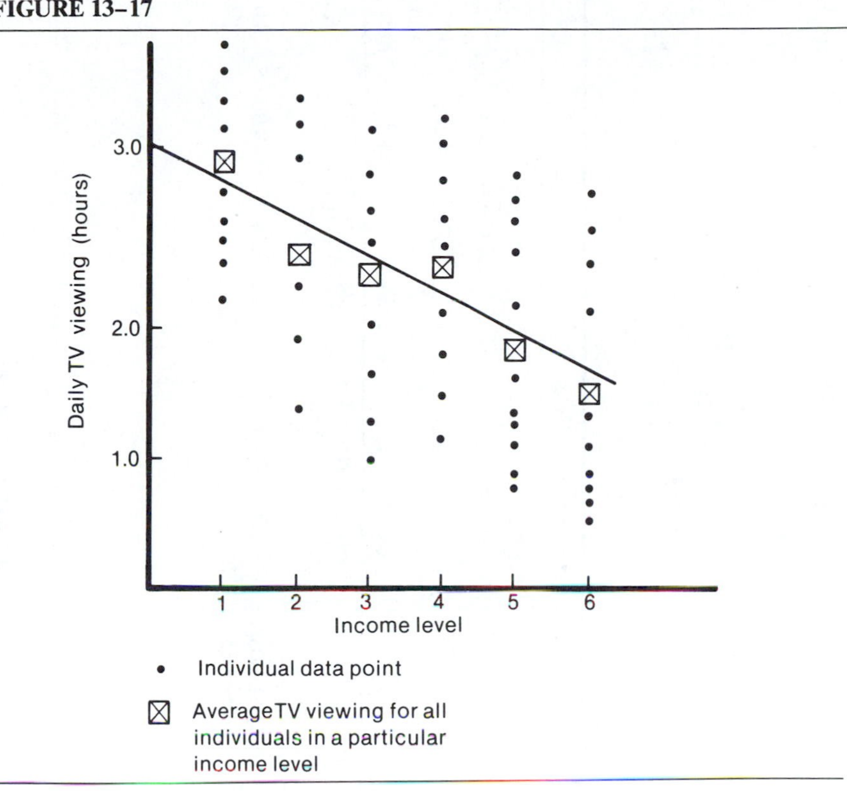

Source: Donald R. Lehmann, "Validity and Goodness of Fit in Data Analysis," in *Advances in Consumer Research*, ed. Mary Jane Schlinger (Ann Arbor, Mich.: Association for Consumer Research, 1975), p. 746.

is to find groups of consumers where concentrating effort would bring a greater average response. Consider the results from a study of 513 housewives. Obviously, knowing a person's income would not make possible an accurate prediction of the amount of time that particular individual spends watching TV. In fact, the R^2 was .048. On the other hand, it is obvious that average behavior is related to income (Figure 13–17). In fact, a regression between income level and average TV viewing behavior produced an R^2 of .878 (Lehmann, 1975). Practically, this shows that very low-income people watched, on average, twice as much TV as high-income people.

A variety of examples concerning the use of regression as a tool for identifying market segments appear in Bass, Tigert, and Lonsdale (1968). Using *Milwaukee Journal* panel data, the authors found the typical low R^2s using demographic variables (age, income, occupation, number of children, education, and TV viewing) as predictors of various frequently purchased products. The differences in average consumption, however, were very noticeable (Figure 13–18). The point, then, is the low R^2s mean that individual predictions cannot be made accurately, not that the results are

FIGURE 13–18 Light and Heavy Buyers by Mean Purchase Rates for Different Socioeconomic Cells

		Description		*Mean Consumption Rate Ranges*		*Ratio of Highest to Lowest Rate*
R^2	*Product*	*Light Buyers*	*Heavy buyers*	*Light Buyers*	*Heavy Buyers*	
.08	Catsup	Unmarried or married over age 50 without children.	Under 50, three or more children.	.74–1.82	2.73–5.79	7.8
.07	Frozen orange juice	Under 35 or over 65, income less than $10,000, not college grads, two or less children.	College grads, income over $10,000, between 35 and 65.	1.12–2.24	3.53–9.00	8.0
.04	Pancake mix	Some college, two or fewer children.	Three or more children, high school or less education.	.48–52	1.10–1.51	3.3
.08	Candy bars	Under 35, no children.	35 or over, three or more children.	1.01–4.31	6.56–22.29	21.9
.08	Cake mix	Not married or under 35, no children. income under $10,000, TV less than $3\frac{1}{2}$ hours.	35 or over, three or more children, income over $10,000.	.55–1.10	2.22–3.80	6.9

R^2	Product	Description: Light Buyers	Description: Heavy buyers	Mean Consumption Rate Ranges: Light Buyers	Mean Consumption Rate Ranges: Heavy Buyers	Ratio of Highest to Lowest Rate
.09	Beer	Under 25 or over 50, college education, nonprofessional, TV less than 2 hours.	Between 25 and 50, not college graduate, TV more than $3\frac{1}{2}$ hours.	0–12.33	17.26–40.30	∞
.02	Cream shampoo	Income less then $8,000, at least some college, fewer than five children.	Income $10,000 or over with high school or less education.	.16–35	.44–.87	5.5
.06	Hair spray	Over 65, under $8,000 income.	Under 65, over $10,000 income, not college graduate.	0–.41	.52–1.68	∞
.09	Toothpaste	Over 50, fewer than three children, income less than $8,000.	Under 50, three or more children, over $10,000 income.	1.41–2.01	2.22–4.39	3.1
.03	Mouthwash	Under 35 or over 65, less than $8,000 income, some college.	Between 35 and 65, income over $8,000, high school or less education.	.46–.85	.98–1.17	2.5

Source: Frank Bass, Douglas Tigert, and Ronald Lonsdale, "Market Segmentation—Group versus Individual Behavior." Reprinted from *Journal of Marketing Research*, published by the American Marketing Association, 5 (August 1968), p. 267.

worthless. In fact, when using survey data, R^2s above .6 usually mean that either the equation is essentially a tautology or that the data were incorrectly analyzed.

Parameter Estimation and Model Selection

In certain circumstances, a model is relatively well established and regression is employed to estimate its parameters. In such a case, the R^2 is of only limited interest. The major concern is with the sign and size of the coefficients. If a prior theory gives a range of acceptable values for the coefficients, then the estimated coefficients may be used as a basis for accepting or rejecting the model.

For example, one might assume (based on some theory or analysis) that the effect of raising price one dollar would be to decrease sales by between one and three units. Hence, in a multiple regression, with sales as the dependent variable and price as one of the independent variables, we would expect the regression coefficient relating price to sales to be between -1 and -3. If the estimated coefficient fell outside the range, then the model would be rejected.

In deciding what model to use to represent a situation, one less "pure" approach is to try several alternatives and see which produces the "best" regression result (high R^2s, plausible and significant coefficients, etc.). While this application of regression is theoretically inferior, in practice it is widely used.

CAUSATION VERSUS CORRELATION

Regression analysis is a correlational procedure which does not directly address the issue of causality. Low R^2s or insignificant regression coefficients may indicate weak causality, bad data, or a poor mathematical representation of the relation between variables. Similarly, high R^2s or significant regression coefficients may indicate bad data or tautologies. Even with good data, a high R^2 can mislead a researcher into imputing causality where none exists. For example, assume a researcher ran the following regression:

$$\text{Fertilizer applied} = B_0 + B_1 \text{ (yield)}$$

Presumably both R^2 and B_1 would be significant. If the data were based on an experiment using equally productive fields, however, the conclusion that yield caused fertilizer application could be exactly wrong.

Numerous examples of strong correlation not necessarily indicating causation can be found. Consider football. NFL football statistics for 1973 indicate that the winning team gained more yards rushing than the losing team. The apparent implication is to stress rushing in the game plan in order to win. On further reflection, however, this may not be so wise. A team with a lead tends to run to use up the clock and avoid turnovers. Therefore, being ahead (which is quite conducive to winning) may lead to rushing yards just as much as rushing yards leads to winning. Another example is the correlation between the stork population and the human birth rate. While the most popular explanation is that more people mean more houses, more houses more chimneys, and more chimneys more storks, the alternatives are quite interesting.

Probably the classic example of correlation is the result attributed to Jevons, who found that sun spot activity was strongly related to business cycles. Obviously, this is purely coincidental say the pundits. On the other hand, it is conceivable that the relationship is causal. Sun spots change the gravitational pull of the sun, which in turn affects the orbit of the earth and its rotation. Changing the rotation of the earth then affects its electromagnetic field. Since individuals' nervous systems function by a type of electricity, this would affect the way people think and behave and, consequently, conduct business. While this may seem like a far-out explanation (or possibly a false one, if you know much about physics), the point is that it is difficult to differentiate causality and correlation. It would not be surprising if astrology turned out to be related to changing gravitational pulls "when Jupiter aligns with Mars," and so forth.

The point of this section, therefore, is that causality is essentially impossible to determine from regressions. Any causal implications must be the result of prior knowledge and judgment. What regression can do for someone interested in causality is to estimate the strength of causality which has been correctly prespecified by the researcher.

Consider again the data on the 50 states (Table 9–1 in Chapter 9). Assuming one were interested in profiling average income per capita, one might run a regression with average income versus the other available variables (population, etc.). Notice this is a "fishing expedition"—which means we may catch an old shoe, rather than a prize trout.

The results, presented in the order of a typical computer output, are shown as Table 13–8. The correlations indicate income is positively related to taxes, percent in urban areas, and forest acreage, and negatively related to being in the South. The regression results bear this out with all the coefficients except South being significant. The failure of the South to be significant can be explained by its collinearity with taxes ($r = -.60$).

The R^2 of .72 is substantial. Yet, obviously, this model is flawed causally. A causal implication of the model would be that, to increase income, you increase taxes, put more people in the city, and leave more land as forests. This is not likely to work. Also, the coefficient of the forest variable bears further discussion. In fact, it could be called the Alaska result, since Alaska has both the highest average income and the most forest acreage. Hence, this regression appears to have been influenced by one unusual data point.

TABLE 13–8 Regression of Average Income

Variables:

- Inc: Average personal income in thousands.
- Pop: Population in millions.
- Popch: Percent population change over last five years.
- Urb: Percent living in metropolitan areas.
- Tax: State and local taxes per capita.
- South: 1 if yes; 0 otherwise.
- Govt: Government employment in thousands.
- Col: College enrollment in thousands.
- Min: Mineral production in millions of dollars.
- For: Forest acreage in millions.
- Mfg: Value added by manufacturers in billions of dollars.
- Farm: Farm cash receipts in millions of dollars.

Simple Correlations

Variable	*Inc.*	*Pop.*	*Popch.*	*Urb.*	*Tax.*	*South*	*Govt.*	*Col.*	*Min.*	*For.*	*Mfg.*	*Farm*
Inc.:	1.00	0.24	−0.10	0.42	0.70	−0.51	0.25	0.28	−0.17	0.32	0.28	0.08
Pop.:	0.24	1.00	−0.29	0.56	0.37	0.03	0.99	0.96	0.33	0.10	0.94	0.52
Popch.:	−0.08	−0.29	1.00	−0.09	−0.16	0.08	−0.27	−0.25	0.03	0.35	−0.42	−0.26
Urb.:	0.42	0.56	−0.09	1.00	0.42	−0.02	0.55	0.53	0.14	−0.02	0.54	0.09
Tax:	0.70	0.37	−0.17	0.42	1.00	−0.60	0.41	0.45	−0.20	−0.03	0.38	0.04
South:	−0.51	0.03	0.08	−0.02	−0.60	1.00	0.01	−0.05	0.35	0.03	−0.09	−0.03
Govt.:	0.25	0.99	−0.27	0.55	0.41	0.01	1.00	0.98	0.31	0.12	0.91	0.52
Col.:	0.28	0.96	−0.25	0.53	0.65	−0.05	0.98	1.00	0.28	0.13	0.87	0.51
Min.:	−0.17	0.33	0.03	0.14	−0.20	0.35	0.31	0.28	1.00	0.12	0.20	0.29
For.:	0.32	0.10	0.35	−0.02	−0.03	0.03	0.12	0.13	0.12	1.00	0.03	−0.00
Mfg.:	0.28	0.94	−0.42	0.54	0.38	−0.09	0.91	0.87	0.20	0.03	1.00	0.46
Farm:	0.08	0.52	−0.25	0.09	0.04	−0.03	0.52	0.51	0.29	−0.00	0.46	1.00

Variables in the Equation

Variable	B	Beta	S_B	F
Pop.	0.16	0.84	0.24	0.47
Popch.	−0.10	−0.12	0.09	1.21
Urb.	0.10	0.30	0.00	7.02
Tax	0.47	0.65	0.00	19.77
South	−0.25	−0.13	0.26	0.95
Govt.	−0.25	−0.90	0.00	0.42
Col.	−0.94	−0.25	0.00	0.17
Min.	−0.24	−0.05	0.00	0.24
For.	0.23	0.46	0.00	23.46
Mfg.	−0.33	−0.04	0.04	0.01
Farm	0.84	0.19	0.00	2.83

Constant: 2.29
R^2: 0.73
Adjusted R^2: 0.65
Standard error: 0.51

Analysis of Variance

	d.f.	Sum of Squares	Mean Square	F
Regression	11	26.71	2.43	9.24
Residual	38	9.95	0.26	

This emphasizes the crucial role that a few outliers (unusual data points) can play in influencing the results of a regression. In summary, then, regression fishing expeditions may find significant coefficients and big R^2s. If not interpreted carefully, however, these results can be misleading—especially if the individual coefficients are interpreted as causal relations.

Simultaneous Equation Regression

In many circumstances, one would posit that two variables are interrelated. For example, consider the relation between advertising and sales. Sales is generally thought to depend on advertising. On the other hand, advertising budgets are often set as a percent of sales, and, therefore, sales affect advertising. This means that a single regression of sales versus advertising would produce an aggregate summary of the advertising to sales and the sales to advertising relations and, hence, be relatively useless. To get around this problem of joint effects, one alternative is to construct two equations:

$$\text{Sales} = f(\text{advertising, other variables})$$

$$\text{Advertising} = f(\text{sales, other variables})$$

By estimating the two equations simultaneously, it is sometimes possible to estimate the separate effects of advertising on sales and sales on advertising. While simultaneous procedures are fairly technical and beyond the scope of this book (see Appendix 13–D), the recognition of the problem of joint causation and the realization that procedures exist for dealing with the problem is very useful. If you think you have encountered such a problem, call an expert.

MAKING REGRESSION USEFUL

A key question is: "How can a researcher use regression without 'putting off' potential users?" This question raises two issues. The first issue concerns how to go about building a useful model. In deciding what variables to include, a variety of considerations/criteria must be weighed:

1. *Parsimony.* The boss is a busy person; don't overtax his or her brain with complicated models.
2. *Data availability.* Use what is readily available, because data collection is both expensive and tedious.
3. *Plausibility.* Try to use variables which are logically related to the dependent variables (sun spots are a no-no).
4. *Goodness of fit.* Try to get a big R^2. Low R^2s may be significant but are hard to sell.

5. *Good coefficients.* Use only variables whose coefficients are significant with plausible signs and coefficients.
6. *Technical limitations.* The entire range of technical issues (multicollinearity, autocorrelation, heteroscedasticity, omitted variables, etc.) should be considered.

Since many of these criteria conflict (e.g., parsimony versus goodness of fit), the researcher must exercise judgment. Building a regression model is, thus, as much a craft as a science.

The other major issue in making regression useful is in communicating the results. In this regard, remember that F tests and Durbin-Watson statistics may be important aids to interpretation but usually become barriers to communication. With rare exception, the users of regressions are, quite properly, not statisticians. Hence, they do not understand or care about statistical jargon and tend to be irritated by it (sometimes as a defense against feeling inadequate). The wise researcher, therefore, attempts to simplify the results. One especially effective trick is the "what if" approach. Rather than simply presenting the resulting equation, calculate estimates for different levels of the key variables by plugging the values into the equation and discuss them (i.e., if we spend $100,000 on advertising, then sales will be X, while if we spend $200,000, sales will be Y). In short, never forget that, for marketing research, regression is only a means to the end of providing more useful information on which to base real decisions.

SUMMARY

Motivation

Regression analysis is an attempt to predict one dependent variable (Y) as a linear combination of a set of k independent variables (Xs). Example:

$$\text{Sales} = f(\text{income, education, age,} \ldots)$$

Model

$$Y = B_0 + B_1 X_1 + B_2 X_2 + \cdots + B_k X_k + \mu$$

(i.e., Sales $= B_0 + B_1(\text{income}) + B_2(\text{education}) + \cdots$.)

Solution

Bs are chosen so as to minimize the sum of the squared differences between the actual and predicted values of Y: $\Sigma(Y - \hat{Y})^2$.

Input

The raw data on the Xs and Y for a number (n) of observations.

Output

1. The regression coefficients (Bs).
2. Index of fit (R^2).
3. Standard error of prediction ($S_{Y.X}$).

Interpretation

1. The Bs are interpreted as the amount of change in Y which would be caused by a change of one unit in each of the Xs. B_0 is the constant (intercept), which is the prediction for Y if all the Xs were zero.
2. R^2 is the percent of the variance in Y explained (1 = all, 0 = none).
3. $S_{Y.X}$ is a measure of how uncertain (inaccurate) predictions made using the results will be.

The Interpretation Is Complicated if —

1. Multicollinearity exists (the Xs are highly correlated).
2. Autocorrelation exists (the μs are correlated, a typical problem in time series data where cycles exist).
3. Certain important variables are omitted.
4. The measurements are biased.
5. Heteroscedasticity exists (the expected error term, μ, is not constant).

Uses

There are many uses, including the following:

1. Forecasting.
2. Segmentation.
3. Parameter estimations and model selection.

Glossary of Equivalent Terms and Symbols

1. Dependent variable, criterion variable, Y.
2. Independent variable, predictor variable, X_i.

3. Intercept, constant, B_0.
4. Slope, regression coefficient, B_i.
5. e, $Y - \hat{Y}$, error, residual, deviation.

PROBLEMS

1. The frequency of purchase of a luxury nondurable may be a function of a person's income. The following sample has been obtained:

Income	*Purchases Per Year*
10	1
15	2
20	2
15	1
20	3
20	4
25	5
5	0
5	1
20	3
15	3
15	2
5	2
10	2
25	3
10	3
10	2
5	2
15	4
15	3

a. Estimate the regression line graphically.
b. Examine the plot of purchase rate versus income to determine if the assumption of homoscedasticity seems warranted. That is, does the variance of the disturbance term appear to be independent of income?
c. Examine the plot of mean purchases for each income level. Does the linear model appear to be adequate or should a nonlinear model be used?

2. In a study, 155 full-page magazine ads were used. The percent of the people who read the ads (as measured by Starch scores) was regressed

against a variety of mechanical layout variables, copy/message variables, and product class. The sixth step of a stepwise regression was as follows:

Variable	*B*	S_B
Bleed	4.05	1.00
Product category 11	−.48	.13
Product category 12	.51	.22
Size	−.40	.22
Product category 5	−1.44	.84
Product category 17	−.24	.16
Constant	10.19	

$R^2 = .24.$

Standard error = 5.87

a. Interpret the results statistically.
b. What managerial conclusions can you draw?

3. Let $X_1, X_2, \ldots, X_{20}$ represent the number of Ph.D. degrees awarded by U.S. universities in the years 1961, 1962, . . . , 1980. Let $Y_1, Y_2, \ldots, Y_{20}$ represent the GNP for the United States in those same years. Assume that we have performed a simple correlation analysis on the time series X versus the time series Y.
   a. What do you feel the approximate value of r will be (both magnitude and sign)? Justify your answer.
   b. What can be said about the causal effect of Ph.D.s on GNP?
4. In using multiple regression, when is collinearity (high correlation among the independent variables) a problem and when is it not a problem?
5. Assume I am interested in the relationship of income to age and height for a sample of 10 males. The data are as follows:

Income	*Age*	*Height (inches)*
$13,000	29	69
20,000	35	76
40,000	37	70
15,000	21	73
8,000	18	64
19,000	29	71
31,000	42	67
5,000	17	72
29,000	45	75
32,000	31	68

Interpret:

a. By tabular analysis.

b. By graphical analysis of the two independent variables separately.

c. By using multiple regression.

6. How might I use regression analysis to estimate b and c if I think $Y = kX^bZ^c$, given a set of measurements on Y, X, Z?
7. Is it possible for all the individual regression coefficients to be nonsignificant and the R^2 to be significant? Why not *or* what would it mean?
8. When will omitted variable bias occur in regression analysis?
9. The following regression model was estimated to explain the annual sales of a mail-order house:

$$S_t = 105 + \underset{(4.2)}{3.0A_t} + \underset{(1.0)}{12.0M_t} + \underset{(1.1)}{.5C_t}; \; R^2 = .95$$

where

S_t = \$ sales in year t.
A_t = \$ advertising expenditure in year t.
M_t = \$ merchandise mailing expenditures in year t.
C_t = Number of catalogs distributed in year t.

The estimated standard errors are in parentheses below the coefficient estimates. The customer service manager suggests that we should increase our mailing expenditures next year by sending more shipments first class, rather than parcel post, since the mailing expenditures coefficient is "significant" in the regression. What would you advise?

10. Joe Planner is in charge of sales forecasting for Trinket Company. He collected 20 monthly variables which he thought might be related to Trinket Company sales. The first was U.S. automobile sales (seasonally adjusted). The 20th was monthly rainfall in Morningside Heights. Joe ran a regression using the 20 monthly variables to explain the monthly sales (dollars) of Trinket Company for the last 96 months. The regression had an R^2 of .95. Joe is predicting sales for this month of \$100, based upon this regression model.

a. Interpret his work. Joe thinks that the R^2 is a good measure of his model's performance. Is it?

b. You now find that the third variable in Joe's regression was the monthly expenditure (dollars) for salespersons entertaining customers. The coefficient of this variable was 5.2, with an estimated standard error of .2. Joe figures that, since we make 40 percent gross margin on sales, it would be profitable to increase the entertaining budget:

Spend	\$ 1	more on entertaining
	× 5	(minimum sales increase/\$) from regression
	\$ 5	sales increase
	× 40%	gross margin
	\$ 2	increase in contribution to profits
	− 1	recover added entertaining cost
	\$ 1	leaves \$1 profit improvement

Is Joe's conclusion correct? Why?

c. Joe's rival suggests that the monthly entertaining budget should be changed monthly and set randomly, based upon the last digit of the winning number in the New Jersey State Lottery. Interpret the recommendation of Joe's rival. What would this recommendation gain us?

11. If my independent variables in a regression are highly correlated,
    a. Are the regression assumptions violated?
    b. What will happen to my coefficient estimates?
    c. What will happen to R?
12. What is a way to detect if the disturbances (errors) in regressions are correlated?
13. What is the difference between predictive, causal, and correlational relationships?

BIBLIOGRAPHY

Bass, Frank M.; Douglas J. Tigert; and Ronald T. Lonsdale. "Market Segmentation—Group versus Individual Behavior." *Journal of Marketing Research* 5 (August 1968), pp. 264–70.

Bass, Frank M., and Dick R. Wittink. "Pooling Issues and Methods in Regression Analysis with Examples in Marketing Research." *Journal of Marketing Research* 12 (November 1975), pp. 414–25.

Belsley, D.; E. Kuh; and R. E. Walsh. *Regression Diagnostics*. New York: John Wiley & Sons, 1980.

Cooil, Bruce; Russell S. Winer; and David L. Rados. "Cross-Validation for Prediction." *Journal of Marketing Research* 24 (August 1987), pp. 271–79.

Draper, N., and H. Smith. *Applied Regression Analysis*. New York: John Wiley & Sons, 1966.

Frank, Ronald E.; William F. Massy; and Yoram Wind. *Market Segmentation*. Englewood Cliffs, N.J.: Prentice-Hall, 1972.

Galton, F. *Natural Inheritance*. London: MacMillan, 1889.

Hoerl, Arthur E., and Robert W. Kennard. "Ridge Regression: Biased Estimation for Nonorthogonal Problems." *Technometrics* 12 (1970), pp. 55–67.

Johnston, J. *Econometric Methods*. 2nd ed. New York: McGraw-Hill, 1972.

Judge, Georg G.; W. E. Griffiths; R. Carter Hill; Helmut Lutkephol; and Tsoung-Chao Lee. *The Theory and Practice of Econometrics*. New York: John Wiley & Sons, 1985.

Krishnamurthi, Lakshman, and Arvind Rangaswamy. "The Equity Estimator for Marketing Research." *Marketing Science* 6 (Fall 1987), pp. 336–57.

Lehmann, Donald R. "Validity and Goodness of Fit in Data Analysis." In *Advances in Consumer Research*, ed., Mary Jane Schlinger. Ann Arbor, Mich.: Association for Consumer Research, 1975, pp. 741–49.

McIntyre, Shelby H.; David B. Montgomery; V. Srinivasan; and Barton A. Weitz. "Evaluating the Statistical Significance of Models Developed by Stepwise Regression." *Journal of Marketing Research* 20 (February 1983), pp. 1–11.

Massy, William F.; Ronald E. Frank; and Thomas M. Lodahl. *Purchasing Behavior and Personal Attributes*. Philadelphia: University of Pennsylvania Press, 1968.

Neter, John; William Wasserman; and Michael H. Kutner. *Applied Linear Regression Models*. Homewood, Ill.: Richard D. Irwin, 1983.

Ofir, Chezy, and Andre Khuri. "Multicollinearity in Marketing Models: Diagnostics and Remedial Measures." *International Journal of Research in Marketing* 3 (1986), pp. 181–205.

Appendix 13–A

Hand Calculation

Hand calculations of regression coefficients are rarely made. Nonetheless, to see how these estimation formulas can be applied is useful. Consider the following data:

X	Y
1	8
3	16
5	19
7	25
9	36
11	34

Assuming we were forced to solve this problem by hand, we could set up Table 13A–1, and get;

$$B_1 = \frac{196}{70} = 2.8$$

$$B_0 = 23 - \frac{196}{70}(6) = 23 - 16.8 = 6.2$$

$$r = \frac{196}{\sqrt{70}\,\sqrt{584}} = .969$$

TABLE 13A–1

	X	Y	$(X - \bar{X})$	$(Y - \bar{Y})$	$(X - \bar{X}) \cdot (Y - \bar{Y})$	$(X - \bar{X})^2$	$(Y - \bar{Y})^2$
	1	8	−5	−15	75	25	225
	3	16	−3	−7	21	9	49
	5	19	−1	−4	4	1	16
	7	25	1	2	2	1	4
	9	36	3	13	39	9	169
	11	34	5	11	55	25	121
Sum	36	138	0	0	196	70	584
Average	6	23					

TABLE 13A–2

	X	Y	XY	X^2	Y^2
	1	8	8	1	64
	3	16	48	9	256
	5	19	95	25	361
	7	25	175	49	625
	9	36	324	81	1,296
	11	34	374	121	1,156
Sum	36	138	1,024	286	3,758
Average	6	23			

TABLE 13A–3

X	Y	$\hat{Y}$	$Y - \hat{Y}$	$(Y - \hat{Y})^2$
1	8	9	−1	1.00
3	16	14.6	1.4	1.96
5	19	20.2	−1.2	1.44
7	25	25.8	−.8	.64
9	36	31.4	4.6	21.16
11	34	37.0	−3.0	9.00
				35.20

Alternatively, we could use the raw data in Table 13A–2. Here the results would be:

$$B_1 = \frac{1{,}024 - 6(6)(23)}{286 - 6(6)^2} = \frac{196}{70} = 2.8$$

$$B_0 = 23 - 2.8(6) = 6.2$$

$$r = \frac{1{,}024 - 6(6)(23)}{\sqrt{286 - 6(6)^2}\,\sqrt{3{,}758 - 6(23)^2}} = \frac{196}{\sqrt{70}\,\sqrt{584}} = .969$$

To calculate the standard error of estimate, we can calculate the values of $\hat{Y} = 6.2 + 2.8X$ (Table 13A–3). Thus:

$$S_{Y.X} \sqrt{\frac{35.20}{4}} = 2.97$$

Appendix 13–B

Formula Derivation

This appendix presents a brief outline of the derivation of the formulas used in regression analysis. As such, it assumes a knowledge of basic matrix algebra. A reader unfamiliar with it should skip this (and most of Appendix 13–E as well). For a more complete treatment, see Johnston (1972).

TWO-VARIABLE CASE

Model:

$$Y = \alpha + \beta X + \mu$$

Procedure: Select $\hat{\alpha}$, $\hat{\beta}$ in order to Min $\sum_{i=1}^{n} (Y_i - \hat{Y}_i)^2 = \Sigma e_i^2$

Method:

$$\sum_{i=1}^{n} \left(Y_i - \hat{Y}\right)^2 = \sum_{i=1}^{n} \left(Y_i - \hat{\alpha} - \hat{\beta} X_i\right)^2$$

Taking partial derivatives with respect to $\hat{\alpha}$ and $\hat{\beta}$, we get:

$$\frac{\partial \Sigma e_i^2}{\partial \hat{\alpha}} = \sum_{i=1}^{n} 2\left(Y_i - \hat{\alpha} - \hat{\beta} X_i\right)(-1)$$

$$\frac{\partial \Sigma e_i^2}{\partial \hat{\beta}} = \sum_{i=1}^{n} 2\left(Y_i - \hat{\alpha} - \hat{\beta} X_i\right)(-X_i)$$

(N.B.: The second-order conditions for a minimum are met.) Setting the partial derivatives equal to 0:

$$\sum_{i=1}^{n} 2(Y_i - \alpha - \beta X_i) = 0$$

$$\sum_{i=1}^{n} 2X_i(Y_i - \hat{\alpha} - \hat{\beta} X_i) = 0$$

These two equations (sometimes called the *normal equations* for some obscure reason) can be solved for $\hat{\alpha}$ and $\hat{\beta}$:

$$\hat{\alpha} = \overline{Y} - \hat{\beta}\overline{X}$$

$$\hat{\beta} = \frac{\sum_{i=1}^{n} X_i Y_i - n\overline{X}\overline{Y}}{\sum_{i=1}^{n} X_i^2 - n\overline{X}^2} = \frac{\sum_{i=1}^{n} (X_i - \overline{X})(Y_i - \overline{Y})}{\sum_{i=1}^{n} (X_i - \overline{X})^2}$$

GENERAL LINEAR MODEL

Model:

$$Y_i = B_0 + B_1 X_{1i} + B_2 X_{2i} + \cdots + B_k X_{ki} + \mu_i$$

Matrix notation:

$$Y = XB + \mu$$

where

$$Y = \begin{bmatrix} Y \\ Y_2 \\ \cdot \\ \cdot \\ \cdot \\ Y_n \end{bmatrix} \qquad X = \begin{bmatrix} 1 & X_{11} & \cdots & X_{k1} \\ 1 & X_{12} & \cdots & X_{k2} \\ \cdot & \cdot & & \cdot \\ \cdot & \cdot & & \cdot \\ \cdot & \cdot & & \cdot \\ 1 & X_{1n} & \cdots & X_{kn} \end{bmatrix}$$

$$B = \begin{bmatrix} B_0 \\ B_1 \\ B_2 \\ \cdot \\ \cdot \\ \cdot \\ B_k \end{bmatrix} \quad \text{and} \quad \mu = \begin{bmatrix} \mu_1 \\ \mu_2 \\ \cdot \\ \cdot \\ \cdot \\ \mu_n \end{bmatrix}$$

Procedure: Selcct $\hat{\beta}$ in order to minimize

$$\sum_{i=1}^{n} (Y_i - \hat{Y}_i)^2$$

In matrix form, this becomes

$$(Y - X\hat{\beta})'(Y - X\hat{\beta}) = e'e$$

In order to

$$\text{Min} \sum_{i=1}^{n} (Y_i - \hat{Y}_i)^2 = \text{Min}[Y'Y - 2\hat{\beta}X'Y + \hat{\beta}X'X\hat{\beta}]$$

we take the first derivative with respect to the vector $\hat{\beta}$.

Therefore,

$$\frac{\partial e'e}{\partial \hat{\beta}} = -2X'Y + 2X'X\hat{\beta}$$

Setting this equal to 0 and solving, we get

$$\hat{\beta} = [X'X]^{-1}X'Y$$

Appendix 13–C

Sample Regression Output

```
STATISTICAL PACKAGE FOR THE SOCIAL SCIENCES SPSSH - VERSION 6.00                    06/27/77        PAGE    1

          SPACE ALLOCATION FOR THIS RUN..

              TOTAL AMOUNT REQUESTED                                     80000 BYTES


              DEFAULT TRANSPACE ALLOCATION                               10000 BYTES


                 MAX NO OF TRANSFORMATIONS PERMITTED             100
                 MAX NO OF RECODE VALUES                         400
                 MAX NO OF ARITHM.OR LOG.OPERATIONS              600

              RESULTING WORKSPACE ALLOCATION                             70000 BYTES

                    VARIABLE LIST   YRBORN,INCOME,FAMSIZE,EXPENSE,
                                    BRAND,INFO,VARIETY,TASTE,OTHERS,DIET,PRICE,
                                    AVAIL,EASE,HABIT,SPECIAL,NUTRI
                    INPUT MEDIUM    DISK
                    N OF CASES      UNKNOWN
                    INPUT FORMAT    FIXED(20X,F2.0,54X,2F1.0/12X,F1.0,1X,
                                    2F1.0,1X,10F1.0/////)

                  ACCORDING TO YOUR INPUT FORMAT, VARIABLES ARE TO BE READ AS FOLLOWS

                  VARIABLE   FORMAT   RECORD     COLUMNS

                  YRBORN     F 2. 0        1      21-  22
                  INCOME     F 1. 0        1      77-  77
                  FAMSIZE    F 1. 0        1      78-  78
                  EXPENSE    F 1. 0        2      13-  13
                  BRAND      F 1. 0        2      15-  15
                  INFO       F 1. 0        2      16-  16
                  VARIETY    F 1. 0        2      18-  18
                  TASTE      F 1. 0        2      19-  19
                  OTHERS     F 1. 0        2      20-  20
                  DIET       F 1. 0        2      21-  21
                  PRICE      F 1. 0        2      22-  22
                  AVAIL      F 1. 0        2      23-  23
                  EASE       F 1. 0        2      24-  24
                  HABIT      F 1. 0        2      25-  25
                  SPECIAL    F 1. 0        2      26-  26
                  NUTRI      F 1. 0        2      27-  27

THE INPUT FORMAT PROVIDES FOR  16 VARIABLES.   16 WILL BE READ
IT PROVIDES FOR  6 RECORDS ('CARDS') PER CASE.  A MAXIMUM OF   78 'COLUMNS' ARE USED ON A RECORD.

                  RECODE           EXPENSE(1=12.5)(2=22.5)(3=37.5)
                                   (4=52.5)(5=70)
                  COMPUTE          AGE=75-YRBORN
                  MISSING VALUES   EXPENSE(0),YRBORN(00),FAMSIZE(0),INCOME(0)/
                                   BRAND,INFO,VARIETY,TASTE,OTHERS,DIET,PRICE,
                                   AVAIL,EASE,HABIT,SPECIAL,NUTRI(0)
                  REGRESSION       VARIABLES=EXPENSE,INCOME,AGE,FAMSIZE,
```

```
STATISTICAL PACKAGE FOR THE SOCIAL SCIENCES SPSSH - VERSION 6.00          06/27/77        PAGE    2
                                        BRAND,INFO,VARIETY,TASTE,OTHERS,DIET,PRICE,
                                        AVAIL,EASE,HABIT,SPECIAL,NUTRI/
                                        REGRESSION=EXPENSE WITH INCOME TO NUTRI(2)/
                                        REGRESSION=EXPENSE WITH INCOME TO NUTRI(1)/
                      STATISTICS        ALL

 ***** REGRESSION PROBLEM REQUIRES   5120 BYTES WORKSPACE, NOT INCLUDING RESIDUALS *****

                      READ INPUT DATA

AFTER READING    940 CASES FROM SUBFILE NONAME  ,  END OF FILE WAS ENCOUNTERED ON LOGICAL UNIT # 8
```

```
STATISTICAL PACKAGE FOR THE SOCIAL SCIENCES SPSSH - VERSION 6.00          06/27/77        PAGE    3

FILE    NONAME    (CREATION DATE = 06/27/77)
```

VARIABLE	MEAN	STANDARD DEV	CASES
EXPENSE	37.5230	15.1153	762
INCOME	2.7520	1.4208	762
AGE	43.7008	16.5416	762
FAMSIZE	3.2874	1.3756	762
BRAND	2.3425	1.4150	762
INFO	1.8740	0.6504	762
VARIETY	2.0407	0.9603	762
TASTE	1.2362	0.5656	762
OTHERS	1.6955	0.8978	762
DIET	3.0433	1.5749	762
PRICE	1.7520	0.9619	762
AVAIL	2.1654	1.1265	762
EASE	2.7546	1.2245	762
HABIT	2.7927	1.1390	762
SPECIAL	2.2559	1.2511	762
NUTRI	1.6745	0.8800	762

STATISTICAL PACKAGE FOR THE SOCIAL SCIENCES SPSSH - VERSION 6.00 06/27/77 PAGE 4

FILE NONAME (CREATION DATE = 06/27/77)

CORRELATION COEFFICIENTS

A VALUE OF 99.00000 IS PRINTED
IF A COEFFICIENT CANNOT BE COMPUTED.

	EXPENSE	INCOME	AGE	FAMSIZE	BRAND	INFO	VARIETY	TASTE	OTHERS	DIET	PRICE	AVAIL
EXPENSE	1.00000	0.41605	-0.08544	0.57810	0.03772	-0.01307	0.00627	-0.02907	-0.01740	0.01790	0.08422	-0.04510
INCOME	0.41605	1.00000	-0.12226	0.27252	-0.00606	-0.03244	0.02474	0.04357	0.01180	0.06882	0.25973	-0.01045
AGE	-0.08544	-0.12226	1.00000	-0.27220	-0.10066	0.06135	-0.02248	-0.01154	-0.02234	-0.15224	0.02787	-0.04620
FAMSIZE	0.57810	0.27252	-0.27220	1.00000	0.09856	0.03318	0.05480	0.03592	0.04967	0.11919	-0.01359	-0.02050
BRAND	0.03772	-0.00606	-0.10066	0.09856	1.00000	-0.14867	-0.01897	0.02355	0.04289	-0.05148	-0.14218	0.00563
INFO	-0.01307	-0.03244	0.06135	0.03318	-0.14867	1.00000	0.11131	0.00956	0.03999	0.10925	0.12432	-0.01097
VARIETY	0.00627	0.02474	-0.02248	0.05480	-0.01897	0.11131	1.00000	0.32582	0.20949	0.14394	0.05362	0.10292
TASTE	-0.02907	0.04357	-0.01154	0.03592	0.02355	0.00956	0.32582	1.00000	0.33071	0.04455	0.04020	0.12194
OTHERS	-0.01740	0.01180	-0.02234	0.04967	0.04289	0.03999	0.20949	0.33071	1.00000	0.13573	0.02808	0.07829
DIET	0.01790	0.06882	-0.15224	0.11919	-0.05148	0.10925	0.14394	0.04455	0.13573	1.00000	0.10772	0.07803
PRICE	0.08422	0.25973	0.02787	-0.01359	-0.14218	0.12432	0.05362	0.04020	0.02808	0.10772	1.00000	0.20125
AVAIL	-0.04510	-0.01045	-0.04620	-0.02050	0.00563	-0.01097	0.10292	0.12194	0.07829	0.07803	0.20125	1.00000
EASE	-0.01904	-0.01162	-0.00577	-0.02516	0.04099	-0.11477	0.05097	0.08001	0.05865	0.02868	0.12452	0.30326
HABIT	-0.12929	-0.08542	-0.00964	-0.05753	0.04413	-0.16303	0.08822	0.11692	0.12709	0.03578	0.05854	0.23015
SPECIAL	0.02835	0.03206	-0.04843	-0.00843	-0.13495	0.13496	0.08648	0.09273	0.07531	0.02238	0.32362	0.17289
NUTRI	0.03267	0.05937	0.00070	0.03938	-0.05916	0.26807	0.25361	0.22594	0.14054	0.27946	0.22741	0.08470

	EASE	HABIT	SPECIAL	NUTRI
EXPENSE	-0.01904	-0.12929	0.02835	0.03267
INCOME	-0.01162	-0.08542	0.03206	0.05937
AGE	-0.00577	-0.00964	-0.04843	0.00070
FAMSIZE	-0.02516	-0.05753	-0.00843	0.03938
BRAND	0.04099	0.04413	-0.13495	-0.05916
INFO	-0.11477	-0.16303	0.13496	0.26807
VARIETY	0.05097	0.08822	0.08648	0.25361
TASTE	0.08001	0.11692	0.09273	0.22594
OTHERS	0.05865	0.12709	0.07531	0.14054
DIET	0.02868	0.03578	0.02238	0.27946
PRICE	0.12452	0.05854	0.32362	0.22741
AVAIL	0.30326	0.23015	0.17289	0.08470
EASE	1.00000	0.28569	0.06163	-0.00837
HABIT	0.28569	1.00000	0.09907	0.02305
SPECIAL	0.06163	0.09907	1.00000	0.18079
NUTRI	-0.00837	0.02305	0.18079	1.00000

```
STATISTICAL PACKAGE FOR THE SOCIAL SCIENCES SPSSH - VERSION 6.00          06/27/77        PAGE    5

FILE    NONAME    (CREATION DATE = 06/27/77)

* * * * * * * * * * * * * * * * * * * * * * * *  M U L T I P L E   R E G R E S S I O N  * * * * * * * * * * * * * *   VARIABLE LIST  1
                                                                                                                        REGRESSION LIST  1
DEPENDENT VARIABLE..    EXPENSE

VARIABLE(S) ENTERED ON STEP NUMBER  1..     NUTRI
                                            INCOME
                                            AGE
                                            FAMSIZE
                                            BRAND
                                            INFO
                                            VARIETY
                                            TASTE
                                            OTHERS
                                            DIET
                                            PRICE
                                            AVAIL
                                            EASE
                                            HABIT
                                            SPECIAL
```

MULTIPLE R	0.65532
R SQUARE	0.42945
ADJUSTED R SQUARE	0.41876
STANDARD ERROR	11.53155

ANALYSIS OF VARIANCE	DF	SUM OF SQUARES	MEAN SQUARE	F
REGRESSION	15.	74667.73002	4977.84867	37.43399
RESIDUAL	746.	99200.61808	132.97670	

---------------- VARIABLES IN THE EQUATION ------------------

VARIABLE	B	BETA	STD ERROR B	F
NUTRI	0.47245	0.02750	0.54198	0.760
INCOME	2.88617	0.27128	0.32247	80.108
AGE	0.07983	0.08737	0.02683	8.851
FAMSIZE	5.85584	0.53293	0.33067	313.608
BRAND	0.00635	0.00059	0.30616	0.000
INFO	-1.08607	-0.04673	0.69705	2.428
VARIETY	0.02149	0.00137	0.47587	0.002
TASTE	-1.39632	-0.05225	0.83180	2.818
OTHERS	-0.28381	-0.01686	0.50323	0.318
DIET	-0.46426	-0.04837	0.28538	2.647
PRICE	0.28637	0.01822	0.49960	0.329
AVAIL	-0.24058	-0.01796	0.40468	0.353
EASE	0.28449	0.02305	0.37152	0.586
HABIT	-1.06932	-0.08058	0.39900	7.182
SPECIAL	0.49106	0.04064	0.36442	1.816
(CONSTANT)	12.76075			

------------- VARIABLES NOT IN THE EQUATION -------------

VARIABLE	BETA IN	PARTIAL	TOLERANCE	F

ALL VARIABLES ARE IN THE EQUATION

```
STATISTICAL PACKAGE FCR THE SOCIAL SCIENCES SPSSH - VERSION 6.00          06/27/77        PAGE    6

FILE    NONAME    (CREATION CATE = 06/27/77)

* * * * * * * * * * * * * * * * * * * * * * * *  M U L T I P L E   R E G R E S S I O N  * * * * * * * * * * * * * *   VARIABLE LIST  1
                                                                                                                        REGRESSION LIST  1

CEPENDENT VARIABLE..    EXPENSE
```

SUMMARY TABLE

VARIABLE	MULTIPLE R	R SQUARE	RSQ CHANGE	SIMPLE R	B	BETA
NUTRI	0.03267	0.00107	0.00107	0.03267	0.47245	0.02750
INCOME	0.41612	0.17316	0.17209	0.41605	2.88617	0.27128
AGE	0.41759	0.17438	0.00122	-0.08544	0.07983	0.08737
FAMSIZE	0.64366	0.41429	C.23992	0.57810	5.85584	0.53293
BRAND	0.64367	0.41431	0.00001	0.03772	0.00635	0.00059
INFO	0.64425	0.41506	0.00075	-0.01307	-1.08607	-0.04673
VARIETY	0.64473	0.41574	0.00067	0.00627	0.02149	0.00137
TASTE	0.64720	0.41887	0.00313	-0.02907	-1.39632	-0.05225
OTHERS	0.64772	0.41954	0.00067	-0.01740	-0.28381	-0.01686
CIET	0.64959	0.42197	0.00243	0.01790	-0.46426	-0.04837
PRICE	0.64991	0.42239	C.00042	0.08422	0.28637	0.01822
AVAIL	0.65029	0.42288	0.00049	-0.04510	-0.24058	-0.01796
EASE	0.65032	0.42292	0.00004	-0.01904	0.28449	0.02305
HABIT	0.65426	0.42806	0.00514	-0.12929	-1.06932	-0.08058
SPECIAL	0.65532	0.42945	0.00139	0.02835	0.49106	0.04064
(CONSTANT)					12.76075	

```
STATISTICAL PACKAGE FOR THE SOCIAL SCIENCES SPSSH - VERSION 5.00          06/27/77        PAGE    7
FILE    NGNAME   (CREATION DATE = 06/27/77)

* * * * * * * * * * * * * * * * * * * * * * M U L T I P L E   R E G R E S S I O N * * * * * * * * * * * * * *   VARIABLE LIST  1
DEPENDENT VARIABLE..    EXPENSE                                                                               REGRESSION LIST  2

VARIABLE(S) ENTERED ON STEP NUMBER  1..     FAMSIZE

MULTIPLE R           0.57810                      ANALYSIS OF VARIANCE     DF      SUM OF SQUARES      MEAN SQUARE            F
R SQUARE             0.33420                      REGRESSION                1.        58106.10040      58106.10040      381.47701
ADJUSTED R SQUARE    0.33420                      RESIDUAL                760.       115762.24769        152.31875
STANDARD ERROR      12.34175

------------------ VARIABLES IN THE EQUATION ------------------       ------------- VARIABLES NOT IN THE EQUATION -------------

VARIABLE              B           BETA      STD ERROR B       F         VARIABLE     BETA IN      PARTIAL    TOLERANCE         F

FAMSIZE            6.35215      0.57810       0.32523      381.477      INCOME       0.27925      0.32927     0.92573      92.298
(CONSTANT)        16.64090                                               AGE          0.07767      0.09159     0.92591       6.421
                                                                         BRAND       -0.01944     -0.02371     0.99029       0.427
                                                                         INFO        -0.03229     -0.03955     0.99890       1.189
                                                                         VARIETY     -0.02548     -0.03119     0.99700       0.739
                                                                         TASTE       -0.04990     -0.06111     0.99871       2.845
                                                                         OTHERS      -0.04622     -0.05658     0.99753       2.438
                                                                         DIET        -0.05174     -0.06296     0.98579       3.021
                                                                         PRICE        0.09209      0.11285     0.99982       9.790
                                                                         AVAIL       -0.03326     -0.04076     0.99958       1.263
                                                                         EASE        -0.00450     -0.00551     0.99937       0.023
                                                                         HABIT       -0.09635     -0.11789     0.99669      10.697
                                                                         SPECIAL      0.03323      0.04072     0.99993       1.261
                                                                         NUTRI        0.00992      0.01215     0.99845       0.112
```

```
STATISTICAL PACKAGE FOR THE SOCIAL SCIENCES SPSSH - VERSION 6.00                 06/27/77        PAGE    8

FILE    NONAME    (CREATION DATE = 06/27/77)

* * * * * * * * * * * * * * * * * * * * * * *  M U L T I P L E   R E G R E S S I O N  * * * * * * * * * * * * * *   VARIABLE LIST  1
                                                                                                                 REGRESSION LIST  2
DEPENDENT VARIABLE..     EXPENSE

VARIABLE(S) ENTERED ON STEP NUMBER  2..     INCOME

MULTIPLE R             0.63748                 ANALYSIS OF VARIANCE    DF     SUM OF SQUARES      MEAN SQUARE          F
R SQUARE               0.40638                 REGRESSION               2.     70657.10393      35328.55197       259.80087
ADJUSTED R SQUARE      0.40560                 RESIDUAL               759.    103211.24416        135.98319
STANDARD ERROR        11.66118

---------------- VARIABLES IN THE EQUATION -----------------      ------------ VARIABLES NOT IN THE EQUATION -------------

VARIABLE              B          BETA      STD ERROR B      F       VARIABLE     BETA IN     PARTIAL   TOLERANCE        F

FAMSIZE           5.51597     0.50200       0.31938    298.281      AGE          0.09242     0.11527     0.92341      10.207
INCOME            2.97087     0.27925       0.30923     92.298      BRAND       -0.01017    -0.01313     0.98912       0.131
(CONSTANT)       11.21403                                           INFO        -0.02073    -0.02687     0.99704       0.548
                                                                    VARIETY     -0.02823    -0.03659     0.99689       1.016
                                                                    TASTE       -0.05942    -0.07702     0.99748       4.523
                                                                    OTHERS      -0.04574    -0.05929     0.99753       2.674
                                                                    DIET        -0.06213    -0.08000     0.98437       4.883
                                                                    PRICE        0.02001     0.02498     0.92485       0.473
                                                                    AVAIL       -0.03190    -0.04140     0.99955       1.301
                                                                    EASE        -0.00317    -0.00411     0.99934       0.013
                                                                    HABIT       -0.07722    -0.09979     0.99144       7.625
                                                                    SPECIAL      0.02367     0.03069     0.99865       0.715
                                                                    NUTRI       -0.00369    -0.00478     0.99589       0.017
```

STATISTICAL PACKAGE FOR THE SOCIAL SCIENCES SPSSH - VERSION 6.00 06/27/77 PAGE 9

FILE NCNAME (CREATION DATE = 06/27/77)

* M U L T I P L E R E G R E S S I O N * * * * * * * * * * * * * * VARIABLE LIST 1
REGRESSION LIST 2

DEPENDENT VARIABLE.. EXPENSE

VARIABLE(S) ENTERED ON STEP NUMBER 3.. AGE

MULTIPLE R	0.64364
R SQUARE	0.41427
ADJUSTED R SQUARE	0.41273
STANDARD ERROR	11.59109

ANALYSIS OF VARIANCE	DF	SUM OF SQUARES	MEAN SQUARE	F
REGRESSION	3.	72028.40852	24009.46951	178.70374
RESIDUAL	758.	101839.93958	134.35348	

---------------- VARIABLES IN THE EQUATION ----------------

VARIABLE	B	BETA	STD ERROR B	F
FAMSIZE	5.77801	0.52585	0.32789	310.535
INCOME	3.02193	0.28405	0.30779	96.396
AGE	0.08445	0.09242	0.02643	10.207
(CONSTANT)	6.52153			

------------- VARIABLES NOT IN THE EQUATION -------------

VARIABLE	BETA IN	PARTIAL	TOLERANCE	F
BRAND	-0.00313	-0.00406	0.98294	0.012
INFO	-0.02719	-0.03539	0.99200	0.949
VARIETY	-0.02758	-0.03598	0.99684	0.981
TASTE	-0.05941	-0.07754	0.99748	4.578
OTHERS	-0.04492	-0.05862	0.99744	2.610
DIET	-0.05185	-0.06670	0.96931	3.383
PRICE	0.01626	0.02041	0.92330	0.316
AVAIL	-0.02717	-0.03545	0.99662	0.952
EASE	-0.00198	-0.00258	0.99916	0.005
HABIT	-0.07459	-0.09700	0.99053	7.190
SPECIAL	0.02827	0.03686	0.99606	1.030
NUTRI	-0.00499	-0.00650	0.99568	0.032

```
STATISTICAL PACKAGE FOR THE SOCIAL SCIENCES SPSSH - VERSION 6.00          06/27/77          PAGE  10

FILE    NGNAME   (CREATION DATE = 06/27/77)

* * * * * * * * * * * * * * * * * * * * * * * *  M U L T I P L E   R E G R E S S I O N  * * * * * * * * * * * * * *   VARIABLE LIST  1
                                                                                                                      REGRESSION LIST  2
DEPENDENT VARIABLE..     EXPENSE

VARIABLE(S) ENTERED ON STEP NUMBER  4..     HABIT

MULTIPLE R           0.64791          ANALYSIS OF VARIANCE     DF     SUM OF SQUARES      MEAN SQUARE           F
R SQUARE             0.41978          REGRESSION               4.      72986.62405      18246.65601      136.91993
ADJUSTED R SQUARE    0.41748          RESIDUAL               757.     100881.72405        133.26516
STANDARD ERROR      11.54405

----------------- VARIABLES IN THE EQUATION ------------------       ------------- VARIABLES NOT IN THE EQUATION --------------

VARIABLE              B          BETA      STD ERROR B        F       VARIABLE     BETA IN      PARTIAL   TOLERANCE         F

FAMSIZE           5.74106     0.52248        0.32685    303.531       BRAND        0.00028      0.00036     0.98090     0.000
INCOME            2.96086     0.27830        0.30739     92.783       INFO        -0.04046     -0.05220     0.96547     2.065
AGE               0.08232     0.09008        0.02634      9.767       VARIETY     -0.02089     -0.02726     0.98831     0.562
HABIT            -0.98989    -0.07459        0.36916      7.190       TASTE       -0.05109     -0.06649     0.98257     3.357
(CONSTANT)        9.66878                                             OTHERS      -0.03584     -0.04659     0.98050     1.645
                                                                      DIET        -0.04873     -0.06293     0.96756     3.006
                                                                      PRICE        0.02278      0.02864     0.91703     0.621
                                                                      AVAIL       -0.01075     -0.01371     0.94461     0.142
                                                                      EASE         0.02088      0.02626     0.91803     0.522
                                                                      SPECIAL      0.03609      0.04705     0.98604     1.677
                                                                      NUTRI       -0.00279     -0.00365     0.99481     0.010
```

STATISTICAL PACKAGE FOR THE SOCIAL SCIENCES SPSSH - VERSION 6.00 06/27/77 PAGE 11

FILE NONAME (CREATION DATE = 06/27/77)

* M U L T I P L E R E G R E S S I O N * * * * * * * * * * * * * * VARIABLE LIST 1
REGRESSION LIST 2

DEPENDENT VARIABLE.. EXPENSE

VARIABLE(S) ENTERED ON STEP NUMBER 5.. TASTE

MULTIPLE R	0.64988
R SQUARE	0.42235
ADJUSTED R SQUARE	0.41929
STANDARD ERROR	11.52613

ANALYSIS OF VARIANCE	DF	SUM OF SQUARES	MEAN SQUARE	F
REGRESSION	5.	73432.55368	14686.51074	110.54826
RESIDUAL	756.	100435.79442	132.85158	

------------------ VARIABLES IN THE EQUATION ------------------

VARIABLE	B	BETA	STD ERROR B	F
FAMSIZE	5.75875	0.52409	0.32646	311.129
INCOME	2.98583	0.28065	0.30721	94.462
AGE	0.08249	0.09028	0.02630	9.840
HABIT	-0.90670	-0.06832	0.37137	5.961
TASTE	-1.36528	-0.05109	0.74520	3.357
(CONSTANT)	10.98957			

------------- VARIABLES NOT IN THE EQUATION -------------

VARIABLE	BETA IN	PARTIAL	TOLERANCE	F
BRAND	0.00110	0.00143	0.98065	0.002
INFO	-0.03893	-0.05030	0.96457	1.915
VARIETY	-0.00527	-0.00654	0.88911	0.032
OTHERS	-0.02174	-0.02684	0.88073	0.544
DIET	-0.04700	-0.06079	0.96639	2.800
PRICE	0.02398	0.03021	0.91657	0.690
AVAIL	-0.00566	-0.00721	0.93542	0.039
EASE	0.02351	0.02961	0.91585	0.662
SPECIAL	0.04048	0.05271	0.97960	2.104
NUTRI	0.00891	0.01140	0.94593	0.098

```
STATISTICAL PACKAGE FOR THE SOCIAL SCIENCES SPSSH - VERSION 6.00                06/27/77        PAGE   19

FILE    NCNAME    (CREATION DATE = 06/27/77)

* * * * * * * * * * * * * * * * * * * * *  M U L T I P L E   R E G R E S S I O N  * * * * * * * * * * * * *   VARIABLE LIST   1
                                                                                                           REGRESSION LIST 2

DEPENDENT VARIABLE..    EXPENSE

VARIABLE(S) ENTERED ON STEP NUMBER 13..    PRICE

MULTIPLE R            0.65532              ANALYSIS OF VARIANCE      DF    SUM OF SQUARES     MEAN SQUARE          F
R SQUARE              0.42945              REGRESSION               13.      74667.40535      5743.64657      43.30854
ADJUSTED R SQUARE     0.42031              RESIDUAL                748.      99200.94275       132.62158
STANDARD ERROR       11.51614

---------------- VARIABLES IN THE EQUATION -----------------       ----------- VARIABLES NOT IN THE EQUATION -----------

VARIABLE              B          BETA       STD ERROR B       F        VARIABLE    BETA IN    PARTIAL   TOLERANCE       F

FAMSIZE            5.65684     0.53302       0.32893     317.038       BRAND       0.00058    0.00073     0.93130     0.000
INCOME             2.88617     0.27128       0.32202      80.331       VARIETY     0.00136    0.00164     0.83697     0.002
AGE                0.07979     0.08732       0.02672       8.920
HABIT             -1.06834    -0.08050       0.39797       7.206
TASTE             -1.30708    -0.05191       0.80594       2.962
DIET              -0.46374    -0.04832       0.28381       2.670
SPECIAL            0.49058     0.04060       0.36205       1.836
INFO              -1.08545    -0.04671       0.69056       2.471
NUTRI              0.47603     0.02771       0.53588       0.789
EASE               0.28493     0.02308       0.37081       0.590
OTHERS            -0.28140    -0.01671       0.50019       0.317
AVAIL             -0.23969    -0.01790       0.40374       0.352
PRICE              0.28491     0.01813       0.49687       0.329
(CONSTANT)        12.79161

F-LEVEL OR TOLERANCE-LEVEL INSUFFICIENT FOR FURTHER COMPUTATION
```

STATISTICAL PACKAGE FOR THE SOCIAL SCIENCES SPSSH - VERSION 6.00 06/27/77 PAGE 20

FILE NCNAME (CREATION DATE = 06/27/77)

* M U L T I P L E R E G R E S S I O N * * * * * * * * * * * * * * VARIABLE LIST 1
REGRESSION LIST 2

DEPENDENT VARIABLE.. EXPENSE

SUMMARY TABLE

VARIABLE	MULTIPLE R	R SQUARE	RSQ CHANGE	SIMPLE R	B	BETA
FAMSIZE	0.57810	0.33420	0.33420	0.57810	5.85684	0.53302
INCOME	0.63748	0.40638	0.07219	0.41605	2.88617	0.27128
AGE	0.64364	0.41427	0.00789	-0.08544	0.07979	0.08732
HABIT	0.64791	0.41978	0.00551	-0.12929	-1.06834	-0.08050
TASTE	0.64986	0.42235	0.00256	-0.02907	-1.38708	-0.05191
DIET	0.65152	0.42448	0.00213	0.01790	-0.46374	-0.04832
SPECIAL	0.65278	0.42612	0.00164	0.02835	0.49058	0.04060
INFO	0.65398	0.42769	0.00157	-0.01307	-1.08545	-0.04671
NUTRI	0.65449	0.42835	0.00066	0.03267	0.47603	0.02771
EASE	0.65478	0.42873	0.00038	-0.01904	0.28493	0.02308
OTHERS	0.65497	0.42899	0.00025	-0.01740	-0.28140	-0.01671
AVAIL	0.65513	0.42920	0.00021	-0.04510	-0.23969	-0.01790
PRICE	0.65532	0.42945	0.00025	0.08422	0.28491	0.01813
(CONSTANT)					12.79161	

Appendix 13–D

Simultaneous Equation Regression

PROBLEM

The basic regression model assumes there is one dependent variable which is affected by a set of independent variables. This is a useful model but often not an accurate assumption about the way the world operates. Consider the issue of the influence of advertising on sales. If we plotted sales versus advertising, we might get Figure 13D–1. It is easy to assume

FIGURE 13D–1

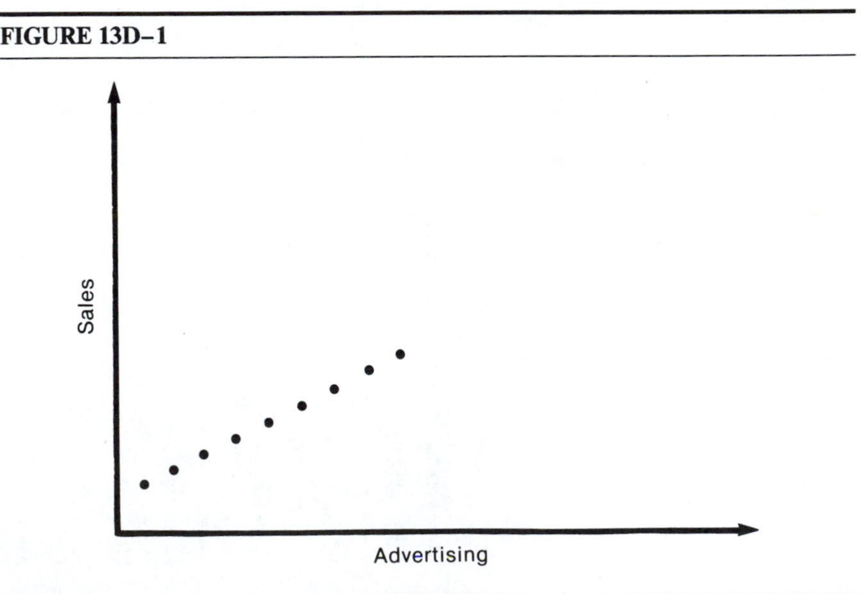

FIGURE 13D–2

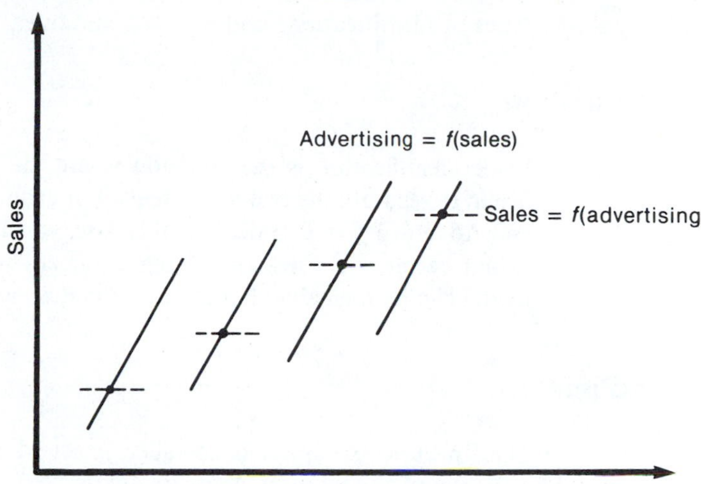

that these data can be approximated by a line which indicates the effect of advertising on sales. Presumably, advertising does indeed affect sales. On the other hand, advertising budgets are traditionally set as a percentage of anticipated sales. Hence, the observed points could well be a set of intersections of lines which indicate how advertising affects sales and how sales affects advertising (Figure 13D–2). In this case, the simple plot of sales versus advertising produces some weighted average of the advertising-to-sales and sales-to-advertising effects.

METHOD

A basic method for disentangling two-way effects among variables is simultaneous equation regression. The trick is to specify one equation for each direction of causation. In the sales-advertising example, that means two equations:

$$\text{Sales} = f(\text{advertising})$$

$$\text{Advertising} = f(\text{sales})$$

The method is then to simultaneously estimate coefficients of both equations.

The key to the success of simultaneous equations estimation is the presence of other (exogenous) variables which act only as independent variables. If these other independent variables are fortuitous, then their influences can be used to disentangle the two-way relations among the basic (endogenous) variables. The ability of a system of equations to separate two-way relations is tied to the concept of identification. There are three types of identification: under, exact, and over.

Underidentification

Underidentification is the situation where the "other" variables are insufficient to separate the two-way effects. For example, Sales = B_1(advertising), and Advertising = B_2(sales). In this case, which comes first (sales or advertising) becomes a chicken-and-egg argument with no solution. Unless the model can be logically altered, no estimates can be obtained.

Exact Identification

The "neatest" situation is so-called exact identification. In this case, the estimates of the two-way relations are derived in a straightforward two-step process. Assume:

$$\text{Sales} = B_1(\text{advertising}) + \gamma_1(\text{GNP})$$

$$\text{Advertising} = B_2(\text{advertising}) + \gamma_2(\text{Competitive advertising})$$

Call

$$\left.\begin{aligned} \text{GNP} &= X_1 \\ \text{Competitive advertising} &= X_2 \end{aligned}\right\} \text{Exogenous variables}$$

$$\left.\begin{aligned} \text{Sales} &= Y_1 \\ \text{Advertising} &= Y_2 \end{aligned}\right\} \text{Endogenous variables}$$

We can now write the two equations in matrix form as:

$$\begin{bmatrix} -1 & B_1 \\ -B_2 & -1 \end{bmatrix} \begin{bmatrix} Y_1 \\ Y_2 \end{bmatrix} + \begin{bmatrix} \gamma_1 & 0 \\ 0 & \gamma_2 \end{bmatrix} \begin{bmatrix} X_1 \\ X_2 \end{bmatrix} = \begin{bmatrix} \mu_1 \\ \mu_2 \end{bmatrix}$$

or

$$BY + \Gamma X = \mu$$

To solve for Y, we multiply both sides by B^{-1}:

$$B^{-1}BY + B^{-1}\Gamma X = B^{-1}\mu$$

or

$$Y = -B^{-1}\Gamma X + B^{-1}\mu$$

Since we assume $B^{-1}\mu = 0$:

$$Y = -B^{-1}\Gamma X$$

Hence, we have now set the endogenous variables as a function of the exogenous variables, often called the reduced form equations. The two-step process first requires one to run regular regression (ordinary least squares—OLS) on the reduced form equations:

$$Y_1 = a_1X_1 + a_2X_2$$
$$Y = a_3X_3 + a_4X_4$$

The next step is to deduce the B_is and γ_is from the a_is:

$$\begin{bmatrix} a_1 & a_2 \\ a_3 & a_4 \end{bmatrix} = -\beta^{-1}\Gamma$$
$$= \frac{-1}{1-\beta_1\beta_2}\begin{bmatrix} -1 & -\beta_1 \\ -\beta_2 & -1 \end{bmatrix}\begin{bmatrix} \gamma_1 & 0 \\ 0 & \gamma_2 \end{bmatrix}$$
$$= \frac{-1}{1-\beta_1\beta_2}\begin{bmatrix} -\gamma_1 & -\beta\gamma_2 \\ -\beta_2\gamma_1 & -\gamma_2 \end{bmatrix}$$

Thus:

$$a_1 = \gamma_1$$
$$a_2 = \beta_1\gamma_2$$
$$a_3 = \beta_2\gamma_2$$
$$a_4 = \gamma_2$$

Therefore, $\beta_1 = \dfrac{a_2}{a_4}$, and so forth. This process is called *indirect least squares* (ILS).

Logically, this "trick" works because each of the exogenous variables influences one and only one of the endogenous variables. Here we can view this as an experiment where we know, for example, that changes in gross national product first affect sales and that changes in competitive advertising first affect advertising. Hence, by varying GNP and advertising (or observing how they vary naturally), we can separate the sales-to-advertising and advertising-to-sales effects. If, for example, GNP affects both sales and advertising, we can no longer logically determine both its impact on sales and advertising and sales and advertising's effects on each other. Thus, the key to simultaneous equation methods is the appropriateness and predictive ability of the exogenous variables.

Overidentification

Overidentification is the situation where the exogenous variables are more than sufficient to identify the two-way causations. For example:

$$\text{Sales} = \beta_1(\text{advertising}) + \gamma_1(\text{GNP}) + \gamma_3(\text{CPI})$$
$$\text{Advertising} = \beta_2(\text{sales}) + \gamma_2(\text{competitive advertising})$$
$$+\gamma_4(\text{share}) + \gamma_5(\text{media rates})$$

Here, no simple solution can be traced from the reduced form back to the original coefficients.

One common estimation procedure in this case is two-stage least squares (TSLS). The steps are:

1. Find A from $Y = AX$ (run the reduced form equations by OLS).
2. Set $Y^* = AX$ (replace the actual values of Y with their predicted values from AX) and then run $BY^* + \Gamma X = \mu$ by OLS.

Identification Checking

In checking for identification, there are the following two common approaches:

Order Condition. The order condition is a necessary but not sufficient condition for identification. It is a counting rule which says for each equation:

$$\text{Number of endogenous variables included} - 1$$

$$\leq \text{Number of exogenous variables excluded}$$

Rank Condition. The rank condition is a sufficient condition for identification. It requires one to form the augmented β, Γ matrix: $\beta\Gamma$. Now for each equation (e.g., the second), remove the row of that equation (e.g., second row) and any column where the equation removed had a nonzero element. If the rank of the reduced matrix is equal to the number of original equations minus 1, then the equation is identified. If the rank is less than that, then the equation is not identified.

Consider the example in the exact identification case. Here the $B\Gamma$ matrix is:

$$\begin{bmatrix} -1 & B_1 & \gamma_1 & 0 \\ -B_2 & 1 & 0 & \gamma_2 \end{bmatrix}$$

To check on the second equation, remove the second row and all columns with a nonzero value in the second row. This leaves:

$$[\gamma_1]$$

Since the reduced matrix is of order $2 - 1 = 1$, then the equation is identified.

ESTIMATION

Estimation problems in simultaneous equation models get very complex. The problem is that all the nice assumptions about the error terms are often false and, hence, OLS may not be the best approach. On the other hand, for recursive[3] models, OLS is the best, and it does quite well in many other situations as well. In short, simultaneous equation estimation is a technical problem which calls for technical help.

---

[3]A recursive model is one in which the direction of causation is in one direction (no feedback exists) such as awareness → attitude → intention → choice. If choice were assumed to also influence attitude, the middle would then be nonrecursive.

Appendix 13–E

The Effect of Collinearity on the Standard Error of a Regression Coefficient

TWO INDEPENDENT VARIABLES

The standard error of a regression coefficient (S_{B_i}) is the product of the standard error of estimate ($S_{Y.X}$) times the ith diagonal element in the inverse of the covariance matrix ($[X'X]_{ii}^{-1}$).

For two independent variables, we know:

$$[X'X] = \begin{bmatrix} S_1^2 & S_{12} \\ S_{12} & S_2^2 \end{bmatrix}$$

Consequently:

$$[X'X]^{-1} = \frac{1}{S_1^2 S_2^2 - S_{12}^2} \begin{bmatrix} S_2^2 & -S_{12} \\ -S_{12} & S_1^2 \end{bmatrix}$$

Thus, the most efficient set of data has $S_{12} = 0$ and the ratio $\dfrac{S_1^2 S_2^2 - S_{12}^2}{S_1^2 S_2^2}$ measures the efficiency of two correlated independent variables versus the efficiency had they been uncorrelated.

ORTHOGONAL AND NONORTHOGONAL DESIGNS

Another way to view the effect of collinearity is to consider the difference between orthogonal and nonorthogonal designs. Here, we use three independent dummy variables in a factorial design of eight observations as the "population," and contrast an orthogonal and a nonorthogonal sample of size four. (Obviously, a bigger example might be "more interesting," but it would also be more unmanageable.)

	Observation	X_1	X_2	X_3
Factorial design:	1	1	1	1
	2	1	1	0
	3	1	0	1
	4	0	1	1
	5	1	0	0
	6	0	1	0
	7	0	0	1
	8	0	0	0
Orthogonal design:	1	1	1	1
	2	0	1	0
	3	1	0	0
	4	0	0	1
Nonorthogonal design:	1	1	1	1
	2	0	1	1
	3	1	0	1
	4	0	0	0

Putting the data in deviation form, we get:

	Observation	X_1	X_2	X_3
Factorial design:	1	.5	.5	.5
	2	.5	.5	−.5
	3	.5	−.5	.5
	4	−.5	.5	.5
	5	.5	−.5	−.5
	6	−.5	.5	−.5
	7	−.5	−.5	.5
	8	−.5	−.5	−.5
Orthogonal design:	1	.5	.5	.5
	2	−.5	.5	−.5
	3	.5	−.5	−.5
	4	−.5	−.5	.5
Nonorthogonal design:	1	.5	.5	.25
	2	−.5	.5	.25
	3	.5	−.5	.25
	4	−.5	−.5	−.75

Thus, for $[X'X]$ and $[X'X]^{-1}$ we get:

	$[X'X]$	$[X'X]^{-1}$
Factorial design:	$\begin{bmatrix} 2 & & \\ & 2 & \\ & & 2 \end{bmatrix}$	$\begin{bmatrix} \frac{1}{2} & & \\ & \frac{1}{2} & \\ & & \frac{1}{2} \end{bmatrix}$
Orthogonal design:	$\begin{bmatrix} 1 & & \\ & 1 & \\ & & 1 \end{bmatrix}$	$\begin{bmatrix} 1 & & \\ & 1 & \\ & & 1 \end{bmatrix}$
Nonorthogonal design:	$\begin{bmatrix} 2 & 0 & .5 \\ 0 & 1 & .5 \\ .5 & .5 & .75 \end{bmatrix}$	$\begin{bmatrix} 2 & 1 & -2 \\ 1 & 2 & -2 \\ -2 & -2 & 4 \end{bmatrix}$

The orthogonal design produces, with a sample half the size, an estimate half as accurate as the full factorial design—exactly what we would expect. By contrast, the nonorthogonal design produces an estimate of the coefficient of the third independent variable $\frac{1}{8}$ as accurate as the factorial design and $\frac{1}{4}$ as accurate as the orthogonal design. Notice that the estimates of the coefficients of the first and second independent variables are also damaged. In summary, nonorthogonal designs hurt the accuracy of regression estimates.

Appendix 13–F

ANOVA and Regression

Having seen how categorical variables can be introduced in regression, the astute (i.e., fanatical) reader may notice a similarity between ANOVA and regression with categorical variables. To make clear the general equivalence, consider again the problem from Chapter 12 of the effect of package color on sales:

Advertising Strategy	*Package Color* A	B	C
I	14	8	8
	10	14	6
II	11	3	5
	9	7	1

These data can be analyzed via regression by first creating a data set with dummy variables to represent the colors and strategies:

$$D_1 = 1 \text{ if package color} = \text{A}, 0 \text{ otherwise}$$

$$D_2 = 1 \text{ if package color} = \text{B}, 0 \text{ otherwise}$$

$$D_3 = 1 \text{ if advertising strategy} = \text{I}, 0 \text{ otherwise}$$

The simple two-way without interaction model can then be estimated from:

$$Y = B_0 + B_1D_1 + B_2D_2 + B_3D_3$$

If both B_1 and B_2 are not significantly different from zero, the package color doesn't matter. Similarly, if B_3 equals zero, the advertising strategy has no impact on sales. We can also add interaction terms (D_1D_3, D_2D_3) to parallel the two-way with interaction model:

$$Y = B_0 + B_1D_1 + B_2D_2 + B_3D_3 + B_4(D_1D_3) + B_5(D_2D_3)$$

Here, if B_4 and B_5 equal zero, then no significant interactions exist.

We can then perform ANOVA-like analysis of the following types:

ANOVA Model	*Regression Equivalent*
"One-way" color only	$Y = B_0 + B_1D_1 + B_2D_2$
"One-way" advertising only	$Y = B_0 + B_1D_3$
"Two-way" without interaction	$Y = B_0 + B_1D_1 + B_2D_2 + B_3D_3$
"Two-way" with interactions	$Y = B_0 + B_1D_1 + B_2D_2 + B_3D_3$ $+ B_4D_1D_3 + B_5D_2D_3$

The model of two-way with interactions will exactly predict the group means as follows:

Advertising Strategy	*Color*		
	A	*B*	*C*
I	$B_0 + B_1 + B_3 + B_4$	$B_0 + B_2 + B_3 + B_5$	$B_0 + B_3$
II	$B_0 + B_1$	$B_0 + B_2$	B_0

"Standard" dummy variable coding (1–0) requires interpretation of the coefficients as the mean difference between the category of the dummy and the category which is omitted. Hence, in this example, the coefficient of D_1 is interpreted as the difference in means between color A and color C (here, $11 - 5 = 6$).

It is also possible to use so-called effect coding. This codes each dummy 1, 0, or -1 where the dummies are coded -1 if the variable falls in the omitted category. Here, if color C is used, D_1 and D_2 are coded -1 instead of the standard 0. The advantage of effect coding is that the resulting coefficients can be interpreted directly as the effect of the particular dummy variable (i.e., the difference in means for that category from the grand mean). Thus, the coefficient of D_1 becomes the difference between the mean of color A and the grand mean (here $11 - 8 = 3$).

TABLE 13F–1 Coding Schemes

I. Dummy variable coding: Raw data.

	Y	D_1	D_2	D_3	$D_1 D_3$	$D_2 D_3$
1	14	1	0	1	1	0
2	8	0	1	1	0	1
3	8	0	0	1	0	0
4	10	1	0	1	1	0
5	14	0	1	1	0	1
6	6	0	0	1	0	0
7	11	1	0	0	0	0
8	3	0	1	0	0	0
9	5	0	0	0	0	0
10	9	1	0	0	0	0
11	7	0	1	0	0	0
12	1	0	0	0	0	0

II. Effect Coding: Raw data.

	Y	D_1	D_2	D_3	$D_1 D_3$	$D_2 D_3$
1	14	1	0	1	1	0
2	8	0	1	1	0	1
3	8	−1	−1	1	−1	−1
4	10	1	0	1	1	0
5	14	0	1	1	0	1
6	6	−1	−1	1	−1	−1
7	11	1	0	−1	−1	0
8	3	0	1	−1	0	−1
9	5	−1	−1	−1	1	1
10	9	1	0	−1	−1	0
11	7	0	1	−1	0	−1
12	1	−1	−1	−1	1	1

III. Dummy variables: Group means.

Y	D_1	D_2	D_3
12	1	0	1
11	0	1	1
7	0	0	1
10	1	0	0
5	0	1	0
3	0	0	0

IV. Effect coding: Group means.

Y	D_1	D_2	D_3
12	1	0	1
11	0	1	1
7	−1	−1	1
10	1	0	−1
5	0	1	−1
3	−1	−1	−1

TABLE 13F–2 ANOVA via Regression

Column effect model color only (raw data):

	Dummy Variable Coding		Effect Coding	
	Coefficient	*t*	*Coefficient*	*t*
D_1: package color A	6	2.52	3	2.18
D_2: package color B	3	1.26	0	0
Constant	5		8	
R^2	.41		.41	
F	3.18		3.18	
ESS	72		72	
TSS	174		174	

Color and advertising without interactions:

	Raw Data				Group Means			
	Dummy Variable Coding		Effect Coding		Dummy Variable Coding		Effect Coding	
	Coefficient	*t*	*Coefficient*	*t*	*Coefficient*	*t*	*Coefficient*	*t*
D_1: package color A	6	3.27	3	2.83	6	4.24	3	3.67
D_2: package color B	3	1.63	0	0	3	2.12	0	0
D_3: advertising strategy	4	2.67	2	2.67	4	3.46	2	3.46
Constant	3		8		3		8	
R^2	.69		.69		.94		.94	
F	5.93		5.93		10.00		10.00	
ESS	120		120		60		60	
TSS	174		174		64		64	

Color and advertising with interactions (raw data):

	Dummy Variable Coding		Effect Coding	
	Coefficient	*t*	*Coefficient*	*t*
D_1: package color A	7	2.53	3	2.65
D_2: package color B	2	0.72	0	0
D_3: advertising strategy	4	1.44	2	2.50
$D_1 D_3$	−2	−0.51	−1	−0.88
$D_2 D_3$	2	0.51	1	.88
Constant	3		8	
R^2	.74		.74	
F	3.34		3.34	
ESS	128		128	
TSS	174		174	

Furthermore, it is possible to perform analysis directly on the group means, instead of the individual observations, as long as the interactions are not used. (If they are, there are no degrees of freedom left and the regression cannot be run.) This will not affect the coefficients if the cell sizes are equal, but will increase the R^2 by removing the within cell variation from consideration.

Alternative coding schemes for raw and group mean data are shown in Table 13F–1. To demonstrate the essential equivalence of ANOVA and regression, several models are shown in Table 13F–2. The "interested reader" can verify that the results are equivalent by simple inspection.

In some cases, each subject (e.g., store, etc.) provides multiple observations, a so-called repeated measure design. One can incorporate this "subject" effect into the analysis by using dummy variables. By using a separate dummy variable for each subject (which basically treats subjects as another factor in the ANOVA), we can both estimate their effects and remove the effect from the assessment of the impact of other variables (e.g., color and advertising) from the error term, thus making the finding of statistically significant results more likely.

Unfortunately, dealing with a large number of subjects requires a large number of dummy variables. As an imperfect but useful substitute, one can compute the average value of the dependent variable for each subject and then include this average value in the regression (e.g., Sales = f(color, advertising, store average). This average variable will then remove much of the subject effect from the error term in the regression. This approach is useful, however, only if each subject is exposed to all the possible treatments.

Appendix 13–G

Increasing the Precision of Estimated Regression Coefficients

The precision of estimated regression coefficients is related to the standard deviation of the ith regression coefficient. This standard deviation (S_{B_i}) has two basic components: the standard error of the regression ($S_{Y.X}$) and an element in the inverse of the covariance matrix of the independent (X) variables $(X'X)^{-1}$. The following scheme summarizes methods for improving the efficiency of estimated coefficients:

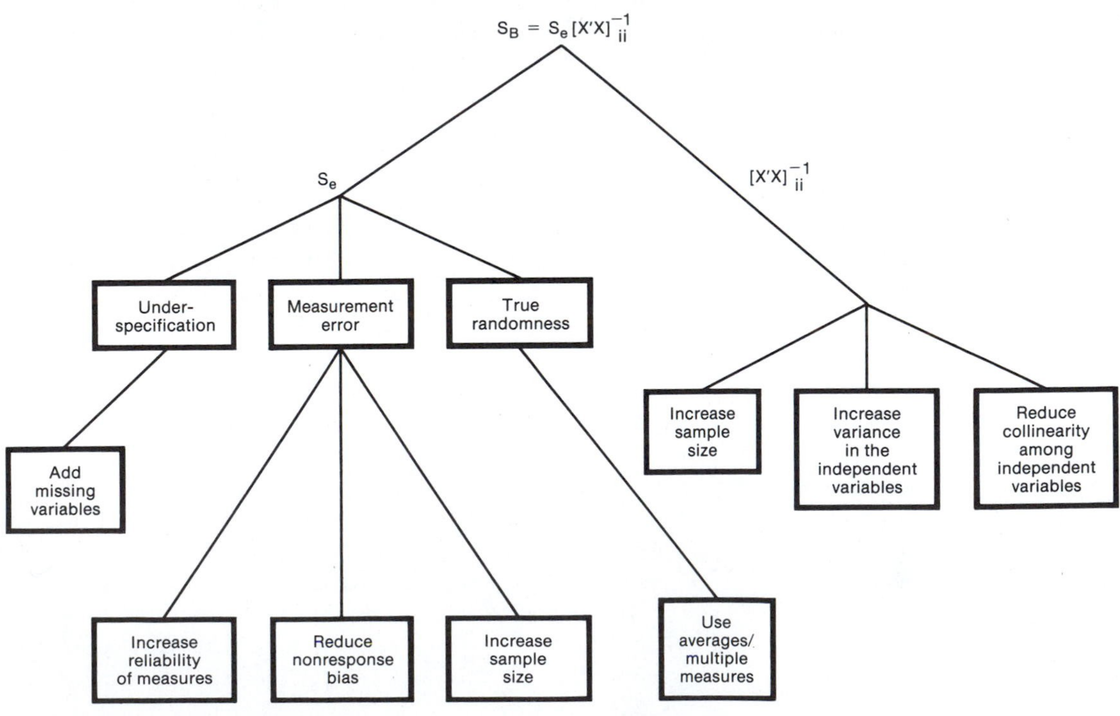

Appendix 13–H

Testing for Significant Improvement

A larger regression model (one which contains more parameters/variables) will outperform a simpler one in terms of R^2. When the larger model contains the smaller one, it is possible to test for the statistical significance of the improvement due to adding the variables. This appendix presents two examples of such tests.

1. TESTING FOR THE SIGNIFICANCE OF A SET OF VARIABLES

In many situations, it is desirable to examine whether a category of variables as a group adds significantly to prediction. For example, one might wonder whether adding general attitudes or values improves prediction over simply using demographics. Because the values may be correlated among themselves as well as with some of the demographics, collinearity makes examination of the individual t statistics of these variables inadequate to determine whether they add anything.

What is needed is to examine the set of variables as a whole. This is done by running the analysis with and without the set of variables as a group and comparing the predictive power of the models/analyses. Consider the following example: Based on a sample of 1,000, we predicted sales of a product based on seven demographic variables alone with an R^2 of .1. When we added 10 values, R^2 increased to .15. In this case, we can compare the R^2s and note that we increase it 5 percent (or alternatively, that we explained 5 percent of the 90 percent which needed to be explained).

To see if the difference/improvement is statistically significant, we compare the errors in prediction, assuming we use both the seven demographic and the 10 values variables with the improvement in prediction resulting from adding the 10 values variables. Specifically, we build a test statistic (index):

$$\frac{\left(\sum\limits_{\substack{\text{Demographics}\\\text{only}}} \text{errors}^2 - \sum\limits_{\substack{\text{Demographics}\\\text{plus values}}} \text{errors}^2\right) \Big/ 10}{\left(\sum\limits_{\substack{\text{Demographics}\\\text{plus values}}} \text{errors}^2\right) \Big/ (1000 - 17 - 1)}$$

or equivalently:

$$\frac{\left(R^2_{\substack{\text{Demographics}\\\text{plus values}}} - R^2_{\substack{\text{Demographics}\\\text{only}}}\right) \Big/ 10}{\left(1 - R^2_{\substack{\text{Demographics}\\\text{plus values}}}\right) \Big/ 982}$$

This index follows the F distribution with 10 and 982 degrees of freedom. If the test statistic is greater than the value in the F table, then we say that the variables added significantly improve prediction. Here, the test statistic =

$$\frac{.15 - .10/10}{.85/982} = 5.78$$

Since $F_{.05,10,\infty} = 1.83$, this difference is statistically significant at the .05 level. This test, sometimes referred to as a *nested model* test, is in general given by:

$$\frac{\sum\limits_{\substack{\text{Nested}\\\text{model}}} \text{errors}^2 - \sum\limits_{\substack{\text{Full}\\\text{model}}} \text{errors}^2 \Big/ k}{\sum\limits_{\substack{\text{Full}\\\text{model}}} \text{error}^2 \Big/ (n - m - 1)}$$

where

n = number of observations.

m = number of parameters (variables) in the full model.

k = number of parameters added to the nested (reduced, smaller) model by the full model.

Equivalently, this can be written as:

$$\frac{\left(R^2_{\text{Full model}} - R^2_{\text{Nested model}}\right) \Big/ k}{\left(1 - R^2_{\text{Full model}}\right) \Big/ (n - m - 1)}$$

2. TESTING FOR DIFFERENCES ACROSS SEGMENTS

In many cases you may be interested in whether a model applies to all segments or whether the segments differ. For example, you may wonder if the impact of price (X_1) and shopping convenience (X_2) in a regression model,

$$Y = B_0 + B_1(\text{Price}) + B_2(\text{Shopping convenience})$$

are the same for low-, middle-, and high-income customers:

Total Sample	*Income Segments* *Low*	*Middle*	*High*
B_0	B_{L0}	B_{M0}	B_{H0}
B_1	B_{L1}	B_{M1}	B_{H1}
B_2	B_{L2}	B_{M2}	B_{H2}

Obviously, you need to run the analyses for the three segments separately and then examine the results. Beyond eyeballing the results (a fairly imprecise approach), if you also run the model for the entire sample the following test can be constructed:

Let:

$$\sum_{\text{In segments}} \text{errors}^2 = \sum_{\substack{\text{Low-income}\\ \text{regression}}} \text{errors}^2 + \sum_{\substack{\text{Middle-income}\\ \text{regression}}} \text{errors}^2 + \sum_{\substack{\text{High-income}\\ \text{regression}}} \text{errors}^2$$

Then we can compare the errors in the separate models with the errors in the model run on the full sample:

$$\frac{\left.\sum_{\substack{\text{Full sample}\\ \text{model}}} \text{errors}^2 - \sum_{\substack{\text{In}\\ \text{segments}}} \text{errors}^2 \middle/ (g-1)k\right.}{\left.\sum_{\substack{\text{In}\\ \text{segments}}} \text{errors}^2 \middle/ (n-gk-1)\right.}$$

where

g = number of segments.
k = number of parameters in the model.

Here, $g = 3$ and $k = 3$. Thus, if the sum of the errors squared were 20, 30, and 15 within the three segment regressions and 100 in the full sample regression, we would have:

$$\frac{100-(20+30+15)/2(3)}{(20+30+15)/(n-9-1)}$$

If the total sample size were 130, this would become:

$$\frac{35/6}{65/120} = 10.77$$

Since $F_{.05,6,120} = 2.18$, this would indicate that the segments were significantly different.

Another way to run this test is to use dummy variables in what is sometimes called a *varying parameter model* and perform a nested model test. First, create two dummy variables: Z_1 if the the person is middle income and Z_2 if he or she has high income. Then run the following regressions:

Full sample model:

$$Y = B_0 + B_1X_1 + B_2X_2$$

Segment model:

$$Y = B_0 + B_0'Z_1 + B_0''Z_2 + B_1X_1 + B_1'(Z_1X_1)$$
$$+B_1''(Z_2X_2) + B_2X_2 + B_2'(Z_1X_2) + B_2''(Z_2X_2)$$

Now, since the segmented model nests (includes) the full sample model, simply compare the results from the two regressions via a nested model test;

$$\frac{\left(R^2_{\substack{\text{Segmented}\\\text{model}}} - R^2_{\substack{\text{Full sample}\\\text{model}}}\right) \Big/ 6}{\left(1 - R^2_{\substack{\text{Segmented}\\\text{model}}}\right) \Big/ n - 9 - 1}$$

Chapter 14

Grouping Procedures

In the past two chapters, various procedures for predicting a criterion variable have been discussed. In this chapter, the focus turns to grouping things—variables, customers, and so forth—together. The purpose of grouping procedures is not prediction but simplification.

The desire to categorize large numbers of data points into a more manageable classification scheme is a basic human trait. It is also a practical necessity for many marketing and marketing research problems. It is simply not feasible to consider each user of toothpaste separately or to use 317 variables in most analyses or presentations. Large amounts of data need to be reduced into more manageable forms. This chapter discusses factor analysis and cluster analysis in some detail, two procedures which attempt to simplify data.

FACTOR ANALYSIS

Basic Notion

The basic purpose of factor analysis is to group together variables which are highly correlated (and thus, to some extent redundant). There are two basic reasons for doing this. First, there is the desire for simplification. For example, while it is possible to analyze 67 variables in detail, it would be much easier, both to analyze and communicate the study, if only 15 variables were used. One use of factor analysis is to reduce the 67 variables to 15 with the minimum possible loss of information (and the resulting low level of collinearity among the 15 variables retained for further analysis). The second reason for using factor analysis is to uncover an underlying

TABLE 14–1 Hypothetical Correlations among Four Variables

	Variable			
Variable	*1*	*2*	*3*	*4*
1	1	.9	.7	.2
2		1	.8	.05
3			1	.1
4				1

structure in the data. This use of factor analysis assumes that the 67 variables are manifestations of a small number (e.g., 10) of key but unmeasured constructs. It then attempts to deduce what the underlying constructs are by examining the relations among the 67 measured variables. These two uses for factor analysis are, though closely related, sufficiently different that they place different emphasis on how the results are interpreted and used. Specifically, the first use leads to a relatively mechanistic use of factor analysis as a means to an end and uses the factors as input into another analysis (e.g., regression) or decision (e.g., questionnaire design). By contrast, the second use treats the results of the factor analysis as the end itself and focuses on interpreting the factors themselves.

In marketing research, the major use of grouping together redundant variables is to help the researcher select a smaller number of variables for further analysis (without excluding variables which contain a substantial amount of information not available from the reduced set of variables). The reduced set of variables are then used (*a*) to more efficiently analyze the results of a given study by reducing the number of variables considered or (*b*) to reduce the amount of data needed in subsequent studies by reducing the number of pieces of information (e.g., questions) collected.

Consider the correlation matrix of Table 14–1. Here we have four variables, which were questions on a pilot study. Assume we need to reduce these four questions to two questions (there is only room for two questions on the next wave of the study or the computer algorithm we want to use can only handle two variables).

The best way to simplify is to have a theory dictating which variables to retain. Absent theory, common sense suggests that I discard those variables which give me the least additional information value if retained. To do this, I might find out which variables are most correlated with each other. In this example, variables 1, 2, and 3 all seem fairly highly correlated with each other, and 4 seems to be different. Hence, I might classify 1, 2, and 3 as type A variables and 4 as a type B variable, and then pick a representative of each type. What factor analysis essentially does (when all the theory is

TABLE 14–2 Hypothetical Two-Factor Assignment Table

	Factor	
Variable	*1*	*2*
1	1	0
2	1	0
3	1	0
4	0	1

TABLE 14–3 Sample Correlation Matrix

	Variable			
Variable	*1*	*2*	*3*	*4*
1	1	1	1	0
2	1	1	1	0
3	1	1	1	0
4	0	0	0	1

stripped aside) is to group together those variables which are highly correlated.

The key output of a factor analysis is what might be called an *assignment matrix*. This matrix indicates which variables belong to each group. In the previous example, the suggested assignment pattern is given in Table 14–2, where a "1" indicates that the variable belongs in the factor and a "0" indicates it does not. Actually, the world is never quite as simple as this example indicates. The previous assignment matrix implies the assignment was perfectly clear-cut and would result from a correlation matrix like that in Table 14–3. The actual correlation matrix showed variable 4 to be

TABLE 14–4 Two-Factor Assignment Matrix

	Factor	
Variable	*1*	*2*
1	.9	.02
2	.92	.05
3	.81	.09
4	.11	.93

somewhat correlated with variables 1, 2, and 3 and variables 1, 2, and 3 less than perfectly correlated with each other. Therefore, a more tentative assignment scheme is likely to result, such as that in Table 14–4.

As we proceed to discuss factor analysis in a more formal manner, it is important to recall that its major output will be an assignment matrix of the type just discussed.

Factor Analysis: Model

The model underlying factor analysis is that observed data (Xs) are really "produced" by some underlying and unobserved factors (fs). This model is essentially adapted from psychology. The objective in psychology is often to understand the structure of the data (e.g., what are the basic determinants of individual scores on an aptitude test), and the method deduces the structure indirectly by naming the factors (e.g., quantitative ability, analytical skill, etc.). Believing this model is not necessary for using factor analysis for some purposes, such as removing redundant variables. Nonetheless, much of the "flavor" of the interpretation of factor analysis for both construct derivation and variable reduction purposes comes from this model. The basic form of the model is:

Observed value of the kth person on the ith variable = f(kth person's scores on the underlying factors and a random element)

Put mathematically, this becomes:

$$X_{ik} = \lambda_{i1} f_{1k} + \lambda_{i2} f_{2k} + \cdots + \lambda_{im} f_{mk} + e_{ik} \tag{14.1}$$

where

X_{ik} = value of variable i for the kth observation.
f_{jk} = value of the jth factor for the kth observation (commonly called *factor scores*).
λ_{ij} = relation of the ith variable with the jth common factor and there are m factors and p variables, $m \leq p$.

The λ_{ij}s (often called *loadings*) indicate how the underlying constructs (factors) are related to the measured variables. More specifically, the loadings are the correlations between the factors and the variables. The loadings, thus, form the assignment matrix (Table 14–5).

TABLE 14–5 Assignment (Loading) Matrix

	Factor			
Variable	*1*	*2*	...	*m*
1	λ_{11}	λ_{12}	...	λ_{1m}
2	λ_{21}	λ_{22}	...	λ_{2m}
⋮	⋮	⋮		⋮
p	λ_{p1}	λ_{p2}	...	λ_{pm}

How a Factor Analysis Program Works

The purpose of factor analysis is to derive a "good" set of λs (assignments). A good set of λs has two basic properties. First, the λs must produce Xs which closely match the observed Xs. Second, the λs must clearly indicate which variables belong with which factors. The problem is that both the factor values and the loadings are unknown. A variety of approaches to deriving the λs can be imagined, including the inelegant (and inefficient) method of trial-and-error guessing. The most common approach, however, requires two basic steps.

1. The Principal Components Are Calculated. Principal components (PCs) are derived from the original Xs by the following model:

$$PC_j = a_{j1}X_1 + a_{j2}X_2 + \cdots + a_{jp}X_p \tag{14.2}$$

where

PC_j = jth principal component.
a_{ji} = the coefficient relating the ith variable to the jth component.

These components are uniquely derived mathematically (see Appendix 14–A), so the first contains as much of the total information in all the p original variables as possible, the second (which is independent of the first) contains as much as possible of the remaining information, and so forth. (In this context, the information in a variable is operationalized as its variance.) Graphically, the first principal component can be viewed as finding a line (plane) which passes through the data so as to most spread out the observations (Figure 14–1). What principal components really do is change the p original variables into p components which are perfectly independent of each other. The greater the collinearity among the original variables, the more of the original variance is accounted for by the first principal component.

It is possible to use the a_{ji} values as a basis for assigning variables to groups. Unfortunately, these results tend to be fairly muddled, with no

FIGURE 14–1 Principal Components of Two Variables

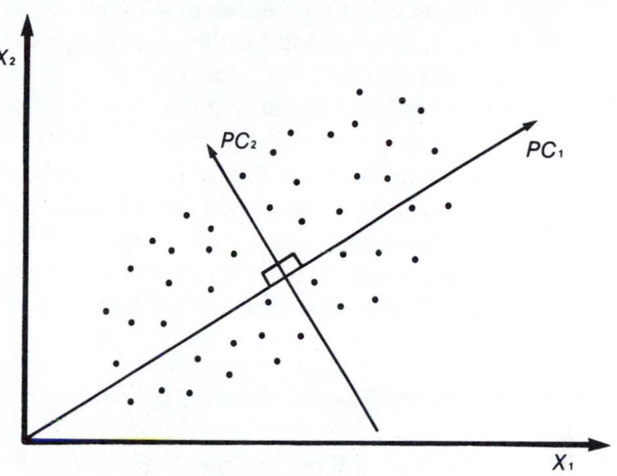

clear-cut pattern of which variable belongs in which groups. For example, it is common to have most of the variables appear to be related to the first component. For this reason, a second step is used.

2. ***The Original Configuration Is Revised.*** Recall that the original goal was to achieve an assignment matrix which is clear in indicating which variables belong in which grouping (factor). Since the a_{ji}s in principal

FIGURE 14–2 Rotated Factors

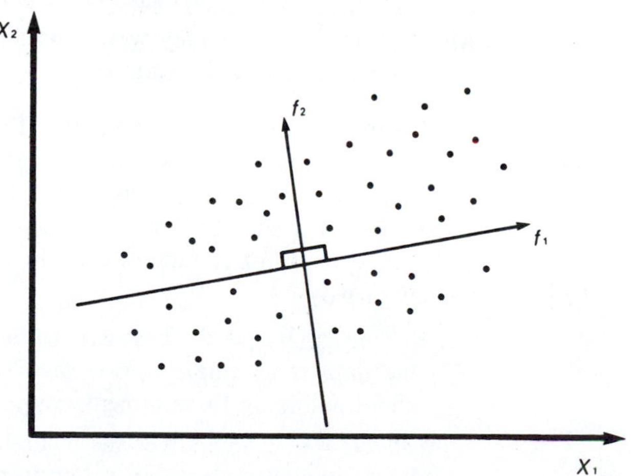

components are not very useful in this regard, the obvious solution is to "improve" them. The method for improving the results is to "massage" the original a_{ji}s so that the new values (λ_{ij}s) are numbers which are closer to 1 or 0. The method for this massaging is to rotate the original components in order to make the λ_{ij}s close to 1s or 0s. This rotation maintains the total information in the original components but reassigns it across the factors and makes interpretation of the factors easier.

Consider again Figure 14–1. By rotating the original components, we can achieve a picture like Figure 14–2. In both cases, the factors are orthogonal (independent) and explain (represent) the original data equally well; but in the rotated case, X_1 and factor 1 and X_2 and factor 2 go together, whereas in the unrotated case factors 1 and 2 both seem to contain both X_1 and X_2.

Using and Interpreting Factor Analysis

Having outlined the basic steps in factor analysis as it is commonly applied, it is now important to delineate what decisions the user makes and how the results are interpreted. The basic decisions are which variables to include, the number of factors to retain, which final solution to use, and naming the factors.

Which Variables to Include. A very important (but often overlooked) step is the selection of variables to be analyzed. Factor analysis can only reduce data present in the original variables; it cannot help indicate what important factors or variables have been omitted. Factor analysis also will reproduce obvious results. For example, if someone factor analyzed participation in two sports, consumption of two wines, and reading of two magazines, such as *Time* and *Newsweek*, he or she might get an interesting cross-fertilization (e.g., *Time*'s readers consume a certain kind of wine). More likely, however, they would obtain three factors: sports, wine consumption, and magazine readership.

Number of Factors to Retain. Principal components analysis produces one component for each variable. Rotating p components will reproduce the original p variables—hardly a simplified result. To be parsimonious, a smaller number of factors ($m < p$) must be retained. The question of how many factors exist in the data is settled in the following variety of ways:

Prior theory. By far the best way to determine how many factors exist in the data is to employ prior theory (e.g., a theory that people think about colors on three dimensions).

Available space. Sometimes the available space on a questionnaire or the limitations of a computer program or analytical procedure will dictate the maximum number of variables to retain.

Examining the results. When prior theory is unavailable (or questionable) as a guide, a researcher must resort to examining the data for a clue about how many factors exist. One approach is to use trial and error, finding the best solution for two factors, three factors, and so forth, and then choosing the solution which is most useful/felicitous/pleasing. Aside from the potential for researcher bias influencing the choice adversely, this method is not very efficient. A more mechanical approach is often desired.

A very common approach for determining the number of factors is to examine the eigenvalues (characteristic values) of the principal components solution. Recall that the principal components solution produced p components for p variables. As a bonus, the eigenvalues indicate what percent of the total variance is accounted for by each of the components. The percent of the variance accounted for by the jth component is given by:

$$\begin{array}{c}\text{Percent total variation in original} \\ p \text{ variables accounted for by } j\text{th} \\ \text{principal component}\end{array} = \frac{\text{Eigenvalue}_j}{\sum_{i=1}^{p} (\text{eigenvalue}_i)} \tag{14.3}$$

When (as is typically done) the correlation matrix is used as the basis for factoring, this becomes:

$$\frac{\text{Eigenvalue}_j}{\text{Number of variables}} \tag{14.4}$$

This formula allows the percent of total variance accounted for to be used as a criterion for determining the number of factors in several ways:

1. By requiring inclusion of enough factors to reach a certain level of total variance explained.

2. By requiring any factor to explain at least the amount of variance which a truly independent variable would explain. If all the original variables were independent, then each component (which would equal one variable) would explain $1/n$ percent of the total variance and have an eigenvalue equal to 1. This criterion is often known as the *eigenvalue-greater-than-one* rule and tends to produce good (interpretable) results.[1]

---

[1] An interesting empirical phenomenon which often occurs in survey research data is that one third of the components will have eigenvalues greater than one, and this one third of the components will account for two thirds of the variance in the original variables. For example, if there are 39 original variables, one would typically get about 13 eigenvalues greater than one. This "rule" also provides a tipoff to the amount of collinearity in the data since one third of the components accounting for 85 percent of the variance means unusually high collinearity, and one third accounting for 50 percent indicates atypically low intercorrelations among the original variables.

TABLE 14–6 Eight-Variable Eigenvalue Analysis

Eigen-value	*Percent of Total Variance Explained*	*Cumulative Percent Explained*
4.0	4/8 = 50%	50
1.2	1.2/8 = 15%	65
.8	.8/8 = 10%	75
.7	.7/8 = 8.75%	83.75
.6	.6/8 = 7.5%	91.25
.4	.4/8 = 5%	96.25
.2	.2/8 = 2.5%	98.75
.1	.1/8 = 1.25%	100
8	100%	

3. By requiring each subsequent factor to explain a substantial and/or significant amount of the residual variance. This sequential testing approach can be done in many ways (Morrison, 1976; Lehmann and Morrison, 1977) but is not widely used in marketing research.

To see how these schemes work, consider the example involving eight variables of Table 14–6. Notice that if I require 70 percent of the variance to be explained, I would use three factors. On the other hand, if I use the eigenvalue-greater-than-one rule, I would use two factors. If I expect the variance explained by a factor to be substantially bigger than that explained by the subsequent factor(s), I might use only one factor. Hence, the correct number of factors is not always easy to deduce.

Which Final Solution to Use. The first step is to decide on how many factors exist. Once this is done, many programs perform an iterative procedure called *principal factoring*, which modifies the principle components to account for the fact that a given number of factors explains less than 100 percent of the variance in the original variables. These components are then rotated to improve interpretation of the factors.

A variety of rotation schemes exist for transforming the original solution into a more clear-cut assignment matrix (commonly called *simple structure*). The major decision is whether the factors can be correlated (in which case they can be rotated obliquely) or are independent (in which case they must be rotated orthogonally). For the occasional/typical user, orthogonal rotation is probably the best choice. Several orthogonal rotation schemes exist, including quartimax, varimax, and so forth. These schemes provide a criterion for rotation which places a premium on having the loadings (λ_{ij}s) close to one or zero. Varimax is the most commonly used, and orthogonal varimax rotation is the default option in most canned computer programs. Put differently, the novice user should simply look at the rotated loadings.

Naming the Factors. It is common practice to try to name factors. This is done by seeing what the variables which load heavily on the factor have in common. Exactly what "load heavily" means is somewhat vague and really depends on the study. However, many people choose an arbitrary cutoff level, such as .5, for the loadings so each variable tends to load on exactly one factor. For example, a factor which includes income, education, and occupational status might be called *well-offness*. The naming of factors is quite subjective but also fun and occasionally produces an interesting insight. Moreover, in some cases, such as segment development, the names themselves may be the key result of the analysis.

Nutritional Example

One of the questions on the now infamous food survey dealt with actual consumption of 30 foods. Specifically, frequency of consumption was asked for these foods (section I, question 14). An obvious question which arises is whether there are patterns of consumption which occur across people. To examine this notion, a factor analysis of the 30 variables was performed. The basic input data were the reported consumption of the 30 foods for the 940 respondents. The actual output appears in Appendix 14–B.

There were seven eigenvalues greater than one, and the first seven factors accounted for 49.2 percent of the variance in the original 30 variables. This indicated a generally low level of collinearity among the variables. These seven variables were then rotated to produce a more interpretable grouping pattern. The results are shown in Table 14–7. To name the factors, we examine those variables with the largest loadings on each factor. The factors appear to be:

1. Junk/convenience foods.
2. Calories/desserts.
3. Skim versus whole milk.
4. Meat substitutes.
5. Alcohol.
6. Beef.
7. Margarine versus butter.

Exactly what this means is unclear. The skim versus whole milk and margarine versus butter factors represent obvious conscious choices. The junk/convenience food, meat substitute, and beef factors are also obvious groupings, as are the desserts. The fact that alcoholic beverages seem to have their own factor is only mildly interesting.

The communalities indicate the portion of the variation in each variable accounted for by the six factors. The communalities are the sum of the squared loadings of a variable with each of the factors (e.g., $.32 = (-.12)^2$

TABLE 14–7 Food Consumption Factor Loadings

	Factor							
Food	*1*	*2*	*3*	*4*	*5*	*6*	*7*	*Communality*
Canned fruit	−.12	.46	.04	.06	.00	.30	−.02	.32
Fresh fruit	−.10	.41	.22	.15	.23	.30	−.15	.41
Bread	.07	.52	−.10	.09	.13	.15	.15	.36
Rice	.05	.17	−.00	.16	.34	.10	.03	.18
Butter	.10	.13	.18	.00	.12	.04	−.49	.32
Margarine	.11	.31	.02	.00	.23	.13	.65	.60
Cheese	.13	.18	−.00	.11	.35	.21	.08	.23
Ice cream	.21	.51	−.05	.01	.08	.05	−.06	.32
Whole milk	.07	.21	−.67	.09	−.02	.05	−.06	.52
Skim milk	.07	.15	.70	.18	.03	.08	.13	.58
Snack foods (potato chips, pretzels)	.62	.11	−.07	.11	.04	.02	.04	.41
Desserts	.22	.58	−.06	.06	.09	−.08	−.01	.40
Alcholic beverages	.14	−.12	−.04	.07	.52	−.01	−.04	.31
Soft drinks	.56	−.06	−.03	.06	.01	.16	−.04	.35
Fish	.00	.16	.14	.41	.34	.22	−.13	.40
Cold cereal	−.03	.43	.03	.14	.02	.07	.05	.22
Frozen vegetables	.05	.18	.13	.05	.31	.27	−.01	.22
Fresh vegetables	−.09	.30	.10	.11	.32	.45	−.04	.43
Canned vegetables	.18	.18	.02	.28	−.04	.39	−.11	.30
Poultry	.10	.15	.00	.41	.26	.30	−.01	.36
Beef (hamburger)	.25	.25	.00	.25	.14	.46	−.12	.43
Steak or roast beef	.24	.09	−.03	.00	.21	.48	−.01	.34
Pork	.32	.12	−.09	.01	.15	.36	−.05	.28
Tuna fish	.20	.01	.08	.49	.25	.09	−.04	.36
Frozen dinners	.30	.06	.03	.22	.07	−.03	.06	.15
Hot dogs	.33	.07	−.07	.38	−.04	.03	.06	.27
Coffee or tea	.04	.18	−.01	.09	.30	.21	.11	.19
Pasta	.43	.14	−.01	.21	.25	.14	.08	.33
Food of fast-food restaurants	.66	.02	.10	.04	−.17	.10	−.10	.50
Food at regular restaurants	.30	.12	.14	−.11	.34	.15	−.15	.30

$+ (.46)^2 + (.04)^2 + (.06)^2 + (.00)^2 + (.30)^2 + (-.02)^2)$. Notice that some of the communalities (portion of variance in each of the variables accounted for by the factors) are extremely low, indicating for example that only 15 percent of the variance in consumption of frozen dinners is accounted for by the seven factors. This suggests that either (*a*) the data are very noisy/unreliable or (*b*) consumption of one food is relatively independent of consumption of other foods.

Uses of Factor Analysis

Factor analysis is a very flexible tool. Nonetheless, there are two major uses: reducing variables to a more manageable number and discovering constructs/variable groups.

Reducing Variables to a More Manageable Number. Early in the study of a problem, a large number of variables (e.g., 70) may appear as candidates for study. Yet such a large number will encumber both survey and model alike. There is a strong desire, therefore, to reduce the 70 variables to a more manageable number. The obvious place to start is to require the variables to be theoretically/logically useful and measurable. Beyond that, it is generally agreed that reducing redundancy is an efficient way to improve the variable set. Since factor analysis groups variables into factors so all the variables in a factor are correlated with each other, it is obviously a useful technique for this problem. The problem comes in deciding how to eliminate variables. There are at least three major approaches:

Pick one variable to represent each factor. The representative should be both a good variable (well measured and understood) and have a high loading on the factor. It is also important to include variables which do not load highly on any factor, since they are unique/unrelated to the other variables. This is the easiest approach and by no means inferior to the more complicated methods.

Build an index based on the major variables on each factor. This index could be a simple sum or some weighted combination of the "big loading" variables. The index method is basically a way to increase reliability by the use of multiple measures of a construct.

Use the factor scores. The scores of each observation on the underlying factors can be estimated and used to represent each factor (see Appendix 14–A). This result can guarantee truly independent variables. Unfortunately, it does not reduce variables to be measured for future studies, since it requires all of them to be included in the score. It also is harder to interpret a factor score than a single variable or a simple sum of two or three variables.

To see how these three methods are used, consider the six-variable example in Appendix 14–A, summarized in Table 14–8. Here the three approaches might be applied as follows:

1. Representative method: Choose husband's education to represent factor 1 and family size to represent factor 2. .

2. Index method: Use total education (wife's education plus husband's education) to represent factor 1 and an index equal to family size plus

TABLE 14–8 Factor Loadings

Variable	Factor 1	Factor 2
Education of wife	.71	.08
Education of husband	.86	.16
Age	−.39	−.40
Income	.53	.37
Family size	.07	.88
Weekly food expenditure	.19	.64

weekly food expenditure (converted to comparable scales) to represent factor 2.

3. Factor score method: Use the factor score coefficients to get:

$$\text{Factor 1 score} = .26(\text{education 1}) + .64(\text{education 2}) - .05(\text{age}) + .13(\text{income}) - .16(\text{family size}) + .01(\text{food expenditure}).$$

$$\text{Factor 2 score} = -.06(\text{education 1}) - .07(\text{education 2}) - .04(\text{age}) + .10(\text{income}) + .73(\text{family size}) + .20(\text{food expenditure}).$$

It is common to use these factor scores as independent variables in a regression to predict some other variable. Using the six original variables we would have:

$$Y = B_0 + B_1X_1 + B_2X_2 + \cdots + B_6X_6$$

Now we get $Y = E_0 + E_1f_1 + E_2f_2$. Using the factor scores reduces collinearity, and thus we are more certain about the regression coefficients. Unfortunately, we are also now unsure what the variables are (Acito and Anderson, 1986). Given the choice between known variables and uncertain coefficients and unknown variables and certain coefficients, many people prefer known variables.

It is also worth pointing out that using the representative method of variable selection is likely to create an omitted variable/specification problem. Assume that I use only husband's education in a regression, but that the wife's education is really the key variable. In this case, the coefficient of husband's education could well lead me to falsely conclude that it is the key variable. Hence, all three methods reduce redundancy—but not without

FIGURE 14–3 Alternative Ways to Deal with Collinear Variables in Regression

Approach	*Model*	*Pros*	*Cons*
Use all variables	$Y = B_0 + B_1X_1 + B_2X_2 + B_3X_3 + B_4X_4 + B_5X_5 + B_6X_6$	Easy to do	Collinearity, need all variables
Representative method	$Y = C_0 + C_1X_2 + C_2X_5$	Simple model	Omitted variable bias
Index method	$Y = D_0 + D_1(X_1 + X_2) + D_2(X_5 + X_6)$	Understandable	Still need 4 variables
Factor scores	$Y = E_0 + E_1(f_1) + E_2(f_2)$	Directly obtainable from computer analysis	Identity of fs unclear No reduction in variables

cost. The regressions run using each of these approaches compared to simply including all six original variables in the equation are shown in Figure 14–3. While none of the methods is universally the best, the index method often proves the most useful.

In using factor analysis to reduce a data set, two other points are crucial. First, if there is a key variable, it is often desirable to retain several variables which are closely related to it. In the six-variable case just mentioned, assume we were interested in explaining food expenditures. In that case, we would keep all variables which loaded heavily on the same factor with it: family size, income, and age. (Actually, a more efficient procedure would be to include all variables which had a simple correlation with food expenditure above some cutoff level.) Second, there is nothing inherently important about the first few factors. They are first because they represent a large number of redundant variables, not because those variables are important or useful per se.

Discovering Constructs / Variable Groups. A major use of factor analysis is to uncover a set of factors which are interpretable and contribute to understanding. Put differently, a researcher can try to name the factors and then see if these names give any insight into a problem. This is a search for an "ah-ha" phenomenon, where a result leads to fairly immediate enlightenment. Recognizing that the factors are bound by the original variables and, thus, in no sense guaranteed to include all important constructs, this "soft" use of factor analysis is both cheap and potentially rewarding.

Confirmatory Factor Analysis

This chapter has focused on the use of factor analysis to discover patterns of redundancy. It is also possible to use something known as confirmatory (as opposed to exploratory) factor analysis to examine whether a prior expectation of the grouping is possible (often using the LISREL package). This essentially requires predicting the assignment (loading) matrix and seeing how well it fits the data. The procedure is not widely used in applied research—partly due to the lack of strong prior expectations—and consequently it will not be discussed further.

A Product Attribute Rating Example

This example involves the ratings given to a particular new small car on 10 product attributes. The data were collected as part of the monitoring of the introduction of a new car. The purpose of this analysis was to see the underlying structure of these ratings so the consumers' basic choice criteria could be understood. Put differently, the question was whether there were really 10 separate attributes of the car. The first three eigenvalues were 5.15, 1.14, and .86; and the first three factors accounted for 71.4 percent of the variance. The rotated loadings matrix is shown in Table 14–9. These three factors tend to delineate "style and drivability," "price," and "resale value" as the three major categories of these car attributes. (When only two factors were rotated, the "price" and "resale value" factors were combined.) Interestingly, the same basic split between style and driving attributes and economy/price attributes occurred for eight different small cars and four

TABLE 14–9 Car Attribute Loading Matrix

	Factor			
Attributes	*1*	*2*	*3*	*Communality*
Resale value	.13	.12	.91	.850
Gas economy	.29	.73	.26	.688
Value for money	.42	.58	.50	.756
Exterior appearance	.74	.04	.44	.736
Easy and fun to drive	.65	.38	.15	.586
Easy maintenance	.43	.52	.41	.618
Reliability and construction	.67	.21	.51	.752
Pickup	.77	.18	.15	.652
Inexpensive	.07	.89	−.03	.793
Features	.81	.21	.02	.706
				7.144

samples of consumers over four waves of data collection. (In all, the factor analyses produced a four-inch pile of computer output and, as a side benefit, a lifetime supply of scrap paper.) Thus, these two factors appear to be enduring, rather than transitory. Incidentally, the same two factors could have been derived by examination of the simple correlations among pairs of attributes.

A Lifestyle Example

Another example of a use of factor analysis involved a study of lifestyle measures (Villani and Lehmann, 1975). A set of 504 housewives had been asked to indicate their degree of agreement with a series of 153 statements both in 1971 and 1973. One issue in the study was whether the structure/pattern of responses remained constant. To measure structure, factor analyses were employed.

Comparing the 1971 and 1973 factor analyses showed a high degree of stability in the structure. Using the eigenvalue-greater-than-one rule, both 1971 and 1973 data sets produced 51 factors accounting for 67 percent of the variance in the original 153 variables. The factors themselves also seemed to be quite stable. The first four factors (subjectively named "creative cook," "attitude toward television," "home cleanliness," and "religious practices and attitudes") were essentially identical (Table 14–10).[2] In all, 34 of the 51 factors appear to be unchanged in content (but did not necessarily appear in the same order). The 17 factors which do not match consisted of factors with only one or two variables in them and, hence, are inherently less stable. The conclusion one can draw from this is that there are underlying lifestyle patterns which do endure over a reasonable length of time. A similar finding of stability exists across geographic areas within the United States (Lesser and Hughes, 1986).

Fifty States Data Example

In previous analyses, it has been clear that various measures of a state (e.g., income, taxes) are correlated. To portray the relation among variables, a factor analysis was performed.[3] Three eigenvalues are greater than one and in total they account for $(5.05 + 2.26 + 1.46)/12 = 73.1$ percent of the

---

[2] Notice that all the signs in the fourth factor change between 1971 and 1973. Since the sign is arbitary (the 1971 factor might be called proreligious and the 1973 factor antireligious), this is unimportant.

[3] The results are taken from an SPSS run of type PA2.

TABLE 14–10 Lifestyle Factors

	Factor Loadings	
	1971	*1973*
Creative cook:		
I look for ways to prepare fancy meals	.62	.74
I like to try new recipes	.66	.62
I think of myself as a creative cook	.70	.69
I am more interested in new food products than most people	.56	.56
I like to make gourmet dishes	.70	.73
Attitude toward television:		
Televison has added a great deal of enjoyment to my life	.70	.69
I don't like watching television and so I rarely do	−.73	−.64
Television is a friendly companion when I am alone	.75	.62
I watch television to be entertained	.56	.66
I watch television more than I should	.53	.40
I like having television on while I do other things around the house	.57	.27
I watch television in order to quietly relax	.39	.67
I watch television to get away from the ordinary cares of the day	.28	.56
Home cleanliness:		
I try to wash the dishes promptly after each meal	.55	.62
I usually keep my house very neat and clean	.58	.68
I am uncomfortable when my house is not completely clean	.73	.66
My idea of housekeeping is "once over lightly"	−.55	−.66
A house should be dusted and polished at least three times a week	.51	.46
I usually have regular days for cleaning, cooking, and shopping	.51	.33
Religious practices and atitudes:		
I pray several times a week	.73	−.75
I go to church regularly	.78	−.80
Women should be allowed to have an abortion they feel necessary	−.56	.50

Source: Kathryn Villani and Donald Lehmann, "An Examination of the Stability of AIO Measures." Reprinted from *1975 Combined Proceedings*, Fall Conference, published by the American Marketing Association, 1975, p. 486.

variance in the original 12 variables. After various iterations and varimax rotation, the factor loading matrix is that of Table 14–11.

In naming the factors, it is useful to underline the largest loadings. This can entail picking an arbitrary cutoff or underlining the largest number in each row. Here, we chose to underline the loadings above .5. Examining the table, it is clear that the first factor is basically a size measure. This factor almost always appears when comparing regions or countries. (In fact, if none of the variables were on a per capita basis, this factor would be even more dominant.) The second factor is clearly a wealth factor and shows that, in 1975, the South was a relatively poor region. The third factor is

TABLE 14–11 Rotated Factor Matrix

	1	*2*	*3*	*Communality*
Income	.23	.77	.28	.73
Population	.99	.05	−.01	.99
Population change	−.29	−.10	.56	.41
Percent urban	.54	.28	.07	.37
Tax per capita	.31	.82	−.04	.78
If South	.06	−.74	.11	.57
Government expenditures	.99	.07	.01	.99
College enrollment	.96	.13	.02	.95
Mineral production	.36	−.40	.16	.32
Forest acreage	.10	.04	.70	.50
Manufacturing output	.92	.15	−.17	.90
Farm output	.53	−.09	−.13	.31
"Name"	Size	Wealth	Population density	
Original eigenvalues	5.05	2.26	1.46	

essentially a single variable—forest acreage—although by combining forest acreage with population change, which can be greater in the smaller, less densely populated states, we could "creatively" name this factor as population density. If we were to reduce the number of variables, one strategy would be to choose one variable to represent each of the factors (I prefer population, income per capita, and forest acreage) plus retain those variables with small communalities (here using .5 as a cutoff that would add population change, percent urban, mineral production, and farm output). Therefore, we could reduce the 11 variables to 7 with little loss of information and to 3 (population, income per capita, and forest acreage) with only moderate information loss.

CLUSTER ANALYSIS

Introduction

Cluster analysis (also known as *classification* or *numerical taxonomy*) is a broad field spanning many disciplines. Much of the literature involves examples from such diverse fields as biology, auditory and visual perception, and linguistics. There is even a professional society, the Classification Society, devoted to the problems of clustering. An excellent historical perspective and introduction is provided by Sokal (1974) and a very complete treatment of the subject is provided by Sneath and Sokal (1973). Its use has, like that of most other multivariate procedures, been greatly facilitated by computers, without which applications become extremely tedious. The common element to these problems is that a large number of objects have been measured on a number of variables, and the objects need to be grouped. In marketing, cluster analysis has been largely used for two basic purposes (Frank and Green, 1968):

1. Clustering (grouping) customers into segments.
2. Clustering/matching potential subjects or study areas (e.g., cities for test markets) to assure a balanced sample or data collection process.

The steps involved in both these cases are:

1. Definition of similarity among items.
2. Creation of clusters.
3. Description of clusters.
4. Use of the clusters to simplify the world and make it more understandable.

This chapter will proceed by first presenting the basic notion of clustering and then describing the major alternative approaches to clustering in terms of defining similarity, creating clusters, and describing clusters.

Cluster Analysis: Basic Notion

If we decided to classify a number of observations based on their values on two variables (X_1 and X_2), the observations could be plotted (Figure 14–4). In this case, three obvious clusters emerge. The reason these clusters are appealing is that the members of each cluster are quite similar to each other and quite different from members of other clusters in terms of the two variables. What cluster analysis algorithms attempt to do is to uncover such distinct clusters.

Unfortunately, the world is rarely as cooperative as the previous example suggests. A more likely situation would be that of Figure 14–5. Here, the "best" clusters are much harder to identify.

To derive clusters other than graphically, first a measure is needed which indicates the closeness of each pair of points (and, therefore, observations). Then some algorithm for grouping observations together based on the measure is required. The next two sections cover some of the alternative measures and algorithms available for use.

FIGURE 14–4 Three "Obvious" Clusters in Two Dimensions

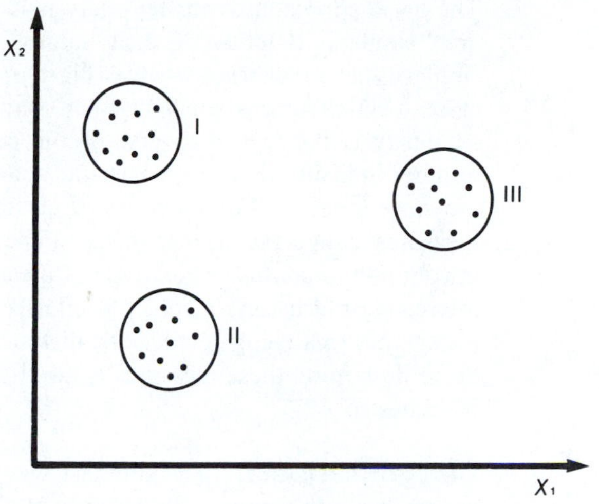

FIGURE 14–5 "Typical" Observations on Two Variables

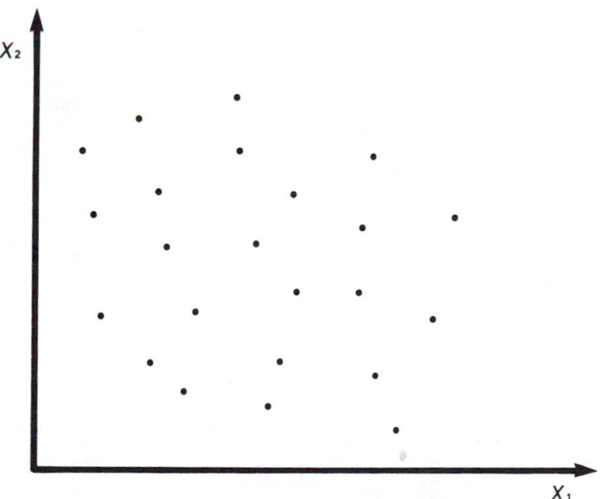

Similarity / Distance Measures

The basic approach of cluster analysis is to group together variables which are "similar" in terms of their values on the variables. Here we define similarity as a construct where a big number indicates that two objects are close together and a small number that two objects are far apart. Thus, similarity is the logical inverse of the concept of distance, where a large number indicates that objects are far apart and a small number that objects are close together. For purposes of clustering, either similarity or distance measures can serve as the basis. (The only problem is that it is not uncommon to confuse which type of measure is being used, leading to some interesting but useless results.) Similarity/distance measures come in three basic types: matching coefficients, distance measures, and pattern measures. Since describing these measures is admittedly tedious, the reader's patience is requested.

Categorical Data. The simplest way to determine if two observations are similar is to compute the number of characteristics on which they match (cleverly called a *matching coefficient*). Such a measure is most appropriate when the variables are categorical. For example, we might use such a measure for classifying furniture buyers, based on their favorite style (early American or modern), pattern (plain, plaid, or floral), and color (blue, yellow, red, or green). Here the data might be as follows:

	Favorite		
Customer	*Style*	*Pattern*	*Color*
1	1	3	1
2	1	2	2
3	2	3	3
4	2	2	3

Unweighted. The simplest matching coefficient counts the number of matches between two objects:

$$S_{ij} = \sum_{c=1}^{p} Z_c \tag{14.5}$$

where

S_{ij} = similarity between objects i and j.

p = number of characteristics (variables) measured.

$Z_c = 1$ if $X_{ic} = X_{jc}$.

$= 0$ otherwise.

In the furniturc example,

$$S_{12} = 1 + 0 + 0 = 1$$

$$S_{13} = 0 + 1 + 0 = 1$$

$$S_{14} = 0 + 0 + 0 = 0$$

$$S_{23} = 0 + 0 + 0 = 0$$

$$S_{24} = 0 + 1 + 0 = 1$$

$$S_{34} = 1 + 0 + 1 = 2$$

Weighted. Simple matching coefficients tend to be dominated by the variables with few categories. (It is much easier to get a match if there are only 2 categories than if there are 20.) For that reason, many researchers choose to weight the matches by their "difficulty." A common way to do this is to weight a match on a characteristic by the number of categories of the characteristic:

$$S_{ij} = \sum_{c=1}^{p} V_c Z_c \tag{14.6}$$

where

V_c = number of values of characteristic c.

In the previous example, this suggests:

$$S_{12} = 2(1) + 3(0) + 4(0) = 2$$

$$S_{13} = 2(0) + 3(1) + 4(0) = 3$$

$$S_{14} = 2(0) + 3(0) + 4(0) = 0$$

$$S_{23} = 2(0) + 3(0) + 4(0) = 0$$

$$S_{24} = 2(0) + 3(1) + 4(0) = 3$$

$$S_{34} = 2(1) + 3(0) + 4(1) = 6$$

Intervally Scaled Data: Distance Measures. Matching coefficients are necessary when data are purely categorical. Whenever data are intervally scaled, however, they tend to produce unappealing results. Consider the data in Table 14–12. Variables 1 through 3 are attitudes measured on a 7-point scale, and variable 4 is an interest scale which ranges between 11

TABLE 14–12 Sample Data

Object Observation Person	Variable / Characteristic 1	2	3	4
1	2	4	6	32
2	5	2	5	36
3	3	3	7	30
4	1	2	3	16
5	4	3	2	30

and 40. The matching coefficients, using Equations 14.5 and 14.6, are as follows:

	Unweighted	*Weighted*
S_{12} =	0	0
S_{13} =	0	0
S_{14} =	0	0
S_{15} =	0	0
S_{23} =	0	0
S_{24} =	1	7
S_{25} =	0	0
S_{34} =	0	0
S_{35} =	2	37
S_{45} =	0	0

These results suggest that objects 3 and 5 are very similar, objects 2 and 4 somewhat similar, and all other pairs completely different. Yet this result is unappealing since objects 2 and 4 seem to be very different, except for the match on variable 2, and objects 1 and 3 very similar on all four variables. The reason for this is that being close is given no credit by a matching coefficient; either two objects match exactly or not at all. For this reason, many people prefer distance measures which explicitly incorporate closeness. Some of the most popular include the following:

Sum of Absolute Deviations.

$$D_{ij} = \sum_{c=1}^{p} |X_{ic} - X_{jc}| \tag{14.7}$$

In this case:

$$D_{12} = |2 - 5| + |4 - 2| + |6 - 5| + |32 - 38|$$
$$= 12$$

$D_{13} = 5$, and so forth

Sum of Squared Differences.

$$D_{ij} = \sum_{c=1}^{p} \left(X_{ic} - X_{jc} \right)^2 \qquad (14.8)$$

Here:

$$D_{12} = (2 - 5)^2 + (4 - 2)^2 + (6 - 5)^2 + (32 - 38)^2$$
$$= 9 + 4 + 1 + 36 = 50$$

$D_{13} = 7$, and so forth.

Minowski Metric. The most general form of distance measures, such as Equations 14.7 and 14.8, is given by:

$$D_{ij} = \left[\sum_{c=1}^{p} W_c \left(X_{ic} - X_{jc} \right)^k \right]^{1/k} \qquad (14.9)$$

This fairly overwhelming formula reduces to Equation 14.7 if we assume that $W_c = 1$ for all characteristics and let $k = 1$, and to the square root of Equation 14.8 if we let $k = 2$. As you can see (Figure 14–6), $k = 2$ produces "as the crow flies" or Euclidean distance. For $k = 1$, this distance measure is sometimes called *city block*, since in New York City to go from 43rd and 5th Avenue to 44th and 7th Avenue you must walk one block north (43rd to 44th) and two blocks west (5th to 7th Avenue) for a total of three blocks (unless, of course, you can find a way through buildings, leap buildings in a single bound, etc.).

FIGURE 14–6 City Block and Euclidean Distance

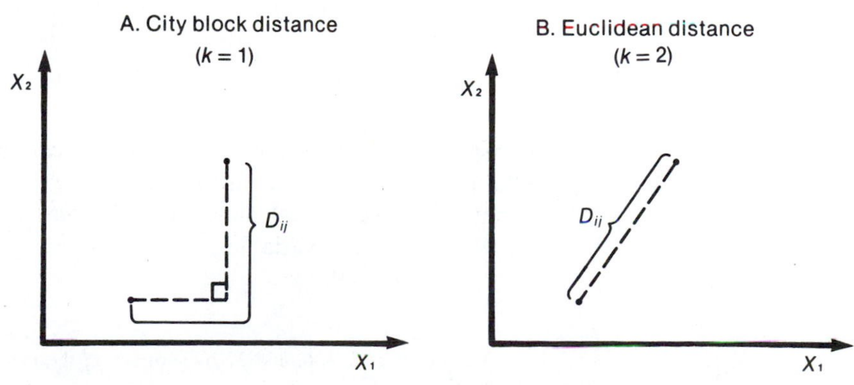

Properties. All these distance measures are affected by the scale of the variables used. In the example presented in Table 14–12, variable 4 tends to dominate the distance measures because it has a bigger range of numbers. To reduce this effect, the variables can be standardized before being input to the clustering program. Alternatively, the distances on each characteristic can be weighted by either using the inverse of the standard deviation $\left(W_c = \frac{1}{s_c}\right)$ or the simpler inverse of the range of the variable $\left(W_c = \frac{1}{\text{range}}\right)$. While this will reduce the scale effect, it does not remove the effect of collinearity. If several of the variables are related to each other, whatever construct/factor they represent will dominate the distance measure. A researcher may desire to have it do so. If such dominance is undesirable, however, the redundancy must be reduced. This can be done by simply omitting redundant variables. Alternatively, Mahalanobis D^2 distance measure can be used. This measure removes both scale and collinearity effects from the distance calculations and is often promoted as *the* measure (Morrison, 1967).

Pattern Measures. Distance measures assume that the absolute values of variables contain useful information. If only the relative values have meaning, then another form of distance measure is needed. Consider again the five-object example of Table 14–12 in terms of S_{14}:

	Variable			
Object	*1*	*2*	*3*	*4*
1	2	4	6	32
4	1	2	3	16

So far, all the matching and distance measures have indicated 1 and 4 as very dissimilar objects. Yet, the values for object 1 are all exactly twice the values for object 4. Hence, in terms of the pattern of responses, 1 and 4 are identical. Two major alternative procedures produce measures which reflect the pattern in the data:

1. The first approach is to standardize each object[4] ahead of time and then use the previously discussed measures.
2. Alternatively, we could calculate a correlation coefficient between objects 1 and 4 over the four variables.[5]

---

[4] That means convert 2, 4, 6, and 32 by subtracting the mean of 11 and dividing by the standard deviation.

[5] That means correlating X_1 (2, 4, 6, and 32) with X_2 (1, 2, 3, and 16).

Summary. In summary, then, there are a variety of similarity and distance measures available. Choice of the best one depends somewhat on technical issues (Green and Rao, 1969) but much more heavily on logical questions. Put differently, the researcher must decide whether exact matches, absolute differences, or patterns of responses are a more meaningful basis for grouping objects. Fortunately, a very strong pattern will tend to be recovered over a broad range of similarity measures and a weak one may be pretty useless, anyway.

Cluster Creation

Assuming a satisfactory similarity measure is developed, a grouping algorithm must be chosen. The choice is typically dictated by available computer algorithms, of which a large number exist (e.g., Spath, 1980, Oliva

TABLE 14–13 Two-Variable Example

	Variable	
Object	*1*	*2*
1	2	4
2	5	2
3	3	3
4	1	2
5	4	3

FIGURE 14–7 Plot of Two-Variable Example

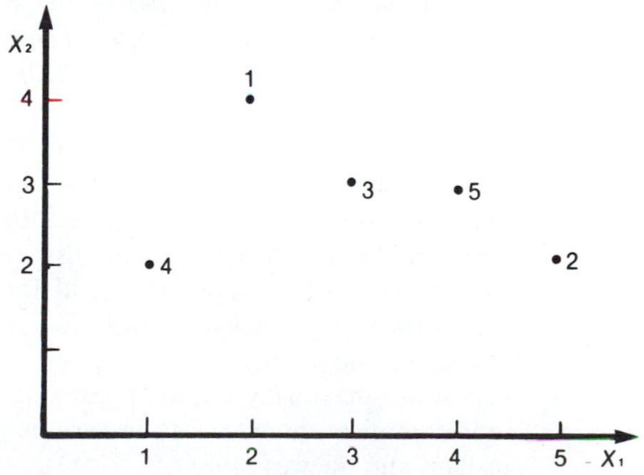

TABLE 14–14 Distance Matrix: Sum of Squared Differences

	Object				
Object	*1*	*2*	*3*	*4*	*5*
1		13	2	5	5
2			5	16	2
3				5	1
4					10
5					

and Reidenbach, 1985). It is still useful, however, to understand how some of these approaches operate.

To facilitate description of the grouping algorithms, the example of Table 14–13 will be used. The example is portrayed graphically in Figure 14–7. Using the sum of squared distances, we can derive a distance matrix (Table 14–14).

The basic approaches to clustering can be described in terms of the following two basic dimensions:

Hierarchical versus Fixed Number. In deciding which objects belong together, the most direct way to begin is to take the two most similar objects and group them together. Next, the similarities between objects (or objects and the newly formed group) are recomputed and, again, the most similar object pairs are combined. This procedure continues until all the objects are clustered. This approach bears the impressive description *hierarchical agglomerative* and is the most widely used procedure. (For culture fans, its opposite is called *hierarchical divisive* and begins with all objects in one cluster and sequentially removes dissimilar objects from groups.)

It is also possible to devise schemes for clustering which are nonhierarchical. The simplest of these would be to define "typical" members of each cluster and then group objects into the cluster whose typical member they were most similar to. (Since this requires a prior conception of what clusters exist, this is not very useful for initial investigations.) Essentially, these procedures (known often as *K-means clustering*) take a fixed number of clusters and attempt to find the best solution, in the sense that the cluster means are maximally different statistically using an ANOVA-type test. A more complete summary of the various procedures and algorithms appears in Punj and Stewart (1983).

FIGURE 14–8 Snake-Type Clusters

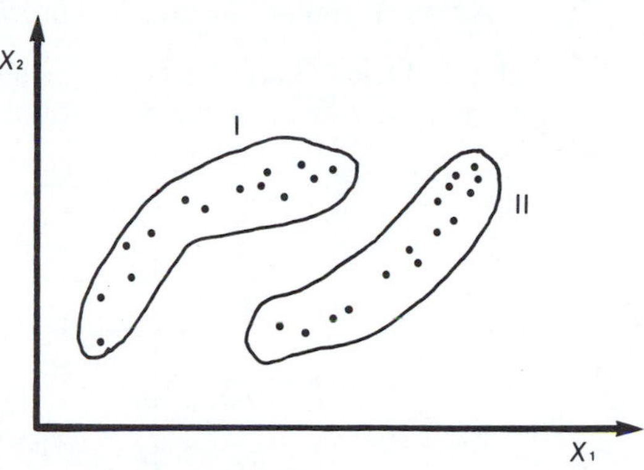

Calculation of Similarity between an Object and a Cluster. Once a cluster is formed, a means must be used for determining how similar an object is to the cluster. The following three basic approaches exist:

As similar as the most similar object (single linkage). This approach says that an object is as similar to a cluster as it is to the nearest object in the cluster. This method is efficient computationally but tends to produce snake-type clusters (Figure 14–8).

As similar as the least similar object (complete linkage). The polar opposite of the first approach is to assume that an object is as similar to a cluster as it is to the object in the cluster with which it is least similar. This tends to produce "nicer" results in most marketing applications. An example of a procedure which uses both of these cluster forming approaches is found in Johnson's Hierarchical Clustering System (Johnson, 1967).

Centroid (average) method. The most widely used approach is the so-called centroid method. Here, once two objects are grouped together, their values on the variables are averaged and the two objects replaced by a new "object" (centroid), which is the average of the objects included in the cluster. Ward's (1963) procedure searches for a clustering solution such that the within cluster variance is minimized. This tends to produce results similar to the *average linkage* method, where the similarity of the object to a cluster is the average of its similarity to each of the items in the cluster.

Hierarchical Clustering Example. To show how these approaches operate, let's return to the example of Table 14–14. This discussion has been provided to show how the computations operate. Obviously, the typical user will be concerned mainly with interpreting and using resulting clusters, rather than actually forming them.

A "most similar" hierarchical procedure would proceed as follows:

Step 1. Object 3 and 5 (the most similar pair) are combined.
Step 2. New distance matrix is formed.[6]

	Object			
Object	*1*	*2*	*3, 5*	*4*
1		13	2	5
2			2	16
3, 5				5
4				

Step 3. Add either object 1 or object 2 (or both) to cluster 3, 5.
Step 4. Assuming we add object 1 to cluster 3, 5, we get a new distance matrix:

	Object		
Object	*2*	*1, 3, 5*	*4*
2		2	16
1, 3, 5			5
4			

Step 5. Add object 2 to cluster 1, 3, 5.
Step 6. Form distance matrix:

	Object	
Object	*1, 2, 3, 5*	*4*
1, 2, 3, 5		5
4		

[6] Since object 1 is 2 from object 3 and 5 from object 5, its distance from the closest object in the cluster is 2.

Step 7. Form final cluster: 1, 2, 3, 4, 5.
Output. The output would then be as follows:

Distance Level	*Groups*
0	1; 2; 3; 4; 5
1	1; 2; 3, 5; 4
2	1, 3, 5; 2; 4
2	1, 2, 3, 5; 4
5	1, 2, 3, 4, 5

Notice, if you plot the cluster on the graph at distance level 2, you get the classic snake-type cluster (Figure 14–9).

The "least similar" hierarchical procedure would proceed as follows:

Step 1. Objects 3 and 5 are combined.
Step 2. New distance matrix is formed.[7]

	Object			
Object	*1*	*2*	*3, 5*	*4*
1		13	5	5
2			5	16
3, 5				10
4				

Step 3. We now have a tie which could be broken in several ways. Assume we group 1 and 4 together (it makes the example work out better).
Step 4. Distance matrix:

	Object		
Object	*1, 4*	*2*	*3, 5*
1, 4		16	10
2			5
3, 5			

[7] Now the distance from object 1 to the cluster of objects 3 and 5 becomes 5, since object 5 is the farthest object from object 1 in the cluster.

FIGURE 14–9 Most Similar Method Result

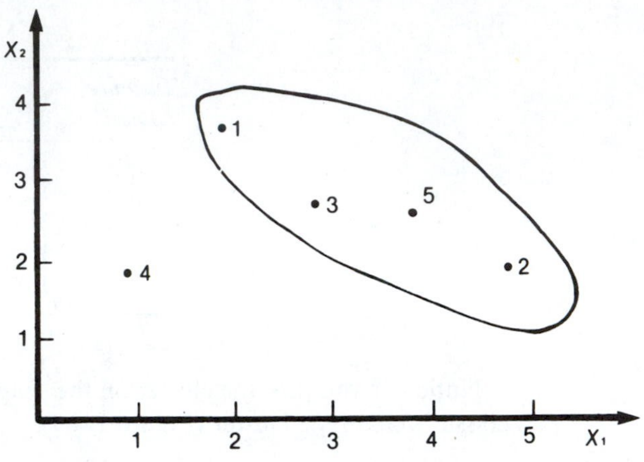

Step 5. Group 2, 3, and 5 together.
Step 6. Distance matrix:

	Object	
Object	*1, 4*	*2, 3, 5*
1, 4		16
2, 3, 5		

Step 7. Group 1, 2, 3, 4, and 5 together.
Output.

Distance Level	*Groups*
0	1; 2; 3; 4; 5
1	1; 2; 3, 5; 4
5	1, 4; 2; 3, 5
5	1, 4; 2, 3, 5
16	1, 2, 3, 4, 5

FIGURE 14–10 Least Similar Method Results

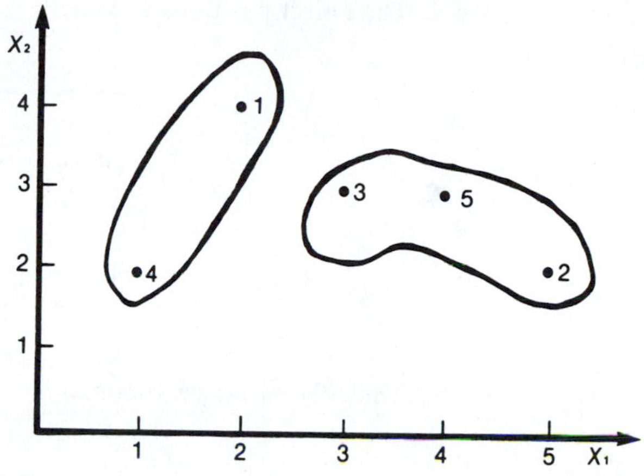

Notice here that, at the distance level of 5, the clusters become, in some sense, more appealing graphically (Figure 14–10).

The centroid (average) method would proceed as follows:

Step 1. Group 3 and 5 together (as before).

Step 2. To calculate distance, we must first replace objects 3 and 5 with their average:

	Variable	
Object	*1*	*2*
1	2	4
2	5	2
3, 5	3.5	3
4	1	2

The distances thus become:

	Object			
Object	*1*	*2*	*3, 5*	*4*
1		13	3.25	5
2			3.25	16
3, 5				7.25
4				

Step 3. Group together either 1 or 2 with 3, 5. Assume we choose 2. (If we choose 1, the answer changes markedly.)

Step 4. The object positions become:

	Variable	
Object	*1*	*2*
2, 3, 5	4	2.67
1	2	4
4	1	2

Thus, the distances become:

Object	*1*	*2, 3, 5*	*4*
1		5.76	5
2, 3, 5			9.45
4			

Step 5. Group 1 and 4 together.

Step 6. The positions are:

	Variable	
Object	*1*	*2*
1, 4	1.5	3
2, 3, 5	4	2.67

Now the distances are:

Object	*1, 4*	*2, 3, 5*
1, 4		6.36
2, 3, 5		

Step 7. Form group 1, 2, 3, 4, 5.

TABLE 14–15

Alternative Clusters		*Means*				
		Cluster I		*Cluster II*		
I	*II*	*Variable 1*	*Variable 2*	*Variable 1*	*Variable 2*	*Total Absolute Difference**
1,2	3,4,5	3.50	3.00	2.67	2.67	1.16
1,3	2,4,5	2.50	3.50	3.33	2.33	2.00
1,4	2,3,5	1.50	3.00	4.00	2.67	2.83
1,5	2,3,4	3.00	3.50	3.00	2.33	1.17
2,3	1,4,5	4.00	2.50	2.33	3.00	2.17
2,4	1,3,5	3.00	2.00	3.00	3.33	1.33
2,5	1,3,4	4.50	2.50	2.00	3.00	3.00
3,4	1,2,5	2.00	2.50	3.67	3.00	2.17
3,5	1,2,4	3.50	3.00	2.67	2.67	1.66
4,5	1,2,3	2.50	2.50	3.33	3.00	1.33

* For example, $|3.5 - 2.67| + |3.00 - 2.67| = 1.16$

The key output in a hierarchical program is a chart indicating how the objects link together at various levels of similarity. An example based on the 50 states data set appears later in this chapter.

Mean-Based Clustering Example. Again returning to the example of Table 14–13, assume I wanted a two-cluster solution and that I also wanted the minimum cluster size to be two. This means there are 10 possible solutions (Table 14–15). To find the "best" solution, I can calculate the means on the two variables for the 10 possible solutions. By comparing the means, I can see which solution produces the greatest total average difference in means.[8] In this case, the solution of 1, 3, 4 versus 2, 5 produces the greatest difference and would be chosen. Notice this produces a different result from the complete linkage hierarchical clustering approach as object 3 shifts clusters. Still, the cluster results are similar, in that you get essentially a low X_1 cluster and a high X_1 cluster, with X_2 being, at best, weakly related to cluster membership.

Other Approaches. A variety of alternative approaches have been developed. One of the most interesting allows the user to include constraints such as "objects A and B will be in the same cluster" (Klastorian, 1983). Another allows a single object to appear in more than one cluster

---

[8] The actual algorithms are typically more complicated and adjust for standard deviations (within cluster variation).

(Arabie, Carroll, DeSarbo, and Wind, 1981). While their MAPCLUS algorithm does not produce the mutually exclusive clusters discussed previously, it does allow for some interesting results. For example, most people who participate in a weight training program, such as Nautilus, would probably classify a workout as both recreation and work. Hence, it would be rated as similar to ditch digging, swimming, and chess. While this would be an "inconvenience" to most clustering routines, since chess and ditch digging are not similar, it would be easily handled in MAPCLUS, which could have ditch digging and Nautilus as one cluster and Nautilus, swimming, and chess as another. Notice, however, that overlapping clusters seem relatively more useful for grouping products, rather than developing segments or strata for sampling.

Cluster Definition

The definition of clusters is a very straightforward task. The usual first step is to define clusters in terms of the cluster member's values of the variables used in the clustering algorithm. As a second step, the cluster members are often compared in terms of other available variables. The two analytical procedures commonly used are:

1. Examination of differences in mean values on each variable separately.
2. Discriminant analysis as a tool to "validate" the clusters. Here, discriminant analysis can be used both to see if the clusters differ significantly and also to indicate (by means of the percent correctly classified) how different the clusters really are. Discriminant analysis is discussed in Chapter 15.

Cluster Usage

Usage of cluster analysis falls into two broad categories. The first is the use of the resulting clusters as input to another problem. One example of this type is using clusters as sampling strata in consumer or industrial data collection. Another example of this use of clusters is as a means to simulate the results of possible marketing programs. Assume the clusters which had been derived were segments of customers who had different demographic and product usage characteristics. By estimating the effect of various possible programs on the type of customer in each segment and then aggregating the estimates, estimates of results of such programs can be obtained.

The other major use of cluster analysis is much less mechanical. Like any other analytical procedure, cluster analysis can be used as a generator of ideas. If the results of a cluster analysis give additional insight into a problem, the analysis must be deemed a success. It is very hard to define exactly what insight is (a light bulb going on, an "ah-ha" response), but it is at least easy to know when it occurs.

Punj and Stewart (1983) discuss five major categories of use for cluster analysis: market segmentation, understanding buyers, new product development, test market selection, and aggregating data. Market segmentation uses entail finding groups of customers who are similar in terms of key variables and then targeting marketing programs to the resulting clusters/segments. Understanding buyers refers to using clusters more as idea generators in terms of how customers buy (see Problem 8 for an example of this). The new product development use of cluster analysis essentially involves grouping similar products together to assess the structure of a market. Test market selection involves grouping regions which are similar in terms of observed characteristics so experiments can be run in comparable areas. Finally, aggregating data refers to grouping data points and using representatives of each cluster in subsequent analyses, generally to fit within size constraints of programs (e.g., if a certain program will only allow 20 observations and you have 1,000, it is possible to use cluster analysis to generate a representative sample of 20). These five uses can be collapsed (clustered?) into three major categories: (1) grouping customers, (2) grouping companies/products, and (3) developing strata for sampling purposes.

Grouping customers into segments is a popular tool in many areas. For example, political scientists often cluster voters into groups. One study based on 4,200 personal interviews came up with 11 clusters with names such as "partisan poor," "enterprisers," and so on (Ornstein, 1987). Two major approaches are used. The first focuses on variables related to the product of interest (e.g., usage, attitude) and creates clusters which are then examined to see if they differ in terms of descriptive variables (e.g., lifestyles). The second focuses on descriptive variables and then examines whether clusters differ in terms of product variables. The first guarantees meaningful clusters but not ones that can be located (e.g., targeted via advertising through certain media or copy), while the second creates targetable segments which do not necessarily differ in terms of product variables. Hence, the choice of variables used in clustering depends on the relative importance of segment "reachability" versus the existence of product use differences.

Issues in Applying Cluster Analysis

Whenever a researcher decides to use cluster analysis, there are several questions he or she should address:

Is a Fancy Approach Needed? Assuming there is a real need to group objects (customers, competing products, etc.), a question which arises is whether a simple grouping procedure will not suffice. Assume I wish to develop segments of customers. An obvious way to approach the problem is to base the grouping on either brand preference or level of usage, or a combination of both:

Brand Used Most Often	*Product Usage Level*		
	Low	*Medium*	*High*
A	1	2	3
B	4	5	6
C	7	8	9
Others	10	11	12

I have thus defined 12 segments which differ in a known, important way. While use of a cluster analysis routine may seem more "unbiased," it really just has hidden the biases (in the choice of variables used, similarity/distance measure employed, etc.) and is certainly not as "natural" a way of developing groups (unless Minkowski metrics and computer algorithms are your concept of nature) as some proponents claim. Some use of cluster analysis can best be described as pseudoscientification. In short, before you roll out a cluster analysis cannon, make sure the problem isn't a mouse.

What Variables to Include? This is the key to the result, so more time should be spent here than typically is. Ideally, relevant nonredundant variables should be used. In practice, care should be taken to include variables which represent the constructs which are assumed to be important without overrepresenting any of the constructs.

What Weights to Use? The issue of how to weight each of the variables informing the similarity or distance measure really encompasses the variable inclusion problem, since exclusion of a variable means a weight of zero has been assigned to that particular variable. In any event, the choice of weights is a logical, rather than a mathematical, problem. Commonly, the simple option of equal weights is employed.

What Computer Program to Use? The answer depends on a combination of program constraints (number of variables, number of objects, etc.) and availability.

What Do I Do with a Big Sample? Even the largest programs rarely handle more than 1,000 objects. Hence, if you have a sample of 3,000, a problem exists. One solution is to cluster a random or representative subsample of 1,000. These results can be used directly or the remaining 2,000 can be brought into the groups by assigning them to the closest group. (A good mechanical way to do this is by calculating discriminant functions on the original sample and then using them to classify the "holdout" sample.)

How Many Clusters are Needed? The issue of how many clusters a researcher uses depends on the problem, taste, and sample size. There is generally no way to get reliable clusters of size less than 30 to 50 from consumer survey data. Therefore, $\frac{n}{50}$ gives a tentative boundary on the maximum number of clusters. Also, the problem may be one in which many clear segments can be expected to exist or one where everything is "mush." Finally, if the goal is insight, some researchers prefer a small number of big segments, while others like to see as many segments as can reasonably be generated.

Reliability Checking. Given the number of choices involved in cluster analysis, one should feel uncomfortable looking at the results of a single approach. For an important problem, sensitivity analysis is called for, and separate results should be generated for alternative similarity measures, numbers of clusters, samples, and so forth (c.f., Doyle and Saunders, 1985). Only when the clusters consistently point the same way can a researcher safely conclude that a "real" set of segments has been uncovered. This is especially true since a small number of outliners (atypical observations) can affect the results noticeably.

Relation to Factor Analysis

Factor analysis can be viewed as a special type of cluster analysis. As it was presented earlier in the chapter, factor analysis attempted to find groups of variables where the similarity measure was the correlation coefficient between pairs of variables. Since in survey data for two variables to be positively correlated, some people must rate both high and some rate both low, the name given to the factor also indicates the presence of a group of respondents who score high on the variables.

Factor analysis computer programs can be used to directly group observations as well as variables. The use of factor analysis to group observations is known as *Q-type factor analysis*. This technique involves "tricking" the factor analysis computer program. The trick goes like this: The computer program expects the data in the form of the left half of Table 14–16. By transposing the data, we can input the data in the right half of Table 14–16. The computer now proceeds thinking the columns are the variables to be factored/group. Since the columns are in fact observations, the program actually groups observations based on their correlations across the p variables.

This approach has some severe problems. For one thing, the number of observations to be grouped is severely limited, often to less than 100 (as, incidentally, are the number of variables in "regular" factor analysis). Second, unless the variables are standardized, the variable with the largest numerical value will tend to dominate the correlations and hence dictate the groups. Still, Q-type factor analysis is occasionally useful.

TABLE 14–16

Typical Factor Analysis Input Data Format					Q-type Factor Analysis Input Data Format				
	Variable					*New Variable (Really the Observation)*			
Observation	*1*	*2*	...	*p*	*New Observation (old variable)*	*1*	*2*	...	*n*
1					1				
2					2				
⋮					⋮				
n					*p*				

An Example: Grouping Customers

In this example, 940 housewives were clustered on the basis of 12 food shopping variables. The variables were as follows:

Importance of variety.
Importance of taste.
Importance of diet restrictions.
Importance of price.
Importance of availability.
Importance of ease of preparation.
Importance of habit.
Importance of advertised specials.
Importance of nutritional value.
Agreement with:
"People need meat to be healthy."
"I feel the need for more nutritional information."
"We entertain more at home than the average family."

In all cases, a "1" is a high value (very important, strongly agree), and a "5" a low value. The Howard-Harris program was used for clustering. Solutions were generated for two, three, four, five, six, and seven clusters. For the sake of simplicity, only the four-cluster solution is discussed. Part of the actual output appears as Appendix 14–C.

The output has two basic parts. The first is the cluster delineations. Specifically, the identification of the members of each of the four clusters is made. Hence, group 1 has persons 9, 11, 16, and so forth, in it. The clusters had 246, 258, 208, and 228 people in them, respectively.

TABLE 14–17 Food Shopping Segments Means

Variable	*Cluster* 1	2	3	4
Importance of variety	1.80	2.18	2.42	1.89
Importance of taste	1.15	1.26	1.62	1.25
Importance of diet restrictions	1.72	4.67	3.49	1.97
Importance of price	1.38	1.63	2.62	1.63
Importance of availability	1.51	1.96	2.80	2.69
Importance of ease of preparation	1.88	2.64	2.91	3.85
Importance of habit	2.38	2.65	3.00	3.37
Importance of advertised specials	1.85	1.72	3.78	2.03
Importance of nutritional value	1.33	1.89	2.28	1.39
Agreement with: "People need meat to be healthy"	2.31	2.43	2.33	2.50
"I feel the need for more nutritional information"	2.00	2.62	2.67	2.12
"We entertain more at home than the average family"	3.86	3.84	3.72	3.67

The other major part of the output contains the means of clusters on the 12 variables. This is the cluster definition stage of the output. The results are shown in Table 14–17. Naming clusters requires as much creative writing as research skill. Nonetheless, the following descriptors were generated:

Cluster 1: This cluster seems to attach great importance to all the attributes. They were called the *all important* cluster.

Cluster 2: This cluster is fairly neutral on all the attributes except diet restrictions (which were unimportant) and advertised specials (which were very important). The lack of importance attributed to other family members' preferences could be due to their not having children at home. This was called the *specials shopper* cluster.

Cluster 3: This cluster is almost the opposite of cluster 1, indicating that all the attributes are relatively unimportant. This may be a sign of caution or lack of interest. In any event, they were called the *unexcited* cluster.

Cluster 4: This cluster is fairly neutral except that it rates both ease of preparation and habit as particularly unimportant. Apparently this group enjoys thinking about and working on food preparation and may contain all the gourmets. This cluster was called the *nonsimplifiers* or *food preparers*.

The results of this study were interesting but failed to produce a great intuitive revelation about food shopping. In fact, the most interesting result was the existence of clusters 1 and 3, who consistently rated all attributes either important or unimportant. This has led to some interesting research on survey response patterns but not much additional knowledge about food consumption decisions.

TABLE 14–18 Similarity Coefficient measures

	Coke	7up	Tab	Like	Pepsi	Sprite	Diet Pepsi
7up	.609						
Tab	.310	.446					
Like	.398	.946	4.457				
Pepsi	.568	.663	.309	.736			
Sprite	.487	1.064	.736	.806	.732		
Diet Pepsi	.324	.291	4.374	2.461	.582	.887	
Fresca	.664	.642	1.592	1.742	.610	1.275	1.820

An Example: Grouping Products

Products can be grouped based on a variety of similarity measures including judged similarity, ratings on attributes, and brand switching. As an example, eight soft drinks with two brands in each possible combination of cola–lemon-lime and nondiet–diet were clustered, based on their brand-switching patterns. Specifically, brand similarity was measured based on:

$$S_{ij} = \frac{\text{Fraction buying } i \text{ and } j \text{ consecutively}}{(\text{Share } i)(\text{Share } j)}$$

(Moore, Pessemier, Lehmann, 1986). These similarity measures (Table 14–18) were then hierarchically clustered. The results (Figure 14–11) indicate a clear partitioning between nondiet and diet segments of the market.

An Example: Grouping Observations

As another example of clustering, the 50 states (we never give up once we have data up on a computer) were analyzed using the SAS clustering program. This program uses the squared distance between objects as the distance measure and proceeds hierarchically. The sum of squared distances between two clusters option was used. This option favors solutions with relatively equally sized clusters. Clustering was done on both unstandardized data (i.e., the raw numbers as they appear in Table 9–1) and standardized data (i.e., each variable was first standardized to have mean 0 and standard deviation 1). As expected, the unstandardized results were dominated by the variable with the biggest numbers—here, forest acreage. Therefore, only the results based on standardized variables are discussed here.

Appendix 14-D shows the pattern of grouping as the analysis moves from 50 distinct states to one large cluster. Notice that the first two states to be grouped together are 17 (Kentucky) and 36 (Oklahoma), followed by 40

FIGURE 14–11 Hierarchical Clustering of Soft Drinks

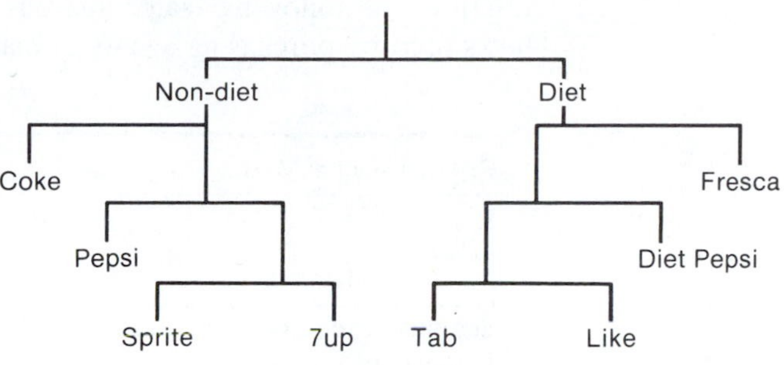

(South Carlolina) and 10 (Georgia). By contrast, the most unique states—those that "resist" clustering the longest—are 2 (Alaska), 5 (California), and 32 (New York). In terms of clusters that emerge, it is desirable to look for groups that form "early" and only combine with other clusters late to find distinct clusters. Here, a 10-group solution seems a reasonable compromise between parsimony (a 3-cluster solution produces 1 group of 25 states, 1 of 17, and 1 of 8) and a trivial solution (e.g., 30 clusters where the largest cluster is 3 states). The clusters and their means on the (standardized) variables appear in Appendix 14-D.

SUMMARY

This chapter has described two grouping procedures which help simplify data. Factor analysis groups together variables which are correlated, and it is used either to simplify analysis or subsequent data collection (by removing redundant variables) or to uncover patterns in the data (by naming the factors). Cluster analysis is a more general procedure that defines segments based on a similarity measure. The similarity or distance measure used depends on the type of data available (categorical data lead to a matching coefficient, intervally scaled data are typically handled with Euclidean distance). Cluster algorithms tend to either gradually link all items together one at a time (hierarchical clustering) or to create a set number of clusters. Cluster analysis is most frequently used to develop segments of customers, to group similar/competing products together to better understand the market structure, or to develop strata for sampling purposes. It is possible to become either turned off by or enamored with the mathematical properties and technical niceties of these techniques. Still, their use is much more of an art form than most people care to admit. Hence, users should concern themselves with ensuring that these (or any other) procedures are (*a*) being used to solve a real problem and (*b*) being used in a way that makes sense.

PROBLEMS

1. Interpret the following factor analysis of the importance of 17 attributes used by purchasing agents in making decisions about suppliers:

Rotated Factor Matrix

	Factor				
Attribute	*1*	*2*	*3*	*4*	*5*
Supplier reputation	.16	.04	.89	.09	−.10
Financing	.15	.79	.08	−.10	−.12
Flexibility	.11	.72	.02	.12	.43
Past experience	.17	.15	.03	.07	.85
Technical service	.47	.42	.22	−.27	.39
Confidence in salespersons	.60	.27	.27	.14	.40
Convenience in ordering	.33	.67	−.20	.03	.14
Reliability data	.57	.02	.29	.21	.46
Price	.08	.06	.03	.84	−.01
Technical specifications	.49	−.03	.07	.43	.59
Ease of use	.52	.19	−.13	−.30	.52
Preference of user	.13	.33	.57	−.43	.38
Training offered	.87	.18	.24	−.12	.06
Reliability of delivery	−.16	.61	.29	.05	.13
Maintenance	.25	.12	−.07	−.18	.77
Sales service	.75	.09	−.28	.29	.13
Training required	.78	.02	.12	−.01	.34
Unrotated eigenvalues	6.30	2.02	1.44	1.37	1.08

2. What is the difference between *Q* and *R* type factor analysis?
3. How would you go about reducing a set of 150 candidate variables for a model of consumer satisfaction to a more manageable number?
4. You have designed a new product and want to advertise its introduction. You want to place advertisements in several different magazines. Your job is to select the particular set of magazines in which the ads should run. Your researcher wants to help you by running a factor analysis of your data. You know which of the 100 largest circulation magazines was read by each person in a sample of 1,000 people during the last month. That is, you have a data matrix which is 100 magazines by 1,000 people in size. Each cell has either zero (person did not read last issue of this magazine) or one (person did read the last issue of this magazine).
   a. If you believe your ad must be seen many times to have any effect, then how can your researcher help you select the magazines? Please be specific about the factor analysis you want the researcher to run and how you will use the results.

b. If you believe, instead, that your ad is so great that people who see it will instantly recognize the benefits of your new product, then how can your researcher use factor analysis to help you select the magazines? Again, please be specific.

c. For your analyses in parts (*a*) and (*b*) above, would you prefer that your researcher provide you the principle components unrotated factor loadings or the rotated factor loadings? Why?

d. If your researcher found that three factors explained 98 percent of variance in the readership data for the 100 magazines, what would you conclude? If only 5 percent?

5. Suppose that you have been collecting opinions about many various aspects of a new product. You notice that people seem to respond similarly to many of the questions.

   a. How would you determine which questions are related to each other?

   b. How would you select the questions which are redundant so they could be eliminated from future studies without loss of most of the information in the original set of questions?

6. You have a set of 38 time series variables, which you wish to use to explain the sales of heavy-duty machine tools. Describe two ways you might use factor analysis before running your regression. What are the advantages and disadvantages of these approaches?

7. The following rotated factor matrix was based on a sample of people who indicated how likely they were to drink wine coolers (measured on a five-point scale) on a number of occasions. Interpret.

	Factor		
	1	*2*	*3*
At lunch	.79	−.03	.02
Between meals	.78	.30	.02
While watching TV	.77	.21	.19
At picnics	.76	.42	.16
At a beach	.73	.37	.18
At dinner	.67	.50	−.04
At cocktail parties	.24	.84	.00
At business meetings	.10	.79	.02
At bars	.31	.79	.21
At restaurants	.31	.77	.16
At breakfast	.04	.03	.92
At sporting events	.44	.41	.50
Original eigenvalue	6.18	1.35	1.07
Rotated eigenvalue	3.85	3.45	1.30

8. Data on the values of a sample of customers were analyzed via factor analysis. Specifically the responses to questions 3 and 4 on the Ownership and Values Survey (Appendix 6–C) were analyzed for some of the respondents. Interpret the results, shown below:

	Factor					
	1	*2*	*3*	*4*	*5*	*6*
SRESPECT	.68	.00	.03	.10	.04	−.09
SECURE	.54	.17	−.03	−.25	.27	.26
WARMREL	.59	−.19	.30	.09	−.03	−.28
ACCOMP	.80	.16	.10	.10	−.03	−.09
SLFFIL	.73	.10	.17	.12	.04	−.01
BELONG	.55	.08	.25	−.19	.20	.41
WRNSPECT	.55	.27	.11	−.12	.17	.20
FUN	.28	.15	.71	−.01	.08	−.01
EXCITE	.18	.24	.71	.00	.03	−.04
PHSFIT	.35	.15	.39	.05	.26	−.14
CONTROL	.30	.50	.05	.01	.31	−.06
KNOW	.56	.16	.04	.21	.34	−.21
COVEN	.22	.31	.26	−.16	.49	.21
OWN	.12	.65	.13	−.21	.21	.19
BEAUTY	.11	.50	.25	.18	.03	.11
GDDEAL	.06	.47	.12	.05	.56	.04
PRACTL	.14	.11	.03	−.00	.76	.06
TRAVEL	.03	.06	.63	.18	.06	.07
VARIETY	.13	.13	.66	.26	.19	−.01
SUCCESS	.32	.67	.13	.11	.09	−.04
WEALTH	.06	.79	.04	−.02	.03	.07
FAME	−.12	.60	.15	.28	.13	.06
UNIQUE	.11	.30	.17	.62	.07	−.02
PGROWTH	.50	.03	.19	.46	.13	−.01
FAIR	.51	−.19	.13	.28	.38	.06
SIMPLE	.11	−.17	.20	.24	.63	.14
PEREXP	−.01	.15	.37	.48	−.09	.26
FINSEC	.00	.17	−.14	.04	.05	.65
FFAME	.01	.65	.04	.29	−.12	.16
STRUGGL	−.00	.07	−.13	.32	.15	.55
INDIV	.05	.16	.00	.71	−.01	−.06
SOCIALLY	.23	−.19	.17	.52	.16	.17
LKRICH	−.10	.52	.13	−.02	−.33	.22
PGROUP	.02	.13	.22	−.06	.02	.55
Variance explained	4.34	3.98	2.80	2.44	2.41	1.77

9. Indicate on a quantitative 1 to 10 scale how similar the following pairs are:
   a. The words "pretty" and "happy."
   The words "ugly" and "homely."
   The words "big" and "important."
   b. The following people: Walter Mondale, George Bush, wife, mother-in-law.
10. Using Table 14–14 as a starting point, produce a graphical summary of the steps in clustering the five objects using the "least similar" method.
11. How would you go about clustering counties in the United States?
12. Assume you were national sales manager for Xerox. How would you proceed to cluster present and potential accounts?
13. Assume a large security dealer asked you to help segment its accounts by means of cluster analysis. What would you do?

BIBLIOGRAPHY

Acito, Frank, and Ronald D. Anderson. "A Simulation Study of Factor Score Indeterminancy." *Journal of Marketing Research* 23 (May 1986), pp. 111–18.

______. "A Monte Carlo Comparison of Factor Analytic Methods." *Journal of Marketing Research* 17 (May 1980), pp. 228–36.

Arabie, P.; J. D. Carroll; W. DeSarbo; and J. Wind. "Overlapping Clustering: A New Method for Product Positioning." *Journal of Marketing Research* 18 (August 1981), pp. 310–17.

Arnold, S. J. "A Test for Clusters." *Journal of Marketing Research* 16 (November 1979), pp. 545–51.

Babakus, Emin; Carl E. Ferguson, Jr.; and Karl G. Jöreskog. "The Sensitivity of Confirmatory Maximum Likelihood Factor Analysis to Violations of Measurement Scale and Distributional Assumptions." *Journal of Marketing Research* 24 (May 1987), pp. 222–28.

Bagozzi, Richard P. *Causal Models in Marketing*. New York: John Wiley & Sons, 1980.

Doyle, Peter, and John Saunders. "Market Segmentation and Positioning in Specialized Industrial Markets." *Journal of Marketing* 49 (Spring 1985), pp. 24–32.

Fornell, Claes, and Fred L. Bookstein. "Two Structural Equation Models: LISREL and PLS Applied to Consumer Exit-Voice Theory." *Journal of Marketing Research* 19 (November 1982), pp. 440–52.

Fornell, Claes, and David F. Larcker. "Evaluating Structural Equation Models with Unobservable Variables and Measurement Error." *Journal of Marketing Research* 18 (February 1981), pp. 39–50.

Frank, Ronald E., and Paul E. Green. "Numerical Taxonomy in Marketing Analysis: A Review Article." *Journal of Marketing Research* 5 (February 1968), pp. 83–94.

Funkhouser, G. Ray. "A Note on the Reliability of Certain Clustering Algorithms." *Journal of Marketing Research* 20 (February 1983), pp. 99–102.

Green, Paul E., and Vithala R. Rao. "A Note on Proximity Measures and Cluster Analysis." *Journal of Marketing Research* 6 (August 1969), pp. 359–64.

Harman, Harry H. *Modern Factor Analysis*. Chicago: University of Chicago Press, 1967.

Howard, N., and Harris, B. "A Hierarchical Grouping Routine, IBM 360/65 FORTRAN IV Program." University of Pennsylvania Computer Center, October 1966.

Johnson, S. C. "Hierarchical Clustering Schemes." *Psychometrika* 32 (September 1967), pp. 241–54.

Jöreskog, Karl G., and Dag Sörbom. "Recent Developments in Structural Equation Modeling." *Journal of Marketing Research* 19 (November 1982), pp. 404–16.

______. *Advances in Factor Analysis and Structural Equation Models*. Cambridge, Mass.: Abt Books, 1979.

Klastorian, T. D. "Assessing Cluster Analysis Results." *Journal of Marketing Research* 20 (February 1983), pp. 92–98.

______. "A Clustering Approach to Systems Design." Unpublished Ph.D. dissertation. Austin, Tex.: The University of Texas, 1973.

Lehmann, Donald R. "Some Alternatives to Linear Factor Analysis for Variable Grouping Applied to Buyer Behavior Variables." *Journal of Marketing Research* 11 (May 1974), pp. 206–13.

Lehmann, Donald R., and Donald G. Morrison. "A Random Splitting Criterion for Selecting the Number of Factors." Working paper. New York: Columbia University Graduate School of Business, 1977.

Lesser, Jack A., and Marie Adele Hughes. "The Generalizability of Psychographic Market Segments across Geographic Locations." *Journal of Marketing* 50 (January 1986), pp. 18–27.

Mahajan, Vijay, and Arun K. Jain. "An Approach to Normative Segmentation." *Journal of Marketing Research* 15 (August 1978), pp. 338–45.

Moore, William L.; Edgar A. Pessemier; and Donald R. Lehmann. "Hierarchical Representations of Market Structures and Choice Processes through Preference Trees." *Journal of Business Research* 14 (1986), pp. 107–11.

Morrison, Donald F. *Multivariate Statistical Methods*. 2nd ed. New York: McGraw-Hill, 1976.

Morrison, Donald G. "Measurement Problems in Cluster Analysis." *Management Science* 13 (August 1967), pp. B775–B780.

Oliva, Terence A., and R. Eric Reidenbach. "Iterative Partitioning Methods: The Use of Mapping Theory as a Clustering Technique." *Journal of Marketing Research* 22 (February 1985), pp. 81–85.

Ornstein, Norman. "How to Win in '88: Meld the Unmeldable." *U.S. News & World Report* 103 (October 12, 1987), pp. 31–33.

Punj, Girish, and David W. Stewart. "Cluster Analysis in Marketing Research: Review and Suggestions for Application." *Journal of Marketing Research* 20 (May 1983), pp. 134–48.

Sneath, P. H. A., and R. R. Sokal. *Numerical Taxonomy*. San Francisco: W. H. Freeman, 1973.

Sokal, R. R. "Numerical Taxonomy." *Science* 185 (September 1974), pp. 1115–23.

Spath, H. *Cluster Analysis Algorithms*. Chichester, England: Ellis Horwood, 1980.

Srivastava, R. K.; R. P. Leone; and A. D. Shocker. "Market Structure Analysis: Hierarchical Clustering of Products Based on Substitution-in-Use." *Journal of Marketing* 45 (Summer 1981), pp. 38–48.

Stewart, David W. "The Application and Misapplication of Factor Analysis in Marketing Research." *Journal of Marketing Research* 18 (February 1981), pp. 51–62.

Villani, Kathryn E. A., and Donald R. Lehmann, "An Examination of the Stability of AIO Measures." *Proceedings*, Fall Conference, American Marketing Association, 1975, pp. 484–88.

Ward, J. "Hierarchical Grouping to Optimize an Objective Function." *Journal of the American Statistical Association* 58 (1963), pp. 236–44.

Wind, Y. "Issues and Advances in Segmentation Research." *Journal of Marketing Research* 15 (August 1978), pp. 317–37.

Wold, Herman. "Soft Modelling: Intermediate Between Traditional Model Building and Data Analysis." *Mathematical Statistics* 6 (1980), pp. 333–46.

Appendix 14–A

Foundations of Factor Analysis

This appendix provides a simple (six-variable) factor analysis example so facility in interpreting results may be improved by careful study of a manageable problem. The basic data and outputs were as follows:

VARIABLES

1. Education of wife.
2. Education of husband.
3. Age.
4. Income.
5. Family size.
6. Weekly food expenditures.

Correlations

	Variable					
Variable	*1*	*2*	*3*	*4*	*5*	*6*
1		61	−.30	.42	.12	.17
2			−.42	.50	.20	.25
3				−.30	−.44	−.27
4					.31	.43
5						.57

Eigenvalues

Eigenvalue	*Percent Variance*	*Cumulative Percent*
2.78	46.4	46.4
1.23	20.5	66.9
.76	12.8	79.7
.50	8.3	88.0
.38	6.3	94.3
.34	5.7	100.0

Principal Components

Variable	Component					
	1	2	3	4	5	6
1	.65	.57	.04	.39	.23	−.21
2	.75	.46	−.03	.03	−.32	.34
3	−.66	.08	.67	.22	.06	.21
4	.74	.10	.41	−.48	.21	−.01
5	.63	−.63	−.14	.19	.28	.28
6	.65	−.53	.35	.16	−.31	−.23

Two-Factor (Unrotated) Solution with Communality ≠ 1

Variable	Factor	
	1	2
1	.58	.41
2	.75	.45
3	−.55	.05
4	.64	.07
5	.63	−.61
6	.57	−.36

Notice here that interpretation is very difficult, due to the fact that all six variables appear to load on factor 1.

Squared Loadings

Variable	Factor		Communalities
	1	2	
1	.34	.17	.51
2	.56	.20	.76
3	.30	.00	.30
4	.41	.00	.41
5	.40	.37	.77
6	.32	.13	.45
Eigenvalue	2.33	.87	3.20
Percent explained	2.33/6 = 38.8%	.87/6 = 14.5%	53.3%

Notice that the 38.8 percent is really the average squared correlation between factor 1 and each of the six original variables. You can also note that the reason the percent of variance explained in the first variable (51 percent) is the sum of the percent explained by the first factor (34 percent) plus the percent explained by the second factor (17 percent) is that the two factors are orthogonal.

Two-Factor (orthogonally rotated) Solution ("loadings")

	Factor	
Variable	*1*	*2*
1	.71	.08
2	.86	.16
3	−.38	−.40
4	.53	.37
5	.07	.88
6	.19	.64

Notice that the interpretation is now much easier. Factor 1 is apparently largely education while factor 2 is mainly family size. Income tends to go with education, and age really doesn't fit either category well.

Squared Loadings

	Factor		
Variable	*1*	*2*	*Communality*
1	.50	.01	.51
2	.74	.03	.77
3	.14	.16	.30
4	.28	.14	.42
5	.00	.77	.77
6	.04	.41	.45
Eigenvalue	1.70	1.52	3.22
Average percent of variance explained	28.3%	25.3%	53.6%

Notice here that the effect of the rotation is to redistribute much of the variance from the first to the second factor. The total variance explained and the communalities, however, are unaffected.

Factor Score Coefficients

Variable	*Factor*	
	1	*2*
1	.27	−.06
2	.64	−.07
3	−.06	−.04
4	.13	.10
5	−.15	.73
6	.01	.20

Notice that these coefficients mean that the first factor score will be largely determined by the value of variable 2 while the second factor is dominated by variable 5, which turn out to be the variables with the biggest loadings on each factor.

Factor scores are estimates of the position of each observation on each unmeasured factor. Several methods of estimation are available (e.g., Harman, 1967). The most widely used form is:

$$f = XS^{-1}\Lambda$$

where

f = matrix of factor scores (an $n \times m$ matrix).

X = raw data (an $n \times p$ matrix).

S^{-1} = inverse of covariance matrix of the original p variables (a $p \times p$ matrix).

Λ = estimated loadings (a $p \times m$ matrix).

Appendix 14–B

Sample Factor Analysis Output

```
STATISTICAL PACKAGE FOR THE SOCIAL SCIENCES SPSSH - VERSION 6.00              03/31/77        PAGE    1

        SPACE ALLOCATION FOR THIS RUN..

            TOTAL AMOUNT REQUESTED                                    80000 BYTES

            DEFAULT TRANSPACE ALLOCATION                              10000 BYTES

               MAX NO OF TRANSFORMATIONS PERMITTED         100
               MAX NO OF RECODE VALUES                     400
               MAX NO OF ARITHM.OR LOG.OPERATIONS          800

            RESULTING WORKSPACE ALLOCATION                            70000 BYTES

                  RUN NAME         FOOD-Q14
                  VARIABLE LIST    V244 TO V273
                  INPUT MEDIUM     DISK
                  N OF CASES       940
                  INPUT FORMAT     FIXED(/43X,30F1.0////)

                 ACCORDING TO YOUR INPUT FORMAT, VARIABLES ARE TO BE READ AS FOLLOWS

                 VARIABLE   FORMAT   RECORD    COLUMNS

                 V244       F 1. 0      2      44-  44
                 V245       F 1. 0      2      45-  45
                 V246       F 1. 0      2      46-  46
                 V247       F 1. 0      2      47-  47
                 V248       F 1. 0      2      48-  48
                 V249       F 1. 0      2      49-  49
                 V250       F 1. 0      2      50-  50
                 V251       F 1. 0      2      51-  51
                 V252       F 1. 0      2      52-  52
                 V253       F 1. 0      2      53-  53
                 V254       F 1. 0      2      54-  54
                 V255       F 1. 0      2      55-  55
                 V256       F 1. 0      2      56-  56
                 V257       F 1. 0      2      57-  57
                 V258       F 1. 0      2      58-  58
                 V259       F 1. 0      2      59-  59
                 V260       F 1. 0      2      60-  60
                 V261       F 1. 0      2      61-  61
                 V262       F 1. 0      2      62-  62
                 V263       F 1. 0      2      63-  63
                 V264       F 1. 0      2      64-  64
                 V265       F 1. 0      2      65-  65
                 V266       F 1. 0      2      66-  66
```

```
FOOD-Q14                                                          03/31/77        PAGE    2

                 ACCORDING TO YOUR INPUT FORMAT, VARIABLES ARE TO BE READ AS FOLLOWS

                 VARIABLE  FORMAT  RECORC    COLUMNS

                 V267      F 1. 0       2    67-  67
                 V268      F 1. 0       2    68-  68
                 V269      F 1. 0       2    69-  69
                 V270      F 1. 0       2    70-  70
                 V271      F 1. 0       2    71-  71
                 V272      F 1. 0       2    72-  72
                 V273      F 1. 0       2    73-  73

THE INPUT FORMAT PRCVIDES FOR  30 VARIABLES.   30 WILL BE READ
IT PROVIDES FOR  6 RECCRDS ('CARDS') PER CASE.  A MAXIMUM OF   73 'COLUMNS' ARE USED ON A RECORD.

                  FACTOR          VARIABLES=V244 TO V273/
                  STATISTICS      2,4,5,6,8

***** FACTCR PROBLEM REQUIRES  16272 BYTES WCRKSPACE *****
```

FOOD-Q14 03/31/77 PAGE 4

FILE NCNAME (CREATION DATE = 03/31/77)

CORRELATION COEFFICIENTS..

	V244	V245	V246	V247	V248	V249	V250	V251	V252	V253
V244	1.00000	0.29938	0.26953	0.12491	0.05573	0.15649	0.14975	0.24135	0.08034	0.10216
V245	0.29938	1.00000	0.27027	0.19368	0.11570	0.12112	0.22934	0.23013	-0.05233	0.22743
V246	0.26953	0.27027	1.00000	0.18648	0.11149	0.34905	0.20291	0.25943	0.18468	0.09629
V247	0.12491	0.19368	0.18648	1.00000	0.08283	0.17819	0.21786	0.15937	0.01512	0.06385
V248	0.05573	0.11570	0.11149	0.08283	1.00000	-0.27590	0.04162	0.10585	0.17725	-0.13395
V249	0.15649	0.12112	0.34905	0.17819	-0.27590	1.00000	0.20701	0.13060	0.03662	0.18192
V250	0.14975	0.22934	0.20291	0.21786	0.04162	0.20701	1.00000	0.18882	0.04174	0.07872
V251	0.24135	0.23013	0.25943	0.15937	0.10585	0.13060	0.18882	1.00000	0.14016	0.04881
V252	0.08034	-0.05233	0.18468	0.01512	0.17725	0.03662	0.04174	0.14016	1.00000	-0.44514
V253	0.10216	0.22743	0.09629	0.06385	-0.13395	0.18192	0.07872	0.04881	-0.44514	1.00000
V254	-0.01356	0.00625	0.10267	0.05924	0.07344	0.14978	0.13223	0.21811	0.12205	0.04400
V255	0.24020	0.21957	0.33804	0.13516	0.13189	0.22486	0.17129	0.39235	0.15206	0.05242
V256	-0.07354	0.05492	0.00973	0.17457	0.09420	0.05625	0.20665	0.02476	0.00208	-0.00810
V257	-0.09618	0.01043	0.05259	0.04880	0.09182	0.05561	0.12934	0.05339	0.07829	0.03625
V258	0.20815	0.32000	0.14672	0.19072	0.10401	0.10710	0.19673	0.10803	-0.00783	0.20187
V259	0.22808	0.23525	0.24611	0.08258	-0.00151	0.18434	0.06295	0.19429	0.18312	0.18151
V260	0.18119	0.22567	0.10889	0.20213	0.05989	0.16110	0.19953	0.13228	0.00499	0.19962
V261	0.27204	0.44751	0.25317	0.18466	0.09800	0.19814	0.26042	0.14452	0.03335	0.16277
V262	0.25284	0.18862	0.20750	0.09468	-0.02925	0.15297	0.20911	0.12957	0.05308	0.12532
V263	0.13637	0.25879	0.19311	0.26622	0.05650	0.15350	0.23673	0.15585	0.09886	0.12033
V264	0.22182	0.24068	0.26118	0.20930	0.03544	0.25112	0.28538	0.25120	0.07462	0.15557
V265	0.17307	0.18156	0.15954	0.16602	0.08876	0.16437	0.18231	0.14222	0.11142	0.08638
V266	0.13482	0.14368	0.17451	0.09787	0.15739	0.13959	0.15987	0.18979	0.11860	0.02303
V267	0.03052	0.16615	0.09219	0.18465	0.05482	0.07401	0.19299	0.07008	0.02993	0.18773
V268	0.07675	0.00490	0.04438	0.09114	0.02303	0.09960	0.12006	0.12035	0.02034	0.09956
V269	0.00265	0.04393	0.12942	0.06016	0.03451	0.10992	0.05782	0.11565	0.11821	0.05786
V270	0.11909	0.20111	0.23886	0.14299	0.03279	0.21038	0.21350	0.11996	0.02690	0.07061
V271	0.03958	0.10143	0.23193	0.20530	0.06352	0.19021	0.23482	0.17592	0.07224	0.12125
V272	-0.01503	0.05140	0.08467	0.14253	0.10802	0.07780	0.14046	0.14556	0.01229	0.10631
V273	0.09322	0.17695	0.08650	0.07461	0.11242	0.08809	0.18305	0.16162	-0.03365	0.09097

FOOD-Q14 03/31/77 PAGE 5

FILE NONAME (CREATION DATE = 03/31/77)

	V254	V255	V256	V257	V258	V259	V260	V261	V262	V263
V244	-0.01356	0.24020	-0.07354	-0.09618	0.20815	0.22808	0.18119	0.27204	0.25284	0.13637
V245	0.00625	0.21957	0.05492	0.01043	0.32000	0.23525	0.22567	0.44751	0.18862	0.25879
V246	0.10267	0.33804	0.00973	0.05259	0.14672	0.24611	0.10889	0.25317	0.20750	0.19311
V247	0.05924	0.13516	0.17457	0.04880	0.19072	0.08258	0.20213	0.18406	0.09468	0.26622
V248	0.07344	0.13189	0.09420	0.09182	0.10401	-0.00151	0.05989	0.09800	-0.02925	0.05650
V249	0.14978	0.22486	0.05625	0.05561	0.10710	0.18434	0.16110	0.19814	0.15297	0.15350
V250	0.13223	0.17129	0.20665	0.12934	0.19673	0.06295	0.19953	0.26042	0.20911	0.23673
V251	0.21811	0.39235	0.02476	0.05339	0.10803	0.19429	0.13228	0.14452	0.12957	0.15585
V252	0.12205	0.15206	0.00208	0.07829	-0.00783	0.18312	0.00499	0.03335	0.05308	0.09886
V253	0.04400	0.05242	-0.00810	0.03625	0.20187	0.18151	0.19962	0.16277	0.12532	0.12033
V254	1.00000	0.20540	0.14567	0.41038	0.04923	0.07234	0.07350	0.00633	0.16682	0.16082
V255	0.20540	1.00000	-0.00135	0.10662	0.12975	0.22106	0.15883	0.20115	0.15220	0.13195
V256	0.14567	-0.00135	1.00000	0.06301	0.17915	-0.03716	0.12454	0.14144	0.00176	0.12525
V257	0.41038	0.10662	0.06301	1.00000	0.07388	-0.03298	0.07071	0.01966	0.16664	0.16750
V258	0.04923	0.12975	0.17915	0.07388	1.00000	0.16373	0.22046	0.31358	0.17794	0.42398
V259	0.07234	0.22106	-0.03716	-0.03298	0.16373	1.00000	0.13541	0.20135	0.11512	0.14843
V260	0.07350	0.15883	0.12454	0.07071	0.22046	0.13541	1.00000	0.31897	0.06664	0.23749
V261	0.00633	0.20115	0.14144	0.01966	0.31358	0.20135	0.31897	1.00000	0.25724	0.29881
V262	0.16682	0.15220	-0.00176	0.16664	0.17794	0.11512	0.06664	0.25724	1.00000	0.23485
V263	0.16082	0.13195	0.12525	0.16750	0.42398	0.14843	0.23749	0.29881	0.23485	1.00000
V264	0.25146	0.24502	0.09624	0.17860	0.24413	0.18786	0.24999	0.31405	0.34909	0.38255
V265	0.16248	0.15409	0.14649	0.17691	0.18744	0.07660	0.23142	0.24716	0.19677	0.24952
V266	0.20917	0.19242	0.12507	0.25694	0.16382	0.02060	0.18624	0.20393	0.21618	0.15268
V267	0.18157	0.04746	0.18474	0.12603	0.34243	0.08510	0.14636	0.14216	0.22626	0.29388
V268	0.21834	0.06824	0.11572	0.14574	0.08989	0.03864	0.04427	0.01494	0.15670	0.12711
V269	0.24157	0.07472	0.06040	0.18610	0.13868	0.05631	0.02476	0.02589	0.18944	0.16453
V270	0.06189	0.14375	0.15882	0.03154	0.19948	0.12455	0.18490	0.21743	0.21783	0.18005
V271	0.28208	0.21900	0.17376	0.25378	0.21904	0.07518	0.18336	0.19882	0.22905	0.19520
V272	0.39123	0.13245	0.13418	0.38530	0.13762	0.04249	0.11553	0.06552	0.14473	0.18389
V273	0.16704	0.17967	0.21563	0.17717	0.20332	0.08568	0.18217	0.18871	0.09255	0.12862

	V264	V265	V266	V267	V268	V269	V270	V271	V272	V273
V244	0.22182	0.17307	0.13482	0.03052	0.07675	0.00265	0.11909	0.03958	-0.01503	0.09322
V245	0.24068	0.18156	0.14368	0.16615	0.00490	0.04393	0.20111	0.10143	0.05140	0.17695
V246	0.26118	0.15994	0.17451	0.09219	0.04438	0.12942	0.23886	0.23193	0.08467	0.08650
V247	0.20930	0.16602	0.09787	0.18465	0.09114	0.06016	0.14299	0.20530	0.14253	0.07461
V248	0.03544	0.08876	0.15739	0.05482	0.02303	0.03451	0.03279	0.06352	0.10802	0.11242
V249	0.25112	0.16437	0.13959	0.07401	0.09960	0.10992	0.21038	0.19021	0.07780	0.08809
V250	0.28538	0.18231	0.15987	0.19239	0.12006	0.05782	0.21350	0.23482	0.14046	0.18305
V251	0.25120	0.14222	0.18979	0.07008	0.12035	0.11565	0.11996	0.17592	0.14556	0.16162
V252	0.07462	0.11142	0.11860	0.02993	0.02034	0.11821	0.02690	0.07224	0.01229	-0.03365
V253	0.15557	0.08638	0.02303	0.18773	0.09956	0.05786	0.07061	0.12125	0.10631	0.09097

FOOD-Q14 03/31/77 PAGE 6

FILE NONAME (CREATION DATE = 03/31/77)

	V264	V265	V266	V267	V268	V269	V270	V271	V272	V273
V254	0.25146	0.16248	0.20917	0.18157	0.21834	0.24157	0.06189	0.28208	0.39123	0.16704
V255	0.24502	0.15409	0.19242	0.04746	0.06824	0.07472	0.14875	0.21900	0.13245	0.17967
V256	0.09624	0.14649	0.12507	0.18474	0.11572	0.06040	0.15882	0.17376	0.13418	0.21563
V257	0.17860	0.17691	0.25694	0.12603	0.14574	0.18610	0.03154	0.25378	0.38530	0.17717
V258	0.24413	0.18744	0.16382	0.34243	0.08989	0.13868	0.19948	0.21904	0.13762	0.20332
V259	0.18786	0.07660	0.02060	0.08510	0.03864	0.05631	0.12455	0.07518	0.04249	0.08568
V260	0.24999	0.23142	0.18624	0.14636	0.04427	0.02476	0.18490	0.18336	0.11553	0.18217
V261	0.31405	0.24716	0.20393	0.14216	0.01494	0.02589	0.21743	0.19882	0.06552	0.18871
V262	0.34939	0.19677	0.21618	0.22626	0.15670	0.18944	0.21783	0.22905	0.14473	0.09255
V263	0.38255	0.24952	0.15268	0.29388	0.12711	0.16453	0.18005	0.19520	0.18389	0.12862
V264	1.00000	0.39771	0.23869	0.22821	0.14915	0.22337	0.23693	0.27550	0.23222	0.14872
V265	0.39771	1.00000	0.32837	0.14931	0.06571	0.09287	0.16500	0.22841	0.25067	0.23887
V266	0.23869	0.32837	1.00000	0.16864	0.05873	0.14875	0.17001	0.28600	0.24074	0.17705
V267	0.22821	0.14931	0.16864	1.00000	0.17039	0.24443	0.14160	0.27634	0.21556	0.14022
V268	0.14915	0.06571	0.05873	0.17039	1.00000	0.21050	0.09934	0.19170	0.23130	0.08858
V269	0.22337	0.09287	0.14875	0.24443	0.21050	1.00000	0.02774	0.24238	0.21251	0.01942
V270	0.23693	0.16500	0.17001	0.14160	0.09934	0.02774	1.00000	0.22244	0.04800	0.17133
V271	0.27550	0.22841	0.28600	0.27634	0.19170	0.24238	0.22244	1.00000	0.39265	0.13650
V272	0.23222	0.25067	0.24074	0.21556	0.23130	0.21251	0.04800	0.39265	1.00000	0.40098
V273	0.14872	0.23887	0.17705	0.14022	0.08858	0.01942	0.17133	0.13650	0.40098	1.00000

DETERMINANT OF CORRELATION MATRIX = 0.0019456(0.19456137D-02)

FOOD-C14 03/31/77 PAGE 7

FILE NCNAME (CREATION DATE = 03/31/77)

VARIABLE	EST COMMUNALITY	FACTOR	EIGENVALUE	PCT OF VAR	CUM PCT
V244	0.26620	1	5.55247	18.5	18.5
V245	0.33675	2	2.23002	7.4	25.9
V246	0.32008	3	1.78448	5.9	31.9
V247	0.17657	4	1.53661	5.1	37.0
V248	0.22846	5	1.30329	4.3	41.4
V249	0.32054	6	1.22577	4.1	45.4
V250	0.21425	7	1.12953	3.8	49.2
V251	0.25511	8	0.99539	3.3	52.5
V252	0.36164	9	0.94962	3.2	55.7
V253	0.37134	10	0.93334	3.1	58.8
V254	0.32592	11	0.86933	2.9	61.7
V255	0.28416	12	0.81081	2.7	64.4
V256	0.18223	13	0.80714	2.7	67.1
V257	0.28941	14	0.77290	2.6	69.7
V258	0.32629	15	0.75752	2.5	72.2
V259	0.21585	16	0.73587	2.5	74.6
V260	0.21455	17	0.70721	2.4	77.0
V261	0.35700	18	0.68020	2.3	79.3
V262	0.26112	19	0.66865	2.2	81.5
V263	0.32966	20	0.64558	2.2	83.7
V264	0.37924	21	0.61143	2.0	85.7
V265	0.27448	22	0.58673	2.0	87.6
V266	0.24483	23	0.57111	1.9	89.6
V267	0.25774	24	0.52931	1.8	91.3
V268	0.14004	25	0.48426	1.6	92.9
V269	0.18575	26	0.47818	1.6	94.5
V270	0.19048	27	0.45340	1.5	96.0
V271	0.32984	28	0.41991	1.4	97.4
V272	0.40546	29	0.39989	1.3	98.8
V273	0.27926	30	0.36986	1.2	100.0

CONVERGENCE REQUIRED 22 ITERATIONS

```
FOOD-C14                                                     03/31/77      PAGE    8

FILE    NCNAME    (CREATION DATE = 03/31/77)

FACTOR MATRIX USING PRINCIPAL FACTOR WITH ITERATIONS
```

	FACTOR 1	FACTOR 2	FACTOR 3	FACTOR 4	FACTOR 5	FACTOR 6	FACTOR 7
V244	0.34996	-0.36230	0.17554	-0.02341	0.09853	0.11869	-0.09118
V245	0.46621	-0.37331	-0.03570	0.16805	0.13041	0.09560	0.01234
V246	0.45987	-0.20029	0.25715	-0.17707	0.00909	-0.00728	0.09363
V247	0.36384	-0.06457	-0.02734	0.08538	-0.09601	-0.09687	0.14170
V248	0.14812	0.12926	0.24052	0.40604	0.18587	0.11559	0.07449
V249	0.40237	-0.18267	-0.01039	-0.51269	-0.17473	-0.33360	0.05353
V250	0.44503	-0.03990	-0.02270	0.05283	-0.06871	-0.15412	0.04292
V251	0.40736	-0.04942	0.25289	-0.09449	0.21850	0.07225	0.14876
V252	0.14069	0.15447	0.64432	0.06355	-0.23397	0.03231	0.02150
V253	0.27216	-0.24084	-0.57397	-0.22069	0.20639	0.16976	0.03545
V254	0.38576	0.46040	0.03925	-0.19230	0.08848	0.04879	0.04475
V255	0.43931	-0.08840	0.30211	-0.14871	0.26343	0.00548	0.13139
V256	0.24834	0.16129	-0.13794	0.25421	-0.11634	-0.29570	0.20243
V257	0.31258	0.46975	-0.04034	-0.06279	0.08505	0.02622	-0.13796
V258	0.48538	-0.13740	-0.17867	0.25640	-0.13773	0.13263	0.10123
V259	0.30270	-0.24083	0.13433	-0.12125	0.04407	0.13931	0.11452
V260	0.40310	-0.13995	-0.08991	0.11858	0.04857	-0.12461	-0.02944
V261	0.51389	-0.32726	-0.01462	0.19087	-0.00111	-0.06772	-0.11731
V262	0.44054	-0.01923	-0.00504	-0.11244	-0.12608	0.17276	-0.22818
V263	0.52107	-0.03756	-0.07318	0.14016	-0.22647	0.11172	-0.01000
V264	0.61051	-0.01432	0.00921	-0.07188	-0.09823	0.04706	-0.20002
V265	0.47846	0.06459	0.02064	0.09296	0.02202	-0.13904	-0.28784
V266	0.43499	0.16383	0.09003	0.06216	0.06489	-0.07828	-0.19485
V267	0.41832	0.13040	-0.22059	0.11691	-0.23671	0.17905	0.13770
V268	0.25573	0.20439	-0.08116	-0.10818	-0.05634	0.09737	0.11832
V269	0.29533	0.25747	-0.00511	-0.13505	-0.17896	0.24406	0.05444
V270	0.38016	-0.11722	-0.00216	0.02389	-0.08663	-0.15397	0.02233
V271	0.50972	0.24415	-0.05088	-0.06604	-0.04749	-0.03510	0.06187
V272	0.44055	0.48931	-0.13678	-0.02193	0.22140	-0.01706	0.01141
V273	0.37733	0.12543	-0.09454	0.15045	0.27604	-0.18530	0.03750

FOOD-Q14 03/31/77 PAGE 9

FILE NCNAME (CREATION CATE = 03/31/77)

VARIABLE	COMMUNALITY	FACTOR	EIGENVALUE	PCT OF VAR	CUM PCT
V244	0.31721	1	4.90524	47.1	47.1
V245	0.41253	2	1.60750	15.4	62.6
V246	0.35798	3	1.23732	11.9	74.5
V247	0.18327	4	0.94044	9.0	83.5
V248	0.31531	5	0.67992	6.5	90.0
V249	0.60291	6	0.59448	5.7	95.7
V250	0.23327	7	0.44347	4.3	100.0
V251	0.31636				
V252	0.51909				
V253	0.58289				
V254	0.41151				
V255	0.40088				
V256	0.31329				
V257	0.35050				
V258	0.35854				
V259	0.21684				
V260	0.22300				
V261	0.42618				
V262	0.30492				
V263	0.36179				
V264	0.43005				
V265	0.34483				
V266	0.27633				
V267	0.36137				
V268	0.15212				
V269	0.26633				
V270	0.19055				
V271	0.33377				
V272	0.50214				
V273	0.30170				

FOOD-Q14 03/31/77 PAGE 10

FILE NONAME (CREATION DATE = 03/31/77)

VARIMAX ROTATED FACTOR MATRIX

	FACTOR 1	FACTOR 2	FACTOR 3	FACTOR 4	FACTOR 5	FACTOR 6	FACTOR 7
V244	-0.11549	0.45781	0.04241	0.06169	0.00379	0.29704	-0.02071
V245	-0.10678	0.40952	0.21542	0.14782	0.23114	0.30065	-0.14609
V246	0.07299	0.52001	-0.09987	0.09165	0.13121	0.15439	0.15104
V247	0.05499	0.16730	-0.00184	0.16312	0.33859	0.09857	0.03582
V248	0.09986	0.12840	-0.17567	0.00354	0.12068	0.04140	-0.49163
V249	0.11125	0.31042	0.02373	0.00804	0.22518	0.12589	0.65345
V250	0.12622	0.17709	-0.00130	0.11410	0.34993	0.21134	0.07639
V251	0.20936	0.50701	-0.04679	0.01600	0.08175	0.05083	-0.06131
V252	0.07156	0.21354	-0.67320	0.08901	-0.02101	0.05408	-0.06228
V253	0.07114	0.15483	0.70382	0.17869	0.02877	0.07881	0.13972
V254	0.61600	0.11152	-0.06651	0.10820	0.03601	0.02342	0.04049
V255	0.21516	0.57625	-0.05771	-0.06261	0.09384	0.07973	-0.01058
V256	0.13960	-0.11658	-0.04034	0.06750	0.52211	-0.00811	-0.03688
V257	0.56116	-0.06237	-0.03217	0.05912	0.01237	0.16135	-0.03718
V258	0.00264	0.16139	0.14440	0.40880	0.34305	0.22304	-0.13221
V259	-0.02513	0.43327	0.03352	0.14215	0.02284	0.06566	0.04816
V260	0.04590	0.17722	0.12687	0.04574	0.31283	0.27066	-0.01325
V261	-0.09372	0.29973	0.10044	0.11458	0.32195	0.44575	-0.04465
V262	0.17558	0.17839	0.01728	0.28122	-0.03632	0.38628	0.11113
V263	0.10100	0.14595	0.00173	0.41154	0.26324	0.30216	-0.01533
V264	0.24735	0.25209	0.00401	0.24859	0.14016	0.45753	0.12052
V265	0.24025	0.09124	-0.03211	0.00453	0.20989	0.48339	-0.00378
V266	0.31872	0.11995	-0.08668	0.00677	0.15421	0.35550	-0.05132
V267	0.20382	0.00989	0.08009	0.49230	0.24834	0.08969	-0.03515
V268	0.29540	0.06274	0.03017	0.22482	0.06886	-0.03306	0.06022
V269	0.32774	0.06660	-0.07558	0.37685	-0.04400	0.02536	0.06458
V270	0.03717	0.18407	-0.00514	0.09005	0.30230	0.20739	0.11293
V271	0.42612	0.13675	-0.01178	0.20809	0.25005	0.14496	0.08065
V272	0.66259	0.02262	0.10144	0.04634	0.17492	0.09554	-0.10218
V273	0.30343	0.12282	0.14384	-0.11760	0.33854	0.14713	-0.15418

Appendix 14–C

Sample Cluster Analysis Output

```
                    LARGE HOWARD HARRIS CLUSTERING PROGRAM
                          THIS VERSION BY C.P.P.C.
                               JULY 9, 1973

            HOWARD-TYPE CLUSTERING ...PROGRAMMED BY WORDLEY AND MODIFIED BY CARMONE

     FOOD CLUSTER

NO OF OBSERVATIONS OR CASES        940
NO OF VRIABLES PER CASE            12
MAX NO OF CLUSTERS                   4
 FORMAT (12F2.0)

INPUT TAPE NO.    8

SCORE WEIGHTS 1.00 1.00 1.00 1.00 1.00 1.00 1.00 1.00 1.00 1.00 1.00 1.00
```

RAW DATA--MEANS--VARIANCES

	1	2	3	4	5	6	7	8	9	10	11	12
1	1.000	1.000	3.000	3.000	3.000	4.000	2.000	1.000	1.000	2.000	2.000	2.000
2	2.000	1.000	1.000	1.000	3.000	3.000	4.000	1.000	1.000	3.000	2.000	4.000
3	2.000	1.000	3.000	1.000	1.000	4.000	3.000	1.000	1.000	2.000	2.000	4.000
4	3.000	1.000	5.000	3.000	2.000	3.000	3.000	2.000	1.000	2.000	3.000	5.000
5	2.000	1.000	1.000	3.000	3.000	3.000	3.000	3.000	1.000	2.000	2.000	4.000
6	2.000	1.000	1.000	1.000	2.000	5.000	5.000	1.000	1.000	1.000	2.000	3.000
7	3.000	3.000	3.000	3.000	3.000	3.000	3.000	3.000	3.000	2.000	3.000	2.000
8	1.000	1.000	1.000	1.000	3.000	5.000	5.000	5.000	1.000	1.000	2.000	5.000
9	1.000	1.000	1.000	1.000	3.000	1.000	5.000	3.000	3.000	1.000	3.000	5.000
10	3.000	1.000	5.000	1.000	1.000	3.000	5.000	1.000	3.000	2.000	3.000	4.000
11	1.000	1.000	3.000	1.000	1.000	1.000	5.000	1.000	1.000	5.000	3.000	5.000
12	3.000	3.000	3.000	1.000	3.000	3.000	3.000	3.000	3.000	2.000	2.000	3.000
13	2.000	1.000	5.000	3.000	3.000	5.000	3.000	1.000	1.000	3.000	3.000	2.000
14	3.000	1.000	5.000	1.000	3.000	3.000	3.000	1.000	1.000	3.000	2.000	4.000
15	1.000	1.000	3.000	3.000	1.000	3.000	3.000	1.000	3.000	1.000	3.000	5.000
16	1.000	1.000	3.000	1.000	3.000	1.000	1.000	1.000	1.000	1.000	1.000	4.000
17	1.000	1.000	1.000	1.000	1.000	3.000	1.000	3.000	1.000	2.000	1.000	3.000
18	1.000	1.000	3.000	1.000	3.000	5.000	5.000	1.000	1.000	5.000	2.000	4.000
19	5.000	3.000	5.000	4.000	3.000	4.000	4.000	3.000	3.000	1.000	2.000	4.000
20	1.000	1.000	2.000	1.000	3.000	3.000	4.000	1.000	2.000	2.000	2.000	3.000
21	3.000	1.000	3.000	2.000	1.000	3.000	2.000	1.000	1.000	5.000	1.000	3.000
22	1.000	1.000	3.000	3.000	3.000	3.000	3.000	3.000	1.000	5.000	4.000	3.000
23	3.000	1.000	1.000	1.000	1.000	3.000	3.000	3.000	1.000	4.000	2.000	2.000
24	3.000	1.000	4.000	3.000	2.000	2.000	2.000	1.000	3.000	2.000	4.000	5.000
25	3.000	1.000	2.000	3.000	2.000	2.000	3.000	3.000	1.000	3.000	2.000	5.000
26	1.000	1.000	3.000	3.000	3.000	5.000	1.000	3.000	1.000	1.000	3.000	3.000
27	1.000	1.000	1.000	1.000	1.000	1.000	1.000	1.000	1.000	2.000	3.000	3.000
28	3.000	1.000	1.000	1.000	1.000	1.000	3.000	5.000	1.000	1.000	1.000	4.000
29	4.000	3.000	5.000	3.000	3.000	3.000	4.000	4.000	3.000	2.000	3.000	5.000
30	1.000	1.000	1.000	2.000	2.000	2.000	2.000	1.000	1.000	1.000	2.000	4.000
31	2.000	1.000	3.000	2.000	3.000	2.000	2.000	3.000	2.000	4.000	3.000	5.000
32	1.000	1.000	3.000	1.000	2.000	2.000	5.000	1.000	1.000	5.000	1.000	5.000
33	2.000	2.000	5.000	3.000	3.000	3.000	3.000	2.000	2.000	5.000	4.000	5.000
34	2.000	1.000	4.000	1.000	2.000	2.000	3.000	3.000	1.000	5.000	3.000	3.000
35	1.000	1.000	1.000	1.000	3.000	3.000	5.000	3.000	1.000	4.000	1.000	3.000
36	2.000	1.000	2.000	1.000	1.000	2.000	3.000	1.000	1.000	1.000	3.000	5.000
37	3.000	3.000	3.000	3.000	1.000	2.000	3.000	3.000	1.000	2.000	3.000	3.000
38	1.000	1.000	3.000	3.000	1.000	3.000	5.000	3.000	1.000	2.000	1.000	3.000
39	1.000	1.000	1.000	3.000	3.000	5.000	3.000	1.000	2.000	1.000	3.000	4.000
40	3.000	3.000	1.000	1.000	4.000	4.000	5.000	1.000	1.000	2.000	2.000	4.000
41	2.000	1.000	3.000	1.000	1.000	1.000	4.000	2.000	1.000	1.000	3.000	2.000
42	3.000	3.000	3.000	3.000	3.000	3.000	3.000	3.000	3.000	2.000	1.000	4.000
43	4.000	1.000	2.000	2.000	3.000	1.000	3.000	1.000	1.000	1.000	2.000	4.000
44	3.000	1.000	3.000	1.000	3.000	3.000	3.000	3.000	3.000	1.000	2.000	3.000
45	3.000	1.000	4.000	3.000	1.000	2.000	1.000	2.000	3.000	1.000	3.000	4.000
46	2.000	1.000	5.000	1.000	1.000	3.000	3.000	2.000	1.000	1.000	2.000	5.000
47	3.000	3.000	1.000	3.000	3.000	1.000	3.000	1.000	1.000	1.000	1.000	3.000
48	3.000	2.000	2.000	2.000	2.000	2.000	2.000	1.000	1.000	3.000	1.000	4.000
49	1.000	1.000	1.000	1.000	1.000	1.000	1.000	1.000	1.000	1.000	1.000	4.000
50	1.000	1.000	3.000	3.000	3.000	3.000	3.000	3.000	3.000	4.000	3.000	5.000
51	1.000	1.000	3.000	2.000	3.000	4.000	4.000	2.000	1.000	2.000	3.000	5.000
52	3.000	1.000	2.000	3.000	2.000	4.000	3.000	3.000	1.000	4.000	2.000	4.000
53	3.000	1.000	2.000	3.000	1.000	3.000	1.000	3.000	2.000	2.000	3.000	4.000
54	1.000	1.000	5.000	1.000	2.000	2.000	1.000	1.000	2.000	1.000	1.000	5.000
55	3.000	1.000	3.000	1.000	2.000	3.000	3.000	2.000	2.000	3.000	3.000	3.000
56	1.000	3.000	1.000	1.000	3.000	3.000	5.000	3.000	1.000	1.000	2.000	3.000
57	3.000	1.000	3.000	1.000	5.000	5.000	3.000	3.000	1.000	4.000	2.000	4.000
58	3.000	2.000	3.000	3.000	3.000	3.000	3.000	4.000	1.000	3.000	3.000	5.000

SPLIT NO. 2

GROUP NO. 1

1	2	3	5	6	9	11	16	17	18	20	21	23	25	27	28	30	32	35	36	39	40	41	43	47
48	49	51	56	60	61	62	63	66	67	69	72	73	76	78	80	81	85	87	90	91	93	94	95	96
97	98	101	113	115	118	119	120	122	123	124	134	135	138	141	142	143	146	148	149	158	159	163	164	166
168	169	170	172	174	175	176	179	183	185	186	190	192	194	195	197	200	205	208	216	221	224	226	227	228
229	231	232	233	234	237	238	239	241	245	247	248	250	252	256	257	258	260	261	262	265	267	268	269	270
271	274	275	280	282	285	289	291	292	298	299	300	307	311	312	319	323	324	325	327	329	330	331	332	334
335	337	340	341	345	351	353	358	359	360	361	363	367	368	369	371	372	375	377	384	385	391	395	398	402
404	410	413	414	417	419	421	423	424	425	426	427	432	433	438	440	442	447	448	450	452	459	463	464	465
468	469	471	479	480	485	488	490	493	497	503	504	506	507	511	516	517	519	520	521	522	523	524	526	534
535	537	543	544	547	552	554	561	562	564	569	571	573	577	579	585	587	588	597	598	600	601	604	610	611
612	615	622	625	628	630	632	634	635	636	638	640	646	647	651	652	654	657	658	660	669	670	674	676	677
678	681	685	687	688	693	695	696	704	708	713	716	719	721	722	723	724	726	730	731	733	737	738	742	743
746	748	749	750	751	752	756	758	759	760	762	763	766	768	771	776	779	782	783	785	787	790	791	792	795
796	797	798	799	800	801	802	809	811	813	816	817	820	821	822	823	825	828	834	835	836	850	851	853	859
860	862	863	867	868	871	872	876	880	881	884	885	887	890	891	894	897	900	907	908	911	912	916	921	923
925	928	931	934	935	940																			

GROUP NO. 2

4	10	13	14	15	24	33	34	45	46	54	55	59	64	65	68	70	74	75	82	84	86	89	92	99
100	106	108	110	111	114	121	126	128	129	130	131	132	144	145	155	161	162	165	177	178	182	188	189	196
198	201	202	209	213	218	220	222	225	236	240	243	244	246	253	254	255	264	266	272	276	277	283	284	288
290	293	295	296	302	303	304	308	309	310	313	315	316	317	320	326	338	339	342	346	347	350	352	357	362
364	366	376	378	379	381	383	387	388	389	390	392	394	396	397	399	401	403	406	407	411	412	415	420	422
430	434	437	439	445	446	451	453	454	461	467	470	475	481	482	484	487	491	492	496	498	499	502	505	508
509	518	528	529	530	532	541	542	545	548	549	555	556	558	559	560	563	565	567	570	572	574	575	576	578
580	582	583	590	593	594	595	596	599	602	605	606	607	608	614	619	623	626	627	629	631	637	642	645	648
649	650	655	656	659	661	662	663	664	666	668	675	680	689	690	694	697	700	701	706	707	711	712	715	725
734	739	740	741	747	753	754	755	765	767	769	774	775	777	778	784	786	794	803	804	812	815	818	819	824
826	827	829	830	831	833	838	840	841	842	844	845	846	847	849	852	854	855	857	864	865	870	873	874	877
882	883	888	889	895	901	903	905	909	910	913	920	922	929	930	933	937	938	939						

GROUP NO. 3

7	8	12	19	22	26	29	31	37	38	42	44	50	52	53	57	58	71	77	79	83	88	102	103	104
105	107	109	112	116	117	125	127	133	136	137	139	140	147	150	151	152	153	154	156	157	160	167	171	173
180	181	184	187	191	193	199	203	204	206	207	210	211	212	214	215	217	219	223	230	235	242	249	251	259
263	273	278	279	281	286	287	294	297	301	305	306	314	318	321	322	328	333	336	343	344	348	349	354	355
356	365	370	373	374	380	382	386	393	400	405	408	409	416	418	428	429	431	435	436	441	443	444	449	455
456	457	458	460	462	466	472	473	474	476	477	478	483	486	489	494	495	500	501	510	512	513	514	515	525
527	531	533	536	538	539	540	546	550	551	553	557	566	568	581	584	586	589	591	592	603	609	613	616	617
618	620	621	624	633	639	641	643	644	653	665	667	671	672	673	679	682	683	684	686	691	692	698	699	702
703	705	709	710	714	717	718	720	727	728	729	732	735	736	744	745	757	761	764	770	772	773	780	781	788
789	793	805	806	807	808	810	814	832	837	839	843	848	856	858	861	866	869	875	878	879	886	892	893	896
898	899	902	904	906	914	915	917	918	919	924	926	927	932	936										

NO. IN EACH GROUP

381	294	265

```
GROUP MEANS BY VARIABLE

     VAR  1          1.7507     2.1939     2.3698
     VAR  2          1.1549     1.2517     1.5925
     VAR  3          1.7C60     4.5714     3.0566
     VAR  4          1.4488     1.6463     2.4189
     VAR  5          1.9265     2.0578     2.7736
     VAR  6          2.6194     2.6973     3.1509
     VAR  7          2.7664     2.6735     3.0943
     VAR  8          1.7008     1.7585     3.7094
     VAR  9          1.2808     1.9048     2.0943
     VAR 10          2.3753     2.4490     2.3585
     VAR 11          1.9895     2.6769     2.4981
     VAR 12          3.7579     3.8605     3.6453


GROUP VARIANCES BY VARIABLE

     VAR  1          C.7508     0.8978     1.0406
     VAR  2          0.2044     0.3244     C.7773
     VAR  3          0.7167     0.5034     1.5704
     VAR  4          0.5518     0.7388     1.1642
     VAR  5          0.8575     1.1701     1.3374
     VAR  6          1.5C08     1.5308     1.1017
     VAR  7          1.1449     1.2199     1.1420
     VAR  8          0.8396     0.707C     C.9307
     VAR  9          0.3437     0.8957     0.9458
     VAR 10          1.4156     1.3494     1.1960
     VAR 11          0.7138     1.0282     0.7934
     VAR 12          1.1534     1.1812     1.1346
```

```
SPLIT NO.    3

     GROUP NO.    1

  9  11  16  17  21  23  25  27  28  30  36  41  43  47  48  49  53  61  62  67  69  72  73  74  76
 78  80  81  87  89  93  94  95  96  97  98 113 114 115 118 119 120 134 143 145 158 164 166 168 170
172 174 183 185 186 195 199 205 206 216 221 224 227 228 229 231 233 240 241 245 247 248 252 256 258
269 270 271 274 275 277 282 291 292 298 299 300 312 315 319 323 324 329 330 334 335 337 341 351 358
359 360 361 363 367 368 371 372 375 377 384 385 391 395 398 402 404 410 413 414 423 425 427 432 433
438 440 452 463 465 468 469 479 480 493 494 516 520 523 524 526 534 535 536 544 552 554 562 564 566
569 573 577 579 600 601 610 612 622 626 628 630 632 634 635 638 640 646 658 660 663 669 676 677 678
681 688 693 696 698 704 708 713 721 722 724 726 730 731 733 735 737 743 746 750 756 758 759 760 762
763 768 771 776 779 780 785 790 791 792 796 797 798 799 800 807 811 813 816 828 834 836 850 853 862
863 867 868 869 871 881 887 890 891 894 897 900 907 911 912 923 925 927 931 934 935

     GROUP NO.    2

  4  10  13  14  15  24  33  34  45  46  54  55  64  65  68  70  75  82  84  92  99 100 108 110 121
126 128 129 130 131 132 141 144 148 155 161 165 177 178 189 196 198 201 202 209 213 218 220 222 225
236 243 244 246 253 254 255 266 272 276 283 284 288 290 293 295 296 302 303 304 309 310 313 316 317
320 326 338 339 342 346 347 350 352 357 362 366 378 379 381 383 387 388 389 390 392 394 396 397 399
401 403 406 407 412 415 420 422 430 434 437 439 445 446 451 454 461 467 470 475 481 482 484 487 491
492 498 502 505 508 509 518 519 528 529 530 532 541 542 545 548 549 555 559 560 565 567 570 572 574
575 576 578 582 583 590 593 594 595 596 599 602 605 606 607 608 614 619 623 629 631 637 642 645 648
649 655 656 659 661 662 664 666 668 679 680 689 690 694 700 701 707 711 712 715 725 734 739 740 741
747 753 754 755 765 767 769 774 775 777 778 784 786 804 812 815 818 819 824 826 827 829 830 831 833
838 840 841 842 844 846 847 854 855 857 865 870 873 877 882 883 888 889 895 901 903 905 909 910 913
920 922 929 930 933 937 938 939

     GROUP NO.    3

  7  12  19  22  29  31  37  42  44  50  58  59  71  77  79  83  88 102 103 104 105 107 109 111 112
116 117 125 127 133 136 137 140 147 151 152 153 156 157 171 173 180 181 182 191 193 203 204 211 214
215 217 219 223 230 235 242 249 251 259 263 273 278 281 286 287 301 305 306 308 314 318 321 322 328
336 344 349 354 356 365 370 373 374 376 380 382 386 393 400 411 416 418 428 431 435 436 441 443 449
455 456 457 458 460 462 466 472 473 474 476 477 478 483 486 489 495 500 501 510 513 531 533 540 545
550 551 553 556 557 568 580 581 584 586 589 591 592 609 613 618 621 624 633 641 644 650 665 667 671
672 673 675 682 683 684 686 691 699 702 705 710 714 717 718 720 728 729 732 745 757 764 772 773 781
789 793 794 805 806 808 810 814 837 839 843 845 858 861 864 866 875 878 879 886 892 893 898 899 902
904 915 917 918 919 926 932 936

     GROUP NO.    4

  1   2   3   5   6   8  18  20  26  32  35  38  39  40  51  52  56  57  60  63  66  85  86  90  91
101 106 122 123 124 135 138 139 142 146 149 150 154 159 160 162 163 167 169 175 176 179 184 187 188
190 192 194 197 200 207 208 210 212 226 232 234 237 238 239 250 257 260 261 262 264 265 267 268 279
280 285 289 294 297 307 311 325 327 331 332 333 340 343 345 348 353 355 364 369 405 408 409 417 419
421 424 426 429 442 444 447 448 450 453 459 464 471 485 488 490 496 497 499 503 504 506 507 511 512
514 515 517 521 522 525 527 537 538 539 543 547 558 561 563 571 585 587 588 597 598 603 604 611 615
616 617 620 625 627 636 639 643 647 651 652 653 654 657 670 674 685 687 692 695 697 703 706 709 716
719 723 727 736 738 742 744 748 749 751 752 761 766 770 782 783 787 788 795 801 802 803 809 817 820
821 822 823 825 832 835 848 849 851 852 856 859 860 872 874 876 880 884 885 896 906 908 914 916 921
924 928 940

NO. IN EACH GROUP
246       258       208       228
```

GROUP VARIANCES BY VARIABLE

VAR 1	0.8156	0.8907	1.0037	0.9431
VAR 2	0.2172	0.3395	C.7559	0.3739
VAR 3	0.7158	0.3669	1.3557	1.0081
VAR 4	0.4881	0.7298	1.1009	0.6888
VAR 5	0.5425	1.0528	1.2092	1.0724
VAR 6	0.6599	1.3767	C.9388	0.7966
VAR 7	0.9759	1.1973	0.9856	1.0573
VAR 8	1.1981	0.6525	0.8646	1.1964
VAR 9	0.4227	0.8982	0.9222	0.4475
VAR 10	1.4915	1.3769	1.1255	1.2851
VAR 11	0.7642	1.0108	0.8178	0.7481
VAR 12	1.1789	1.1906	1.0494	1.1959

GROUP MEANS BY VARIABLE

VAR 1	1.8C49	2.1783	2.4231	1.8860
VAR 2	1.1504	1.2597	1.6154	1.2544
VAR 3	1.7154	4.6744	3.4904	1.9737
VAR 4	1.3821	1.6279	2.6202	1.6316
VAR 5	1.5122	1.9612	2.7981	2.6930
VAR 6	1.8780	2.6434	2.9087	3.8465
VAR 7	2.3821	2.6473	2.9952	3.3684
VAR 8	1.8537	1.7171	3.7788	2.0307
VAR 9	1.3252	1.8876	2.2788	1.3860
VAR 10	2.3130	2.4302	2.3317	2.4956
VAR 11	2.C000	2.6202	2.6683	2.1228
VAR 12	3.8577	3.8372	3.7163	3.6667

Appendix 14–D

SAS Clustering Results, 50 States Data

```
                         CLUSTER ANALYSIS: STATES DATA                   11:32 WEDNESDAY, APRIL 11, 1984     7

                                                NUMBER

      4 4 1 3 4 1 3 4   2 1 3 2 1 2 4 5 3 4       3 4     2 2 3 3   1 2 1 2 2 4 4 1 1 2   3 1 2 3 3 1 4
    1 2 0 0 3 6 7 6 8 4 4 2 1 9 9 6 5 0 4 1 3 9 6 7 4 2 7 0 1 0 9 8 1 8 4 5 3 7 9 5 6 7 5 2 3 2 8 5 8 3
 1 +XXXXXXXXXXXXXXXXXXXXXXXXXXXXXXXXXXXXXXXXXXXXXXXXXXXXXXXXXXXXXXXXXXXXXXXXXXXXXXXXXXXXXXXXXXXXXXXXXXX
 2 +XXXXXXXXXXXXXXXXXXXXXXXXXXXXXXXXXXXXXXXXXXXXXXXXXXXXXXXXXXXXXXXXXXXXXXXXXXXXXXXXXXXXXXXXXXXXXXXXXXX
 3 +XXXXXXXXXXXXXXXXXXXXXXXXXXXXXXXXXXXXXXXXXXXXXXXXX XXXXXXXXXXXXXXXXXXXXXXXXXXXXXXXXX XXXXXXXXXXXXXXX
 4 +XXXXXXXXXXXXXXXXXXXXXXXXXXXXXXXXXXXXXXXXXXXXXXXXX . XXXXXXXXXXXXXXXXXXXXXXXXXXXXXXX XXXXXXXXXXXXXXX
 5 +XXXXXXXXXXXXXXXXXXXXXXXXXXXXXXXXXXXXXXXXXXXXXXXXX . XXXXXXXXXXXXXXXXXXXXXXXXXXXXXXX XXXXXXXXXXXXXXX
 6 +XXXXXXXXXXXXXXXXXXXXXXXXXXXXXXXXXXXXXXXXXXXXXXXXX . XXXXXXXXXXXXXXXXXXXXXXXXXXXXXXX XXX XXXXXXXXXXX
 7 +XXXXXXXXXXXXXXXXXXXXXXXXXXXXXXXXXXXXXXXXXXXXXXXXX . XXXXXXXXXXXXXXXXXXXXXXXXXXXXXXX XXX XXXXXXX XXX
 8 +XXXXXXXXXXXXXXXXXXXXXXXXXXXXXXXXXXXXXXXXXXXXXXXXX . XXXXXXXXXXXXXXX XXXXXXXXXXXXXXX XXX XXXXXXX XXX
 9 +XXXXXXXXXXXXXXXXXXXXXXXXXXXXXXXXXXXXXXX XXXXXXXXX . XXXXXXXXXXXXXXX XXXXXXXXXXXXXXX XXX XXXXXXX XXX
10 +XXXXXXXXXXXXXXXXXXXXXXXXXXX XXXXXXXXXXX XXXXXXXXX . XXXXXXXXXXXXXXX XXXXXXXXXXXXXXX XXX XXXXXXX XXX
11 +XXXXXXXXXXXXXXXXXXXXXXXXXXX XXXXXXXXXXX XXXXXXXXX . XXXXXXXXX XXXXX XXXXXXXXXXXXXXX XXX XXXXXXX XXX
12 +XXXXXXXXXXXXXXXXXXXXXXXXXXX XXXXXXXXXXX XXXXXXXXX . XXXXXXXXX XXXXX XXXXXXXXXXXXXXX . . XXXXXXX XXX
13 +XXXXXXXXXXXXXXXXX XXXXXXXXX XXXXXXXXXXX XXXXXXXXX . XXXXXXXXX XXXXX XXXXXXXXXXXXXXX . . XXXXXXX . .
14 +XXXXXXXXXXXXXXXXX XXXXXXXXX XXXXXXXXXXX XXXXXXXXX . XXXXXXXXX XXXXX XXXXXXXXXXXXXXX . . XXXXXXX . .
15 +XXXXXXXXXXXXXXXXX XXXXXXXXX XXXXXXXXXXX XXX XXXXX . XXXXXXXXX XXXXX XXXXXXXXX XXXXX . . XXXXXXX . .
16 +XXXXXXXXXXXXXXXXX XXXXXXXXX XXXXXXXXXXX XXX XXXXX . XXXXXXXXX XXXXX XXXXXXXXX XXXXX . . XXXXXXX . .
17 +XXXXXXXXXXX XXXXX XXXXXXXXX XXXXXXXXXXX XXX XXXXX . XXXXXXXXX XXXXX XXXXXXXXX XXXXX . . . XXXXX . .
18 +XXXXXXXXXXX XXXXX XXXXXXXXX XXXXXXXXXXX XXX XXXXX . XXXXXXX . XXXXX XXXXXXXXX XXXXX . . . XXXXX . .
19 +XXXXXXXXXXX XXXXX XXXXXXXXX XXXXXXX XXX XXX XXXXX . XXXXXXX . XXXXX XXXXXXXXX XXXXX . . . XXXXX . .
20 +XXXXXXXXXXX XXXXX XXX XXXXX XXXXXXX XXX XXX XXXXX . XXXXXXX . XXXXX XXXXXXXXX XXXXX . . . XXXXX . .
21 +XXXXXXXXXXX XXXXX XXX XXXXX XXXXXXX XXX XXX XXXXX . XXXXXXX . XXXXX XXX XXXXX XXXXX . . . XXXXX . .
22 +XXXXXXXXXXX XXXXX XXX XXXXX XXXXXXX XXX XXX XXXXX . XXXXXXX . XXX . XXX XXXXX XXXXX . . . XXXXX . .
23 +XXXXXXXXXXX XXXXX XXX XXXXX XXXXXXX XXX XXX XXXXX . XXXXXXX . XXX . XXX XXXXX . XXX . . . XXXXX . .
24 +XXXXXXXXXXX XXXXX XXX XXXXX XXXXXXX XXX . . XXXXX . XXXXXXX . XXX . XXX XXXXX . XXX . . . XXXXX . .
25 +XXXXXXXXXXX XXXXX XXX XXXXX XXXXX . XXX . . XXXXX . XXXXXXX . XXX . XXX XXXXX . XXX . . . XXXXX . .
26 +XXXXXXXXXXX XXXXX XXX XXXXX XXXXX . XXX . . XXXXX . XXX XXX . XXX . XXX XXXXX . XXX . . . XXXXX . .
27 +XXXXXXXXXXX XXXXX XXX XXXXX XXXXX . XXX . . XXX . . XXX XXX . XXX . XXX XXXXX . XXX . . . XXXXX . .
28 +XXXXX XXXXX XXXXX XXX XXXXX XXXXX . XXX . . XXX . . XXX XXX . XXX . XXX XXXXX . XXX . . . XXXXX . .
29 +XXXXX XXXXX XXXXX XXX XXXXX XXXXX . XXX . . XXX . . XXX XXX . XXX . XXX XXXXX . XXX . . . XXXXX . .
30 +XXXXX XXX . XXXXX XXX XXXXX XXXXX . XXX . . XXX . . XXX XXX . XXX . XXX XXXXX . XXX . . . XXX . . .
31 +XXXXX XXX . XXXXX XXX XXXXX XXX . . XXX . . XXX . . XXX XXX . XXX . XXX XXXXX . XXX . . . XXX . . .
32 +XXXXX XXX . XXXXX XXX XXXXX XXX . . XXX . . XXX . . XXX XXX . XXX . XXX XXXXX . XXX . . . XXX . . .
33 +XXXXX XXX . XXXXX XXX XXX . XXX . . XXX . . XXX . . XXX XXX . XXX . XXX . XXX . XXX . . . XXX . . .
34 +XXXXX XXX . XXXXX XXX XXX . XXX . . XXX . . XXX . . XXX XXX . . . . XXX . XXX . XXX . . . XXX . . .
35 +XXXXX XXX . XXXXX XXX XXX . XXX . . XXX . . . . . . XXX XXX . . . . XXX . XXX . XXX . . . XXX . . .
36 +XXXXX XXX . XXXXX XXX . . . XXX . . XXX . . . . . . XXX XXX . . . . XXX . XXX . XXX . . . XXX . . .
37 +XXXXX XXX . XXX . XXX . . . XXX . . XXX . . . . . . XXX XXX . . . . XXX . XXX . XXX . . . XXX . . .
38 +XXXXX XXX . XXX . XXX . . . XXX . . XXX . . . . . . XXX XXX . . . . XXX . XXX . XXX . . . XXX . . .
39 +XXXXX XXX . XXX . XXX . . . XXX . . XXX . . . . . . XXX XXX . . . . XXX . . . . XXX . . . XXX . . .
40 +XXXXX XXX . XXX . XXX . . . XXX . . XXX . . . . . . XXX XXX . . . . XXX . . . . XXX . . . . . . . .
41 +XXX . XXX . XXX . XXX . . . XXX . . XXX . . . . . . XXX . . . . . . XXX . . . . XXX . . . . . . . .
42 +XXX . XXX . XXX . . . . . . XXX . . XXX . . . . . . XXX . . . . . . XXX . . . . XXX . . . . . . . .
43 +XXX . XXX . XXX . . . . . . XXX . . XXX . . . . . . XXX . . . . . . XXX . . . . XXX . . . . . . . .
44 +XXX . XXX . XXX . . . . . . XXX . . . . . . . . . . XXX . . . . . . . . . . . . XXX . . . . . . . .
45 +XXX . XXX . XXX . . . . . . . . . . . . . . . . . . XXX . . . . . . . . . . . . XXX . . . . . . . .
46 +XXX . XXX . XXX . . . . . . . . . . . . . . . . . . . . . . . . . . . . . . . . XXX . . . . . . . .
47 +XXX . XXX . XXX . . . . . . . . . . . . . . . . . . . . . . . . . . . . . . . . XXX . . . . . . . .
48 +. . . XXX . XXX . . . . . . . . . . . . . . . . . . . . . . . . . . . . . . . . . . . . . . . . . .
49 +. . . . . . XXX . . . . . . . . . . . . . . . . . . . . . . . . . . . . . . . . . . . . . . . . . .
50 +. . . . . . . . . . . . . . . . . . . . . . . . . . . . . . . . . . . . . . . . . . . . . . . . . .
```

NUMBER OF CLUSTERS

CLUSTER ANALYSIS: STATES DATA   11:32 WEDNESDAY, APRIL 11, 1984   8

OBS	NUMBER	INC	POP	POPCH	URBAN	TAX	GOVT	COLLEGE	MINERAL	FOREST	MFG	FAR1	CLUSTER	CLUSNAME
1	17	-1.0684	-0.18941	-0.2364	-0.4279	-1.1009	-0.28207	-0.32639	0.83825	-0.17422	-0.16659	-0.16324	1	CL12
2	36	-0.7215	-0.34614	-0.1411	-0.0765	-1.2102	-0.25252	-0.24081	0.59832	-0.32744	-0.57112	0.04943	1	CL12
3	10	-0.7215	0.14643	0.1449	-0.0375	-0.7983	0.22678	-0.13812	-0.36410	0.59189	0.05124	0.16956	1	CL12
4	33	-0.9528	0.28076	0.0496	-0.5059	-0.9328	0.09218	-0.00976	-0.47723	0.31382	0.46615	0.35058	1	CL12
5	1	-1.1840	-0.14463	-0.3317	0.1577	-1.5885	-0.15403	-0.20658	-0.14440	0.38192	-0.23919	-0.26981	1	CL12
6	42	-0.9528	-0.01030	-0.0457	0.1968	-1.2438	-0.05883	-0.08677	-0.34607	-0.11180	0.07199	-0.39982	1	CL12
7	16	0.4348	-0.43569	-0.9988	-0.5840	0.0087	-0.37399	-0.31355	-0.07663	-0.78144	-0.48814	1.27992	2	CL13
8	27	0.6660	-0.61481	-0.4270	-0.5450	-0.2435	-0.52500	-0.51465	-0.50839	-0.79846	-0.63336	1.10622	2	CL13
9	7	1.4754	-0.25658	-0.8082	1.2118	0.9839	-0.36742	-0.14668	-0.54336	-0.73036	-0.02137	-0.88455	3	CL17
10	20	0.8973	-0.03269	-0.4270	1.0556	0.8578	-0.01287	-0.07394	-0.46794	-0.68496	-0.29106	-0.66613	3	CL17
11	19	-0.9528	-0.70436	-0.0457	-1.3258	0.2105	-0.70556	-0.64302	-0.54282	0.14925	-0.67485	-0.74622	4	CL18
12	26	-0.2590	-0.79392	0.1449	-1.3258	0.1264	-0.73183	-0.66869	-0.24824	0.43867	-0.78895	-0.38342	4	CL18
13	34	0.3191	-0.81631	-0.7129	-1.7942	-0.4620	-0.73183	-0.67725	-0.47560	-0.83251	-0.80969	0.26841	4	CL18
14	41	-0.7215	-0.79392	-0.7129	-1.7161	-0.4620	-0.75152	-0.67297	-0.50620	-0.75874	-0.76820	0.01978	4	CL18
15	14	-0.0278	0.23598	-0.8082	0.3139	-0.2098	0.10203	0.06298	-0.32148	-0.63389	0.86031	0.70162	2	CL13
16	25	-0.2590	0.12404	-0.9035	0.2358	-0.5965	0.08890	0.03303	-0.18484	-0.00965	0.10310	0.49308	2	CL13
17	4	-1.4153	-0.48047	0.5261	-0.7792	-1.5801	-0.53485	-0.54888	-0.34006	0.18330	-0.50888	0.33602	1	CL12
18	24	-1.8778	-0.43569	-0.1411	-1.2477	-1.2354	-0.43308	-0.45475	-0.34880	0.10385	-0.47777	-0.14919	1	CL12
19	40	-1.2996	-0.32375	0.3355	-0.3888	-1.2607	-0.33131	-0.31783	-0.50511	-0.14585	-0.22882	-0.51687	1	CL12
20	21	0.6660	0.34793	-0.7129	1.1337	1.6396	0.30886	0.67913	-0.52861	-0.65659	0.37279	-0.88715	3	CL17
21	30	1.1285	0.68377	-0.8082	1.3679	0.9335	0.55836	0.33683	-0.48543	-0.71334	1.00553	-0.81071	3	CL17
22	22	0.6660	1.10916	-0.6176	0.9385	0.8998	1.08034	0.85028	0.00589	0.24005	1.98056	-0.10915	5	CL15
23	38	0.3191	1.69128	-1.1894	0.8995	0.3618	1.32656	1.02143	0.73550	0.15493	1.93907	-0.20848	5	CL15
24	47	0.6660	-0.16702	-0.5223	0.5091	0.4207	-0.03257	-0.08677	-0.48379	0.45570	-0.24957	-0.07015	2	CL13
25	49	-0.0278	0.07926	-0.4270	0.0796	1.0428	0.02653	-0.01831	-0.49964	-0.00965	0.27944	0.33862	2	CL13
26	48	-0.9528	-0.54764	-0.6176	-0.8182	-1.0253	-0.57425	-0.50182	0.75080	-0.16287	-0.54000	-0.90900	1	CL12
27	12	-0.7215	-0.77153	1.3839	-1.5990	-0.7815	-0.73511	-0.64302	-0.44827	0.37057	-0.73708	-0.24748	1	CL12
28	31	-1.2996	-0.70436	1.0026	-0.9354	-0.7394	-0.61036	-0.57455	0.49886	0.18330	-0.79932	-0.60736	1	CL12
29	6	0.2035	-0.39092	1.2885	0.8995	0.1264	-0.25252	-0.23225	-0.15260	0.42165	-0.56075	0.07807	6	CL14
30	37	-0.0278	-0.43569	0.4308	0.1187	-0.0165	-0.36086	-0.31783	-0.50565	0.86996	-0.39478	-0.40662	6	CL14
31	8	1.3598	-0.81631	-0.1411	0.3919	0.8998	-0.79748	-0.66441	-0.55976	-0.83251	-0.69559	-0.85491	7	CL21
32	11	0.8973	-0.74914	0.9073	0.8995	1.6228	-0.68915	-0.63018	-0.53954	-0.74171	-0.78895	-0.87103	7	CL21
33	29	-0.4903	-0.77153	0.7167	-0.8573	-0.7479	-0.74824	-0.65157	-0.55484	-0.56579	-0.68522	-0.95008	1	CL12
34	23	0.2035	-0.07747	-0.6176	0.1968	1.0428	-0.06540	-0.08249	-0.00176	0.22302	-0.14584	1.48378	2	CL13
35	45	-0.8371	-0.83870	-0.1411	-2.2627	0.7485	-0.81061	-0.66869	-0.54336	-0.60551	-0.76820	-0.87519	4	CL18
36	46	0.0879	0.16881	0.0496	0.3139	-0.5209	0.22678	0.08866	0.01573	0.07548	-0.12509	-0.45239	1	CL12
37	35	0.3191	1.46739	-0.9988	0.8604	-0.6302	1.14600	0.79466	0.04306	-0.48634	2.39546	0.39895	5	CL15
38	44	-0.9528	-0.68198	1.1932	0.8214	-0.8403	-0.56440	-0.46759	-0.04220	0.01305	-0.71634	-0.81695	6	CL14
39	50	0.3191	-0.86109	1.0026	-2.2627	0.1517	-0.82046	-0.71148	0.22286	-0.28204	-0.82006	-0.80134	4	CL18
40	3	-0.3746	-0.45808	2.9088	0.6262	0.0844	-0.41995	-0.22369	0.29118	0.20032	-0.59186	-0.34786	6	CL14
41	9	-0.1434	0.93005	2.6228	1.0166	-0.4368	0.74876	0.39673	0.00808	0.16060	-0.16659	0.06663	6	CL14
42	15	0.3191	-0.30136	-0.9035	-0.8182	0.1517	-0.31818	-0.34350	-0.46576	-0.71334	-0.25994	3.01483	2	CL13
43	28	1.0129	-0.81631	2.3369	0.8604	1.3958	-0.78435	-0.70292	-0.42149	-0.41824	-0.82006	-0.91524	7	CL21
44	39	0.3191	-0.74914	-1.6660	1.2898	0.2862	-0.73183	-0.53605	-0.55921	-0.83251	-0.64373	-0.97556	3	CL17
45	13	1.3598	1.53456	-1.0941	0.8995	1.0680	1.36595	1.21398	0.06546	-0.63956	2.20876	2.26491	5	CL15
46	18	-1.0684	-0.09986	-0.4270	0.1968	-0.6386	-0.13105	-0.18519	3.89003	0.01873	-0.34292	-0.33433	8	CL11
47	43	-0.2590	1.78084	0.4308	0.7823	-0.8824	1.62858	1.38085	4.90219	0.51244	0.99515	2.11513	8	CL11
48	5	1.1285	3.79537	-0.1411	1.3679	1.5976	4.15642	4.82527	0.96613	1.55095	2.96596	3.28214	9	CL10
49	32	1.1285	3.10180	-1.2847	1.2118	3.1949	3.40463	3.32769	-0.32148	0.13223	2.64441	-0.19548	9	CL10
50	2	3.6723	-0.86109	1.5745	-0.5450	0.3282	-0.79420	-0.72859	-0.31765	5.90361	-0.82006	-0.98596	10	

2

CLUSTER MEANS: STATES DATA 11:32 WEDNESDAY, APRIL 11, 1984 19

OBS	CLUSTER	INCM	POPM	POPCHM	URBANM	TAXM	GOVTM	COLLEGEM	MINERALM	FORESTM	MFGM	FARMM
1	1	-0.96927	-0.29496	0.19252	-0.5004	-1.0547	-0.29778	-0.32944	-0.05907	0.05116	-0.32069	-0.26855
2	2	0.24686	-0.14463	-0.70098	-0.0765	0.2021	-0.13721	-0.15791	-0.31779	-0.28346	-0.06675	1.04349
3	3	0.89725	-0.00134	-0.88445	1.2118	0.9402	-0.04898	0.05186	-0.51691	-0.72355	0.08443	-0.84482
4	4	-0.35536	-0.80138	-0.07752	-1.7812	0.0522	-0.75864	-0.67368	-0.34889	-0.31515	-0.77166	-0.42066
5	5	0.66600	1.45060	-0.97499	0.8995	0.4249	1.22971	0.97009	0.21248	-0.18273	2.13096	0.58656
6	6	-0.25900	-0.20732	1.68883	0.6964	-0.2166	-0.16979	-0.16893	-0.08024	0.33312	-0.48606	-0.28534
7	7	1.08996	-0.79392	1.03439	0.7173	1.3062	-0.75699	-0.66584	-0.50693	-0.66415	-0.76820	-0.88039
8	8	-0.66369	0.84049	0.00191	0.4895	-0.7605	0.74876	0.59783	4.39611	0.26559	0.32612	0.89040
9	9	1.12851	3.44883	-0.71289	1.2898	2.3962	3.78053	4.07648	0.32233	0.94159	2.80519	1.54333
10	10	3.67227	-0.86109	1.57447	-0.5450	0.3282	-0.79420	-0.72859	-0.31765	5.30361	-0.82006	-0.98596

Chapter 15

Multiattribute Modeling

This chapter discusses geometric representation (mapping) of alternatives (e.g., brands) in a multidimensional space. Portraying brands (and customers) in a spatial representation assists in the understanding of the basis for brand preferences and the competitive structure of a market. This chapter presents two major alternative procedures for creating maps: representations based on ratings of the similarity of pairs of alternatives (decompositional) and representations based on direct ratings of brands on prespecified attributes (compositional). In addition, maps developed based on usage data, such as those available from scanner panels, are discussed.

This chapter also discusses a means for assessing the value (utility) of different positions on the attributes, conjoint analysis. Unlike the mapping procedures, conjoint analysis assumes that the attributes and positions on the attributes are known. Thus, attribute mapping studies often logically precede conjoint studies.

BASIC CONCEPT

A basic tenet of much of the research in marketing is that consumers evaluate alternative products on a series of relevant *attributes*. These attributes (which are also called *characteristics* or *dimensions*—the terms are used interchangeably) vary from product category to product category. Hence, for toothpaste one would expect attributes such as decay prevention and tooth whitening to be relevant, while for a machine tool attributes such as accuracy, downtime, and initial price would be expected to be important. Preference (and subsequently choice) is presumed to be determined by each customer selecting the brand which has the best combination of the relevant attributes.

These models are essentially rational economic man models and have been developed in most branches of social science. Models in the same spirit include those of Fishbein (1967) and Rosenberg (1956) in social psychology, Lancaster (1966) in microeconomics, and the expectancy theory models in organizational behavior. It is important to note that such models are designed to help explain/understand preferences or attitudes. To predict choice, a single preference or attitude measure will often do as well as a more complex measure. The advantage of these models is that they attempt to explain why preferences exist and, thus, suggest what can be done to change them.

To use such a multiattribute model, the following three basic pieces of information are needed:

1. The identity of the relevant attributes.
2. The positions of the alternatives (brands) on the attributes.
3. The desired (ideal) levels of each attribute.

From these three pieces of information, an overall value (utility, attitude, preference) for each of the alternatives is derived. Usually, value is assumed to be a function of the position of the alternatives on the relevant attributes. Often value is obtained by simply multiplying the positions on the attributes by the importances (weights) of the attributes.

Multiattribute models can be viewed graphically. (This helps explain why they are often called *spatial models*, *geometric models*, or *perceptual maps*.) Consider Figure 15–1, with two attributes (brilliantly labeled 1 and 2) and nine alternatives (labeled A–I). In this example, alternative C has the most of attribute 1, and alternative A has the most of attribute 2. If you assume alternative I represents the ideal (desired) level on the attributes, then the most preferred brand(s) should be the ones closest to I. In this case, that means alternatives C and G. Whether C or G is most preferred depends on whether attribute 1 or 2 is more important.

FIGURE 15–1 Brand Locations in Two Dimensions

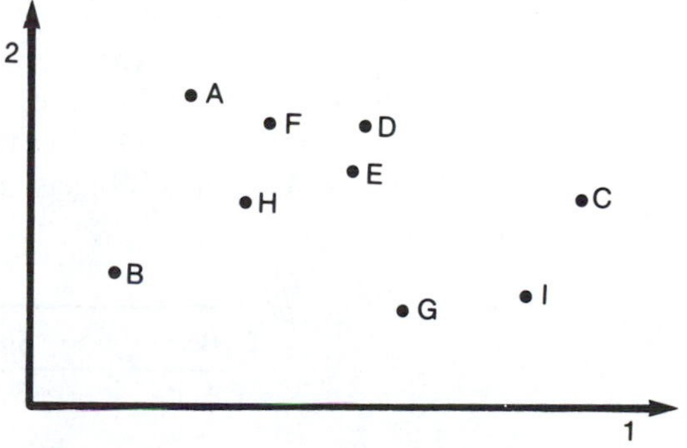

Attribute models are conceptually models of individual consumers. Yet the practicality of their use in marketing usually depends on some form of aggregation. Therefore, most users of such techniques assume some things are constant across customers (at least those in a given segment), such as the attributes and the positions of the alternatives on the attributes.

Attribute models can be developed in a number of ways. One inelegant but interesting approach is seat-of-the-pants executive judgment. In other words, a knowledgeable person may be able to directly draw such a model.

Assuming such a savant is unavailable (or at least needs to be checked up on), a researcher must resort to an analytical procedure to generate attribute models. The remainder of this chapter is devoted to describing some of the major analytical techniques for developing and utilizing such models.

MULTIDIMENSIONAL SCALING (MDS)

Multidimensional scaling is a procedure which decomposes overall similarity rankings to generate a map. The identities of the relevant attributes and the positions of alternatives on the attributes are an output of analysis. This technique was developed by psychometricians, notably Shepard (1962) and Kruskal (1964), and has received great attention in marketing (Green and Carmone, 1970; Green and Rao, 1972). An excellent summary of the use of MDS in marketing appears in Cooper (1983). Its purpose is to deduce indirectly the dimensions a respondent uses to evaluate alternatives. The reason for using the indirect approach is that, in many cases, the attributes may be unknown and respondents unable (what attributes do you use to evaluate paintings?) or unwilling (why do you yell at your kids?) to accurately represent their reasons. The term *multidimensional scaling* has come to refer to a variety of procedures for deducing attribute models from simple (and seemingly innocent) input data. This section will proceed to examine these procedures.

Simple Space: Brand Maps

The basic type of multidimensional scaling involves deducing graphical models of alternatives alone (hence, simple space) from similarity judgments. Here, we ask a respondent to rate pairs of objects in terms of their overall similarity. For three objects, this would require the following as input:

Pair	*Similarity Rating*
A, B	3 (most similar)
A, C	1
B, C	2

FIGURE 15–2 Initial Solution

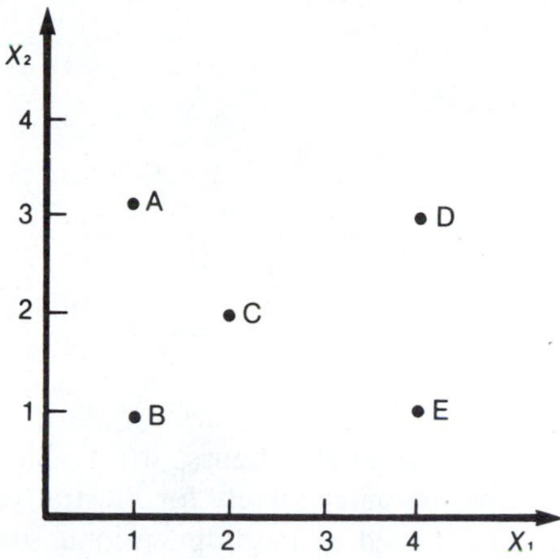

The procedure then deduces the positions of the alternatives on a prespecified number of attributes as output. The purpose of the next two sections is to give an indication of how this "magic" (translation: big computer program) works.

Initial Solution. Simple space analysis proceeds in two basic stages. The first is to develop an initial solution. One alternative is to randomly place points on the desired number of dimensions. This, however, is so horribly inefficient that other procedures are used.

An intuitively appealing starting rule is a variation on the old navigation by triangulation trick. Consider Figure 15–2. If distance data were gener-

TABLE 15–1 Input Data

Pair	*Approximate Distance*
A, B	2
A, C	1.4
A, D	3.0
A, E	3.6
B, C	1.4
B, D	3.5
B, E	3.2
C, D	2.4
C, E	2.3
D, E	2

FIGURE 15–3 Initial Points

A •

D •

ated from this figure, we might have the input data (note we are using metric input merely for illustrative purposes) of Table 15–1. The question addressed by multidimensional scaling is how to go from data such as that in Table 15–1 to a picture, such as Figure 15–2.

To get an initial solution, we can arbitrarily pick any two points, preferably two which are fairly far apart. Here we use A and D and plot them (Figure 15–3). Now choose one more point (C) and draw circles

FIGURE 15–4 Third Point Added

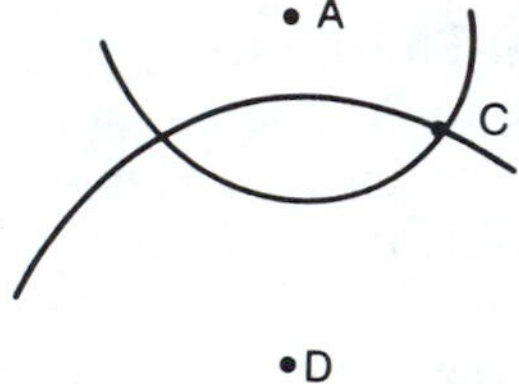

FIGURE 15–5 Four-Point Solution

A •

D •

FIGURE 15–6 Five-Point Solution

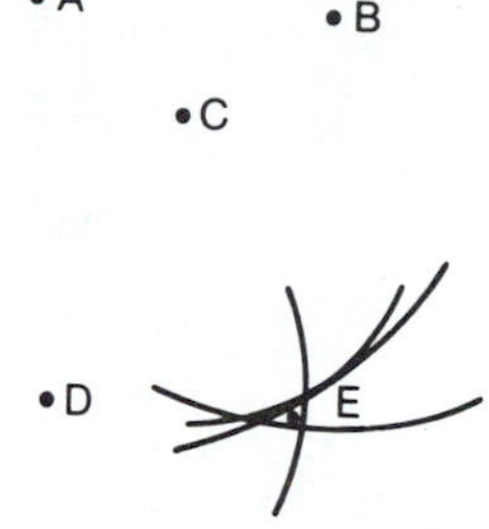

around A and D of length 1.4 and 2.4, respectively (Figure 15–4). You will notice that these circles meet in two places. Arbitrarily choose one point and label it C. Now add the next point (B), by drawing arcs around A, C, and D of appropriate lengths and see where they intersect (Figure 15–5). If the input measures were perfect, they will meet in one point. If the input data contain some error, then the three arcs will almost meet in a small area. Choose the center of the area for the point's location and continue.[1] Finally, adding E we have Figure 15–6. Notice that this configuration is approximately the original one, the difference being due to the error in the input data, although the picture has been rotated 90 degrees and reflected (the mirror image to Figure 15–2 appears in Figure 15–6). Hence, we see that what is preserved is the original orientation among the points and not their exact positions.

Second Stage. Stage two consists of taking the initial solution and trying to improve it. This is accomplished by a procedure known as the *gradient* (for math fans) or *hill-climbing* (for poets) approach. To see how this works, return to the original three-alternative example:

Input:

Pair	*Similarity Rating*
A, B	3 (most similar)
A, C	1
B, C	2

[1]This method depends on the three original points being "good" ones in terms of the accuracy with which the input data represent their distances.

FIGURE 15–7 Three-Brand Model

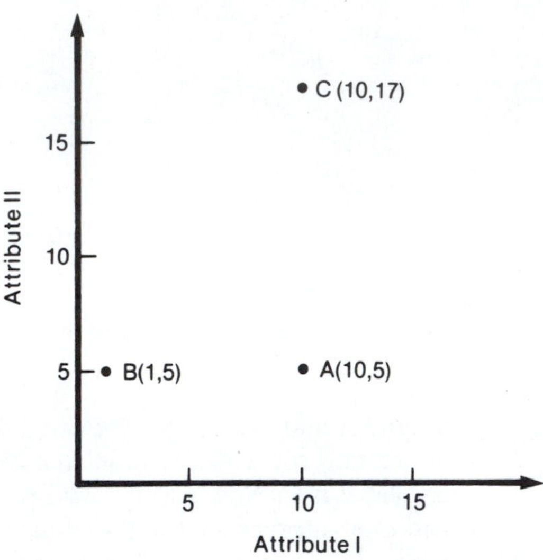

Assume the initial solution is that of Figure 15–7. At this point, one might wish to evaluate how good a solution this is. One way to do this is to calculate the distances between points and see if they match the original input data, in that the most similar pair of alternatives should have the smallest distance between them and so forth. Here we obtain the following:

Pair	*Similarity*	*Distance*	*"Error"*
A, B	3	9	0
A, C	1	12	−1.5
B, C	2	15	+1.5

As hoped, the most similar pair (A,B) is closest together. The other two pairs, unfortunately, are "messed up" since B,C should be closer together than A,C. One way to see how bad the solution is, is to try to "fudge" the distance data so that the similarity data and the derived distances are consistent. The easiest way to do this would be to move both the A,C and B,C distances to 13.5, and hence the error terms are 0, −1.5, and +1.5, respectively. To see how much fudging was required, we can construct an error index:

$$\frac{\Sigma \text{ errors squared}}{\Sigma \text{ distances squared}}$$

$$= \frac{(0)^2 + (1.5)^2 + (1.5)^2}{81 + 225 + 144} \approx .01$$

This index can then be used as a criterion for when a new solution is better or worse than the old solution (the smaller the index, the better the solution).

One way to improve the original solution in this example is to move alternative C a little to the left, making it simultaneously closer to alternative B and farther from alternative A. The second stage of an MDS program would do this. Next the program recomputes the index and again moves points to improve the index. Thus, stage two consists of moving the points around until the distances match the original similarity data well enough or the maximum number of iterations is reached.

Output

The results which are output and interpreted are the positions of the alternatives on the attributes. Assuming the initial picture (Figure 15–7) represented the final output, we would get as the output Table 15–2.

The results are missing one very important fact: the names of the dimensions. Developing the names of the dimensions is an art form akin to labeling factors in factor analysis. Here, we look for a common characteristic of alternatives which fall on the extremes of a dimension. In this example, whatever dimension I is, A and C have a lot of it and B has very little of it. Similarly, C has a lot of whatever is represented by dimension II and A and B not much of it. One popular "trick" for aiding in naming the dimensions is to also collect similarities between the alternatives and various key words which are thought to be related to the major dimensions.

TABLE 15–2 Output of Multidimensional Scaling

	Dimension	
Alternative	*I*	*II*
A	10	5
B	1	5
C	10	17

By scaling both alternatives and words simultaneously, the words then appear in the picture and may facilitate the task of naming the dimensions.

It is also possible to collect ratings of the brands on prespecified attributes separately. These ratings can then be correlated with the positions of the brands on the derived dimensions. If ratings on a particular attribute are highly correlated with positions on a derived dimension, then that helps "name" the dimension.

Some Semitechnical Issues

In using simple space MDS procedures, several points are important to keep in mind.

The Results Are Tentative, Not Conclusive. Some early applications of MDS accepted the apparent dimensions as "truth" without question or validation, which often proved to be disastrous. It is advisable to use MDS as a generator of hypotheses, rather than as a final model of a market. Any important result should be confirmed on a separate sample with a separate method, such as direct questioning, before the results are given too much credence.

The Dimensions Are Not Unique. MDS generates a configuration in which the relative positions of the brands are unique. The picture can be changed by several operations without changing the relationship among the interpoint distances in some of the algorithms (assuming Euclidean distance is used, which it almost always is). These operations are portrayed in Figure 15–8. Hence, the dimensions that appear in the output are not unique. (Still, it is fortunate how often the dimensions which are output from the analysis turn out to be useful/interpretable ones.)

Determining the Number of Dimensions Is Sometimes Difficult. A prior theory about the number of dimensions is the best place to start. Absent a good theory, the most common approach is to examine the results of solutions in several dimensions (e.g., 2, 3, 4) and choose the best one. There are two basic criteria for best. The first involves getting the index used as a criterion for fit to some predetermined level. (When Kruskal's stress is used, many researchers attempt to get stress below .05, with anything above .1 being unacceptable.) The second approach involves plotting the stress values and seeing where the addition of a dimension stops significantly (in a visual sense) improving the index (see Figure 15–9). In this case the index seems to improve substantially going from a one- to two-dimensional solution. Similarly, the index improves going from a two- to three-dimensional solution. The addition of a fourth dimension, on the

FIGURE 15–8 Equivalent Multidimensional Scaling Results

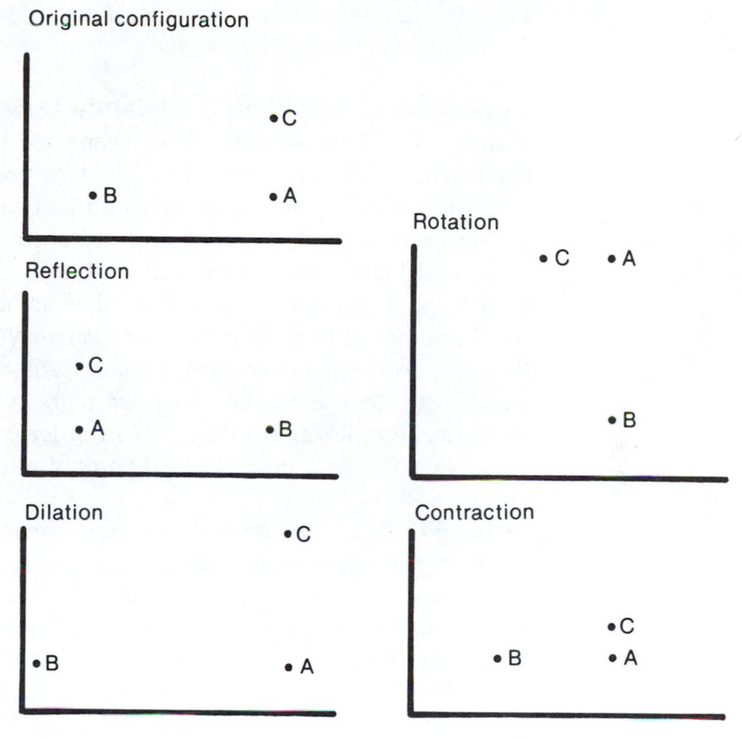

FIGURE 15–9 Badness of Fit Index versus Number of Dimensions

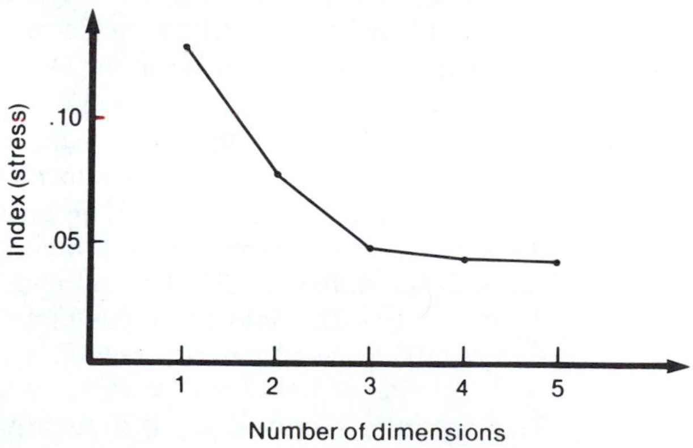

other hand, seems to aid the solution very little. Consequently, most researchers would say there are three dimensions for this set of alternatives. Finding the point where the plot of the index turns flat is often called *looking for the "elbow" in the plot.*

Collection of Similarity / Distance Data Can Be Done in Many Ways. A variety of means have been used for collecting similarity data (McIntyre and Ryans, 1977). The following are among the most useful:

Card Sorting. A common approach used in personal interviewing is to physically produce a separate card for each possible pair of alternatives (e.g., for 10 alternatives, there will be 45 cards). Subjects are then asked to go through a two-step process. First, they are asked to sort the cards into a small number of piles, based on the similarity between the pair of alternatives (e.g., very similar, somewhat similar, somewhat dissimilar, very dissimilar). Next, they are asked to rank pairs within each pile in terms of similarity. By picking up the cards in order (and not dropping them), the researcher obtains a ranking of all pairs of alternatives in terms of similarity.

Ratings. For situations where card sorting is impractical (e.g., mail surveys), respondents are asked to rate pairs of brands on a scale (e.g., an eight-point scale from "very similar" to "very dissimilar"). Alternatively, some researchers prefer to get similarity ratings with respect to a reference brand. By rotating the reference brand, all pairs can be obtained.

Derived Similarity Data. In many studies, similarity measures are derived from other data. For example, ratings of a series of brands on a set of attributes (e.g., rating G.E., Zenith, and other TVs on quality of picture, service, style, etc.) can form the basis of a similarity measure. The basic method of deriving similarity is to compute a distance measure which assesses the similarity of the different brand profiles on the attributes. Any of the similarity or distance measures discussed in the cluster analysis section of the previous chapter can be used, although the two most commonly used are a matching coefficient (when the attributes are categorical) or Euclidean distance (when the attribute ratings are intervally scaled).

Burden on Respondents. A major problem in data collection is the burden on respondents as the number of alternatives increases (e.g., 20 alternatives requires 190 pairs). If respondents are "homogeneous" (have the same similarity perceptions), however, it is possible to have different subjects rate different pairs. For example, in a sample of 1,000, we could divide the 190 pairs into 10 subsets of 19 pairs and have one tenth of the sample (100 subjects) rate each subset.

The Results Depend on the Alternatives. The dimensions which appear are a direct function of the alternatives used in the study. Leaving out an important set of alternatives (e.g., unsweetened cereal from a study of breakfast foods) means that a key dimension (e.g., sweetness) may not appear in the results. Similarly, defining the competition too broadly will result in trivial solutions. For example, studying cereals, dinner entrees, and drinks together will generally produce three clusters of alternatives: cereals, dinner entrees, and drinks. Hence, care must be taken to include (or represent) all "real" competitive alternatives if the results are to be useful (c.f., Malhotra, 1987).

The Number of Alternatives Needed Is Substantial. The number of alternatives needed to produce a certain dimensional solution is much greater than the number of dimensions. While a variety of rules exist, a useful requirement[2] is:

$$\text{Number of alternatives} > 3(\text{number of dimensions})$$

This suggests (as one may have suspected) that there are an infinite number of "perfect" solutions for the three-alternative, two-dimensional example used here for pedagogical purposes.

Variety Seeking Is Not Considered. As it is used in marketing, MDS attempts to model how a consumer chooses the best alternative at a given point in time. In doing so, it does not explicitly take into account immediate past behavior. Assuming my favorite drink were Coke, it seems likely that after 103 straight Cokes I might at least temporarily prefer something (anything) else. The notion of variety-seeking is not easily incorporated into MDS models.

Some Examples

The best way to get a grasp of how MDS works is to examine several examples. The solutions shown tend to be two-dimensional, since (*a*) many of them actually appear to be two-dimensional and (*b*) it is hard to draw three-dimensional solutions on a piece of paper.

Figure 15–10 comes from one of Green's earliest published examples and is based on housewives' ratings of breakfast foods. In playing the name-the-dimensions game, we might call the horizontal dimension *preparation*

---

[2]The reason for this requirement is that there are $\binom{n}{2} = \frac{n(n-1)}{2}$ pairs of alternatives, and hence $\frac{n(n-1)}{2} - 1$ constraints on the solutions. The solution has $n(d)$ degrees of freedom. Therefore, to get a constrained solution, $\frac{n(n-1)}{2} - 1 > n(d)$. Hence, $n \geq 3d$ allows a safety margin to get a well-constrained solution.

FIGURE 15–10 Breakfast Foods Map

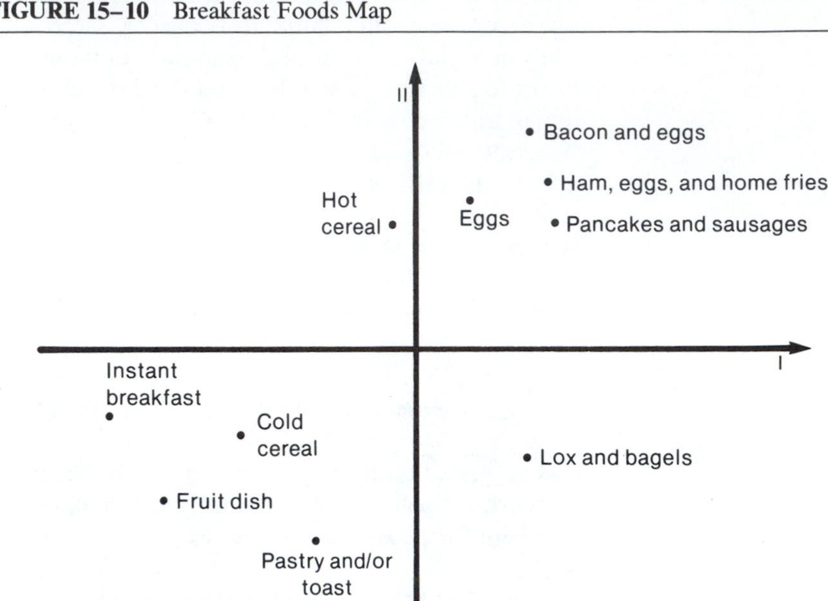

Source: Reprinted with permission of Professor Paul E. Green, Wharton School, University of Pennysylvania.

time. The vertical dimension could well be called *nutritional value*. On the other hand, it could also be called *hot-cold*. Hence, this brings up a crucial point: many names may fit the same dimension. It is important to use other methods (e.g., focus groups, ratings on prespecified attributes) to check which name is really appropriate. Otherwise, we might spend our entire advertising budget stressing how nutritional our brand was when all consumers care about is its temperature. Assuming advertising copy matters, this is a good way to get burned.

Figure 15–11 was based on similarity judgments of 264 subjects collected in the summer of 1969. The purpose of the analysis was to confirm the design of an experiment which included two each of the four possible combinations of lemon-lime versus cola and diet versus nondiet soft drinks (Bass, Pessemier, and Lehmann, 1972). The results clearly indicate cola versus lemon-lime as the horizontal and dominant dimension. The vertical dimension is calories (diet versus nondiet) with one key exception. Like, the name of a diet lemon-lime soft drink at the time, was positioned with the nondiet lemon-limes. Given this mispositioning, it is not surprising that the product failed. It is also not surprising that the product was reintroduced as Sugar Free 7up, making such a misperception highly unlikely.

FIGURE 15–11 Soft Drinks: Judged Similarity Based MDS Output

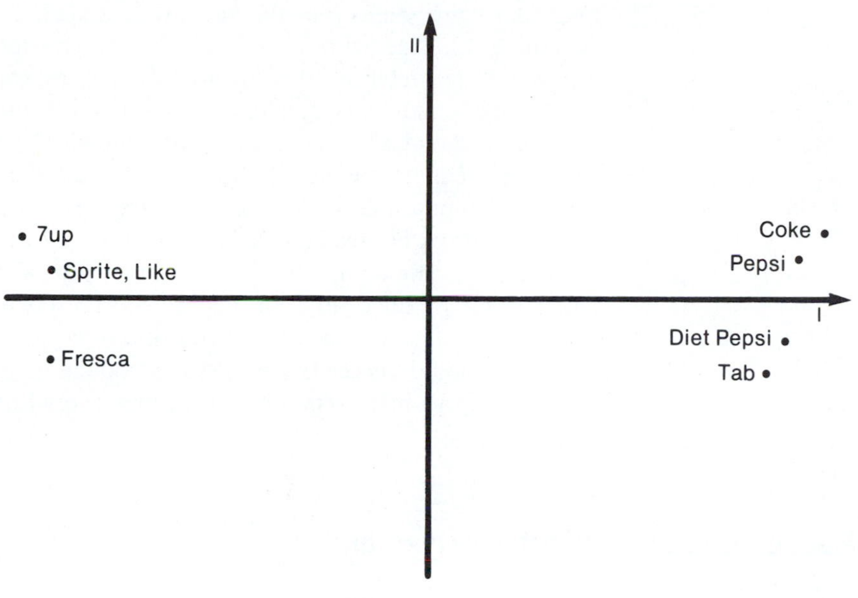

Source: Donald Lehmann, "Judged Similarity and Brand-Switching Data as Similarity Measures." Reprinted from *Journal of Marketing Research*, published by the American Marketing Association, 9 (August 1972), p. 332.

FIGURE 15–12 Soft Drinks with Ideal Brand

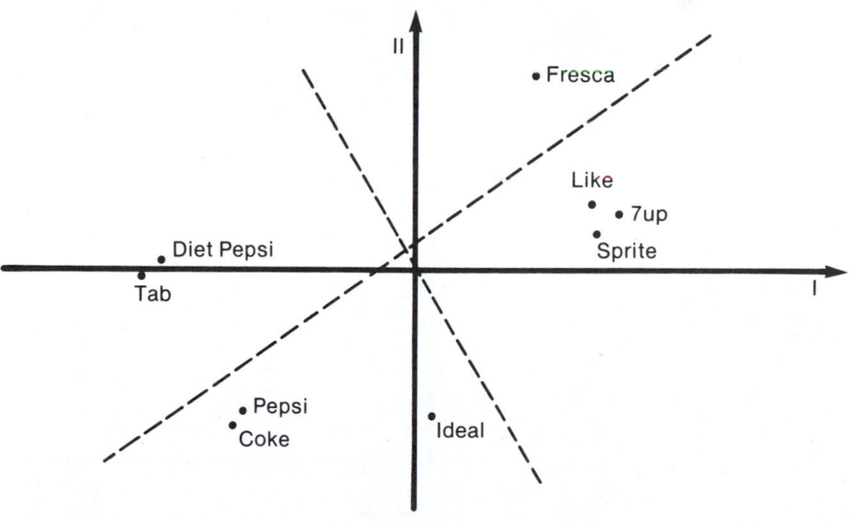

In the same set of data, respondents were also asked to rate how similar the eight brands were to their ideal brand. Using these data, nine alternatives (the eight brands plus the ideal) were scaled. The results are shown in Figure 15–12. This figure indicates several interesting things. First, to get a "proper" interpretation, the dimensions must be rotated to reproduce the lemon-lime versus cola and diet versus nondiet dimensions. Second, the position of the ideal brand suggests that the ideal soft drink would be cola with some lemon-lime added. This may well be the result of an averaging fallacy. Compute the average temperature that tea should be served from those who drink hot tea and those who drink iced tea and you will find that room temperature tea is "best"—not a very appealing result. On the other hand, given products like Dr Pepper (cherry coke taste with prunes as content) and cream soda (basically vanilla soda), it is conceivable that such a product could succeed. The 1976 introduction of Pepsi-Lite was consistent with this interpretation (except that Pepsi-Lite was partly diet).

Representations of Alternatives and Individuals

The approach for jointly positioning subjects and alternatives in the same map is known as *joint space analysis*. The direct method of getting such a space is known as *unfolding* and requires that respondents rank the alternatives in terms of preference. The procedure then attempts to simultaneously

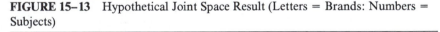

FIGURE 15–13 Hypothetical Joint Space Result (Letters = Brands: Numbers = Subjects)

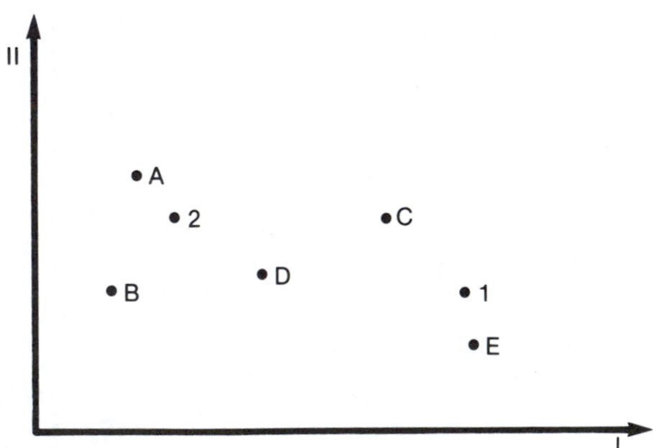

place both alternatives and subjects in a given dimensional space so that people are close to their preferred alternatives and far from their nonpreferred alternatives. Consider the hypothetical example of Figure 15–13, where brands are represented by letters and subjects by numbers. This picture suggests that person 1 would rank E most preferred, C second, D third, and so forth. On the other hand, subject 2's preference order is presumably A, then B, then D, and so forth.

This unfolding type of procedure is very appealing. Unfortunately, the results tend to be disappointing or confusing as well as very unstable. For these reasons many researchers do not employ this approach. In short, don't use unfolding unless you (*a*) are well versed in scaling and (*b*) use a second method to check the results.

The indirect approach to joint space analysis requires that the positions of alternatives on the attributes be established as a first step. As the second step, preference data are gathered and then subjects are overlayed on the picture based on their preference ranking. The most commonly used procedure of this type is PREFMAP, which places subjects on the map in four ways. The two commonly used ways are to represent subjects as vectors, where, the further along the vector a brand appears, the more preferred it is (Phase III) or as an actual ideal point (Phase IV).

Other Approaches

There are a large number of alternative scaling procedures (e.g., CANDECOMP, Carroll and Chang, 1970). One of the most appealing is INDSCAL, which assumes all subjects have the same perceptions but weight the dimensions differently. The derived weights can then be used to cluster subjects.

ALSCAL is a package (now included in the SAS system) which includes a variety of options. It can handle individual differences (à la INDSCAL), asymetric data (e.g., similarity of A to B not equal to the similarity of B to A), unfolding analysis, missing observations, and nominal, ordinal, interval, or ratio scaled input data. It can also take data which consist of ratings of alternatives on attributes and create a similarity measure from them.

ATTRIBUTE-RATING BASED MAPS

The major alternative to similarity-based maps uses direct ratings of alternatives on attributes as the key input data. These ratings can be directly plotted on a graph. The main steps involved are attribute identification and obtaining ratings. In addition, the determination of ideal levels and the value of positions on the attributes is also discussed.

Attribute Identification

Identification of the relevant attributes can be done in many ways. Since multidimensional scaling is essentially a dimension discovery procedure, MDS study can be used to uncover key dimensions. The most commonly used commercial approach is to begin with focus groups. The focus groups are used to generate a list of potential attributes. This list of attributes is then submitted to a sample of customers who each indicate (check off) the important attributes. The commonly checked attributes are then identified as the relevant attributes. An alternative approach is the so-called protocol procedure. In a protocol procedure, customers are asked to describe in detail the steps they went through in buying a particular product. Attributes mentioned are then recorded and compiled as the relevant attributes. It is also common to have subjects list attributes in response to an open-ended question (often called *free elicitation*). A less elegant but useful alternative is to have the researcher and/or manager specify the attributes based on experience. This method is (*a*) inexpensive and (*b*) full of researcher bias.

Deriving Positions of Alternatives on the Attributes

The positions of the alternatives on the attributes are obtained by direct ratings. These ratings are typically done on six- to ten-point bipolar adjective scales, although more elaborate graphical scales are occasionally used. Ratings can be obtained in two basic ways:

Rating a single alternative on all the dimensions at one time:

	Very Low					*Very High*
Crest:						
Decay prevention	1	2	3	4	5	6
Tooth whitening	1	2	3	4	5	6
. . .						
Colgate:						
Decay prevention	1	2	3	4	5	6
Tooth whitening	1	2	3	4	5	6
. . .						

Rating all the alternatives on a single dimension:

	Very Low					*Very High*
Decay prevention:						
Crest	1	2	3	4	5	6
Colgate	1	2	3	4	5	6
Aim	1	2	3	4	5	6
. . .						
Tooth whitening:						
Crest	1	2	3	4	5	6
Colgate	1	2	3	4	5	6
Aim	1	2	3	4	5	6
. . .						

There is strong evidence that respondents tend to "halo" their responses toward brands by rating the brands they like high on all attributes, and vice versa. Hence, the first approach is not very desirable because it makes it very easy for the respondent to think only of the alternative and not about the attribute; thus, all the ratings may be repeated measures of how well the respondent likes the alternative. The second approach makes the attribute the focus of attention. This causes (hopefully) a respondent to place his or her rating of an alternative in the context of the rating of other alternatives on the attribute. It also may be less boring (McLauchlan, 1987). Hence, it makes it less likely that alternative A will be rated higher on the attribute than alternative B unless it really is higher (at least in the view of the respondent).

Determination of Desired (Ideal) Levels

The determination of ideal levels can be obtained by direct questioning. Unfortunately, the results have often been discouraging (Lehmann, 1971; Neidell, 1972). For one thing, many of the attributes used tend to be of the "more is better" type (e.g., decay prevention) and, hence, the ideal logically belongs at the end of the scale. Moreover, respondents seem to have difficulty with the ideal concept on nonobjective attributes and tend to confuse the ideal position on an attribute with, among other things, the importance they give to the attribute. Consequently, many researchers use attributes where one end of the scale is clearly preferred or, alternatively, try to deduce the ideal points indirectly (see the section on multidimensional scaling).

Determination of Value of Positions on the Attribute

The determination of the value of different positions on the attributes has typically centered on finding the importances (weights) consumers attach to the relevant attributes. A common model indicating the overall evaluation of an alternative is:

$$\begin{matrix}\text{Overall}\\\text{evaluation}\\\text{of an}\\\text{alternative}\end{matrix} = \sum_{\substack{\text{all}\\\text{relevant}\\\text{attributes}}} \begin{pmatrix}\text{Weight of}\\\text{attribute}\end{pmatrix} \left| \begin{matrix}\text{Position}\\\text{on the}\\\text{attribute}\end{matrix} - \begin{matrix}\text{Ideal level}\\\text{on the}\\\text{attribute}\end{matrix} \right|$$

or

$$A_j = \sum_{i=1}^{n} W_i |P_{ji} - I_i| \tag{15.1}$$

The weights are usually obtained by using six- to eight-point bipolar adjective scales scaled from *very important* to *very unimportant*. This approach has two major problems. First, respondents have a strong tendency to rate all attributes as at least somewhat important, leading to difficulty in separating the attributes in terms of importance because many end up with the same rating. Second, the weights obtained are at best intervally scaled, whereas the model requires ratio scaled data.[3] Although this usually does not change the predictive power significantly, ratio scaled importances (and position ratings) should be sought, probably by means of constant sum scales. Perhaps fortunately, the weights seem to make very little difference in the predictive power of the models (Beckwith and Lehmann, 1973). This suggests that equal weighting of the attributes is often sufficient. An alternative approach uses a constant sum scale to assess attribute importance. A more extensive approach, conjoint analysis, is discussed later in the chapter.

The direct approach to obtaining attribute models is easy to use and communicate. Further, the results are often "good" in terms of both predictive power and insight. Nonetheless, several problems do exist with these procedures. First, it is very hard to be sure if all the relevant dimensions for respondents have been obtained. Second, there is a tendency for respondents to give socially acceptable answers in terms of both the identity of the relevant dimensions and their importance (i.e., obviously, for a food product, it is "right" to say that nutrition is important). Third,

---

[3] If I multiply together two intervally scaled variables, the result depends on the arbitrary zero value and on the size of the interval involved. This means that not only are the attitude scores not unique but also that the order of predicted preference may be incorrect.

respondents have a strong tendency to halo their responses about the alternatives. This means that they respond mainly in terms of whether they like the alternative regardless of the attribute in question and, hence, the value of the direct ratings is substantially decreased (Beckwith and Lehmann, 1975). For these and other reasons, many researchers use alternative methods to obtain attribute models.

Discriminant Analysis

An alternative way to generate a perceptual map is to use discriminant analysis (see Chapter 16). The basic input data are direct ratings of the alternatives on a set of prespecified attributes. Rather than plotting the results directly, however, multiple group discriminant analysis (the canonical correlate type) is used to generate compound dimensions which explain the ratings. The trick is to generate input data by using the brands as groups. The brands thus appear as the groups in the output. The location of the brands on the attributes is given by the group centroids (means on the discriminant functions). The discriminant functions themselves are combinations of the original dimensions. These compound dimensions are relatively easy to name, since how closely related each of the original attributes is to each of the derived dimensions is part of the output. Since they are totally dependent on the prespecified attributes, however, discriminant analysis only simplifies the direct rating approach and does not deduce unknown dimensions.

Some of the best examples of this approach appear in the work of Richard Johnson (Johnson, 1971). One of his classic examples involved brands of beer. The two-dimensional solution consisted of a "premium-local" dimension and a "heavy" (Budweiser) versus "light" (Miller) dimension. Interestingly, in terms of some ingredients, Miller is heavier than Budweiser. The message here is that "there is naught but thinking makes it so." If you advertise with the Clydesdales, Ed McMahon, and a squat brown bottle you can convince people you're heavier than a "champagne of bottle beer" which is sold in a tall, clear bottle. Another classic example of Johnson's (1970) involved the 1968 presidential campaign. The two-dimensional picture which included both candidates and voter segments provides an interesting vantage point for studying the strategies of the major candidates.

One example of the way discriminant analysis can be used to generate a map uses the by now infamous soft drink study again (Lehmann and Pessemier, 1973). The alternatives become the eight brands, and the eight attributes come from the questionnaire which was used (Table 15–3). The results can be viewed in three parts: the basic map, the relation of the original attributes to the derived dimensions, and (by means of PREFMAP) the location of 10 major segments in the derived space.

TABLE 15–3 Input Format for the Discriminant Analysis Approach for Deriving Attribute Models

	Attribute Rating			
	1	*2*		*8*
	Flavor	*Sweetness*	...	*Thirst Quenching*
Group 1: Brand 1 (Coke)				
Subject				
1				
2				
.				
.				
.				
n				
Group 2: Brand 2 (7up)				
Subject				
1				
2				
.				
.				
.				
n				
.				
.				
.				
Group 8: Brand 8 (Fresca)				
Subject				
1				
2				
.				
.				
.				
n				

Basic Map. The basic map appears as Figure 15–14 and suggests that calories is the key dimension.

Relation of the Original Attributes to the Derived Dimensions. To represent the relation of the original attributes to derived dimensions, the correlations between the attributes and dimensions can be used to plot the attributes in the space[4] (Figure 15–15). These attributes clearly indicate

[4]This is done by using a vector to represent the original attributes. The length of the vector is proportional to the ability of the two derived dimensions to explain the original attributes.

FIGURE 15–14 Basic Map

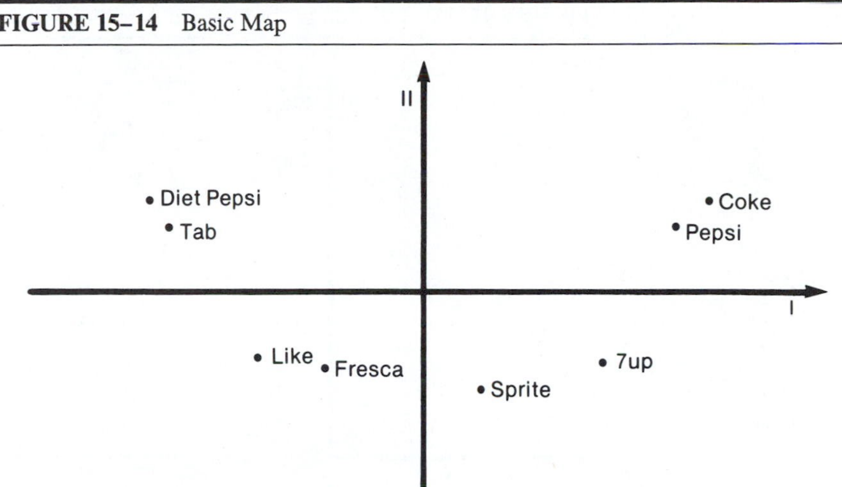

the vertical axis is flavor (lemon-lime versus cola). The horizontal axis is highly correlated with two attributes: calories (diet versus nondiet) and popularity with others. It is the appearance of the popularity with others attribute which is most surprising. This suggests that subjects may have been at least as concerned about the general acceptability of their choice (or its availability) as they were about its caloric content.

Joint Space Map. Subjects were grouped into 10 major segments, based on their frequency of purchase of the eight brands. The segments were then overlayed on the basic map by means of PREFMAP (Phase III). The segments (indicated by the letters) and their sizes are shown in Figure 15–16. For example, the biggest segment (I) appears to prefer Coke and then Pepsi. These results clearly indicate that Coke and Pepsi will do well (they are the two biggest sellers) and that Like is left out in the cold.

Factor Analysis

It is also possible to produce dimensional representations based on factor analyses of direct ratings on prespecified attributes. This produces compound dimensions based on the redundancy of the original attributes. This

---

The correlation between the attribute and the discriminant functions is used to determine the direction of the vector by using a form of $r = \cos(\text{angle})$.

FIGURE 15–15 Relation of the Original Attributes to the Discriminant Functions

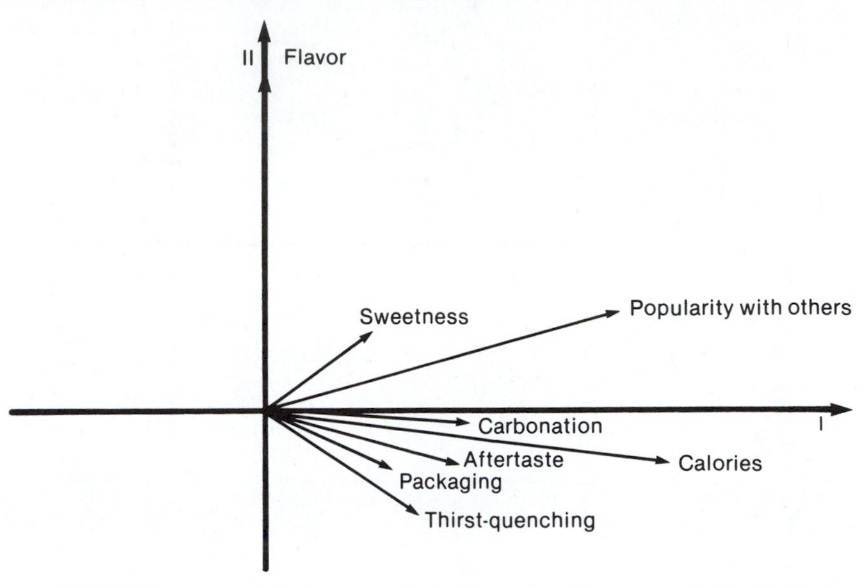

FIGURE 15–16 PREFMAP Results

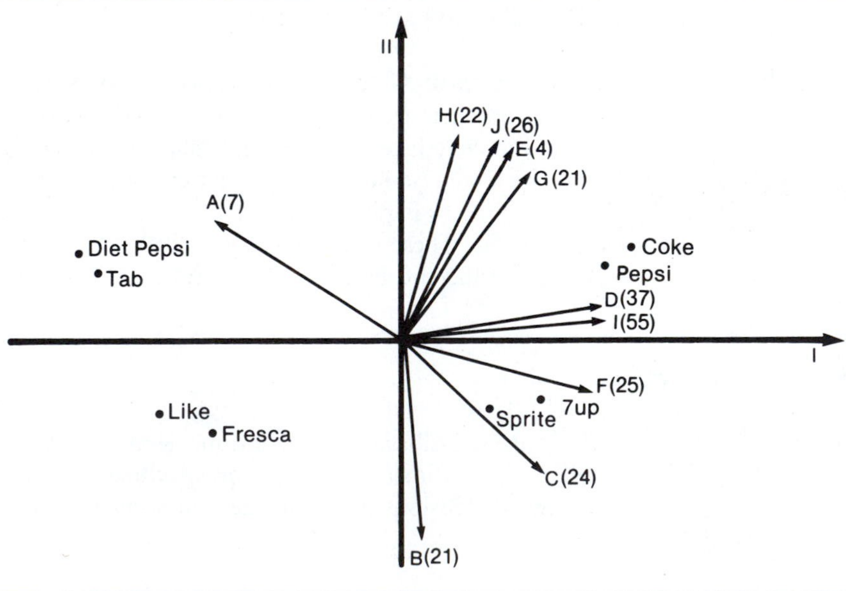

approach often seems to work as well or better than similarity scaling or discriminant analysis (e.g., Hauser and Koppelman, 1979). The attributes derived via factor analysis tend to be those on which there is the most variance in ratings across brands, whereas those based on discriminant analysis are those which distinguish between brands (Huber and Holbrook, 1979).

Derived Distance Based MDS

One approach to deriving maps is to use ratings on attributes as the input data, but to then use derived distances between the alternatives as input into a MDS routine. This is typically done by computing the average distance between the brands on the attributes.

For example, we will consider again some data from the food consumption survey discussed frequently in this book. Specifically, the final question dealt with how similar different pairs of foods are perceived to be. The percent of the sample who checked each pair as similar appear in Table 15–4. Simple inspection of the results indicates that the foods were rated according to the four basic food groups. (Actually, this result could have been at least partially influenced by the design, where the four column-heading foods represent the four basic food groups.)

To use multidimensional scaling on the data, it was necessary to build an index of similarity between all pairs of food. As a first pass, the 4 reference brands were ignored and the 14 other foods used as alternatives. Distances

TABLE 15–4 Foods Similar in Benefits to the Body

	Whole Milk	*Beef*	*Tomatoes*	*Enriched Bread*
A. Oatmeal	22.6%	14.6%	2.2%	75.6%
B. Fish	21.3	76.1	6.3	7.6
C. Rice	11.1	12.1	3.4	78.8
D. Navy beans	10.9	59.1	8.3	37.8
E. Chicken	14.6	82.4	3.0	11.2
F. Potatoes	11.0	6.6	14.4	77.1
G. Eggs	44.4	61.0	2.9	11.4
H. Macaroni	9.6	6.9	1.3	83.3
I. Pork and lamb	11.4	82.9	2.8	6.7
J. String beans	7.3	9.2	73.5	6.3
K. Carrots	17.9	5.9	72.4	6.3
L. Bananas	24.8	11.1	43.2	24.5
M. Peanut butter	26.0	73.8	4.0	19.9
N. Cottage cheese	76.7	36.3	4.8	10.7

between pairs of brands were defined based on the difference in the percent who rated the brands similar to each of the four reference brands. For example, the distance between oatmeal and fish was derived based on the difference in the percent who rated each similar to whole milk, beef, tomatoes, and enriched bread.[5] The resulting distance measures were then input to the KYST program and the output indicated the following:

Number of Dimensions	*Stress*
4	.010
3	.018
2	.071

This seems to suggest a three-dimensional solution, since the fourth dimension does not improve stress noticeably. Since the third dimension was not easily interpretable, the two-dimensional solution is shown as Figure 15–17.

The exact names of these dimensions are unclear, but the horizontal attribute appears to be a protein content dimension. The vertical dimension seems to separate dairy products and fruits and vegetables from meat and starch. Hence, the four basic food groups do seem to be the basis of this sample's food similarity judgments.

As another example of this approach, the data on the 50 states (Table 9–1, with the exception of the variable "South") were used as a basis for forming distances between the 50 states. Each variable was first standardized to remove the effects of differences in scales of the variables from the analysis. Next, Euclidean distance was computed between each pair of states and input to the ALSCAL routine in SAS.

A one-dimensional solution produced a squared correlation between input and derived distances of .875, while a two-dimensional solution increased the squared correlation to .925. The two-dimensional solution is shown in Appendix 15–A and Table 15–5. The first dimension separates states such as Alaska, Idaho, Nevada, New Hampshire, Vermont, and Wyoming from California, Illinois, New York, Ohio, Pennsylvania, and Texas, and appears to reflect the industrial versus rural character of the states. The second dimension separates Louisiana, Mississippi, South Dakota, and Texas from Alaska, California, and New York and appears to be an income dimension.

[5] The distance from oatmeal to fish was given by $(|226 - 213| + |146 - 761| + |22 - 63| + |756 - 76|)/4$.

FIGURE 15–17

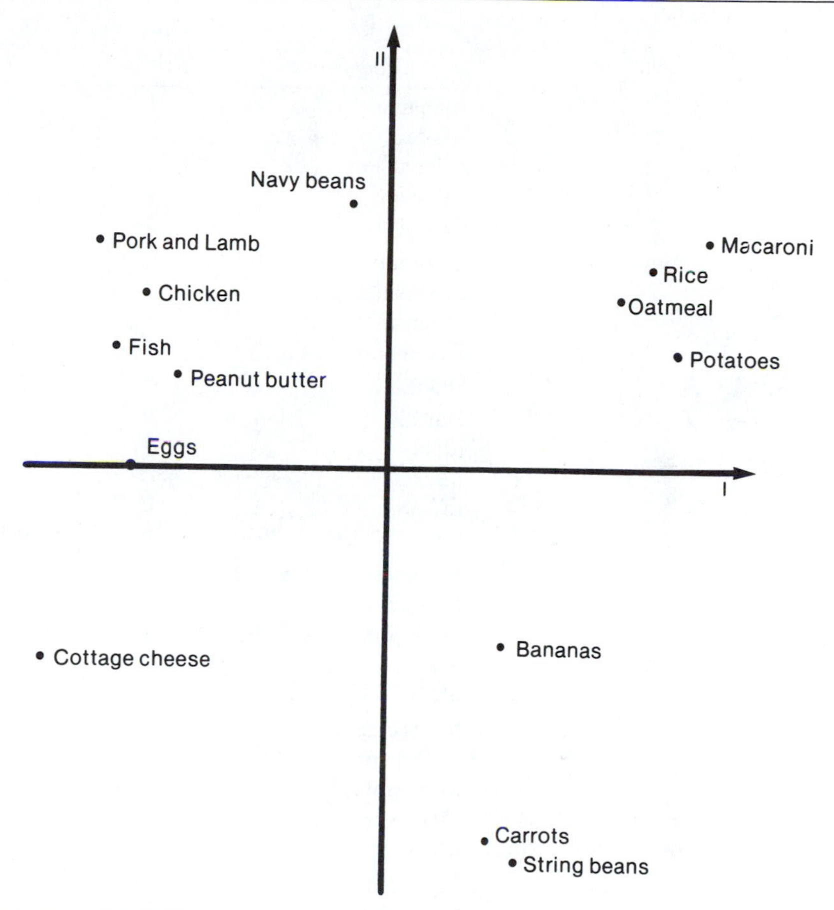

While such subjective naming of dimensions is appropriate, both as a check and as a means of actually developing the names, it is often useful to use a more formal approach. Since the distance measure used is based on locations in the attributes, it is possible to examine the correlation between the states' values on these attributes (income, etc.) and their positions on the two derived dimensions. Here, the ALSCAL program was used to regress each of the 11 original variables used in forming the distance measures against the two derived dimensions. The regression coefficients are shown in Table 15–6, and they (fortunately) generally confirm the names arrived at earlier.

TABLE 15–5 Two-Dimensional MDS for 50 States Data

State Name	Plot Symbol	Dimension 1	Dimension 2
Alabama	1	0.22	0.40
Alaska	2	3.08	−2.11
Arizona	3	0.72	0.03
Arkansas	4	0.72	0.70
California	5	−5.32	−1.90
Colorado	6	0.15	−0.29
Connecticut	7	0.06	−0.51
Delaware	8	0.77	−0.16
Florida	9	−0.39	−0.42
Georgia	A	−0.13	−0.17
Hawaii	B	0.76	−0.30
Idaho	C	1.14	0.45
Illinois	D	−1.68	−0.46
Indiana	E	−0.52	−0.10
Iowa	F	−0.38	0.65
Kansas	G	−0.05	0.18
Kentucky	H	0.11	0.48
Louisiana	I	−0.16	1.33
Maine	J	0.90	0.30
Maryland	K	−0.12	−0.34
Massachusetts	L	−0.52	−0.46
Michigan	M	−0.92	−0.50
Minnesota	N	−0.38	−0.28
Mississippi	O	0.68	0.83
Missouri	P	−0.32	−0.11
Montana	Q	0.84	0.13
Nebraska	R	0.29	0.16
Nevada	S	1.13	−0.29
New Hampshire	T	1.03	0.47
New Jersey	U	−0.63	−0.47
New Mexico	V	0.89	0.60
New York	W	−3.35	−1.80
North Carolina	X	−0.22	−0.06
North Dakota	Y	0.86	0.55
Ohio	Z	−1.18	−0.20
Oklahoma	1	0.15	0.41
Oregon	2	0.30	−0.28
Pennsylvania	3	−1.15	−0.37
Rhode Island	4	0.60	0.32
South Carolina	5	0.46	0.47

TABLE 15–5 *(continued)*

State Name	*Plot Symbol*	*Dimension 1*	*Dimension 2*
South Dakota	6	0.87	0.74
Tennessee	7	0.01	0.16
Texas	8	−2.51	0.99
Utah	9	0.73	0.40
Vermont	A	1.19	0.61
Virginia	B	−0.18	−0.21
Washington	C	−0.11	−0.37
West Virginia	D	0.63	0.65
Wisconsin	E	−0.32	−0.30
Wyoming	F	1.22	0.42

TABLE 15–6 Regressions of Original Variables versus the Two Derived Dimensions

Variable	*Dimension 1*	*Dimension 2*	R^2
Income	.14	−1.24	.61
Population	−.68	−.30	.92
Population change	.35	−.26	.17
Percent urban	−.33	−.54	.42
Tax	−.10	−.94	.46
Government expenditures	−.67	−.35	.94
College students	−.66	−.39	.94
Mineral production	−.42	.74	.34
Forest acreage	−.27	−.94	.35
Manufacturing output	−.61	−.33	.78
Farm output	−.55	.28	.43

Correspondence Analysis

One approach for generating maps uses cross-classification data (e.g., brands rated as having or not having a set of attributes) as a basis (Hoffman and Franke, 1986). In this approach, both brands and attributes are simultaneously portrayed in a single space. While development of this approach continues (c.f., Carroll, Green, and Schaffer, 1986; DeSarbo and Hoffman, 1987), it has shown promise.

A nice example of the use of correspondence analysis portrays snacks based on ratings of snack foods against activities, user characteristics, and attributes of the snacks (Rogus, 1987, Figures 15–18A, B, and C).

FIGURE 15–18A

HOMEMADE PIES
ICE CREAM
When skipping a meal
HOMEMADE COOKIES
FRESH FRUIT
SOFT COOKIES
Before exercise
Watching TV
TOAST/MUFFINS
Before dinner
When dieting
NUTS
When feeling good about yourself
CRACKERS
When concerned about digestion

FIGURE 15–18B

HOMEMADE PIES
ICE CREAM
HOMEMADE COOKIES
FRESH FRUIT
SOFT COOKIES
Healthy
Athletic
Better educated
TOAST/MUFFINS
Older
Slim
NUTS
CRACKERS
Buy health foods
Read ingredients

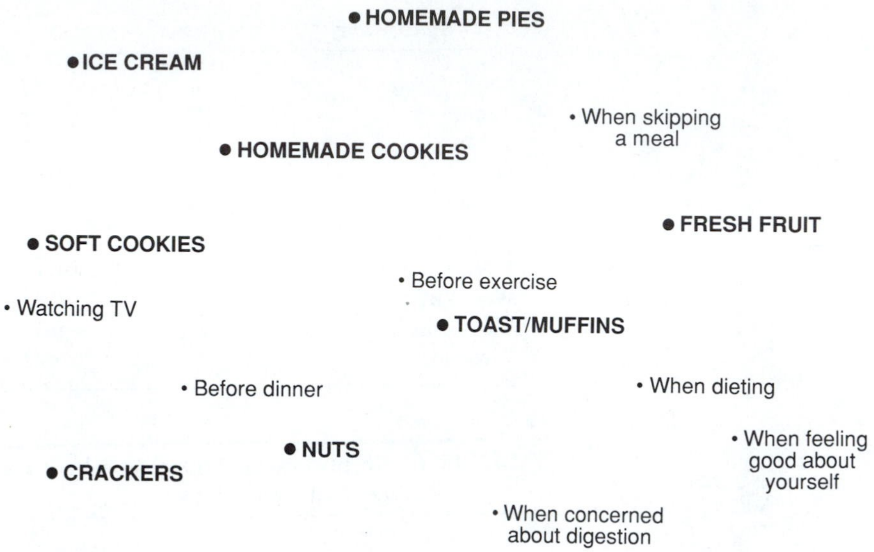

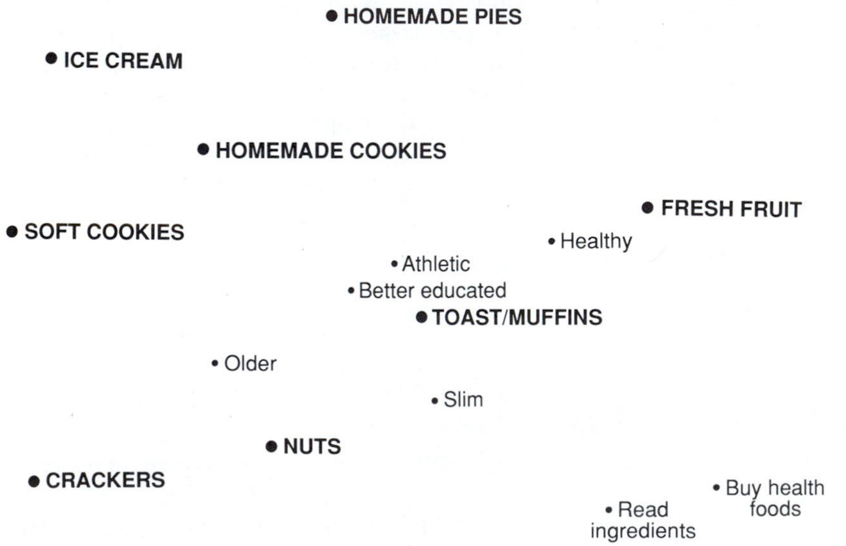

FIGURE 15–18C

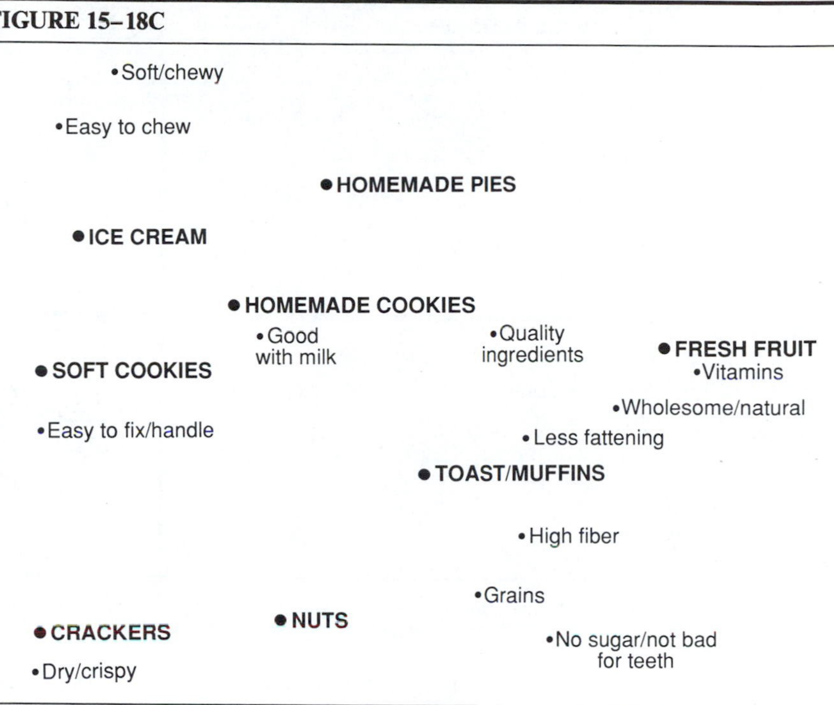

BRAND CHOICE AND SWITCHING BASED MAPS

There is nothing sacred about using judged similarities or derived distances as an input to MDS programs. One would expect more brand switching among similar brands, as they are closer substitutes. Hence, by using brand-switching probabilities as similarity measures, a behavior-based map can be derived. (Since clearly some switching among different brands can be expected due to variety seeking, exactly how to interpret the map is unclear.) The results in the case of the soft drink study are shown in Figure 15–19 (Lehmann, 1972). The major (horizontal) axis appears to be diet-nondiet, and the cola–lemon-lime dimension is somewhat muddled. This suggests (as in fact happened) that consumers would be more likely to give up flavor than to switch from a nondiet to a diet drink, or vice versa. It also indicates that preference dimensions may be different from the dimensions on which consumers make similarity judgments portrayed in Figure 15–11.

Scanner panel data have been used to generate market maps (e.g., Shugan, 1987). Panel data on brand usage have also been used to simultaneously develop market segments based on brand shares by person and market structure based on brand switching (Grover and Srinivasan, 1987) and to examine the impact of marketing variables such as promotion on the resulting market maps (Moore and Winer, 1987).

FIGURE 15–19 Soft Drinks Based on Brand Switching

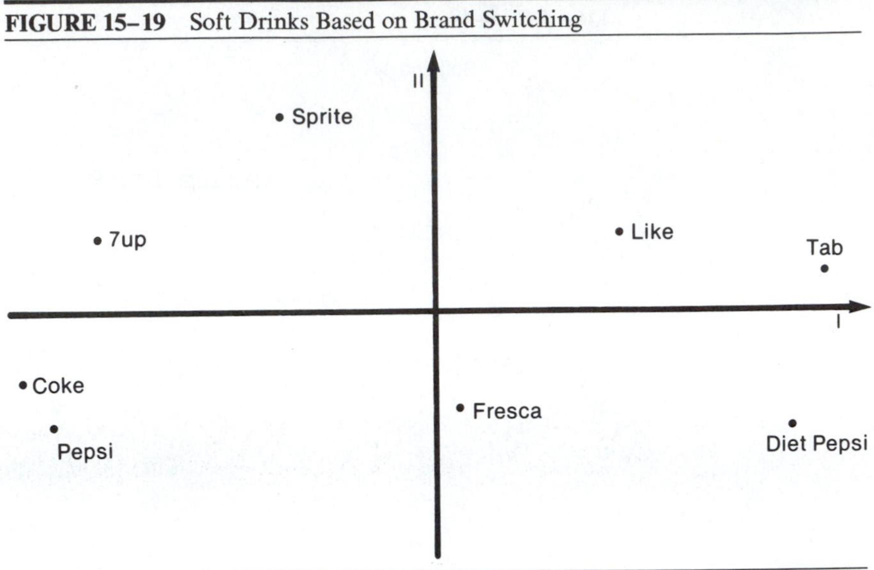

Source: Donald Lehmann, "Judged Similarity and Brand-Switching Data as Similarity Measures." Reprinted from *Journal of Marketing Research*, published by the American Marketing Association, 9 (August 1972), p. 333.

USES FOR MAPS

Attribute-based market maps can be used for a variety of purposes. Among the uses are new product idea generation, potential estimation, and advertising/promotional strategy selection. To see how attribute models might be used in these ways, consider the hypothetical example of Figure 15–20, where the numbers represent segments and the letters represent existing alternatives. Quick perusal of this graph suggests that alternative B is in excellent shape, having segment 1 representing 30 percent of the total market essentially to itself. By contrast, alternative A seems to appeal mainly to segment 6 with 10 percent of the market. To see how this picture could be used to stimulate the results of marketing decisions, consider the following two problems:

New Product Identification

Assume you were assigned to develop a new product for this market. Technical/production problems aside, the following two major alternatives exist:

Target on segment 2 by making a product which is a "2" on attribute I and a "2.7" on attribute II. Since E, C, and D are all somewhat removed from segment 2, it appears there is a reasonable chance of

FIGURE 15–20 Hypothetical Joint Spacc Configuration

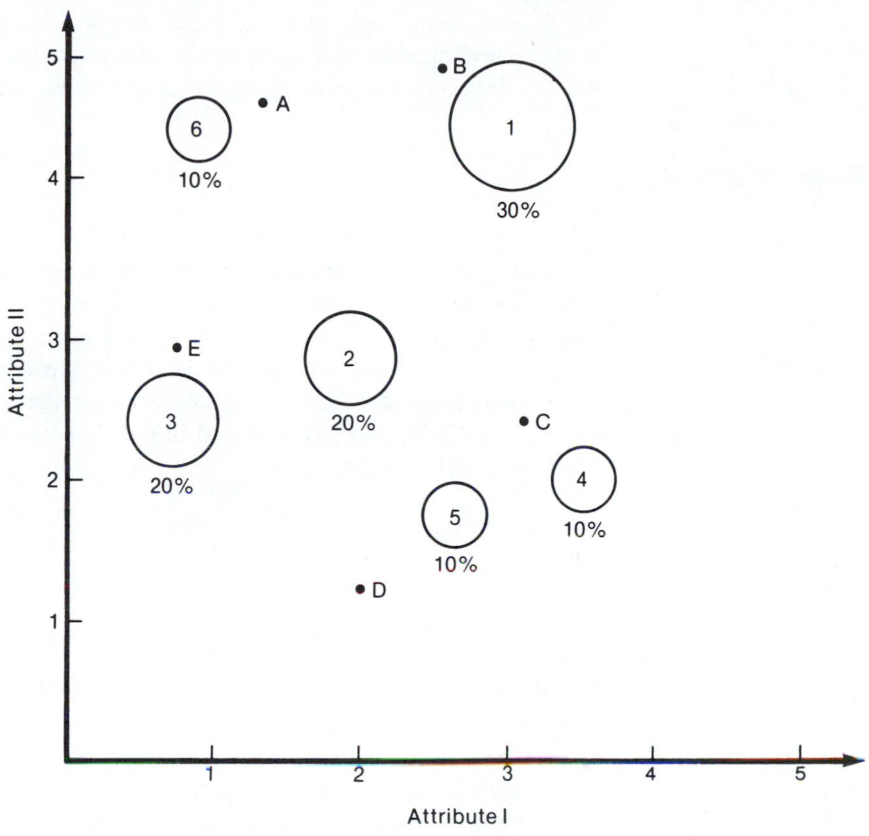

capturing the bulk of this segment and, hence, close to 20 percent of the market. (Also, since the product lies between E and C, it is probably a feasible product to produce.)

Target on segment 1 by making a product which is "3" on attribute I and "4.5" on attribute II. The advantage is that this segment has 30 percent of the market. The disadvantage is that B already is there, and, if they are a strong competitor, you are going to be in a big war if you target here.

Now complicate the problem somewhat by assuming your company already makes C, D, and E. If we still go for segment 2, we will largely cannibalize sales of our own products. Hence, segment 1 looks more appealing. Actually, however, the decision about which (if any) to produce depends heavily on likely competitors' actions and reactions. If we "attack" alternative B, the makers of alternative B may well attack us by going for segment 2. On the other hand, if we fail to attack, there is no guarantee that competitors will do likewise. What the map does is provide a good focus for highlighting some implications of these strategic decisions. An example of a product developed in this fashion was Maxim coffee, which came from an R & D effort targeted to produce rich *and* convenient coffee.

Repositioning

Assume you were put in charge of alternative D. After updating your résumé in anticipation of possible termination, you might consider trying to reposition the product. While many repositionings are theoretically possible, moving D up on attribute II to appeal to segment 2 seems most promising. This could be done by changing the actual product. Alternatively or additionally, advertising could stress that "product D is full of attribute II." If product D is an old brand, "new product D with attribute II added" might be introduced.

Limitations

The point of the two previous examples is to suggest that attribute-based maps can serve as market simulators for the purpose of considering various product policy and promotional strategy decisions. In such use, however, it is important to recognize some of the major limitations of these maps:

Their reliability is not perfect. To use such maps, it is important to have the basic dimensions constant over time. Yet changes in the market often make assumptions of constant maps over time untenable.

The dimensions must be usable. Often, dimensions appear which are either uninterpretable or so compound/abstract that it is unclear exactly what they are, much less how we give a product more of them (e.g., what gives a toothpaste more sex appeal?).

Many products are infeasible. The general state of technology as well as company strengths and weaknesses often preclude many "obvious" strategies. (While a segment usually exists which wants a low-cost and high-quality product, producing one may prove an elusive goal.)

The rational model may be wrong. Choice may not be determined by this mapping/trade-off type of decision making. Consequently, predictions of behavior based on this type of model can be quite deceptive.

SUMMARY

This chapter has presented several methods for producing maps of alternatives. More detail on them is available (c.f., Cooper, 1983; Shocker, 1987; Dillon, Frederick, and Tangpanichdee, 1985). While more elegant procedures exist for developing maps (e.g., correspondence analysis), for most applied users either MDS based on similarity data or derived distances or some simplification of direct ratings (e.g., factor analysis) will generally prove adequate.

The major uses of mapping models are twofold. First, they are very useful for generating hypotheses/ideas (which then should be further investigated). Even small samples (i.e., 15 office workers) occasionally produce interesting results. While MDS-based attribute models can be used to track markets over time (Moore and Lehmann, 1982), they are usually most appropriate as exploratory devices. Second, these maps are extremely useful communication devices. They often serve to get a room full of people to agree on a general plan of attack and this agreement, sometimes more than the plan, can lead to improved performance.

MDS AND CLUSTER ANALYSIS

Both multidimensional scaling and cluster analysis "operate" on a similarity matrix and put similar objects together. The main difference is that MDS attempts to geometrically portray the objects in a space of two or more dimensions, while cluster analysis either simply indicates groups of similar objects or produces a tree representing the similarities. The best approach to use in a particular situation depends on how customers think about the alternatives (Johnson and Fornell, 1987). Nonetheless, the information obtainable is relatively similar.

In addition to being alternative ways to analyze similarity data, MDS and cluster analysis can often be used in conjunction with each other. For example, a researcher facing a large database (e.g., a sample of 800) may first want to cluster observations based on similarity judgments and then produce a separate MDS picture for each derived segment. Alternatively, a small (pilot) sample might be asked to generate similarity measures for a large number of brands. By clustering these brands, a sample of brands could be drawn for use in a large-scale survey such that all the major types of brands would be represented. The major point, therefore, is that MDS and cluster analysis (and any of the other multivariate procedures as well) can be viewed as alternatives for a particular task or as complementary components of a complete analysis plan.

CONJOINT ANALYSIS

An interesting alternative to deriving dimensions is to assume they are known. Conjoint analysis assumes that both the attributes and the positions of the alternatives on the attributes are known. The procedure then attempts to attach values (utilities) to the levels of each of the various

TABLE 15–7 Assumed Underlying (unmeasured) Utility for Various Combinations

Usable Trunk Space (cubic feet)	Fuel Economy (mpg)			
	11–15	*16–20*	*21–25*	*26–30*
7–10	1.4	1.8	2.1	2.6
11–14	1.5	1.9	2.2	2.7
15–18	1.6	2.0	2.3	2.8

attributes. Input data are typically rankings of various combinations of attribute levels, and the output is the utility of the different levels on the various attributes. Consider the problem of assessing how customers trade off price and performance. Obviously, customers prefer the lowest price and the highest performance. To make intelligent marketing decisions, however, we need to know how much extra customers are willing to pay to get a given improvement in performance. Conjoint analysis attempts to answer such a question by treating price and performance as two attributes of a product.

For example, assume we are interested in cars and believe two attributes —fuel economy (which reflects operating cost) and trunk space—are the key attributes. If there are four levels of fuel economy and three of trunk space, there are 12 combinations of attribute levels. Assume the respondent has a value (utility) for each of the possible 12 combinations (Table 15–7). Unfortunately, we suspect the respondent cannot/will not accurately give us those utilities (often called *part-worths*) in response to a direct question. However, we feel that the respondent would be willing to rank the combinations from most to least preferred. Hence, I could collect data by asking respondents to rank order the 12 combinations of attributes. By observing how they trade off the attributes (Table 15–8) I attempt to deduce their underlying utilities for the attribute levels.

TABLE 15–8 Preference Ranking Input Data for Conjoint Analysis

Usable Trunk Space (cubic feet)	Fuel Economy (mpg)			
	11–15	*16–20*	*21–25*	*26–30*
7–10	12	10	6	3
11–14	11	9	5	2
15–18	8	7	4	1

Computationally, utilities are derived by means of a computer algorithm. One very commonly used special algorithm is MONANOVA (Kruskal, 1965), which assumes that overall utility for an alternative is an additive function (with no interactions) of the attribute level utilities:

$$\text{Utility for an alternative} = \sum_{\substack{\text{all} \\ \text{attributes}}} \left(\begin{array}{c} \text{Utility for level of the} \\ \text{alternative on an attribute} \end{array} \right)$$

In this algorithm, utility values are chosen to produce overall utilities which match the original preference ranking. It is also possible and in some ways preferable to use dummy variable regression analysis to get estimates of the utilities of the various characteristics (see Appendix 15–B).

Obviously, maximum trunk space and fuel economy will be the most preferred, and the minimum trunk space and fuel economy will be least preferred. The issue is how a respondent will trade off trunk space and fuel economy as they move from most preferred to least preferred. In Table 15–8, it appears that fuel economy is quite a bit more important than trunk space since the respondent prefers maximum fuel economy (26 to 30 mpg) and minimum trunk space (7 to 10 cubic feet) to "almost maximum" fuel economy (21 to 25 mpg) and maximum trunk space (15 to 18 cubic feet). This trade-off provides the key data which drive subsequent analysis.

The subject's utility levels for each of the attributes might be those of Table 15–9. This table can be used directly to reconstruct the utilities of Table 15–7. For example, the utility of a car with fuel economy 11 to 15 mpg and trunk space of 7 to 10 cubic feet would be .5 + .9 = 1.4. In this hypothetical example, the reconstruction is without error, something which almost never occurs in practice. In addition to using the derived utilities of the levels to estimate the overall utility of existing and potential new

TABLE 15–9 Output of Conjoint Analysis

Fuel Economy Level (mpg)	*Utility*
11–15	.5
16–20	.9
21–25	1.2
26–30	1.7
Trunk Space Level	*Utility*
7–10	.9
11–14	1.0
15–18	1.1

products, the derived utilities on the levels are also used to indicate the relative importance of the attributes. Most commonly, the range of utility levels on an attribute is used as a measure of attribute importance. In the car example, the importance of fuel economy would be estimated as 1.2 = 1.7 − .5, while that of trunk space as .2 = 1.1 − .9. Hence, this respondent is apparently more concerned about economy than carrying capacity.

Disjoint Analysis

Conjoint analysis essentially decomposes ratings data to find the utility (part-worth) values. An alternative approach is to ask subjects to directly rate importances or part-worths one attribute at a time. Returning to the car example, we could generate ratings via constant sum scales:

MPG	11–15	10
	16–20	20
	21–25	30
	26–30	40
		100
Trunk space	7–10	25
	11–14	35
	15–18	40
		100

Such ratings have appeal (Akaah and Korgaonkar, 1983) and are useful for clustering subjects with similar preferences (Green, Carroll, and Goldberg, 1981). Unfortunately, they are not likely to work well for some attributes (e.g., price, where the low price will tend to get all 100 points), and hence trade-off questions are still needed. *Self-explicated* weights have been combined with conjoint results in an attempt to get better estimates of the part-worths (Cattin, Gelfand, and Danes, 1983; Green, Goldberg, and Montemayor, 1981).

An Example

The example presented here is due to Green who has also applied the technique to air carrier selection, tire replacement decisions, and bar soaps (Green and Wind, 1975). It involves preference for spot removers for

TABLE 15–10 Data Collected

Product					
Package Design	*Brand Name*	*Price*	*Good Housekeeping Seal?*	*Money-Back Guarantee?*	*Respondent's Evaluation (ranking)*
A	K2R	1.19	No	No	13
A	Glory	1.39	No	Yes	11
A	Bissell	1.59	Yes	No	17
B	K2R	1.39	Yes	Yes	2
B	Glory	1.59	No	No	14
B	Bissell	1.19	No	No	3
C	K2R	1.59	No	Yes	12
C	Glory	1.19	Yes	No	7
C	Bissell	1.39	No	No	9
A	K2R	1.59	Yes	No	18
A	Glory	1.19	No	Yes	8
A	Bissell	1.39	No	No	15
B	K2R	1.19	No	No	4
B	Glory	1.39	Yes	No	6
B	Bissell	1.59	No	Yes	5
C	K2R	1.39	No	No	10
C	Glory	1.59	No	No	16
C	Bissell	1.19	Yes	Yes	1

Source: Paul Green and Yoram Wind, "New Way to Measure Consumers' Judgments," *Harvard Businesses Review* 53 (July–August 1975), p. 108.

upholstery and carpets. The following attributes were analyzed:

Package design (A, B, C).

Brand names (K2R, Glory, Bissell).

Price ($1.19, $1.39, $1.59).

Good Housekeeping seal (yes or no).

Money-back guarantee (yes or no).

Since there are $3 \times 3 \times 3 \times 2 \times 2 = 108$ possible combinations, it seemed infeasible to test all possible products. Hence, an orthogonal array of 18 combinations was used (translation: a representative subset of the original 108 products was selected). This data from one subject appear in Table 15–10. The resulting utilities appear in Table 15–11.

The results indicate a strong preference for package design B and (surprise) a low price. A money-back guarantee also seems to help, while the brand name and Good Housekeeping seal seem to be relatively unimportant. The results are useful for comparing the relative utility of various existing and new products.

Measurement Phase

Conjoint analysis really has two phases: measurement and analysis. The measurement phase deals with the design of the alternatives to be presented to subjects as well as actual data collection. Design entails several steps:

1. The attributes to be used must be chosen. This may require managerial judgment, focus groups, and/or pilot studies of subjects rating attribute importances.

2. The levels of each attribute must be chosen. The range must be broad enough to include all reasonable alternatives (e.g., car mpg from 15 to 50), but not so broad as to be beyond reasonable expectation (e.g., mpg from 1 to 300). The number of levels chosen should depend on the assumed shape of the utility curve on the attribute:

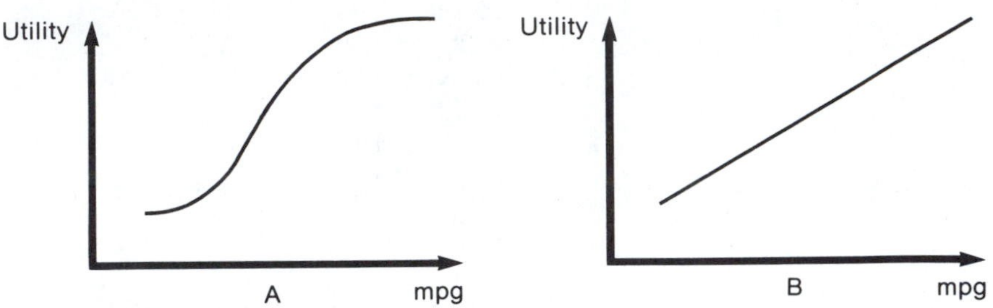

In case A, utility and mpg are nonlinearly related, requiring several points (levels) to recover the curve. In case B, by contrast, two points (levels) are sufficient to recover the curve. In practice, the number of levels used is typically 2 or 3 per attribute.

3. The actual combinations to be given respondents must be selected. Whereas a factorial design is most desirable, it is impractical. If there are 6 attributes of 3 levels each, there are $3^6 = 729$ possible products—far too many to ask one subject to rate. Consequently, one must either (*a*) assume all subjects have the same utility for each product feature (normally a bad assumption) and have different subjects rate different products, or (*b*) give a reduced number of products to each subject. In reducing the number of products, the most common approach is to use *orthogonal* designs on the assumption that there are no interactions between the attributes. [If a *few* interactions are expected, this can be accommodated in the design (Carmone and Green, 1981).] This leads to designs such as that used by Green and Wind in the cleaner example (Table 15–10). An excellent source of orthogonal designs was provided by Addelman (1962). Designs that take a problem with up to 7 attributes with 3 levels each and up to 7 attributes with 2 levels each and produce (by using the appropriate columns) an orthogonal design of 18 products can be seen in Table 15–12 (along with an orthogonal design of 20 products based on 19 attributes of 2 levels each). The design used in the cleaner example comes from columns 1, 2, and 3 for the 3-level attributes and columns 4 and 5 for the 2-level attributes in Basic Plan 7.

TABLE 15–11 Utilities for Spot Remover Attributes

Feature	*Utility*
Package design:	
A	.1
B	1.0
C	.6
Brand name:	
K2R	.3
Glory	.2
Bissell	.5
Price:	
1.19	1.0
1.39	.7
1.59	.1
Good Housekeeping seal:	
Yes	.3
No	.2
Money-back guarantee:	
Yes	.7
No	.2

Source: Paul Green and Yoram Wind, "New Way to Measure Consumers' Judgments." *Harvard Business Review* 53 (July–August, 1975), p. 110.

The design values are converted into product attribute levels as follows:

	Design Value	*Product Attribute Level*
Three-level Attributes	Column 1 = 0	Package design = A
	= 1	= B
	= 2	= C
	Column 2 = 0	Brand name = K2R
	= 1	= Glory
	= 2	= Bissell
	Column 3 = 0	Price = 1.19
	= 1	= 1.39
	= 2	= 1.59
Two-level Attributes	Column 4 = 0	Seal = No
	= 1	= Yes
	Column 5 = 0	Guarantee = No
	= 1	= Yes

TABLE 15–12 Some Orthogonal Designs

BASIC PLAN 7:3^7; 2^7; 18 trials

1234567	1234567
0000000	0000000
0112111	0110111
0221222	0001000
1011120	1011100
1120201	1100001
1202012	1000010
2022102	0000100
2101210	0101010
2210021	0010001
0021011	0001011
0100122	0100100
0212200	0010000
1002221	1000001
1111002	1111000
1220110	1000110
2010212	0010010
2122020	0100000
2201101	0001101

BASIC PLAN 8:2^{19}; 20 trials

00000 12345	00001 67890	11111 12345	1111 6789
00000	00000	00000	0000
11001	11101	01000	0110
01100	11110	10100	0011
10110	01111	01010	0001
11011	00111	10101	0000
01101	10011	11010	1000
00110	11001	11101	0100
00011	01100	11110	1010
00001	10110	01111	0101
10000	11011	00111	1010
01000	01101	10011	1101
10100	00110	11001	1110
01010	00011	01100	1111
10101	00001	10110	0111
11010	10000	11011	0011
11101	01000	01101	1001
11110	10100	00110	1100
01111	01010	00011	0110
00111	10101	00001	1011
10011	11010	10000	1101

Source: Sidney Addleman, "Orthogonal Main-Effect Plans for Asymmetrical Factorial Experiments," *Technometrics* 4 (February 1962), pp. 21–46.

It is also common to add to the orthogonal array a few particularly interesting combinations (e.g., ones the boss favors) or ones which allow the estimation of interactions and sometimes to delete nonsensical ones (e.g., 200 percent increase in output at no additional cost). Put differently, an orthogonal array is efficient statistically and, thus, is a good starting point but not necessarily a requirement for the design phase.

4. The form of the presentation must be selected. This can range from strictly verbal descriptions to pictures or even actual products. Clearly, the more realistic the stimulus, the better the quality of the data gathered. Also, care must be taken to describe attributes in customer- rather than engineer-oriented language. Currently, most researchers present subjects with a "full profile" description—that is, with a hypothetical (or real) product described on all attributes.

A less common alternative is to have respondents trade off on two attributes at a time, essentially filling in a table like 15–8 for each pair of attributes (Johnson, 1974). In the case of the car example, this means ranking the 12 combinations of fuel economy and trunk space in the matrix, then ranking the possible combinations of fuel economy and price, and so forth, until each pair of attributes has been presented. The results can produce both utilities on individual attributes (in Johnson's model, utilities are multiplicative, rather than additive) and simple one-way interactions.

Notice that it is possible to use computer aided interviewing for conjoint analysis. Moreover, since part-worths can be computed after data are partially gathered, the design can be altered so that respondents make judgments on trade-offs where the part-worths are least certain (i.e., the estimates have the largest variances). In this way, the survey can be made both more relevant to the subject and efficient for the analyst. This is a real advantage if only a few key customers are to be studied (and, conversely, may not be worth the trouble for frequently purchased consumer products).

Analysis Phase

The analysis phase is generally carried out by dummy variable regression analysis (Appendix 15–B), although many alternatives exist (Wittink and Cattin, 1981; Acito and Jain, 1980). When the pattern of part-worths (values of the levels) is known in advance, it is possible to constrain the solution to follow the pattern, thereby somewhat improving the estimates (Srinivasan, Jain, and Malhotra, 1983). It is also possible to estimate the values of the various levels of the attributes by mathematical programming (c.f., LINMAP—Srinivasan and Shocker, 1973).

The major decision at the analysis phase has to do with the level of aggregation. Moore (1980) found that treating all subjects as having the same part-worths greatly reduced both predictive power (R^2) and interpretability. In general, we expect different individuals will have different part-worths for the attribute levels. Analyzing each person separately is inefficient in terms of both analysis and interpretation (how does one summarize 1,127 conjoint analyses?). Consequently, segmentation is typically performed by clustering respondents together (c.f., Hagerty, 1985). This can be done based on (*a*) other characteristics (e.g., income) or (*b*) attribute importances as measured by either self-ratings or derived results. The results are then derived for each of the segments.

Actual Use of Conjoint

Conjoint analysis has been widely used in market research in all fields: consumer, industrial, services, and so on (Green and Srinivasan, 1978; Page and Rosenbaum, 1987). A study of commercial use by Cattin and Wittink (1986) produced the following highlights:

1. The most common purposes were new product/concept identification (47 percent), competitive analysis (40 percent), and pricing (38 percent).
2. Most studies used the full-profile approach, as opposed to trading off two attributes at a time.
3. Verbal descriptions of the alternatives and paragraphs account for 70 percent of the applications, with less than 10 percent using actual products.
4. Subjects are asked for preference (41 percent) or intention to buy (39 percent) most often.
5. Rating scales are used more often than rankings (49 versus 36 percent).
6. Regression/ANOVA or logit are the most common approaches to analysis.
7. A typical study uses a sample of about 300.

Pros and Cons

The advantages of conjoint measurement include the following:

The data explicitly require respondents to consider trade-offs on attributes.

The results are easy to interpret, and the key attributes readily established. (The range of the utilities on an attribute is typically taken as a measure of attribute importance.)

The attributes can be categorical (e.g., colors, styles) *as well as intervally scaled constructs.*

The major disadvantages are:

The relevant attributes and key levels must be known in advance. This means not just the physical attributes which are important to engineers but also the attributes consumers actually use to make decisions need to be specified. Choosing the correct levels may seem trivial, but the author encountered one study involving prices of 5, 7, and 9 when the actual price tended to be less than 2. This cast serious doubt on the interpretation of the whole study. Also, the attributes should probably be objective (e.g., horsepower), rather than subjective (e.g., power), whenever possible.[6]

The additive utility function may not be appropriate. At least for objects of art, one could question whether the "whole is the sum of its parts." (With nonorthogonal designs, interaction effects can be estimated.)

The approach gets messy with many attributes and levels. Since the alternatives are essentially factorial combinations of the attributes, the number of possible alternatives quickly gets out of hand. This has led researchers like Green to resort to using orthogonal subsets of the possible alternatives (Green, 1974). As long as there is no complex interaction effect, this approach works quite well. Also, it appears that respondents may focus on one or two key attributes as a means of completing the task when more attributes are actually important (Huber, 1987).

SUMMARY

This chapter has introduced a collection of techniques aimed at aiding understanding of consumers' thinking. Geometric modeling portrays brands (and customers) in a graphical manner based on either judged similarity data or direct ratings on attributes. Conjoint analysis deduces the values of various attribute levels based on ratings of products described in terms of combinations of levels on several attributes. Thus, geometric modeling is useful for discovering or portraying market structure, whereas conjoint analysis evaluates the desirability of various positions (brands) in a market.

For many frequently purchased products, however, it is unlikely that consumers actively process information about many brands on many attributes before making a choice. Rather, their behavior is likely to be relatively routinized. Hence, these models are useful for explaining preference formation and indicating likely long-run equilibrium positions but are not necessarily good models of repetitive decision making.

In-depth knowledge of these methods requires considerable additional investigation. A good starting point is provided by Green and Wind (1975). A serious student of these procedures, however, will want to consult an informal trilogy: Green and Carmone (1970), Green and Rao (1972), and Green and Wind (1973), as well as some of the works of Carroll (e.g.,

---

[6]It may well be that some innovative results can be generated by using soft attributes but these are harder to interpret.

Carroll and Chang, 1970) and others at Bell Labs. It is difficult to gauge the practical utility of these techniques. There is no question that the techniques (*a*) have been used in the real world and (*b*) have been involved in decisions which turned out both well and badly. Suffice it to say that these techniques (*a*) have generated a lot of computer output, (*b*) have not revolutionized marketing, and (*c*) have the potential to be useful in some situations.

PROBLEMS

1. Assume you were brand manager for Lay's potato chips. Also assume people make choices based on multiattribute models. What data would you collect and how would you analyze them if you had:
   a. A budget of $10,000 and two months?
   b. A budget of $100,000 and four months?
   c. A budget of $250,000 and eight months?
2. Assume you had the following distance data:

	Object					
Objects	*1*	*2*	*3*	*4*	*5*	*6*
1		4	6	5	6.5	3.5
2			4.5	6	9	8
3				3.5	7	8
4					4	6
5						4.5
6						

   What is the underlying configuration? (Hint: Try graphing by hand.)
3. Your boss indicates an interest in conjoint analysis, which the boss says is "better than MDS." Outline a 15-minute talk you would give to explain the two techniques and their relations.
4. A series of subjects rated soft drinks on the following:
   1. Carbonation.
   2. Calories.
   3. Sweetness.
   4. Thirst quenching.
   5. Popularity with others.

   These ratings were on 1 to 6 scales, where 6 represented a rating of very high and 1 a rating of very low. They also rated importances of the attributes on a scale of 1 to 6, where 6 represents very important. Given the following data for two individuals:

			Brand								
Respond-dent	*Attri-bute*	*Impor-tance*	*Coke*	*7up*	*Tab*	*Like*	*Pepsi*	*Sprite*	*Diet Pepsi*	*Fresca*	*Ideal*
A	1	3	5	3	2	2	6	5	3	4	3
	2	2	3	5	2	4	6	2	6	5	3
	3	2	6	5	6	5	6	5	5	5	4
	4	1	3	6	5	5	1	4	5	3	6
	5	6	5	5	2	4	4	6	2	1	6
	Preference ranking		2	5	7	6	1	4	3	8	
B	1	3	5	4	2	2	4	4	3	3	3
	2	2	4	4	4	4	4	3	3	5	2
	3	2	3	4	5	4	3	4	5	3	4
	4	2	4	5	5	4	4	4	4	3	6
	5	3	5	5	2	5	3	4	3	3	4
	Preference ranking		6	3	8	4	2	1	7	5	

a. Using the attitude model, $\sum_{1}^{5}$ (importance) · |Brand rating − Ideal|, calculate the predicted ranking of the 8 brands and compare it with the actual ranking.

b. If you drop the ideal point and importances from the model, what are the results?

5. Professional launderers prefer different detergents for different types of clothing. The preferred level of "harshness" and "color fastness" and also the fraction of each type of business are as follows:

		Preferred Level	
Clothing	*Share of Total*	*Harshness*	*Color Fastness*
Heavy whites	50	1	5
Fine whites	10	5	5
Heavy colors	20	2	1
Fine colors	20	5	1

The four present brands have the following properties:

Brand	*Harshness*	*Color Fastness*
A	2	4
B	4	5
C	2	2
D	4	2

a. Estimate the shares of sales of each brand by assuming:
   (1) Distance to brand = Σ|actual − preferred level|
   (2) $\text{Share}_j = (1/\text{distance to } j)/\sum_{i=1}^{4}(1/\text{distance to } i)$

b. Estimate the share of sales which a new "general-purpose" detergent might achieve if it had a harshness level of 3 and a color-fastness level of 3.

c. What does your model assume? What does your model ignore? Can you think of a new model which you like better for addressing question (*b*)?

6. Assume you had to design the data collection instrument to do conjoint analysis in a situation where there were two attributes, both with three levels. What would the instrument be?
7. Assume you were to analyze the results of a conjoint analysis on a single subject (the chief executive officer) for type of desk preferred. Two attributes were employed: size (regular, massive) and material (plastic, metal, wood). The six combinations were as follows:

	Size	*Material*
A	Regular	Plastic
B	Regular	Metal
C	Regular	Wood
D	Massive	Plastic
E	Massive	Metal
F	Massive	Wood

   The data were ranked by your boss from most to least preferred, as F, E, C, B, D, A. Try to deduce the boss's utility function.
8. Assume you were to design a conjoint study on home stereo systems. How would you proceed?

BIBLIOGRAPHY

Acito, Franklin, and Arun K. Jain. "Evaluation of Conjoint Analysis Results: A Comparison of Methods." *Journal of Marketing Research"* 17 (February 1980), pp. 106–12.

Addleman, Sidney. "Orthogonal Main-Effect Plans for Asymmetrical Factorial Experiments." *Technometrics* 4 (February 1962), pp. 21–46.

Akaah, Ishmael P., and Pradeep K. Korgaonkar. "An Empirical Comparison of the Predictive Validity of Self-Explicated, Huber-Hybrid, Tradional Conjoint, and Hybrid Conjoint Models." *Journal of Marketing Research* 20 (May 1983), pp. 187–97.

Bass, Frank M.; Edgar A. Pessemier; and Donald R. Lehmann. "An Experimental Study of Relationships between Attitudes, Brand Preference, and Choice." *Behavioral Science* 17 (November 1972), pp. 532–41.

Beckwith, Neil E., and Donald R. Lehmann. "The Importance of Halo Effects in Multi-Attitude Models." *Journal of Marketing Research* 12 (August 1975), pp. 265–75.

______. "The Importance of Differential Weights in Multiple Attribute Models of Consumer Attitude." *Journal of Marketing Research* 10 (May 1973), pp. 141–45.

Carmone, Frank J., and Paul E. Green. "Model Misspecification in Multiattribute Parameter Estimation." *Journal of Marketing Research* 18 (February 1981), pp. 87–93.

Carroll, J. Douglas, and Jih-Jie Chang. "Analysis of Individual Differences in Multidimensional Scaling Via an N-Way Generalization of 'Eckart-Young' Decomposition." *Psychometrika* 35 (January 1970), pp. 283-320.

Carroll, J. Douglas; Paul E. Green; and Catherine M. Schaffer. "Interpoint Distance Comparisons in Correspondence Analysis." *Journal of Marketing Research* 23 (August 1986), pp. 271–80.

Cattin, Philippe; Alan E. Gelfand; and Jeffrey Danes. "A Simple Bayesian Procedure for Estimation in a Conjoint Model." *Journal of Marketing Research* 20 (February 1983), pp. 29–35.

Cattin, Philippe, and Dick R. Wittink. "Commercial Use of Conjoint Analysis: An Update." Working paper, 1986.

______. "Commercial Use of Conjoint Analysis: A Survey." *Journal of Marketing* 46 (Summer 1982), pp. 44–53.

Cooper, Lee G. "A Review of Multidimensional Scaling in Marketing Research." *Applied Psychological Measurement* 7 (Summer 1983).

DeSarbo, Wayne S., and Donna L. Hoffman. "Constructing MDS Joint Spaces from Binary Choice Data: A Multidimensional Unfolding Threshold Model for Marketing Research." *Journal of Marketing Research* 24 (February 1987), pp. 40–54.

Dillon, William R.; Donald G. Frederick; and Vanchai Tangpanichdee. "Decision Issues in Building Perceptual Product Spaces with Multi-Attribute Rating Data." *Journal of Consumer Research* 12 (June 1985), pp. 47–63.

Dillon, William R., and Stuart Westin. "Scoring Frequency Data for Discriminant Analysis: Perhaps Discrete Procedures Can Be Avoided." *Journal of Marketing Research* 19 (February 1982), pp. 44–56.

Fishbein, Martin. "Attitude and the Prediction of Behavior." *Readings in Attitude Theory and Measurement*, ed. Martin Fishbein. New York: John Wiley & Sons, 1967, pp. 477–92.

Green, Paul E. "On the Analysis of Interactions in Marketing Research Data." *Journal of Marketing Research* 10 (November 1973), pp. 410–20.

______. "On the Design of Choice Experiments Involving Multifactor Alternatives." *Journal of Consumer Research* 1 (September 1974), pp. 61–68.

Green, Paul E., and Frank J. Carmone. *Multidimensional Scaling and Related Techniques in Marketing Analysis*. Boston: Allyn & Bacon, 1970.

Green, Paul E.; J. Douglas Carroll; and Stephen M. Goldberg. "A General Approach to Product Design Optimization Via Conjoint Analysis." *Journal of Marketing* 45 (Summer 1981), pp. 17–37.

Green, Paul E.; Stephen M. Goldberg; and Mila Montemayor. "A Hybrid Utility Estimation Model for Conjoint Analysis." *Journal of Marketing* 45 (Winter 1981), pp. 33–41.

Green, Paul E., and Vithala R. Rao. *Applied Multidimensional Scaling: A Comparison of Approaches and Algorithms*. New York: Holt, Rinehart & Winston, 1972.

Green, Paul E.; Vithala R. Rao; and Wayne S. DeSarbo. "Incorporating Group-Level Similarity Judgments in Conjoint Analysis." *Journal of Consumer Research* 5 (December 1978), pp. 187–93.

Green, Paul E., and V. Srinivasan. "Conjoint Analysis in Consumer Research: Issues and Outlook." *Journal of Consumer Research* 5 (September 1978), pp. 103–23.

Green, Paul E., and Yoram Wind. "New Way to Measure Consumers' Judgments." *Harvard Business Review* 53 (July–August 1975), pp. 107–17.

______. *Multiattribute Decisions in Marketing, a Measurement Approach*. Hinsdale, Ill.: Dryden, 1973.

Grover, Rajiv, and V. Srinivasan. "A Simultaneous Approach to Market Segmentation and Market Structuring." *Journal of Marketing Research* 24 (May 1987), pp. 139–53.

Hagerty, Michael R. "Improving the Predictive Power of Conjoint Analysis: The Use of Factor Analysis and Cluster Analysis." *Journal of Marketing Research* 22 (May 1985), pp. 168–84.

Hauser, John R., and Frank S. Koppelman. "Alternative Perceptual Mapping Techniques: Relative Accuracy and Usefulness." *Journal of Marketing Research* 16 (November 1979), pp. 495–506.

Hoffman, Donna L., and George R. Franke. "Correspondence Analysis: Graphical Representation of Categorical Data in Marketing Research." *Journal of Marketing Research* 23 (August 1986), pp. 213–27.

Holbrook, Morris B., and William L. Moore. "Using Canonical Correlation to Construct Product Spaces for Objects with Known Feature Structures." *Journal of Marketing Research* 19 (February 1982), pp. 87–98.

Holbrook, Morris B.; William L. Moore; and Russell S. Winer. "Constructing Joint Spaces from Pick-Any Data: A New Tool for Consumer Analysis." *Journal of Consumer Research* 9 (June 1982), pp. 99–105.

Huber, Joel. "Conjoint Analysis: How We Got Here and Where We Are." *Proceedings of the Sawtooth Software Conference on Perceptual Mapping, Conjoint Analysis, and Computer Interviewing*, 1987, pp. 237–52.

Huber, Joel, and Morris B. Holbrook. "Using Attribute Ratings for Product Positioning: Some Distinctions Among Compositional Approaches." *Journal of Marketing Research* 16 (November 1979), pp. 507–16.

Johnson, Michael D., and Claes Fornell. "The Nature and Methodological Implications of the Cognitive Representation of Products." *Journal of Consumer Research* 14 (September 1987), pp. 214–28.

Johnson, Richard M. "Trade-Off Analysis of Consumer Durables." *Journal of Marketing Research* 11 (May 1974), pp. 121–27.

______. "Market Segmentation: A Strategic Management Tool." *Journal of Marketing Research* 8 (February 1971), pp. 13–18.

______. "Political Segmentation." *Marketing Review* 25 (February 1970), pp. 20–24.

Kruskal, J. B. "Analysis of Factorial Experiments by Estimating Monotone Transformations of the Data." *Journal of the Royal Statistical Society*, series B, 27 (1965), pp. 251–63.

______. "Multidimensional Scaling by Optimizing Goodness of Fit to a Nonmetric Hypothesis." *Psychometrika* 29 (March 1964), pp. 1–27.

______. "Nonmetric Multidimensional Scaling: A Numerical Method." *Psychometrika* 29 (June 1964), pp. 115–29.

Lancaster, Kelvin J. "A New Approach to Consumer Theory." *Journal of Political Economy* 74 (April 1966), pp. 132–57.

Lehmann, Donald R. "Judged Similarity and Brand-Switching Data as Similarity Measures." *Journal of Marketing Research* 9 (August 1972), pp. 331–34.

______. "Television Show Preference: Application of a Choice Model." *Journal of Marketing Research* 8 (February 1971), pp. 47–55.

Lehmann, Donald R., and Edgar A. Pessemier. "Predicted Probability of Brand Choice Market Segments and Discriminant Attribute Configurations in Joint Space Market Analyses." Presented at Annual Meeting, Operations Research Society of America, Milwaukee, May 1973.

McIntyre, Shelby H., and Adrian B. Ryans. "Time and Accuracy Measures for Alternative Multidimensional Scaling Data Collection Methods: Some Additional Results." *Journal of Marketing Research* 14 (November 1977), pp. 607–10.

McLauchlan, Bill. "How to Design a Perceptual Mapping Study." *Proceedings of the Sawtooth Software Conference on Perceptual Mapping, Conjoint Analysis, and Computer Interviewing*, 1987, pp. 179–88.

Malhotra, Naresh K. "Validity and Structural Reliability of Multidimensional Scaling." *Journal of Marketing Research* 24 (May 1987), pp. 164–73.

Moore, William L. "Levels of Aggregation in Conjoint Analysis: An Empirical Comparison." *Journal of Marketing Research* 17 (November 1980), pp. 516–23.

Moore, William L., and Morris B. Holbrook. "On the Predictive Validity of Joint Space Models in Consumer Evaluations of New Concepts." *Journal of Consumer Research* 9 (September 1982), pp. 206–10.

Moore, William L., and Donald R. Lehmann. "Effects of Usage and Name on Perceptions of New Products." *Marketing Science* 1 (Fall 1982), pp. 351–70.

Moore, William L., and Russell S. Winer. "A Panel-Data Based Method for Merging Joint Space and Market Response Function Estimation." *Marketing Science* 6 (Winter 1987), pp. 25–42.

Neidell, Lester A. "Procedures for Obtaining Similarities Data." *Journal of Marketing Research* 9 (August 1972), pp. 335–37.

Page, Albert L., and Harold F. Rosenbaum. "Redesigning Product Lines with Conjoint Analysis: How Sunbeam Does It." *Journal of Product Innovation Management* 4 (1987), pp. 120–37.

Pessemier, Edgar A. "Single Subject Discriminant Configurations." Institute Paper #406, Institute for Research in the Behavioral, Economic, and Management Sciences, Krannert Graduate School of Industrial Administration, Purdue University, 1973.

Rogus, Carol Ann. "Correspondence Analysis Revisited: Procedures That Enhance Large-Scale Research." *Marketing Review* 42 (May 1987), pp. 21–26.

Rosenberg, M. J. "Cognitive Structure and Attitudinal Affect." *Journal of Abnormal and Social Psychology* 53 (November 1956), pp. 367–72.

Shepard, Roger N. "The Analysis of Proximities: Multidimensional Scaling with an Unknown Distance Function I." *Psychometrika* 27 (June 1962), pp. 125–39.

______. "The Analysis of Proximities: Multidimensional Scaling with an Unknown Distance Function II." *Psychometrika* 27 (September 1962), pp. 219–46.

Shocker, Allan D. "Perceptual Mapping: Its Origins, Methods, and Prospects." *Proceedings of the Sawtooth Software Conference on Perceptual Mapping, Conjoint Analysis, and Computer Interviewing*, 1987, pp. 121–42.

Shugan, Steven M. "Estimating Brand Positioning Maps Using Supermarket Scanning Data." *Journal of Marketing Research* 24 (February 1987), pp. 1–18.

Srinivasan, V.; Arun K. Jain; and Naresh K. Malhotra. "Improving Predictive Power of Conjoint Analysis by Constrained Parameter Estimation." *Journal of Marketing Research* 20 (November 1983), pp. 433–38.

Scrinivasan, V., and A. D. Shocker. "Linear Programming Techniques for Multidimensional Analysis of Preferences." *Psychometrika* 38 (September 1973), pp. 337–69.

Steffler, Volney. "Market Structure Studies: New Products for Old Markets and New Markets (Foreign) for Old Products." In *Applications of the Sciences in Marketing Management*, ed. Frank M. Bass, Charles W. King, and Edgar A. Pessemier. New York: John Wiley & Sons, 1968, pp. 251–68.

Winer, B. J. *Statistical Principles in Experimental Design*. New York: McGraw-Hill, 1973.

Wittink, Dick R., and Philippe Cattin. "Alternative Estimation Methods for Conjoint Analysis: A Monte Carlo Study." *Journal of Marketing Research* 18 (February 1981), pp. 101–6.

Wright, Peter, and Mary Ann Kriewall. "State-of-Mind Effects on the Accuracy with Which Utility Functions Predict Marketplace Choice." *Journal of Marketing Research* 17 (August 1980), pp. 277–93.

Appendix 15–A

SAS ALSCAL on 50 States Data

MDS: STATES DATA

ITERATION HISTORY FOR THE 2 DIMENSIONAL SOLUTION (IN SQUARED DISTANCES)
YOUNGS S-STRESS FORMULA 1 IS USED.

ITERATION	S-STRESS	IMPROVEMENT
1	0.40427	
2	0.20003	0.20423
3	0.18702	0.01302
4	0.18680	0.00022

ITERATIONS STOPPED BECAUSE
S-STRESS IMPROVEMENT LESS THAN 0.001000

STRESS AND SQUARED CORRELATION (RSQ) IN DISTANCES

RSQ VALUES ARE THE PROPORTION OF VARIANCE OF THE SCALED DATA (DISPARITIES) IN THE PARTITION (ROW, MATRIX, OR ENTIRE DATA) WHICH IS ACCOUNTED FOR BY THEIR CORRESPONDING DISTANCES.

STRESS VALUES ARE KRUSKAL'S STRESS FORMULA 1.

STRESS = 0.233 RSQ = 0.925

MDS: STATES DATA

CONFIGURATION DERIVED IN 2 DIMENSIONS

STIMULUS COORDINATES

STIMULUS NUMBER	PLOT SYMBOL	DIMENSION 1	DIMENSION 2
1	1	0.2194	0.4004
2	2	3.0832	-2.1087
3	3	0.7186	0.0264
4	4	0.7210	0.7048
5	5	-5.3162	-1.8998
6	6	0.1511	-0.2865
7	7	0.0628	-0.5075
8	8	0.7661	-0.1555
9	9	-0.3858	-0.4179
10	A	-0.1318	-0.1665
11	B	0.7642	-0.3043
12	C	1.1436	0.4483
13	D	-1.6750	-0.4567
14	E	-0.5154	-0.0954
15	F	-0.3804	0.6474
16	G	-0.0498	0.1781
17	H	0.1125	0.4773
18	I	-0.1559	1.3328
19	J	0.9011	0.3031
20	K	-0.1162	-0.3391
21	L	-0.5178	-0.4593
22	M	-0.9198	-0.5035
23	N	-0.3763	-0.2833
24	O	0.6755	0.8266
25	P	-0.3222	-0.1067
26	Q	0.8419	0.1302
27	R	0.2881	0.1603
28	S	1.1294	-0.2948
29	T	1.0279	0.4748
30	U	-0.6274	-0.4670
31	V	0.8944	0.5985
32	W	-3.3451	-1.7976
33	X	-0.2157	-0.0580
34	Y	0.8608	0.5515
35	Z	-1.1828	-0.1953
36	1	0.1498	0.4115
37	2	0.2951	-0.2752
38	3	-1.1489	-0.3743
39	4	0.5978	0.3199
40	5	0.4587	0.4741
41	6	0.8662	0.7380
42	7	0.0062	0.1609
43	8	-2.5099	0.9938
44	9	0.7307	0.4002
45	A	1.1883	0.6066
46	B	-0.1811	-0.2127
47	C	-0.1053	-0.3743
48	D	0.6278	0.6480
49	E	-0.3203	-0.2959
50	F	1.2173	0.4220

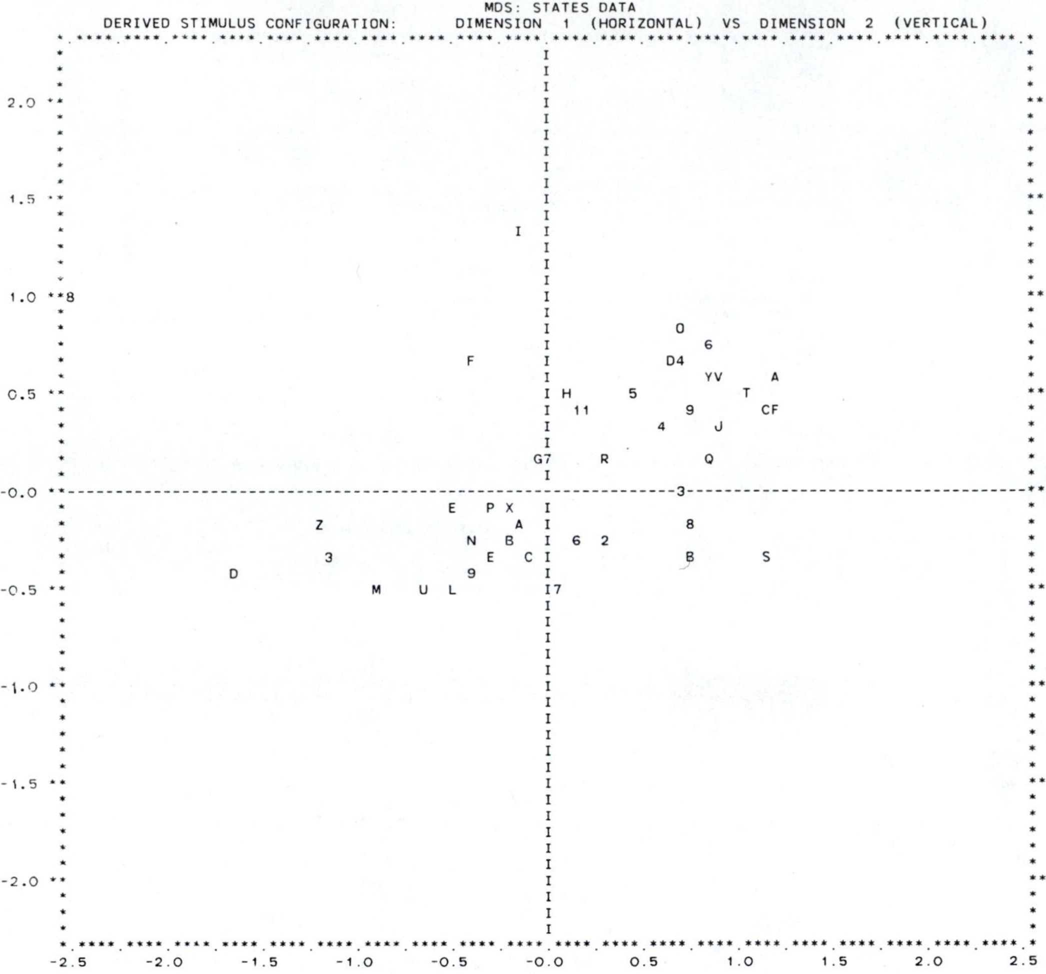
MDS: STATES DATA
DERIVED STIMULUS CONFIGURATION: DIMENSION 1 (HORIZONTAL) VS DIMENSION 2 (VERTICAL)
2.0
1.5
1.0
0.5
-0.0
-0.5
-1.0
-1.5
-2.0
-2.5
-2.0
-1.5
-1.0
-0.5
-0.0
0.5
1.0
1.5
2.0
2.5

Appendix 15–B

Derivation of Attribute Utilities in Conjoint Analysis

Conjoint analysis really consists of two stages. The first stage is data collection, which attempts to efficiently uncover utilities for attribute levels using as few alternatives as possible. The trick to doing this is to understand experimental design well, and to have a copy of a book such as Winer (1973) readily available.

The second stage of conjoint analysis involves estimating the utilities for each level of each attribute. This is usually done by dummy variable regression. To do this, the attribute levels are converted into a series of dummy variables. The stated ranking is then inverted so that a big number indicates high utility. For example, the cleaning product example of Green and Wind (1975) can be converted to a regression problem with 18 observations (one for each alternative) and 8 dummy variables (Table 15B–1). By running a regression on this data, utilities can be estimated. (Notice also that, if the data are sufficient, dummy variables representing interactions can also be created and estimated.)

Assuming no interactions, the regression model becomes:

$$\begin{aligned}\text{Rating} = \text{B}_0 &+ \text{B}_1(\text{Package A}) + \text{B}_2(\text{Package B}) + \text{B}_3(\text{K2R}) \\ &+ \text{B}_4(\text{Glory}) + \text{B}_5(\text{Price 1.19}) + \text{B}_6(\text{Price 1.39}) \\ &+ \text{B}_7(\text{Good Housekeeping Seal}) \\ &+ \text{B}_8(\text{Money-Back Guarantee}).\end{aligned}$$

B_1 then becomes the difference in utility between Package A and Package C (the "left out" package), etc. If we thought that a particular combination of attibutes was particularly effective (e.g., Package Design A and Glory), we could add an interaction term to the regression model to estimate it [e.g., B_9(Package A)(Glory)]. Generally, however, researchers have not found interaction terms to be particularly useful in most conjoint studies.

In the special case when the alternatives are derived according to a full factorial design or an orthogonal array, it is possible to estimate the utilities by hand calculation using the following steps:

1. Estimate the average value of the dependent variable for each level of each attribute. For example, Package Design A appears in 6 combinations and the average score is given by $(6 + 8 + 2 + 1 + 11 + 4)/6 = 5.33$ (Table 15B–2).
2. If you wish to place utilities on a particular scale, convert the average scores to a utility scale. In this case, the averages were rescaled from their range of 5.3 to 13.33 to a range of .1 to 1.0.[7] The results appear in Table 15B–3, along with the results presented by Green and Wind (1975). Notice the close but imperfect correspondence between the two results, especially in terms of the range of utilities on each attribute.

To check on the consistency of these results with the data, the predicted utilities were calculated for both the simple sums and MONANOVA utilities and compared with the stated rankings (Table 15B–4). The results indicate (*a*) that the MONANOVA results are consistent with the rankings and (*b*) that the simple sum results are also consistent and very similar to the MONANOVA. The point, therefore, is that dummy variable regression (or in certain circumstances even average scores) can be used to get quite good approximations of attribute utilities.

[7]This was done by linear interpolation so that 5.33 = .1, 6.22 = .2, 7.11 = .3, and so forth.

TABLE 15B–1 Dummy Coding Scheme

Dependent Variable (19-ranking)	Package Design A	Package Design B	Brand K2R	Brand Glory	Price 1.19	Price 1.39	Good House-keep-ing Seal	Money-back Guar-antee
6	1	0	1	0	1	0	0	0
8	1	0	0	1	0	1	0	1
2	1	0	0	0	0	0	1	0
17	0	1	1	0	0	1	1	1
5	0	1	0	1	0	0	0	0
16	0	1	0	0	1	0	0	0
7	0	0	1	0	0	0	0	1
12	0	0	0	1	1	0	1	0
10	0	0	0	0	0	1	0	0
1	1	0	1	0	0	0	1	0
11	1	0	0	1	1	0	0	1
4	1	0	0	0	0	1	0	0
15	0	1	1	0	1	0	0	0
13	0	1	0	1	0	1	1	0
14	0	1	0	0	0	0	0	1
9	0	0	1	0	0	1	0	0
3	0	0	0	1	0	0	0	0
18	0	0	0	0	1	0	1	1

TABLE 15B–2 Average Score for Attribute Levels

	Score
Package design:	
A	5.33
B	13.33
C	9.83
Brand name:	
K2R	9.17
Glory	8.67
Bissell	10.67
Price:	
1.19	13.00
1.39	10.17
1.59	5.33
Good Housekeeping seal:	
Yes	10.50
No	9.00
Money-back guarantee:	
Yes	12.50
No	8.00

TABLE 15B–3 Attribute Utilities

	Simple Sums	*MONANOVA*
Package design:		
A	.1	.1
B	1.0	1.0
C	.6	.6
Brand name:		
K2R	.5	.3
Glory	.5	.2
Bissell	.7	.5
Price:		
1.19	1.0	1.0
1.39	.6	.7
1.59	.1	.1
Good Housekeeping seal:		
Yes	.7	.3
No	.5	.2
Money-back guarantee:		
Yes	.9	.7
No	.4	.2

TABLE 15B–4 Predicted Utilities from Conjoint Results

Predicted Utility: MONANOVA	*Predicted Utility: Simple Sum*	*Predicted Rank: MONANOVA*	*Predicted Rank: Simple Sum*	*Stated Rank*
1.8	2.5	13	13.5	13
1.9	2.6	11.5	11	11
1.2	2.0	17	17	17
3.0	3.7	2	2	2
1.7	2.5	14.5	13.5	14
2.9	3.6	3	3	3
1.9	2.6	11.5	11	12
2.4	3.2	6.5	6	7
2.2	2.8	8.5	9	9
1.0	1.8	18	18	18
2.2	3.0	8.5	8	8
1.7	2.3	14.5	15	15
2.7	3.4	4	4	4
2.4	3.2	6.5	6	6
2.5	3.2	5	6	5
2.0	2.6	10	11	10
1.3	2.1	16	16	16
3.1	3.9	1	1	1

Chapter 16

Additional Predictive Procedures

Chapter 13 spent a considerable amount of time detailing what regression analysis is and how it can be used. Regression analysis is a very flexible tool which can be used in a wide variety of situations. Nonetheless, there are other predictive procedures which also are used in marketing research. This chapter, therefore, is devoted to describing two such procedures: discriminant analysis and logit analysis. These procedures can deal with situations where the dependent variable is categorical. A brief description of some other procedures—AID, Canonical Correlation, Structural Equation Modeling, and Log-Linear Analysis—appear as Appendixes D through G.

TWO-GROUP LINEAR DISCRIMINANT ANALYSIS

Basic Notion

Many marketing situations revolve around two distinct groups of consumers. For example, we often are concerned with the differences between users and nonusers of a particular product or brand. In such situations, we are often interested in identifying the characteristics (e.g., age, income, education) of users versus nonusers of the product. One technique for analyzing which characteristics "discriminate" members of the two groups and their relative importance is imaginatively called *discriminant analysis*.

To understand how discriminant analysis works, consider the following graph representing the incomes and ages of purchasers (P) and non-

FIGURE 16–1 Purchasers (P) versus Nonpurchasers (N) by Age and Income

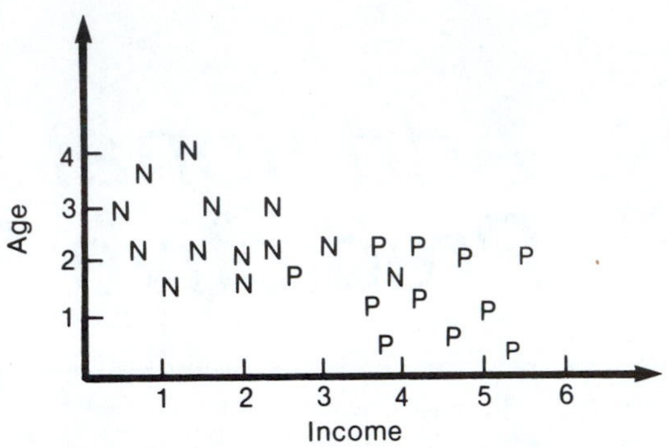

purchasers (N) of a particular product (Figure 16–1). Purchasers of this product appear to be younger and richer than nonpurchasers. Hence, if a 30-year-old drove up to my store in a Mercedes, he (assuming he hadn't stolen it) would be a good prospect for my product, whereas a 65-year-old pensioner would not be. In this case, both age and income discriminate between purchasers and nonpurchasers.

Now consider Figure 16–2. In this situation, height is apparently a perfect discriminator between purchasers and nonpurchasers, while liking of yogurt is essentially worthless as a discriminator.

FIGURE 16–2 Purchasers (P) versus Nonpurchasers (N) by Height and Liking of Yogurt

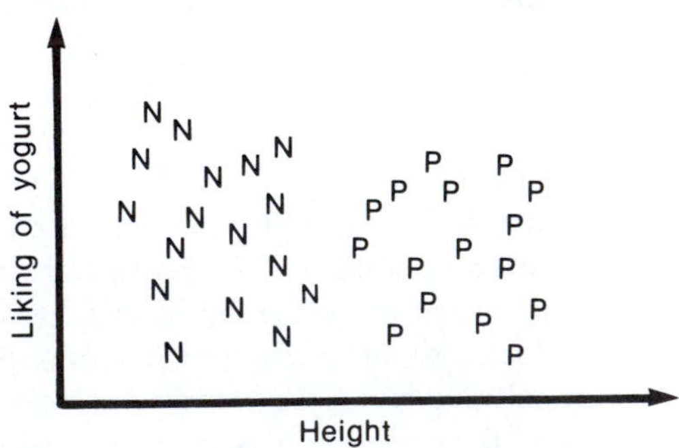

The process of plotting members of the two groups on axes to find out which variables discriminate has some severe limitations. First, it allows for considering only two independent variables at once. Second, it is tedious. And third, it does not give concise results which indicate quantitatively the effect of each of the characteristics on group membership. Therefore, a more formal approach is usually employed.

The Discriminant Function

An effective way to analyze which variables discriminate between members of two groups is to build an index which separates the two groups on the basis of their values on the measured characteristics. When the procedure called discriminant analysis is used, the index is called (again ingeniously) the discriminant function, and the characteristics become the independent variables:

$$f = w_1x_1 + w_2x_2 + \cdots + w_kx_k \tag{16.1}$$

where

$x_1, x_2, \ldots, x_k$ = the measured characteristics (variables).
f = the index (discriminant function).
w_i = the weight (discriminant coefficient) of the ith characteristic in discriminating between the two groups.

Discriminant analysis finds the set of weights which spreads apart the values of index for the two groups as far as possible. Returning to the example involving purchasers (group 2) and nonpurchasers (group 1) (see Figure 16–1), we see that the best index involving income and age might be as follows:

$$f = 3(\text{income}) - 2(\text{age})$$

We can represent this graphically, as in Figure 16–3. Consider the person with both age and income equal to 2. The value of the index for this person would be 3(2) − 2(2) = 2. Similarly, the person with age of 1 and income of 5 would have an index of 3(5) − 2(1) = 13. In fact, all the people in the sample can now be represented by a position on the new index (Figure 16–4). Thus, we can predict group membership based on a person's score on the discriminant function. If the score is closer to the mean of the purchasers, the person would be classified as a purchaser, and vice versa. This is equivalent to drawing a "cutoff" line through the space such that, as much as possible, the purchasers lie on one side of the line and the

FIGURE 16–3 Purchasers (P) versus Nonpurchasers (N): Discriminant Function

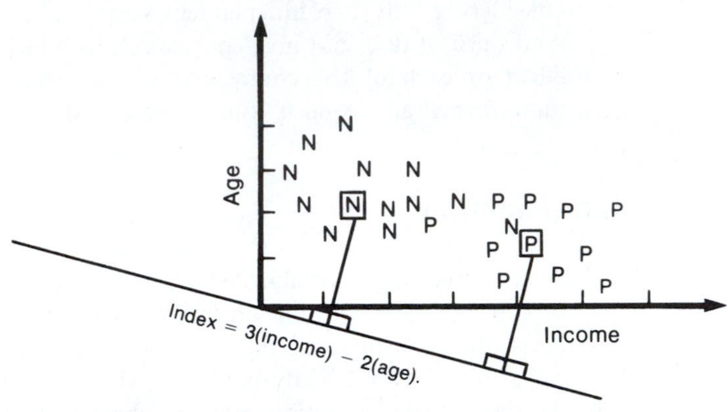

FIGURE 16–4 Positions on the Discriminant Function

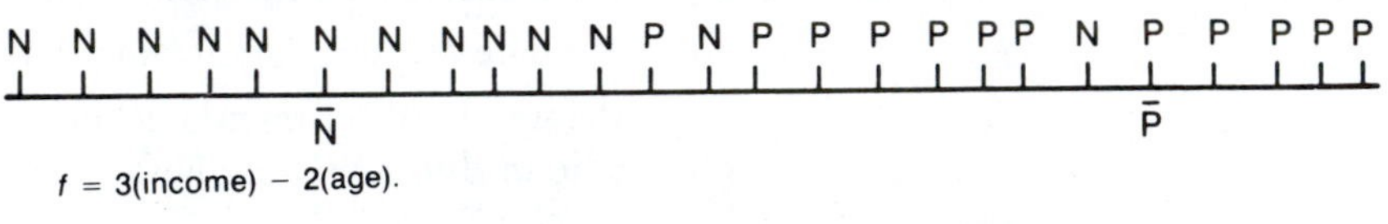

nonpurchasers on the other side. (For a more complete discussion of the weights and the use of discriminant analysis for classification, see Appendix 16–B.)

Relation to Regression Analysis. The basic approach of linear discriminant analysis is identical to that of linear regression analysis: using a weighted linear combination of independent variables to predict a dependent variable. The only difference is that the dependent variable in regression is a "real" variable (at least intervally scaled), whereas in discriminant analysis the dependent variable is group membership (and, hence, only nominally scaled). For two groups, however, it is easy to generate a dummy variable to represent group membership (i.e., code 1 for group 1 membership and 0 for group 2 membership). By using such a dummy variable as the dependent variable, a regression can be run. The resulting regression coefficients will be proportional to the weights which would have been obtained from discriminant analysis. Hence, two-group discriminant analysis is essentially equivalent to regression analysis using a dummy dependent variable.

Using Discriminant Analysis: Basics

The basic purpose of discriminant analysis is to identify what variables are the best predictors of group membership. Since this usually requires a computer program, the key questions are what to input and what to look at in the output.

Input. The input consists of a set of observations for both groups. Values of the predictor variables for both groups are the actual input. Group membership is identified a priori. (Discriminant analysis describes existing groups; it does not find groups.)

Output. Like most computer output, there is more information given than can be profitably used (see Appendix 16–A). This overload is the result of two causes: (*a*) to "debug" a program, a lot of intermediate calculations are output to make it easy to see if the program is working correctly and (*b*) the desire to output enough so specialized uses can be made of the results. While much of this output has some purpose, the general user will find the information that follows sufficient in most applications.

Means of the Variables for the Two Groups. The profiles of the groups in terms of means on the variables serve two basic purposes. First, they are useful to check whether the data were input correctly (a mean of 5.4 on a variable scaled 1 to 5 indicates the input is "messed up"). More important, they give the first indication of which variables distinguish between members of the two groups. Large differences in means on a particular variable suggest that the variable is an important discriminator between the groups. If all the variables have approximately the same standard deviation and there is relatively little correlation among the independent variables, the size of the differences between the means will provide the same ranking of the importances of the variables in discriminating as the size of the discriminant coefficients.

To summarize the results, a profile chart is often very effective. Returning to our hypothetical example, we could plot the purchaser and nonpurchaser groups as in Figure 16–5. Such a plot is very useful in understanding how the two groups differ.

The Discriminant Coefficients (w_is). The discriminant coefficients indicate the relative contribution of a unit on each of the independent variables to the discriminant function. A large discriminant coefficient means that a one-unit change in that particular variable produces a large change in the

FIGURE 16–5 Profile of Purchasers versus Nonpurchasers

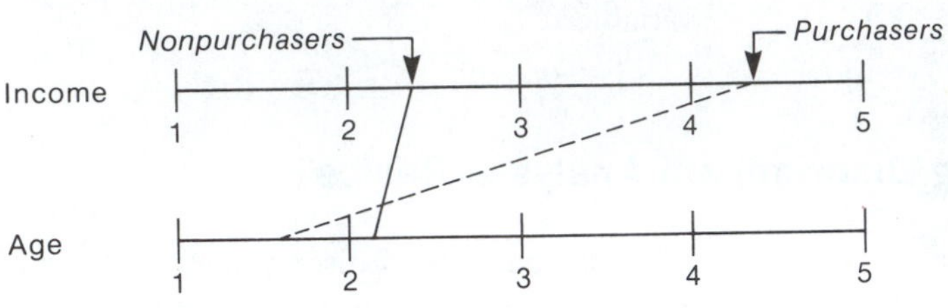

discriminant function, and vice-versa. In short, discriminant coefficients are interpreted exactly the same way as regression coefficients.

Discriminant coefficients (like regression coefficients) are affected by the scale of the independent variable. To remove this scale effect, many researchers either standardize the variables before inputting or multiply each discriminant coefficient (w_i) by the standard deviation of the variable (s_i). The resulting coefficients indicate how much a change of one standard deviation in each of the independent variables would affect the discriminant function. Whenever the scales of the independent variables vary widely (causing large differences in the size of the standard deviations), the unstandardized discriminant coefficients and the standardized discriminant coefficients may give very different importance ratings to the variables.

Discriminant coefficients are not proportional to the simple t values testing differences in means between the two groups for the particular variable when there is multicollinearity among the independent variables. In multiple regression, an independent variable may have a high simple correlation with the dependent variable, but the regression coefficient may be small and/or insignificant if the independent variable is also highly correlated with other independent variables. In discriminant analysis, a variable may be significantly different between two groups, but the discriminant coefficient insignificant due to collinearity with other independent variables. In other words, collinearity among the independent variables makes interpreting discriminant coefficients difficult exactly the way collinearity makes regression coefficients unreliable and hard to interpret.

Returning to the example in Figure 16–1, we see that income is measured on a larger scale than age. Assuming these scales produce standard deviations of income and age equal to 1 and 2, respectively, we can compute the standardized discriminant coefficients by multiplying the "regular" discriminant coefficients by the appropriate standard deviations, obtaining $+3$ and -2. The resulting measure of importance is shown in Table 16–1. In this hypothetical case, the relative importance of the variables in discriminating depends on your definition of importance.

TABLE 16–1 Alternative Measures of the Importance of a Variable

Variable	*Raw Difference in Mean*	*Standard Deviation*	*Unstandardized Discriminant Coefficient*	*Standardized Discriminant Coefficient*
Income	2.0	2	1.5	3.0
Age	−.5	1	−2	−2.0

The Hit-miss Table. Most discriminant analysis programs produce a hit-miss table (also known as a *classification table* or *confusion matrix*). This table indicates how successful the discriminant function would have been in classifying the same observations used to form the function back into their respective groups. (Usually, these tables are constructed under the assumption of equal prior probabilities of group membership.) Such a table might look like the following:

	Predicted Group	
Actual Group	*1*	*2*
1	21	12
2	56	111

The percent correctly classified is often used as a summary measure of the value of the independent variables in predicting group membership. Hence, the percent correctly classified in discriminant analysis is somewhat analogous to R^2 in regression. In this case, the number of correct predictions is 21 + 111 = 132. Since there were 200 observations in all, $\frac{132}{200} = 66$ percent is a measure of how effective the independent variables were in predicting group membership.

Statistical Aspects of Interpretation

Differences in Means. The differences in means between the groups for each variable can be tested by the "old fashioned" t test or the equivalent one-way ANOVA F test:

$$\frac{\bar{x}_{1j} - \bar{x}_{2j}}{s_{1j-2j}} \text{ is } t_{\alpha,\, n_1+n_2-2}$$

or

$$\frac{(\bar{x}_{1j} - \bar{x}_{2j})^2}{s^2_{1j-2j}} \text{ is } F_{\alpha,1,n_1+n_2-2}$$

Such a test can be applied to each of the independent variables.[1]

Rather than test the variables separately, it is possible to test all the variables simultaneously. This test examines whether the means on all the variables (e.g., income, age) are the same for the two groups. This multivariate analysis of variance test produces a variety of equivalent test statistics, the most common of which are an F statistic and the Mahalanobis D^2 (which turns out to be approximately chi-square distributed). A "large" (significant) F or D^2 indicates the means of the two groups are different on the variables and hence that the variables are helpful in separating the groups. A small F (or D^2) indicates that the independent variables are essentially worthless as predictors of group membership.

The Percent Correctly Classified. By examining this hit-miss table, the number of correct classifications can be calculated. The percent correctly classified can be compared statistically against the following four main criteria:

Random. The easiest test to beat is to compare the percent correctly classified (p) with the result of random classification. In the two-group case, that means 50 percent. The one-tail test statistic is:

$$z = \frac{p - 50}{\sqrt{(50)(50)}}\sqrt{n_1 + n_2}$$

where z is standard normally distributed. Hence, when z is big (greater than 2), the independent variables have made a significant contribution to prediction. Returning to our previous example, we had the following:

	Predicted Group	
Actual Group	*1*	*2*
1	21	12
2	56	111

[1]Since many computer programs do not automatically produce these tests (a definite oversight in my opinion), they may require some effort to perform. The differences in means on the jth variable $\bar{x}_{1j} - \bar{x}_{2j}$ is easily computed from the means of the variables. The standard deviation is not directly available and must be obtained from the square root of the jth diagonal element in the pooled variance-covariance matrix.

We can compare 66 percent with 50 percent as follows:

$$z = \frac{66 - 50}{\sqrt{(50)(50)}}\sqrt{200} = \frac{16}{50}\sqrt{200} = 4.5 > 2$$

Thus, we have done significantly better than random at the 95 percent level. If this test fails to be significant, all the others will also.

The Largest Group Criterion. The toughest test is to compare the percent correctly classified with the percent that would be correctly classified by assuming everyone was a member of the largest group. This criterion becomes extremely hard to beat as one group becomes dominant. In the previous example, 167 = 83.5 percent of the people are in the largest group (nonpurchasers). Simply saying everyone is a nonpurchaser will give the fewest misclassifications since 83.5 is greater than 66. This criterion is somewhat inappropriate in a practical sense, however, since we are much more concerned with finding purchasers than with avoiding contacting nonpurchasers. Beating the largest group criterion is sufficient to demonstrate the worth of the independent variables but is not necessary for the variables to be useful.

Proportional Chance Criterion. A compromise between random and largest group criteria is the proportional chance criterion (Morrison, 1969). This criterion is:

$$C_{\text{pro}} = P_1^2 + P_2^2 \tag{16.2}$$

In the previous example, this becomes:

$$C_{\text{pro}} = \left(\frac{33}{200}\right)^2 + \left(\frac{167}{200}\right)^2 = 72.7 \text{ percent}$$

Comparison of the actual percent with this percent gives a "fairer" measure of the predictive power of the variables than comparison with the largest group. (This should also be tested for statistical significance.)

The "Fairest" Criterion. In some sense, the fairest criterion is to assume that likelihood of correct classification is dependent on both the probability of group membership (P_i) and the fraction assigned to each group (f_i) (Mostellar and Bush, 1954). The criterion is:

$$C_{\text{fair}} = f_1(P_1) + f_2(P_2) \tag{16.3}$$

In the previous example, that would be:

$$C_{\text{fair}} = \frac{77}{200}\left(\frac{33}{200}\right) + \frac{123}{200}\left(\frac{167}{200}\right) = 58 \text{ percent}$$

Therefore, we would compare the 66 percent correctly classified with 58 percent.

The Bias Problem. Using the same observations to examine the ability of the discriminant function to correctly classify observations as were used to create the discriminant function produces an upward bias in the percent correctly classified. The obvious way to remove the bias is to split the sample into an analysis sample, which is used to construct the discriminant function, and a *holdout sample*. The holdout sample is then classified into groups based on the discriminant function derived from the analysis sample, eliminating the bias. The problem with this approach is that for a large sample ($n > 300$), the bias is relatively small. For a small sample ($n < 50$), on the other hand, there are probably not enough observations to split the data into two groups. Consequently, the "split-half" approach is useful mainly for moderate sample sizes.

An extreme but effective way to remove the bias in classifying is to run $n_1 + n_2$ separate discriminant analyses. In each of these analyses, one observation is the holdout observation. Hence, we use the discriminant function based on the $n_1 + n_2 - 1$ observations to classify the holdout observation. By rotating the holdout observation, one can estimate the percent correctly classified. Fortunately, for most problems such an extreme remedy is unnecessary.

Issues in Applications

Where. Two-group discriminant analysis can be applied anywhere the criterion variable can be divided into two groups. This means situations including purchasers versus nonpurchasers, buyers of brand A versus buyers of all other brands, good risks versus bad risks, and so forth are candidates for two-group discriminant analysis.

In everyday life, one need only apply for a credit card or a loan to be subjected to the results of discriminant analysis. Your income, age, length of residence, and so forth are all considered (and appropriately weighted) in deciding whether to give you a loan. The weights are often rounded to even numbers so a clerk can easily calculate your "score." If your score is above a certain level, you get the credit card or loan. If not, you have literally been discriminated against.

How. Building a discriminant model is equivalent to building a regression model. All the caveats and suggestions about model building made in the regression chapter apply here as well. Two other issues often are raised by users of discriminant analysis. One question is whether the two groups must be of equal size. As long as the objective is to find the best discriminant function possible, given a sample has already been drawn, the best approach is to use all the data points available. In short, the groups do not have to be of equal size. In designing a sample, on the other hand, guaranteeing relatively equal sample sizes in the two groups for a fixed total sample size will somewhat improve the reliability of the results.

Another issue is what will happen when the two basic assumptions of normality and equal covariances in the two groups are violated. Violation of the basic assumptions makes statistical interpretation of the results very difficult. If the covariances in the two groups are sufficiently unequal, the optimal discriminant function becomes nonlinear. Nonetheless, for the purpose of finding interesting relations, discriminant analysis is remarkably robust. Therefore, such relaxations as using binary (dummy) variables as independent variables can be done in practice if not in theory.

Examples

Innovators versus Noninnovators. The first example concerns the difference between personalities of innovators and noninnovators in the purchase of a new home appliance (Robertson and Kennedy, 1968). In this study, 60 innovators were compared with 40 noninnovators on seven personality variables (Table 16–2). The two groups are profiled in Figure 16–6. The discriminant coefficients indicate that venturesomeness is the best discriminator (among the seven personality measures studied) and that interest range is the worst. You may notice that the size of the discriminant coefficients produces a ranking different from what would be generated by looking at the differences in the means on the variables. The reasons for this are (*a*) unequal variances of the variables and/or (*b*) multicollinearity among the predictor variables.

TABLE 16–2 Differences between Innovators and Noninnovators

	Innovator Mean	*Noninnovator Mean*	*Discriminant Coefficient*
Venturesomeness	4.88	4.12	3.59
Social mobility	3.93	3.20	3.08
Privilegedness	3.68	3.25	2.04
Social integration	4.13	3.78	2.44
Status concern	2.00	1.73	.95
Interest range	5.27	5.00	.59
Cosmopolitanism	2.77	3.03	−2.86

Source: Thomas Robertson and James Kennedy, "Prediction of Consumer Innovators: Application of Multiple Discriminant Analysis." Adapted from *Journal of Marketing Research*, published by the American Marketing Association, 5 (February 1968), pp. 66–67.

FIGURE 16–6 Profile of Innovators and Noninnovators

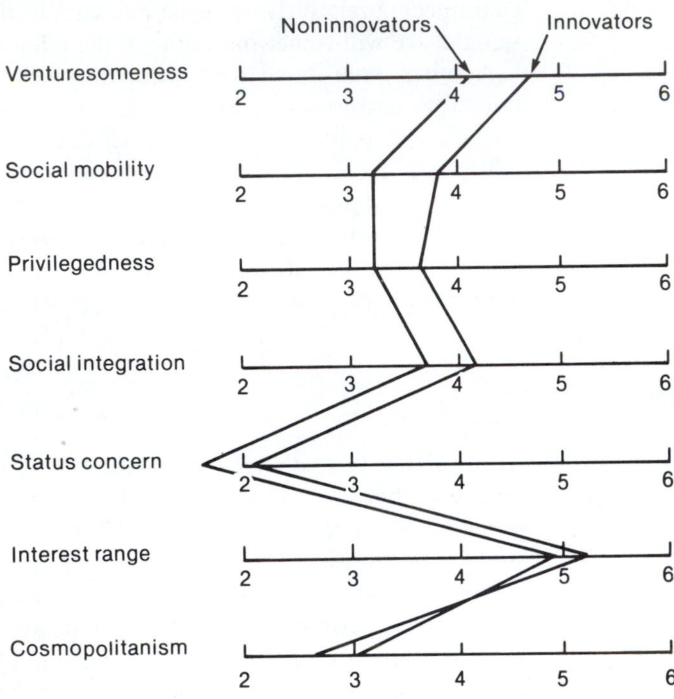

U.S. versus U.K. Purchasing Agents. This example deals with industrial purchasing agents (Lehmann and O'Shaughnessy, 1974). To compare purchasing agents in the United Kingdom with those in the United States, the importances they attributed to 17 attributes for four product types were analyzed. One part of the analysis involved discriminant analysis between U.S. and U.K. purchasing agents. Four two-group discriminant analyses were performed, one for each of the four product types. The resulting discriminant functions are shown in Table 16–3. Notice here that unstandardized discriminant coefficients are reported. Since the 17 attributes were all rated on the same scale and had approximately the same standard deviations, the standardized coefficients would be expected to be very similar to the unstandardized coefficients.

In interpreting these results, it is important to recognize that the function arbitrarily placed U.K. purchasing agents at the top of the scale. (This can be ascertained by either looking at the group means on the discriminant functions or by simply examining the group means on the separate vari-

TABLE 16–3 Discriminant Functions: U.K. versus U.S. Purchasing Agents

	Product Type			
Attribute	*I*	*II*	*III*	*IV*
Reputation	−1.10	−.16	−.95	−1.02
Financing	−.01	.50	.85	1.64
Flexibility	−.19	.53	1.07	−1.73
Past experience	−1.16	−.11	−.27	−1.05
Technical service	.19	2.38	1.57	−.96
Confidence in salespersons	.81	.42	−.55	.48
Convenience in ordering	1.13	1.11	−.01	.18
Reliability data	−.58	−.67	−.24	.44
Price	−.81	−2.10	−.21	.27
Technical specifications	1.33	−.66	−.69	−.30
Ease of use	−.09	.18	.87	−1.17
Preference of user	−.45	−2.02	−.09	.88
Training offered	.15	−2.63	−.96	−1.16
Training required	−1.55	.39	−.45	−.12
Reliability of delivery	2.41	2.60	.64	1.36
Maintenance	.87	1.04	.42	1.50
Sales service	−.39	1.03	1.30	1.96

ables and then deducing which way the function goes.) With this in mind, it is possible to interpret the results by looking for big (relatively) discriminant coefficients. In this example, any coefficient greater than 1 in absolute size was identified as "big" in interpreting the results.

U.K. purchasing agents place greater emphasis on reliability of delivery and maintenance for all four product types, on convenience in ordering for Type I and II products, and on sales service and financing for products which give rise to procedural (Type III) or political (Type IV) problems. U.S. purchasing agents, on the other hand, tend to stress reputation for Type I, III, and IV products, past experience for Type I and IV, training offered for Type II, III, and IV products, and price for Type I and II products. Hence, one might conclude that U.K. purchasing agents are relatively more service oriented and U.S. agents somewhat more experience/reputation oriented. Interestingly, these results largely reinforce the results of simple t tests for differences in mean importance on the 17 attributes.

To get a measure of how well the 17 attributes predict group membership, there are two common approaches. The first is to test whether the independent variables taken as a whole differ significantly across the groups. Most canned programs calculate an F statistic to test this significance. In the current example, the test statistic used was a Mahalanobis D^2. This formidable sounding statistic is approximately chi-square (χ^2) distributed with (Number of groups − 1)(Number of variables) degrees of freedom. Here there were (2 − 1)(17) = 17 degrees of freedom. The Mahalanobis D^2s were 41.0, 50.8, 29.2, and 45.6, respectively, for the four product types. Since at the .05 significance level the cutoff for a significant chi-square with 17 degrees of freedom is 27.6, the independent variables contribute significantly (if not spectacularly) to predicting group membership. In other words, U.S. and U.K. purchasing agents attribute significantly different importances to product attributes.

The other way to see how well the discriminant function performs is to use it to classify some observations and see how well it does in terms of correct classifications. Ideally, a fresh sample of observations should be classified. Since the purchasing agent project budget was exhausted, a fresh sample was not feasible. The next best approach is to use a holdout sample for classifications which was not used to compute the discriminant functions. Given the small sample size here (26 in one group, 19 in the other), this was not feasible. The least desirable approach is to see how well the discriminant function performs in classifying the observations used in constructing the functions. In spite of the inflated value this can give in terms of the percent correctly classified, the fact that canned programs do this automatically makes this a common way to look at the results. In this case, the percent correctly reclassified was 84.4 percent, 86.7 percent, 77.8 percent, and 84.4 percent, respectively, for the four product types. These are "pretty good" results and again support the notion that product attribute importances differ between U.S. and U.K. purchasing agents.

50 States Example. As a final example of two-group discriminant analysis, the 50 states in Table 9–1 were broken into two groups—15 in the South and the 35 others. The two groups were then compared, based on the other available variables (income, etc.). The first step in examining the results in Table 16–4 is to examine the means of the two groups. The big differences appear to be that the South is (or was in 1973) lower in income and taxes and higher in mineral production. This is confirmed by the univariate F tests, which have 1 numerator and 48 denominator degrees of freedom. College enrollment differs on average, but apparently the within group variation is so large that the difference is not statistically significant.

In examining the discriminant functions, we note that the most important discriminator is population. The reason this and not income, taxes, or mineral production is the best discriminator is multicollinearity among the variables. This emphasizes the point that the discriminant coefficients are not deducible from the means alone. It also suggests a more parsimonious model would probably predict group membership as well as this model.

Several other parts of the output are of some interest. The canonical correlation is a measure of the multiple correlation we would have obtained if we had run a regression with the dependent variable a dummy variable. Hence, $(.80)^2 = .64$ is the R^2.

TABLE 16–4 Discriminant Analysis of Southern versus non-Southern States

Variable	*Variable Means South*	*Non-South*	*One-Way F*	*Unstandardized Disc. Function*	*Standardized Disc. Function*
Average income	4.95	5.91	17.13	−0.43	−0.32
Population	4.45	4.19	0.05	0.92	4.15
Population change	1.37	1.19	0.30	−0.37	−0.39
Percent urban	57.00	58.37	0.03	0.02	0.33
Tax per capita	464.13	618.23	26.97	−0.01	−0.87
Government expenditures	286.13	281.54	0.00	0.00	0.75
College enrollment	165.20	192.45	0.14	−0.01	−2.03
Mineral production	2006.27	610.49	6.84	0.00	0.03
Forest acres	15.93	14.70	0.05	0.01	0.15
Manufacturing output	6.77	8.66	0.40	−0.27	−2.65
Farm receipts	1801.73	1943.37	0.06	−0.00	−0.40
Canonical correlation	.80				
Wilks Lambda	.37				
Chi-square	42.71				
Degrees of freedom	11				

Wilks Lambda is the ratio of within group to total variance. Therefore, it is essentially equal to $1 - R^2$, here $1 - .63 = .37$.

The chi-square value tests whether, overall, the variables help discriminate. Here the 42.71 is compared with the chi-square table and 11 (the number of independent variables) degrees of freedom. Since the .001 level is 31.3, we have very strong evidence that the variables are significantly related to whether a state is in the South or not.

The classification matrix which results is, thus, not surprisingly fairly impressive:

	Predicted Group	
Actual Group	*Non-South*	*South*
Non-South	32	3
South	1	14

Consequently, 92 percent of the observations are correctly classified—much better than random (50 percent), largest group (70 percent), or proportional chance ($(.7)^2 + (.3)^2 = 58$ percent) criteria. Obviously, this percent is somewhat overstated, since there are 11 predictor variables and only 15 southern states. A prudent researcher might, therefore, redo the analysis with fewer independent variables (e.g., population, college enrollment, and manufacturing output).

MULTIPLE GROUP DISCRIMINANT ANALYSIS

The major approach to more than two-group discriminant analysis is to first attempt to find a single function which simultaneously spreads all groups apart as far as possible. Next, a second function (independent of the first) is found which best further explains differences in group membership and so forth. For g groups, there will be $g - 1$ such functions. This can be viewed graphically as Figure 16–7. The functions are mathematically derived by canonical correlation.

FIGURE 16–7 Simultaneous Approach to More than Two-Group Discriminant Analysis

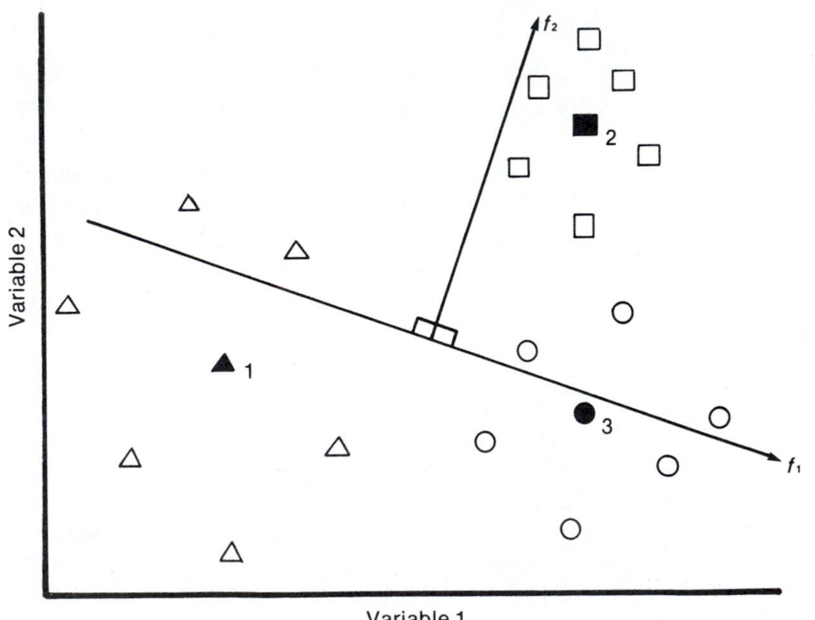

A Nutritional Example

Returning to the nutrition study, assume we are again interested in explaining weekly food consumption expenditures in terms of other characteristics. Since there were five response categories to the food expenditure question, we have five groups of respondents, ranging from those who spend less than $15 per week to those who spend over $60 per week. (These data are really at least as well suited to regression—the alert reader will notice that food expenditure was the dependent variable in the regression example in the previous chapter—since food expenditure is at least ordinally and probably intervally scaled. This example is used, therefore, mainly for pedagogical purposes.)

The SPSS input and output appear in Appendix 16–A. The 853 respondents provided complete data in terms of education of both husband and wife, age, income, family size, how often they shopped, the number of alternatives considered (section I of the questionnaire, question 6), and information receptivity (section II, question 6), as well as food expenditures. Examination of the mean values shows "reasonable numbers" and relatively equal standard deviations. The group means are shown in Table 16–5. These means indicate that larger spenders tend to be more educated, younger, have higher incomes and larger family size, and to shop more extensively.

The significance of the differences among the five groups on a variable-by-variable basis are given by the F tests, which appear next in the output. The 106.0 for family size is the largest, with the 49.1 for income next biggest, indicating that these variables are the most important in separating the five groups. Interestingly, education, age, and how often they shop are all also significantly ($F > 4$) related to food expenditures. (Alas, my favorite variables—number of brands shopped and information sought—are not significantly related to food expenditures.)

TABLE 16–5 Variable Averages for Five Food Expenditure Level Groups

	Group				
	1	*2*	*3*	*4*	*5*
	< $15	*$15–$29*	*$30–$44*	*$45–$59*	*> $60*
Education of wife	3.32	4.11	4.29	4.47	4.49
Education of husband	2.79	3.75	4.08	4.57	4.69
Age	4.09	3.46	3.06	2.50	2.72
Income	1.62	2.06	2.75	3.47	3.75
Family size	2.09	2.52	3.13	4.14	5.11
How often they shop	1.91	2.18	2.27	2.29	2.62
Number of brands shopped for	1.82	2.25	2.34	2.25	2.72
Information sought	1.91	1.91	1.81	1.84	1.87
Sample size	34	284	293	181	61

The program then (after giving some gratuitous information) proceeds to enter variables stepwise into a discriminant analysis in the following order:

1. Family size.
2. Income.
3. How often they shop.
4. Age.
5. Education of the wife.
6. Number of brands shopped for.

This order differs substantially from what the size of simple *F*s indicates due to multicollinearity.

Next, the classification function coefficients are output (Table 16–6). These functions can be used for (*a*) classification and (*b*) finding the two-group discriminant function (unstandardized) between a particular pair of groups (see Appendix 16–B). Here, for example, the function which best discriminates between groups 1 and 2 is:

−.43	Education of wife
+.20	Age
−.02	Income
−.25	Family size
−.73	How often they shop
−.17	Number of brands shopped for

while that between 2 and 3 is:

+.07	Education of wife
+.05	Age
−.39	Income
−.44	Family size
−.27	How often they shop
−.01	Number of brands shopped for

It appears that the variable which best discriminates between those who spend under \$15 and those who spend \$15–\$29 is how often they shopped, while what separates the \$15–29 from the \$30–\$44 spenders is income and family size.

The multiple discriminant functions are also output in both standardized and unstandardized forms. The first function is the most useful, the second next most useful, and so forth. The output indicated (by means of a

TABLE 16–6 Classification Functions

	Group				
	1	*2*	*3*	*4*	*5*
Education of wife	2.92	3.35	3.28	3.21	3.22
Age	3.61	3.41	3.36	3.32	3.70
Income	.42	.44	.83	1.21	1.38
Family size	3.13	3.38	3.82	4.55	5.48
How often they shop	2.83	3.56	3.83	4.00	4.69
Number of brands shopped for	1.18	1.33	1.34	1.24	1.44
Constant	−19.61	−22.89	−25.23	−28.80	−37.02

chi-square test of Wilks Lambda) that three functions are significant at the .05 (or .01, for that matter) level. The most important variables in the first function are family size, income, and how often they shop. The second function is related to age and family size. The results can be portrayed graphically as Figure 16–8. Hence, these results largely reinforce the analysis of the means and simple *F* tests as well as the ANOVA and regression results of previous chapters.

FIGURE 16–8 Group Means on First Two Discriminant Functions

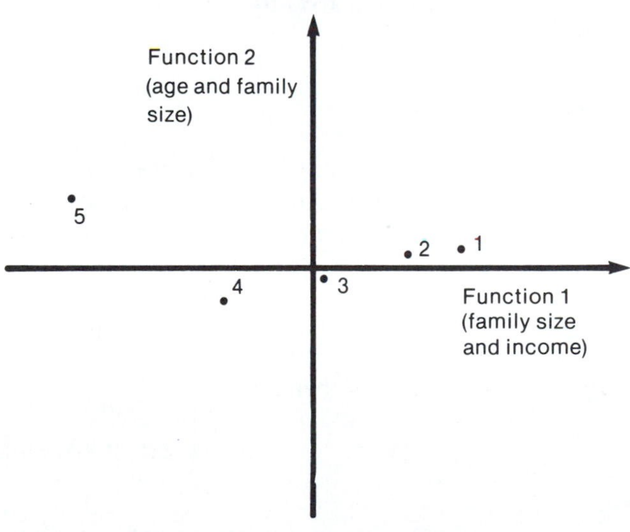

LOGIT MODELS

Logit models were developed to predict the probability that an event would occur.

Model

The general form of the logit model assumes for each response category (outcome) that the probability of the outcome is equal to:

$$P_i = \frac{\exp[BX_i]}{\sum_j \exp[BX_j]} \tag{16.4}$$

where

$$\begin{aligned} BX_i &= B_0 + B_1 X_{i1} + B_2 X_{i2} + \cdots \\ &= \text{value of } BX_i \text{ for observation } i. \end{aligned}$$

Notice that this model is "logically consistent," in that the sum of the predicted probabilities (the P_is) is equal to one. No matter how large the BX_i function gets, P_i can only approach one, and no matter how small BX_i gets, P_i will still be positive (but close to zero). In the case of choice among alternatives (e.g., brands), BX_i is often interpreted as the value or utility of alternative i (c.f., Gensch, 1985; Guadagni and Little, 1983). The use of a logit model to predict choice among alternatives is the major use of these models in marketing.

Estimation

The model predicts that the probability of a series of (independent) outcomes occurring in a set of observations is the product of the probabilities of the events:

$$\begin{aligned} &\begin{pmatrix}\text{Probability of} \\ \text{observation 1}\end{pmatrix} \cdot \begin{pmatrix}\text{Probability of} \\ \text{observation 2}\end{pmatrix} \cdots \\ &= \left(\frac{\exp BX_i}{\sum_j \exp BX_j}\right)\left(\frac{\exp BX_k}{\sum_j \exp BX_j}\right) \cdots \end{aligned} \tag{16.5}$$

where outcome i occurs in the first observation.
outcome k occurs in the second observation.
etc.

FIGURE 16–9 Binary Logit

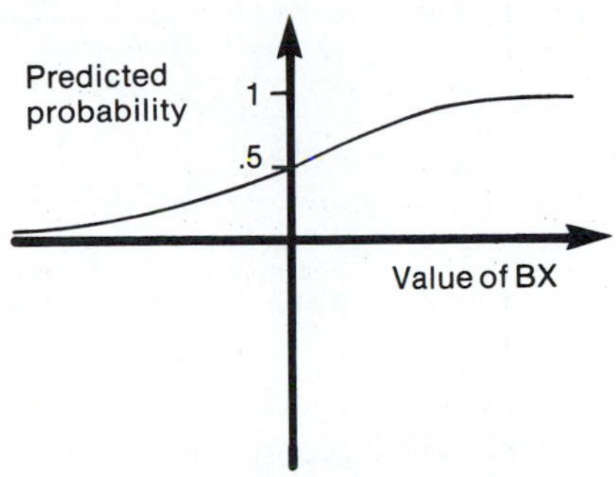

This formula is known as the *likelihood function*. To select values for the Bs, an appropriate criterion is to pick those Bs which maximize the probability of the series of events. This approach is known, not surprisingly, as *maximum likelihood estimation* (translation: find a computer program to get results).

For the special case of a binary (two-category) dependent variable, this model becomes:

$$\frac{P_1}{P_2} = \frac{\exp BX_1}{\exp BX_2}$$

or

$$\left(\frac{P_1}{1 - P_1}\right) = \exp B(X_1 - X_2)$$

Thus,

$$\ln\left(\frac{P_1}{1 - P_1}\right) = B(X_1 - X_2) = BX^* \qquad (16.6)$$

The term $\frac{P}{1 - P}$ is referred to as the *logit*. This leads to models, such as Equation 16.6, being called (binary) *logit models* and the multiple category version in 16.4 as *multinomial logit*. The binary logit model produces an s-shaped curve relating the value of BX^* to probability (Figure 16–9).

Example

When the X variables are continuous (i.e., take on numerous values), then Equation 16.5 is estimated directly. If, on the other hand, the X variables are categorical themselves (or are grouped into categories), *and* there are

TABLE 16–7 Probability of Adoption

	High School Education		*College Education*	
Income	*Nonmobile*	*Mobile*	*Nonmobile*	*Mobile*
≤ 12,500	.071	.199	.069	.214
> 12,500	.108	.254	.149	.270

Source: Paul E. Green, Frank J. Carmone, and David P. Wachspress, "On the Analysis of Qualitative Data in Marketing Research," *Journal of Marketing Research*, February 1977, p. 53.

only two categories of the dependent variable, then we can use an aggregate table which reports the probability of occurrence in each cell to estimate the Bs. Consider the data in Table 16–7, taken from Green, Carmone, and Wachspress (1977), concerning adoption of a phone service. For each of the 10,524 respondents we could create a term to represent the likelihood of adopting or not adopting. (In fact, if we used education in terms of number of years and income to the nearest dollar, we would have to.) However, since the data are categorical, we can use the logit of the probabilities in each of the eight cells as the observations and dummy variables on the levels of education, mobility, and income as the independent variables. The results (which weighted the data to get more efficient estimates using a procedure known, cleverly, as *weighted least squares*) were:

$$\ln\frac{P}{1-P} = -.903 - .164(\text{low education}) - .986(\text{low mobility}) - .438(\text{low income})$$

The results indicate, as the table suggests, mobility has the largest impact on adoption and education the smallest. (A more general procedure for dealing with cross-classified data, log-linear analysis, is briefly described in Appendix 16–G.)

SUMMARY

This chapter has discussed two other predictive procedures: discriminant analysis and logit. These procedures complement previously discussed predictive procedures: tabular analysis, ANOVA, and regression. They do not complete the list of predictive procedures. In addition to these, there are canonical correlation, multiple classification analysis (MCA), which is very much like a dummy variable regression program, and probit analysis, which treats both the dependent and the independent variables as nonintervally scaled. In fact, one could fill several volumes with such procedures. Such an all-inclusive approach is not useful for marketing research. Given time constraints and computer limitations, it is unrealistic to expect researchers to know all the possible techniques well. It is much more profitable to understand one well (I vote for regression) and to know enough about the others (especially ANOVA and discriminant analysis) to know when their special properties make their use advantageous.

Put differently, predictive procedures have severely diminishing marginal utility. Running multiple predictive procedures on the same set of data is more likely to increase the computer bill than understanding. Also, very few people really understand these procedures. To really understand them requires a start-up cost in terms of time and trial-and-error learning. Finally, don't be afraid to ask the "professional" a question; good ones can provide answers which are at least partially intelligible.

PROBLEMS

1. Assume I run a discriminant analysis on business school majors using aptitude scores as independent variables and get the following classification matrix:

	Predicted Group				
Actual Group	*International Business*	*Marketing*	*Finance*	*Production*	*Others*
International business	70	40	30	20	40
Marketing	50	90	30	10	20
Finance	20	20	80	60	20
Production	20	30	40	80	30
Others	20	20	40	20	100

   a. How well have I done (statistically)?
   b. What do the results indicate?
2. Explain the difference between discriminant analysis and classification.
3. In two-group discriminant analysis, could the *sign* of a discriminant coefficient and the *sign* of the difference between means on the variable differ? What would it mean?
4. Explain the difference between discriminant analysis and cluster analysis. Give an example of the type of marketing problems for which each is useful.
5. Your researcher wants to use a discriminant analysis to see if he or she can "predict the people who try a new brand" compared to those who do not try the new brand. You know that the market share of the new brand is only 5 percent and observe that you can predict 95 percent of the population correctly by simply assuming each person did not try the new brand. Yet you are bothered by this assumption because it

suggests that the market share of the new brand should be zero. You do not think your researcher will be able to predict 95 percent correctly with his or her discriminant analysis model, so you are reluctant to pay for such an investigation. Can anything possibly come out of the discriminant analysis research which might justify the cost of the investigation? What?

6. The following are the income (in $1,000) and age of a sample of 20 purchasers of an expensive automobile brand. A particular accessory was purchased by 12 of the sample but was not purchased by 8 of the sample. The age and income of the sample were as follows:

Twelve Purchasers		*Eight Nonpurchasers*	
Age	*Income ($000)*	*Age*	*Income ($000)*
30	20	30	50
40	50	40	30
40	60	40	40
50	40	40	40
50	70	50	20
60	30	50	30
60	40	60	20
60	40	60	50
60	50		
60	60		
60	70		
70	20		

a. Graphically determine a linear discriminant function which will well predict the purchase of the accessory.

b. Determine the values of the discriminant function which correspond to nonpurchase, and the values which correspond to purchase of the accessory.

c. How well does the function discriminate?

7. Of what use are the following outputs of a discriminant analysis?

a. Mahalanobis D^2 test statistic.

b. The discriminant function in a two-group analysis.

c. The first discriminant function in a three-group analysis.

d. The second discriminant function in a three-group analysis.

e. The hit-miss classification table for the estimation sample.

f. The hit-miss classification table for a holdout sample.

BIBLIOGRAPHY

Aldrich, John H., and Forrest D. Nelson. "Linear Probability, Logit, and Probit Models." Sage University Paper #45. Beverly Hills, Calif.: Sage Publications, 1984.

Assael, Henry. "Segmenting Markets by Group Purchasing Behavior: An Application of the AID Technique." *Journal of Marketing Research* 7 (May 1970), pp. 153–58.

Bagozzi, R. P. *Causal Models in Marketing*. New York: John Wiley & Sons, 1980.

Blattberg, Robert C., and Robert J. Dolan. "An Assessment of the Contribution of Log-Linear Models to Marketing Research." *Journal of Marketing* 45 (Spring 1981), pp. 89–97.

Cooley, William W., and Paul R. Lohnes. *Multivariate Data Analysis*. New York: John Wiley & Sons, 1971.

DeSarbo, Wayne S., and David K. Hildebrand. "A Marketer's Guide to Log-Linear Models for Qualitative Data Analysis." *Journal of Marketing* 44 (Summer 1980), pp. 40–51.

Dillon, William R. "The Performance of the Linear Discriminant Function in Nonoptimal Situations and the Estimation of Classification Error Rates: A Review of Recent Findings." *Journal of Marketing Research* 16 (August 1979), pp. 370–81.

Dillon, William R., and Stuart Westin. "Scoring Frequency Data for Discriminant Procedures Can Be Avoided." *Journal of Marketing Research* 19 (February 1982), pp. 44–56.

Flath, David, and E. W. Leonard. "A Comparison of Two Logit Models in the Analysis of Qualitative Marketing Data." *Journal of Marketing Research* 16 (November 1979), pp. 533–38.

Fornell, Claes, and Fred L. Bookstein. "Two Structural Equation Models: LISREL and PLS Applied to Consumer Exit-Voice Theory." *Journal of Marketing Research* 19 (November 1982), pp. 440–52.

Fornell, Claes, and D. F. Larcker. "Evaluating Structural Equation Models with Unobservable Variables and Measurement Error." *Journal of Marketing Research* 18 (February 1981), pp. 39–50.

Gensch, Dennis H. "Empirically Testing a Disaggregate Choice Model for Segments." *Journal of Marketing Research* 22 (November 1985), pp. 462–67.

Gensch, Dennis H., and Wilfred W. Recker. "The Multinomial, Multiattribute Logit Choice Model." *Journal of Marketing Research* 14 (February 1979), pp. 124–32.

Green, Paul E.; Frank J. Carmone; and David P. Wachspress. "On the Analysis of Qualitative Data in Marketing Research." *Journal of Marketing Research* 14 (February 1977), pp. 52–59.

Guadagni, Peter M., and John D. C. Little. "A Logit Model of Brand Choice Calibrated on Scanner Data." *Marketing Science* 2 (Summer 1983), pp. 203–38.

Holbrook, Morris B., and William L. Moore. "Using Canonical Correlation to Construct Product Spaces for Objects with Known Feature Structures." *Journal of Marketing Research* 19 (February 1982), pp. 87–98.

Hora, Stephen C., and James B. Wilcox. "Estimation of Error Rates in Several-Population Discriminant Analysis." *Journal of Marketing Research* 19 (February 1982), pp. 57–61.

Jöreskog, Karl G., and Dag Sörbom. "Recent Developments in Structural Equation Modeling." *Journal of Marketing Research* 19 (November 1982), pp. 404–16.

______. *LISREL IV: Analysis of Linear Structural Relations by the Method of Maximum Likelihood*. Chicago: National Education Resources, 1978.

Knoke, David, and Peter J. Burke. "Log-Linear Models." Sage University Paper #20. Beverly Hills, Calif.: Sage Publications, 1981.

Lehmann, Donald R., and John O'Shaughnessy. "Difference in Attribute Importance for Different Industrial Products." *Journal of Marketing* 38 (April 1974), pp. 36–42.

McFadden, Daniel. "Conditional Logit Analysis of Qualitative Choice Behavior." In *Frontiers in Economics*, ed. P. Zarenika. New York: Academic Press, 1973.

McLachlan, Douglas L., and Johny K. Johansson. "Market Segmentation with Multivariate AID." *Journal of Marketing* 45 (Winter 1981), pp. 74–84.

Morgan, J. N., and J. A. Sonquist. *The Determination of Interaction Effects*. Monograph No. 35. Ann Arbor: Survey Research Center, Institute for Social Research, University of Michigan, 1964.

Morrison, Donald F. *Multivariate Statistical Methods*. 2nd ed. New York: McGraw-Hill, 1976.

Morrison, Donald G. "On the Interpretation of Discriminant Analysis." *Journal of Marketing Research* 6 (May 1969), pp. 156–63.

Mostellar, Frederich, and Robert R. Bush. "Selective Quantitative Techniques." In *Handbook of Social Psychology*, vol. 1, ed. Gardner Lindzey. Reading, Mass.: Addison-Wesley, 1954.

Reynolds, H. T. "Analysis of Nominal Data." Sage University Paper Series on Quantitative Applications in the Social Sciences, #07-007. Beverly Hills, Calif.: Sage Publications, 1977.

Robertson, Thomas S., and James N. Kennedy. "Prediction of Consumer Innovators: Application of Multiple Discriminant Analysis." *Journal of Marketing Research* 5 (February 1968), pp. 64–69.

Ryans, Adrian B., and Charles B. Weinberg. "Territory Sales Response." *Journal of Marketing Research* 16 (November 1979), pp. 453–65.

Simon, Hermann. "Dynamics of Price Elasticity and Brand Life Cycles: An Empirical Study." *Journal of Marketing Research* 16 (November 1979), pp. 439–52.

Wold, Herman A. "Estimation and Evaluation of Models Where Theoretical Knowledge is Scarce: An Example of Partial Least Squares." In *Evaluation of Econometric Models*, ed. J. Ramsey and J. Kmenta. New York: Academic Press, 1979.

Appendix 16–A

Sample Discriminant Analysis Output

```
STATISTICAL PACKAGE FOR THE SOCIAL SCIENCES SPSSH - VERSION 6.00                    10/19/76        PAGE    1

         SPACE ALLOCATION FOR THIS RUN..

            TOTAL AMOUNT REQUESTED                                    80000 BYTES

            DEFAULT TRANSPACE ALLOCATION                              10000 BYTES

               MAX NO OF TRANSFORMATIONS PERMITTED            100
               MAX NO OF RECODE VALUES                        400
               MAX NO OF ARITHM.OR LOG.OPERATIONS             800

            RESULTING WORKSPACE ALLOCATION                            70000 BYTES

                  FILE NAME        LEHNUTRI
                  VARIABLE LIST    EDUC1,EDUC2,AGE,INCOME,FAMSIZE,HOWOFTEN,EXPENSE,
                                   BRAND,INFO
                  INPUT MEDIUM     DISK
                  N OF CASES       UNKNOWN
                  INPUT FORMAT     FIXED(56X,2F1.0,17X,3F1.0/9X,F1.0,2X,F1.0,X,2F1.0////)

                 ACCORDING TO YOUR INPUT FORMAT, VARIABLES ARE TO BE READ AS FOLLOWS

                 VARIABLE   FORMAT   RECORD     COLUMNS

                 EDUC1      F 1. 0        1     57-  57
                 EDUC2      F 1. 0        1     58-  58
                 AGE        F 1. 0        1     76-  76
                 INCOME     F 1. 0        1     77-  77
                 FAMSIZE    F 1. 0        1     78-  78
                 HOWOFTEN   F 1. 0        2     10-  10
                 EXPENSE    F 1. 0        2     13-  13
                 BRAND      F 1. 0        2     15-  15
                 INFO       F 1. 0        2     16-  16

THE INPUT FORMAT PROVIDES FOR   9 VARIABLES.    9 WILL BE READ
IT PROVIDES FOR  6 RECORDS ('CARDS') PER CASE.  A MAXIMUM OF    78 'COLUMNS' ARE USED ON A RECORD.

                 MISSING VALUES EDUC1 TO EXPENSE (C)
                 READ INPUT DATA

AFTER READING     940 CASES FROM SUBFILE LEHNUTRI,  END OF FILE WAS ENCOUNTERED ON LOGICAL UNIT # 8


STATISTICAL PACKAGE FOR THE SOCIAL SCIENCEE SPSSH - VERSION 6.00                    10/19/76        PAGE    2

                  DISCRIMINANT     GROUPS=EXPENSE(1,5)/VARIABLES=EDUC1 TO HOWOFTEN,BRAND,
                                   INFO/METHOD=WILKS/
                  OPTIONS          5,7,11,12,13,14
                  STATISTICS       ALL

FIRST ANALYSIS LIST IS MISSING. ALL VARIABLES WILL BE  USED WITH INCLUSION LEVELS OF ONE.

***** WARNING *****       OPTIONS 13 THRU 19  AND STATISTICS 7, 8  ARE NOT YET IMPLEMENTED AND WILL BE IGNORED.

 ***** THIS DISCRIMINANT ANALYSIS REQUIRES    5624 BYTES OF WORKSPACE *****
```

STATISTICAL PACKAGE FOR THE SOCIAL SCIENCES SPSSH - VERSION 6.00 10/19/76 PAGE 3

FILE LEHNUTRI (CREATION DATE = 10/19/76)

GROUP COUNTS

	GROUP 1	GROUP 2	GROUP 3	GROUP 4	GROUP 5	TOTAL
COUNT	34.0000	284.0000	293.0000	181.0000	61.0000	853.0000

MEANS

	GROUP 1	GROUP 2	GROUP 3	GROUP 4	GROUP 5	TOTAL
EDUC1	3.3235	4.1092	4.2901	4.4696	4.4918	4.2438
EDUC2	2.7941	3.7465	4.0751	4.5691	4.6885	4.0633
AGE	4.0882	3.4648	3.0648	2.4972	2.7213	3.0938
INCOME	1.6176	2.0634	2.7543	3.4696	3.7541	2.7022
FAMSIZE	2.0882	2.5211	3.1331	4.1381	5.1148	3.2427
HOWOFTEN	1.9118	2.1831	2.2730	2.2873	2.6230	2.2567
BRAND	1.8235	2.2465	2.3379	2.2541	2.7213	2.2966
INFO	1.9118	1.9120	1.8089	1.8398	1.8689	1.8581

STANDARD DEVIATIONS

	GROUP 1	GROUP 2	GROUP 3	GROUP 4	GROUP 5	TOTAL
EDUC1	1.3645	1.2854	1.1912	1.2044	1.1493	1.2500
EDUC2	1.6838	1.6769	1.5331	1.4495	1.4668	1.6202
AGE	1.5249	1.6156	1.4308	1.0986	0.8969	1.4634
INCOME	0.9539	1.3008	1.3451	1.2847	1.2471	1.4366
FAMSIZE	0.2879	0.8834	1.3083	1.2054	1.4503	1.3987
HOWOFTEN	0.6682	0.6685	0.6829	0.7034	0.7564	0.6977
BRAND	1.2666	1.3797	1.4185	1.4069	1.4734	1.4067
INFO	0.7535	0.7251	0.6807	0.6598	0.6449	0.6919

STATISTICAL PACKAGE FOR THE SOCIAL SCIENCES SPSSH - VERSION 6.00 10/19/76 PAGE 4

WILKS' LAMBDA (U-STATISTIC) AND UNIVARIATE F-RATIO WITH 4 AND 848 DEGREES OF FREEDOM

VARIABLE	WILKS' LAMBDA	F
EDUC1	0.9643	7.8525
EDUC2	0.9314	15.6173
AGE	0.9201	18.4185
INCOME	0.8119	49.1218
FAMSIZE	0.6667	106.0062
HOWOFTEN	0.9662	7.4155
BRAND	0.9880	2.5646
INFO	0.9958	0.8873

WITHIN GROUPS COVARIANCE MATRIX

	EDUC1	EDUC2	AGE	INCOME	FAMSIZE	HOWOFTEN	BRAND	INFO
EDUC1	1.5138							
EDUC2	1.1412	2.4565						
AGE	-0.4561	-0.8300	1.9795					
INCOME	0.6210	0.9189	-0.3880	1.6835				
FAMSIZE	0.0594	0.1346	-0.5932	0.1254	1.3103			
HOWOFTEN	-0.0036	-0.0498	0.2460	0.0426	-0.0979	0.4726		
BRAND	0.0959	0.2142	-0.3385	-0.0120	0.1527	-0.0106	1.9644	
INFO	-0.0890	-0.0988	0.0798	-0.0126	0.0043	0.0188	-0.1537	0.4789

WITHIN GROUPS CORRELATION MATRIX

	EDUC1	EDUC2	AGE	INCOME	FAMSIZE	HOWOFTEN	BRAND	INFO
EDUC1	1.0000							
EDUC2	0.5918	1.0000						
AGE	-0.2635	-0.3764	1.0000					
INCOME	0.3890	0.4519	-0.2125	1.0000				
FAMSIZE	0.0422	0.0750	-0.3683	0.0844	1.0000			
HOWOFTEN	-0.0042	-0.0462	0.2544	0.0478	-0.1244	1.0000		
BRAND	0.0556	0.0975	-0.1717	-0.0066	0.0952	-0.0110	1.0000	
INFO	-0.1046	-0.0910	0.0820	-0.0140	0.0055	0.0395	-0.1584	1.0000

STATISTICAL FACKACE FCF THE SOCIAL SCIENCES SPSSH - VERSION 6.00 10/19/76 PAGE 5

TOTAL COVARIANCE MATRIX

	ECUC1	ECUC2	AGE	INCCME	FAMSIZE	HOWOFTEN	BRAND	INFO
EDUC1	1.5625							
ECUC2	1.2322	2.6251						
AGF	-0.5428	-C.5966	2.1414					
INCOME	0.7429	1.1668	-0.634C	2.CE38				
FAMSIZE	C.2C64	C.4482	-0.8878	0.6134	1.9563			
HOWOFTEN	C.02C7	-C.0045	0.2C63	0.1C59	-0.0056	0.4868		
BRAND	0.1213	C.2570	-0.3662	0.C450	0.2331	0.0083	1.9788	
INFO	-0.C945	-C.1084	0.C968	-C.C294	-0.0113	0.0165	-0.1551	0.4787

STATISTICAL FACKAGE FCR THE SOCIAL SCIENCES SPSSH - VERSION 6.00 10/19/76 PAGE 7

\- -

VARIABLE ENTEREC CN STEP NUMBER 1.. FAMSIZE

				DEGREES OF FREEDOM		SIGNIFICANCE
WILKS' LAMBDA	C.66665	APPROXIMATE F	1C6.C0616	4	848.00	0.000
RAO'S V	424.C1978	CHANGE IN V	424.01978	4		0.0

F MATRIX - DECREES CF FREECCM: 1, 848

	GROUP 1	GROLP 2	GROUP 3	GROLP 4
GROUP 2	4.34259			
GROUP 3	25.38301	41.21944		
GROUP 4	91.79C56	22C.58722	86.24487	
GROUP 5	152.61307	257.78857	151.3C998	33.21054

\-------- VARIABLES IN THE ANALYSIS ---------

VARIABLE	ENTRY CRITEFION	F TO REMOVE
FAMSIZE	1C6.CC616	106.00616

\---------- VARIABLES NOT IN THE ANALYSIS -----------

VARIABLE	TOLERANCE	F TO ENTER	ENTRY CRITERION
EDUC1	0.99822	5.11005	7.85246
EDUC2	0.99437	7.94118	15.61726
AGE	0.86432	4.42566	18.41850
INCOME	0.99287	26.45332	49.12177
HOWOFTEN	0.98452	10.83165	7.41548
BRANC	0.99094	1.48431	2.56460
INFO	0.99997	0.86361	0.88735

```
STATISTICAL PACKAGE FCR THE SOCIAL SCIENCES SPSSH - VERSION 6.00                10/19/76        PAGE   12
-----------------------------------------------------------------------------------------------------------

VARIABLE ENTERED CN STEP NUMBER  6..    BRAND

                                                                DEGREES OF FREEDOM      SIGNIFICANCE
WILKS' LAMBDA          C.55C66     APPROXIMATE F     22.86526      24      2942.09           0.000
RAO'S V              658.01665     CHANGE IN V        6.45825       4                        0.167

F MATRIX - DEGREES CF FREEDCM:      6,   843

             GROUP     1   GROLP     2   GROUP      3   GROLP     4
GROUP   2      4.25634
GRCUP   3     11.24604     13.42533
GROUP   4     26.76987     55.89760     19.24010
GROUP   5     39.71443     60.87253     34.04955     10.43001

------- VARIABLES IN THE ANALYSIS ---------          ----------- VARIABLES NOT IN THE ANALYSIS ------------

VARIABLE          ENTRY            F TO              VARIABLF   TOLERANCE        F TO         ENTRY
                 CRITERION         REMOVE                                        ENTER        CRITERICN

EDUC1              2.08856          2.02444          EDUC2       0.54819         0.84227      0.89131
AGE                3.39772          2.99604          INFO        0.96163         0.84561      0.81323
INCCME            26.45332         21.00511
FAMSIZE          106.00616         71.84845
HOWOFTEN           8.69083          7.48479
BRAND              1.55753          1.55752

F LEVEL INSUFFICIENT FOR FURTHER COMPUTATICN
```

STATISTICAL PACKAGE FOR THE SOCIAL SCIENCES SPSSH - VERSION 6.00 10/19/76 PAGE 13

FILE LEHNUTRI (CREATION DATE = 10/19/76)

- D I S C R I M I N A N T A N A L Y S I S -

SUMMARY TABLE

STEP NUMBER	VARIABLE ENTERED REMOVED	F TO ENTER OR REMOVE	NUMBER INCLUDED	WILKS' LAMBDA	SIG.	RAO'S V	CHANGE IN RAO'S V	SIG. OF CHANGE
1	FAMSIZE	106.00616	1	0.66665	0.000	424.01978	424.01978	0.0
2	INCOME	26.45332	2	0.59262	0.000	577.29126	153.27148	0.0
3	HOWOFTEN	8.69083	3	0.56923	0.000	628.94336	51.65210	0.000
4	AGE	3.39772	4	0.56022	0.000	642.81152	13.86816	0.008
5	EDUC1	2.08856	5	0.55473	0.000	651.55859	8.74707	0.068
6	BRAND	1.55753	6	0.55066	0.000	658.01685	6.45825	0.167

CLASSIFICATION FUNCTION COEFFICIENTS

	GROUP 1	GROUP 2	GROUP 3	GROUP 4	GROUP 5
EDUC1	2.91970	3.35136	3.28176	3.20768	3.21836
AGE	3.60870	3.40733	3.36344	3.31698	3.69674
INCOME	0.41949	0.44196	0.82507	1.21068	1.37844
FAMSIZE	3.12835	3.38411	3.81591	4.55318	5.47836
HOWOFTEN	2.82546	3.56189	3.82936	3.99922	4.69368
BRAND	1.18224	1.32601	1.33864	1.23757	1.47313
CONSTANT	-19.61284	-22.88771	-25.23024	-28.79979	-37.01587

DISCRIMINANT FUNCTION	EIGENVALUE	RELATIVE PERCENTAGE	CANONICAL CORRELATION	:	FUNCTIONS DERIVED	WILKS' LAMBDA	CHI-SQUARE	DF	SIGNIFICANCE
				:	0	0.5507	505.055	24	0.0
1	0.72246	93.10	0.648	:	1	0.9485	44.769	15	0.000
2	0.02870	3.70	0.167	:	2	0.9757	20.820	8	0.008
3	0.02188	2.82	0.146	:	3	0.9971	2.499	3	0.475
4	0.00296	0.38	0.054	:					

REMAINING COMPUTATIONS WILL BE BASED ON 4 DISCRIMINANT FUNCTION(S)

STATISTICAL PACKAGE FOR THE SOCIAL SCIENCES SPSSH – VERSION 6.00 10/19/76 PAGE 14

STANDARDIZED DISCRIMINANT FUNCTION COEFFICIENTS

	FUNC 1	FUNC 2	FUNC 3	FUNC 4
EDUC1	0.02931	0.01147	-0.70139	0.52128
AGE	-0.01743	0.80563	0.29404	-0.20102
INCOME	-0.41692	-0.42982	0.30218	-0.89749
FAMSIZE	-0.77391	0.56026	0.29381	0.53745
HOWOFTEN	-0.20329	0.24330	-0.56126	-0.17733
BRAND	-0.01463	0.37179	-0.37260	-0.42580

UNSTANDARDIZED DISCRIMINANT FUNCTION COEFFICIENTS

	FUNC 1	FUNC 2	FUNC 3	FUNC 4
EDUC1	0.02345	0.00918	-0.56111	0.41702
AGE	-0.01191	0.55054	0.20093	-0.13737
INCOME	-0.29021	-0.29919	0.21035	-0.62473
FAMSIZE	-0.55331	0.40056	0.21006	0.38425
HOWOFTEN	-0.29136	0.34870	-0.80440	-0.25415
BRAND	-0.01040	0.26430	-0.28487	-0.30270
CONSTANT	3.19721	-3.62650	2.93368	0.36612

CENTROIDS OF GROUPS IN REDUCED SPACE

	FUNC 1	FUNC 2	FUNC 3	FUNC 4
GROUP 1	1.02553	0.15579	0.64837	-0.05555
GROUP 2	0.59904	0.06620	-0.06331	0.04861
GROUP 3	0.04177	-0.05837	-0.06789	-0.06798
GROUP 4	-0.71423	-0.19783	0.08964	0.04585
GROUP 5	-1.44158	0.47234	-0.00654	-0.00484

STATISTICAL PACKAGE FOR THE SOCIAL SCIENCES SPSSH - VERSION 6.00 10/19/76 PAGE 17

PREDICTION RESULTS -

ACTUAL GROUP	NO. OF CASES	PREDICTED GROUP MEMBERSHIP GP. 1	GP. 2	GP. 3	GP. 4	GP. 5
GROUP 1	34.	20. 58.8%	13. 38.2%	1. 2.9%	0. 0.0%	0. 0.0%
GROUP 2	284.	86. 30.3%	106. 37.3%	59. 20.8%	24. 8.5%	9. 3.2%
GROUP 3	293.	50. 17.1%	65. 22.2%	90. 30.7%	57. 19.5%	31. 10.6%
GROUP 4	181.	7. 3.9%	7. 3.9%	33. 18.2%	84. 46.4%	50. 27.6%
GROUP 5	61.	2. 3.3%	1. 1.6%	6. 9.8%	12. 19.7%	40. 65.6%

PERCENT OF "GROUPED" CASES CORRECTLY CLASSIFIED: 39.86%

Appendix 16–B

Technical Aspects of Discriminant Analysis

THE DISCRIMINANT FUNCTION

The discriminant coefficients can be expressed as a matrix product as follows:

$$d = W^{-1}(\bar{x}_1 - \bar{x}_2) \tag{16B.1}$$

where

$W =$ the pooled within group covariance matrix.

$\bar{x}_1 =$ vector of means of the first group on all k variables.

$\bar{x}_2 =$ vector of means of the second group on all k variables.

This formulation can be better understood by considering the special case where the predictor variables are perfectly independent of each other. In this case, the discriminant function becomes

$$d = \left[\frac{\bar{x}_{11} - \bar{x}_{21}}{s_1^2}\right]x_1 + \left[\frac{\bar{x}_{12} - \bar{x}_{22}}{s_2^2}\right]x_2 + \cdots + \left[\frac{\bar{x}_{1k} - \bar{x}_{2k}}{s_k^2}\right]x_k$$

Hence, the weight assigned a particular variable depends on (a) the

TABLE 16B–1 The Effect of Difference in Mean and Variance on Discriminant Coefficients

Difference in Means	*Variance*	*Discriminant Coefficient*
Small	Small	Moderate
Small	Large	Close to zero
Large	Small	Large
Large	Large	Moderate

difference in means between the two groups on that variable and (*b*) the variance of that variable. Practically, this means that variables on which the two groups differ significantly will be weighted heavily by the discriminant function. The relation between the differences in mean between groups and standard deviation on a particular variable and the discriminant coefficient is summarized in Table 16B–1.

OPTIMAL CLASSIFICATION

The basic motivation of discriminant analysis is to determine which of a set of characteristics are most important as discriminators between members of the two groups. Discriminant analysis, therefore, is not primarily addressed to the objective of classifying an individual into one of two groups based on the values the individual has on the predictor variables. The resulting discriminant function can, however, be used to optimally classify observations.

The basic approach in most classification procedures is to assign an individual to the group where the expected opportunity cost of misclassification is the smallest. This requires taking the following three pieces of information into account:

1. The cost of misclassifying a member of one group as a member of another:

$C(1|2)$ = cost of classifying a person as a member of group 1 given he or she is really a member of group 2 (e.g., classifying a customer as a noncustomer).

$C(2|1)$ = cost of classifying a person as a member of group 2 given the person is really a member of group 1.

2. The relative likelihoods that a person in the two groups would exhibit the values on the variables of the individual who is to be classified:

$L(Z|1)$ = likelihood that a person in group 1 would exhibit a set of characteristics equal to Z.

$L(Z|2)$ = likelihood that a person in group 2 would exhibit a set of characteristics equal to Z.

3. The overall (prior) probability that any individual will be a member of each of the two groups:

$P(1)$ = probability that an individual is a member of group 1.
$P(2)$ = probability that an individual is a member of group 2.

To classify a person as a member of group 1, the following inequality must hold:

$$\text{Expected cost of classifying as a 1} < \text{Expected cost of classifying as a 2} \tag{16B.2}$$

or

$$[P(1)]\,[C(2\,|\,1)]\,[L(Z|\,1)] > [P(2)]\,[C(1\,|\,2)]\,[L(Z\,|\,2)]$$

This can be rewritten as:

$$\frac{[P(2)]\,[C(1|2)]}{[P(1)]\,[C(2|1)]} < \frac{L(Z|1)}{L(Z|2)}$$

For the case with equal priors and costs of misclassification, the formula reduces to classify an observation as a member of group 1 if $L(Z|1) > L(Z|2)$.

To this point nothing has depended on performing discriminant analysis. The likelihoods can be evaluated directly. Direct evaluation, however, is not very easy without a computer, given the messy formulas involved. Fortunately, the discriminant function can be used to get optimal classification if the following two assumptions are met:

1. The predictor variables are normally distributed.
2. The variances are equal in the two groups.

In this case, the linear discriminant function will provide optimal classification if the following rule is followed:

Let

$$K = \frac{[P(2)]\,[C(1|2)]}{[P(1)]\,[C(2|1)]}. \tag{16B.3}$$

$\bar{f}_1, \bar{f}_2$ = mean value of the groups on the discriminant function which are calculated by multiplying the discriminant weights (w_is) times the means of the variables for each group.

$$\bar{f}_1 = w_1\bar{x}_{11} + w_2\bar{x}_{12} + \cdots + w_k\bar{x}_{1k}. \tag{16B.4}$$

$$\bar{f}_2 = w_1\bar{x}_{21} + w_2\bar{x}_{22} + \cdots + w_k\bar{x}_{2k}.$$

n = total number of observations ($n_1 + n_2$).

$$f = w_1Z_1 + w_2Z_2 + \cdots + w_kZ_k \tag{16B.5}$$

= value of the person to be classified on the discriminant function.

Then (assuming $\bar{f}_1 < \bar{f}_2$) we would classify an observation as a member of group 1 if:

$$f < \frac{\bar{f}_1 + \bar{f}_2}{2} - \log_e k \tag{16B.6}$$

For equal priors and costs of misclassifying, this reduces to:

$$f < \frac{\bar{f}_1 + \bar{f}_2}{2} \tag{16B.7}$$

USING THE DISCRIMINANT FUNCTION FOR CLASSIFICATION

Recalling the earlier example involving nonpurchasers and purchasers measured in terms of age and income, we had:

$$f = 3(\text{income}) - 2(\text{age})$$

If the group means on income and age were 2.5 and 2, respectively, for nonpurchasers, and the group means for purchasers were 4.5 and 1.5, the mean values for the two groups on the discriminant function are as follows:

$$\bar{f}_1 = 3(2.5) - 2(2) = 3.5$$

and

$$\bar{f}_2 = 3(4.5) - 2(1.5) = 10.5$$

Thus, the "cutoff" can be derived from Formula 16B.7 as:

$$\frac{\bar{f}_1 + \bar{f}_2}{2} = \frac{3.5 + 10.5}{2} = 7$$

Now assume we wished to classify a person as a member of group one or two based on the person's income of 3 and age of 2. In this case, $f = 3(3) - 2(2) = 5$. Since $5 < 7$, we would classify this person as a nonpurchaser.

Appendix 16–C

Classification Functions and Discriminant Analysis

Discriminant analysis is closely related to classification. Optimal classification can be performed (assuming the variables are normally distributed) by computing the value of a classification function for each group. The bigger the value of a particular classification function, the more likely a person is a member of the group.

Assume for a moment I had three groups with the following classification functions:

Variable	CF_1	CF_2	CF_3
1	7	5	4
2	5	3	1
Constant	2	5	9

If I were to try and classify an observation with values 2 and 3 on the two variables into one of the three groups, I could directly use the multivariate normal distribution and a computer algorithm to find the likelihood that an observation with values 2 and 3 came from each of the three groups. A shortcut is available, however, by using the three classification functions:

$$\text{Value of } CF_1 = 7(2) + 5(3) + 2 = 31$$

$$\text{Value of } CF_2 = 5(2) + 3(3) + 5 = 24$$

$$\text{Value of } CF_3 = 4(2) + 1(3) + 9 + 20$$

Since the value of CF_1 is largest, it turns out that this particular observation is most likely to belong to the first group.

Classification functions are occasionally interpreted directly, with a big value attributed to a variable which is a major contributor to group membership. The classification functions can also be used to derive the two-group discriminant functions between pairs of groups. For g groups, there are $\binom{g}{2} = g(g-1)/2$ two-group discriminant functions, one for each pair of groups. Mathematically, the discriminant functions turn out to be the differences between pairs of classification functions (e.g., $f_{12} = CF_1 - CF_2$).

Returning to our previous example we would derive the two-group discriminant function between groups 1 and 3 (f_{13}) as follows:

$$f_{13} = (7 - 4)X_1 + (5 - 1)X_2 = 3X_1 + 4X_2$$

The constant is usually ignored. (It turns out, however, that the difference in the constant term produces the cutoff point for maximum likelihood classification. Hence, in this case, the cutoff point would be $2 - 9 = -7$. Alternatively, retaining the constant term makes the cutoff point equal to zero.)

Appendix 16–D

Automatic Interaction Detector (AID)

Another predictive technique which enjoyed a brief period of popularity in marketing is AID. This technique assumes that the dependent variables are intervally scaled but that all the independent variables are only nominally scaled (as opposed to regression, which assumes they are intervally scaled). The technique proceeds by a stepwise procedure to "explain" the dependent variable.

METHOD

A hypothetical example is the best way to explain AID. Assume I were interested in explaining beer consumption among business school professors in terms of their weight, age, number of articles published, outside income, and degree of sports-mindedness. If I collected data on these variables and consumption from 439 professors, AID would proceed as follows:

1. It computes average beer consumption (assume here it is 3.4 liters/class).

2. It looks at each variable separately to see which "best" explains beer consumption, by using each possible combination of categories to break the total sample into two groups. For example, if age is distributed:

$$1 = \text{under } 30 \quad (n = 112)$$
$$2 = 30 - 45 \quad (n = 201)$$
$$3 = \text{over } 45 \quad (n = 126)$$

we can compare average beer consumption of those under 30 (1s) with those over 30 (2s and 3s):

Under 30	*Over 30*
4.0	3.2

Alternatively, we could compare those under 45 (1s and 2s) with those over 45 (3s). These are the only two possible monotonic (ordered) splits. If we are willing to accept any combination (such as 1s and 3s—under 30 and over 45s versus 2s), more splits are possible. The program computes the amount explained by each possible age split based on a between sum of squares calculation:

$$\text{BSS} = n_1\overline{Y}_1^2 + n_2\overline{Y}_2^2 - (n_1 + n_2)\overline{\overline{Y}}^2$$

FIGURE 16D–1 Hypothetical AID Analysis of Professors' Beer Consumption

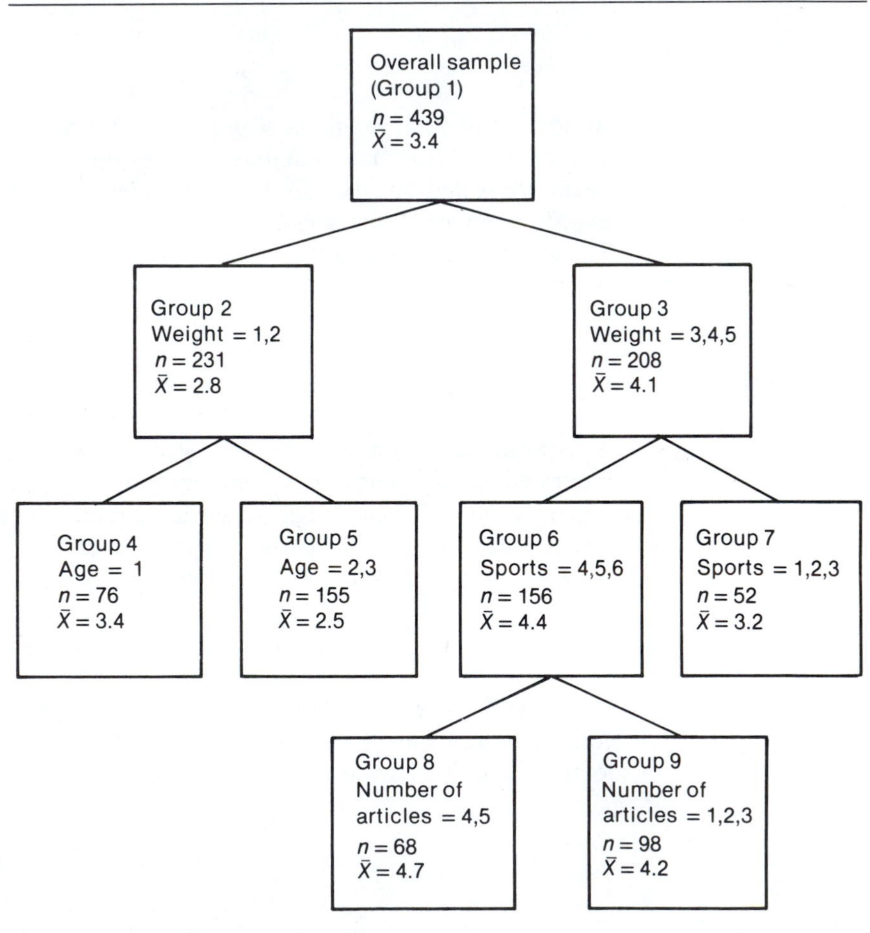

where

$\overline{\overline{Y}}$ = mean beer consumption of the overall groups.

$\overline{Y}_1$ and $\overline{Y}_2$ = means of the two groups.

n_1 and n_2 =sizes of the two groups.

(In essence, AID performs ANOVA on each possible way to split the sample.) The "best" split is then retained for this variable.

3. The program proceeds to get the best split for each independent variable separately. Next, it selects that variable which best spreads out beer consumption and splits the sample accordingly. For example, we might split on weight as follows:

Group 2: (weight = 1, 2) n = 231

Average consumption = 2.3

Group 3: (weight = 3, 4, 5) n = 208

Average consumption = 4.1

4. The program takes each resulting group (here groups 2 and 3) and goes back to step 2 to see if each group can be further subdivided and still

FIGURE 16D–2 AID Analysis of Monthly Phone Bills

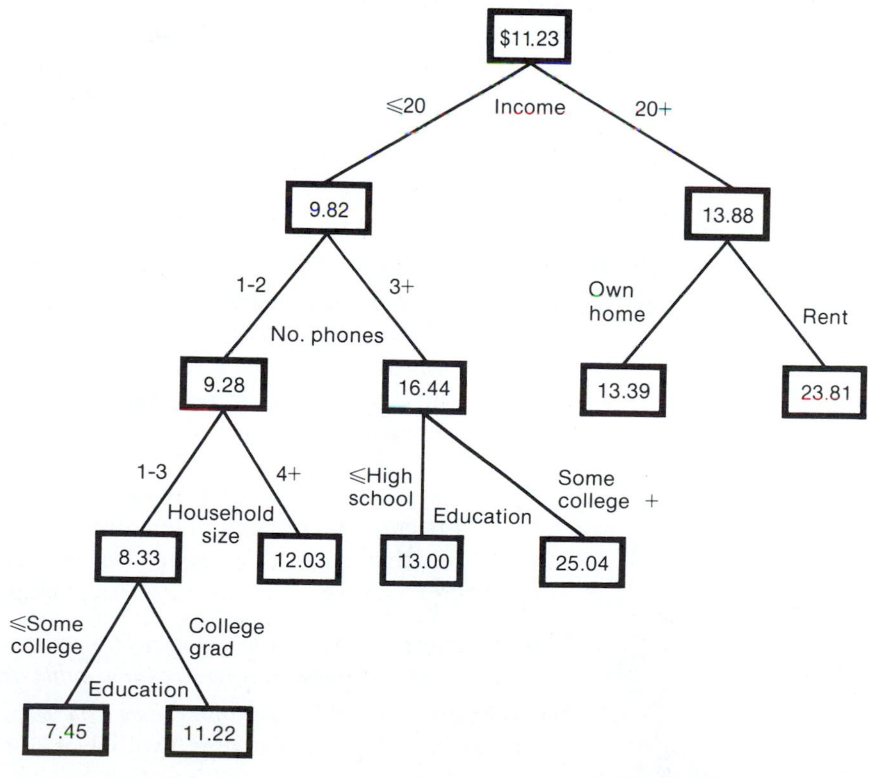

explain a minimum amount of the variance and/or retain a minimum group size. Every time a subsample is formed, an attempt is made to see if the group can be further separated.

5. The results are output. Typically, they are summarized in a chart, such as Figure 16D–1. Here, the heaviest consumers of beer (4.7 liters/class) are heavy, sports-minded, and publish a lot (possibly under the influence of their consumption).

A "real" example of AID is based on a sample of 862 families. MacLachlan and Johansson (1981) segmented families based on total phone bills. The results appear as Figure 16D–2.

SUMMARY OF AID

The AID procedure has several properties:

It is a segmenting process which begins with the entire sample and then subdivides it into segments which differ in terms of the dependent variable.

The splitting process is binary. Each group is split into exactly two subgroups.

After the first split, variables may enter in different orders down the various branches of the "tree." In this example, the lightweights (group 2) split on age, while the heavier professors were split on the basis of sports-mindedness. This feature is where the *interaction* in AID comes from: A variable may be important only in conjunction with another, something a standard stepwise regression program would not uncover.

The process may split on the same variable more than once. For example, the procedure might next split group 7 on the basis of weight into weight category 3 versus weight categories 4 and 5.

At some point, the program stops splitting. There are two basic stopping rules:

1. The sample size in a cell (either the original or one of the resulting segments) is too small to be split.
2. Not enough variance is accounted for by the split.

AID is really an elaborate tabular approach. It is used mainly to search for identifiable segments who respond differently with respect to some criterion (dependent) variable, such as consumption, attitude, and so forth. Like most procedures, however, it has some shortcomings:

Because it requires "physically" splitting the sample, the procedure needs a massive sample if more than two or three splits are sought.

The technique, like all stepwise procedures, is very sensitive to collinearity and, hence, is unstable. Running two halves of a sample through AID programs separately often creates quite different looking results and consequently different interpretations.

The computer program itself tends to be among the most difficult to decipher.

Unless discipline is exercised, it is possible to allow the program to continue to split into groups of size 2 or 3, which are more likely to be misleading than informative.

In short, then, AID is a tool for generating hypotheses about segments and is very useful in exploratory studies. To use it for other purposes, however, is to invite trouble.

Appendix 16–E

Canonical Correlation

Canonical correlation is the extension of regression to the case of multiple dependent variables. It produces sets of weights (regression coefficients) such that an index of the independent variables is "maximally correlated" with an index of the dependent variables:

$$a_1Z_1 + \cdots + a_kZ_k = b_1X_1 + \cdots + b_gX_g$$

Assuming the sets of variables are not perfectly redundant (collinear), the procedure will produce the minimum of k and g canonical sets of weights.

Canonical correlation has been mainly used as a means of performing multiple group discriminant analysis, although it has been used to generate perceptual maps by using dummy variable coding for group membership as the dependent variables (Holbrook and Moore, 1982). It also can be viewed as the special case of so-called structural equation or causal modeling where there are two constructs, as shown below.

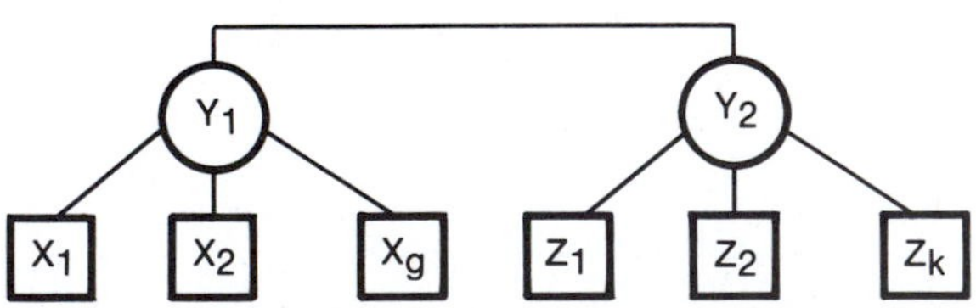

Appendix 16–F

Structural Equation Modeling

A number of researchers have become interested in so-called structural equation modeling (i.e., the entire November 1982 issue of the *Journal of Marketing Research* was devoted to this topic). These approaches essentially blend two basic procedures:

1. Simultaneous equation regression.
2. Factor analysis.

Essentially, they use both multiple measures to improve reliability and simultaneous equation models to estimate "causal" impact. Consider the following simple example:

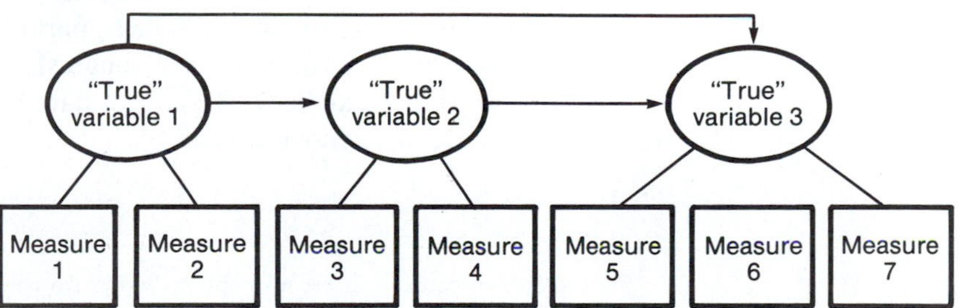

A simple approach to this situation is to first form indexes of the variables based on the measures and then run regressions on the indexes. The index formation can be done via factor analysis or simply averaging the measures (assuming their scales are comparable):

$$\text{Index 1} = \frac{\text{Measure 1} + \text{Measure 2}}{2}$$

$$\text{Index 2} = \frac{\text{Measure 3} + \text{Measure 4}}{2}$$

$$\text{Index 3} = \frac{\text{Measure 5} + \text{Measure 6} + \text{Measure 7}}{3}$$

Then regressions are run:

$$\text{Index 2} = B_{02} + B_{12}\ (\text{Index 1})$$

$$\text{Index 3} = B_{03} + B_{13}\ (\text{Index 1}) + B_{23}\ (\text{Index 2})$$

Since the indexes are based on multiple measures, they are generally more reliable than a single measure.

In many situations, however, the measures themselves may be correlated. For example, if measures 2 and 5 are both measured on six-point scales, response style would tend to increase the correlation between the variables. To take into account such relations, as well as to more efficiently (in a statistical sense) estimate the parameters, some relatively elaborate procedures have been developed.

The essence of these procedures is that the true variables (constructs) are unobserved. Therefore, the "game" is to estimate both the relations of the measures to the constructs and the causal relations among the constructs simultaneously.

Two different approaches to estimating the parameters of these models exist.[2] The first is that of Jöreskog and Sörbom (1982) and Bagozzi (1980), known as LISREL, which is now available as part of the SPSS package. The second is known as PLS (partial least squares), and derives from Wold (1979) and Fornell and Larcker (1981). Both have considerable promise but are not recommended for novice users.

---

[2] They differ conceptually in the assumption they make about whether the measures are *caused* by the true variables or combine to form them. LISREL relies on a maximum likelihood estimation procedure, whereas PLS does least squares estimation. The major advantage of these procedures is that they focus attention on both measurement issues and the structural/causal relations. At present, their use is largely restricted to academics.

Appendix 16–G

Log-Linear Models

Log-linear models are an alternative to traditional cross-tabulations and chi-square analysis of tabular data (i.e., the observed frequencies of various combinations of two or more categorical variables). Recalling the material in Chapter 11 (or turning back there, as most of us do), we compute the probability of being in a cell in a two-dimensional table as the product of the probability of being in the row by the probability of being in the column. The log-linear approach decomposes the frequency in each cell into simple (row and column) effects plus an interaction effect, using a regression (ANOVA) model. For a three-way table (reported frequencies on the various combinations of three categorical variables), the log-linear model is:

$$\log\begin{pmatrix}\text{observed}\\ \text{frequency}\\ \text{in each}\\ \text{cell}\end{pmatrix} = \text{Constant} + \text{Simple effects} + \text{2-way interactions} + \text{3-way interactions}$$

or

$$\log(F_{ijk}) = \mu + \mu_i^X + \mu_j^Y + \mu_k^Z + \mu_{ij}^{XY} + \mu_{ik}^{XZ} + \mu_{jk}^{YZ} + \mu_{ijk}^{XYZ}$$

where

$$\sum_i \mu_i^X = \sum_j \mu_j^Y = \sum_k \mu_k^Z = \sum_i \sum_j \mu_{ij}^{XY} = \sum_i \sum_k \mu_{ik}^{XZ} = \sum_j \sum_k \mu_{jk}^{YZ}$$

$$= \sum_i \sum_j \sum_k \mu_{ijk}^{XYZ} = 0$$

The value of this model is that the simple main effects model ($\log F_{ijk} = \mu + \mu_i^X + \mu_j^Y + \mu_k^Z$) is based on the assumption of independence. Hence, if there is an association among variables, some of the interaction terms must be significant. Thus, testing for association requires showing that the more complete model is superior predictively to the simple main effects model. Moreover, by examining which interaction terms are significant, one can determine the source of the association—something that a standard chi-square analysis does not provide. Anyone interested in pursuing this procedure should consult additional sources, such as DeSarbo and Hildebrand (1980), Dillon (1979), Reynolds (1977), Blattberg and Dolan (1981), and Knoke and Burke (1981).

Part 4

Applications

This section provides some brief discussion of how the methods of the previous chapters can be applied to particular problems, such as forecasting and segmentation. This is by no means intended to be complete but, rather, to demonstrate the applicability of research beyond a research course.

Chapter 17

Market Potentials and Sales Forecasting

Mention of the term *forecasting* brings forth a myriad of images, including complex computerized models, planning, and bad guesses. To some people, forecasting and marketing research are nearly synonymous. The diversity of associations that the term forecasting brings forth immediately suggests that forecasting encompasses many different problems and approaches. The purpose of this chapter is to briefly suggest what marketing forecasting is and how one might go about producing forecasts.

One general point about forecasting is very important. When asking for a forecast, most people want a single number. Providing a best-guess number is important. However, it is also important to provide a range of likely outcomes. In many cases, the range may be at least as important as the best guess. The range gives the user of the forecast a notion of how tightly he or she can plan. For example, if a sales forecast range is provided, the user can count on needing production capacity for meeting the low end of the range and can develop contingency plans for meeting demand up to the higher end of the range. Hence, artificially tightening the range of a forecast may increase its credibility but damages its usefulness. One final point is worth making: Avoid silly precision in the forecasts. A result of 11,172.13 cases may sound better than 11,000 but is usually misleadingly precise. In short, there may be more initial selling required to gain acceptance for a forecast with a range (e.g., 11,000 ± 3,000 cases) but in the long run such forecasts are usually better.

PURPOSES

Probably the best place to begin a discussion of forecasting is by considering the various purposes of forecasting. Four of the most salient are evaluation of a market (market potential estimation), planning and budgeting, developing standards for evaluating performance, and answering "what if" questions.

Evaluation of a Market (Market Potential Estimation)

One of the most common forecasting problems involves assessing the potential sales of a product or service in a particular market. The market in question may be defined in terms of a set of competing products or a geographical area. The purposes of such estimates are usually (*a*) to determine whether a product or service has sufficient promise to warrant further effort or (*b*) to decide which region is more attractive and should receive more attention.

Planning and Budgeting

In conjunction with a company's planning cycle, key inputs into the plan are forecasts of sales broken by product type, region, time period, and so forth. These forecasts are needed to schedule production, purchasing, and financial arrangements as well as to aid in allocating marketing effort. Note that it is important to separate dollar sales, unit sales, and market share since an increase in dollar sales may mask a decline in unit sales or market share.

Developing Standards for Evaluating Performance

Given the popularity of bonus/incentive compensation systems, an obvious question which arises is what performance level serves as a base figure. Forecasts of the likely results under typical conditions provide a bench mark against which actual results can be compared.

Answering "What If" Questions

Many times a forecast is requested to estimate the effect of various marketing policies (i.e., if advertising is cut 30 percent, what will happen to sales?). Such forecasts are especially prevalent in the areas of pricing policy and advertising/promotional strategy. This type of forecasting requires a model in which the independent/predictor variables are under the control of management. As such, it is qualitatively different from most forecasting, which tends to be concerned with extrapolating past trends.

QUALITY/ACCURACY NEEDED IN THE FORECAST

The effort needed to generate a forecast depends on the benefits and costs of a good or bad forecast. The following are some of the major determinants of that value.

Magnitude of the Item Forecast. If the item is large either in absolute terms or relative to the size of the business ($10,000 may not be much to General Foods, but it surely is to a corner grocery store), a good forecast becomes more important.

Variability/Uncertainty in the Item. For forecasting effort to pay off, there must be variability in the item's value.

Cost of an Error. The greater the opportunity cost of a bad forecast, the greater the need for a good forecast. Reorder cost and time, cost of out-of-stock (which may simply delay the sale, create a lost sale, or even lead to a permanently lost customer), and inventory carrying costs all influence the cost of an error in forecasting.

Number of Items Forecast. A model/method which is practical for a major product may be economically unfeasible to apply to 20,000 or more individual items.

Cost of Forecast. Both the time and the monetary costs of a forecast must be considered.

Ease of Communication and Use. Forecasts which are hard to interpret or communicate have an important hidden cost associated with them.

MARKET POTENTIALS

Market potentials play a major role in deciding how much effort to allocate to a product or region. Potential can be defined in terms of the most optimistic notion (maximum potential), some reasonable potential estimate (a best-guess potential), or the minimum potential ("guaranteed" potential).

Moreover, potential depends on the state of the economy and marketing mix decisions (e.g., price). Thus, before undertaking any potential study, it is important to first decide which kind of potential measure is needed.

Simple Methods

Obtaining a good market potential estimate may require some fairly sophisticated analysis. Given the time and budget pressures under which many decisions are made, however, most complicated methods are not used. This section outlines three approaches which can be used for getting an answer relatively quickly.

Successive Ratio. The successive ratio method consists of beginning with the universe as all potential customers and then reducing this by conditional probabilities to get an estimate of "real" potential customers. The process works equally well for consumer or industrial goods. For the sake of illustration, the potential for a consumer good—diet scotch (if light beer, why not light scotch?)—and an industrial good—a new copying system—might be estimated as follows:

Diet scotch potential = (population)(percent diet conscious)(percent scotch drinkers)(per capita consumption of liquor)(expected share of diet scotch)

New copying system potential = (number of businesses)(percent have copiers)(percent "need" fancy features)(share attainable)

Notice that this approach depends on the accuracy of the ratios (e.g., percent diet conscious) used. These ratios can be derived from survey results (e.g., agree-disagree with "I am very concerned about my weight"), past experience (e.g., the percent share obtained by light beer), or executive judgment. Given the limited accuracy of all these approaches, sensitivity analysis in which the ratios are varied is usually desirable.

Segment Buildup. A second procedure for estimating market potential is the so-called segment buildup approach. Using this approach requires that the market be split into segments which are readily identifiable. Sales to each segment are estimated separately and then totaled to get overall sales. This method is often used in industrial marketing, with SIC codes as the basis for segments. Examples of this approach are shown in Table 17–1. Notice that, in estimating sales in each segment, a successive ratio type approach was used. This brings up the important point: that these methods may be used as complements as well as substitutes for each other.

TABLE 17–1 Segment Buildup Approach to Market Potential Estimation

Segment	*(A)* *Size*	*(B)* *Amount Consumed per Capita*	*(C)* *Share Attainable*	*(A × B × C)* *Segment Potential*
Diet scotch:				
Single males < 30				
Single females < 30				
Married males < 30				
Married females < 30				
Single males ≥ 30				
Single females ≥ 30				
Married males ≥ 30				
Married females ≥ 30				
	(A) *Number*	*(B)* *Percent Need This Type*	*(C)* *Share Attainable*	*(A × B × C)* *Segment Potential*
New copying system:				
Schools				
Retail businesses				
Banks				
Offices				
Warehouses				
Manufacturing facilities				
Other businesses				

Potential by Area. The third approach is quite different from the other two. First, it is designed to measure relative, rather than absolute, potential. Second, it assumes that several factors contribute to potential. It derives an index, which is a weighted combination of the factors that are thought to contribute to potential. The weights may be derived subjectively or by formal analysis of past data, such as regression analysis, with sales as the dependent variable and factors such as population and income as independent variables. Typically, the weights are chosen so they sum to one. For example, the relative potential for a region could be estimated as:

Diet scotch: Percent total population in region (P).
Percent retail sales in region (R).
Percent disposable income in region (DI).

$$\text{Index} = W_1P + W_2R + W_3DI$$

New copying system: Percent population in region (P).
Percent schools in region (S).
Percent retail businesses in region (RB).
Percent banks in region (B).
Percent offices in region (O).
Percent warehouses in region (WH).
Percent manufacturing facilities in region (MF).
Percent other businesses in region (OB).
Percent Xerox sales in region (XS).
Percent other copier sales in region (CS).

$$\text{Index} = W_1P + W_2S + W_3RB + W_4B + W_5O + W_5WH + W_7MF + W_8OB + W_9XS + W_{10}CS$$

The diet scotch index is a general one which could be applied to a variety of products. In fact, if the weights are .2 for population, .3 for retail sales, and .5 for disposable income, this becomes the *Sales and Marketing Management* buying power index. By contrast, the index for the new copying system has many more factors included. This is done to allow the main target of the product (e.g., offices) to be given a major weight and other secondary targets (e.g., schools) to be included but at a lower weight. Also, this index attempts to include sales of analogous products, in this case Xerox and other copier sales. Sales of analogous products often give the best indication of market potential.

Uses

The most common use of market potential estimates is for evaluating product potential. Put differently, having adequate market potential is a requirement before proceeding with new product development or testing.

Market potential can also be used as a control device for evaluating performance. For example, assume I had market potential estimates and sales data for several regions (Figure 17–1). In this case, the relation between potential and actual sales is quite close. Hence, I could use the sales versus potential curve for evaluating performance. Those regions whose sales fall above the upper control limit would be classified as "good," while those whose sales fall below the lower control limit would be "bad." While these results could then be tied directly to compensation for regional managers, this might not be appropriate. For example, a region which did very well could have done so because an important competitor folded or a major promotion was staged. Similarly, a region which did badly could have done so because of increased competitive pressure. Therefore, the best use of market potential estimates for control is as a warning device to indicate

FIGURE 17–1 Hypothetical Sales versus Market Potential Data

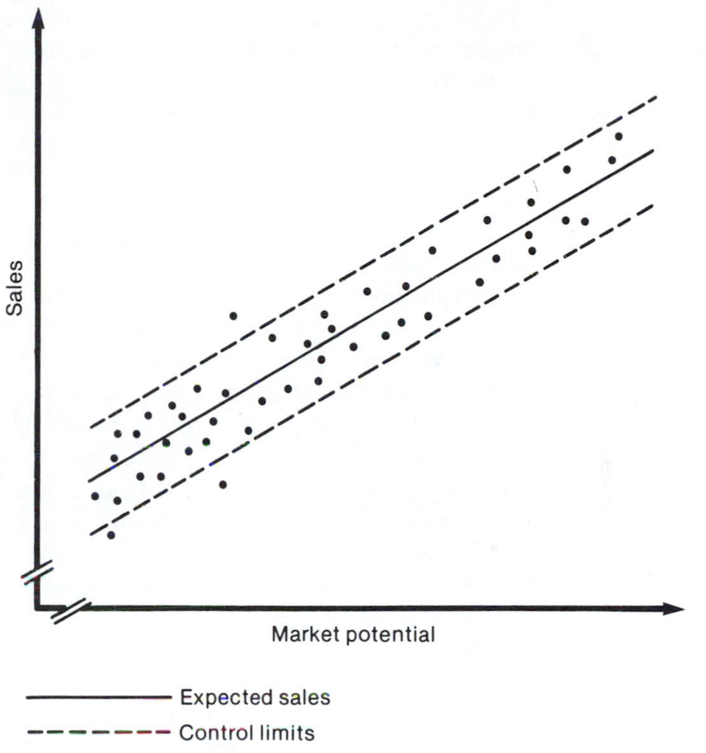

when a region is doing especially well or poorly. One should then attempt to determine why (good management, competition, luck, etc.) the region had an exceptional performance and learn something from it.

One final word of caution is in order regarding using market potential estimates. For relatively un-new new products (e.g., an unsweetened cereal or a new tractor) the measures of market potential just described will do fairly well. For genuinely new products (sometimes called *discontinuous innovations*), however, it is possible for market potential forecasts, especially those based on sales of other products, to be grossly in error. Some classic cases of underestimation of potential have occurred, notably in the case of IBM computers (would you believe a worldwide potential of 20 to 30 machines was forecast in the early 1950s?) and Xerox copiers. The point, therefore, is that while market potential estimates based on these approaches are likely to outperform blue-sky guessing, they are hardly foolproof.

FORECASTING METHODS

There are three basic types of forecasting: qualitative, extrapolative, and model based. This section will outline some of the major alternatives of these three types.

Qualitative

Judgment. The least complicated forecasting method is the use of expert judgment (guessing might be a more appropriate description). Here, we simply ask someone what the future will be and record the answer. If the expert chosen happens to know the Delphic Oracle or be a mystic, the forecast may be excellent. Unfortunately, it is hard to know whether someone can predict the future a priori. The key to the value of expert judgment is the ability of the expert to recall from memory relevant data and assimilate the data in making a guess. While judgment is often unsystematic, it can be a very useful tool and can overcome some of the limitations of quantitative techniques. Probably the best use of judgment, however, is to adjust the results of quantitative procedures, rather than as the sole forecasting tool.

Much has been written concerning the limitations of intuitive judgments as predictors (e.g., Einhorn and Hogarth, 1978). Still, many people are convinced that judgment-based models (often called *decision calculus models*) are useful predictors of market behavior (e.g., Little and Lodish, 1981). Also, in many situations, judgments have proven to be as accurate predictors as more complicated procedures (e.g., Armstrong, 1978). A number of procedures have been developed for removing the bias from executive judgment (Cox and Summers, 1987; Moriarty, 1985).

Polling of Experts. The polling of experts method is really an extension of expert judgment under a safety-in-numbers assumption. Rather than trust a single expert, this approach collects forecasts from a number of experts. This is often done by conducting surveys of managers, sales forces, and customer expectations. The forecasts are then combined in some manner, such as a simple or weighted average (since some experts are presumably more expert than others, their forecasts are weighted more heavily). This method thus produces a forecast which is "neutral" and will (like most methods) avoid the unusual/radically different result. In fact, the most useful information from polling experts may be the range of the forecasts and the reasons given to support the forecasts, rather than their average. Companies in Canada were found to rely most heavily on executive opinion juries and sales force composite estimates (Small, 1980) in their forecasts.

Panel Consensus. The panel consensus method of forecasting consists of putting a group of experts in a room and waiting for them to agree on a forecast. Aside from problems with dominant group members, this method will generally produce (assuming the panel members eventually agree) the conventional wisdom. Since experts have a nasty habit of being wrong (e.g., remember the new math, stock market forecasts, and the impossibility of an international oil cartel?), the experts' opinions can be deceptively impressive.

Extrapolation: Qualitative

As a starting point for or an alternative to expert judgment, a variety of extrapolation procedures exist. Two of these are essentially qualitative/judgmental in nature—last period + *X* percent and graphical eyeball.

Last Period + *X* Percent. One of the most common approaches to forecasting is to estimate the percent change expected in the variable to be forecast. This is especially common in deriving annual sales forecasts for major product breakdowns. For example, we may forecast dishwasher sales in dollars as last year's plus 6 percent.

Graphical Eyeball. Similar to the last period + *X* percent method, the graphical eyeball approach requires that past data be plotted. Then the next value is "eyeballed" to match the past pattern (Figure 17–2). As should be obvious, this method does by graph what many quantitative techniques do by number crunching.

FIGURE 17–2 Graphical Eyeball Forecasting

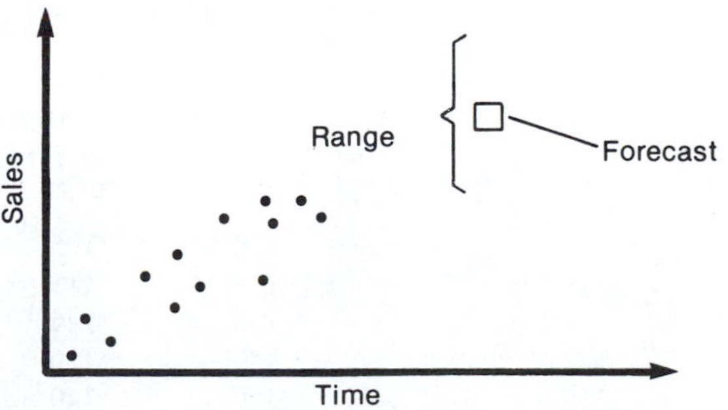

Extrapolation: Quantitative

A variety of quantitative extrapolation procedures are also available. Some of the most commonly used are discussed here.

Moving Average. Moving averages, an old forecasting standby, are widely used as a means of reducing the noise in data to uncover the underlying pattern. In doing so, it is important to recognize that past data have at least four major components:

1. Base value.
2. Trend.
3. Cycles (seasonality).
4. Random.

What moving averages essentially do is to smooth out random variation to make the patterns (trends and cycles) more obvious.

Complex moving-average models are available for estimating trends and cycles. For purposes of introduction, however, we will consider only the simple moving-average approach. A three-period moving average of sales at time t is given by:

$$\hat{S}_t = \frac{S_{t-1} + S_t + S_{t+1}}{3} \tag{17.1}$$

Note this implies that (a) each data point used is weighted equally and (b) no trend or cycle is accounted for. To see how this method works, consider the three-month moving average for the eight periods of data in Table 17–2. As can be seen readily, the fluctuation in values is much less in the moving averages than in the raw data, and a consistent trend of increase of about 10 units per period becomes quite apparent. Forecasts would now be based on the pattern of the moving averages, rather than the raw data.

Moving-average methods can be extended to track trends and seasonal patterns as well. As we can see in Table 17–2, a three-period average of the

TABLE 17–2 Hypothetical Data

Period	*Sales*	*Three-Month Moving Average*	*Trend*	*Three-Period Average Trend*
1	100			
2	110	105	+10	
3	105	115	−5	+10
4	130	125	+25	+10
5	140	130	+10	+5
6	120	140	−20	+10
7	160	152	+40	+11.67
8	175		+15	

trend indicates approximately a 10-unit increase per period. Recently, regression analysis (to be discussed later) has begun to replace moving averages as a forecasting tool for all but the simplest situations.

Exponential Smoothing. A second major approach to extrapolation is exponential smoothing. As in the case of moving averages, this approach literally smooths out the random variation in period-to-period values. Also like moving averages, trends and cycles must be estimated (smoothed) separately. The simplest form of exponential smoothing produces a forecast which is a weighted combination of last period's results and last period's forecast. The formula for this is:

$$\hat{S}_{t+1} = \alpha S_t + (1 - \alpha)\hat{S}_t \tag{17.2}$$

where the smoothing constant α = weight of last period sales and $(1 - \alpha)$ = weight of the last forecast. Notice that when α equals 1, we are simply using last period results as a forecast. When $\alpha = 0$, on the other hand, we are completely ignoring last period sales and keeping the forecast constant. Typically, the "right" value of α is somewhere in between.[1]

---

[1]The term *exponential smoothing* comes from the property of this method which weights the most recent period most heavily, the next most recent next most heavily, and so forth in an exponential manner. This property can be seen by examining the simple model:

$$\hat{S}_{t+1} = \alpha S_t + (1 - \alpha)\hat{S}_t$$

But:

$$\hat{S}_t = \alpha S_{t-1} + (1 - \alpha)\hat{S}_{t-1}$$

Therefore,

$$\begin{aligned}\hat{S}_{t+1} &= \alpha S_t + (1 - \alpha)\left[\alpha S_{t-1} + (1 - \alpha)\hat{S}_{t-1}\right] \\ &= \alpha S_t + \alpha(1 - \alpha)S_{t-1} + (1 - \alpha)^2\hat{S}_{t-1}\end{aligned}$$

Similarly, we can substitute for $\hat{S}_{t-1}$ and get:

$$\hat{S}_{t+1} = \alpha S_t + \alpha(1 - \alpha)S_{t-1} + \alpha(1 - \alpha)^2 S_{t-2} + (1 - \alpha)^3\hat{S}_{t-2}$$

By extension this becomes:

$$\begin{aligned}\hat{S}_{t+1} = {} & \alpha S_t + \alpha(1 - \alpha)S_{t-1} + \alpha(1 - \alpha)^2 S_{t-2} \\ & + \alpha(1 - \alpha)^3 S_{t-3} + \cdots + \alpha(1 - \alpha)^n S_{t-n} + \cdots\end{aligned}$$

Hence, the data points are weighted exponentially where the exponent indicates the age of the data.

TABLE 17–3 Exponential Smoothing Example

	$\alpha = .2$			$\alpha = .8$		
Sales	$\hat{S}_t$	$.2S_t$	$.8\hat{S}_t$	$\hat{S}_t$	$.8S_t$	$.2\hat{S}_{t-1}$
100	100	20	80	100	80	20
110	100	22	80	100	88	20
105	102	21	81.6	108	84	21.6
130	102.6	26	82.1	105.6	104	21.1
140	108.1	28	86.5	125.1	112	25.0
120	114.5	24	91.6	137.0	96	27.4
160	115.6	32	92.5	123.4	128	25.7
175	124.6	35	99.6	153.7	140	30.7
	134.6			170.7		

Searching for the right α is really a trial-and-error process. Using the eight-period example of Table 17–2, we can see how a small α (.2) produces a slowly changing forecast, while a large α (.8) tracks last period sales much more closely (Table 17–3). In both cases, a value of 100 was arbitrarily used for the first forecast. (The effect of this value on the forecast gradually decreases as more periods are included.) For $\alpha = .2$, the forecast for the second period becomes:

$$\hat{S}_2 = .2(S_1) + .8(\hat{S}_1)$$
$$= .2(100) + .8(100) = 100$$

Similarly, the third period forecast becomes:

$$\hat{S}_3 = .2(S_2) + .8(\hat{S}_2)$$
$$= .2(110) + .8(100) = 102$$

Notice that both sets of forecasts lag behind actual sales. The reason for this is that the trend was ignored. To account for both trend and seasonality by means of exponential smoothing requires a more complex model:

$$\hat{S}_{t+1} = \frac{\alpha S_t}{F_{t-L}} + (1 - \alpha)(\hat{S}_t + R_{t-1}) \tag{17.3}$$

where the seasonality is given by:

$$F_t = \beta \frac{S_t}{\hat{S}_{t+1}} + (1 - \beta) F_{t-L} \tag{17.4}$$

TABLE 17–4 Time Series Regression Example

Input Data			*Output*
Time	Sales		$\hat{S}$
1	100		94.3
2	110	Computer/calculator	105.2
3	105	→	115.0
4	130		124.9
5	140		134.8
6	120		144.7
7	160	↓	154.6
8	175	Sales = 85.4 + 9.88 (time) →	164.4

where L is the periodicity (length) of the seasonal pattern and the trend is obtained from:

$$R_{t+1} = \gamma(S_{t+1} - S_t) + (1 - \gamma)R_t \tag{17.5}$$

and α, β, and γ are three separately estimated smoothing constants. Generally, data involving cycles and trends are handled by means of regression analysis, rather than by exponential smoothing.

Time Series Regression. A third way to extrapolate data is by using regression analysis with time (period) as the independent variable. Time series regression produces estimates of the base level (intercept) and trend (slope). Seasonal patterns can be handled outside the regression (i.e., by removing the estimated seasonal component from the values of the dependent variable before performing the regression) or by various "tricks" within the regression (e.g., using dummy variables, as in the fuel oil example in Chapter 13, see Wildt, 1977). Ignoring seasonality, the model is simply:

$$\text{Sales} = a + b(\text{time})$$

Addressing the same eight-period example in this manner produces the result of Table 17–4. The forecast for period 10 based on this model would be:

$$\hat{S}_{10} = 85.4 + 9.88(10) = 184.2$$

Actually, all three methods (moving average, exponential smoothing, and time series regression) are very similar. They do weight data differently: moving average weights some of the data points equally, exponential smoothing weights all the data points unequally, and regression typically weights all the points equally, although unequal weights can be used. Choice among the three is, hence, a matter of taste, availability, and experience. Since the reader is presumably already familiar with regression at this point, he or she might be well advised to use time series regression when the choice arises.

Box-Jenkins. The Box-Jenkins methodology is a complicated statistical procedure for extrapolating time series data. The basic approach is to assume that sales in the current period are based on a combination of random "shocks" (called *white noise*) and past sales. It encompasses several different approaches:

1. AR (autoregressive), where the variable to be forecast can be written as a linear combination of previous values of the variable:

$$S(t) = a_1 S(t-1) + a_2 S(t-2) + \cdots + a_k S(t-k) \qquad (17.6)$$

2. MA (moving average), where the variable to be forecast can be written as a linear combination of previous random shocks:

$$S(t) = b_1 e(t-1) + b_2 e(t-2) + \cdots + b_p e(t-p) \qquad (17.7)$$

3. ARMA (autoregressive moving average), where the variable to be forecast can be expressed is expressed as a combination of Equations 17.6 and 17.7.

4. ARIMA (autoregressive integrated moving average) where the variable to be forecast is expressed as differences in Equations 17.6 and 17.7 to make the series stationary (i.e., a fixed mean).

The whole forecasting process can be viewed as a three-stage trial-and-error process. First, a tentative model is identified. Second, that model is estimated, and third, some diagnostic checking is performed. If a model performs adequately, it can be used for forecasting; if it does not perform well, a new model is then tested. The advantage of the model is that it is often an accurate predictor in stable environments. The disadvantages are that it requires many periods of data to be estimated, and that choice of the appropriate model requires considerable expertise. Put differently, it is not a tool for the unitiated.

Additive versus Multiplicative Models. One final point is important in considering extrapolation procedures. In building a model of sales as a function of base values, trends, and cycles, these components may be combined in more than one way. The best way to decide how to combine them is to look at a graph of the data, such as Figure 17–3. In case A, the cycle "explodes" and, hence, a multiplicative model is appropriate:

$$\text{Sales} = (\text{base})(\text{trend})(\text{seasonality})$$

FIGURE 17–3 Hypothetical Sales Patterns over Time

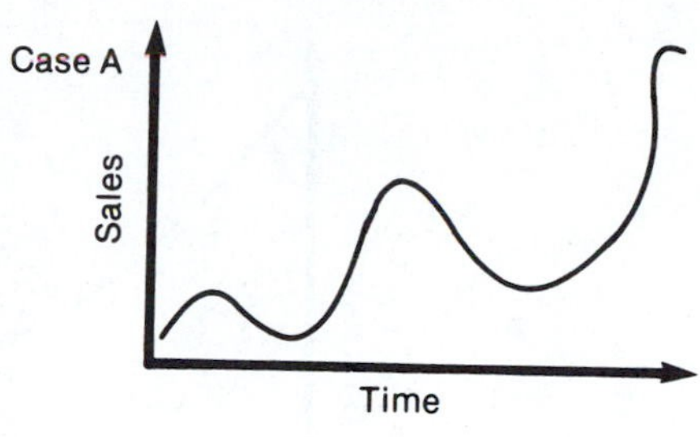

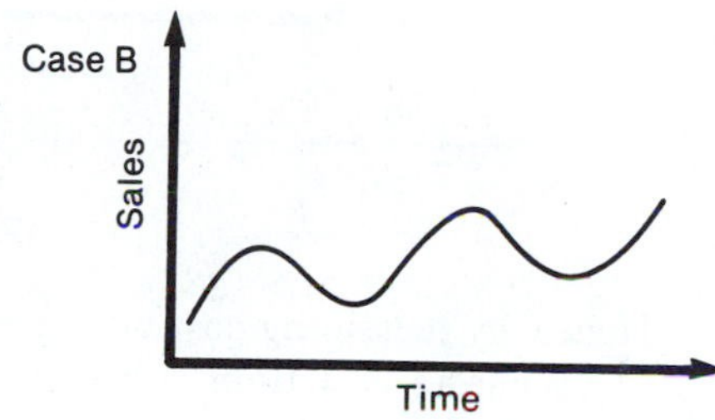

In case B, on the other hand, the spread of the cycle is constant, indicating a linear model:

$$\text{Sales} = \text{Base} + \text{Trend} + \text{Seasonality}$$

Generally, an additive type model will suffice.

Model Based

Model based forecasting approaches are distinguished from extrapolation procedures in that, in addition to using past data for the item being forecast, they assume that future results will occur based on either a particular pattern or set of influences. Some of the most common model forms include experience models, epidemic models, input-output models, single equation regression models, and simultaneous equation models.

Experience Models. A basic pattern which occurs in many areas is that the cost of an operation (e.g., producing a product) decreases as cumulative experience increases. The shape of the cost versus experience curve, often called a *learning curve*, is typically exponential (Figure 17–4).

FIGURE 17–4 Experience Curve

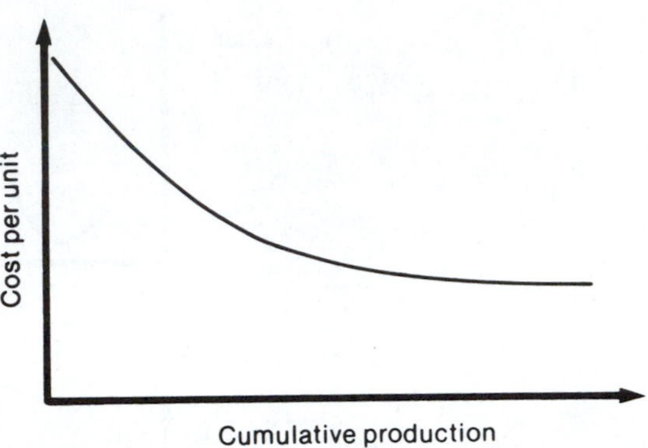

Hence, by measuring cost during initial production and estimating the rate of decline in cost from either limited data or subjective estimation, costs can be forecast for various times and production levels in the future.

Epidemic Models. An approach to forecasting sales of a new product is to assume that initial sales of the product will follow the same shape curve (Figure 17–5) as an epidemic (which, given some new products, may be an apt analogy). This curve implies that there will be a slow start, during

FIGURE 17–5 Trial over Time for a New Product

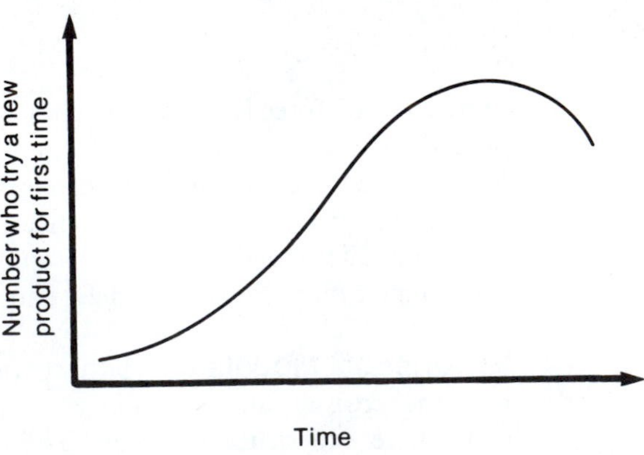

FIGURE 17–6 Cumulative Trial over Time

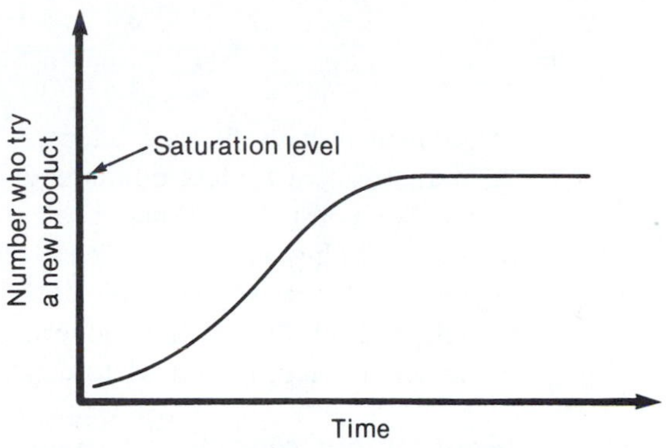

which the innovators become "infected," followed by a growth period in which sales of the product (or the disease) spread rapidly through the population. Sales then slow down as the number of eventual buyers (people susceptible to the disease) is approached (Figure 17–6). Such a model has been presented by Bass (1969) and used in companies such as Eastman Kodak to forecast sales of new consumer durables in terms of when they would peak and how big the peak would be.

The model used by Bass has the following form:

$$p(t) = p + \frac{q}{M} Y(t)$$

where

$p(t)$ = probability of purchase given no previous purchase was made.
$Y(t)$ = total number who have tried up to time t.
M = total number of potential buyers (saturation level).
q = parameter reflecting the rate of diffusion of the product (coefficient of imitation).
p = initial probability of purchase (coefficient of innovation).

Thus,

$$\begin{aligned} S(t) &= [M - Y(t)]\, p(t) \\ &= pM + [q - p] Y(t) - \frac{q}{M} [Y(t)]^2 \end{aligned}$$

The model can be estimated by running a regression of current versus past sales:

$$S(t) = c_0 + c_1Y(t) + c_2[Y(t)]^2$$

These models have fit past adoption patterns quite well. Unfortunately, they are sensitive to data points and, hence, are unreliable when only four or five data points (e.g., years of sales) are available. The simple models also ignore marketing variables. For example, the saturation level M probably depends on price, which often declines over time, and the purchase rate $p(t)$ depends on distribution, advertising, etc. Recent extensions of the Bass model allow for p, q, and M to depend on price, advertising, and so forth.

Input-Output Models. An input-output model is essentially a model which balances production resources used with final products produced. These models are generally used to model an entire economy with different sectors of the economy (steel, etc.) used as the elements of the analysis. In general, these models are not used in marketing research.

Single Equation Regression Models. Single equation regression models are the most widely used form of models in marketing research. These models are developed in three stages.

First, the variables which are assumed to affect the dependent variable are specified:

$$\text{Sales} = f(\text{our price, competitors' prices, our advertising, competitor's advertising, disposable income})$$

Next, a model which indicates the form of the relation between the independent variables and sales is specified. These models are generally linear, such as:

$$\begin{aligned} \text{Sales in cartons } (S) = {} & \text{constant} \\ & + B_1 \text{ (our price)} \\ & + B_2 \text{ (our advertising)} \\ & + B_3 \text{ (disposable income)} \end{aligned}$$

The model is then estimated by means of regression analysis:

$$\begin{aligned} S = {} & 1.2 - .2(\text{price in \$}) + 1.3(\text{advertising in \$}) \\ & + .1(\text{disposable income in billions of \$}) \end{aligned}$$

These models serve two basic uses:

Straight forecasting. $\tilde{S} \pm 2S_{Y.X}$. Notice that to use regression models to forecast one must first forecast the values of the independent variables. If this is difficult, then regression becomes less useful as a straight forecasting device. Put differently, in building a multiple regression model for purposes of forecasting, make sure that the independent variables are easily forecast.

Answering "what if" questions. In our example,
B_1 = marginal effect of changing our price.
B_2 = marginal effect of changing our advertising share.
If you make the rather large assumption that the relation between price and sales is causal, rather than just correlational, you can answer questions like, "What if I increase advertising by $10?" In this case, a $10 increase in advertising would lead to a (1.3)(10) = 13 carton change in sales.

The criteria for which variables to include in a regression model are numerous, including the following:

1. Parsimony (bosses like simple models).
2. Data availability (available data typically dictate variable selection).
3. Plausibility (do the independent variables logically affect the dependent variable?).
4. Goodness of fit (does the independent variable help predict the dependent variable? Bosses hate low R^2s).
5. "Good" coefficients (are the signs and magnitudes of the coefficients reasonable?).

Given these multiple criteria, it is not surprising that building regression models is a trial-and-error process.

Two major variations of the linear sales model exist. One makes the model multiplicative, rather than linear:

$$\text{Sales} = B_0(\text{price})^{B_1}(\text{advertising})^{B_2}(\text{income})^{B_3}$$

This model is typically estimated by taking logarithms of both sides and running a regression as follows:

$$\text{log sales} = B_0 + B_1(\text{log price}) + B_2(\text{log advertising}) + B_3(\text{log income})$$

The other major variation is to build market share models in either linear or multiplicative forms. These models are widely used for mature product categories, where sales of one product come mainly at the expense of another. These models tend to be defined in terms of relative values of the independent variables, e.g.:

$$\text{Share } A = B_0 + B_1 \frac{\text{Price } A}{\text{Average price}} + B_2 \frac{\text{Advertising } A}{\text{Total advertising}} + \cdots$$

One final point in using single equation regression models is that most sales and share levels have substantial inertia. Therefore, it is often desirable to include a lagged value of the dependent variable in the equation. Failure to do so may bias the coefficients of the independent variables (e.g., make the advertising coefficient bigger than it "should" be) and, consequently, lead to poor decisions.

Simultaneous Equation Models. To improve the accuracy of a forecast for a particularly important variable (e.g., oil prices), it is often necessary to take into account the interdependency between this variable and other variables. For example, the price of oil influences the price of food and the price of food influences the price of oil. To model such interdependency, systems of equations are specified. The parameters of these models are then estimated by simultaneous equation regression. Using these models requires considerable development cost and technical know-how and, hence, they are used only in limited circumstances.

CHOICE OF FORECASTING METHOD

Time Horizon

The time horizon has a major effect on the forecasting method that is appropriate and on the accuracy of the forecast. Put bluntly, anything will do to predict next week (with exceptions—e.g., umbrellas), and nothing can predict 30 years ahead. The relation between the time horizon of the forecast and the method to be used can be summarized as follows:

Term of Forecast	*"Best" Method*
1. Super short (less than 6 months)	Any method: The die is cast already
2. Short (6 months)	Simple extrapolation
3. Medium (1–5 years)	Quantitative (regression)
4. Long (5–30 years)	Model building
5. Super long (30 years and up)	FAC*

*Flip a coin; no one knows.

Use of Quantitative Procedures

Using quantitative procedures may at times seem tedious. Still, there are several reasons why quantitative methods are beneficial:

1. They simplify routine, repetitive situations.
2. They force explicit statements of assumptions.
3. They provide a bench mark for qualitative thinking.
4. They are a way to start when the situation seems hopelessly complex.

When using quantitative procedures, remember:

If possible, graph the data. (A picture may be worth a thousand analyses.) As an example of how important a picture can be, consider again the eight-period example of Table 17–2. Graphed, the data look like Figure 17–7. An interesting pattern thus emerges: two up periods followed by a down period. While this pattern is only three cycles old, it does suggest that a forecast in the 130–40 area for period 9 would be supportable. This pattern can be overlooked by simple number crunching.

Do sensitivity analysis. Only when a result seems to be stable over method and data points (drop one or two points and rerun the analysis) can the forecast be advanced with much conviction.

Use scenarios. Single estimates are not very useful, partly because the values of the independent variables in the future are uncertain. However, quantitative models can be used to provide forecasts under alternative values for the independent variables. At the minimum, a best guess, worst case (e.g., poor economic conditions), and best case scenario should be presented.

Examine big "residuals." By examining the characteristics of those periods (data points) when the forecast was bad, omitted variables can often be uncovered.

Avoid silly precision. This means rounding off the forecast and giving an honest plus or minus range.

Be tolerant of errors. Expect the methods to improve your odds of making a good forecast, not to guarantee them.

Remember you will generally miss all the turning points. Quantitative (as well as qualitative) forecasting methods work well as long as the patterns which occurred in the past extend into the future. Whenever a major change occurs, however, most forecasts will be way off. Put differently, most forecasting methods are generally useless for pre-

FIGURE 17–7 Plot of Sales Data Example

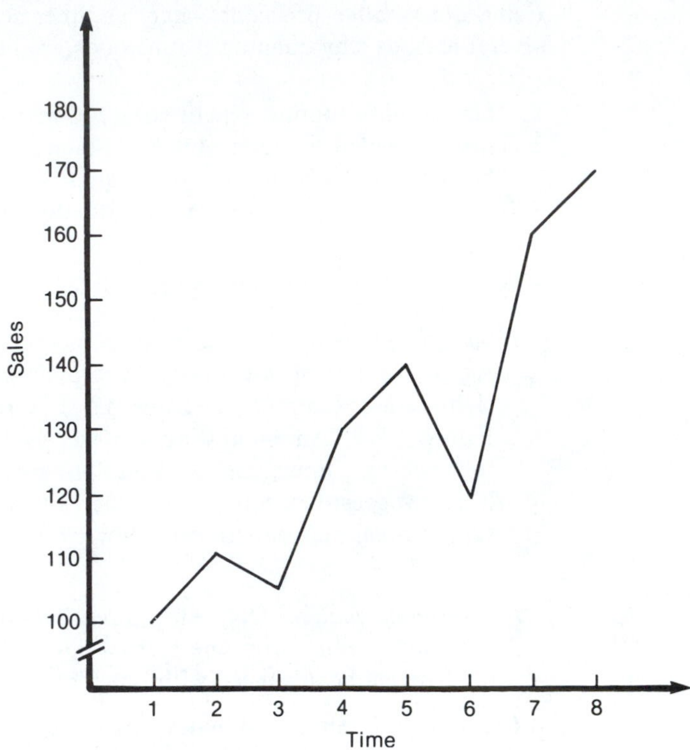

dicting major changes in the way the world operates (oil embargoes, changes in social values, etc.) and so the effects of these are not included in most forecasts.

Combining Forecasts

So far this chapter has described a number of forecasting methods and their strengths and weaknesses. In practice, when making an important forecast it is both common and prudent to make several forecasts and then combine them. Put differently, the issue is not to decide which is the best forecast but to create a forecast that combines the available forecasts. For example, in producing an industry forecast, one should generally:

1. Plot the data and extrapolate. Normally, for mature industries a linear extrapolation will suffice; whereas, for new industries a nonlinear procedure (such as the Bass model), which explicitly recognizes the eventual saturation level, is often useful.

2. Build a regression model which includes independent variables which are, as much as possible:

a. Good predictors.

b. Uncorrelated with each other.

c. Easy to forecast themselves.

This model will usually include general economic variables (e.g., GNP, population) as well as industry variables (e.g., average price, if it has been changing).

3. Collect forecasts available from others (e.g., security analysts).

4. Provide a subjective forecast based on considering likely future changes and their impact on sales.

5. Create a bottom-up forecast (e.g., by summing up district managers' forecasts).

The range of these forecasts provides a useful indication of the uncertainty faced. Moreover, deciding how to combine these forecasts forces one to make explicit assumptions.

Recently, a number of researchers have addressed the issue of the optimal way to combine forecasts. The best way is to weight forecasts based on their relative accuracy. Unless there is great variation in accuracy, therefore, an equal weighting works quite well.

EXAMPLE: THE YEAR 2000

In 1970, a problem was posed which was, in essence, "What will the effect of different U.S. populations be on U.S. industries in the year 2000?" Given this rather nebulous topic, the decision was made to build a model of unit sales for 19 industries based on, among other things, population. A variety of approaches were considered and rejected:

1. Input-output analysis. (The researcher didn't know enough about it.)
2. Simultaneous equation regression models. (Insufficient time and budget.)
3. Index numbers. (Not enough experience with, too subjective.)

That left two approaches:

1. Single equation regression.
2. Polling of experts.

The major thrust was to use a single equation model for each of the 19 industries. Also, 35 experts were asked to indicate what they felt would happen to sales in the 19 industries under different population assumptions (Howard and Lehmann, 1972). These judgments were used mainly to backstop the quantitative methods and served to help eliminate predictions which would not be believable. (Having believable predictions tends to increase the speed with which a consultant gets paid.)

A wide variety of potential regression models are available. There being no particular reason for choosing one, a number were investigated[2] (Table 17–5). The results were then examined and the best model chosen. Almost without exception, the lagged models and first difference models produced "funny" results when extrapolated 30 years into the future based on the data used (1948–69 and 1959–69). In fact, the "best" results seemed to come from using the 1959–69 data on model (2):

$$Sales = B_0 + B_1(\text{POP}_t) + B_2\frac{\text{DI}_t}{\text{CPI}_t}$$

The resulting equations were then used for forecasting unit sales in the year 2000 under two population estimates and two disposable income estimates. The results clearly illustrate the frustration of forecasting 30 years into the future based on 11 years' worth of data. First, the supposedly low population estimate at the time was 266,281,000, a number which currently appears, if anything, high. Second, it is hard to believe that some of the projections will come true. The best example of this is automobile sales, where the forecasts for the year 2000 based on the lower population and disposable income estimates were as follows:

Domestic	1.2 million
Imported	19 million

This result is hard to believe on two counts. First, given oil shortages, it is difficult to project sales of 20 million cars in the year 2000 (at least cars as we know them today). Secondly, it seems unlikely that imported cars will be allowed (either by GM, etc., or the U.S. government) to so totally dominate the market. (It may be, however, that small cars will have such a dominant share.) This prediction is the result of the linear extrapolation of the past trend over a long time period. While linear extrapolations work well in the

[2]Actually, many more could have been used if either more variables were used or if population were broken down by age groups.

TABLE 17–5 Alternative Models of Sales as a Function of Population

	Model
	1. $S_t = B_0 + B_1(\mathrm{POP}_t)$
	2. $S_t = B_0 + B_1(\mathrm{POP}_t) + B_2\left(\frac{\mathrm{DI}_t}{\mathrm{CPI}_t}\right)$
	3. $S_t = B_0 + B_1(\mathrm{POP}_t) + B_2\left(\frac{\mathrm{DI}_t}{\mathrm{CPI}_t} \Big/ \mathrm{POP}_t\right)$
	4. $S_t = B_0 + B_1(t) + B_2(\mathrm{POP}_t) + B_3(\mathrm{DI}_t/\mathrm{CPI}_t)$
	5. $S_t = B_0 + B_1(t) + B_2(\mathrm{POP}_t) + B_3\left(\frac{\mathrm{DI}_t}{\mathrm{CPI}_t} \Big/ \mathrm{POP}_t\right)$
	6. $S_t = B_0 + B_1(t) + B_2(\mathrm{POP}_t)$
One-year lags	7. $S_t = B_0 + B_1(\mathrm{POP}_{t-1})$
	8. $S_t = B_0 + B_1(\mathrm{POP}_{t-1}) + B_2(\mathrm{DI}_{t-1}/\mathrm{CPI}_{t-1})$
	9. $S_t = B_0 + B_1(\mathrm{POP}_{t-1}) + B_2\left(\frac{\mathrm{DI}_t}{\mathrm{CPI}_t} \Big/ \mathrm{POP}_{t-1}\right)$
	10. $S_t = B_0 + B_1(t-1) + B_2(\mathrm{POP}_{t-1}) + B_3(\mathrm{DI}_{t-1}/\mathrm{CPI}_{t-1})$
	11. $S_t = B_0 + B_1(t-1) + B_2(\mathrm{POP}_{t-1}) + B_3\left(\frac{\mathrm{DI}_{t-1}}{\mathrm{CPI}_{t-1}} \Big/ \mathrm{POP}_{t-1}\right)$
	12. $S_t = B_0 + B_1(t-1) + B_2(\mathrm{POP}_{t-1})$
Five-year lags	13. $S_t = B_0 + B_1(\mathrm{POP}_{t-5})$
	14. $S_t = B_0 + B_1(\mathrm{POP}_{t-5}) + B_2(\mathrm{DI}_{t-5}/\mathrm{CPI}_{t-5})$
	15. $S_t = B_0 + B_1(\mathrm{POP}_{t-5}) + B_2\left(\frac{\mathrm{DI}_{t-5}}{\mathrm{CPI}_{t-5}} \Big/ \mathrm{POP}_{t-5}\right)$
	16. $S_t = B_0 + B_1(t-5) + B_2(\mathrm{POP}_{t-5}) + B_3(\mathrm{DI}_{t-5}/\mathrm{CPI}_{t-5})$
	17. $S_t = B_0 + B_1(t-5) + B_2(\mathrm{POP}_{t-5}) + B_3\left(\frac{\mathrm{DI}_{t-5}}{\mathrm{CPI}_{t-5}} \Big/ \mathrm{POP}_{t-5}\right)$
	18. $S_t = B_0 + B_1(t-5) + B_2(\mathrm{POP}_{t-5})$
First differences	19. $(S_t - S_{t-1}) = B_0 + B_1(\mathrm{POP}_t - \mathrm{POP}_{t-1})$
	20. $(S_t - S_{t-1}) = B_0 + B_1(\mathrm{POP}_t - \mathrm{POP}_{t-1}) + B_2\left(\frac{\mathrm{DI}_t}{\mathrm{CPI}_t} - \frac{\mathrm{DI}_{t-1}}{\mathrm{CPI}_{t-1}}\right)$
	21. $(S_t - S_{t-1}) = B_0 + B_1(\mathrm{POP}_t - \mathrm{POP}_{t-1}) + B_2\left(\frac{\mathrm{DI}_t}{\mathrm{CPI}_t} \Big/ \mathrm{POP}_t - \frac{\mathrm{DI}_{t-1}}{\mathrm{CPI}_{t-1}} \Big/ \mathrm{POP}_{t-1}\right)$
Logs*	22. $\log S_t = B_0 + B_1 \log(\mathrm{POP}_t) + B_2 \log(\mathrm{DI}_t/\mathrm{CPI}_t)$
	23. $\log S_t = B_0 + B_1 \log(\mathrm{POP}_t) + B_2 \log\left(\frac{\mathrm{DI}_t}{\mathrm{CPI}_t} \Big/ \mathrm{POP}_t\right)$
Logs, one-year lags	24. $\log S_t = B_0 + B_1 \log(\mathrm{POP}_{t-1}) + B_2 \log(\mathrm{DI}_{t-1}/\mathrm{CPI}_{t-1})$
	25. $\log S_t = B_0 + B_1 \log(\mathrm{POP}_{t-1}) + B_2 \log\left(\frac{\mathrm{DI}_{t-1}}{\mathrm{CPI}_{t-1}} \Big/ \mathrm{POP}_{t-1}\right)$
Logs, five-year lags	26. $\log S_t = B_0 + B_1 \log(\mathrm{POP}_{t-5}) + B_2 \log(\mathrm{DI}_{t-5}/\mathrm{CPI}_{t-5})$
	27. $\log S_t = B_0 + B_1 \log\left(\frac{\mathrm{DI}_{t-5}}{\mathrm{CPI}_{t-5}} \Big/ \mathrm{POP}_{t-5}\right)$

Key: S = sales.
POP = population.
DI = disposable income.
CPI = total consumer price index.
t = time (year).

*This implies $S_t = B_0(\mathrm{POP}_t)^{B_1}(\mathrm{DI}_t/\mathrm{CPI}_t)^{B_2}$

short run, they tend to be off in the long run. The point, therefore, is that these estimates cannot be maintained with much certainty (would you believe a confidence interval of zero to infinity?). That doesn't mean that long-range forecasts aren't important; airports, utilities, and so forth, all need to plan many years in the future. What it does mean is that anyone doing long-range forecasting deserves credit for courage and some sympathy.

SUMMARY

Forecasting is a trying undertaking. Besides a sense of security and humor, the following are useful tools:

1. Understanding of:
  a. The problem.
  b. The situation.

2. Common sense.

3. Willingness to live with uncertainty. (False precision costs money since it doesn't encourage proper contingency planning.)

4. A number cruncher (the ability to use quantitative methods).

5. A coin. At some point in the forecasting process, a guess will need to be made. By using a coin, you can blame the result on someone or something else. If that won't do, hire a consultant. At least then when the forecast is bad you can have the satisfaction of firing him or her.

PROBLEMS

1. Prepare an estimate of diswasher sales for:
   a. Next year.
   b. Five years from now.
   c. 2010.

   Use whatever sources of information and data are available (with appropriate citations) as well as any quantitative techniques you feel are relevant. Limit the report (exclusive of exhibits) to five pages.
2. A utility plans to introduce a new small appliance aimed at homeowners which costs about $80. The product is essentially a decorative version of the basic equipment used by 90 percent of the homes and businesses.
   a. Using the information given, indicate the absolute and relative potential of the product in the two sales districts.

b. What other information would you find useful?

	A (Center City)	*B (Suburban County)*
Number residential customers	61,200	48,200
Number businesses	16,000	6,600
Amount spent by residential customers on the service	1,400,000	1,240,000
Amount spent by business customers on the service	6,990,000	1,180,000
Income per capita	6,700	6,000
Population	146,000	141,000
Retail sales	60,000,000	47,000,000
Furniture/appliance sales	3,360,000	2,220,000

3. Given the following data:

Year	*Sales*
1970	28.2
1971	31.4
1972	30.3
1973	34.5
1974	37.8
1975	33.9
1976	38.6
1977	40.1
1978	37.8
1979	41.2

Forecast 1980 sales by:

a. Graphical eyeball.
b. Regression.
c. Extrapolating three period moving averages.
d. Using exponential smoothing to estimate the trend for $\alpha = .2$ and $\alpha = .8$.

4. Assume you were responsible for forecasting sales of Alcort Sunfish (a small sailboat). How would you proceed?
5. Assume you were assigned to model annual sales of beer for Schlitz.
a. What would your model look like and how would you proceed?
b. What would you do differently to forecast monthly beer sales?

BIBLIOGRAPHY

Armstrong, J. Scott. "Forecasting with Econometric Methods." *Journal of Business* 51 (1978), pp. 549–61.

Armstrong, J. Scott; Roderick J. Brodie; and Shelby McIntyre. "Forecasting Methods for Marketing: Review of Empirical Research." *Singapore Marketing Review* 2 (1987), pp. 7–23.

Bass, Frank M. "A New Product Growth for Model Consumer Durables." *Management Science* 15 (January 1969), pp. 215–27.

Chakravarti, Dipankar; Andrew Mitchell; and Richard Staelin. "Judgment Based Marketing Decision Models: Problems and Possible Solutions." *Journal of Marketing* 45 (Fall 1981), pp. 13–23.

Chambers, John C.; Satinder K. Mullick; and Donald D. Smith. *An Executive's Guide to Forecasting*. New York: John Wiley & Sons, 1974.

______. "How to Choose the Right Forecasting Technique." *Harvard Business Review* 49 (July–August 1971), pp. 45–74.

Cox, Anthony D., and John O. Summers. "Heuristics and Biases in the Intuitive Projection of Retail Sales." *Journal of Marketing Research* 24 (August 1987), pp. 290–297.

Cox, William E., Jr. *Industrial Marketing Research*. New York: John Wiley & Sons, Inc., 1979.

Draper, N., and H. Smith, *Applied Regression Analysis*. New York: John Wiley & Sons, 1966.

Einhorn, Hillel J.; Robin M. Hogarth; and Eric Kelmpner. "Quality of Group Judgment." *Psychological Bulletin* 84 (1977), pp. 158–72.

Einhorn, Hillel J., and Robin M. Hogarth. "Confidence in Judgment: Persistence of the Illusion of Validity." *Psychological Review* 85 (1978), pp. 395–416.

Georgoff, David M., and Robert G. Murdick. "Manager's Guide to Forecasting." *Harvard Business Review* 64 (January–February 1986), pp. 110–20.

Howard, John A., and Donald R. Lehmann. "The Effect of Different Populations on Selected Industries in the Year 2000." Commission on Population Growth and the American Future, Research Reports II. In *Economic Aspects of Population Change*, ed. Elliot R. Morss and Ritchie H. Reed, 1972, pp. 145–58.

Kapoor, S. G.; P. Madhok; and S. M. Wu. "Modeling and Forecasting Sales Data by Time Series." *Journal of Marketing Research* 18 (February 1981), pp. 94–100.

Larréché, Jean-Claude, and Reza Moinpour. "Managerial Judgment in Marketing: The Concept of Expertise." *Journal of Marketing Research* 20 (May 1983), pp. 110–21.

Lawton, S. B., and W. H. Lawton. "An Autocatalytic Model for the Diffusion of Educational Innovations." *Educational Administration Quarterly* 15 (Winter 1979), pp. 19–46.

Little, John D. C., and Leonard M. Lodish. "Commentary on Judgment Based Marketing Decision Models." *Journal of Marketing* 45 (Fall 1981), pp. 24–29.

McLaughlin, Robert L. "The Breakthrough in Sales Forecasting." *Journal of Marketing* 27 (April 1963), pp. 46–54.

McLaughlin, Robert L., and J. J. Boyle. *Short Term Forecasting.* Chicago: American Marketing Association, 1968.

Moriarty, Mark M. "Design Features of Forecasting Systems Involving Management Judgments." *Journal of Marketing Research* 22 (November 1985), pp. 353–64.

Small, Lawrence R. "Sales Forecasting in Canada: A Survey of Practices." Ottawa: The Conference Board of Canada, 1980.

Wheelwright, S. C., and S. Makridakis. *Forecasting Methods for Management*. New York: John Wiley & Sons, 1977.

Wildt, Albert R. "Estimating Models of Seasonal Market Response Using Dummy Variables." *Journal of Marketing Research* 14 (February 1977), pp. 34–41.

Chapter 18

Product Research

The purpose of this chapter is to give a brief overview of the types of research which are commonly carried out for a product. More complete coverage is available elsewhere (e.g., Urban and Hauser, 1980; Pessemier, 1977; and Wind, 1982). This chapter will begin by covering the major types of research done in conjunction with an existing brand and then describe the typical stages of new product research.

EXISTING PRODUCTS

Monitoring the Overall Market

The most common type of research is designed to simply monitor a market. This serves as a control mechanism for the annual plan so unexpected changes are detected early. The most general type of monitoring concerns the state of the total market. Total market monitoring concerns three major categories: size, growth, and competition.

Size. Size is usually studied with secondary data (trade association, government data). Analysis is typically restricted to simple description (sales were *X*, etc.). Seasonality/cycles are also monitored.

Growth. Market growth projections are sometimes available from secondary data, especially for basic industries. For more narrowly defined categories, however (e.g., scented antidandruff shampoos), secondary projections are likely to be nonexistent or unreliable. In such cases, both secondary and internal data are used to build forecasting schemes/models, ranging from graphical eyeball to complex regression models.

Competition. A major source of information on competition is audits (such as Nielsen) where shares are reported by area, and so forth. Probably the best early warning system for competitive moves is a good competitive intelligence system. When this intelligence system fails, field salespersons are usually the first to encounter the effects of the competitive maneuver. Panel data are useful for analyzing switching patterns and, by implication, defining competition. Similarly, survey data can be used both for analyzing switching (i.e., by comparing brand bought last time with brand bought the time before that) and for direct questioning of which brands compete and how. In addition to corporate competition, patterns in the elements of the marketing mix are also monitored.

Developing the Annual Plan

The basic tool of coordination for many products is the annual plan. This plan reviews past results and then gives a blueprint for marketing programs for the upcoming years. Development of these plans typically takes from five to six months (e.g., July to January). The major steps are as follows.

Updating the Fact Book. The fact book is a compilation of statistical data on such items as sales by customer type, profits, marketing programs, and so forth. Much of the monitoring data collected during the year end up in the fact book.

Doing a Situation Analysis. The situation analysis is the major research step in the plan development process. This step of marketing planning attempts to translate the fact book into a concise summary of the status of the market in terms of its current and future size, customer segments and preferences, present and future market shares, and present and projected elements of the marketing mix of the company and its major competitors. In addition, the analysis attempts to pinpoint opportunities for the company to improve performance by changing various elements of the marketing mix (e.g., advertising copy).

Reviewing Long-Run Objectives. The long-run objectives for a product are typically set in advance. Nonetheless, past and projected performance provide inputs which can be used to modify objectives (e.g., if the objective is to be a dominant member of a given market and the company's share is 2 percent after five years, the objective is probably in need of alteration).

Setting Strategy and Operational Objectives. First, the key market segments are defined and basic appeals to be used to reach those segments are designed. This is usually called an *annual strategy*, and includes the general notion of product positioning. In this context, positioning includes defining strategy in terms of:

1. Characteristics (attributes) of the product to stress.
2. Target customers.
3. Which competitors to challenge.

Next, specific operational objectives are set. These include the following:

1. Overall sales/share/profit.
2. Product positioning on key attributes.
3. Pricing.
4. Advertising (awareness, recall, etc.)
5. Promotion.
6. Sales (by segment, product, district, salespersons).
7. Distribution (percent distribution coverage, etc.).
8. Product development.
9. Research (information needed to produce next year's plan).

Specifying Market Programs. This stage in the planning cycle involves specifying the programs (tactics) which will lead to meeting the operational objectives. These programs include the various elements of the marketing mix:

1. Pricing policy.
2. Advertising.
   a. Copy strategy.
   b. Media schedule.
   c. Timing.
3. Promotions.
4. Sales.
5. Distribution.
6. R & D.
7. Market research.

Preparing a Budget and Pro Forma Profit and Loss and Cash Flow Statements. This stage consists of summarizing the financial consequences of the marketing programs and sales forecasts.

Devising Control Procedures and Contingency Plans. The control procedures usually require collecting data to monitor the market. If the results begin to differ substantially from the objectives, then alternative (contingency) plans are implemented.

Role of Research

The major role of marketing research in the planning process (besides fighting for a bigger budget for next year) is in the situation analysis phase. The purpose here is to analyze the market so that the marketing programs next year will be more effective than they are this year. (The obvious hope is to achieve an optimal program, but attainment of this for any sustained period is the impossible dream.) The role of marketing programs can be seen in terms of an analogy. Assume you sat in front of a control panel on which were dials for the various elements of the marketing mix (Figure 18–1). Further, assume each dial had a number of fine-tuning features (e.g., advertising has fine-tuning for copy strategy, media mix, timing). The game is to set the dials in the correct positions. In doing so, however, there are several problems:

Competitive reaction. All the competitors also have control boards. These boards are similar but not identical, due to patents, channels of distribution used, and so forth. When competitors change their settings, your results change.

Trends. There are trends in the market which make it impossible for a constant setting to be optimal.

Exogenous events. Exogenous events, such as economic trends, shortages, and government regulations can produce such a strong reaction that they swamp the effect of the settings on the control panel. (Ever tried to watch TV in a lightning storm?)

Execution. The dials set the desired levels of the elements of the marketing mix. Unfortunately, the execution of this plan is usually less than perfect. In fact, many marketers feel good execution is at least as important as a good plan.

One way to go about setting the marketing mix panel is to initially set all the dials to zero (analogous to zero-based budgeting). Assuming things are going fairly well, however, this seems inefficient since the dials may well be somewhere near their optimal settings already. Hence, the more common approach is to develop a plan which involves only slight changes from last year's. (Such a plan is also easier to sell, since your boss may be the person who wrote last year's plan.)

As mentioned before, the role of research in this process is to provide the analysis upon which marketing program selection is based. It does this in several ways: testing elements of the marketing mix, fire fighting, and forecasting.

Testing Elements of the Marketing Mix. A major question in budget setting is how much should be allocated to each of the general elements of the mix. Attempts to compare different elements of the mix

FIGURE 18–1 Marketing Program Control Board

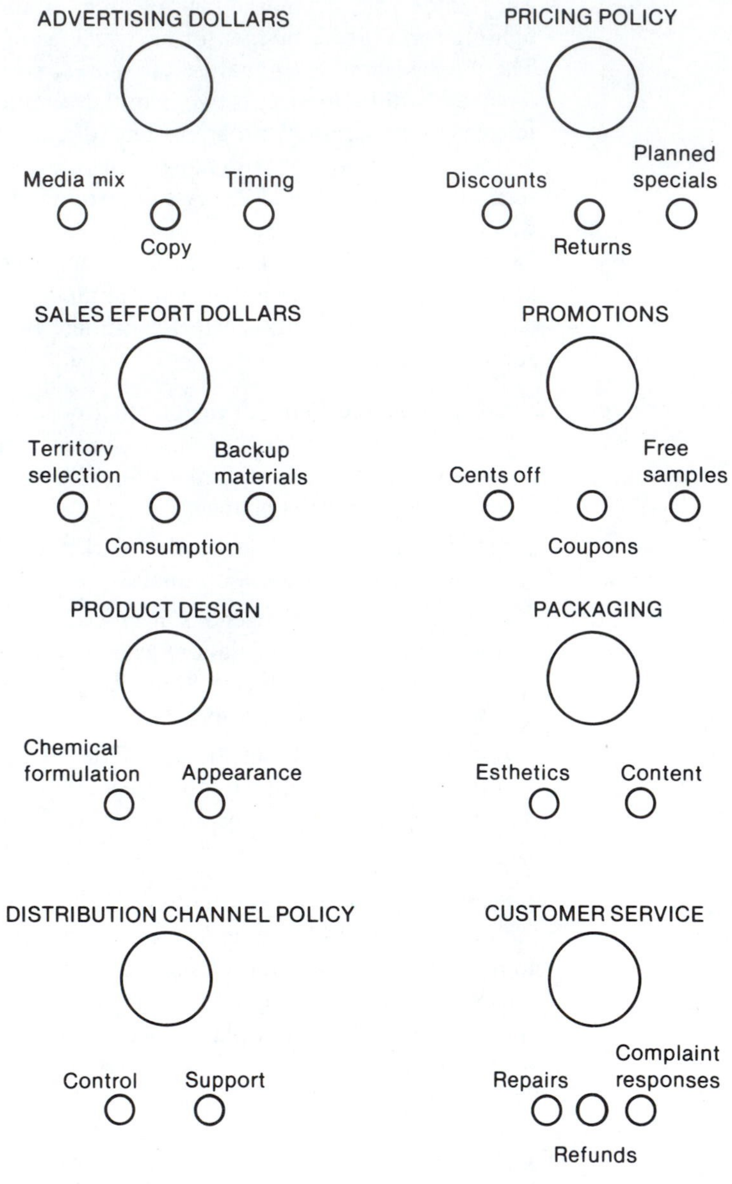

appear in both academic publications and company practices (Prasad and Ring, 1976). Typically, however, each element of the mix is studied separately:

Advertising Budgeting. Partly because of its size in relation to the total budget for many consumer products, the size of the advertising budget often has a large impact on profits. Investigation of the effectiveness of different advertising budgets has generally been done either by field experiment (these are hard to implement, partly because of the obvious resistance of a regional manager to cutting the ad budget in his or her region) or by means of simultaneous equation regression analysis (Bass, 1969; Beckwith, 1972). In addition, operations research models of the type first proposed by Vidale and Wolfe (1957) have been used to estimate advertising effects over time. More recently, effort has centered on estimating the length of time that advertising affects sales (Palda, 1964; Bass and Clarke, 1972; Parsons, 1975; Clarke, 1976; Dhalla, 1978; Assmus, Farley, and Lehmann, 1984). Decisions concerning choice of media are often made in conjunction with a model, such as ADBUDG (Little and Lodish, 1969).

Pricing. Pricing studies fall into three major categories. The first category is experiments. Here, in either field or controlled settings, consumers are exposed to prices in a "real" setting and the results analyzed to estimate price elasticity. The second basic type of study employs regression models. Here, sales versus price data in different regions, time periods, and so forth are used to estimate price elasticity. The problem in this type of study is in controlling for the other variables (e.g., advertising, competitive prices) which also varied. The third basic type of price study involves survey data. In its simplest form, this involves a "would you buy X at price Y?" type question. One problem with this approach is that the resulting data are unreliable as predictors of actual behavior. Moreover, the practice, when a demand curve is being sought, is to ask the respondent "would you buy" at several prices (e.g., "Would you buy at $10, $15, $20, . . . ?"). The problem with this is that respondents quickly perceive the "game" and tend to "hold out" for the low price. A more subtle way to get at price sensitivity is through conjoint measurement. In conjoint measurement, the data collected provide an indication of consumers' utility for various product characteristics, including price and, by deduction, a measure of price elasticity.

Promotions. The response to promotions could be estimated by using past results as bench marks and predicting accordingly. Alternatively, consumers could be asked to indicate their likely response to a promotion. While the absolute response may not be meaningful, by comparing the indicated response with the actual results of cases with similar responses, the actual results may be estimated. It is also important to consider the effects of a promotion both on the trade (wholesalers stocking up on the product) and on ultimate consumers (who may stockpile the product or increase consumption). Finally, the effect of promotions can be estimated by experiments. In fact, promotional response is generally very well suited to experiments, especially of the controlled store variety.

Advertising Copy. The likely response to advertising copy is an often-studied topic. The typical procedure is laboratory based, where a group of consumers view a commercial (usually embedded in a larger context, such as a TV show) and then indicate their reaction (*a*) to the brand itself and (*b*) to the ad. By comparing before-after values, the impact of the ad can be gauged. (Again, remember that it is not absolute values but the values in comparison to the values of known "good" ads that is important.) Some of the typical measurements include awareness of copy points, overall attitude, and intention to buy. One interesting trick is to measure attitude on a constant sum scale compared to the major competitive brands. Ads are also sometimes judged by consumer juries directly in terms of their appeal. Here, the jury views the ad and, like a focus group, proceeds to describe its reactions. Consumer juries are especially useful in evaluating strategies in mock-up/unfinalized form. It is also possible to evaluate ads by actual field experiments. This tends to be prohibitively expensive. However, special facilities exist (such as split-cable TV setups, where half the panel can see one ad and half another) which make such tests feasible. The actual conducting of advertising studies is typically done by the advertising agency which handles the product.

Fire Fighting. Fire fighting research is called for when something goes wrong. The something that went wrong is usually failure of a program to reach its objective (e.g., sales are off 30 percent in the West). The other major thing that inspires emergency research is a major competitive move (e.g., a new product introduction, a major promotional campaign). Here much primary data collection is often impossible due to time and budget constraints. Besides looking at standard monitoring tools (scanner panel data, etc.), the best recourse tends to be a combination of interrogation of salespersons and people in the channels and consumer contact through phone interviews.

Forecasting. The plan that is adopted has a series of operational goals (Sales = *X*, etc.). These goals are really forecasts of what will happen, given the particular set of marketing programs that are employed. Development of the forecasts is clearly a marketing research task. The general approach to obtaining the forecast is iterative. The first step is often to get forecasts at a very disaggregated level by, for example, asking salespersons or district managers how much they think that they will sell of the product. One of the major benefits of this is that it involves more people in the planning process and, therefore, should increase commitment to the plan which is finally adopted. Also, being close to the market, salespersons or district managers may have information about the current state of the market which is not yet known at corporate headquarters. These forecasts are then aggregated. At the same time, forecasts are prepared independently by staff personnel using quantitative techniques. Since the two forecasts typically differ noticeably (some salespersons sandbag, etc.) not only from each other but from long-range objectives, a series of adjustments and negotiations are then carried out for the purposes of gaining broad agreement for the final forecast.

SEGMENTATION

Segmenting markets is widely accepted as one of the requirements for successful marketing. By dividing the market into relatively homogeneous submarkets, both strategy formulation and tactical decision making (e.g., choice of media for advertising) can be simplified. Unfortunately, the desirability of segmentation does not guarantee its doability, much less give much guidance on how to do it.

The first thing to recognize is that market segmentation is usually a figment (albeit a useful one) of a researcher's or manager's imagination. While customers are different, a particular segmentation scheme is one of an infinite number that could be created. Since a segmentation scheme's value is more in the insight it provides than in the statistical precision with which it was founded, there is no one correct way to do segmentation. This section briefly describes desirable characteristics of segments, bases for forming segments, and how some of the analytical methods described in this book can be combined to produce a segmentation study.

Desirable Criteria

While there is no single way to evaluate a segmentation scheme, the following five criteria provide a useful standard for evaluation:

1. *Sizable.* Segments must be of sufficient size in terms of potential sales (but not in terms of number of customers) to be worth worrying about. (As a rule billion-dollar companies don't care much about J. R. Smith at 1188 Maple Street—or all the people on Maple Street, for that matter.)

2. *Identifiable.* Segments should be identifiable so that when presenting results they can be referred to by more pleasing titles than segment A, segment B (e.g., the 35 to 50 segment, the sports-minded, companies in New York).

3. *Reachable.* It may be sufficient for strategic purposes to identify a segment. For purposes of planning the marketing mix (e.g., advertising), however, it is useful to be able to target efforts on a segment. Therefore, a sports-minded segment tends to be reachable through the media (e.g., *Sports Illustrated*), whereas people who prefer the color blue, though identified, may be hard to reach (except by labels on blue towels, or by copy that employs the color blue).

4. *Respond differently.* Ideally, segments should respond differently to at least some of the elements of the offering. If all segments respond the same, then no specialized programs can be used. For example, some customers may be sensitive to advertising but not price, whereas others are concerned about price but unaffected by advertising, and still others care about a single attribute, such as downtime. The sensitivity to changes in market offering forms a useful basis for both describing the overall market and defining segments. It also makes the "why they buy" part of the analysis particularly crucial.

5. *Stable.* Since future plans are based on past data, segments (and hopefully but not necessarily the members of those segments) should be fairly stable over time.

While it would be nice for segments to satisfy all these criteria, in general one has to make trade-offs in choosing a segmentation scheme.

Bases for Segmentation

There are two basic categories of variables which can be used for segmenting:

1. *Descriptor variables.* These variables describe customers in general terms (e.g., demographics). They include the entire gamut of variables which can be used to profile individuals (or businesses). Basically, they indicate *who* the customers are and *where* they are.

2. *Product category variables.* These variables describe the customer in terms of how he or she relates to the product of interest. They include measures of *what* they bought or will buy (e.g., intention), *when* they buy, *where* they buy (e.g., distribution channel), *how* they buy (i.e., information sources and shopping behavior) and *why* they buy (e.g., benefits sought).

Segmentation based on descriptor variables guarantees definable and reachable segments, but not those that respond differently. Product category variable based segmentation guarantees segments which respond differently, but not that are definable or reachable. Therefore, you either have to pick one (or try both and see which works) or create a hybrid, using some of each type of variable (e.g., age of customer and brand bought last).

Analytical Approaches

The analytical approaches available are numerous but group into three basic categories:

1. *Cluster analysis.* These approaches, which basically use factor or cluster analysis, or both, begin by amassing a set of available (and hopefully relevant) variables (e.g., 150 lifestyle questions) on a sample of customers (e.g., by means of a survey or through secondary data sources). If there are many variables, an attempt is often made to reduce the number of variables (e.g., through factor analysis). The reduced number of variables (if we choose a representative variable for each factor) or factor scores are then input into a clustering algorithm.

The clusters are then compared/profiled in terms of the variables which were used to form them (e.g., by simple analysis of means, ANOVAs, or discriminant analysis). The clusters are also compared in terms of other variables (e.g., lifestyle based clusters are compared in terms of product usage data).

2. *A priori grouping.* This approach produces segments based on managerial judgment. For example, an obvious segmentation scheme exists for many products by combining usage rates for the product category (low, medium, high) with brand bought/preferred (e.g., ours, our major competitor's, other). Other obvious segmentation plans include other product category variables (e.g., where they shop or purchase) plus the full range of descriptor variables (age, income, . . .). The segments are then profiled the same way as segments based on cluster analysis.

While not elegant, a priori based clusters are often more useful than so-called natural clusters because they are readily identifiable and reachable and obviously have responded differently to the product offering. In fact, it is always advisable to use such segmentation strategy as at least a basis for comparison with the results of more "data-massaging"-oriented approaches.

3. *Regression analysis.* Rather than treat all the variables available as "equals," as in cluster analysis, this method assumes one variable is the criterion (e.g., product class usage) and then attempts to find which other variables (e.g., age, income) are most highly related to it. The market is then segmented on the basis of these variables.

A variety of statistical procedures are available for such studies, including cross-tabulation, analysis of variance, and AID (see Table 18–1 for a list of analytical methods for examining customer differences). At least for the first stages of such research, however, some form of regression analysis is frequently used. In performing such regressions it is often useful to treat the variables as "categorical" (by using a series of so-called dummy variables). In any event, these regressions (at least for frequently purchased consumer products) tend to produce poor fits with individual behavior. Yet, in spite of the low Rs, these regressions often point to useful bases for segmentation. For example, Bass, Tigert, and Lonsdale (1968) found significant differences in product category usage based on demographics such as age and income (Table 13–18). Similar results were found by Assael and Roscoe (1976) in segmenting the market of long-distance phone expenditures. Tollefson and Lessig (1978) suggest segments should be formed based on response to marketing mix variables. A more elegant form of criterion-based segmentation is to first assess the way individual customers value

TABLE 18–1 Analytical Methods for Examining Customer Differences

Identifying relations among two variables:
- Cross-tabs (categorical variables).
- Correlations (continuous variables).

Predicting a criterion variable based on several other variables:
- ANOVA.
- Regression.
- Discriminant analysis.
- AID (Automatic Interaction Detector).

Simplifying a database:
- Factor analysis: identifying redundant variables.
- Cluster analysis: forming segments.
- Multidimensional scaling: graphically representing a number of alternatives on a small number of dimensions.

different attributes of the product (e.g., through a constant-sum assessment of attribute importance or by conjoint analysis). Clusters are then formed based on these values. As an example of this, Elrod and Winer (1982) grouped customers based on their relative responses to price changes estimated from individual level regressions.

NEW PRODUCTS

The distinction between new and existing products is not as obvious as it appears to be. Part of the confusion has to do with perspective: If Bernie C. formed a detergent company, the detergent would be a new product for him, hardly the case for Proctor and Gamble. There are also degrees of newness: Is another toothpaste with fluoride really a new product? In fact, it is safe to say that the vast majority of so-called new products are really new brands and not new in a technological sense at all. Nonetheless, tradition dictates defining new brands as new and, hence, this section will focus on new brands at least as much as really new products.

Idea Generation

The first stage in the development of a new product is idea generation. Many ideas appear as intuitive leaps. Some ideas are the result of technological or R & D breakthroughs (e.g., Teflon). Others are brought by outsiders. When a company is under a deadline to come up with a new idea, however, serendipity cannot be relied on. Four major approaches are available for generating ideas:

1. Focus groups.
2. Brainstorming.
3. Examining customer complaints.
4. Attribute-based analysis.

Of these approaches, only the last requires much analytical skill. The notion of designing products which satisfy particular consumer wants has been called *benefit segmentation* (Kuehn and Day, 1962; Haley, 1968). Sometimes this involves geometric mapping procedures, such as multidimensional scaling.

Concept Tests

Concept tests are initial screens of consumer reactions to new product concepts. The purposes of a concept test are to (*a*) choose the most promising from a set of alternatives, (*b*) get an initial notion of the commercial prospects of a concept, (*c*) find out who is most interested in the concept, and (*d*) indicate what direction further development work should take. Samples are often convenience oriented. Common sample sources include community groups, employees, and central locations (shopping centers).

The most common approach is to present consumers with a verbal/written statement of the product idea and then record their reactions. Recently, many researchers have chosen to also include physical mockups and advertising statements in the concept test. (These are really prototype or prototype/concept tests.) The data gathered are both diagnostic (why do you like/not like the product?) and predictive (would you buy it if it cost $_____?). Including a concrete "would you buy" question is crucial if the results are to be at all useful predictively. The data collection procedures fall into the following three major categories:

Surveys. Surveys are useful for getting large samples for projection purposes. On the other hand, it is often difficult to properly convey a concept in a survey, especially an impersonal one. Some different mail concept tests taken from an NFO brochure are shown in Appendix 18–A.

Focus Groups. Focus groups' strength is their diagnostic power, in that they can be used to get detailed discussions of various aspects of the concept. As predictors of actual sales, they are fairly inaccurate due to their small sample sizes.

Demonstrations. A popular way to present a concept is to gather a group of consumers, present them with a "story" about the new product, and record their reaction. Questions asked are typically related to:

1. Do they understand the concept?
2. Do they believe the concept?
3. Is the concept different from other products in an important way?
4. Is the difference beneficial?
5. Do they like or dislike the concept and why?
6. What could be done to make the product more acceptable?
7. How would they like to see the product (color, size, etc.)?
8. Would they buy it?
9. What price would they expect to pay for it?
10. What would their usage be in terms of volume, purpose, source of purchase, and so forth?

Actually, concept tests themselves vary. The most basic concept test is a concept screening test where many concepts are described briefly and subjects are asked for an overall evaluation (e.g., intention to buy). These tests are used to reduce the concepts under consideration to a manageable number. Next, concept generation tests (often involving focus groups) are used to refine the concept statements. This is typically followed by concept evaluation tests. These tests are based on larger samples and attempt to quantitatively assess demand for the concept based on samples of 200 to 300. These tests are typically done competitively, in the sense that other new concepts and/or existing products are also evaluated at the same time. For a more complete discussion of concept tests, see Moore (1982).

Product Use Tests

This type of research consists of physically producing the product[1] and then getting consumers to use it. The purpose of a product test is to (*a*) uncover product shortcomings, (*b*) evaluate commercial prospects, (*c*) evaluate alternative formulations, (*d*) uncover the appeal of the product to various market segments, and (*e*) if lucky, to gain ideas for other elements of the marketing program. Such tests may be either branded (best for estimating sales) or unbranded/blind (best for focusing directly on physical formulation).

---

[1] Note that the product used in this phase is typically specially produced and may not match the quality of the product under mass production. For example, Knorr soup product test samples were produced in Europe, while the actual mass-produced product was made in a new computerized plant in Argo, Illinois, which produced a product of different quality. Hence, the success or failure of the test product does not necessarily imply success or failure of the actual product.

There are three major types of product use tests. Initially such tests are usually conducted with small samples (often using convenience samples, such as employees). These initial tests are diagnostic and are directed toward eliminating serious problems with the product (e.g., the jar won't fit in the door of a refrigerator), as well as getting a rough idea of how good it is vis-à-vis competitive products. This phase also allows the company to find out how the product is actually used and, potentially, to change the target appeal. Employee testing is commonly used in connection with food products.

The second type of use test includes a limited time horizon forced trial situation where customers are given the product to use and asked for their reactions to it. At the end, a simulated purchase occasion is also used. This may consist of a hypothetical "would you buy" type question or, better, an actual choice situation, where the customer either chooses one of a set of products including the new product (usually at a reduced price) or simply chooses to "buy" or not buy the new product. To get a result which is meaningful, many researchers tend to use a stratified sample. The strata are usually either product category usage rate (heavy, medium, light, none) or brand usually used. This stratification ensures adequate sample size to predict the effect of the product on the key market segments.

The most elaborate form of product use test requires placement of the product in homes for an extended period. For packaged goods, this is usually a period of about two months. The advantage of this extended period is that the results allow for both the wear-out of initial expectations and the development of problems which only manifest themselves over time (e.g., food which goes stale). Subjects are required to complete before and after questionnaires, as well as maintain a diary of actual use of the new and competitive products over the period of the test. Here again, the inclusion at the end of the test of an actual choice situation helps to give the results a bottom-line orientation.

Preference Tests

The best known preference tests are the taste tests conducted for food products. Here the purpose is to experiment with alternative formulations which are supposed to (*a*) taste better or (*b*) cut costs. The problem is greatly complicated by carryover effects (does the second beer ever taste as good as the first?) and the lack of discriminatory power for most consumers (try to tell Schlitz from Bud in a blind test). Taste tests fall into several categories:

Monadic. The respondent uses one product once and then evaluates it.

Successive monadic. The respondent uses several products sequentially and rates each one.

Paired comparison. Respondents use two products at the same occasion and then indicate which they prefer.

Replicated comparisons. To get a better fix on consumers' ability to discriminate and their preference, it is common to replicate the paired test. It is also possible to use groups of three products—called *triangles* or *triads* where two of the products are identical—to better estimate the ability of consumers to discriminate. To see why a replicated test is useful, consider the following situation (Johnson).

A set of subjects is presented with a pair of products (A and B) on two different occasions. We will assume there are three kinds of consumers:

1. Those who can tell the difference and prefer A.
2. Those who can tell the difference and prefer B.
3. Those who cannot distinguish among A and B and who randomly indicate preference.

The key is to estimate these three fractions. First we must observe the actual reported preference table:

Second Preference	*First Preference*	
	A	*B*
A	48%	15%
B	13	24

The naive interpretation is that 48 percent prefer A (since they consistently choose it) and 24 percent prefer B. As we will see, however, this is a bad estimate. Returning to the three kinds of consumers, we have the conditional probabilities of test result given true consumer preference shown in Table 18–2. Hence, the expressed percent is a function of true preference as follows:

$$\%AA_e = \%A_t + \tfrac{1}{4}(\%\text{ Neither}_t)$$

$$\%BB_e = \%B_t + \tfrac{1}{4}(\%\text{ Neither}_t)$$

$$\%\text{Neither}_e = \tfrac{1}{2}(\%\text{ Neither}_t)$$

TABLE 18–2 Probability of Expressed Preference, Given True Preference

"True" Consumer Preference	*Expressed Preference*		
	AA	*BB*	*AB, BA (neither)*
A	1	0	0
B	0	1	0
Neither	$\frac{1}{4}$	$\frac{1}{4}$	$\frac{1}{2}$

where

$\%AA_e$ = the expressed percent who choose A both times.

$\%A_t$ = true percent who prefer A

Solving this for the true fractions gives:

$$\%\text{Neither}_t = 2(\%\text{Neither}_e)$$

$$\%A_t = \%AA_e - \tfrac{1}{4}(\%\text{Neither}_t)$$

$$\%B_t = \%BB_e - \tfrac{1}{4}(\%\text{Neither}_t)$$

For our example, we get:

$$\%\text{Neither}_t = 2(13\% + 15\%) = 56\%$$

$$\%A_t = 48\% - \tfrac{1}{4}(56\%) = 34\%$$

$$\%B_t = 24\% - \tfrac{1}{4}(56\%) = 10\%$$

The correct interpretation of the results is thus (*a*) most people don't perceive a difference and (*b*) B is in trouble. For a discussion of the interpretation of triangle tests, see Morrison (1981); Buchanan and Morrison (1985); and Buchanan, Givon, and Goldman (1987).

Factor Tests. Factor tests involve separately testing for the effect of varying elements of the marketing program, such as price, advertising copy, and so forth. These tests are conducted in essentially the same way for new products as they are for existing products. Most such tests are conducted in central locations or labs and involve exposing consumers to different treatments and seeing how they respond.

One of the most interesting ways to do this is through a controlled store test (Hardin, 1966). This entails testing a product in an actual store, in which complete control over price, facings, point-of-purchase displays, and so forth is maintained (several suppliers offer these services). As such, this procedure falls somewhere between a lab and field experiment in both realism and cost. This method is especially useful in testing packaging, pricing, facings, and point-of-purchase displays.

Market Tests. The ultimate in realism is a market test. The purpose of such a test is (*a*) to predict sales and profits from a major product launch and (*b*) to "practice up" so marketing, distribution, and production skills are developed before entering full-scale operations. Projections are typically made for both share and actual sales, appropriately adjusted to national levels. The major sources of concern are as follows:

1. Trial rate.
2. Repeat rate (for frequently purchased goods).
3. Usage rate/number bought per customer.

In addition, awareness, attitudes, and distribution are usually monitored. Given these measures, a projected sales estimate can be made.

In designing a market test, it is important to clearly delineate what information is to be gathered and why before proceeding. Several decisions must be made.

Action standards. Standards for evaluating the results should be set up in advance. These standards should specify when the various possible decisions (e.g., stop the test, continue the test, revamp the product, go national) will be implemented.

Where. The choice of where to test market is a serious problem. Most market tests are done in two to three cities. (This further emphasizes that the "test" is not designed to try out numerous strategies—at most two to three alternatives can be used.) Cities are chosen on the basis of representativeness of the population, the ability of the firm to gain distribution and media exposure in the area, and availability of good research suppliers in the area. Also, areas which are self-contained in terms of media (especially TV) are preferred. The result is that certain medium-sized cities are often chosen, such as Syracuse, New York; Fresno, California; and Fort Wayne, Indiana.

What to do? The best test market designers are careful to make the effort in the area proportional to what would reasonably be expected in a national launch. Notice here we mean effort and not budget. If a city has particularly expensive (the usual case, when buying spot TV ads) or inexpensive media costs, allocating budget on a population basis would result in a media schedule which had either too few or too many exposures. The goal is to make distribution, price to consumers (price breaks to retailers and wholesalers are needed to gain distribution), and so forth as representative as possible. What typically happens, however, is that the effort afforded the product (including the people talent) is somewhat greater than the comparable national effort.

How long? The question of how long to run a test is not easily answered. Obviously, a longer run gives more information; but it also costs more and gives competitors more time to formulate a counterattack. Consumer packaged goods typically stay in test markets between 6 and 12 months. The reason for the length of the test market is to include several purchase cycles, so repeat usage as well as trial can be accurately assessed. (It is not uncommon for a product to gain a big initial share, due to trial, and then lose share as repeat business fails to live up to trial.)

How much? For a consumer-packaged good, test marketing costs run close to $1 million. Advertising and promotion typically account for 65 to 70 percent of the budget, with the rest of the budget divided between information gathering and analysis and miscellaneous administrative and other expenses.

Information gathering. During a test market, a variety of information is gathered, most of it related to actual sales. In monitoring sales, it is important to recognize that a large percentage of first-year factory sales (e.g., 30 percent) represent a one-time stocking up by the channels of distribution, and not sales to final consumers. The three major data sources are (*a*) actual sales (typically at least 40 stores per area) plus distribution, promotion, and so forth; (*b*) surveys which measure awareness, attitude, and so forth; and (*c*) panels which report actual purchase and allow monitoring of trial and repeat rates.

Sales Forecasting

Forecasting sales from a test market is always difficult. (If it weren't, all products which went national after test marketing would succeed.) However, at least for frequently purchased consumer products, some fairly widely used procedures have been developed. It is possible to simply wait and see at what levels sales stabilize. Unfortunately, this takes a fairly long period (up to two years) and, hence, a lot of money. Therefore, what is really desired is an early warning system which forecasts the eventual sales level of a new product before it is attained. Assuming such a new product is really a new brand which fits into an existing product category, three basic factors are the keys to eventual sales:

1. The eventual proportion of consumers who will try the product.
2. The proportion of triers who remain with the brand.
3. The usage rate of the product category among the eventual users.

In fact, the repeat rate alone is often a good predictor of success, as Figure 18–2, based on 120 products studied by NPD, demonstrates.

A large number of models exist which attempt to project these three factors early in the introduction.

Fourt-Woodlock. The earliest of the new product models which attained widespread interest was that of Fourt and Woodlock (1960). This model was intended to predict the market success of grocery products.

The first stage in the model attempts to predict penetration (eventual level of trial). It assumes that (*a*) there is an eventual penetration level (P)

FIGURE 18–2

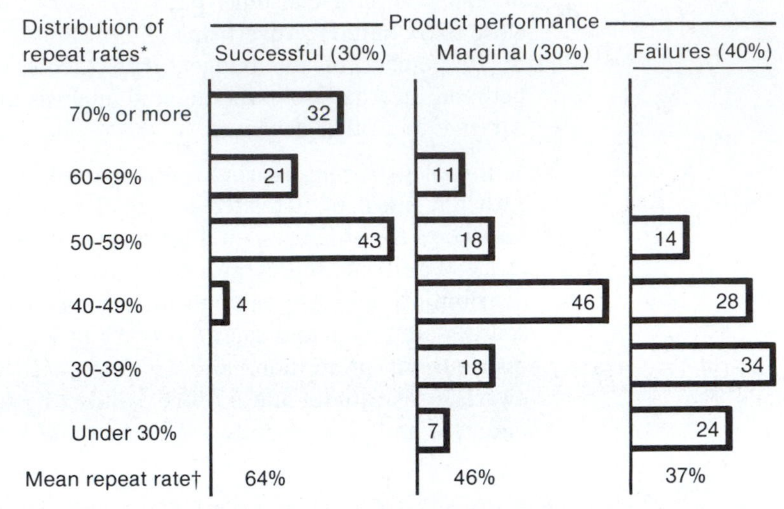

* Based upon 120 new products.
†Percent of triers who will ever repeat.

Source: "We Make the Answers to Your Marketing Questions Perfectly Clear." New York: NPD Research, 1982.

and that (*b*) each period some percentage of the nonbuyers who eventually will buy the product buy it. The second stage in this model focuses on repeat purchase. Specifically, it focuses on the repeat ratios, the portion of initial buyers who repeat purchase once (N_1/N_F), the portion of first repeat purchasers who repeat purchase a second time (N_2/N_1), and so forth. This stage is used for forecasting sales in the next period as the sum of new buyers plus first repeaters plus second repeaters, and so forth. This model has proved to be somewhat cumbersome in application. It also assumes that the market is constant in terms of advertising, distribution, pricing, and so forth, a very troublesome albeit useful assumption.

Parfitt–Collins. Parfitt and Collins (1968) produced a simpler model than Fourt and Woodlock. Their approach focuses on predicting market share, rather than actual sales. The three key elements in using their model are (*a*) to estimate eventual penetration (P), (*b*) to estimate the ultimate share of their purchases that buyers of the new brand will make of the new brand (M), and (*c*) to estimate the relative product category usage rate of buyers of the new brand (U). The estimated eventual share is, thus, simply the product $P \cdot M \cdot U$.

Eventual penetration is usually estimated by simply plotting the fraction who have bought the product over time and graphically eyeballing the eventual result (Figure 18–3). Alternatively, the saturation level can be estimated by running a regression of cumulative sales:

$$S(t) = a + be^{-t}$$

Similarly, eventual repeat rate can be deduced graphically (Figure 18–4). Finally, the relative product category usage rate of buyers of the new brand is obtained by either using purchase panel data to estimate it (the usual way) or judgmentally. Assuming this were .8 (eventual users of the product buy 80 percent as much as an average product category user), we would estimate the ultimate share to be $P \cdot M \cdot U$ = (45 percent)(15 percent)(.8) = 5.4 percent.

N. W. Ayer. Both the Fourt-Woodlock and Parfitt-Collins approaches are based on observing repeat purchasing from panel data. The Ayer model, on the other hand, is based on the notion that the adoption of a product follows a series of stages. More specifically, three main stages are used: awareness, initial/trial purchase, and repeat purchase/loyalty. Using data from several product introductions, this model estimated the relationship between marketing variables and these three variables. This was done by means of three regressions:

$$
\begin{aligned}
\text{Awareness} = {} & a_1 + b_{11}\,(\text{product positioning}) \\
& + b_{12}\sqrt{(\text{media impressions})(\text{copy execution})} \\
& + b_{13}(\text{ad message containing consumer promotions}) \\
& + b_{14}(\text{category interest}) + e_1 \\
\text{Initial purchase} = {} & a_2 + b_{21}(\text{estimated awareness}) \\
& + b_{22}\{(\text{distribution})(\text{packaging})\} \\
& + b_{23}(\text{if a family brand}) \\
& + b_{24}(\text{consumer promotion}) \\
& + b_{25}(\text{satisfaction with product samples}) \\
& + b_{26}(\text{category usage}) + e_2 \\
\text{Repeat purchase} = {} & f(\text{initial purchase, relative price, product satisfaction,} \\
& \text{purchase frequency})
\end{aligned}
$$

Source: Henry Claycamp and Lucien Liddy, "Prediction of New Product Performance: An Analytical Approach." Adapted from *Journal of Marketing Research*, published by the American Marketing Association, 4 (November 1969), p. 416.

By inputting data to the estimated model, sales projections can be derived. Notice that many of the variables are marketing variables, which is,

FIGURE 18–3 Typical Penetration for New Brand over Time

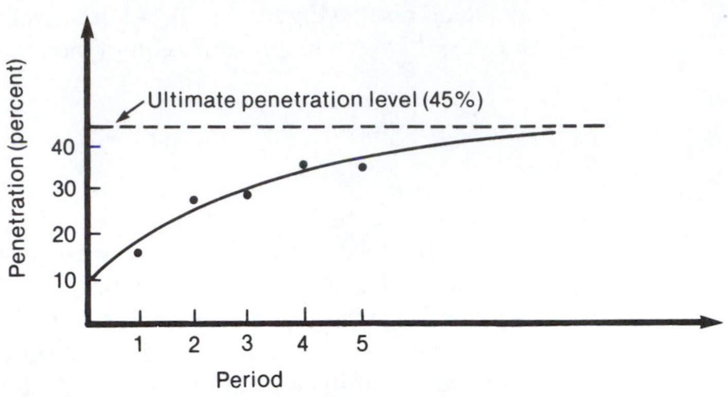

in some sense, an improvement over the previous models. Notice also, however, that many of these variables (e.g., copy execution) must be subjectively estimated; hence, making the results potentially more subject to researcher bias (Claycamp and Liddy, 1969).

Extensions of Parfitt–Collins. The NEWS Model (Pringle, Wilson, and Brody, 1982) is ad agency BBD & O's model for predicting sales of a new consumer product. As such, it competes with Assmus's (1975) NEW-PROD and Blattberg and Golanty's (1978) TRACKER (used by the Leo Burnett advertising agency). These models use consumer survey data and explicitly include the impact of controllable marketing variables, mainly focusing on

FIGURE 18–4 Typical Repeat Rate for New Brand over Time

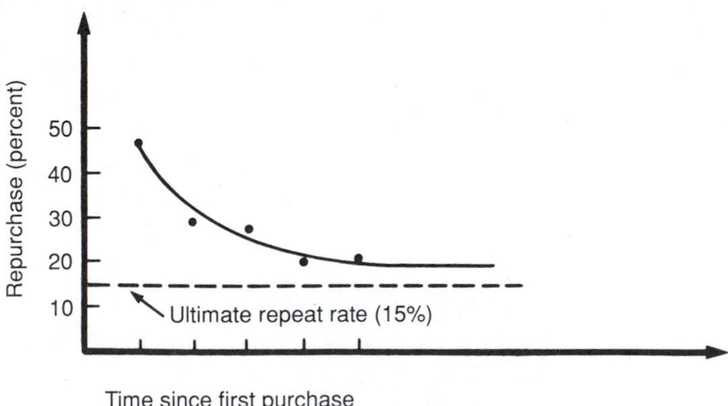

advertising as it impacts awareness and trial. As such, they are extensions of the Parfitt–Collins approach.

The awareness and trial stages of the TRACKER model are:

Awareness:

$$\ln\left(\frac{1 - A_t}{1 - A_{t-1}}\right) = a - bG_t$$

where

A_t = cumulative awareness in period t.
G_t = gross rating points in period t.

Trial:

$$T_t - T_{t-1} = \alpha(A_t - A_{t-1}) + \beta(A_{t-1} - T_{t-1})$$

where

T_t = cumulative trial in period t.

The NEWS Model awareness stage breaks apart awareness due to advertising and promotion. Similarly, the trial model is also different from TRACKER. Experience with the model has been quite good, with predicted share within 1 percent of actual share, when test market data are used as input, and within 2 percent, when only pretest market data are used (Pringle, Wilson, and Brody, 1982).

Laboratory experiment based models. Silk and Urban's (1978) ASSESOR, Burke's BASES, and Blackburn and Clancy's (1980) LITMUS models use pretest market data to estimate sales. Specifically, ASSESOR uses a simulated shopping trip following advertising exposure and an in-home use period. In most cases the market share estimates are within one share point of the share observed in the market. With LITMUS, movement from awareness to trial and trial to repeat is estimated based on a laboratory experiment. These are, not surprisingly, both less expensive and somewhat less reliable than models based on actual market experience. They have grown substantially in popularity during the 1980s.

Other Models. A variety of other models exist for forecasting new product sales, including Sprinter (Urban, 1970) and those of Massy (1969), Ehrenberg (1972), and Eskin (1973). A summary of many of these models is available in Kotler (1971), Urban and Hauser (1980), Wind and Mahajan (1981), Narasimhan and Sen (1983), and Shocker and Hall (1986).

In summary, test marketing is a major undertaking, which entails both time and money expenses as well as a loss of surprise. Given notice of a test market, a competitor will often react by (a) trying to protect sales in the test market area by advertising or promotional programs, which also serve to confuse the interpretation of the test market; (b) doing whatever possible to mess up the results of the test; and (c) planning a counteroffensive for a possible national launch. Also, there are many causes where test marketing is not practical. For example, any major durable where extensive tooling is required is not suitable for test marketing. For these and other reasons, many researchers and companies use less costly and more controlled alternatives to test marketing (Klompmaker, Hughes, and Haley, 1976).

SUMMARY

Figure 18–5 depicts a chronology for research through the development of a new product. The out-of-pocket costs increase as the stages unfold, with major out-of-pocket costs involved in product development for a product test (especially for high technology products), test marketing, and national launching. In some companies, these or similar steps must be followed in a lock-step manner, with research required at each step before going ahead to

FIGURE 18–5 Sequential New Product Evaluation

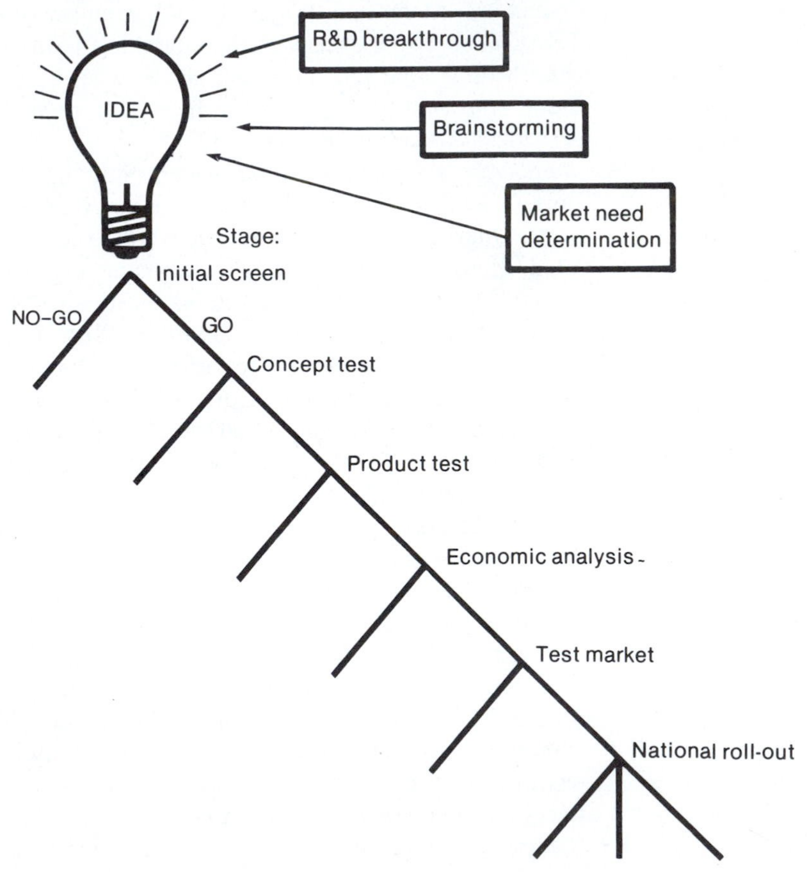

the next. In other companies, the steps are much more likely to be reordered, combined, or eliminated. What is most important, therefore, is to follow a procedure which (*a*) makes sense and (*b*) is tied to some bench mark so that comparative judgments can be made.

PROBLEMS

1. A large manufacturer, Ajax, Inc., is considering the average price levels ($1.00, $1.10, and $1.20) for a product which presently sells for $1.10. Particularly troublesome is the response of the single large competitor, Acme Corporation. It is not known whether it will follow the price change or not. The problem is made more troublesome by the presence of a single large customer, who now buys over half of both Ajax and Acme production of this particular product. Discuss a *methodology* for selecting the best price level for Ajax. Be specific about how you would use this methodology at Ajax. Exactly what would you *do* if you were at Ajax?
2. What are the major decisions which face the product manager of a well-established brand and what research might help him or her make each of the decisions?
3. Assume I ran a repeat pair test on two different formulations of Zonko, an alcoholic beverage where formula A was 70 proof and formula B was 100 proof (the old formula). The results were as follows:

Preferred Second Time	*Preferred First Time*	
	A	*B*
A	22%	14%
B	12	52

   Interpret statistically and managerially.
4. How would you go about selecting a magazine in which to advertise:
   a. A specialty fashion item.
   b. Catsup.
   c. A new car.
   d. A machine tool.
   e. A copying machine.
5. Assume sales of a new product followed the following pattern:

	Monthly Period						
	1	*2*	*3*	*4*	*5*	*6*	*7*
Percent who have tried (panel data)	18	19	23	24	27	33	34
Share among past triers (panel data)	75	59	44	36	37	35	30
Share (audit data)	1.2	1.9	3.7	3.6	3.9	4.1	3.8

What is your projection for eventual share, and what are the assumptions of this projection?

6. Assume you were in charge of monitoring the progress of a new convenience food.
   a. What would you monitor?
   b. How would you combine the measures in a coherent systems framework?
7. Consider the screening of new product ideas. Two product ideas, A and B, were evaluated using six criteria:

Decision Criterion	*Relative Weight*	*Committee's Average Rating 5 = Very Good 1 = Very Poor* A	B	*Minimum Rating Acceptable*
Sales volume	.30	4.2	3.2	3.5
Profit objective	.20	3.5	4.0	3
Insulation from competition	.15	2.3	2.6	3
Availability of capital	.15	5.0	4.0	4
Availability of raw materials	.10	4.3	2.8	4
Effect on present products	.10	3.0	3.5	2
	1.00			

For each product idea, compute the quantity:

$$S = \Sigma \text{ relative weight} \times \text{Average rating}$$

Which product ideas are accepted under the following rules?

a. Accept if S is greater than 3.
b. Accept if the product idea achieves the minimum acceptable rating on *all* criteria.
c. Accept if the product idea achieves the minimum acceptable rating on four or more criteria.
d. What other decision rules can you think of?
e. Which decision method is better?
f. What other factors are ignored in trying to put numbers in the decision process?

8. HPG, Inc., is planning to market test a new frozen toaster product: Baconeggs. Baconeggs is an all-synthetic textured vegetable protein (largely soybeans) which is sold frozen, in a sealed aluminum foil package. The homemaker places the frozen package in the toaster to warm, then removes the product from the aluminum foil package to

serve. The product then looks and tastes like scrambled eggs with two strips of (fake) bacon on top. The product has succeeded (more or less) in a long succession of concept, product, and advertising tests, and now HPG will market test the item in Fort Wayne, Indiana. Describe the market test methodology. Exactly what data will you collect? How will you collect it? How (specifically) will you analyze it? What decisions are you trying to make for next year's annual marketing plan which will be facilitated by these analyses?

9. In market research home tests of new products, two waves of trials are often done on the same sample of households. For example, each household may be given two plain, numbered boxes of different detergents and asked to choose its favorite after using both boxes. These same households are then given two more boxes, numbered differently but containing the same products, as on the first trial. You have been asked to interpret results from two such tests, each with a sample of 1,000 people.

	Trial 1		
Trial 2	*No. Households Choosing Brand A*	*No. Households Choosing Brand B*	*Total*
No. households choosing brand A	280	220	500
No. households choosing brand B	260	240	500
Total	540	460	1,000

(The table is read as follows: 280 people chose brand A on both trials, 240 chose B both times, 260 chose A first, then B; and 220 chose B first and then A.)

a. Your supervisor wants to know whether consumers can discriminate clearly between A and B. What do you conclude and why? (Warning—think carefully about what you want to test!)

b. Suppose a pound of B costs twice as much to manufacture as a pound of A. What should management do? Why?

BIBLIOGRAPHY

Assael, Henry, and A. Marvin Roscoe, Jr. "Approaches to Market Segmentation Analysis." *Journal of Marketing* 40 (October 1976), pp. 67–76.

Assmus, Gert. "NEWPROD: The Design and Implementation of a New Product Model." *Journal of Marketing* 39 (January 1975), pp. 16–23.

Assmus, Gert; John U. Farley; and Donald R. Lehmann. "How Advertising Affects Sales: Meta-Analysis of Econometric Results." *Journal of Marketing Research* 21 (February 1984), pp. 65–74.

Bass, Frank M. "A Simultaneous Regression Study of Advertising and Sales of Cigarettes." *Journal of Marketing Research* 6 (August 1969), pp. 291–300.

Bass, Frank M., and Darral G. Clarke. "Testing Distributed Lag Models of Advertising Effect." *Journal of Marketing Research* 9 (August 1972), pp. 298–308.

Bass, Frank M.; Douglas J. Tigert; and Ronald T. Lonsdale. "Market Segmentation—Group versus Individual Behavior." *Journal of Marketing Research* 5 (August 1968), pp. 264–70.

Beckwith, Neil E. "Multivariate Analysis of Sales Response of Competing Brands to Advertising." *Journal of Marketing Research* 9 (May 1972), pp. 168–76.

Blattberg, Robert, and John Golanty. "TRACKER: An Early Test Market Forecasting and Diagnostic Model for New Product Planning." *Journal of Marketing Research* 15 (May 1978), pp. 192–202.

Blackburn, Joseph D., and Kevin J. Clancy. "LITMUS: A New Product Planning Model." In *Proceedings: Market Measurement and Analysis*, ed. Robert P. Leone. Providence, R.I.: Institute of Management Sciences, 1980, pp. 182–93.

Buchanan, Bruce; Moshe Givon; and Arieh Goldman. "Measurement of Discrimination Ability in Taste Tests: An Empirical Investigation." *Journal of Marketing Research* 24 (May 1987), pp. 154–63.

Buchanan, Bruce S., and Donald G. Morrison. "Measuring Simple Preferences: An Approach to Blind, Forced Choice Product Testing." *Marketing Science* 4 (Spring 1985), pp. 93–109.

Clarke, Darral G. "Econometric Measurement of the Duration of Advertising Effect on Sales." *Journal of Marketing Research* 13 (November 1976), pp. 345–57.

Claycamp, Henry J., and Lucien E. Liddy. "Prediction of New Product Performance: An Analytical Approach." *Journal of Marketing Research* 4 (November 1969), pp. 414–20.

Dhalla, Nairman K. "Assessing the Long-Term Value of Advertising." *Harvard Business Review* 56 (January–February, 1978), pp. 87–95.

Ehrenberg, A. S. C. *Repeat-Buying: Theory and Application*. New York: North-Holland, 1972.

Elrod, Terry, and Russell S. Winer. "An Empirical Evaluation of Aggregation Approaches for Developing Market Segments." *Journal of Marketing* 46 (Fall 1982), pp. 65–74.

Eskin, Gerald J. "Dynamic Forecasts of New Product Demand Using a Depth of Repeat Model." *Journal of Marketing Research* 10 (May 1973), pp. 115–19.

Fourt, Louis A., and Joseph W. Woodlock. "Early Prediction of Market Success for New Grocery Products." *Journal of Marketing* 25 (October 1960), pp. 31–38.

Haley, R. I. "Benefit Segmentation: A Decision-Oriented Research Tool." *Journal of Marketing* 32 (July 1968), pp. 30–35.

Hardin, David K. "A New Approach to Test Marketing." *Journal of Marketing* 31 (October 1966), pp. 28–31.

Johnson, Richard M. "Simultaneous Measurement of Discrimination and Preference." Chicago: Market Facts (no date).

Klompmaker, Jay E.; G. David Hughes; and Russell I. Haley. "Test Marketing in New Product Development." *Harvard Business Review* 54 (May–June 1976), pp. 128–38.

Kotler, Philip. *Marketing Decision Making: A Model Building Approach*. New York: Holt, Rinehart & Winston, 1971.

Kuehn, Alfred A., and Ralph Day. "Strategy of Product Quality." *Harvard Business Review* 40 (November–December 1962), pp. 100–10.

Little, John D. C., and Leonard M. Lodish. "A Media Planning Calculus." *Operations Research* 17 (January–February 1969), pp. 1–35.

Mahajan, Vijay, and Eitan Muller. "Innovation Diffusion and New Product Growth Models in Marketing." *Journal of Marketing* 43 (Fall 1979), pp. 55–68.

Massy, William F. "Forecasting the Demand for New Convenience Products." *Journal of Marketing Research* 6 (November 1969), pp. 405–12.

Massy, William F.; Ronald E. Frank; and Yoram Wind. *Market Segmentation*. Englewood Cliffs, N.J.: Prentice-Hall, 1972.

Moore, William L. "Concept Testing." *Journal of Business Research* 10 (1982), pp. 279–94.

Morrison, Donald G. "Triangle Taste Tests: Are the Subjects Who Respond Correctly Lucky or Good?" *Journal of Marketing* 45 (Summer 1981), pp. 111–19.

Narasimhan, Chakravarthi, and Subrata K. Sen. "New Product Models for Test Market Data." *Journal of Marketing* 47 (Winter 1983), pp. 11–24.

Palda, Kristian S. *The Measurement of Cumulative Advertising Effects*. Englewood Cliffs, N.J.: Prentice-Hall, 1964.

Parfitt, J. H., and B. J. K. Collins. "Use of Consumer Panels for Brand-Share Prediction." *Journal of Marketing Research* 5 (May 1968), pp. 131–45.

Parsons, Leonard J. "The Product Life Cycle and Time-Varying Advertising Elasticities." *Journal of Marketing Research* 12 (November 1975), pp. 476–80.

Pessemier, Edgar A. *Product Management*. New York: John Wiley & Sons, 1977.

Prasad, V. Kanti, and L. Winston Ring. "Measuring Sales Effects of Some Marketing Mix Variables and Their Interactions." *Journal of Marketing Research* 13 (November 1976), pp. 391–96.

Pringle, Lewis G.; R. Dale Wilson; and Edward I. Brody. "News: A Decision-Oriented Model for New Product Analysis and Forecasting." *Marketing Science* 1 (Winter 1982), pp. 1–29.

Shocker, Alan D. and William G. Hall, "Pretest Market Models: A Critical Evaluation", *Journal of Product Innovation Management*, 3, (1986), pp. 86–107.

Shocker, Alan D., and V. Srinivasan. "Multiattribute Approaches for Product Concept Evaluation and Generation: A Critical Review." *Journal of Marketing Research* 16 (May 1979), pp. 159–80.

Silk, Alvin J., and Glen L. Urban. "Pre-Test Market Evaluation of New Packaged Goods: A Model and Measurement Methodology." *Journal of Marketing Research* 15 (May 1978), pp. 171–91.

Tollefson, John O., and V. Parker Lessig. "Aggregation Criteria in Normative Market Segmentation Theory." *Journal of Marketing Research* 15 (August 1978), pp. 346–55.

Urban, Glen L. "Sprinter Mod. III: A Model for the Analysis of New Frequently Purchased Consumer Products." *Operations Research* 18 (September–October 1970), pp. 805–54.

Urban, Glen L., and John R. Hauser. *Design and Marketing of New Products*. Englewood Cliffs, N.J.: Prentice-Hall, 1980.

Vidale, M. L., and H. B. Wolfe. "An Operations-Research Study of Sales Response to Advertising." *Operations Research* 5 (June 1957), pp. 370–81.

"We Make the Answers to Your Marketing Questions Perfectly Clear." New York: NPD Research, 1982.

Wind, Yoram. *Product Policy*. Reading, Mass.: Addison-Wesley, 1982.

Wind, Yoram, and Vijay Mahajan. "A Reexamination of New Product Forecasting Models." In *The Changing Marketing Environment: New Theories and Applications*, ed. Kenneth Bernhardt, Ira Dolich, Michael Etzel, William Kehoe, Thomas Kinnear, William Perreault, Jr., and Kenneth Roering. Chicago: American Marketing Association, 1981, pp. 358–63.

Appendix 18–A

Sample Concept Test Formats*

*Source: National Family Opinion, Inc., *Concept Testing*, New York, 1975.

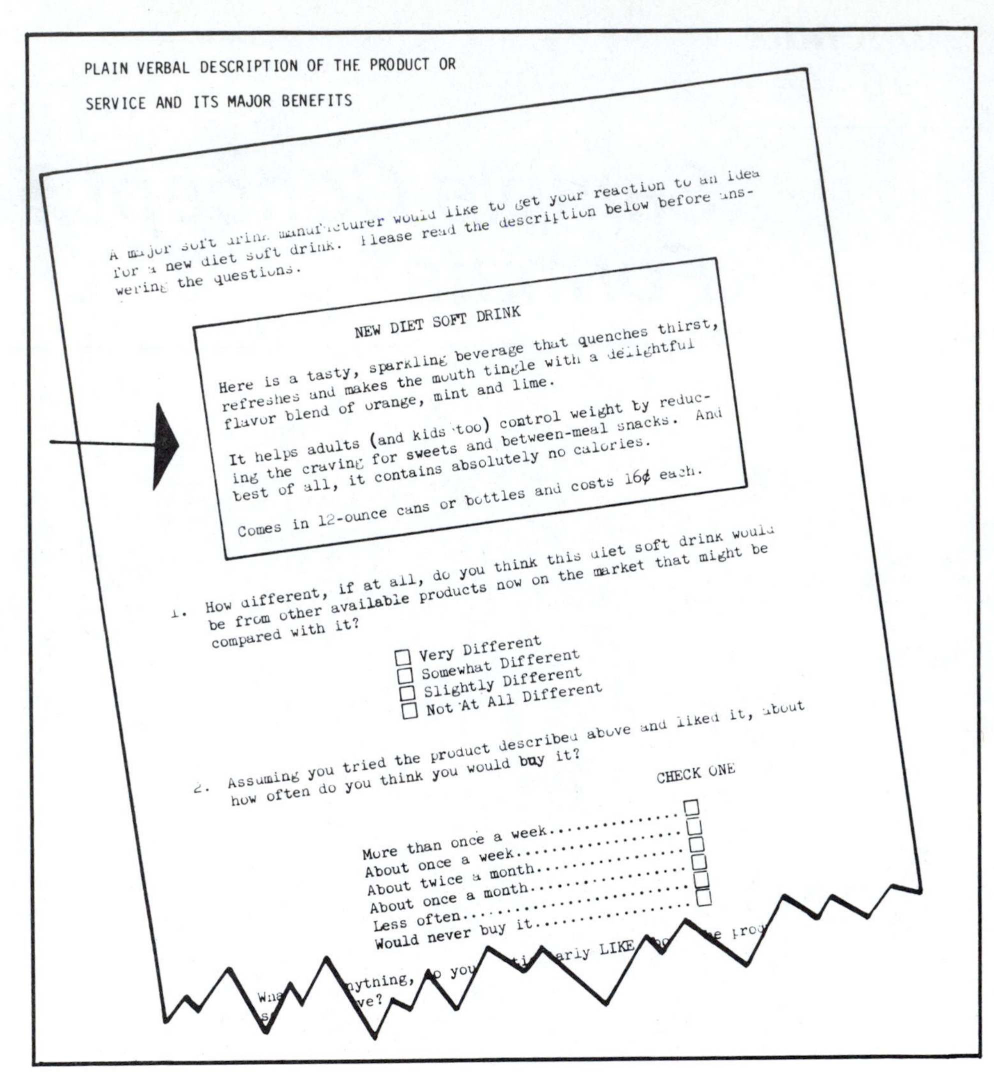
PLAIN VERBAL DESCRIPTION OF THE PRODUCT OR

SERVICE AND ITS MAJOR BENEFITS

A major soft drink manufacturer would like to get your reaction to an idea for a new diet soft drink. Please read the description below before answering the questions.

NEW DIET SOFT DRINK

Here is a tasty, sparkling beverage that quenches thirst, refreshes and makes the mouth tingle with a delightful flavor blend of orange, mint and lime.

It helps adults (and kids too) control weight by reducing the craving for sweets and between-meal snacks. And best of all, it contains absolutely no calories.

Comes in 12-ounce cans or bottles and costs 16¢ each.

1. How different, if at all, do you think this diet soft drink would be from other available products now on the market that might be compared with it?

☐ Very Different
☐ Somewhat Different
☐ Slightly Different
☐ Not At All Different

2. Assuming you tried the product described above and liked it, about how often do you think you would buy it?

CHECK ONE

More than once a week.................. ☐
About once a week...................... ☐
About twice a month.................... ☐
About once a month..................... ☐
Less often............................. ☐
Would never buy it..................... ☐

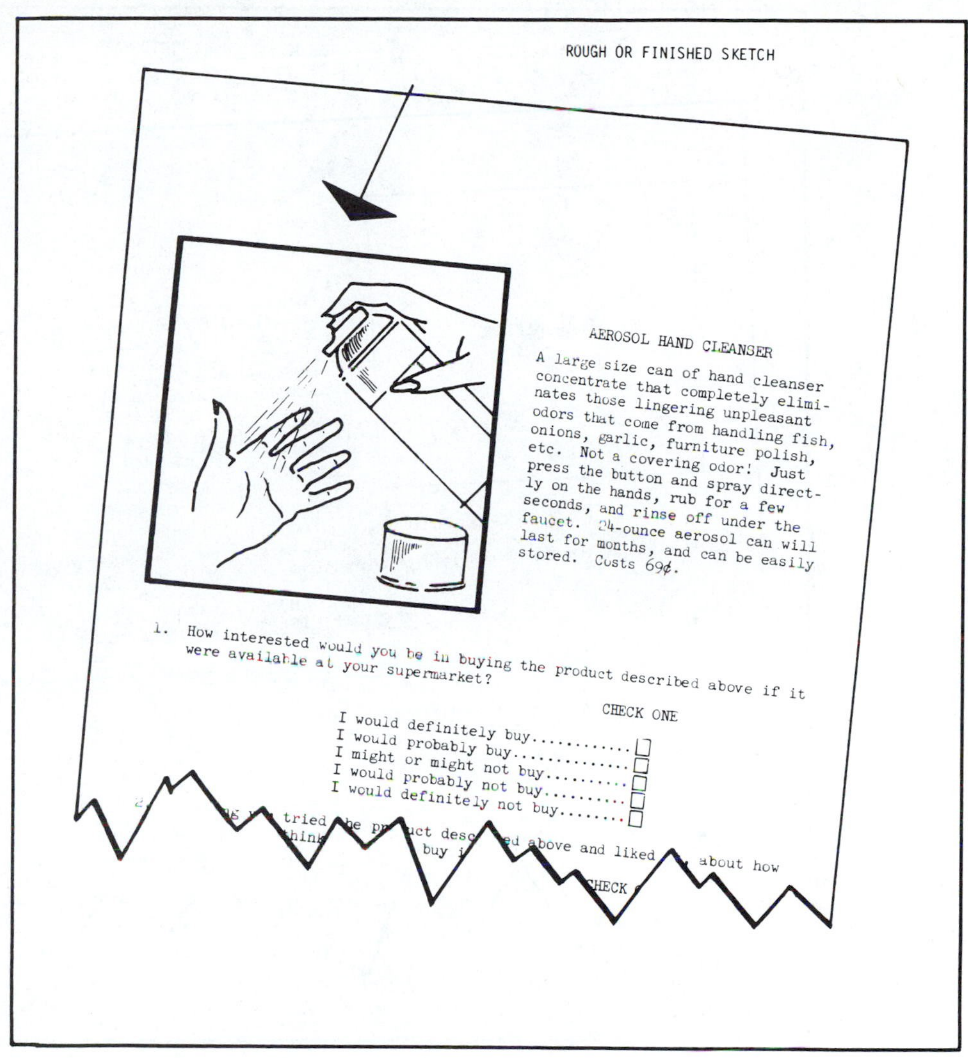
ROUGH OR FINISHED SKETCH
AEROSOL HAND CLEANSER
A large size can of hand cleanser concentrate that completely eliminates those lingering unpleasant odors that come from handling fish, onions, garlic, furniture polish, etc. Not a covering odor! Just press the button and spray directly on the hands, rub for a few seconds, and rinse off under the faucet. 24-ounce aerosol can will last for months, and can be easily stored. Costs 69¢.
1. How interested would you be in buying the product described above if it were available at your supermarket?
CHECK ONE
I would definitely buy..........
I would probably buy............
I might or might not buy.........
I would probably not buy.........
I would definitely not buy.......

COLOR SKETCH OR PHOTOGRAPH

COLOR HALFTONE

THE NEW TWO-SUITER

For college vacations. For pleasure trips. For business trips. It's made of a new expandable vinyl that actually breathes and stretches to accommodate the load. Room for two suits inside, incidentals in two outside pockets. Combination lock you set for yourself. 49½" x 13" x 8".

1. Based on what you have read above about this product, how would you compare the New Two-Suiter to conventional luggage in terms of:

	FAR SUPERIOR	MUCH BETTER	ABOUT THE SAME	NOT AS GOOD
Durability..................	☐	☐	☐	☐
Weather proof...............	☐	☐	☐	☐
Easy to carry...............	☐	☐	☐	☐
Appearance..................	☐	☐	☐	☐
Size........................	☐	☐	☐	☐

2. What are some of the things you like about the New Two-Suiter?

____

____

3. What are some of the things you do not like about the New Two-Suiter?

Chapter 19

Industrial Marketing Research

The area of industrial marketing is often overlooked in discussions of research. Yet industrial products constitute a far larger part of the economy than consumer goods. Here, industrial marketing is defined as marketing of a product or service to an intermediate customer. This broad definition means that industrial marketing includes not only such obvious examples as machine tools but computers, textbooks, and ethical drugs as well. Hence the first point to be made is that there is no such thing as "typical" industrial marketing.

TYPES OF INDUSTRIAL MARKETING

Industrial marketing can be broken into categories in several ways. One method of categorizing industrial products is based on the complexity of the result of buying the product from the buyer's point of view. Four categories have been identified (Lehmann and O'Shaughnessy, 1974):

1. Routine products, where both the technical performance features of the product and application procedures are known.
2. Procedural problem products, where the technical performance is known but application procedures need to be developed.
3. Performance problem products, where the technical performance of the product is unknown.

4. Political problem products, where the product is a major buy affecting many organization units and costing a lot of money and both technical performance and application procedures are unclear.

Numerous other bases exist for categorizing industrial products. Among these are the following:

1. Price.
2. Criticalness of the product to the overall operation and appearance of the system as a whole.
3. Distribution method (direct sales versus wholesaler).
4. Amount of custom engineering involved (standard versus special order products).
5. Number of key customers.
6. Expertise of purchasing agents (high, e.g., doctor, versus low, e.g., clerk).

Given certain combinations of these characteristics, an industrial good can be quite similar to a consumer good and, hence, the marketing and marketing research problems and methods become very similar (Figure 19–1). The point is that many consumer goods have characteristics similar to industrial goods. By considering the family as the customer, the analogy is even closer. The purchasing agent role is even repeated, in that whoever does the food shopping is really a purchasing agent for the household. Similarly, big decisions (houses, cars, etc.) tend to involve many family members (organizational units) in the decision process. The result of this similarity is that industrial marketing research can use many of the techniques and procedures of consumer marketing research.

Industrial marketing researchers can learn from consumer product marketing research, partly because consumer product marketing has had the benefit (albeit often a dubious one) of fancy techniques being routinely applied. There is a great reluctance on the part of many industrial marketers to believe that they have anything to learn from either consumer product marketers or academics. In fact, there is an amazing amount of defensiveness and resentment toward marketing researchers on the part of industrial marketers. Perhaps this defensiveness has something to do with the sales orientation of industrial marketing. Still, the defensiveness seems unfounded. In the first place, industrial marketing is in many ways superior to consumer marketing. It accounts for a larger share of GNP and pays at least as well as consumer marketing. Moreover, the products are, at least on an engineering level, more interesting than consumer products (somehow I find design of a computer or machine tool more interesting than design of a bar of soap). Still there tends to be a fairly provincial attitude that suggests consumer and industrial marketing are completely different. While there are differences, there are at least as many similarities.

FIGURE 19–1 Similarity of Consumer and Industrial Products

Sample Products		*Characteristics of the Industrial Product*						
Consumer	*Industrial*	*Type*	*Price*	*Criticalness*	*Distribution*	*Custom Engineering*	*Number of Customers*	*Expertise of Decision Maker*
Frequently purchased good (canned soup)	Bolt	I	Low	Low (unless fails)	Wholesale	None	Many	Low
Durable (dishwasher)	Machine tool	II	Moderate	Moderate	Direct	None	Many	Moderate
Electric car	New copying system	III	High	Moderate (unless fails)	Direct	Little	Moderate	Varies
House	Computer system	IV	Very high	High	Direct	Some	Few	Committee decision

KEY FEATURES

Having argued that industrial marketing (and, therefore, industrial marketing research) is not that different from consumer marketing, we now turn to some of the features of industrial marketing which affect the research done. The major problems remain the same: preparing annual plans, assessing market potential, allocating effort to different elements of the marketing program, and so forth. Differences result from the environmental conditions, which affect (*a*) the amount of different types of research done and (*b*) the form of the research. Some of the most important features are purchasing agents and the buying process, identifying the buying center, direct (personal) sales, custom engineering, few key customers, hard-to-obtain interviews, and the general absence of test marketing.

Purchasing Agents and the Buying Process

The formal institution of a purchasing agent separates industrial marketing from consumer marketing. Here someone is charged as his or her major reason for existence with making good buys (i.e., low price, reliable performance, delivered on time). The purchasing agent becomes the principal contact point for sellers of routine order products (bolts, paper, etc.). The agents also have influence in more complex product selection. Moreover they tend to serve a gate-keeper role, in which they screen sellers from the person or persons who make the actual buying decision. Therefore the important research problems are (*a*) to find out who the purchasing agents are, (*b*) to find out what their preferences are, and (*c*) to find out for whom, if anyone, they are "fronting."

Identifying the Buying Center

Industrial marketing often involves finding out who has impact on a decision. For example, typewriter selection by a company may be influenced by users, superior(s), and purchasing agents. The first task is often to try to locate these people. This is typically done by "snowballing," which consists of asking people in the organization to identify those who are involved in the decision. By asking several different people and comparing responses, a core of key people typically emerges.

In addition to identifying who has influence on a decision, it is useful to understand the kind of influence they have. Returning to the typewriter decision, some operating manager is likely to have the budget and, hence, signature authorization power. Such a person can block a decision but rarely makes a choice (e.g., IBM versus Xerox) unilaterally. On the other hand, users often have strong preferences but no authority. Consequently, it is useful to try to understand who has authority (budget), who has interest/preferences, and who is perceived of as being expert.

Direct (Personal) Sales

Personal selling is used for many consumer goods (insurance, encyclopedias, Avon products, etc.). In industrial marketing, however, the salesperson is typically accorded more prestige, power, and pay. Also, the salesperson tends to serve something of a technical consulting role to the client. In fact to many people, industrial marketing is synonymous with sales and sales management. Hence, research related to sales management is a big part of industrial marketing research. Some of the most common types of research which relate to salespersons are:

1. Overall sales forecasting.
2. Potential estimation (by territory).
3. Sales effectiveness estimation.
4. Selection of salespersons.
5. Territory boundaries and salespersons' assignments.
6. Salespersons' time allocation scheduling.
7. Salespersons' compensation schedules.

Interestingly, much of the research on these topics takes on an operations research orientation, especially territory boundary, and assignment problems, time allocation scheduling, and compensation schedules (e.g., Farley, 1964), which are amenable to mathematical programming approaches. An excellent overview of the sales management area is available in Wotruba (1971). An example of a model which has been developed to aid in managing salespersons is CALL-PLAN (Lodish, 1971).

Custom Engineering

Many large-ticket industrial products such as power generators require custom engineering for each sale. Thus the technical expertise of the sales (or technical back-up) staff plays a large role in the sales effort. For this reason research centering on (*a*) determining the importance of custom engineering, (*b*) determining the types of custom engineering needed, and (*c*) assessing the perceived competence of the sales staff is common. Similarly, the importance of after-sales service becomes more crucial, and perceived competence in this area is also a key area of interest.

Few Key Customers

For many consumer products, the potential customers number in the millions. For specialized industrial goods, the number of key customers may be more in the range of 10 to 30 and can be as small as 1 or 2, so many of the statistical procedures which depend on large samples are not useful. The result of this is that analytical techniques to study customers tend to be small-sample oriented, including mainly tabular procedures such as cross-tabs.

Hard-to-Obtain Interviews

For consumer products, it is relatively easy to find consumers who are willing to provide information about their preferences and usage patterns as well as to try out products. For many industrial products, it is sometimes hard to decide who to interview. Once the key individual is uncovered, getting an appointment and uninterrupted responses from busy executives is extremely difficult. Reliable data are also hard to obtain. For example, most executives or purchasing agents correctly perceive it is to their advantage to have many products available. Consequently, respondents tend to indicate more interest in new products than they really may have.

Absence of Test Marketing

Possibly the most obvious distinguishing characteristic of much of industrial marketing research is the absence of test marketing. This is often explainable by the fact that, unlike most frequently purchased products, the costs of developing and making prototypes are usually very high. This makes potential estimates the crucial numbers in go-no-go decisions and, hence, places particular emphasis on market potential estimation. The closest analogy to test marketing is the design and sale of a custom designed and manufactured product. Depending on how well it works, this may develop into a "mass-produced" product.

DATA SOURCES

The sources of data used by industrial marketing researchers tend to lean heavily toward published data contained in either government reports or syndicated services. Besides reliance on secondary data, such as the Census of Manufacturers data and trade association sources, most research relies on interviews of key prospects. This is often done informally by sales personnel who, acting as application specialists, are often called upon to diagnose customer problems and recommend solutions. The solutions are often the source of new product ideas. Hence sales personnel often play a role that straddles sales, market research, and new product development. In getting formal interviews, a common approach is to use salespersons as interviewers. This section will proceed to discuss some of the pros and cons of this approach.

Salespersons as Interviewers

The appropriateness of using salespersons as interviewers depends on a variety of conditions.

Type of research and salespersons. If the research is fairly mundane (e.g., penetration studies designed to find out if a particular product is being used or questions about product line extensions) and the interview is very structured, ordinary salespersons are adequate. When the problem becomes more complex (new product concept tests, etc.), however, the salesperson needs to have some special skills to fruitfully complete the task.

Time available. Salespersons will push research to the back of their agenda (commissions are paid on the basis of sales, not completed questionnaires). Hence, super busy (and good) salespersons generally are poor interviewers.

Type of customers. Some customers may resent interviews. When this is the case, the potential lost sales are probably not worth the information obtained, which will be of dubious value at best.

Access to right people. The thought of using salespersons as interviewers is appealing in that it is apparently a cost-saving approach. However if the people to be interviewed are not regularly contacted by the salespersons, the apparent economies vanish.

Control of sample and interviewer cheating. Assuming a salesperson is given a quota of interviews to collect, he or she will typically (*a*) talk to best friends among the clients and (*b*) be tempted to cheat by personally filling out the questionnaires.

With these points in mind, the following are keys to successful salesperson interviewing:

1. Having a good questionnaire (pretested).
2. Training the sales force.
3. Having only a few surveys per year and limited time per survey.

In summary, then, the pros of salespersons' interviewing include speed, ease of implementation, and spin-off knowledge, which the salespersons may acquire by being involved in the research. The cons include time diverted from sales calls, potential annoyance to salespersons and customers, and lack of training.

SUMMARY

This chapter has argued that many of the approaches used in consumer product marketing research are equally applicable to industrial marketing research. Still, there are some unique features which make industrial marketing research a special field. This chapter is short because the differences are more environmental than analytical. Nonetheless, someone interested in industrial marketing research will want to consult some other sources (e.g., Rawnsley, 1978; Cox, 1979; Choffray and Lilien, 1980).

BIBLIOGRAPHY

Beswick, Charles A., and David W. Cravens. "A Multistage Decision Model for Salesforce Management." *Journal of Marketing Research* 14 (May 1977), pp. 135–44.

Cardozo, Richard N., and James W. Cagley. "Experimental Study of Industrial Buyer Behavior." *Journal of Marketing Research* 8 (August 1971), pp. 329–34.

Choffray, Jean-Marke, and Gary L. Lilien. *Market Planning for New Industrial Products*. New York: John Wiley & Sons, 1980.

Cox, William E., Jr. *Industrial Marketing Research*. New York: John Wiley & Sons, 1979.

Cox, William E., Jr., and George N. Havens. "Determination of Sales Potentials and Performance for an Industrial Goods Manufacturer." *Journal of Marketing Research* 14 (November 1977), pp. 574–78.

Farley, John U. "An Optimal Plan for Salesmen's Compensation." *Journal of Marketing Research* 1 (May 1964), pp. 39–43.

Lamont, Lawrence M., and William J. Lundstrom. "Identifying Successful Industrial Salesmen by Personality and Personal Characteristics." *Journal of Marketing Research* 14 (November 1977), pp. 517–29.

Lehmann, Donald R., and John O'Shaughnessy. "Difference in Attribute Importance for Different Industrial Products." *Journal of Marketing* 38 (April 1974), pp. 36–42.

Lodish, Leonard M. "CALLPLAN: An Interactive Salesman's Call Planning System." *Management Science* 18 (December 1971), pp. P24–P40.

O'Shaughnessy, John. "Industrial Buying Behavior: Implications for Individual Account Planning." Working paper, Columbia University Graduate School of Business, 1977.

Ozanne, Urban B., and Gilbert A. Churchill, Jr. "Five Dimensions of the Industrial Adoption Process." *Journal of Marketing Research* 8 (August 1971), pp. 322–28.

Rawnsley, Allan, ed. *Manual of Industrial Marketing Research*. New York: John Wiley & Sons, 1978.

Sheth, J. N. "A Model of Industrial Buyer Behavior." *Journal of Marketing* 37 (October 1973), pp. 50–56.

Walker, Orville C., Jr.; Gilbert A. Churchill, Jr.; and Neil M. Ford. "Motivation and Performance in Industrial Selling: Present Knowledge and Needed Research." *Journal of Marketing Research* 14 (May 1977), pp. 156–68.

Webster, Frederick E., Jr., and Yoram Wind. "A General Model for Understanding Organizational Buying Behavior." *Journal of Marketing* 36 (April 1972), pp. 12–19.

Weingard, Robert E. "Why Studying the Purchasing Agent is Not Enough." *Journal of Marketing* 32 (January 1968), pp. 41–45.

Wotruba, Thomas R. *Sales Management*. New York: Holt, Rinehart & Winston, 1971.

Chapter 20

Final Comments

Having reached the end of this book, the reader may wonder if there is anything else worth saying about marketing research. Actually, there is a lot more to be covered. Nonetheless, for a variety of reasons (including a blister on the author's finger) this book has come to its end. The purpose of this chapter is to delineate a variety of topics which have not been covered: research in international marketing, political, legal, and ethical issues, and some forecasts about the future of marketing research.

THE EXPANDING WORLD OF MARKET RESEARCH

International

The need to consider international markets and competition is widely recognized, but the dimensions of the issue are not. During the last 20 years, the U.S. has gone from having about 400 of the Fortune 500 companies to about 200. The average age in the U.S. and Europe is over 30 and rising; in the less-developed areas it is stable at 15. It is in these developing countries where much of the opportunity for growth exists.

The marketing research portrayed in this book has been that of the United States. Exporting the methodology becomes increasingly difficult as differences become more apparent.

In other developed countries, the major differences are twofold. First, the existing suppliers differ although many U.S. suppliers, such as Nielsen and I.M.S., also offer services abroad. Second, cultural differences are very important. In addition to social and legal taboos on certain behavior, subtle nuances of tradition and language make transfer of methodologies, especially survey based, very difficult. Simultaneous back and forth translation is a minimum for a U.S. researcher trying to gather data in a foreign culture. So is employment of a natural citizen to avoid some of the classic blunders which have occurred in the past. Even with safeguards, time pressures and communication breakdowns can lead to some serious shortcomings. This author well remembers a survey monitoring a test market done in Argentina in which a fairly key question—intention to buy the product—was inadvertently/sloppily omitted.

In developing countries, the problems become even more basic. Often accurate basic data on population, industry, and so forth are unavailable. That, combined with the low literacy rates and the rural nature of many populations, makes many of the standard techniques useless. (Random digit dialing doesn't work too well when only 2 percent of the population have phones.) For a careful discussion of the problems of conducting international marketing research, see Douglas and Craig (1983).

Legal

Another arena which has recently experienced a boom in marketing research is the legal area (e.g., Frey and Kinnear, 1979). Led by the Federal Trade Commission, regulatory agencies have increasingly required "proof" of various types. For example, the FTC required claim substantiation for ads which in turn required marketing research. Research results have become crucial to various agency rulings. For example, the FTC has the power to order corrective advertising when deceptive advertising practices have created lasting false impressions. The role for research in such a case is to find out (*a*) whether the ads deceived people and (*b*) whether the deception persists. In point of fact, the hearings often feature expert witness testimony on both sides, with FTC witnesses arguing both that the ads were deceptive and that the deception will persist, and the company witnesses arguing that the ads aren't all that deceptive and, anyway, their effects are short-lived. (Not infrequently, this conflicting testimony is based on the same studies.)

Another problem is that, during legal proceedings, presumably confidential studies may be forced to be disclosed. This typically occurs during the discovery phase of a legal action, where the two parties to the action can request from the opposite side the data and analysis on which they based their claims. Hence, all research reports are potentially subject to scrutiny in a legal setting.

The standards-of-evidence questions raised by legal cases are nontrivial. For example, the natural level of confusion/deception is clearly not zero. (Try to understand federal tax laws or the Bible, for example.) What, then, is the level of deception required to be called deception? Moreover, sampling procedures which managers accept as useful are criticizable as unrepresentative. Thus marketing research (like most of the rest of us) is still struggling to find its way in legal proceedings.

Recently marketing research has played a key role in areas ranging from trademark infringement cases to evaluating applications to the FCC for cellular mobile phone licenses. In fact, it appears that the expert witness business has been one of the real growth fields of the 1980s.

One final point is worth noting. Forecasts and research results matter. Decisions are made based on them. This importance (plus the continuing trend to settling disputes in court) led Beecham in 1987 to sue Saatchi and Saatchi for $24 million based on an "overoptimistic" forecast for Delicare cold water wash by Yankelovich, Skelly and White/Clancy, Shulman (Alter, 1987). Delicare, a product designed to compete against Woolite, was introduced and captured 17.4 percent of the market. However, the $75,000 controlled test market predicted a share of 45.4 to 52.3, given media spending of $18 million and 21.2 to 24.9, given spending of $8 million. Beecham pointed to the difference in household penetration figures (basically potential) used in the forecast as a cause for the error: 75 percent, while Beecham believed it was 30 percent.

What does all this suggest? Be careful using forecasts. By checking on the details of the method (e.g., penetration level), mistakes can be avoided. Also be aware that forecasts are just that, and not guarantees. Finally, if you are providing forecasts, make your assumptions explicit and communicate them to your clients.

Ethical

A related but separate issue is the ethical conduct of market research. Clearly, claiming that a sales call is marketing research is inappropriate. Also when for the purposes of an experiment a subject is deceived, it is incumbent upon the researcher to correct the misimpression before "releasing" the subject into the world, a process somewhat inhumanely called *debriefing*. More subtle issues involve the level of privacy invasion deemed acceptable. Probably the best advice is, if you wouldn't want it done to you or your friends, don't do it to anyone else (somewhere I've heard a pithier version of this).

Political

Study any recent national political campaign and all the elements of marketing and marketing research are in evidence. Strategists worry about "positioning" candidates on attributes. Voters' (consumers') views on issues are monitored carefully. Target segments are identified which are vulnerable and programs are designed to reach them. Many of the top people in campaign organizations are marketing researchers. In short, political campaigns are run like businesses, with marketing and marketing research their key elements. (Perhaps this explains why most candidates are as bland as the TV shows on which their "paid political announcements" are aired.)

THE FUTURE

Projecting the future, as the chapter on forecasting hopefully conveyed, is a hazardous and uncertain business. Nonetheless, the author (partially on the assumption that most readers have given up by now and, therefore, bad forecasts cannot cause too much damage) feels the following trends will be evident.

Research Will Be More Quantitative

This seems to be the general trend of all disciplines, and marketing is no more likely to be an exception than were physics or sociology.

Legal Considerations Will Increase

On one hand, more research will be required for various regulatory purposes. On the other hand, new constraints in areas such as privacy protection will affect the type of research which can be done.

Technological Changes Will Affect Research Methods

For example, innovations such as two-way cable TV will make a new type of in-home personal interview (without an interviewer physically present) possible. Similarly, automated checkout systems provide an extremely useful source of information. The increasing availability of data will lead to:

1. More analysis of disaggregated data.
2. More integrated databases, as the trend toward "single-source" data suppliers suggests.
3. More research which is decision support system oriented than purely analytical/number crunching.

Planning

Marketing research will continue to become more integrated in the strategic planning process. In fact, marketing research can be viewed as the external intelligence function of a company. An enlightened (or at least different) organization chart might be something like the following:

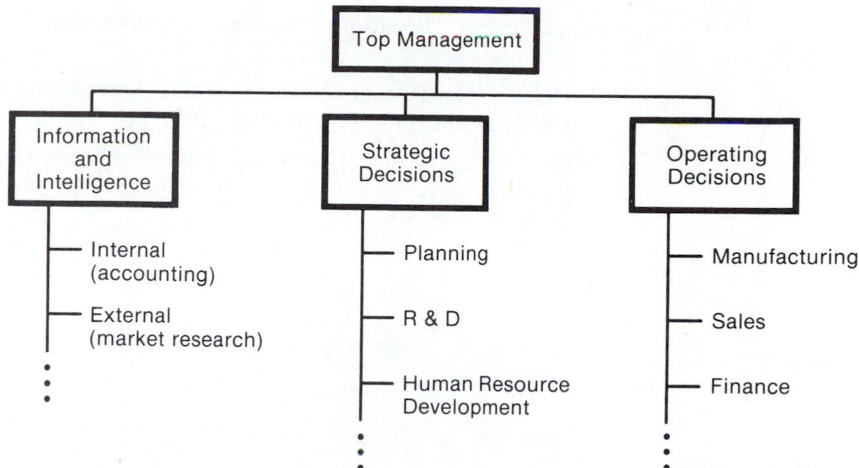

Given such a view, marketing research can be seen as a service function supporting both long-run decisions (e.g., five-year plans, new product development through R & D), and short-term (operating) decisions (e.g., promotions).

Research and Management Functions Will Become More Integrated

An increasingly complex world makes increased technical sophistication a likely requirement of managers. Similarly, researchers have been found to occasionally have an idea as well as a number. Hence, more of a team relationship is likely to evolve. Similarly, more rotational assignments between management and research are likely to occur.

CONCLUSION

The conclusion to a research book really is more of a commencement than a conclusion. This book has merely introduced the subject; it is up to the reader to pursue it in detail. There are some who claim research (and especially quantitative research) is worthless, others who believe it is the end itself. Both are foolish. Research can be a valuable tool, the kind of tool which an adept person uses as a competitive advantage. The way to learn about it is to think, ask questions, and observe. Hopefully, this book (or at least its references) will help. As we say at the close of the course, "May you have good samples, big R^2s, and low collinearity."

BIBLIOGRAPHY

Alter, Stewart. "Beecham vs. Saatchi." *Advertising Age* 58 (July 13, 1987), pp. 1 and 86.

Douglas, Susan P., and C. Samuel Craig. *International Marketing Research*. Englewood Cliffs, N.J.: Prentice-Hall, 1983.

Frey, Cynthia J., and Thomas C. Kinnear. "Legal Constraints and Marketing Research: Review and Call to Action." *Journal of Marketing Research* 16 (August 1979), pp. 295–302.

Appendixes

Appendix A

Random Numbers

56970	10799	52098	04184	54967	72938	50834	23777	08392
83125	85077	60490	44369	66130	72936	69848	59973	08144
55503	21383	02464	26141	68779	66388	75242	82690	74099
47019	06683	33203	29603	54553	25971	69573	83854	24715
84828	61152	79526	29554	84580	37859	28504	61980	34997
08021	31331	79227	05748	51276	57143	31926	00915	45821
36458	28285	30424	98420	72925	40729	22337	48293	86847
05752	96065	36847	87729	81679	59126	59437	33225	31280
26768	02513	58454	56958	20575	76746	40878	06846	32828
42613	72456	43030	58085	06766	60227	96414	32671	45587
95457	12176	65482	25596	02678	54592	63607	82096	21913
95276	67524	63564	95958	39750	64379	46059	51666	10433
66954	53574	64776	92345	95110	59448	77249	54044	67942
17457	44151	14113	02462	02798	54977	48340	66738	60184
03704	23322	83214	59337	01695	60666	97410	55064	17427
21538	16997	33210	60337	27976	70661	08250	69509	60264
57178	16730	08310	70348	11317	71623	55510	64750	87759
31048	40058	94953	55866	96283	40620	52087	80817	74533
69799	83300	16498	80733	96422	58078	99643	39847	96884
90595	65017	59231	17772	67831	33317	00520	90401	41700
33570	34761	08039	78784	09977	29398	93896	78227	90110
15340	82760	57477	13898	48431	72936	78160	87240	52710
64079	07733	36512	56186	99098	48850	72527	08486	10951
63491	84886	67118	62063	74958	20946	28147	39338	32109
92003	76568	41034	28260	79708	00770	88643	21188	01850
52360	46658	66511	04172	73085	11795	52594	13287	82531
74622	12142	68355	65635	21828	39539	18988	53609	04001
04157	50070	61343	64315	70836	82857	35335	87900	36194
86003	60070	66241	32836	27573	11479	94114	81641	00496
41208	80187	20351	09630	84668	42486	71303	19512	50277
06433	80674	24520	18222	10610	05794	37515	48619	62866
39298	47829	72648	37414	75755	04717	29899	78817	03509
89884	59651	67533	68123	17730	95862	08034	19473	63971
61512	32155	51906	61662	64430	16688	37275	51262	11569
99653	47635	12506	88535	36553	23757	34209	55803	96275
95913	11085	13772	76638	48423	25018	99041	77529	81360
55804	44004	13122	44115	01601	50541	00147	77685	58788
35334	82410	91601	40617	72876	33967	73830	15405	96554
57729	88646	76487	11622	96297	24160	09903	14047	22917
86648	89317	63677	70119	94739	25875	38829	68377	43918
30574	06039	07967	32422	76791	30725	53711	93385	13421
81307	13114	83580	79974	45929	85113	72268	09858	52104
02410	96385	79067	54939	21410	86980	91772	93307	34116
18969	87444	52233	62319	08598	09066	95288	04794	01534
87863	80514	66860	62297	80198	19347	73234	86265	49096
08397	10538	15438	62311	72844	60203	46412	65943	79232
28520	45247	58729	10854	99058	18260	38765	90038	94209
44285	09452	15867	70418	57012	72122	36634	97283	95943
86299	22510	33571	23309	57040	29285	67870	21913	72958
84842	05748	90894	61658	15001	94005	36308	41161	37341

Appendix B

Standard Normal Distribution Areas

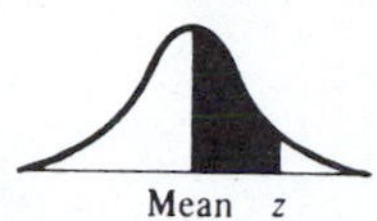

z	.00	.01	.02	.03	.04	.05	.06	.07	.08	.09
0.0	.0000	.0040	.0080	.0120	.0160	.0199	.0239	.0279	.0319	.0359
0.1	.0398	.0438	.0478	.0517	.0557	.0596	.0636	.0675	.0714	.0753
0.2	.0793	.0832	.0871	.0910	.0948	.0987	.1026	.1064	.1103	.1141
0.3	.1179	.1217	.1255	.1293	.1331	.1368	.1406	.1443	.1480	.1517
0.4	.1554	.1591	.1628	.1664	.1700	.1736	.1772	.1808	.1844	.1879
0.5	.1915	.1950	.1985	.2019	.2054	.2088	.2123	.2157	.2190	.2224
0.6	.2257	.2291	.2324	.2357	.2389	.2422	.2454	.2486	.2518	.2549
0.7	.2580	.2612	.2642	.2673	.2704	.2734	.2764	.2794	.2823	.2852
0.8	.2881	.2910	.2939	.2967	.2995	.3023	.3051	.3078	.3106	.3133
0.9	.3159	.3186	.3212	.3238	.3264	.3289	.3315	.3340	.3365	.3389
1.0	.3413	.3438	.3461	.3485	.3508	.3531	.3554	.3577	.3599	.3621
1.1	.3643	.3665	.3686	.3708	.3729	.3749	.3770	.3790	.3810	.3830
1.2	.3849	.3869	.3888	.3907	3925	.3944	.3962	.3980	.3997	.4015
1.3	.4032	.4049	.4066	.4082	.4099	.4115	.4131	.4147	.4162	.4177
1.4	.4192	.4207	.4222	.4236	.4251	.4265	.4279	.4292	.4306	.4319
1.5	.4332	.4345	.4357	.4370	.4382	.4394	.4406	.4418	.4429	.4441
1.6	.4452	.4463	.4474	.4484	.4495	.4505	.4515	.4525	.4535	.4545
1.7	.4554	.4564	.4573	.4582	.4591	.4599	.4608	.4616	.4625	.4633
1.8	.4641	.4649	.4656	.4664	.4671	.4678	.4686	.4693	.4699	.4706
1.9	.4713	.4719	.4726	.4732	.4738	.4744	.4750	.4756	.4761	.4767
2.0	.4772	.4778	.4783	.4788	.4793	.4798	.4803	.4808	.4812	.4817
2.1	.4821	.4826	.4830	.4834	.4838	.4842	.4846	.4850	.4854	.4857
2.2	.4861	.4864	.4868	.4871	.4875	.4878	.4881	.4884	.4887	.4890
2.3	.4893	.4896	.4898	.4901	.4904	.4906	.4909	.4911	.4913	.4916
2.4	.4918	.4920	.4922	.4925	.4927	.4929	.4931	.4932	.4934	.4936
2.5	.4938	.4940	.4941	.4943	.4945	.4946	.4948	.4949	.4951	.4952
2.6	.4953	.4955	.4956	.4957	.4959	.4960	.4961	.4962	.4963	.4964
2.7	.4965	.4966	.4967	.4968	.4969	.4970	.4971	.4972	.4973	.4974
2.8	.4974	.4975	.4976	.4977	.4977	.4978	.4979	.4979	.4980	.4981
2.9	.4981	.4982	.4982	.4983	.4984	.4984	.4985	.4985	.4986	.4986
3.0	.49865	.4987	.4987	.4988	.4988	.4989	.4989	.4989	.4990	.4990
4.0	.4999683									

Source: *Fundamental Statistics for Business and Economics*, 4th ed. by John Neter, William Wasserman, and G. A. Whitmore, Copyright © 1973 by Allyn and Bacon, Inc. Reprinted with permission.

Appendix C

The t Distribution

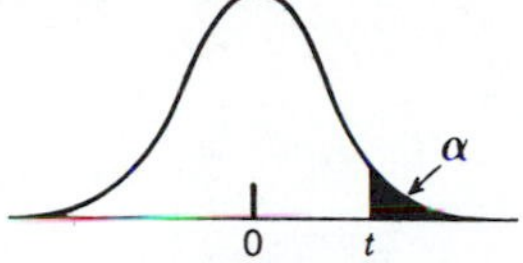

α / d.f.	.10	.05	.025	.01	.005
1	3.078	6.314	12.706	31.821	63.657
2	1.886	2.920	4.303	6.965	9.925
3	1.638	2.353	3.182	4.541	5.841
4	1.533	2.132	2.776	3.747	4.604
5	1.476	2.015	2.571	3.365	4.032
6	1.440	1.943	2.447	3.143	3.707
7	1.415	1.895	2.365	2.998	3.499
8	1.397	1.860	2.306	2.896	3.355
9	1.383	1.833	2.262	2.821	3.250
10	1.372	1.812	2.228	2.764	3.169
11	1.363	1.796	2.201	2.718	3.106
12	1.356	1.782	2.179	2.681	3.055
13	1.350	1.771	2.160	2.650	3.012
14	1.345	1.761	2.145	2.624	2.977
15	1.341	1.753	2.131	2.602	2.947
16	1.337	1.746	2.120	2.583	2.921
17	1.333	1.740	2.110	2.567	2.898
18	1.330	1.734	2.101	2.552	2.878
19	1.328	1.729	2.093	2.539	2.861
20	1.325	1.725	2.086	2.528	2.845
21	1.323	1.721	2.080	2.518	2.831
22	1.321	1.717	2.074	2.508	2.819
23	1.319	1.714	2.069	2.500	2.807
24	1.318	1.711	2.064	2.492	2.797
25	1.316	1.708	2.060	2.485	2.787
26	1.315	1.706	2.056	2.479	2.779
27	1.314	1.703	2.052	2.473	2.771
28	1.313	1.701	2.048	2.467	2.763
29	1.311	1.699	2.045	2.462	2.756
30	1.310	1.697	2.042	2.457	2.750
40	1.303	1.684	2.021	2.423	2.704
60	1.296	1.671	2.000	2.390	2.660
120	1.289	1.658	1.980	2.358	2.617
∞	1.282	1.645	1.960	2.326	2.576

Source: Hoel, *Elementary Statistics*, 3rd ed. New York: John Wiley & Sons, 1971 c.

Appendix D

The χ^2 Distribution

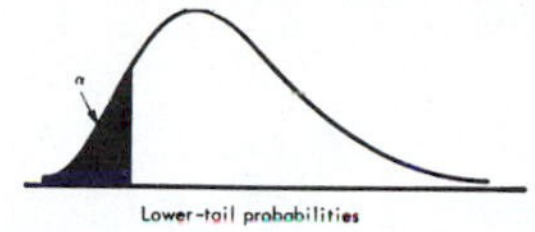

df \ α	.001	.005	.010	.025	.050	.100
1	.000	.000	.000	.001	.004	.016
2	.002	.010	.020	.051	.103	.211
3	.024	.072	.115	.216	.352	.584
4	.091	.207	.297	.484	.711	1.06
5	.210	.412	.554	.831	1.15	1.61
6	.381	.676	.872	1.24	1.64	2.20
7	.598	.989	1.24	1.69	2.17	2.83
8	.857	1.34	1.65	2.18	2.73	3.49
9	1.15	1.73	2.09	2.70	3.33	4.17
10	1.48	2.16	2.56	3.25	3.94	4.87
11	1.83	2.60	3.05	3.82	4.57	5.58
12	2.21	3.07	3.57	4.40	5.23	6.30
13	2.62	3.57	4.11	5.01	5.89	7.04
14	3.04	4.07	4.66	5.63	6.57	7.79
15	3.48	4.60	5.23	6.26	7.26	8.55
16	3.94	5.14	5.81	6.91	7.96	9.31
17	4.42	5.70	6.41	7.56	8.67	10.1
18	4.90	6.26	7.01	8.23	9.39	10.9
19	5.41	6.84	7.63	8.91	10.1	11.7
20	5.92	7.43	8.26	9.59	10.9	12.4
21	6.45	8.03	8.90	10.3	11.6	13.2
22	6.98	8.64	9.54	11.0	12.3	14.0
23	7.53	9.26	10.2	11.7	13.1	14.8
24	8.08	9.89	10.9	12.4	13.8	15.7
25	8.65	10.5	11.5	13.1	14.6	16.5
26	9.22	11.2	12.2	13.8	15.4	17.3
27	9.80	11.8	12.9	14.6	16.2	18.1
28	10.4	12.5	13.6	15.3	16.9	18.9
29	11.0	13.1	14.3	16.0	17.7	19.8
30	11.6	13.8	15.0	16.8	18.5	20.6
35	14.7	17.2	18.5	20.6	22.5	24.8
40	17.9	20.7	22.2	24.4	26.5	29.1
45	21.3	24.3	25.9	28.4	30.6	33.4
50	24.7	28.0	29.7	32.4	34.8	37.7
55	28.2	31.7	33.6	36.4	39.0	42.1
60	31.7	35.5	37.5	40.5	43.2	46.5
65	35.4	39.4	41.4	44.6	47.4	50.9
70	39.0	43.3	45.4	48.8	51.7	55.3
75	42.8	47.2	49.5	52.9	56.1	59.8
80	46.5	51.2	53.5	57.2	60.4	64.3
85	50.3	55.2	57.6	61.4	64.7	68.8
90	54.2	59.2	61.8	65.6	69.1	73.3
95	58.0	63.2	65.9	69.9	73.5	77.8
100	61.9	67.3	70.1	74.2	77.9	82.4

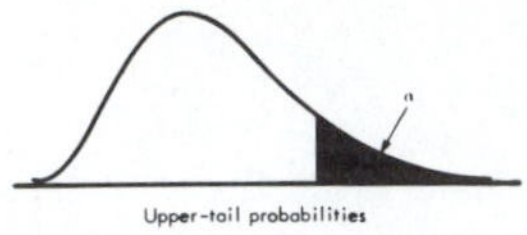

df \ α	.100	.050	.025	.010	.005	.001
1	2.71	3.84	5.02	6.63	7.88	10.8
2	4.61	5.99	7.38	9.21	10.6	13.8
3	6.25	7.81	9.35	11.3	12.8	16.3
4	7.78	9.49	11.1	13.3	14.9	18.5
5	9.24	11.1	12.8	15.1	16.7	20.5
6	10.6	12.6	14.4	16.8	18.5	22.5
7	12.0	14.1	16.0	18.5	20.3	24.3
8	13.4	15.5	17.5	20.1	22.0	26.1
9	14.7	16.9	19.0	21.7	23.6	27.9
10	16.0	18.3	20.5	23.2	25.2	29.6
11	17.3	19.7	21.9	24.7	26.8	31.3
12	18.5	21.0	23.3	26.2	28.3	32.9
13	19.8	22.4	24.7	27.7	29.8	34.5
14	21.1	23.7	26.1	29.1	31.3	36.1
15	22.3	25.0	27.5	30.6	32.8	37.7
16	23.5	26.3	28.8	32.0	34.3	39.3
17	24.8	27.6	30.2	33.4	35.7	40.8
18	26.0	28.9	31.5	34.8	37.2	42.3
19	27.2	30.1	32.9	36.2	38.6	43.8
20	28.4	31.4	34.2	37.6	40.0	45.3
21	29.6	32.7	35.5	38.9	41.4	46.8
22	30.8	33.9	36.8	40.3	42.8	48.3
23	32.0	35.2	38.1	41.6	44.2	49.7
24	33.2	36.4	39.4	43.0	45.6	51.2
25	34.4	37.7	40.6	44.3	46.9	52.6
26	35.6	38.9	41.9	45.6	48.3	54.1
27	36.7	40.1	43.2	47.0	49.6	55.5
28	37.9	41.3	44.5	48.3	51.0	56.9
29	39.1	42.6	45.7	49.6	52.3	58.3
30	40.3	43.8	47.0	50.9	53.7	59.7
35	46.1	49.8	53.2	57.3	60.3	66.6
40	51.8	55.8	59.3	63.7	66.8	73.4
45	57.5	61.7	65.4	70.0	73.2	80.1
50	63.2	67.5	71.4	76.2	79.5	86.7
55	68.8	73.3	77.4	82.3	85.7	93.2
60	74.4	79.1	83.3	88.4	92.0	99.6
65	80.0	84.8	89.2	94.4	98.1	106.0
70	85.5	90.5	95.0	100.4	104.2	112.3
75	91.1	96.2	100.8	106.4	110.3	118.6
80	96.6	101.9	106.6	112.3	116.3	124.8
85	102.1	107.5	112.4	118.2	122.3	131.0
90	107.6	113.1	118.1	124.1	128.3	137.2
95	113.0	118.8	123.9	130.0	134.2	143.3
100	118.5	124.3	129.6	135.8	140.2	149.4

Appendix
E

Critical Values of the F Distribution

Appendix E: Five Percent Level of Significance

Degrees of freedom for denominator	Degrees of freedom for numerator																		
	1	2	3	4	5	6	7	8	9	10	12	15	20	24	30	40	60	120	∞
1	161	200	216	225	230	234	237	239	241	242	244	246	248	249	250	251	252	253	254
2	18.5	19.0	19.2	19.2	19.3	19.3	19.4	19.4	19.4	19.4	19.4	19.4	19.4	19.5	19.5	19.5	19.5	19.5	19.5
3	10.1	9.55	9.28	9.12	9.01	8.94	8.89	8.85	8.81	8.79	8.74	8.70	8.66	8.64	8.62	8.59	8.57	8.55	8.53
4	7.71	6.94	6.59	6.39	6.26	6.16	6.09	6.04	6.00	5.96	5.91	5.86	5.80	5.77	5.75	5.72	5.69	5.66	5.63
5	6.61	5.79	5.41	5.19	5.05	4.95	4.88	4.82	4.77	4.74	4.68	4.62	4.56	4.53	4.50	4.46	4.43	4.40	4.37
6	5.99	5.14	4.76	4.53	4.39	4.28	4.21	4.15	4.10	4.06	4.00	3.94	3.87	3.84	3.81	3.77	3.74	3.70	3.67
7	5.59	4.74	4.35	4.12	3.97	3.87	3.79	3.73	3.68	3.64	3.57	3.51	3.44	3.41	3.38	3.34	3.30	3.27	3.23
8	5.32	4.46	4.07	3.84	3.69	3.58	3.50	3.44	3.39	3.35	3.28	3.22	3.15	3.12	3.08	3.04	3.01	2.97	2.93
9	5.12	4.26	3.86	3.63	3.48	3.37	3.29	3.23	3.18	3.14	3.07	3.01	2.94	2.90	2.86	2.83	2.79	2.75	2.71
10	4.96	4.10	3.71	3.48	3.33	3.22	3.14	3.07	3.02	2.98	2.91	2.85	2.77	2.74	2.70	2.66	2.62	2.58	2.54
11	4.84	3.98	3.59	3.36	3.20	3.09	3.01	2.95	2.90	2.85	2.79	2.72	2.65	2.61	2.57	2.53	2.49	2.45	2.40
12	4.75	3.89	3.49	3.26	3.11	3.00	2.91	2.85	2.80	2.75	2.69	2.62	2.54	2.51	2.47	2.43	2.38	2.34	2.30
13	4.67	3.81	3.41	3.18	3.03	2.92	2.83	2.77	2.71	2.67	2.60	2.53	2.46	2.42	2.38	2.34	2.30	2.25	2.21
14	4.60	3.74	3.34	3.11	2.96	2.85	2.76	2.70	2.65	2.60	2.53	2.46	2.39	2.35	2.31	2.27	2.22	2.18	2.13
15	4.54	3.68	3.29	3.06	2.90	2.79	2.71	2.64	2.59	2.54	2.48	2.40	2.33	2.29	2.25	2.20	2.16	2.11	2.07
16	4.49	3.63	3.24	3.01	2.85	2.74	2.66	2.59	2.54	2.49	2.42	2.35	2.28	2.24	2.19	2.15	2.11	2.06	2.01
17	4.45	3.59	3.20	2.96	2.81	2.70	2.61	2.55	2.49	2.45	2.38	2.31	2.23	2.19	2.15	2.10	2.06	2.01	1.96
18	4.41	3.55	3.16	2.93	2.77	2.66	2.58	2.51	2.46	2.41	2.34	2.27	2.19	2.15	2.11	2.06	2.02	1.97	1.92
19	4.38	3.52	3.13	2.90	2.74	2.63	2.54	2.48	2.42	2.38	2.31	2.23	2.16	2.11	2.07	2.03	1.98	1.93	1.88
20	4.35	3.49	3.10	2.87	2.71	2.60	2.51	2.45	2.39	2.35	2.28	2.20	2.12	2.08	2.04	1.99	1.95	1.90	1.84
21	4.32	3.47	3.07	2.84	2.68	2.57	2.49	2.42	2.37	2.32	2.25	2.18	2.10	2.05	2.01	1.96	1.92	1.87	1.81
22	4.30	3.44	3.05	2.82	2.66	2.55	2.46	2.40	2.34	2.30	2.23	2.15	2.07	2.03	1.98	1.94	1.89	1.84	1.78
23	4.28	3.42	3.03	2.80	2.64	2.53	2.44	2.37	2.32	2.27	2.20	2.13	2.05	2.01	1.96	1.91	1.86	1.81	1.76
24	4.26	3.40	3.01	2.78	2.62	2.51	2.42	2.36	2.30	2.25	2.18	2.11	2.03	1.98	1.94	1.89	1.84	1.79	1.73
25	4.24	3.39	2.99	2.76	2.60	2.49	2.40	2.34	2.28	2.24	2.16	2.09	2.01	1.96	1.92	1.87	1.82	1.77	1.71
30	4.17	3.32	2.92	2.69	2.53	2.42	2.33	2.27	2.21	2.16	2.09	2.01	1.93	1.89	1.84	1.79	1.74	1.68	1.62
40	4.08	3.23	2.84	2.61	2.45	2.34	2.25	2.18	2.12	2.08	2.00	1.92	1.84	1.79	1.74	1.69	1.64	1.58	1.51
60	4.00	3.15	2.76	2.53	2.37	2.25	2.17	2.10	2.04	1.99	1.92	1.84	1.75	1.70	1.65	1.59	1.53	1.47	1.39
120	3.92	3.07	2.68	2.45	2.29	2.18	2.09	2.02	1.96	1.91	1.83	1.75	1.66	1.61	1.55	1.50	1.43	1.35	1.25
∞	3.84	3.00	2.60	2.37	2.21	2.10	2.01	1.94	1.88	1.83	1.75	1.67	1.57	1.52	1.46	1.39	1.32	1.22	1.00

Appendix E: One Percent Level of Significance

Degrees of freedom for numerator

Degrees of freedom for denominator	1	2	3	4	5	6	7	8	9	10	12	15	20	24	30	40	60	120	∞
1	4,052	5,000	5,403	5,625	5,764	5,859	5,928	5,982	6,023	6,056	6,106	6,157	6,209	6,235	6,261	6,287	6,313	6,339	6,366
2	98.5	99.0	99.2	99.2	99.3	99.3	99.4	99.4	99.4	99.4	99.4	99.4	99.4	99.5	99.5	99.5	99.5	99.5	99.5
3	34.1	30.8	29.5	28.7	28.2	27.9	27.7	27.5	27.3	27.2	27.1	26.9	26.7	26.6	26.5	26.4	26.3	26.2	26.1
4	21.2	18.0	16.7	16.0	15.5	15.2	15.0	14.8	14.7	14.5	14.4	14.2	14.0	13.9	13.8	13.7	13.7	13.6	13.5
5	16.3	13.3	12.1	11.4	11.0	10.7	10.5	10.3	10.2	10.1	9.89	9.72	9.55	9.47	9.38	9.29	9.20	9.11	9.02
6	13.7	10.9	9.78	9.15	8.75	8.47	8.26	8.10	7.98	7.87	7.72	7.56	7.40	7.31	7.23	7.14	7.06	6.97	6.88
7	12.2	9.55	8.45	7.85	7.46	7.19	6.99	6.84	6.72	6.62	6.47	6.31	6.16	6.07	5.99	5.91	5.82	5.74	5.65
8	11.3	8.65	7.59	7.01	6.63	6.37	6.18	6.03	5.91	5.81	5.67	5.52	5.36	5.28	5.20	5.12	5.03	4.95	4.86
9	10.6	8.02	6.99	6.42	6.06	5.80	5.61	5.47	5.35	5.26	5.11	4.96	4.81	4.73	4.65	4.57	4.48	4.40	4.31
10	10.0	7.56	6.55	5.99	5.64	5.39	5.20	5.06	4.94	4.85	4.71	4.56	4.41	4.33	4.25	4.17	4.08	4.00	3.91
11	9.65	7.21	6.22	5.67	5.32	5.07	4.89	4.74	4.63	4.54	4.40	4.25	4.10	4.02	3.94	3.86	3.78	3.69	3.60
12	9.33	6.93	5.95	5.41	5.06	4.82	4.64	4.50	4.39	4.30	4.16	4.01	3.86	3.78	3.70	3.62	3.54	3.45	3.36
13	9.07	6.70	5.74	5.21	4.86	4.62	4.44	4.30	4.19	4.10	3.96	3.82	3.66	3.59	3.51	3.43	3.34	3.25	3.17
14	8.86	6.51	5.56	5.04	4.70	4.46	4.28	4.14	4.03	3.94	3.80	3.66	3.51	3.43	3.35	3.27	3.18	3.09	3.00
15	8.68	6.36	5.42	4.89	4.56	4.32	4.14	4.00	3.89	3.80	3.67	3.52	3.37	3.29	3.21	3.13	3.05	2.96	2.87
16	8.53	6.23	5.29	4.77	4.44	4.20	4.03	3.89	3.78	3.69	3.55	3.41	3.26	3.18	3.10	3.02	2.93	2.84	2.75
17	8.40	6.11	5.19	4.67	4.34	4.10	3.93	3.79	3.68	3.59	3.46	3.31	3.16	3.08	3.00	2.92	2.83	2.75	2.65
18	8.29	6.01	5.09	4.58	4.25	4.01	3.84	3.71	3.60	3.51	3.37	3.23	3.08	3.00	2.92	2.84	2.75	2.66	2.57
19	8.19	5.93	5.01	4.50	4.17	3.94	3.77	3.63	3.52	3.43	3.30	3.15	3.00	2.92	2.84	2.76	2.67	2.58	2.49
20	8.10	5.85	4.94	4.43	4.10	3.87	3.70	3.56	3.46	3.37	3.23	3.09	2.94	2.86	2.78	2.69	2.61	2.52	2.42
21	8.02	5.78	4.87	4.37	4.04	3.81	3.64	3.51	3.40	3.31	3.17	3.03	2.88	2.80	2.72	2.64	2.55	2.46	2.36
22	7.95	5.72	4.82	4.31	3.99	3.76	3.59	3.45	3.35	3.26	3.12	2.98	2.83	2.75	2.67	2.58	2.50	2.40	2.31
23	7.88	5.66	4.76	4.26	3.94	3.71	3.54	3.41	3.30	3.21	3.07	2.93	2.78	2.70	2.62	2.54	2.45	2.35	2.26
24	7.82	5.61	4.72	4.22	3.90	3.67	3.50	3.36	3.26	3.17	3.03	2.89	2.74	2.66	2.58	2.49	2.40	2.31	2.21
25	7.77	5.57	4.68	4.18	3.86	3.63	3.46	3.32	3.22	3.13	2.99	2.85	2.70	2.62	2.53	2.45	2.36	2.27	2.17
30	7.56	5.39	4.51	4.02	3.70	3.47	3.30	3.17	3.07	2.98	2.84	2.70	2.55	2.47	2.39	2.30	2.21	2.11	2.01
40	7.31	5.18	4.31	3.83	3.51	3.29	3.12	2.99	2.89	2.80	2.66	2.52	2.37	2.29	2.20	2.11	2.02	1.92	1.80
60	7.08	4.98	4.13	3.65	3.34	3.12	2.95	2.82	2.72	2.63	2.50	2.35	2.20	2.12	2.03	1.94	1.84	1.73	1.60
120	6.85	4.79	3.95	3.48	3.17	2.96	2.79	2.66	2.56	2.47	2.34	2.19	2.03	1.95	1.86	1.76	1.66	1.53	1.38
∞	6.63	4.61	3.78	3.32	3.02	2.80	2.64	2.51	2.41	2.32	2.18	2.04	1.88	1.79	1.70	1.59	1.47	1.32	1.00

Source: This table is reproduced from M. Merrington and C. M. Thompson, "Tables of Percentage Points of the Inverted Beta *(F)* Distribution," *Biometrika* 33 (1943), by permission of the Biometrika trustees.

Index

A

B

C

D

E

F

G

H

I

J

K

L

M

N

O

P

Q

R

U

V

W

Y

Z